FOURTH EDITION

BUSINESS INTELLIGENCE, ANALYTICS, AND DATA SCIENCE:

A Managerial Perspective

Ramesh Sharda
Oklahoma State University

Dursun Delen
Oklahoma State University

Efraim Turban
University of Hawaii

With contributions to previous editions by

J. E. Aronson
The University of Georgia

Ting-Peng Liang
National Sun Yat-sen University

David King
JDA Software Group, Inc.

 **Pearson**

330 Hudson Street, NY NY 10013

VP Editorial Director: Andrew Gilfillan
Senior Portfolio Manager: Samantha Lewis
Content Development Team Lead: Laura Burgess
Content Developer: Stephany Harrington
Program Monitor: Ann Pulido/SPi Global
Editorial Assistant: Madeline Houpt
Product Marketing Manager: Kaylee Carlson
Project Manager: Revathi Viswanathan/Cenveo
  Publisher Services
Text Designer: Cenveo Publisher Services

Cover Designer: Brian Malloy/Cenveo Publisher
  Services
Cover Art: Olga Morkotun/Shutterstock
Full-Service Project Management: Cenveo
  Publisher Services
Composition: Cenveo Publisher Services
Printer/Binder: LSC Communications
Cover Printer: LSC Communications
Text Font: 10/12 Times LT Pro

Credits and acknowledgments borrowed from other sources and reproduced, with permission, in this textbook appear on the appropriate page within text.

Microsoft and/or its respective suppliers make no representations about the suitability of the information contained in the documents and related graphics published as part of the services for any purpose. All such documents and related graphics are provided as is without warranty of any kind. Microsoft and/or its respective suppliers hereby disclaim all warranties and conditions with regard to this information, including all warranties and conditions of merchantability, whether express, implied or statutory, fitness for a particular purpose, title and non-infringement.

In no event shall Microsoft and/or its respective suppliers be liable for any special, indirect or consequential damages or any damages whatsoever resulting from loss of use, data or profits, whether in an action of contract, negligence or other tortious action, arising out of or in connection with the use or performance of information available from the services. The documents and related graphics contained herein could include technical inaccuracies or typographical errors. Changes are periodically added to the information herein. Microsoft and/or its respective suppliers may make improvements and/or changes in the product(s) and/or the program(s) described herein at any time. Partial screen shots may be viewed in full within the software version specified.

Microsoft® Windows®, and Microsoft Office® are registered trademarks of the Microsoft Corporation in the U.S.A. and other countries. This book is not sponsored or endorsed by or affiliated with the Microsoft Corporation.

Library of Congress Cataloging-in-Publication Data

Names: Sharda, Ramesh, author. | Delen, Dursun, author. | Turban, Efraim, author.
Title: Business intelligence, analytics, and data science : a managerial perspective / Ramesh Sharda, Oklahoma State
  University, Dursun Delen, Oklahoma State University, Efraim Turban, University of Hawaii ; with contributions by J.
  E. Aronson, The University of Georgia, Ting-Peng Liang, National Sun Yat-sen University, David King, JDA Software
  Group, Inc.
Other titles: Business intelligence
Description: Fourth edition. | Boston : Pearson, [2016] | Earlier edition published as: Business intelligence : a
  managerial perspective on analytics. | Includes index.
Identifiers: LCCN 2016031095| ISBN 9780134633282 | ISBN 0134633288
Subjects: LCSH: Business intelligence. | Industrial management.
Classification: LCC HD38.7 .B8714 2016 | DDC 658.4/72–dc23 LC record available at https://lccn.loc.gov/2016031095

ISBN-10:   0-13-463328-8
ISBN-13: 978-0-13-463328-2

Brief Contents

Preface xix
About the Authors xxv

Chapter 1 **An Overview of Business Intelligence, Analytics, and Data Science** 3

Chapter 2 **Descriptive Analytics I: Nature of Data, Statistical Modeling, and Visualization** 53

Chapter 3 **Descriptive Analytics II: Business Intelligence and Data Warehousing** 127

Chapter 4 **Predictive Analytics I: Data Mining Process, Methods, and Algorithms** 189

Chapter 5 **Predictive Analytics II: Text, Web, and Social Media Analytics** 247

Chapter 6 **Prescriptive Analytics: Optimization and Simulation** 319

Chapter 7 **Big Data Concepts and Tools** 369

Chapter 8 **Future Trends, Privacy and Managerial Considerations in Analytics** 417

Glossary 467
Index 475

Contents

Preface   xix

About the Authors   xxv

Chapter 1 An Overview of Business Intelligence, Analytics, and Data Science   3

1.1 OPENING VIGNETTE: Sports Analytics—An Exciting Frontier for Learning and Understanding Applications of Analytics   4

1.2 Changing Business Environments and Evolving Needs for Decision Support and Analytics   11

1.3 Evolution of Computerized Decision Support to Analytics/Data Science   13

1.4 A Framework for Business Intelligence   15

Definitions of BI   16

A Brief History of BI   16

The Architecture of BI   16

The Origins and Drivers of BI   16

▶ APPLICATION CASE 1.1 Sabre Helps Its Clients through Dashboards and Analytics   18

A Multimedia Exercise in Business Intelligence   19

Transaction Processing versus Analytic Processing   19

Appropriate Planning and Alignment with the Business Strategy   20

Real-Time, On-Demand BI Is Attainable   21

Developing or Acquiring BI Systems   21

Justification and Cost–Benefit Analysis   22

Security and Protection of Privacy   22

Integration of Systems and Applications   22

1.5 Analytics Overview   22

Descriptive Analytics   24

▶ APPLICATION CASE 1.2 Silvaris Increases Business with Visual Analysis and Real-Time Reporting Capabilities   24

▶ APPLICATION CASE 1.3 Siemens Reduces Cost with the Use of Data Visualization   25

Predictive Analytics   25

▶ APPLICATION CASE 1.4 Analyzing Athletic Injuries   26

Prescriptive Analytics   26

Analytics Applied to Different Domains   27

▶ APPLICATION CASE 1.5 A Specialty Steel Bar Company Uses Analytics to Determine Available-to-Promise Dates   27

Analytics or Data Science?   28

1.6 Analytics Examples in Selected Domains 29

Analytics Applications in Healthcare—Humana Examples 29

Analytics in the Retail Value Chain 33

1.7 A Brief Introduction to Big Data Analytics 35

What Is Big Data? 35

    ▶ **APPLICATION CASE 1.6 CenterPoint Energy Uses Real-Time Big Data Analytics to Improve Customer Service 37**

1.8 An Overview of the Analytics Ecosystem 37

Data Generation Infrastructure Providers 39

Data Management Infrastructure Providers 39

Data Warehouse Providers 40

Middleware Providers 40

Data Service Providers 40

Analytics-Focused Software Developers 41

Application Developers: Industry Specific or General 42

Analytics Industry Analysts and Influencers 43

Academic Institutions and Certification Agencies 44

Regulators and Policy Makers 45

Analytics User Organizations 45

1.9 Plan of the Book 46

1.10 Resources, Links, and the Teradata University Network Connection 47

Resources and Links 47

Vendors, Products, and Demos 48

Periodicals 48

The Teradata University Network Connection 48

The Book's Web Site 48

    Chapter Highlights 49

    Key Terms 49

    Questions for Discussion 49

    Exercises 50

    References 51

Chapter 2	**Descriptive Analytics I: Nature of Data, Statistical Modeling, and Visualization 53**

2.1 OPENING VIGNETTE: SiriusXM Attracts and Engages a New Generation of Radio Consumers with Data-Driven Marketing 54

2.2 The Nature of Data 57

2.3 A Simple Taxonomy of Data 61

    ▶ **APPLICATION CASE 2.1 Medical Device Company Ensures Product Quality While Saving Money 63**

2.4 The Art and Science of Data Preprocessing 65

> ▶ **APPLICATION CASE 2.2 Improving Student Retention with Data-Driven Analytics** 68

2.5 Statistical Modeling for Business Analytics 74

Descriptive Statistics for Descriptive Analytics 75

Measures of Centrality Tendency (May Also Be Called Measures of Location or Centrality) 76

Arithmetic Mean 76

Median 77

Mode 77

Measures of Dispersion (May Also Be Called Measures of Spread Decentrality) 77

Range 78

Variance 78

Standard Deviation 78

Mean Absolute Deviation 78

Quartiles and Interquartile Range 78

Box-and-Whiskers Plot 79

The Shape of a Distribution 80

> ▶ **APPLICATION CASE 2.3 Town of Cary Uses Analytics to Analyze Data from Sensors, Assess Demand, and Detect Problems** 84

2.6 Regression Modeling for Inferential Statistics 86

How Do We Develop the Linear Regression Model? 87

How Do We Know If the Model Is Good Enough? 88

What Are the Most Important Assumptions in Linear Regression? 89

Logistic Regression 90

> ▶ **APPLICATION CASE 2.4 Predicting NCAA Bowl Game Outcomes** 91

Time Series Forecasting 96

2.7 Business Reporting 98

> ▶ **APPLICATION CASE 2.5 Flood of Paper Ends at FEMA** 100

2.8 Data Visualization 101

A Brief History of Data Visualization 101

> ▶ **APPLICATION CASE 2.6 Macfarlan Smith Improves Operational Performance Insight with Tableau Online** 103

2.9 Different Types of Charts and Graphs 106

Basic Charts and Graphs 106

Specialized Charts and Graphs 107

Which Chart or Graph Should You Use? 108

2.10 The Emergence of Visual Analytics 110

Visual Analytics 112

High-Powered Visual Analytics Environments 112

2.11 Information Dashboards   117

▶ **APPLICATION CASE 2.7 Dallas Cowboys Score Big with Tableau and Teknion**   118

Dashboard Design   119

▶ **APPLICATION CASE 2.8 Visual Analytics Helps Energy Supplier Make Better Connections**   119

What to Look for in a Dashboard   121

Best Practices in Dashboard Design   121

Benchmark Key Performance Indicators with Industry Standards   121

Wrap the Dashboard Metrics with Contextual Metadata   121

Validate the Dashboard Design by a Usability Specialist   122

Prioritize and Rank Alerts/Exceptions Streamed to the Dashboard   122

Enrich Dashboard with Business-User Comments   122

Present Information in Three Different Levels   122

Pick the Right Visual Construct Using Dashboard Design Principles   122

Provide for Guided Analytics   122

Chapter Highlights   *123*
Key Terms   *123*
Questions for Discussion   *124*
Exercises   *124*
References   *126*

Chapter 3   **Descriptive Analytics II: Business Intelligence and Data Warehousing**   **127**

3.1 OPENING VIGNETTE: Targeting Tax Fraud with Business Intelligence and Data Warehousing   128

3.2 Business Intelligence and Data Warehousing   130

What Is a Data Warehouse?   131

A Historical Perspective to Data Warehousing   132

Characteristics of Data Warehousing   133

Data Marts   134

Operational Data Stores   135

Enterprise Data Warehouses (EDW)   135

Metadata   135

▶ **APPLICATION CASE 3.1 A Better Data Plan: Well-Established TELCOs Leverage Data Warehousing and Analytics to Stay on Top in a Competitive Industry**   135

3.3 Data Warehousing Process   137

3.4 Data Warehousing Architectures   139

Alternative Data Warehousing Architectures   142

Which Architecture Is the Best?   144

3.5 Data Integration and the Extraction, Transformation, and Load (ETL)
Processes   145

Data Integration   146

▶ **APPLICATION CASE 3.2 BP Lubricants Achieves BIGS
Success**   146

Extraction, Transformation, and Load   148

3.6 Data Warehouse Development   150

▶ **APPLICATION CASE 3.3 Use of Teradata Analytics
for SAP Solutions Accelerates Big Data Delivery**   151

Data Warehouse Development Approaches   153

Additional Data Warehouse Development Considerations   156

Representation of Data in Data Warehouse   156

Analysis of Data in Data Warehouse   158

OLAP versus OLTP   158

OLAP Operations   159

3.7 Data Warehousing Implementation Issues   160

Massive Data Warehouses and Scalability   162

▶ **APPLICATION CASE 3.4 EDW Helps Connect State
Agencies in Michigan**   163

3.8 Data Warehouse Administration, Security Issues, and Future
Trends   164

The Future of Data Warehousing   165

3.9 Business Performance Management   170

Closed-Loop BPM Cycle   171

▶ **APPLICATION CASE 3.5 AARP Transforms Its BI
Infrastructure and Achieves a 347% ROI in Three
Years**   173

3.10 Performance Measurement   175

Key Performance Indicator (KPI)   175

Performance Measurement System   176

3.11 Balanced Scorecards   177

The Four Perspectives   177

The Meaning of Balance in BSC   179

3.12 Six Sigma as a Performance Measurement System   179

The DMAIC Performance Model   180

Balanced Scorecard versus Six Sigma   180

Effective Performance Measurement   181

▶ **APPLICATION CASE 3.6 Expedia.com's Customer
Satisfaction Scorecard**   182

Chapter Highlights   183
Key Terms   184
Questions for Discussion   184
Exercises   185
References   187

Chapter 4 **Predictive Analytics I: Data Mining Process, Methods, and Algorithms** 189

4.1 OPENING VIGNETTE: Miami-Dade Police Department Is Using Predictive Analytics to Foresee and Fight Crime 190

4.2 Data Mining Concepts and Applications 193

▶ **APPLICATION CASE 4.1 Visa Is Enhancing the Customer Experience While Reducing Fraud with Predictive Analytics and Data Mining** 194

Definitions, Characteristics, and Benefits 196

How Data Mining Works 197

▶ **APPLICATION CASE 4.2 Dell Is Staying Agile and Effective with Analytics in the 21st Century** 198

Data Mining versus Statistics 203

4.3 Data Mining Applications 203

▶ **APPLICATION CASE 4.3 Predictive Analytic and Data Mining Help Stop Terrorist Funding** 205

4.4 Data Mining Process 206

Step 1: Business Understanding 207

Step 2: Data Understanding 208

Step 3: Data Preparation 208

Step 4: Model Building 209

▶ **APPLICATION CASE 4.4 Data Mining Helps in Cancer Research** 209

Step 5: Testing and Evaluation 212

Step 6: Deployment 212

Other Data Mining Standardized Processes and Methodologies 212

4.5 Data Mining Methods 215

Classification 215

Estimating the True Accuracy of Classification Models 216

▶ **APPLICATION CASE 4.5 Influence Health Uses Advanced Predictive Analytics to Focus on the Factors That Really Influence People's Healthcare Decisions** 223

Cluster Analysis for Data Mining 225

Association Rule Mining 227

4.6 Data Mining Software Tools 231

▶ **APPLICATION CASE 4.6 Data Mining Goes to Hollywood: Predicting Financial Success of Movies** 233

4.7 Data Mining Privacy Issues, Myths, and Blunders 237

▶ **APPLICATION CASE 4.7 Predicting Customer Buying Patterns—The Target Story** 238

Data Mining Myths and Blunders 238

Chapter Highlights 241

Key Terms 242

Questions for Discussion 242

Exercises 243

References 245

Chapter 5   **Predictive Analytics II: Text, Web, and Social Media Analytics   247**

5.1 OPENING VIGNETTE: Machine versus Men on Jeopardy!: The Story of Watson   248

5.2 Text Analytics and Text Mining Overview   251
> ► **APPLICATION CASE 5.1 Insurance Group Strengthens Risk Management with Text Mining Solution   254**

5.3 Natural Language Processing (NLP)   255
> ► **APPLICATION CASE 5.2 AMC Networks Is Using Analytics to Capture New Viewers, Predict Ratings, and Add Value for Advertisers in a Multichannel World   257**

5.4 Text Mining Applications   261
Marketing Applications   261
Security Applications   261
> ► **APPLICATION CASE 5.3 Mining for Lies   262**

Biomedical Applications   264
Academic Applications   266
> ► **APPLICATION CASE 5.4 Bringing the Customer into the Quality Equation: Lenovo Uses Analytics to Rethink Its Redesign   266**

5.5 Text Mining Process   268
Task 1: Establish the Corpus   269
Task 2: Create the Term–Document Matrix   269
Task 3: Extract the Knowledge   271
> ► **APPLICATION CASE 5.5 Research Literature Survey with Text Mining   273**

5.6 Sentiment Analysis   276
> ► **APPLICATION CASE 5.6 Creating a Unique Digital Experience to Capture the Moments That Matter at Wimbledon   277**

Sentiment Analysis Applications   280
Sentiment Analysis Process   282
Methods for Polarity Identification   284
Using a Lexicon   284
Using a Collection of Training Documents   285
Identifying Semantic Orientation of Sentences and Phrases   286
Identifying Semantic Orientation of Documents   286

5.7 Web Mining Overview   287
Web Content and Web Structure Mining   289

5.8 Search Engines   291
Anatomy of a Search Engine   292
1. Development Cycle   292

2. Response Cycle   293

Search Engine Optimization   294

Methods for Search Engine Optimization   295

▶ **APPLICATION CASE 5.7 Understanding Why Customers Abandon Shopping Carts Results in a $10 Million Sales Increase**   297

5.9 Web Usage Mining (Web Analytics)   298

Web Analytics Technologies   299

Web Analytics Metrics   300

Web Site Usability   300

Traffic Sources   301

Visitor Profiles   302

Conversion Statistics   302

5.10 Social Analytics   304

Social Network Analysis   304

Social Network Analysis Metrics   305

▶ **APPLICATION CASE 5.8 Tito's Vodka Establishes Brand Loyalty with an Authentic Social Strategy**   305

Connections   308

Distributions   308

Segmentation   309

Social Media Analytics   309

How Do People Use Social Media?   310

Measuring the Social Media Impact   311

Best Practices in Social Media Analytics   311

Chapter Highlights   313
Key Terms   314
Questions for Discussion   315
Exercises   315
References   316

Chapter 6   **Prescriptive Analytics: Optimization and Simulation**   **319**

6.1 OPENING VIGNETTE: School District of Philadelphia Uses Prescriptive Analytics to Find Optimal Solution for Awarding Bus Route Contracts   320

6.2 Model-Based Decision Making   322

Prescriptive Analytics Model Examples   322

▶ **APPLICATION CASE 6.1 Optimal Transport for ExxonMobil Downstream through a DSS**   323

Identification of the Problem and Environmental Analysis 324

Model Categories 324

▶ **APPLICATION CASE 6.2 Ingram Micro Uses Business Intelligence Applications to Make Pricing Decisions** 325

6.3 Structure of Mathematical Models for Decision Support 328

The Components of Decision Support Mathematical Models 328

The Structure of Mathematical Models 329

6.4 Certainty, Uncertainty, and Risk 330

Decision Making under Certainty 330

Decision Making under Uncertainty 331

Decision Making under Risk (Risk Analysis) 331

6.5 Decision Modeling with Spreadsheets 331

▶ **APPLICATION CASE 6.3 American Airlines Uses Should-Cost Modeling to Assess the Uncertainty of Bids for Shipment Routes** 332

▶ **APPLICATION CASE 6.4 Pennsylvania Adoption Exchange Uses Spreadsheet Model to Better Match Children with Families** 333

▶ **APPLICATION CASE 6.5 Metro Meals on Wheels Treasure Valley Uses Excel to Find Optimal Delivery Routes** 334

6.6 Mathematical Programming Optimization 336

▶ **APPLICATION CASE 6.6 Mixed-Integer Programming Model Helps the University of Tennessee Medical Center with Scheduling Physicians** 337

Linear Programming Model 338

Modeling in LP: An Example 339

Implementation 344

6.7 Multiple Goals, Sensitivity Analysis, What-If Analysis, and Goal Seeking 346

Multiple Goals 346

Sensitivity Analysis 347

What-If Analysis 348

Goal Seeking 348

6.8 Decision Analysis with Decision Tables and Decision Trees 349

Decision Tables 350

Decision Trees 351

6.9 Introduction to Simulation 352

Major Characteristics of Simulation 352

▶ **APPLICATION CASE 6.7 Simulating Effects of Hepatitis B Interventions** 353

Advantages of Simulation 354

Disadvantages of Simulation 355

The Methodology of Simulation 355

Simulation Types   356

Monte Carlo Simulation   357

Discrete Event Simulation   358

▶ **APPLICATION CASE 6.8 Cosan Improves Its Renewable Energy Supply Chain Using Simulation**   358

6.10 Visual Interactive Simulation   359

Conventional Simulation Inadequacies   359

Visual Interactive Simulation   359

Visual Interactive Models and DSS   360

Simulation Software   360

▶ **APPLICATION CASE 6.9 Improving Job-Shop Scheduling Decisions through RFID: A Simulation-Based Assessment**   361

Chapter Highlights   364
Key Terms   364
Questions for Discussion   365
Exercises   365
References   367

Chapter 7 **Big Data Concepts and Tools**   **369**

7.1 OPENING VIGNETTE: Analyzing Customer Churn in a Telecom Company Using Big Data Methods   370

7.2 Definition of Big Data   373

The "V"s That Define Big Data   374

▶ **APPLICATION CASE 7.1 Alternative Data for Market Analysis or Forecasts**   377

7.3 Fundamentals of Big Data Analytics   378

Business Problems Addressed by Big Data Analytics   381

▶ **APPLICATION CASE 7.2 Top Five Investment Bank Achieves Single Source of the Truth**   382

7.4 Big Data Technologies   383

MapReduce   383

Why Use MapReduce?   385

Hadoop   385

How Does Hadoop Work?   385

Hadoop Technical Components   386

Hadoop: The Pros and Cons   387

NoSQL   389

▶ **APPLICATION CASE 7.3 eBay's Big Data Solution**   390

▶ **APPLICATION CASE 7.4 Understanding Quality and Reliability of Healthcare Support Information on Twitter**   392

7.5 Big Data and Data Warehousing   393

Use Cases for Hadoop   393

Use Cases for Data Warehousing   394

The Gray Areas (Any One of the Two Would Do the Job)   395

Coexistence of Hadoop and Data Warehouse   396

7.6 Big Data Vendors and Platforms   397

IBM InfoSphere BigInsights   398

▶ **APPLICATION CASE 7.5 Using Social Media for Nowcasting the Flu Activity   400**

Teradata Aster   401

▶ **APPLICATION CASE 7.6 Analyzing Disease Patterns from an Electronic Medical Records Data Warehouse   402**

7.7 Big Data and Stream Analytics   406

Stream Analytics versus Perpetual Analytics   408

Critical Event Processing   408

Data Stream Mining   408

7.8 Applications of Stream Analytics   409

e-Commerce   409

Telecommunications   409

▶ **APPLICATION CASE 7.7 Salesforce Is Using Streaming Data to Enhance Customer Value   410**

Law Enforcement and Cybersecurity   411

Power Industry   411

Financial Services   411

Health Sciences   411

Government   412

Chapter Highlights   412
Key Terms   413
Questions for Discussion   413
Exercises   413
References   414

Chapter 8 **Future Trends, Privacy and Managerial Considerations in Analytics   417**

8.1 OPENING VIGNETTE: Analysis of Sensor Data Helps Siemens Avoid Train Failures   418

8.2 Internet of Things   419

▶ **APPLICATION CASE 8.1 SilverHook Powerboats Uses Real-Time Data Analysis to Inform Racers and Fans   420**

▶ **APPLICATION CASE 8.2 Rockwell Automation Monitors Expensive Oil and Gas Exploration Assets   421**

IoT Technology Infrastructure   422

RFID Sensors 422

Fog Computing 425

IoT Platforms 426

▶ **APPLICATION CASE 8.3 Pitney Bowes Collaborates with General Electric IoT Platform to Optimize Production** 426

IoT Start-Up Ecosystem 427

Managerial Considerations in the Internet of Things 428

8.3 Cloud Computing and Business Analytics 429

Data as a Service (DaaS) 431

Software as a Service (SaaS) 432

Platform as a Service (PaaS) 432

Infrastructure as a Service (IaaS) 432

Essential Technologies for Cloud Computing 433

Cloud Deployment Models 433

Major Cloud Platform Providers in Analytics 434

Analytics as a Service (AaaS) 435

Representative Analytics as a Service Offerings 435

Illustrative Analytics Applications Employing the Cloud Infrastructure 436

▶ **MD Anderson Cancer Center Utilizes Cognitive Computing Capabilities of IBM Watson to Give Better Treatment to Cancer Patients** 436

▶ **Public School Education in Tacoma, Washington, Uses Microsoft Azure Machine Learning to Predict School Dropouts** 437

▶ **Dartmouth-Hitchcock Medical Center Provides Personalized Proactive Healthcare Using Microsoft Cortana Analytics Suite** 438

▶ **Mankind Pharma Uses IBM Cloud Infrastructure to Reduce Application Implementation Time by 98%** 438

▶ **Gulf Air Uses Big Data to Get Deeper Customer Insight** 439

▶ **Chime Enhances Customer Experience Using Snowflake** 440

8.4 Location-Based Analytics for Organizations 441

Geospatial Analytics 441

▶ **APPLICATION CASE 8.4 Great Clips Employs Spatial Analytics to Shave Time in Location Decisions** 443

▶ **APPLICATION CASE 8.5 Starbucks Exploits GIS and Analytics to Grow Worldwide** 444

Real-Time Location Intelligence 445

▶ **APPLICATION CASE 8.6 Quiznos Targets Customers for Its Sandwiches** 446

Analytics Applications for Consumers 446

8.5 Issues of Legality, Privacy, and Ethics   448

   Legal Issues   448

   Privacy   449

   Collecting Information about Individuals   449

   Mobile User Privacy   450

   Homeland Security and Individual Privacy   450

   Recent Technology Issues in Privacy and Analytics   451

   Who Owns Our Private Data?   452

   Ethics in Decision Making and Support   452

8.6 Impacts of Analytics in Organizations: An Overview   453

   New Organizational Units   454

   Redesign of an Organization through the Use of Analytics   455

   Analytics Impact on Managers' Activities, Performance, and Job
     Satisfaction   455

   Industrial Restructuring   456

   Automation's Impact on Jobs   457

   Unintended Effects of Analytics   458

8.7 Data Scientist as a Profession   459

   Where Do Data Scientists Come From?   459

      Chapter Highlights   *462*

      Key Terms   *463*

      Questions for Discussion   *463*

      Exercises   *463*

      References   *464*

Glossary   *467*

Index   *475*

Preface

Analytics has become the technology driver of this decade. Companies such as IBM, SAP, IBM, SAS, Teradata, SAP, Oracle, Microsoft, Dell and others are creating new organizational units focused on analytics that help businesses become more effective and efficient in their operations. Decision makers are using more computerized tools to support their work. Even consumers are using analytics tools, either directly or indirectly, to make decisions on routine activities such as shopping, health/healthcare, travel, and entertainment. The field of business intelligence and business analytics (BI & BA) has evolved rapidly to become more focused on innovative applications for extracting knowledge and insight from data streams that were not even captured some time back, much less analyzed in any significant way. New applications turn up daily in healthcare, sports, travel, entertainment, supply-chain management, utilities, and virtually every industry imaginable. The term *analytics* has become mainstream. Indeed, it has already evolved into other terms such as data science, and the latest incarnation is deep learning and Internet of Things.

This edition of the text provides a managerial perspective to business analytics continuum beginning with descriptive analytics (e.g., the nature of data, statistical modeling, data visualization, and business intelligence), moving on to predictive analytics (e.g., data mining, text/web mining, social media mining), and then to prescriptive analytics (e.g., optimization and simulation), and finally finishing with Big Data, and future trends, privacy, and managerial considerations. The book is supported by a Web site (pearsonhighered.com/sharda) and also by an independent site at dssbibook.com. We will also provide links to software tutorials through a special section of the Web sites.

The purpose of this book is to introduce the reader to these technologies that are generally called *business analytics* or *data science* but have been known by other names. This book presents the fundamentals of the techniques and the manner in which these systems are constructed and used. We follow an EEE approach to introducing these topics: **Exposure**, **Experience**, and **Exploration**. The book primarily provides **exposure** to various analytics techniques and their applications. The idea is that a student will be inspired to learn from how other organizations have employed analytics to make decisions or to gain a competitive edge. We believe that such **exposure** to what is being done with analytics and how it can be achieved is the key component of learning about analytics. In describing the techniques, we also introduce specific software tools that can be used for developing such applications. The book is not limited to any one software tool, so the students can **experience** these techniques using any number of available software tools. Specific suggestions are given in each chapter, but the student and the professor are able to use this book with many different software tools. Our book's companion Web site will include specific software guides, but students can gain **experience** with these techniques in many different ways. Finally, we hope that this **exposure** and **experience** enable and motivate readers to **explore** the potential of these techniques in their own domain. To facilitate such **exploration**, we include exercises that direct them to Teradata University Network and other sites as well that include team-oriented exercises where appropriate. We will also highlight new and innovative applications that we learn about on the book's Web site.

Most of the specific improvements made in this fourth edition concentrate on four areas: reorganization, new chapters, content update, and a sharper focus. Despite the many changes, we have preserved the comprehensiveness and user friendliness that have made the text a market leader. Finally, we present accurate and updated material that is not available in any other text. We next describe the changes in the fourth edition.

What's New in the Fourth Edition?

With the goal of improving the text, this edition marks a major reorganization of the text to reflect the focus on business analytics. This edition is now organized around three major types of business analytics (i.e., descriptive, predictive, and prescriptive). The new edition has many timely additions, and the dated content has been deleted. The following major specific changes have been made.

- **New organization.** The book recognizes three types of analytics: descriptive, predictive, and prescriptive, a classification promoted by INFORMS. Chapter 1 introduces BI and analytics with an application focus in many industries. This chapter also includes an overview of the analytics ecosystem to help the user explore all the different ways one can participate and grow in the analytics environment. It is followed by an overview of statistics, importance of data, and descriptive analytics/ visualization in Chapter 2. Chapter 3 covers data warehousing and data foundations including updated content, specifically data lakes. Chapter 4 covers predictive analytics. Chapter 5 extends the application of analytics to text, Web, and social media. Chapter 6 covers prescriptive analytics, specifically linear programming and simulation. It is totally new content for this book. Chapter 7 introduces Big Data tools and platforms. The book concludes with Chapter 8, emerging trends and topics in business analytics including location analytics, Internet of Things, cloud-based analytics, and privacy/ethical considerations in analytics. The discussion of an analytics ecosystem recognizes prescriptive analytics as well.

- **New chapters.** The following chapters have been added:

  Chapter 2. *Descriptive Analytics I: Nature of Data, Statistical Modeling, and Visualization*   This chapter aims to set the stage with a thorough understanding of the nature of data, which is the main ingredient for any analytics study. Next, statistical modeling is introduced as part of the descriptive analytics. Data visualization has become a popular part of any business reporting and/or descriptive analytics project; therefore, it is explained in detail in this chapter. The chapter is enhanced with several real-world cases and examples (75% new material).

  Chapter 6. *Prescriptive Analytics: Optimization and Simulation*   This chapter introduces prescriptive analytics material to this book. The chapter focuses on optimization modeling in Excel using linear programming techniques. It also introduces the concept of simulation. The chapter is an updated version of material from two chapters in our DSS book, 10th edition. For this book it is an entirely new chapter (99% new material).

  Chapter 8. *Future Trends, Privacy and Managerial Considerations in Analytics*   This chapter examines several new phenomena that are already changing or are likely to change analytics. It includes coverage of geospatial analytics, Internet of Things, and a significant update of the material on cloud-based analytics. It also updates some coverage from the last edition on ethical and privacy considerations (70% new material).

- **Revised Chapters.**   All the other chapters have been revised and updated as well. Here is a summary of the changes in these other chapters:

  Chapter 1. *An Overview of Business Intelligence, Analytics, and Data Science*   This chapter has been rewritten and significantly expanded. It opens with a new vignette covering multiple applications of analytics in sports. It introduces the three types of analytics as proposed by INFORMS: descriptive, predictive, and prescriptive analytics. A noted earlier, this classification is used in guiding the complete reorganization of the book itself (earlier content but with a new figure). Then it includes several new examples of analytics in healthcare and in the retail industry. Finally, it concludes with significantly expanded and updated coverage of the analytics ecosystem to give the students a sense of the vastness of the analytics and data science industry (about 60% new material).

Chapter 3. *Descriptive Analytics II: Business Intelligence and Data Warehousing* This is an old chapter with some new subsections (e.g., data lakes) and new cases (about 30% new material).

Chapter 4. *Predictive Analytics I: Data Mining Process, Methods, and Algorithms* This is an old chapter with some new content organization/ flow and some new cases (about 20% new material).

Chapter 5. *Predictive Analytics II: Text, Web, and Social Media Analytics* This is an old chapter with some new content organization/flow and some new cases (about 25% new material).

Chapter 7. *Big Data Concepts and Analysis* This was Chapter 6 in the last edition. It has been updated with a new opening vignette and cases, coverage of Teradata Aster, and new material on alternative data (about 25% new material).

- **Revamped author team.** Building on the excellent content that has been prepared by the authors of the previous editions (Turban, Sharda, Delen, and King), this edition was revised primarily by Ramesh Sharda and Dursun Delen. Both Ramesh and Dursun have worked extensively in analytics and have industry as well as research experience.

- **Color print!** We are truly excited to have this book appear in color. Even the figures from previous editions have been redrawn to take advantage of color. Use of color enhances many visualization examples and also the other material.

- **A live, updated Web site.** Adopters of the textbook will have access to a Web site that will include links to news stories, software, tutorials, and even YouTube videos related to topics covered in the book. This site will be accessible at dssbibook.com.

- **Revised and updated content.** Almost all the chapters have new opening vignettes that are based on recent stories and events. In addition, application cases throughout the book have been updated to include recent examples of applications of a specific technique/model. New Web site links have been added throughout the book. We also deleted many older product links and references. Finally, most chapters have new exercises, Internet assignments, and discussion questions throughout.

- **Links to Teradata University Network (TUN).** Most chapters include new links to TUN (teradatauniversitynetwork.com).

- **Book title.** As is already evident, the book's title and focus have changed substantially.

- **Software support.** The TUN Web site provides software support at no charge. It also provides links to free data mining and other software. In addition, the site provides exercises in the use of such software.

The Supplement Package: www.pearsonhighered.com/sharda

A comprehensive and flexible technology-support package is available to enhance the teaching and learning experience. The following instructor and student supplements are available on the book's Web site, pearsonhighered.com/sharda:

- **Instructor's Manual.** The Instructor's Manual includes learning objectives for the entire course and for each chapter, answers to the questions and exercises at the end of each chapter, and teaching suggestions (including instructions for projects). The Instructor's Manual is available on the secure faculty section of pearsonhighered. com/sharda.

- *Test Item File and TestGen Software.* The Test Item File is a comprehensive collection of true/false, multiple-choice, fill-in-the-blank, and essay questions. The questions are rated by difficulty level, and the answers are referenced by book page number. The Test Item File is available in Microsoft Word and in TestGen. Pearson Education's test-generating software is available from www.pearsonhighered.com/ irc. The software is PC/MAC compatible and preloaded with all the Test Item File questions. You can manually or randomly view test questions and drag-and-drop to create a test. You can add or modify test-bank questions as needed. Our TestGens are converted for use in BlackBoard, WebCT, Moodle, D2L, and Angel. These conversions can be found on pearsonhighered.com/sharda. The TestGen is also available in Respondus and can be found on www.respondus.com.

- *PowerPoint slides.* PowerPoint slides are available that illuminate and build on key concepts in the text. Faculty can download the PowerPoint slides from pearson-highered.com/sharda.

Acknowledgments

Many individuals have provided suggestions and criticisms since the publication of the first edition of this book. Dozens of students participated in class testing of various chapters, software, and problems and assisted in collecting material. It is not possible to name everyone who participated in this project, but our thanks go to all of them. Certain individuals made significant contributions, and they deserve special recognition.

First, we appreciate the efforts of those individuals who provided formal reviews of the first through third editions (school affiliations as of the date of review):

Ann Aksut, Central Piedmont Community College
Bay Arinze, Drexel University
Andy Borchers, Lipscomb University
Ranjit Bose, University of New Mexico
Marty Crossland, MidAmerica Nazarene University
Kurt Engemann, Iona College
Badie Farah, Eastern Michigan University
Gary Farrar, Columbia College
Jerry Fjermestad, New Jersey Institute of Technology
Christie M. Fuller, Louisiana Tech University
Martin Grossman, Bridgewater State College
Jahangir Karimi, University of Colorado, Denver
Huei Lee, Eastern Michigan University
Natalie Nazarenko, SUNY Fredonia
Joo Eng Lee-Partridge, Central Connecticut State University
Gregory Rose, Washington State University, Vancouver
Khawaja Saeed, Wichita State University
Kala Chand Seal, Loyola Marymount University
Joshua S. White, PhD, State University of New York Polytechnic Institute
Roger Wilson, Fairmont State University
Vincent Yu, Missouri University of Science and Technology
Fan Zhao, Florida Gulf Coast University

We also appreciate the efforts of those individuals who provided formal reviews of this text and our other DSS book—*Business Intelligence and Analytics: Systems for Decision Support*, 10th Edition, Pearson Education, 2013.

Second, several individuals contributed material to the text or the supporting material. Susan Baskin of Teradata and Dr. David Schrader provided special help in identifying new TUN and Teradata content for the book and arranging permissions for the same. Dr. Dave Schrader contributed the opening vignette for the book. This vignette also included material developed by Dr. Ashish Gupta of Auburn University and Gary Wilkerson of the University of Tennessee–Chattanooga. It will provide a great introduction to analytics. We also thank INFORMS for their permission to highlight content from *Interfaces*. We also recognize the following individuals for their assistance in developing this edition of the book: Pankush Kalgotra, Prasoon Mathur, Rupesh Agarwal, Shubham Singh, Nan Liang, Jacob Pearson, Kinsey Clemmer, and Evan Murlette (all of Oklahoma State University). Their help for this edition is gratefully acknowledged. Teradata Aster team, especially Mark Ott, provided the material for the opening vignette for Chapter 7. Aster material in Chapter 7 is adapted from other training guides developed by John Thuma and Greg Bethardy. Dr. Brian LeClaire, CIO of Humana Corporation led with contributions of several real-life healthcare case studies developed by his team at Humana. Abhishek Rathi of vCreaTek contributed his vision of analytics in the retail industry. Dr. Rick Wilson's excellent exercises for teaching and practicing linear programming skills in Excel are also gratefully acknowledged. Matt Turck agreed to let us adapt his IoT ecosystem material. Ramesh also recognizes the copyediting assistance provided by his daughter, Ruchy Sharda Sen. In addition, the following former PhD students and research colleagues of ours have provided content or advice and support for the book in many direct and indirect ways:

Asil Oztekin, Universality of Massachusetts-Lowell
Enes Eryarsoy, Sehir University
Hamed Majidi Zolbanin, Ball State University
Amir Hassan Zadeh, Wright State University
Supavich (Fone) Pengnate, North Dakota State University
Christie Fuller, Boise State University
Daniel Asamoah, Wright State University
Selim Zaim, Istanbul Technical University
Nihat Kasap, Sabanci University

Third, for the previous edition, we acknowledge the contributions of Dave King (JDA Software Group, Inc.). Other major contributors to the previous edition include J. Aronson (University of Georgia), who was our coauthor, contributing to the data warehousing chapter; Mike Goul (Arizona State University), whose contributions were included in Chapter 1; and T. P. Liang (National Sun Yet-Sen University, Taiwan), who contributed material on neural networks in the previous editions. Judy Lang collaborated with all of us, provided editing, and guided us during the entire project in the first edition.

Fourth, several vendors cooperated by providing case studies and/or demonstration software for the previous editions: Acxiom (Little Rock, Arkansas), California Scientific Software (Nevada City, California), Cary Harwin of Catalyst Development (Yucca Valley, California), IBM (San Carlos, California), DS Group, Inc. (Greenwich, Connecticut), Gregory Piatetsky-Shapiro of KDnuggets.com, Gary Lynn of NeuroDimension Inc. (Gainesville, Florida), Palisade Software (Newfield, New York), Promised Land Technologies (New Haven, Connecticut), Salford Systems (La Jolla, California), Sense Networks (New York, New York), Gary Miner of StatSoft, Inc. (Tulsa, Oklahoma), Ward Systems Group, Inc. (Frederick, Maryland), Idea Fisher Systems, Inc. (Irving, California), and Wordtech Systems (Orinda, California).

Fifth, special thanks to the Teradata University Network and especially to Susan Baskin, Program Director; Hugh Watson, who started TUN; and Michael Goul, Barb Wixom, and Mary Gros for their encouragement to tie this book with TUN and for providing useful material for the book.

Finally, the Pearson team is to be commended: Samantha Lewis, who has worked with us on this revision and orchestrated the color rendition of the book; and the production team, Ann Pulido, and Revathi Viswanathan and staff at Cenveo, who transformed the manuscript into a book.

We would like to thank all these individuals and corporations. Without their help, the creation of this book would not have been possible.

R.S.

D.D.

E.T.

Note that Web site URLs are dynamic. As this book went to press, we verified that all the cited Web sites were active and valid. Web sites to which we refer in the text sometimes change or are discontinued because companies change names, are bought or sold, merge, or fail. Sometimes Web sites are down for maintenance, repair, or redesign. Most organizations have dropped the initial "www" designation for their sites, but some still use it. If you have a problem connecting to a Web site that we mention, please be patient and simply run a Web search to try to identify the new site. Most times, the new site can be found quickly. We apologize in advance for this inconvenience.

About the Authors

Ramesh Sharda (MBA, PhD, University of Wisconsin–Madison) is the Vice Dean for Research and Graduate Programs, Watson/ConocoPhillips Chair, and a Regents Professor of Management Science and Information Systems in the Spears School of Business at Oklahoma State University (OSU). He cofounded and directed OSU's PhD in Business for the Executives Program. About 200 papers describing his research have been published in major journals, including *Operations Research, Management Science, Information Systems Research, Decision Support Systems,* and the *Journal of MIS.* He cofounded the AIS SIG on Decision Support Systems and Knowledge Management (SIGDSA). Dr. Sharda serves on several editorial boards, including those of *Decision Sciences Journal, Decision Support Systems,* and *ACM Data Base.* He has authored and edited several textbooks and research books and serves as the coeditor of several Springer book series (Integrated Series in Information Systems, Operations Research/ Computer Science Interfaces, and Annals of Information Systems) with Springer. He is also currently serving as the Executive Director of the Teradata University Network. His current research interests are in decision support systems, business analytics, and technologies for managing information overload.

Dursun Delen (PhD, Oklahoma State University) is the Spears Endowed Chair in Business Administration, Patterson Foundation Endowed Chair in Business Analytics, Director of Research for the Center for Health Systems Innovation, and Regents Professor of Management Science and Information Systems in the Spears School of Business at Oklahoma State University (OSU). Prior to his academic career, he worked for a privately owned research and consultancy company, Knowledge Based Systems Inc., in College Station, Texas, as a research scientist for 5 years, during which he led a number of decision support and other information systems–related research projects funded by several federal agencies including the Department of Defense (DoD), National Aeronautics and Space Administration (NASA), National Institute for Standards and Technology (NIST), Ballistic Missile Defense Organization (BMDO), and Department of Energy (DOE). Dr. Delen has published more than 100 peer-reviewed articles, some of which have appeared in major journals like *Decision Sciences, Decision Support Systems, Communications of the ACM, Computers and Operations Research, Computers in Industry, Journal of Production Operations Management, Artificial Intelligence in Medicine, International Journal of Medical Informatics, Expert Systems with Applications,* and *IEEE Wireless Communications.* He recently authored/coauthored seven textbooks in the broad areas of business analytics, data mining, text mining, business intelligence, and decision support systems. He is often invited to national and international conferences for keynote addresses on topics related to data/text mining, business analytics, decision support systems, business intelligence, and knowledge management. He served as the General Cochair for the Fourth International Conference on Network Computing and Advanced Information Management (September 2–4, 2008, in Seoul, South Korea) and regularly chairs, tracks, and minitracks at various information systems and analytics conferences. He is currently serving as Editor-in-Chief, Senior Editor, Associate Editor, or Editorial Board Member for more than a dozen academic journals. His research and teaching interests are in data and text mining, business analytics, decision support systems, knowledge management, business intelligence, and enterprise modeling.

Efraim Turban (MBA, PhD., University of California, Berkeley) is a Visiting Scholar at the Pacific Institute for Information System Management, University of Hawaii. Prior to this, he was on the staff of several universities, including City University of Hong Kong; Lehigh University; Florida International University; California State University, Long Beach; Eastern Illinois University; and the University of Southern California. Dr. Turban is the author of more than 100 refereed papers published in leading journals, such as *Management Science, MIS Quarterly,* and *Decision Support Systems.* He is also the author of 20 books, including *Electronic Commerce: A Managerial Perspective* and *Information Technology for Management.* He is also a consultant to major corporations worldwide. Dr. Turban's current areas of interest are Web-based decision support systems, social commerce, and collaborative decision making.

BUSINESS INTELLIGENCE, ANALYTICS, AND DATA SCIENCE

A MANAGERIAL PERSPECTIVE

This book deals with a collection of computer technologies that support managerial work—essentially, decision making. These technologies have had a profound impact on corporate strategy, performance, and competitiveness. Collectively, these technologies are called *business intelligence, business analytics,* and *data science*. Although the evolution of the terms is discussed, these names are also used interchangeably. This book tells stories of how smart people are employing these techniques to improve performance, service, and relationships in business, government, and non-profit worlds.

An Overview of Business Intelligence, Analytics, and Data Science

LEARNING OBJECTIVES

- Understand the need for computer-ized support of managerial decision making
- Recognize the evolution of such computerized support to the current state—analytics/data science
- Describe the business intelligence (BI) methodology and concepts
- Understand the different types of ana-lytics and see selected applications
- Understand the analytics ecosystem to identify various key players and career opportunities

The business environment (climate) is constantly changing, and it is becoming more and more complex. Organizations, both private and public, are under pres-sures that force them to respond quickly to changing conditions and to be inno-vative in the way they operate. Such activities require organizations to be agile and to make frequent and quick strategic, tactical, and operational decisions, some of which are very complex. Making such decisions may require considerable amounts of relevant data, information, and knowledge. Processing these, in the framework of the needed decisions, must be done quickly, frequently in real time, and usually requires some computerized support.

This book is about using business analytics as computerized support for managerial decision making. It concentrates on the theoretical and conceptual foundations of deci-sion support, as well as on the commercial tools and techniques that are available. This book presents the fundamentals of the techniques and the manner in which these sys-tems are constructed and used. We follow an EEE approach to introducing these topics: **Exposure**, **Experience**, and **Exploration**. The book primarily provides exposure to var-ious analytics techniques and their applications. The idea is that a student will be inspired to learn from how other organizations have employed analytics to make decisions or to gain a competitive edge. We believe that such **exposure** to what is being done with analytics and how it can be achieved is the key component of learning about analytics. In describing the techniques, we also give examples of specific software tools that can be used for developing such applications. The book is not limited to any one software tool, so students can **experience** these techniques using any number of available software tools. We hope that this exposure and experience enable and motivate readers to explore the potential of these techniques in their own domain. To facilitate such **exploration**, we include exercises that direct the reader to Teradata University Network (TUN) and other sites that include team-oriented exercises where appropriate.

This introductory chapter provides an introduction to analytics as well as an overview of the book. The chapter has the following sections:

1.1   Opening Vignette: Sports Analytics—An Exciting Frontier for Learning and Understanding Applications of Analytics   4

1.2   Changing Business Environments and Evolving Needs for Decision Support and Analytics   11

1.3   Evolution of Computerized Decision Support to Analytics/Data Science   13

1.4   A Framework for Business Intelligence   15

1.5   Analytics Overview   22

1.6   Analytics Examples in Selected Domains   29

1.7   A Brief Introduction to Big Data Analytics   35

1.8   An Overview of the Analytics Ecosystem   37

1.9   Plan of the Book   46

1.10 Resources, Links, and the Teradata University Network Connection   47

1.1   OPENING VIGNETTE: Sports Analytics—An Exciting Frontier for Learning and Understanding Applications of Analytics

The application of analytics to business problems is a key skill, one that you will learn in this book. Many of these techniques are now being applied to improve decision making in all aspects of sports, a very hot area called sports analytics. Sports analytics is the art and science of gathering data about athletes and teams to create insights that improve sports decisions, such as deciding which players to recruit, how much to pay them, who to play, how to train them, how to keep them healthy, and when they should be traded or retired. For teams, it involves business decisions such as ticket pricing, as well as roster decisions, analysis of each competitor's strengths and weaknesses, and many game-day decisions.

Indeed, sports analytics is becoming a specialty within analytics. It is an important area because sports is a big business, generating about $145B in revenues each year, plus an additional $100B in legal and $300B in illegal gambling, according to Price Waterhouse.[1] In 2014, only $125M was spent on analytics (less than 0.1% of revenues). This is expected to grow at a healthy rate to $4.7B by 2021.[2]

---

[1] "Changing the Game: Outlook for the Global Sports Market to 2015," Price Waterhouse Coopers Report, appears at https://www.pwc.com/gx/en/hospitality-leisure/pdf/changing-the-game-outlook-for-the-global-sports-market-to-2015.pdf. Betting data from https://www.capcredit.com/how-much-americansspend-on-sports-each-year/.

[2] "Sports Analytics Market Worth $4.7B by 2021," Wintergreen Research Press Release, covered by PR Newswire at http://www.prnewswire.com/news-releases/sports-analytics-market-worth-47-billion-by-2021-509869871.html, June 25, 2015.

The use of analytics for sports was popularized by the *Moneyball* book by Michael Lewis in 2003 and the movie starring Brad Pitt in 2011. It showcased Oakland A's general manager Billy Beane and his use of data and analytics to turn a losing team into a winner. In particular, he hired an analyst who used analytics to draft players able to get on base as opposed to players who excelled at traditional measures like runs batted in or stolen bases. These insights allowed them to draft prospects overlooked by other teams at reasonable starting salaries. It worked—they made it to the playoffs in 2002 and 2003.

Now analytics are being used in all parts of sports. The analytics can be divided between the front office and back office. A good description with 30 examples appears in Tom Davenport's survey article.[3] Front-office business analytics include analyzing fan behavior ranging from predictive models for season ticket renewals and regular ticket sales, to scoring tweets by fans regarding the team, athletes, coaches, and owners. This is very similar to traditional customer relationship management (CRM). Financial analysis is also a key area, where salary caps (for pros) or scholarship limits (colleges) are part of the equation.

Back-office uses include analysis of both individual athletes as well as team play. For individual players, there is a focus on recruitment models and scouting analytics, analytics for strength and fitness as well as development, and PMs for avoiding overtraining and injuries. Concussion research is a hot field. Team analytics include strategies and tactics, competitive assessments, and optimal roster choices under various on-field or on-court situations.

The following representative examples illustrate how three sports organizations use data and analytics to improve sports operations, in the same way analytics have improved traditional industry decision making.

Example 1: The Business Office

Dave Ward works as a business analyst for a major pro baseball team, focusing on revenue. He analyzes ticket sales, both from season ticket holders as well as single-ticket buyers. Sample questions in his area of responsibility include why season ticket holders renew (or do not renew) their tickets, as well as what factors drive last-minute individual seat ticket purchases. Another question is how to price the tickets.

Some of the analytical techniques Dave uses include simple statistics on fan behavior like overall attendance and answers to survey questions about likelihood to purchase again. However, what fans say versus what they do can be different. Dave runs a survey of fans by ticket seat location ("tier") and asks about their likelihood of renewing their season tickets. But when he compares what they say versus what they do, he discovers big differences. (See Figure 1.1.) He found that 69% of fans in Tier 1 seats who said on the

Tier	Highly Likely	Likely	Maybe	Probably Not	Certainly Not
1	92	88	75	69	45
2	88	81	70	65	38
3	80	76	68	55	36
4	77	72	65	45	25
5	75	70	60	35	25

FIGURE 1.1   Season Ticket Renewals—Survey Scores.

---

[3]Thomas Davenport, "Analytics in Sports: The New Science of Winning," International Institute for Analytics White paper, sponsored by SAS, February 2014. On the SAS Web site at: http://www.sas.com/content/dam/SAS/ en_us/doc/whitepaper2/iia-analytics-in-sports-106993.pdf. (Accessed July 2016)

survey that they would "probably not renew" actually did. This is useful insight that leads to action—customers in the green cells are the most likely to renew tickets, so require fewer marketing touches and dollars to convert, for example, compared to customers in the blue cells.

However, many factors influence fan ticket purchase behavior, especially price, which drives more sophisticated statistics and data analysis. For both areas, but especially single-game tickets, Dave is driving the use of dynamic pricing—moving the business from simple static pricing by seat location tier to day-by-day up-and-down pricing of individual seats. This is a rich research area for many sports teams and has huge upside potential for revenue enhancement. For example, his pricing takes into account the team's record, who they are playing, game dates and times, which star athletes play for each team, each fan's history of renewing season tickets or buying single tickets, as well as factors like seat location, number of seats, and real-time information like traffic congestion historically at game time and even the weather. See Figure 1.2.

Which of these factors are important? How much? Given his extensive statistics background, Dave builds regression models to pick out key factors driving these historic behaviors and create PMs to identify how to spend marketing resources to drive revenues. He builds churn models for season ticket holders to create segments of customers who will renew, won't renew, or are fence-sitters, which then drives more refined marketing campaigns.

In addition, he does sentiment scoring on fan comments like tweets that help him segment fans into different loyalty segments. Other studies about single-game attendance drivers help the marketing department understand the impact of giveaways like bobble-heads or T-shirts, or suggestions on where to make spot TV ad buys.

Beyond revenues, there are many other analytical areas that Dave's team works on, including merchandising, TV and radio broadcast revenues, inputs to the general manager on salary negotiations, draft analytics especially given salary caps, promotion effectiveness including advertising channels, and brand awareness, as well as partner analytics. He's a very busy guy!

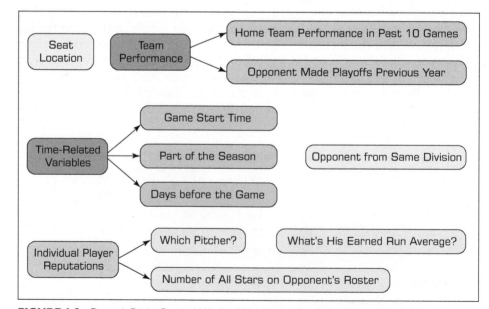

FIGURE 1.2 Dynamic Pricing Previous Work—Major League Baseball. *Source:* Adapted from C. Kemper and C. Breuer, "How Efficient is Dynamic Pricing for Sports Events? Designing a Dynamic Pricing Model for Bayern Munich", *Intl. Journal of Sports Finance*, 11, pp. 4-25, 2016.

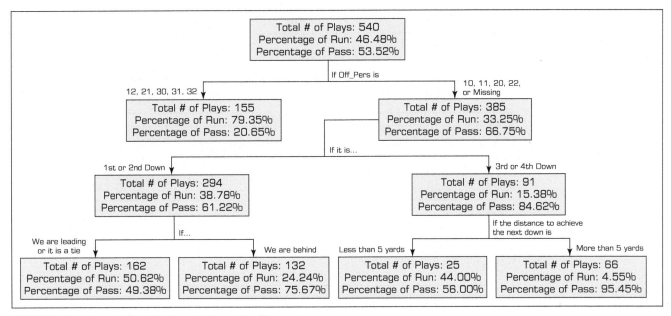

FIGURE 1.3 Cascaded Decision Tree for Run or Pass Plays.

Example 2: The Coach

Bob Breedlove is the football coach for a major college team. For him, it's all about winning games. His areas of focus include recruiting the best high school players, developing them to fit his offense and defense systems, and getting maximum effort from them on game days. Sample questions in his area of responsibility include: Who do we recruit? What drills help develop their skills? How hard do I push our athletes? Where are opponents strong or weak, and how do we figure out their play tendencies?

Fortunately, his team has hired a new team operations expert, Dar Beranek, who specializes in helping the coaches make tactical decisions. She is working with a team of student interns who are creating opponent analytics. They used the coach's annotated game film to build a cascaded decision tree model (Figure 1.3) to predict whether the next play will be a running play or passing play. For the defensive coordinator, they have built heat maps (Figure 1.4) of each opponent's passing offense, illustrating their tendencies to throw left or right and into which defensive coverage zones. Finally, they built some time series analytics (Figure 1.5) on explosive plays (defined as a gain of more than 16 yards for a passing play or more than 12 yards for a run play). For each play, they compare the outcome with their own defensive formations and the other team's offensive formations, which helps Coach Breedlove react more quickly to formation shifts during a game. We will explain the analytical techniques that generated these figures in much more depth in Chapters 2–5 and Chapter 7.

New work that Dar is fostering involves building better high school athlete recruiting models. For example, each year the team gives scholarships to three students who are wide receiver recruits. For Dar, picking out the best players goes beyond simple measures like how fast athletes run, how high they jump, or how long their arms are to newer criteria like how quickly they can rotate their heads to catch a pass, what kinds of reaction times they exhibit to multiple stimuli, and how accurately they run pass routes. Some of her ideas illustrating these concepts appear on the TUN Web site; look for the BSI Case of Precision Football.[4]

[4]Business Scenario Investigation BSI: The Case of Precision Football (video). (Fall 2015). Appears on http://www.teradatauniversitynetwork.com/About-Us/Whats-New/BSI–Sports-Analytics—Precision-Football//,Fall 2015. (Accessed September 2016)

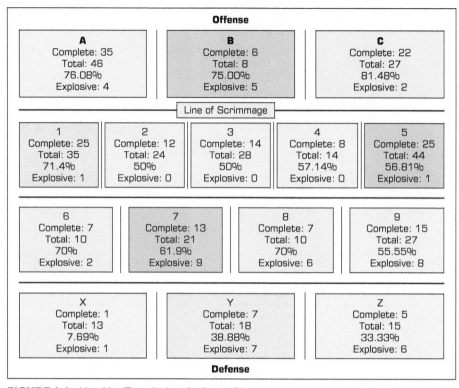

FIGURE 1.4 Heat Map Zone Analysis for Passing Plays.

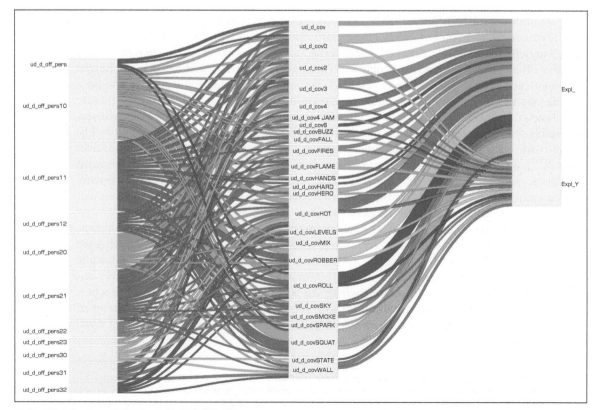

FIGURE 1.5 Time Series Analysis of Explosive Plays.

FIGURE 1.6   Soccer Injury Models.[5]

Example 3: The Trainer

Dr. Dan Johnson is the trainer for a women's college soccer team. His job is to help the players stay healthy and to advise the coaches on how much load to put on players during practices. He also has an interest in player well-being, including how much they sleep and how much rest they get between heavy and light practice sessions. The goal is to ensure that the players are ready to play on game days at maximum efficiency.

Fortunately, because of wearables, there is much more data for Dr. Dan to analyze. His players train using vests that contain sensors that can measure internal loads like heartbeats, body temperature, and respiration rates. The vests also include accelerometers that measure external loads like running distances and speeds as well as accelerations and decelerations. He knows which players are giving maximal effort during practices and those who aren't.

His focus at the moment is research that predicts or prevents player injuries (Figure 1.6). Some simple tasks like a Single Leg Squat Hold Test—standing on one foot, then the other—with score differentials of more than 10% can provide useful insights on body core strengths and weaknesses (Figure 1.7). If an athlete is hit hard during a match, a trainer can conduct a sideline test, reacting to a stimulus on a mobile device, which adds to traditional concussion protocols. Sleep sensors show who is getting adequate rest (or who partied all night). He has the MRI lab on campus do periodic brain scans to show which athletes are at risk for brain injury.

---

[5] "Women's Soccer Injuries," National Center for Catastrophic Sports Injury Research Report, NCAA. NCAA Sport Injury fact sheets are produced by the Datalys Center for Sports Injury Research and Prevention in collaboration with the National Collegiate Athletic Association, and STOP Sports Injuries. Appears at https://www.ncaa.org/sites/default/files/NCAA_W_Soccer_Injuries_WEB.pdf. (Accessed November 2016).

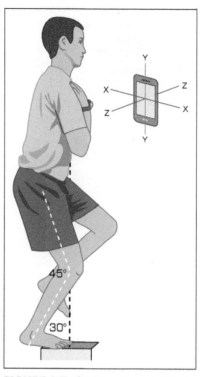

FIGURE 1.7   Single Leg Squat Hold Test–
Core Body Strength Test
(*Source:* Figure adapted from Gary Wilkerson
and Ashish Gupta).

QUESTIONS ABOUT THESE EXAMPLES

1. What are three factors that might be part of a PM for season ticket renewals?
2. What are two techniques that football teams can use to do opponent analysis?
3. How can wearables improve player health and safety? What kinds of new analytics can trainers use?
4. What other analytics uses can you envision in sports?

What Can We Learn from These Vignettes?

Beyond the front-office business analysts, the coaches, trainers, and performance experts, there are many other people in sports who use data, ranging from golf groundskeepers who measure soil and turf conditions for PGA tournaments, to baseball and basketball referees who are rated on the correct and incorrect calls they make. In fact, it's hard to find an area of sports that is *not* being impacted by the availability of more data, especially from sensors.

Skills you will learn in this book for business analytics will apply to sports. If you want to dig deeper into this area, we encourage you to look at the Sports Analytics section of the Teradata University Network (TUN) a free resource for students and faculty. On this Web site, you will find descriptions of what to read to find out more about sports analytics, compilations of places where you can find publically available data sets for analysis, as well as examples of student projects in sports analytics and interviews of sports professionals who use data and analytics to do their jobs. Good luck learning analytics!

Source and Credits: Contributed by Dr. Dave Schrader, who retired after 24 years in advanced development and marketing at Teradata. He has remained on the Board of Advisors of the Teradata University Network, where he spends his retirement helping students and faculty learn more about sports analytics. The football visuals (Figures 1.3–1.5) were constructed by Peter Liang and Jacob Pearson, graduate students at Oklahoma State University, as part of a student project in the spring of 2016. The training visuals (Figures 1.6 and 1.7) are adapted from the images provided by Prof. Gary Wilkerson of the University of Tennessee at Chattanooga and Prof. Ashish Gupta of Auburn University.

1.2   Changing Business Environments and Evolving Needs for Decision Support and Analytics

The opening vignette illustrates how an entire industry can employ analytics to develop reports on what is happening, predict what is likely to happen, and then also make decisions to make the best use of the situation at hand. These steps require an organization to collect and analyze vast stores of data. From traditional uses in payroll and bookkeeping functions, computerized systems have now penetrated complex managerial areas ranging from the design and management of automated factories to the application of analytical methods for the evaluation of proposed mergers and acquisitions. Nearly all executives know that information technology is vital to their business and extensively use information technologies.

Computer applications have moved from transaction processing and monitoring activities to problem analysis and solution applications, and much of the activity is done with cloud-based technologies, in many cases accessed through mobile devices. Analytics and BI tools such as data warehousing, data mining, online analytical processing (OLAP), dashboards, and the use of the cloud-based systems for decision support are the cornerstones of today's modern management. Managers must have high-speed, networked information systems (wireline or wireless) to assist them with their most important task: making decisions. In many cases, such decisions are routinely being automated, eliminating the need for any managerial intervention.

Besides the obvious growth in hardware, software, and network capacities, some developments have clearly contributed to facilitating growth of decision support and analytics in a number of ways, including the following:

- **Group communication and collaboration.** Many decisions are made today by groups whose members may be in different locations. Groups can collaborate and communicate readily by using collaboration tools as well as the ubiquitous smartphones. Collaboration is especially important along the supply chain, where partners—all the way from vendors to customers—must share information. Assembling a group of decision makers, especially experts, in one place can be costly. Information systems can improve the collaboration process of a group and enable its members to be at different locations (saving travel costs). More critically, such supply chain collaboration permits manufacturers to know about the changing patterns of demand in near real time and thus react to marketplace changes faster.
- **Improved data management.** Many decisions involve complex computations. Data for these can be stored in different databases anywhere in the organization and even possibly outside the organization. The data may include text, sound, graphics, and video, and these can be in different languages. Many times it is necessary to transmit data quickly from distant locations. Systems today can search, store, and transmit needed data quickly, economically, securely, and transparently.
- **Managing giant data warehouses and Big Data.** Large data warehouses (DWs), like the ones operated by Walmart, contain humongous amounts of data. Special

methods, including parallel computing, Hadoop/Spark, and so on, are available to organize, search, and mine the data. The costs related to data storage and mining are declining rapidly. Technologies that fall under the broad category of Big Data have enabled massive data coming from a variety of sources and in many different forms, which allows a very different view into organizational performance that was not possible in the past.

- **Analytical support.** With more data and analysis technologies, more alternatives can be evaluated, forecasts can be improved, risk analysis can be performed quickly, and the views of experts (some of whom may be in remote locations) can be collected quickly and at a reduced cost. Expertise can even be derived directly from analytical systems. With such tools, decision makers can perform complex simulations, check many possible scenarios, and assess diverse impacts quickly and economically. This, of course, is the focus of several chapters in the book.

- **Overcoming cognitive limits in processing and storing information.** According to Simon (1977), the human mind has only a limited ability to process and store information. People sometimes find it difficult to recall and use information in an error-free fashion due to their cognitive limits. The term *cognitive limits* indicates that an individual's problem-solving capability is limited when a wide range of diverse information and knowledge is required. Computerized systems enable people to overcome their cognitive limits by quickly accessing and processing vast amounts of stored information.

- **Knowledge management.** Organizations have gathered vast stores of information about their own operations, customers, internal procedures, employee interactions, and so forth, through the unstructured and structured communications taking place among the various stakeholders. Knowledge management systems have become sources of formal and informal support for decision making to managers, although sometimes they may not even be called *KMS*. Technologies such as text analytics and IBM Watson are making it possible to generate value from such knowledge stores.

- **Anywhere, anytime support.** Using wireless technology, managers can access information anytime and from anyplace, analyze and interpret it, and communicate with those involved. This perhaps is the biggest change that has occurred in the last few years. The speed at which information needs to be processed and converted into decisions has truly changed expectations for both consumers and businesses. These and other capabilities have been driving the use of computerized decision support since the late 1960s, but especially since the mid-1990s. The growth of mobile technologies, social media platforms, and analytical tools has enabled a different level of information systems (IS) support for managers. This growth in providing data-driven support for any decision extends to not just the managers but also to consumers. We will first study an overview of technologies that have been broadly referred to as BI. From there we will broaden our horizons to introduce various types of analytics.

SECTION 1.2 REVIEW QUESTIONS

1. What are some of the key system-oriented trends that have fostered IS-supported decision making to a new level?

2. List some capabilities of information systems that can facilitate managerial decision making.

3. How can a computer help overcome the cognitive limits of humans?

1.3 Evolution of Computerized Decision Support to Analytics/Data Science

The timeline in Figure 1.8 shows the terminology used to describe analytics since the 1970s. During the 1970s, the primary focus of information systems support for decision making focused on providing structured, periodic reports that a manager could use for decision making (or ignore them). Businesses began to create routine reports to inform decision makers (managers) about what had happened in the previous period (e.g., day, week, month, quarter). Although it was useful to know what had happened in the past, managers needed more than this: They needed a variety of reports at different levels of granularity to better understand and address changing needs and challenges of the business. These were usually called management information systems (MIS). In the early 1970s, Scott-Morton first articulated the major concepts of DSS. He defined DSSs as "interactive computer-based systems, which help decision makers utilize *data* and *models* to solve unstructured problems" (Gorry and Scott-Morton, 1971). The following is another classic DSS definition, provided by Keen and Scott-Morton (1978):

> Decision support systems couple the intellectual resources of individuals with the capabilities of the computer to improve the quality of decisions. It is a computer-based support system for management decision makers who deal with semistructured problems.

Note that the term *decision support system*, like *management information system* and several other terms in the field of IT, is a content-free expression (i.e., it means different things to different people). Therefore, there is no universally accepted definition of DSS.

During the early days of analytics, data was often obtained from the domain experts using manual processes (i.e., interviews and surveys) to build mathematical or knowledge-based models to solve constrained optimization problems. The idea was to do the best with limited resources. Such decision support models were typically called operations research (OR). The problems that were too complex to solve optimally (using linear or nonlinear mathematical programming techniques) were tackled using heuristic methods such as simulation models. (We will introduce these as prescriptive analytics later in this chapter and in a bit more detail in Chapter 6.)

In the late 1970s and early 1980s, in addition to the mature OR models that were being used in many industries and government systems, a new and exciting line of models had emerged: rule-based expert systems. These systems promised to capture experts' knowledge in a format that computers could process (via a collection of if–then–else rules or heuristics) so that these could be used for consultation much the same way that one

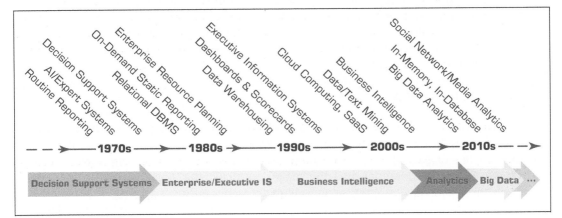

FIGURE 1.8 Evolution of Decision Support, Business Intelligence, and Analytics.

would use domain experts to identify a structured problem and to prescribe the most probable solution. ESs allowed scarce expertise to be made available where and when needed, using an "intelligent" DSS.

The 1980s saw a significant change in the way organizations captured business-related data. The old practice had been to have multiple disjointed information systems tailored to capture transactional data of different organizational units or functions (e.g., accounting, marketing and sales, finance, manufacturing). In the 1980s, these systems were integrated as enterprise-level information systems that we now commonly call enterprise resource planning (ERP) systems. The old mostly sequential and nonstandardized data representation schemas were replaced by relational database management (RDBM) systems. These systems made it possible to improve the capture and storage of data, as well as the relationships between organizational data fields while significantly reducing the replication of information. The need for RDBM and ERP systems emerged when data integrity and consistency became an issue, significantly hindering the effectiveness of business practices. With ERP, all the data from every corner of the enterprise is collected and integrated into a consistent schema so that every part of the organization has access to the single version of the truth when and where needed. In addition to the emergence of ERP systems, or perhaps because of these systems, business reporting became an on-demand, as-needed business practice. Decision makers could decide when they needed to or wanted to create specialized reports to investigate organizational problems and opportunities.

In the 1990s, the need for more versatile reporting led to the development of executive information systems (EISs; DSSs designed and developed specifically for executives and their decision-making needs). These systems were designed as graphical dashboards and scorecards so that they could serve as visually appealing displays while focusing on the most important factors for decision makers to keep track of the key performance indicators. To make this highly versatile reporting possible while keeping the transactional integrity of the business information systems intact, it was necessary to create a middle data tier known as a DW as a repository to specifically support business reporting and decision making. In a very short time, most large to medium-sized businesses adopted data warehousing as their platform for enterprise-wide decision making. The dashboards and scorecards got their data from a DW, and by doing so, they were not hindering the efficiency of the business transaction systems mostly referred to as (ERP) systems.

In the 2000s, the DW-driven DSSs began to be called BI systems. As the amount of longitudinal data accumulated in the DWs increased, so did the capabilities of hardware and software to keep up with the rapidly changing and evolving needs of the decision makers. Because of the globalized competitive marketplace, decision makers needed current information in a very digestible format to address business problems and to take advantage of market opportunities in a timely manner. Because the data in a DW is updated periodically, it does not reflect the latest information. To elevate this information latency problem, DW vendors developed a system to update the data more frequently, which led to the terms *real-time data warehousing* and, more realistically, *right-time data warehousing*, which differs from the former by adopting a data-refreshing policy based on the needed freshness of the data items (i.e., not all data items need to be refreshed in real time). DWs are very large and feature rich, and it became necessary to "mine" the corporate data to "discover" new and useful knowledge nuggets to improve business processes and practices, hence the terms *data mining* and *text mining*. With the increasing volumes and varieties of data, the needs for more storage and more processing power emerged. Although large corporations had the means to tackle this problem, small to medium-sized companies needed more financially manageable business models. This need led to service-oriented architecture and software and infrastructure-as-a-service analytics business models. Smaller companies, therefore, gained access to analytics capabilities on an as-needed basis and paid only for what they used, as opposed to investing in financially prohibitive hardware and software resources.

In the 2010s, we are seeing yet another paradigm shift in the way that data is captured and used. Largely because of the widespread use of the Internet, new data generation mediums have emerged. Of all the new data sources (e.g., radio-frequency identification [RFID] tags, digital energy meters, clickstream Web logs, smart home devices, wearable health monitoring equipment), perhaps the most interesting and challenging is social networking/social media. This unstructured data is rich in information content, but analysis of such data sources poses significant challenges to computational systems, from both software and hardware perspectives. Recently, the term *Big Data* has been coined to highlight the challenges that these new data streams have brought on us. Many advancements in both hardware (e.g., massively parallel processing with very large computational memory and highly parallel multiprocessor computing systems) and software/algorithms (e.g., Hadoop with MapReduce and NoSQL) have been developed to address the challenges of Big Data.

It's hard to predict what the next decade will bring and what the new analytics-related terms will be. The time between new paradigm shifts in information systems and particularly in analytics has been shrinking, and this trend will continue for the foreseeable future. Even though analytics is not new, the explosion in its popularity is very new. Thanks to the recent explosion in Big Data, ways to collect and store this data, and intuitive software tools, data-driven insights are more accessible to business professionals than ever before. Therefore, in the midst of global competition, there is a huge opportunity to make better managerial decisions by using data and analytics to increase revenue while decreasing costs by building better products, improving customer experience, and catching fraud before it happens, improving customer engagement through targeting and customization all with the power of analytics and data. More and more companies are now preparing their employees with the know-how of business analytics to drive effectiveness and efficiency in their day-to-day decision-making processes.

The next section focuses on a framework for BI. Although most people would agree that BI has evolved into analytics and data science, many vendors and researchers still use that term. So Section 1.4 pays homage to that history by specifically focusing on what has been called BI. Following the next section, we introduce analytics and will use that as the label for classifying all related concepts.

SECTION 1.3 REVIEW QUESTIONS

1. List three of the terms that have been predecessors of analytics.
2. What was the primary difference between the systems called MIS, DSS, and Executive Support Systems?
3. Did DSS evolve into BI or vice versa?

1.4   A Framework for Business Intelligence

The decision support concepts presented in Sections 1.2 and 1.3 have been implemented incrementally, under different names, by many vendors that have created tools and methodologies for decision support. As noted in Section 1.3, as the enterprise-wide systems grew, managers were able to access user-friendly reports that enabled them to make decisions quickly. These systems, which were generally called EISs, then began to offer additional visualization, alerts, and performance measurement capabilities. By 2006, the major *commercial* products and services appeared under the term *business intelligence* (BI).

Definitions of BI

Business intelligence (BI) is an umbrella term that combines architectures, tools, databases, analytical tools, applications, and methodologies. It is, like DSS, a content-free expression, so it means different things to different people. Part of the confusion about BI lies in the flurry of acronyms and buzzwords that are associated with it (e.g., business performance management [BPM]). BI's major objective is to enable interactive access (sometimes in real time) to data, to enable manipulation of data, and to give business managers and analysts the ability to conduct appropriate analyses. By analyzing historical and current data, situations, and performances, decision makers get valuable insights that enable them to make more informed and better decisions. The process of BI is based on the *transformation* of data to information, then to decisions, and finally to actions.

A Brief History of BI

The term *BI* was coined by the Gartner Group in the mid-1990s. However, as the history in the previous section points out, the concept is much older; it has its roots in the MIS reporting systems of the 1970s. During that period, reporting systems were static, were two dimensional, and had no analytical capabilities. In the early 1980s, the concept of EISs emerged. This concept expanded the computerized support to top-level managers and executives. Some of the capabilities introduced were dynamic multidimensional (ad hoc or on-demand) reporting, forecasting and prediction, trend analysis, drill-down to details, status access, and critical success factors. These features appeared in dozens of commercial products until the mid-1990s. Then the same capabilities and some new ones appeared under the name BI. Today, a good BI-based enterprise information system contains all the information executives need. So, the original concept of EIS was transformed into BI. By 2005, BI systems started to include *artificial intelligence* capabilities as well as powerful analytical capabilities. Figure 1.9 illustrates the various tools and techniques that may be included in a BI system. It illustrates the evolution of BI as well. The tools shown in Figure 1.9 provide the capabilities of BI. The most sophisticated BI products include most of these capabilities; others specialize in only some of them.

The Architecture of BI

A BI system has four major components: a *DW*, with its source data; *business analytics*, a collection of tools for manipulating, mining, and analyzing the data in the DW; *BPM* for monitoring and analyzing performance; and a *user interface* (e.g., a **dashboard**). The relationship among these components is illustrated in Figure 1.10.

The Origins and Drivers of BI

Where did modern approaches to data warehousing and BI come from? What are their roots, and how do those roots affect the way organizations are managing these initiatives today? Today's investments in information technology are under increased scrutiny in terms of their bottom-line impact and potential. The same is true of DW and the BI applications that make these initiatives possible.

Organizations are being compelled to capture, understand, and harness their data to support decision making to improve business operations. Legislation and regulation (e.g., the Sarbanes-Oxley Act of 2002) now require business leaders to document their business processes and to sign off on the legitimacy of the information they rely on and report to stakeholders. Moreover, business cycle times are now extremely compressed; faster, more informed, and better decision making is, therefore, a competitive imperative. Managers need the *right information* at the *right time* and in the *right place*. This is the mantra for modern approaches to BI.

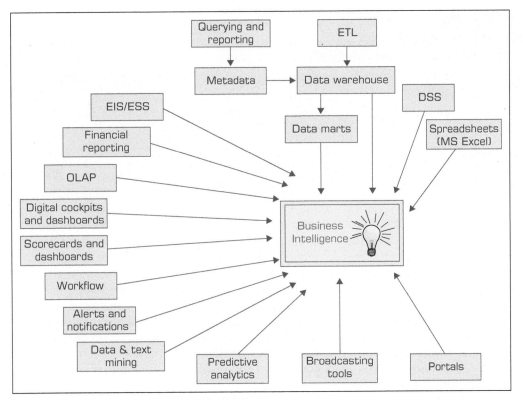

FIGURE 1.9   Evolution of Business Intelligence (BI).

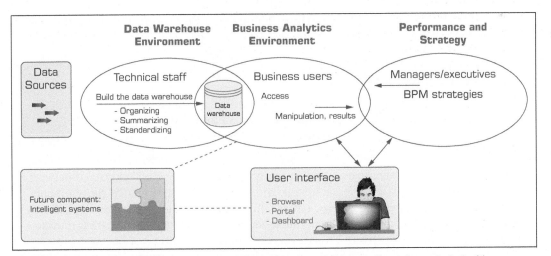

FIGURE 1.10   A High-Level Architecture of BI.   (*Source:* Based on W. Eckerson, *Smart Companies in the 21st Century: The Secrets of Creating Successful Business Intelligent Solutions.* The Data Warehousing Institute, Seattle, WA, 2003, p. 32, Illustration 5.)

Organizations have to work smart. Paying careful attention to the management of BI initiatives is a necessary aspect of doing business. It is no surprise, then, that organizations are increasingly championing BI and under its new incarnation as analytics. Application Case 1.1 illustrates one such application of BI that has helped many airlines as well as, of course, the companies offering such services to the airlines.

Application Case 1.1

Sabre Helps Its Clients Through Dashboards and Analytics

Sabre is one of the world leaders in the travel industry, providing both business-to-consumer services as well as business-to-business services. It serves travelers, travel agents, corporations, and travel suppliers through its four main companies: Travelocity, Sabre Travel Network, Sabre Airline Solutions, and Sabre Hospitality Solutions. The current volatile global economic environment poses significant competitive challenges to the airline industry. To stay ahead of the competition, Sabre Airline Solutions recognized that airline executives needed enhanced tools for managing their business decisions by eliminating the traditional, manual, time-consuming process of aggregating financial and other information needed for actionable initiatives. This enables real-time decision support at airlines throughout the world to maximize their (and in turn Sabre's) return on information by driving insights, actionable intelligence, and value for customers from the growing data.

Sabre developed an Enterprise Travel Data Warehouse (ETDW) using Teradata to hold its massive reservations data. ETDW is updated in near-real time with batches that run every 15 minutes, gathering data from all of Sabre's businesses. Sabre uses its ETDW to create Sabre Executive Dashboards that provide near real-time executive insights using a Cognos BI platform with Oracle Data Integrator and Oracle Goldengate technology infrastructures. The Executive Dashboards offer their client airlines' top-level managers and decision makers a timely, automated, user-friendly solution, aggregating critical performance metrics in a succinct way and providing at a glance a 360-degree view of the overall health of the airline. At one airline, Sabre's Executive Dashboards provide senior management with a daily and intraday snapshot of key performance indicators in a single application replacing the once-a-week, 8-hour process of generating the same report from various data sources. The use of dashboards is not limited to the external customers; Sabre also uses them for their assessment of internal operational performance.

The dashboards help Sabre's customers to have a clear understanding of the data through the visual displays that incorporate interactive drill-down capabilities. It replaces flat presentations and allows for a more focused review of the data with less effort and time. This facilitates team dialog by making the data/metrics pertaining to sales performance available to many stakeholders, including ticketing, seats sold and flown, operational performance including the data on flight movement and tracking, customer reservations, inventory, and revenue across an airline's multiple distribution channels. The dashboard systems provide scalable infrastructure, graphical user interface support, data integration, and aggregation that empower airline executives to be more proactive in taking actions that lead to positive impacts on the overall health of their airline.

With its ETDW, Sabre could also develop other Web-based analytical and reporting solutions that leverage data to gain customer insights through analysis of customer profiles and their sales interactions to calculate customer value. This enables better customer segmentation and insights for value-added services.

QUESTIONS FOR DISCUSSION

1. What is traditional reporting? How is it used in the organization?
2. How can analytics be used to transform the traditional reporting?
3. How can interactive reporting assist organizations in decision making?

What We Can Learn from This Application Case

This case shows that organizations that earlier used reporting only for tracking their internal business activities and meeting the compliance requirements set out by the government are now moving toward generating actionable intelligence from their transactional business data. Reporting has become broader as organizations are now trying to analyze the archived transactional data to understand the underlying hidden trends and patterns that will enable them to make better decisions by gaining insights into problematic areas and resolving them to pursue current and future market opportunities. Reporting has advanced to interactive online reports, which enable the users to pull and build quick custom reports and even present the reports aided by visualization tools that have the ability to connect to the database, providing the capabilities of digging deep into summarized data.

Source: Teradata.com, "Sabre Airline Solutions," Terry, D. (2011), "Sabre Streamlines Decision Making," http://www.teradatamaga zine.com/v11n04/Features/Sabre-Streamlines-Decision-Making/ (Accessed July 2016).

A Multimedia Exercise in Business Intelligence

TUN includes videos (similar to the television show *CSI*) to illustrate concepts of analytics in different industries. These are called "BSI Videos (Business Scenario Investigations)." Not only are these entertaining, but they also provide the class with some questions for discussion. For starters, please go to http://www.teradatauniversitynetwork.com /Library/Items/BSI–The-Case-of-the-Misconnecting-Passengers/ or www.youtube.com /watch?v=NXEL5F4_aKA. Watch the video that appears on YouTube. Essentially, you have to assume the role of a customer service center professional. An incoming flight is running late, and several passengers are likely to miss their connecting flights. There are seats on one outgoing flight that can accommodate two of the four passengers. Which two passengers should be given priority? You are given information about customers' profiles and relationships with the airline. Your decisions might change as you learn more about those customers' profiles.

Watch the video, pause it as appropriate, and answer the questions on which passengers should be given priority. Then resume the video to get more information. After the video is complete, you can see the slides related to this video and how the analysis was prepared on a slide set at www.slideshare.net/teradata/bsi-how-we-did-it-the -case-of-the-misconnecting-passengers.

This multimedia excursion provides an example of how additional available information through an enterprise DW can assist in decision making.

Although some people equate DSS with BI, these systems are not, at present, the same. It is interesting to note that some people believe that DSS is a part of BI—one of its analytical tools. Others think that BI is a special case of DSS that deals mostly with reporting, communication, and collaboration (a form of data-oriented DSS). Another explanation (Watson, 2005) is that BI is a result of a continuous revolution, and as such, DSS is one of BI's original elements. Further, as noted in the next section onward, in many circles BI has been subsumed by the new terms *analytics* or *data science*.

Transaction Processing versus Analytic Processing

To illustrate the major characteristics of BI, first we will show what BI is not—namely, transaction processing. We're all familiar with the information systems that support our transactions, like ATM withdrawals, bank deposits, cash register scans at the grocery store, and so on. These *transaction processing* systems are constantly involved in handling updates to what we might call *operational databases*. For example, in an ATM withdrawal transaction, we need to reduce our bank balance accordingly; a bank deposit adds to an account; and a grocery store purchase is likely reflected in the store's calculation of total sales for the day, and it should reflect an appropriate reduction in the store's inventory for the items we bought, and so on. These **online transaction processing (OLTP)** systems handle a company's routine ongoing business. In contrast, a DW is typically a distinct system that provides storage for data that will be used for *analysis*. The intent of that analysis is to give management the ability to scour data for information about the business, and it can be used to provide tactical or operational decision support, whereby, for example, line personnel can make quicker and/or more informed decisions. We will provide a more technical definition of DW in Chapter 2, but suffice it to say that DWs are intended to work with informational data used for **online analytical processing (OLAP)** systems.

Most operational data in enterprise resources planning (ERP) systems—and in its complementary siblings like *supply chain management* (SCM) or *CRM*—are stored in an OLTP system, which is a type of computer processing where the computer responds immediately to user requests. Each request is considered to be a *transaction*, which is a computerized record of a discrete event, such as the receipt of inventory or a customer order. In other words, a transaction requires a set of two or more database updates that must be completed in an all-or-nothing fashion.

The very design that makes an OLTP system efficient for transaction processing makes it inefficient for end-user ad hoc reports, queries, and analysis. In the 1980s, many business users referred to their mainframes as "black holes " because all the information went into them, but none ever came back. All requests for reports had to be programmed by the IT staff, whereas only "precanned" reports could be generated on a scheduled basis, and ad hoc real-time querying was virtually impossible. Although the client/server-based ERP systems of the 1990s were somewhat more report-friendly, it has still been a far cry from a desired usability by regular, nontechnical, end users for things such as operational reporting, interactive analysis, and so on. To resolve these issues, the notions of DW and BI were created.

DWs contain a wide variety of data that present a coherent picture of business conditions at a single point in time. The idea was to create a database infrastructure that was always online and contained all the information from the OLTP systems, including historical data, but reorganized and structured in such a way that it was fast and efficient for querying, analysis, and decision support. Separating the OLTP from analysis and decision support enables the benefits of BI that were described earlier.

Appropriate Planning and Alignment with the Business Strategy

First and foremost, the fundamental reasons for investing in BI must be aligned with the company's business strategy. BI cannot simply be a technical exercise for the information systems department. It has to serve as a way to change the manner in which the company conducts business by improving its business processes and transforming decision-making processes to be more data driven. Many BI consultants and practitioners involved in successful BI initiatives advise that a framework for planning is a necessary precondition. One framework, developed by Gartner, Inc. (2004), decomposes planning and execution into *business, organization, functionality*, and *infrastructure* components. At the business and organizational levels, strategic and operational objectives must be defined while considering the available organizational skills to achieve those objectives. Issues of organizational culture surrounding BI initiatives and building enthusiasm for those initiatives and procedures for the intra-organizational sharing of BI best practices must be considered by upper management—with plans in place to prepare the organization for change. One of the first steps in that process is to assess the IS organization, the skill sets of the potential classes of users, and whether the culture is amenable to change. From this assessment, and assuming there is justification and the need to move ahead, a company can prepare a detailed action plan. Another critical issue for BI implementation success is the integration of several BI projects (most enterprises use several BI projects) among themselves and with the other IT systems in the organization and its business partners.

If the company's strategy is properly aligned with the reasons for DW and BI initiatives, and if the company's IS organization is or can be made capable of playing its role in such a project, and if the requisite user community is in place and has the proper motivation, it is wise to start BI and establish a BI Competency Center within the company. The center could serve some or all of the following functions (Gartner, 2004):

- The center can demonstrate how BI is clearly linked to strategy and execution of strategy.
- A center can serve to encourage interaction between the potential business user communities and the IS organization.
- The center can serve as a repository and disseminator of best BI practices between and among the different lines of business.
- Standards of excellence in BI practices can be advocated and encouraged throughout the company.
- The IS organization can learn a great deal through interaction with the user communities, such as knowledge about the variety of types of analytical tools that are needed.
- The business user community and IS organization can better understand why the DW platform must be flexible enough to provide for changing business requirements.
- It can help important stakeholders like high-level executives see how BI can play an important role.

Another important success factor of BI is its ability to facilitate a real-time, on-demand agile environment, introduced next.

Real-Time, On-Demand BI Is Attainable

The demand for instant, on-demand access to dispersed information has grown as the need to close the gap between the operational data and strategic objectives has become more pressing. As a result, a category of products called *real-time BI applications* has emerged. The introduction of new data-generating technologies, such as RFID and other sensors is only accelerating this growth and the subsequent need for real-time BI. Traditional BI systems use a large volume of *static* data that has been extracted, cleansed, and loaded into a *DW* to produce reports and analyses. However, the need is not just reporting because users need business monitoring, performance analysis, and an understanding of why things are happening. These can assist users, who need to know (virtually in real time) about changes in data or the availability of relevant reports, alerts, and notifications regarding events and emerging trends in social media applications. In addition, business applications can be programmed to act on what these real-time BI systems discover. For example, an SCM application might automatically place an order for more "widgets" when real-time inventory falls below a certain threshold or when a CRM application automatically triggers a customer service representative and credit control clerk to check a customer who has placed an online order larger than $10,000.

One approach to real-time BI uses the DW model of traditional BI systems. In this case, products from innovative BI platform providers provide a service-oriented, near-real-time solution that populates the DW much faster than the typical nightly *extract/transfer/load* batch update does (see Chapter 3). A second approach, commonly called *business activity management* (BAM), is adopted by pure-play BAM and/or hybrid BAM-middleware providers (such as Savvion, Iteration Software, Vitria, webMethods, Quantive, Tibco, or Vineyard Software). It bypasses the DW entirely and uses **Web services** or other monitoring means to discover key business events. These software monitors (or **intelligent agents**) can be placed on a separate server in the network or on the transactional application databases themselves, and they can use event- and process-based approaches to proactively and intelligently measure and monitor operational processes.

Developing or Acquiring BI Systems

Today, many vendors offer diversified tools, some of which are completely preprogrammed (called *shells*); all you have to do is insert your numbers. These tools can be purchased or leased. For a list of products, demos, white papers, and more current product information, see product directories at tdwi.org. Free user registration is required. Almost all BI applications are constructed with shells provided by vendors who may themselves create a custom solution for a client or work with another outsourcing provider. The issue that companies face is which alternative to select: purchase, lease, or build. Each of these alternatives has several options. One of the major criteria for making the decision is justification and cost–benefit analysis.

Justification and Cost–Benefit Analysis

As the number of potential BI applications increases, the need to justify and prioritize them arises. This is not an easy task due to the large number of intangible benefits. Both direct and intangible benefits need to be identified. Of course, this is where the knowledge of similar applications in other organizations and case studies is extremely useful. For example, The Data Warehousing Institute (tdwi.org) provides a wealth of information about products and innovative applications and implementations. Such information can be useful in estimating direct and indirect benefits.

Security and Protection of Privacy

This is an extremely important issue in the development of any computerized system, especially BI that contains data that may possess strategic value. Also, the privacy of employees and customers needs to be protected.

Integration of Systems and Applications

With the exception of some small applications, all BI applications must be integrated with other systems such as databases, legacy systems, enterprise systems (particularly ERP and CRM), e-commerce (sell side, buy side), and many more. In addition, BI applications are usually connected to the Internet and many times to information systems of business partners.

Furthermore, BI tools sometimes need to be integrated among themselves, creating synergy. The need for integration pushed software vendors to continuously add capabilities to their products. Customers who buy an all-in-one software package deal with only one vendor and do not have to deal with system connectivity. But, they may lose the advantage of creating systems composed from the "best-of-breed" components.

SECTION 1.4 REVIEW QUESTIONS

1. Define *BI*.
2. List and describe the major components of BI.
3. Define *OLTP*.
4. Define *OLAP*.
5. List some of the implementation topics addressed by Gartner's report.
6. List some other success factors of BI.

1.5 Analytics Overview

The word *analytics* has largely replaced the previous individual components of computerized decision support technologies that have been available under various labels in the past. Indeed, many practitioners and academics now use the word *analytics* in place of BI. Although many authors and consultants have defined it slightly differently, one can view **analytics** as the process of developing actionable decisions or recommendations for actions based on insights generated from historical data. According to the Institute for Operations Research and Management Science (INFORMS), analytics represents the combination of computer technology, management science techniques, and statistics to solve real problems. Of course, many other organizations have proposed their own interpretations and motivations for analytics. For example, SAS Institute Inc. proposed eight levels of analytics that begin with standardized reports from a computer system. These reports essentially provide a sense of what is happening with an organization. Additional technologies have enabled us to create more customized reports that can be generated on an ad hoc basis. The next extension of reporting takes us to OLAP-type queries that allow a user to dig deeper and determine specific sources of concern or opportunities. Technologies available today can also automatically issue alerts for a decision maker when performance warrants such alerts. At a consumer level we see such alerts for weather or other issues. But similar alerts can also be generated in specific settings when sales fall above or below a certain level within a certain time period or when the inventory for a specific product is running low. All of these applications are made possible through analysis and queries on data being collected by an organization. The next level of analysis might entail statistical analysis to better understand patterns. These can then be taken a step further to develop forecasts or models for predicting how customers might respond to a specific marketing campaign or ongoing service/product offerings. When an organization has a good view of what is happening and what is likely to happen, it can also employ other techniques to make the best decisions under the circumstances. These eight levels of analytics are described in more detail in a white paper by SAS (sas.com/news/sascom/analytics_levels.pdf).

This idea of looking at all the data to understand what is happening, what will happen, and how to make the best of it has also been encapsulated by INFORMS in proposing three levels of analytics. These three levels are identified (informs.org/Community/Analytics) as descriptive, predictive, and prescriptive. Figure 1.11 presents a graphical view of these three levels of analytics. It suggests that these three are somewhat independent steps and one type of analytics applications leads to another. It also suggests that there is actually some overlap across these three types of analytics. In either case, the interconnected nature of different types of analytics applications is evident. We next introduce these three levels of analytics.

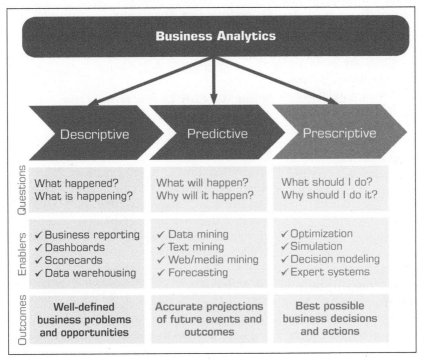

FIGURE 1.11 Three Types of Analytics.

Descriptive Analytics

Descriptive (or reporting) analytics refers to knowing what is happening in the organization and understanding some underlying trends and causes of such occurrences. First, this involves the consolidation of data sources and availability of all relevant data in a form that enables appropriate reporting and analysis. Usually, the development of this data infrastructure is part of DWs. From this data infrastructure we can develop appropriate reports, queries, alerts, and trends using various reporting tools and techniques.

A significant technology that has become a key player in this area is visualization. Using the latest visualization tools in the marketplace, we can now develop powerful insights in the operations of our organization. Application Cases 1.2 and 1.3 highlight some such applications. Color renderings of visualizations discussed in these applications are available online or the book's companion Web site (dssbibook.com).

Application Case 1.2

Silvaris Increases Business with Visual Analysis and Real-Time Reporting Capabilities

Silvaris Corporation was founded in 2000 by a team of forest industry professionals to provide technological advancement in the lumber and building material sector. Silvaris is the first e-commerce platform in the United States specifically for forest products and is headquartered in Seattle, Washington. It is a leading wholesale provider of industrial wood products and surplus building materials.

Silvaris sells its products and provides international logistics services to more than 3,500 customers. To manage various processes that are involved in a transaction, they created a proprietary online trading platform to track information flow related to transactions between traders, accounting, credit, and logistics. This allowed Silvaris to share its real-time information with its customers and partners. But due to the rapidly changing prices of materials, it became necessary for Silvaris to get a real-time view of data without moving data into a separate reporting format.

Silvaris started using Tableau because of its ability to connect with and visualize live data. Due to dashboards created by Tableau that are easy to understand and explain, Silvaris started using Tableau for reporting purposes. This helped Silvaris in pulling out information quickly from the data and identifying issues that impact their business. Silvaris succeeded in managing online versus offline orders with the help of reports generated by Tableau. Now,

Silvaris keeps track of online orders placed by customers and knows when to send renew pushes to which customers to keep them purchasing online. Also, analysts of Silvaris can save time by generating dashboards instead of writing hundreds of pages of reports by using Tableau.

Questions for Discussion

1. What was the challenge faced by Silvaris?
2. How did Silvaris solve its problem using data visualization with Tableau?

What We Can Learn from This Application Case

Many industries need to analyze data in real time. Real-time analysis enables the analysts to identify issues that impact their business. Visualization is sometimes the best way to begin analyzing the live data streams. Tableau is one such data visualization tool that has the capability to analyze live data without bringing live data into a separate reporting format.

Sources: Tableau.com, "Silvaris Augments Proprietary Technology Platform with Tableau's Real-Time Reporting Capabilities," http://www.tableau.com/sites/default/files/case-studies/silvaris-business-dashboards_0.pdf (accessed July 2016); Silvaris.com, "Overview," http://www.silvaris.com/About/ (accessed July 2016).

Application Case 1.3

Siemens Reduces Cost with the Use of Data Visualization

Siemens is a German company headquartered in Berlin, Germany. It is one of the world's largest companies focusing on the areas of electrification, automation, and digitalization. It has an annual revenue of 76 billion euros.

The visual analytics group of Siemens is tasked with end-to-end reporting solutions and consulting for all of Siemens internal BI needs. This group was facing the challenge of providing reporting solutions to the entire Siemens organization across different departments while maintaining a balance between governance and self-service capabilities. Siemens needed a platform that could analyze their multiple cases of customer satisfaction surveys, logistic processes, and financial reporting. This platform should be easy to use for their employees so that they can use this data for analysis and decision making. In addition, the platform should be easily integrated with existing Siemens systems and give employees a seamless user experience.

They started using Dundas BI, a leading global provider of BI and data visualization solutions. It allowed Siemens to create highly interactive dashboards that enabled Siemens to detect issues early and thus save a significant amount of money. The dashboards developed by Dundas BI helped Siemens

global logistics organization answer questions like how different supply rates at different locations affect the operation, thus helping them to reduce cycle time by 12% and scrap cost by 25%.

QUESTIONS FOR DISCUSSION

1. What challenges were faced by Siemens visual analytics group?
2. How did the data visualization tool Dundas BI help Siemens in reducing cost?

What We Can Learn from This Application Case

Many organizations want tools that can be used to analyze data from multiple divisions. These tools can help them improve performance and make data discovery transparent to their users so that they can identify issues within the business easily.

Sources: Dundas.com, "How Siemens Drastically Reduced Cost with Managed BI Applications," http://www.dundas.com/resource/getcasestudy?caseStudyName=09-03-2016-Siemens%2FDundas-BI-Siemens-Case-Study.pdf (accessed July 2016); Wikipedia.org, "SIEMENS," https://en.wikipedia.org/wiki/Siemens (accessed July 2016); Siemens.com, "About Siemens," http://www.siemens.com/about/en/ (accessed July 2016).

Predictive Analytics

Predictive analytics aims to determine what is likely to happen in the future. This analysis is based on statistical techniques as well as other more recently developed techniques that fall under the general category of **data mining**. The goal of these techniques is to be able to predict if the customer is likely to switch to a competitor ("churn"), what the customer would likely buy next and how much, what promotions a customer would respond to, whether this customer is a creditworthy risk, and so forth. A number of techniques are used in developing predictive analytical applications, including various classification algorithms. For example, as described in Chapters 4 and 5, we can use classification techniques such as logistic regression, decision tree models, and neural networks to predict how well a motion picture will do at the box office. We can also use clustering algorithms for segmenting customers into different clusters to be able to target specific promotions to them. Finally, we can use association mining techniques to estimate relationships between different purchasing behaviors. That is, if a customer buys one product, what else is the customer likely to purchase? Such analysis can assist a retailer in recommending or promoting related products. For example, any product search on Amazon.com results in the retailer also suggesting other similar products that a customer may be interested in. We will study these techniques and their applications in Chapters 3 through 6. Application Case 1.4 illustrates one such application in sports.

Application Case 1.4

Analyzing Athletic Injuries

Any athletic activity is prone to injuries. If the injuries are not handled properly, then the team suffers. Using analytics to understand injuries can help in deriving valuable insights that would enable coaches and team doctors to manage the team composition, understand player profiles, and ultimately aid in better decision making concerning which players might be available to play at any given time.

In an exploratory study, Oklahoma State University analyzed American football-related sports injuries by using reporting and predictive analytics. The project followed the CRISP-DM methodology (to be described in Chapter 4) to understand the problem of making recommendations on managing injuries, understanding the various data elements collected about injuries, cleaning the data, developing visualizations to draw various inferences, building PMs to analyze the injury healing time period, and drawing sequence rules to predict the relationships among the injuries and the various body part parts afflicted with injuries.

The injury data set consisted of more than 560 football injury records, which were categorized into injury-specific variables—body part/site/laterality, action taken, severity, injury type, injury start and healing dates—and player/sport-specific variables—player ID, position played, activity, onset, and game location. Healing time was calculated for each record, which was classified into different sets of time periods: 0–1 month, 1–2 months, 2–4 months, 4–6 months, and 6–24 months.

Various visualizations were built to draw inferences from injury data set information depicting the healing time period associated with players' positions, severity of injuries and the healing time period, treatment offered and the associated healing time period, major injuries afflicting body parts, and so forth.

Neural network models were built to predict each of the healing categories using IBM SPSS Modeler. Some of the predictor variables were current status of injury, severity, body part, body site, type of injury, activity, event location, action taken, and position played. The success of classifying the healing category was quite good: Accuracy was 79.6% percent. Based on the analysis, many business recommendations were suggested, including employing more specialists' input from injury onset instead of letting the training room staff screen the injured players; training players at defensive positions to avoid being injured; and holding practice to thoroughly safety-check mechanisms.

QUESTIONS FOR DISCUSSION

1. What types of analytics are applied in the injury analysis?
2. How do visualizations aid in understanding the data and delivering insights into the data?
3. What is a classification problem?
4. What can be derived by performing sequence analysis?

What We Can Learn from This Application Case

For any analytics project, it is always important to understand the business domain and the current state of the business problem through extensive analysis of the only resource—historical data. Visualizations often provide a great tool for gaining the initial insights into data, which can be further refined based on expert opinions to identify the relative importance of the data elements related to the problem. Visualizations also aid in generating ideas for obscure problems, which can be pursued in building PMs that could help organizations in decision making.

Source: Sharda, R., Asamoah, D., & Ponna, N. (2013). "Research and Pedagogy in Business Analytics: Opportunities and Illustrative Examples." *Journal of Computing and Information Technology, 21*(3), 171–182.

Prescriptive Analytics

The third category of analytics is termed **prescriptive analytics**. The goal of prescriptive analytics is to recognize what is going on as well as the likely forecast and make decisions to achieve the best performance possible. This group of techniques has historically been studied under the umbrella of OR or management sciences and are generally aimed at optimizing the performance of a system. The goal here is to provide a decision or a recommendation for a specific action. These recommendations can be in the form of a specific yes/no decision for a problem, a specific amount (say, price for a specific item or airfare to charge), or a complete set of production plans. The decisions may be presented to a decision maker in a report or may be used directly in an automated decision rules system (e.g., in airline pricing systems). Thus, these types of analytics can also be termed **decision or normative analytics**. Application Case 1.5 gives an example of such prescriptive analytic applications. We will learn about some aspects of prescriptive analytics in Chapter 6.

Analytics Applied to Different Domains

Applications of analytics in various industry sectors have spawned many related areas or at least buzzwords. It is almost fashionable to attach the word *analytics* to any specific industry or type of data. Besides the general category of text analytics—aimed at getting value out of text (to be studied in Chapter 5)—or Web analytics—analyzing Web data

Application Case 1.5

A Specialty Steel Bar Company Uses Analytics to Determine Available-to-Promise Dates

This application case is based on a project that includes one of us. A company that does not wish to disclose its name (or even the precise industry) was facing a major problem of making decisions on which inventory of raw materials to use to satisfy which customers. This company supplies custom configured steel bars to its customers. These bars may be cut into specific shapes or sizes and may have unique material and finishing requirements. The company procures raw materials from around the world and stores them in its warehouse. When a prospective customer calls the company to request a quote for the specialty bars meeting specific material requirements (composition, origin of the metal, quality, shapes, sizes, etc.), the salesperson usually has just a little bit of time to submit such a quote including the date when the product can be delivered and, of course, prices, and so on. It must make available-to-promise (ATP) decisions, which determine in real time the dates when it can promise delivery of products that customers requested during the quotation stage. Previously, a salesperson had to make such decisions by analyzing reports on available inventory of raw materials. Some of the available raw material may have already been committed to another customer's order. Thus the inventory in stock may not really be the free inventory available. On the other hand, there may be raw material that is expected to be delivered in the near future that could also be used for satisfying the order

from this prospective customer. Finally, there might even be an opportunity to charge a premium for a new order by repurposing previously committed inventory to satisfy this new order while delaying an already committed order. Of course, such decisions should be based on the cost–benefit analyses of delaying a previous order. The system should thus be able to pull real-time data about inventory, committed orders, incoming raw material, production constraints, and so on.

To support these ATP decisions, a real-time DSS was developed to find an optimal assignment of the available inventory and to support additional what-if analysis. The DSS uses a suite of mixed-integer programming models that are solved using commercial software. The company has incorporated the DSS into its enterprise resource planning system to seamlessly facilitate its use of business analytics.

QUESTIONS FOR DISCUSSION

1. Why would reallocation of inventory from one customer to another be a major issue for discussion?

2. How could a DSS help make these decisions?

Source: Pajouh Foad, M., Xing, D., Hariharan, S., Zhou, Y., Balasundaram, B., Liu, T., & Sharda, R. (2013). "Available-to-Promise in Practice: An Application of Analytics in the Specialty Steel Bar Products Industry." *Interfaces*, *43*(6), 503–517. http://dx.doi.org/10.1287/inte.2013.0693 (accessed July 2016).

streams (also in Chapter 5)—many industry- or problem-specific analytics professions/ streams have been developed. Examples of such areas are marketing analytics, retail analytics, fraud analytics, transportation analytics, health analytics, sports analytics, talent analytics, behavioral analytics, and so forth. For example, Section 1.1 introduced the phrase *sports analytics*. Application Case 1.1 could also be termed a case study in airline analytics. The next section will introduce health analytics and market analytics broadly. Literally, any systematic analysis of data in a specific sector is being labeled as "(fill-in-blanks)" analytics. Although this may result in overselling the concept of analytics, the benefit is that more people in specific industries are aware of the power and potential of analytics. It also provides a focus to professionals developing and applying the concepts of analytics in a vertical sector. Although many of the techniques to develop analytics applications may be common, there are unique issues within each vertical segment that influence how the data may be collected, processed, analyzed, and the applications implemented. Thus, the differentiation of analytics based on a vertical focus is good for the overall growth of the discipline.

Analytics or Data Science?

Even as the concept of analytics is receiving more attention in industry and academic circles, another term has already been introduced and is becoming popular. The new term is *data science*. Thus, the practitioners of data science are data scientists. D. J. Patil of LinkedIn is sometimes credited with creating the term *data science*. There have been some attempts to describe the differences between data analysts and data scientists (e.g., see emc.com/collateral/about/news/emc-data-science-study-wp.pdf). One view is that *data analyst* is just another term for professionals who were doing BI in the form of data compilation, cleaning, reporting, and perhaps some visualization. Their skill sets included Excel, some SQL knowledge, and reporting. You would recognize those capabilities as descriptive or reporting analytics. In contrast, a data scientist is responsible for predictive analysis, statistical analysis, and more advanced analytical tools and algorithms. They may have a deeper knowledge of algorithms and may recognize them under various labels—data mining, knowledge discovery, or machine learning. Some of these professionals may also need deeper programming knowledge to be able to write code for data cleaning/analysis in current Web-oriented languages such as Java or Python and statistical languages such as R. Many analytics professionals also need to build significant expertise in statistical modeling, experimentation, and analysis. Again, our readers should recognize that these fall under the predictive and prescriptive analytics umbrella. However, prescriptive analytics also includes more significant expertise in OR including optimization, simulation, decision analysis, and so on. Those who cover these fields are more likely to be called data scientists than analytics professionals.

Our view is that the distinction between analytics and data scientist is more of a degree of technical knowledge and skill sets than functions. It may also be more of a distinction across disciplines. Computer science, statistics, and applied mathematics programs appear to prefer the data science label, reserving the analytics label for more business-oriented professionals. As another example of this, applied physics professionals have proposed using *network science* as the term for describing analytics that relate to groups of people—social networks, supply chain networks, and so forth. See http://barabasi.com/networksciencebook/ for an evolving textbook on this topic.

Aside from a clear difference in the skill sets of professionals who only have to do descriptive/reporting analytics versus those who engage in all three types of analytics, the distinction is fuzzy between the two labels, at best. We observe that graduates of our analytics programs tend to be responsible for tasks which are more in line with data science professionals (as defined by some circles) than just reporting analytics. This book is clearly aimed at introducing the capabilities and functionality of all analytics (which include data science), not just reporting analytics. From now on, we will use these terms interchangeably.

SECTION 1.5 REVIEW QUESTIONS

1. Define *analytics*.
2. What is descriptive analytics? What are the various tools that are employed in descriptive analytics?
3. How is descriptive analytics different from traditional reporting?
4. What is a DW? How can data warehousing technology help to enable analytics?
5. What is predictive analytics? How can organizations employ predictive analytics?
6. What is prescriptive analytics? What kinds of problems can be solved by prescriptive analytics?
7. Define modeling from the analytics perspective.
8. Is it a good idea to follow a hierarchy of descriptive and predictive analytics before applying prescriptive analytics?
9. How can analytics aid in objective decision making?

1.6   Analytics Examples in Selected Domains

You will see examples of analytics applications throughout various chapters. That is one of the primary approaches (exposure) of this book. In this section, we highlight two application areas—healthcare and retail, where there have been the most reported applications and successes.

Analytics Applications in Healthcare—Humana Examples

Although healthcare analytics span a wide variety of applications from prevention to diagnosis to efficient operations and fraud prevention, we focus on some applications that have been developed at a major health insurance company, Humana. According to the company Web site, "The company's strategy integrates care delivery, the member experience, and clinical and consumer insights to encourage engagement, behavior change, proactive clinical outreach and wellness. . . ." Achieving these strategic goals includes significant investments in information technology in general, and analytics in particular. Brian LeClaire is senior vice president and CIO of Humana, a major health insurance provider in the United States. He has a PhD in MIS from Oklahoma State University. He has championed analytics as a competitive differentiator at Humana—including cosponsoring the creation of a center for excellence in analytics. He described the following projects as examples of Humana's analytics initiatives, led by Humana's Chief Clinical Analytics Officer, Vipin Gopal.

Example 1: Preventing Falls in a Senior Population— An Analytic Approach

Accidental falls are a major health risk for adults age 65 years and older with one-third experiencing a fall every year.[1] Falls are also the leading factor for both fatal and nonfatal injuries in older adults, with injurious falls increasing the risk of disability by up to 50%.[2] The costs of falls pose a significant strain on

---

[1]http://www.cdc.gov/homeandrecreationalsafety/falls/adultfalls.html.

[2]Gill, T. M., Murphy, T. E., Gahbauer, E. A., et al. (2013). Association of injurious falls with disability outcomes and nursing home admissions in community living older persons. *American Journal of Epidemiology, 178*(3), 418–425.

the U.S. healthcare system, with the direct costs of falls estimated at $34 billion in 2013 alone.[1] With the percent of seniors in the U.S. population on the rise, falls and associated costs are anticipated to increase. According to the Centers for Disease Control and Prevention (CDC), "Falls are a public health problem that is largely preventable."[1]

Humana is the nation's second-largest provider of Medicare Advantage benefits with approximately 3.2 million members, most of whom are seniors. Keeping their senior members well and helping them live safely at their homes is a key business objective, of which prevention of falls is an important component. However, no rigorous methodology was available to identify individuals most likely to fall, for whom falls prevention efforts would be beneficial. Unlike chronic medical conditions such as diabetes and cancer, a fall is not a well-defined medical condition. In addition, falls are usually underreported in claims data as physicians typically tend to code the consequence of a fall such as fractures and dislocations. Although many clinically administered assessments to identify fallers exist, they have limited reach and lack sufficient predictive power.[3] As such, there is a need for a prospective and accurate method to identify individuals at greatest risk of falling, so that they can be proactively managed for fall prevention. The Humana analytics team undertook the development of a Falls Predictive Model in this context. It is the first comprehensive PM reported that utilizes administrative medical and pharmacy claims, clinical data, temporal clinical patterns, consumer information, and other data to identify individuals at high risk of falling over a time horizon.

Today, the Falls PM is central to Humana's ability to identify seniors who could benefit from fall mitigation interventions. An initial proof-of-concept with Humana consumers, representing the top 2% of highest risk of falling, demonstrated that the consumers had increased utilization of physical therapy services, indicating consumers are taking active steps to reduce their risk for falls. A second initiative utilizes the Falls PM to identify high-risk individuals for remote monitoring programs. Using the PM, Humana was able to identify 20,000 consumers at a high risk of falls, who benefited from this program. Identified consumers wear a device that detects falls and alerts a 24/7 service for immediate assistance.

This work was recognized by the Analytics Leadership Award by Indiana University Kelly School of Business in 2015, for innovative adoption of analytics in a business environment.

---

[3]Gates, S., Smith, L. A., Fisher, J. D., et al. (2008). Systematic review of accuracy of screening instruments for predicting fall risk among independently living older adults. *Journal of Rehabilitation Research and Development, 45*(8), 1105–1116.

Contributors: Harpreet Singh, PhD; Vipin Gopal, PhD; Philip Painter, MD.

Example 2: Humana's Bold Goal—Application of Analytics to Define the Right Metrics

In 2014, Humana, Inc. announced its organization's Bold Goal to improve the health of the communities it serves by 20% by 2020 by making it easy for people to achieve their best health. The communities that Humana serves can be defined in many ways, including geographically (state, city, neighborhood), by product (Medicare Advantage, employer-based plans, individually purchased), or by clinical profile (priority conditions including diabetes, hypertension, CHF [congestive heart failure], CAD [coronary artery disease], COPD [chronic obstructive pulmonary disease], or depression). Understanding the health of these communities and how they track over time is critical not only for the evaluation of the goal, but also in crafting strategies to improve the health of the whole membership in its entirety.

A challenge before the analytics organization was to identify a metric that captures the essence of the Bold Goal. Objectively measured traditional health insurance metrics such as hospital admissions or ER visits per 1,000 persons would not capture the spirit of this new mission. The goal was to identify a metric that captures health and its improvement in a community, but was also relevant to Humana as a business. Through rigorous analytic evaluations, Humana eventually selected "Healthy Days," a four-question, quality-of-life questionnaire originally developed by the CDC to track and measure their overall progress toward the Bold Goal.

It was critical to make sure that the selected metric was highly correlated to health and business metrics, such that any improvement in Healthy Days resulted in improved health and better business results. Some examples of how "Healthy Days" is correlated to metrics of interest include the following:

- Individuals with more unhealthy days (UHDs) exhibit higher utilization and cost patterns. For a 5-day increase in UHDs, there is (a) an $82 increase in average monthly medical and pharmacy costs, (b) an increase of 52 inpatient admits per 1000 patients, and (c) a 0.28-day increase in average length of stay.[1]
- Individuals who exhibit healthy behaviors and have their chronic conditions well managed have fewer UHDs. For example, when we look at individuals with diabetes, UHDs are lower if they obtained an LDL screening (–4.3 UHDs) or a diabetic eye exam (–2.3 UHDs). Likewise, if they have controlled blood sugar levels measured by HbA1C (–1.8 UHDs) or LDL levels (–1.3 UHDs).[2]
- Individuals with chronic conditions have more UHDs than those who do not have: (a) CHF (16.9 UHDs), (b) CAD (14.4 UHDs), (c) hypertension (13.3 UHDs), (d) diabetes (14.7 UHDs), (e) COPD (17.4 UHDs), or (f) depression (22.4 UHDs).[1,3,4]

Humana has since adopted Healthy Days as their metric for the measurement of progress toward Bold Goal.[5]

Contributors: Tristan Cordier, MPH; Gil Haugh, MS; Jonathan Peña, MS; Eriv Havens, MS; Vipin Gopal, PhD.

[1]Havens, E., Peña, J., Slabaugh, S., Cordier, T., Renda, A., & Gopal, V. (2015, October). Exploring the relationship between health-related quality of life and health conditions, costs, resource utilization, and quality measures. Podium presentation at the ISOQOL 22nd Annual Conference, Vancouver, Canada.

[2]Havens, E., Slabaugh, L., Peña J., Haugh G., & Gopal, V. (2015, February). Are there differences in Healthy Days based on compliance to preventive health screening measures? Poster presentation at Preventive Medicine 2015, Atlanta, GA.

[3]Chiguluri, V., Guthikonda, K., Slabaugh, S., Havens, E., Peña, J., & Cordier, T. (2015, June). Relationship between diabetes complications and health related quality of life among an elderly population in the United States. Poster presentation at the American Diabetes Association 75th Annual Scientific Sessions. Boston, MA.

[4]Cordier, T., Slabaugh, L., Haugh, G., Gopal, V., Cusano, D., Andrews, G., & Renda, A. (2015, September). Quality of life changes with progressing congestive heart failure. Poster presentation at the 19th Annual Scientific Meeting of the Heart Failure Society of America, Washington, DC.

[5]http://populationhealth.humana.com/wp-content/uploads/2016/05/BoldGoal2016ProgressReport_1.pdf.

Example 3: Predictive Models to Identify the Highest Risk Membership in a Health Insurer

The 80/20 rule generally applies in healthcare, that is, roughly 20% of consumers account for 80% of healthcare resources due to their deteriorating health and chronic conditions. Health insurers like Humana have typically enrolled the highest-risk enrollees in clinical and disease management programs to help manage the chronic conditions the members have.

Identification of the right members is critical for this exercise, and in the recent years, PMs have been developed to identify enrollees with the high future risk. Many of these PMs were developed with heavy reliance on medical claims data, which results from the medical services that the enrollees use. Because of the lag that exists in submitting and processing claims data, there is a corresponding lag in identification of high-risk members for clinical program enrollment. This issue is especially relevant when new members join a health insurer, as they would not have a claims history with an insurer. A claims-based PM could take on average of 9–12 months after enrollment of new members to identify them for referral to clinical programs.

In the early part of this decade, Humana attracted large numbers of new members in its Medicare Advantage products and needed a better way to clinically manage this membership. As such, it became extremely important that a different analytic approach be developed to rapidly and accurately identify high-risk new members for clinical management, to keep this group healthy and costs down.

Humana's Clinical Analytics team developed the New Member Predictive Model (NMPM) that would quickly identify at-risk individuals soon after their new plan enrollments with Humana, rather than waiting for sufficient claim history to become available for compiling clinical profiles and predicting future health risk. Designed to address the unique challenges associated with new members, NMPM developed a novel approach that leveraged and integrated broader data sets beyond medical claims data such as self-reported health risk assessment data and early indicators from pharmacy data, employed advanced data mining techniques for pattern discovery, and scored every MA consumer daily based on the most recent data Humana has to date. The model was deployed with a cross-functional team of analytics, IT, and operations to ensure seamless operational and business integration.

Ever since NMPM was implemented in January 2013, it has been rapidly identifying high-risk new members for enrollment in Humana's clinical programs. The positive outcomes achieved through this model have been highlighted in multiple senior leader communications from Humana. In the first quarter 2013 earnings release presentation to investors, Bruce Broussard, CEO of Humana, stated the significance of "improvement in new member PMs and clinical assessment processes," which resulted in 31,000 new members enrolled in clinical programs, compared to 4,000 in the same period a year earlier, a 675% increase. In addition to the increased volume of clinical program enrollments, outcome studies showed that the newly enrolled consumers identified by NMPM were also referred to clinical programs sooner, with over 50% of the referrals identified within the first 3 months after new MA plan enrollments. The consumers identified also participated at a higher rate and had longer tenure in the programs.

Contributors: Sandy Chiu, MS; Vipin Gopal, PhD.

These examples illustrate how an organization explores and implements analytics applications to meet its strategic goals. You will see several other examples of healthcare applications throughout various chapters in the book.

Analytics in the Retail Value Chain

The retail sector is where you would perhaps see the most applications of analytics. This is the domain where the volumes are large but the margins are usually thin. Customers' tastes and preferences change frequently. Physical and online stores face many challenges in succeeding. And market dominance at one time does not guarantee continued success. So investing in learning about your suppliers, customers, employees, and all the stakeholders that enable a retail value chain to succeed and using that information to make better decisions has been a goal of the analytics industry for a long time. Even casual readers of analytics probably know about Amazon's enormous investments in analytics to power their value chain. Similarly, Walmart, Target, and other major retailers have invested millions of dollars in analytics for their supply chains. Most of the analytics technology and service providers have a major presence in retail analytics. Coverage of even a small portion of those applications to achieve our exposure goal could fill a whole book. So this section just highlights a few potential applications. Most of these have been fielded by many retailers and are available through many technology providers, so in this section we will take a more general view rather than point to specific cases. This general view has been proposed by Abhishek Rathi, CEO of vCreaTek.com. vCreaTek, LLC is a boutique analytics software and service company that has offices in India, the United States, the United Arab Emirates (UAE), and Belgium. The company develops applications in multiple domains, but retail analytics is one of their key focus areas.

Figure 1.12 highlights selected components of a retail value chain. It starts with suppliers and concludes with customers, but illustrates many intermediate strategic and operational planning decision points where analytics—descriptive, predictive, or prescriptive—can play a role in making better data-driven decisions. Table 1.1 also illustrates some of the important areas of analytics applications, examples of key questions that can be answered through analytics, and of course, the potential business value derived from fielding such analytics. Some examples are discussed next.

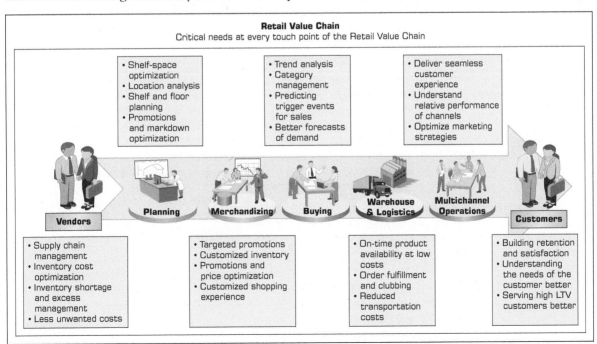

FIGURE 1.12   Example of Analytics Applications in a Retail Value Chain. Contributed by Abhishek Rathi, CEO, vCreaTek.com

TABLE 1.1	Examples of Analytics Applications in the Retail Value Chain	
Analytic Application	**Business Question**	**Business Value**
Inventory Optimization	1. Which products have high demand? 2. Which products are slow moving or becoming obsolete?	1. Forecast the consumption of fast-moving products and order them with sufficient inventory to avoid a stock-out scenario. 2. Perform fast inventory turnover of slow-moving products by combining them with one in high demand.
Price Elasticity	1. How much net margin do I have on the product? 2. How much discount can I give on this product?	1. Markdown prices for each product can be optimized to reduce the margin dollar loss. 2. Optimized price for the bundle of products is identified to save the margin dollar.
Market Basket Analysis	1. What products should I combine to create a bundle offer? 2. Should I combine products based on slow-moving and fast-moving characteristics? 3. Should I create a bundle from the same category or different category line?	1. The affinity analysis identifies the hidden correlations between the products, which can help in following values: a) Strategize the product bundle offering based on focus on inventory or margin. b) Increase cross-sell or up-sell by creating bundle from different categories or the same categories, respectively.
Shopper Insight	1. Which customer is buying what product at what location?	1. By customer segmentation, the business owner can create personalized offers resulting in better customer experience and retention of the customer.
Customer Churn Analysis	1. Who are the customers who will not return? 2. How much business will I lose? 3. How can I retain them? 4. What demography of customer is my loyal customer?	1. Businesses can identify the customer and product relationships that are not working and show high churn. Thus can have better focus on product quality and reason for that churn. 2. Based on the customer lifetime value (LTV), the business can do targeted marketing resulting in retention of the customer.
Channel Analysis	1. Which channel has lower customer acquisition cost? 2. Which channel has better customer retention? 3. Which channel is more profitable?	1. Marketing budget can be optimized based on insight for better return on investment.
New Store Analysis	1. What location should I open? 2. What and how much opening inventory should I keep?	1. Best practices of other locations and channels can be used to get a jump start. 2. Comparison with competitor data can help to create a differentiator/USP factor to attract the new customers.
Store Layout	1. How should I do store layout for better topline? 2. How can I increase my in-store customer experience?	1. Understand the association of products to decide store layout and better alignment with customer needs. 2. Workforce deployment can be planned for better customer interactivity and thus satisfying customer experience.
Video Analytics	1. What demography is entering the store during the peak period of sales? 2. How can I identify a customer with high LTV at the store entrance so that a better personalized experience can be provided to this customer?	1. In-store promotions and events can be planned based on the demography of incoming traffic. 2. Targeted customer engagement and instant discount enhances the customer experience resulting in higher retention.

An online retail site usually knows its customer as soon as the customer signs in, and thus they can offer customized pages/offerings to enhance the experience. For any retail store, knowing its customer at the store entrance is still a huge challenge. By combining the video analytics and information/badge issued through their loyalty program, the store may be able to identify the customer at the entrance itself and thus enable an extra opportunity for a cross-sell or up-sell. Moreover, a personalized shopping experience can be provided with more customized engagement during the customer's time in the store.

Store retailers invest lots of money in attractive window displays, promotional events, customized graphics, store decorations, printed ads, and banners. To discern the effectiveness of these marketing methods, the team can use shopper analytics by observing closed-circuit television (CCTV) images to figure out the demographic details of the in-store foot traffic. The CCTV images can be analyzed using advanced algorithms to derive demographic details such as age, gender, and mood of the person browsing through the store.

Further, the customer's in-store movement data when combined with shelf layout and planogram can give more insight to the store manager to identify the hot-selling/profitable areas within the store. Moreover, the store manager can use this information to also plan the workforce allocation for those areas for peak periods.

Market basket analysis has commonly been used by the category managers to push the sale of the slowly moving SKUs. By using advanced analytics of data available, the product affinity can be done at the lowest level of SKU to drive better ROIs on the bundle offers. Moreover, by using price elasticity techniques, the markdown or optimum price of the bundle offer can also be deduced, thus reducing any loss in the profit margin.

Thus by using data analytics, a retailer can not only get information on its current operations but can also get further insight to increase the revenue and decrease the operational cost for higher profit. A fairly comprehensive list of current and potential retail analytics applications that a major retailer such as Amazon could use is proposed by a blogger at Data Science Central. That list is available at http://www.datasciencecentral.com/profiles/blogs/20-data-science-systems-used-by-amazon-to-operate-its-business. As noted earlier, there are too many examples of these opportunities to list here, but you will see many examples of such applications throughout the book.

SECTION 1.6 REVIEW QUESTIONS

1. Why would a health insurance company invest in analytics beyond fraud detection? Why is it in their best interest to predict the likelihood of falls by patients?
2. What other applications similar to prediction of falls can you envision?
3. How would you convince a new health insurance customer to adopt healthier lifestyles (Humana Example 3)?
4. Identify at least three other opportunities for applying analytics in the retail value chain beyond those covered in this section.
5. Which retail stores that you know of employ some of the analytics applications identified in this section?

1.7 A Brief Introduction to Big Data Analytics

What Is Big Data?

Any book on analytics and data science has to include significant coverage of what is called **Big Data analytics**. We will cover it in Chapter 7 but here is a very brief introduction. Our brains work extremely quickly and efficiently and are versatile in processing large amounts of all kinds of data: images, text, sounds, smells, and video. We process all different forms of data relatively easily. Computers, on the other hand, are still finding it hard to keep up with the pace at which data is generated, let alone analyze it fast. This is why we have the problem of Big Data. So, what is Big Data? Simply put, Big Data is data that cannot be stored in a single storage unit. Big Data typically refers to data that comes in many different forms: structured, unstructured, in a stream, and so forth. Major sources of such data are clickstreams from Web sites, postings on social media sites such as Facebook, and data from traffic, sensors, or weather. A Web search engine like Google needs to search and index billions of Web pages to give you relevant search results in a fraction of a second. Although this is not done in real time, generating an index of all the Web pages on the Internet is not an easy task. Luckily for Google, it was able to solve this problem. Among other tools, it has employed Big Data analytical techniques.

There are two aspects to managing data on this scale: storing and processing. If we could purchase an extremely expensive storage solution to store all this at one place on one unit, making this unit fault tolerant would involve a major expense. An ingenious solution was proposed that involved storing this data in chunks on different machines connected by a network—putting a copy or two of this chunk in different locations on the network, both logically and physically. It was originally used at Google (then called the Google File System) and later developed and released as an Apache project as the Hadoop Distributed File System (HDFS).

However, storing this data is only half the problem. Data is worthless if it does not provide business value, and for it to provide business value, it has to be analyzed. How can such vast amounts of data be analyzed? Passing all computation to one powerful computer does not work; this scale would create a huge overhead on such a powerful computer. Another ingenious solution was proposed: Push computation to the data, instead of pushing data to a computing node. This was a new paradigm and gave rise to a whole new way of processing data. This is what we know today as the MapReduce programming paradigm, which made processing Big Data a reality. MapReduce was originally developed at Google, and a subsequent version was released by the Apache project called Hadoop MapReduce.

Today, when we talk about storing, processing, or analyzing Big Data, HDFS and MapReduce are involved at some level. Other relevant standards and software solutions have been proposed. Although the major toolkit is available as an open source, several companies have been launched to provide training or specialized analytical hardware or software services in this space. Some examples are HortonWorks, Cloudera, and Teradata Aster.

Over the past few years, what was called Big Data changed more and more as Big Data applications appeared. The need to process data coming in at a rapid rate added velocity to the equation. An example of fast data processing is algorithmic trading. This uses electronic platforms based on algorithms for trading shares on the financial market, which operates in microseconds. The need to process different kinds of data added variety to the equation. Another example of a wide variety of data is sentiment analysis, which uses various forms of data from social media platforms and customer responses to gauge sentiments. Today, Big Data is associated with almost any kind of large data that has the characteristics of volume, velocity, and variety. Application Case 1.6 illustrates an application of Big Data analytics in the energy industry. We will study Big Data technologies and applications in Chapter 7.

SECTION 1.7 REVIEW QUESTIONS

1. What is Big Data analytics?
2. What are the sources of Big Data?
3. What are the characteristics of Big Data?
4. What processing technique is applied to process Big Data?

Application Case 1.6

CenterPoint Energy Uses Real-Time Big Data Analytics to Improve Customer Service

CenterPoint Energy is a *Fortune* 500 energy delivery company based in Houston, Texas. Its primary business includes electric transmission and distribution, natural gas distribution, and natural gas sales and service. It has over five million metered customers in the United States.

CenterPoint Energy uses smart grids to collect real-time information about the health of various aspects of the grid like meters, transformers, and switches that are used in providing electricity. This real-time power usage information is analyzed with Big Data analytics and allows for a much quicker diagnosis and solution. For example, the data can predict and potentially help prevent a power outage.

In addition, the tool collects weather information allowing historical data to help predict the magnitude of an outage from a storm. This insight will act as a guide for putting the right resources out before a storm occurs to avoid an outage.

Second, to better understand their customers, CenterPoint Energy utilizes sentiment analysis, which examines a customer's opinion by way of emotion (happiness, anger, sadness, etc.). The company segments their customers based on the sentiment and is able to market to these groups in a more personalized way, providing a more valuable customer service experience.

As a result of using Big Data analytics, CenterPoint Energy has saved 600,000 gallons of fuel in the last 2 years by resolving six million service requests remotely. In addition, they have saved $24 million for their customers in this process.

QUESTIONS FOR DISCUSSION

1. How can electric companies predict a possible outage at a location?
2. What is customer sentiment analysis?
3. How does customer sentiment analysis help companies provide a personalized service to their customers?

What We Can Learn from This Application Case

With the use of Big Data analytics, energy companies can better solve customer issues like outages and electric faults within a shorter span of time compared to the earlier process. Also sentiment analysis can help target their customers according to their needs.

Sources: Sap.com, "A 'Smart' Approach to Big Data in the Energy Industry," http://www.sap.com/bin/sapcom/cs_cz/downloadasset .2013-10-oct-09-20.a-smart-approach-to-big-data-in-the-energy-industry-pdf.html (accessed June 2016); centerpointenergy .com, "Electric Transmission & Distribution (T&D)," http://www .centerpointenergy.com/en-us/Corp/Pages/Company-overview .aspx (accessed June 2016); YouTube.com, "CenterPoint Energy Talks Real Time Big Data Analytics," https://www.youtube.com/ watch?v=s7CzeSlIEfI (accessed June 2016).

1.8 An Overview of the Analytics Ecosystem

So you are excited about the potential of analytics and want to join this growing industry. Who are the current players, and what to do they do? Where might you fit in? The objective of this section is to identify various sectors of the analytics industry, provide a classification of different types of industry participants, and illustrate the types of opportunities that exist for analytics professionals. Eleven different types of players are identified in an **analytics ecosystem**. An understanding of the ecosystem also gives the reader a broader view of how the various players come together. A secondary purpose of understanding the analytics ecosystem for the BI professional is also to be aware of organizations and new offerings and opportunities in sectors allied with analytics. The section concludes with some observations about the opportunities for professionals to move across these clusters.

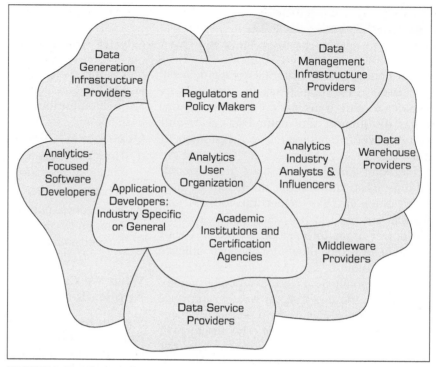

FIGURE 1.13 Analytics Ecosystem.

Although some researchers have distinguished business analytics professionals from data scientists (Davenport and Patil, 2012), as pointed out previously, for the purpose of understanding the overall analytics ecosystem, we treat them as one broad profession. Clearly, skill needs can vary between a strong mathematician to a programmer to a modeler to a communicator, and we believe this issue is resolved at a more micro/individual level rather than at a macro level of understanding the opportunity pool. We also take the widest definition of analytics to include all three types as defined by INFORMS—descriptive/reporting/visualization, predictive, and prescriptive as described earlier.

Figure 1.13 illustrates one view of the analytics ecosystem. The components of the ecosystem are represented by the petals of an analytics flower. Eleven key sectors or clusters in the analytics space are identified. The components of the analytics ecosystem are grouped into three categories represented by the inner petals, outer petals, and the seed (middle part) of the flower.

The outer six petals can be broadly termed as the technology providers. Their primary revenue comes from providing technology, solutions, and training to analytics user organizations so they can employ these technologies in the most effective and efficient manner. The inner petals can be generally defined as the analytics accelerators. The accelerators work with both technology providers and users. Finally, the core of the ecosystem comprises the analytics user organizations. This is the most important component, as every analytics industry cluster is driven by the user organizations.

The metaphor of a flower is well-suited for the analytics ecosystem as multiple components overlap each other. Similar to a living organism like a flower, all these petals grow and wither together. We use the terms *components, clusters, petals,* and *sectors* interchangeably to describe the various players in the analytics space. We introduce each of the industry sectors next and give some examples of players in each sector. The list of company names included in any petal is not exhaustive. The representative list of companies in each cluster is just to illustrate that cluster's unique offering to describe where analytics talent may be used or hired away. Also, mention of a company's name or its capability in one specific group does not imply that it is the only activity/offering of that organization. The main goal is to focus on the different analytic capabilities within each component of the analytics space. Many companies play in multiple sectors within the analytics industry and thus offer opportunities for movement within the field both horizontally and vertically.

Matt Turck, a venture capitalist with FirstMark has also developed and updates an analytics ecosystem focused on Big Data. His goal is to keep track of new and established players in various segments of the Big Data industry. A very nice visual image of his interpretation of the ecosystem and a comprehensive listing of companies is available through his Web site: http://mattturck.com/2016/02/01/big-data-landscape/ (accessed August 2016). We will also see a similar ecosystem in the context of the Internet of Things (IoT) in the last chapter.

Data Generation Infrastructure Providers

Perhaps the first place to begin identifying the clusters is by noting a new group of companies that enable generating and collection of data that may be used for developing analytical insights. Although this group could include all the traditional point-of-sale systems, inventory management systems, and technology providers for every step in a company's supply/value chain and operations, we mainly consider new players where the primary focus has been on enabling an organization to develop new insights into its operations as opposed to running its core operations. Thus this group includes companies creating the infrastructure for collecting data from different sources.

One of the emerging components of such an infrastructure is the "sensor." Sensors collect a massive amount of data at a faster rate and have been adopted by various sectors such as healthcare, sports, and energy. For example, health data collected by the sensors is generally used to track the health status of the users. Some of the major players manufacturing sensors to collect health information are AliveCor, Google, Shimmer, and Fitbit. Likewise, the sports industry is using sensors to collect data from the players and field to develop strategies and improve team play. Examples of the companies producing sports-related sensors include Sports Sensors, Zepp, Shockbox, and others. Similarly, sensors are used for traffic management. These help in taking real-time actions to control traffic. Some of the providers are Advantech B+B SmartWorx, Garmin, and Sensys Network.

Sensors play a major role in the Internet of Things and are an essential part of smart objects. These make machine-to-machine communication possible. The leading players in the infrastructure of IoT are Intel, Microsoft, Google, IBM, Cisco, Smartbin, SIKO Products, Omega Engineering, Apple, and SAP. This cluster is probably the most technical group in the ecosystem. We will review an ecosystem for IoT in Chapter 8. Indeed, there is an ecosystem around virtually each of the clusters we identify here.

Data Management Infrastructure Providers

This group includes all of the major organizations that provide hardware and software targeting the basic foundation for all data management solutions. Obvious examples of these include all major hardware players that provide the infrastructure for database computing—IBM, Dell, HP, Oracle, and so on; storage solution providers like EMC (recently bought by Dell) and NetApp; companies providing indigenous hardware and software platforms such as IBM, Oracle, and Teradata; and data solution providers offering hardware and platform independent database management systems like the SQL Server family of Microsoft and specialized integrated software providers such as SAP fall under this group. This group also includes other organizations such as database appliance providers, service providers, integrators, developers, and so on, that support each of these companies' ecosystems.

Several other companies are emerging as major players in a related space, thanks to the network infrastructure enabling cloud computing. Companies such as Amazon

(Amazon Web Services), IBM (Bluemix), and Salesforce.com pioneered to offer full data storage and analytics solutions through the cloud, which now have been adopted by several companies listed earlier.

A recent crop of companies in the Big Data space are also part of this group. Companies such as Cloudera, Hortonworks, and many others do not necessarily offer their own hardware but provide infrastructure services and training to create the Big Data platform. This would include Hadoop clusters, MapReduce, NoSQL, Spark, Kafka, Flume, and other related technologies for analytics. Thus they could also be grouped under industry consultants or trainers enabling the basic infrastructure. Full ecosystems of consultants, software integrators, training providers, and other value-added providers have evolved around many of the large players in the data management infrastructure cluster. Some of the clusters listed below will identify these players because many of them are moving to analytics as the industry shifts its focus from efficient transaction processing to deriving analytical value from the data.

Data Warehouse Providers

Companies with a data warehousing focus provide technology and services aimed toward integrating data from multiple sources, thus enabling organizations to derive and deliver value from its data assets. Many companies in this space include their own hardware to provide efficient data storage, retrieval, and processing. Companies such as IBM, Oracle, and Teradata are major players in this arena. Recent developments in this space include performing analytics on the data directly in memory. Another major growth sector has been data warehousing in the cloud. Examples of such companies include Snowflake and Redshift. Companies in this cluster clearly work with all the other sector players in providing DW solutions and services within their ecosystem and hence become the backbone of the analytics industry. It has been a major industry in its own right and, thus, a supplier and consumer of analytics talent.

Middleware Providers

Data warehousing began with a focus on bringing all the data stores into an enterprise-wide platform. Making sense of this data has become an industry in itself. The general goal of the middleware industry is to provide easy-to-use tools for reporting or descriptive analytics, which forms a core part of BI or analytics employed at organizations. Examples of companies in this space include Microstrategy, Plum, and many others. A few of the major players that were independent middleware players have been acquired by companies in the first two groups. For example, Hyperion became a part of Oracle, SAP acquired Business Objects, and IBM acquired Cognos. This sector has been largely synonymous with the BI providers offering dashboarding, reporting, and visualization services to the industry, building on top of the transaction processing data and the database and DW providers. Thus many companies have moved into this space over the years, including general analytics software vendors such as SAS or new visualization providers such as Tableau, or many niche application providers. A product directory at TDWI.org lists 201 vendors just in this category (http://www.tdwidirectory.com/category/business-intelligence-services) as of June 2016, so the sector has been robust. This is clearly also the sector attempting to move to a more data science segment of the industry.

Data Service Providers

Much of the data an organization uses for analytics is generated internally through its operations, but there are many external data sources that play a major role in any organization's decision making. Examples of such data sources include demographic data, weather data,

data collected by third parties that could inform an organization's decision making, and so on. Several companies realized the opportunity to develop specialized data collection, aggregation, and distribution mechanisms. These companies typically focus on a specific industry sector and build on their existing relationships in that industry through their niche platforms and services for data collection. For example, Nielsen provides data sources to their clients on customer retail purchasing behavior. Another example is Experian, which includes data on each household in the United States. Omniture has developed technology to collect Web clicks and share such data with their clients. Comscore is another major company in this space. Google compiles data for individual Web sites and makes a summary available through Google Analytics services. Other examples are Equifax, TransUnion, Acxiom, Merkle, Epsilon, and Avention. This can also include organizations such as ESRI.org, which provides location-oriented data to their customers. There are hundreds of other companies that are developing niche platforms and services to collect, aggregate, and share such data with their clients. As noted earlier, many industry-specific data aggregators and distributors exist and are moving to offer their own analytics services. Thus this sector is also a growing user and potential supplier of analytics talent, especially with specific niche expertise.

Analytics-Focused Software Developers

Companies in this category have developed analytics software for general use with data that has been collected in a DW or is available through one of the platforms identified earlier (including Big Data). It can also include inventors and researchers in universities and other organizations that have developed algorithms for specific types of analytics applications. We can identify major industry players in this space using the three types of analytics: descriptive, predictive, and prescriptive analytics.

REPORTING/DESCRIPTIVE ANALYTICS Reporting or descriptive analytics is enabled by the tools available from the middleware industry players identified earlier, or unique capabilities offered by focused providers. For example, Microsoft's SQL Server BI toolkit includes reporting as well as predictive analytics capabilities. On the other hand, specialized software is available from companies such as Tableau for visualization. SAS also offers a Visual Analytics tool with similar capacity. There are many open source visualization tools as well. Literally hundreds of data visualization tools have been developed around the world, and many such tools focus on visualization of data from a specific industry or domain. Because visualization is the primary way thus far for exploring analytics in industry, this sector has witnessed the most growth. Many new companies are being formed. For example, Gephi, a free and open source software, focuses on visualizing networks. A Google search will show the latest list of such software providers and tools.

PREDICTIVE ANALYTICS Perhaps the biggest recent growth in analytics has been in this category, and there are a large number of companies that focus on predictive analytics. Many statistical software companies such as SAS and SPSS embraced predictive analytics early on, and developed software capabilities as well as industry practices to employ data mining techniques and classical statistical techniques for analytics. IBM-SPSS Modeler from IBM and Enterprise Miner from SAS are some of the examples of tools used for predictive analytics. Other players in this space include KXEN, Statsoft (recently acquired by Dell), Salford Systems, and scores of other companies that may sell their software broadly or use it for their own consulting practices (next group of companies).

Three open source platforms (R, RapidMiner, and KNIME) have also emerged as popular industrial-strength software tools for predictive analytics and have companies that support training and implementation of these open source tools. Revolution Analytics is an example of a company focused on R development and training. R integration is possible with most analytics software. A company called Alteryx uses R extensions for reporting and predictive analytics, but its strength is in shared delivery of analytics solutions processes to customers and other users. Similarly, RapidMiner and KNIME are also examples of open source providers. Companies like Rulequest that sell proprietary variants of Decision Tree software and NeuroDimensions, a Neural Network software company, are examples of companies that have developed specialized software around a specific technique of data mining.

PRESCRIPTIVE ANALYTICS Software providers in this category offer modeling tools and algorithms for optimization of operations usually called management science/operations research software. This field has had its own set of major software providers. IBM, for example, has classic linear and mixed integer programming software. Several years ago, IBM also acquired a company called ILOG, which provides prescriptive analysis software and services to complement their other offerings. Analytics providers such as SAS have their own OR/MS tools—SAS/OR. FICO acquired another company called XPRESS that offers optimization software. Other major players in this domain include companies such as AIIMS, AMPL, Frontline, GAMS, Gurobi, Lindo Systems, Maximal, NGData, Ayata, and many others. A detailed delineation and description of these companies' offerings is beyond the scope of our goals here. Suffice it to say that this industry sector has seen much growth recently.

Of course, there are many techniques that fall under the category of prescriptive analytics, and each has their own set of providers. For example, simulation software is provided by major companies like Rockwell (ARENA) and Simio. Palisade provides tools that include many software categories. Similarly, Frontline offers tools for optimization with Excel spreadsheets, as well as predictive analytics. Decision analysis in multiobjective settings can be performed using tools such as Expert Choice. There are also tools from companies such as Exsys, XpertRule, and others for generating rules directly from data or expert inputs.

Some new companies are evolving to combine multiple analytics models in the Big Data space including social network analysis and stream mining. For example, Teradata Aster includes its own predictive and prescriptive analytics capabilities in processing Big Data streams. Several companies have developed complex event processing (CEP) engines that make decisions using streaming data, such as IBM's Infosphere Streams, Microsoft's StreamInsight, and Oracle's Event Processor. Other major companies that have CEP products include Apache, Tibco, Informatica, SAP, and Hitachi. It is worthwhile to note again that the provider groups for all three categories of analytics are not mutually exclusive. In most cases, a provider can play in multiple components of analytics.

We next introduce the "inside petals" of the analytics flower. These clusters can be called analytics accelerators. Although they may not be involved in developing the technology directly, these organizations have played a key role in shaping the industry.

Application Developers: Industry Specific or General

The organizations in this group use their industry knowledge, analytical expertise, solutions available from the data infrastructure, DW, middleware, data aggregators, and analytics software providers to develop custom solutions for a specific industry. Thus, this industry group makes it possible for analytics technology to be used in a specific industry. Of course, such groups may also exist in specific user organizations. Most major analytics technology providers like IBM, SAS, and Teradata clearly recognize the opportunity to connect to a specific industry or client and offer analytic consulting services. Companies that have traditionally provided application/data solutions to specific sectors are now developing industry-specific analytics offerings. For example, Cerner provides electronic medical records solutions to medical providers, and their offerings now include many analytics reports and visualizations. Similarly, IBM offers a fraud detection engine for the health insurance industry, and is working with an insurance company to employ their famous Watson analytics platform in assisting medical providers and insurance companies with diagnosis and disease management. Another example of a vertical application provider is Sabre Technologies, which provides analytical solutions to the travel industry including fare pricing for revenue optimization and dispatch planning.

This cluster also includes companies that have developed their own domain-specific analytics solutions and market them broadly to a client base. For example, Nike, IBM, and Sportvision develop applications in sports analytics to improve the play and increase the viewership. Acxiom has developed clusters for virtually all households in the United States based on the data they collect about households from many different sources. Credit score and classification reporting companies (FICO, Experian, etc.) also belong in this group. IBM and several other companies offer pricing optimization solutions in the retail industry.

This field represents an entrepreneurial opportunity to develop industry-specific applications. Many emerging in Web/social media/location analytics are trying to profile users for better targeting of promotional campaigns in real time. Examples of such companies and their activities include: YP.com employs location data for developing user/ group profiles and targeting mobile advertisements, Towerdata profiles users on the basis of e-mail usage, Qualia aims to identify users through all device usage, and Simulmedia targets advertisements on TV on the basis of analysis of a user's TV watching habits.

The growth of smartphones has spawned a complete industry focused on specific analytics applications for consumers as well as organizations. For example, smartphone apps such as Shazam, Soundhound, or Musixmatch are able to identify a song on the basis of the first few notes and then let the user select it from their song base to play/download /purchase. Waze uses real-time traffic information shared by users, in addition to the location data, for improving navigation. Voice recognition tools such as Siri on the iPhone, Google Now, and Amazon Alexa are leading to many more specialized analytics applications for very specific purposes in analytics applied to images, videos, audio, and other data that can be captured through smartphones and/or connected sensors. Smartphones have also elevated the shared economy providers such as Uber, Lyft, Curb, and Ola. Many of these companies are exemplars of analytics leading to new business opportunities.

Online social media is another hot area in this cluster. Undoubtedly, Facebook is the leading player in the space of online social networking followed by Twitter and LinkedIn. Moreover, the public access to their data has given rise to multiple other companies that analyze their data. For example, Unmetric analyzes Twitter data and provides solutions to their clients. Similarly, there are several other companies that focus on social network analysis.

A trending area in the application development industry is the IoT. Several companies are building applications to make smart objects. For example, SmartBin has developed intelligent remote monitoring systems for the waste and recycling sectors. Several other organizations are working on building smart meters, smart grids, smart cities, connected cars, smart homes, smart supply chains, connected health, smart retail, and other smart objects.

This start-up activity and space is growing and is in major transition due to technology/venture funding and security/privacy issues. Nevertheless, the application developer sector is perhaps the biggest growth industry within analytics at this point. This cluster provides a unique opportunity for analytics professionals looking for more entrepreneurial career options.

Analytics Industry Analysts and Influencers

The next cluster of the analytics industry includes three types of organizations or professionals. The first group is the set of professional organizations that provide advice to the analytics industry providers and users. Their services include marketing analyses, coverage of new developments, evaluation of specific technologies, and development of training/white papers/ and so on. Examples of such players include organizations such as the Gartner Group, The Data Warehousing Institute, Forrester, McKinsey, and many of the general and technical publications and Web sites that cover the analytics industry. Gartner Group's Magic Quadrants are highly influential and are based on industry surveys. Similarly, TDWI.org professionals provide excellent industry overviews and are very aware of current and future trends of this industry.

The second group includes professional societies or organizations that also provide some of the same services but are membership based and organized. For example, INFORMS, a professional organization, has now focused on promoting analytics. Special Interest Group on Decision Support and Analytics, a subgroup of the Association for Information Systems, also focuses on analytics. Most of the major vendors (e.g., Teradata and SAS) also have their own membership-based user groups. These entities promote the use of analytics and enable sharing of the lessons learned through their publications and conferences. They may also provide recruiting services, and are thus good sources for locating talent.

A third group of analytics industry analysts is what we call analytics ambassadors, influencers, or evangelists. These analysts have presented their enthusiasm for analytics through their seminars, books, and other publications. Illustrative examples include Steve Baker, Tom Davenport, Charles Duhigg, Wayne Eckerson, Bill Franks, Malcolm Gladwell, Claudia Imhoff, Bill Inman, and many others. Again, the list is not inclusive. All of these ambassadors have written books (some of them bestsellers!) and/or given many presentations to promote the analytics applications. Perhaps another group of evangelists to include here is the authors of textbooks on BI/analytics who aim to assist the next cluster to produce professionals for the analytics industry. Clearly, it will take some time for an analytics student to become a member of this cluster, but they could be working with members of this cluster as researchers or apprentices.

Academic Institutions and Certification Agencies

In any knowledge-intensive industry such as analytics, the fundamental strength comes from having students who are interested in the technology and choosing that industry as their profession. Universities play a key role in making this possible. This cluster, then, represents the academic programs that prepare professionals for the industry. It includes various components of business schools such as information systems, marketing, management sciences, and so on. It also extends far beyond business schools to include computer science, statistics, mathematics, and industrial engineering departments across the world. The cluster also includes graphics developers who design new ways of visualizing information. Universities are offering undergraduate and graduate programs in analytics in all of these disciplines, though they may be labeled differently. A major growth frontier has been certificate programs in analytics to enable current professionals to retrain and retool themselves for analytics careers. Certificate programs enable practicing analysts to gain basic proficiency in specific software by taking a few critical courses from schools that offer these programs. TUN includes a list of analytics programs. It includes almost 150 programs, and there are likely many more such programs, with new ones being added daily.

Another group of players assists with developing competency in analytics. These are certification programs that award a certificate of expertise in specific software. Virtually every major technology provider (IBM, Microsoft, Microstrategy, Oracle, SAS, Tableau, and Teradata) has their own certification programs. These certificates ensure that potential new hires have a certain level of tool skills. On the other hand, INFORMS offers a Certified Analytics Professional certificate program that is aimed at testing an individual's general analytics competency. Any of these certifications give a college student additional marketable skills.

The growth of academic programs in analytics is staggering. Only time will tell if this cluster is overbuilding the capacity that can be consumed by the other clusters, but at this point, the demand appears to outstrip the supply of qualified analytics graduates, and this is the most obvious place to find at least entry-level analytics hires.

Regulators and Policy Makers

The players in this component are responsible for defining rules and regulations for protecting employees, customers, and shareholders of the analytics organizations. The collection and sharing of the users' data require strict laws for securing privacy. Several organizations in this space regulate the data transfer and protect users' rights. For example, the Federal Communications Commission (FCC) regulates interstate and international communications. Similarly, the Federal Trade Commission (FTC) is responsible for preventing data-related unfair business practices. The International Telecommunication Union (ITU) regulates the access to information and communication technologies (ICTs) to underserved communities worldwide. On the other hand, a nonregulatory federal agency named the National Institute of Standards and Technology (NIST), helps advance the technology infrastructure. There are several other organizations across the globe that regulate the data security and accelerate the analytics industry. This is a very important component in the ecosystem so that no one can misuse consumers' information.

For anyone developing or using analytics applications, it is perhaps crucial to have someone on the team who is aware of the regulatory framework. These agencies and professionals who work with them clearly offer unique analytics talents and skills.

Analytics User Organizations

Clearly, this is the economic engine of the whole analytics industry, and therefore, we represent this cluster as the core of the analytics flower. If there were no users, there would be no analytics industry. Organizations in every industry, regardless of size, shape, and location, are using or exploring the use of analytics in their operations. These include the private sector, government, education, military, and so on. It includes organizations around the world. Examples of uses of analytics in different industries abound. Others are exploring similar opportunities to try and gain/retain a competitive advantage. Specific companies are not identified in this section; rather, the goal here is to see what type of roles analytics professionals can play within a user organization.

Of course, the top leadership of an organization, especially in the information technology group (chief information officer, etc.), is critically important in applying analytics to its operations. Reportedly, Forrest Mars of the Mars Chocolate Empire said that all management boiled down to applying mathematics to a company's operations and economics. Although not enough senior managers subscribe to this view, the awareness of applying analytics within an organization is growing everywhere. A health insurance company executive once told us that his boss (the CEO) viewed the company as an IT-enabled organization that collected money from insured members and distributed it to the providers. Thus efficiency in this process was the premium they could earn over a competitor. This led the company to develop several analytics applications to reduce fraud and overpayment to providers, promote wellness among those insured so they would use the providers less often, generate more efficiency in processing, and thus be more profitable.

Virtually all major organizations in every industry that we are aware of are hiring analytical professionals under various titles. Figure 1.14 is a word cloud of the selected titles of our program graduates at Oklahoma State University from 2013 to 2016. It clearly shows that Analytics and Data Science are popular titles in the organizations hiring graduates of such programs. Other key words appear to include terms such as Risk, Database, Security, Revenue, Marketing, and so on.

FIGURE 1.14   Word Cloud of Job Titles of Analytics Program Graduates.

Of course, user organizations include career paths for analytics professionals moving into management positions. These titles include project managers, senior managers, and directors, all the way up to the chief information officer or chief executive officer. This suggests that user organizations exist as a key cluster in the analytics ecosystem and thus can be a good source of talent. It is perhaps the first place to find analytics professionals within the vertical industry segment.

The purpose of this section has been to present a map of the landscape of the analytics industry. Eleven different groups that play a key role in building and fostering this industry were identified. More petals/components can be added over time in the analytics flower/ecosystem. Because data analytics requires a diverse skill set, understanding of this ecosystem provides you with more options than you may have imagined for careers in analytics. Moreover, it is possible for professionals to move from one industry cluster to another to take advantage of their skills. For example, expert professionals from providers can sometimes move to consulting positions, or directly to user organizations. Overall, there is much to be excited about the analytics industry at this point.

SECTION 1.8 REVIEW QUESTIONS

1. List the 11 categories of players in the analytics ecosystem.
2. Give examples of companies in each of the 11 types of players.
3. Which companies are dominant in more than one category?
4. Is it better to be the strongest player in one category or be active in multiple categories?

1.9   Plan of the Book

The previous sections have given you an understanding of the need for information technology in decision making, the evolution of BI, and now into analytics and data science. In the last several sections we have seen an overview of various types of analytics and their applications. Now we are ready for a more detailed managerial excursion into these topics, along with some deep hands-on experience in some of the technical topics. Figure 1.15 presents a plan on the rest of the book.

In this chapter, we have provided an introduction, definitions, and overview of DSSs, BI, and analytics, including Big Data analytics and data science. We also gave you an

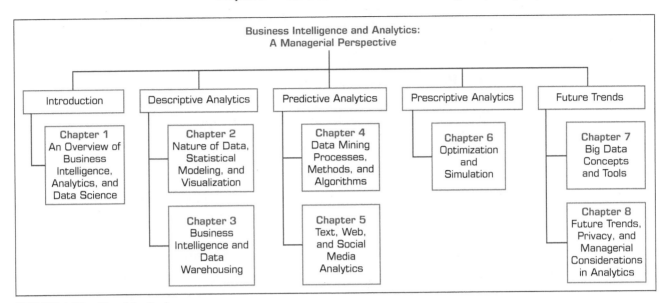

FIGURE 1.15 Plan of the Book.

overview of the analytics ecosystem to have you appreciate the breadth and depth of the industry. Chapters 2 and 3 cover descriptive analytics and data issues. Data clearly form the foundation for any analytics application. Thus we cover an introduction to data warehousing issues, applications, and technologies. This section also covers business reporting and visualization technologies and applications. This is followed by a brief overview of BPM techniques and applications—a topic that has been a key part of traditional BI.

The next section covers predictive analytics. Chapter 4 provides an introduction to predictive analytics applications. It includes many of the common data mining techniques: classification, clustering, association mining, and so forth. Chapter 5 focuses on text mining applications as well as Web analytics, including social media analytics, sentiment analysis, and other related topics. Chapter 6 covers prescriptive analytics. Chapter 7 includes more details of Big Data analytics. Chapter 8 includes a discussion of emerging trends. The ubiquity of wireless and GPS devices and other sensors is resulting in the creation of massive new databases and unique applications. A new breed of analytics companies is emerging to analyze these new databases and create a much better and deeper understanding of customers' behaviors and movements. It is leading to the automation of analytics and has also spanned a new area called the "Internet of Things." The chapter also covers cloud-based analytics, Finally, Chapter 8 also attempts to integrate all the material covered in this book and concludes with a brief discussion of security/privacy dimensions of analytics.

1.10 Resources, Links, and the Teradata University Network Connection

The use of this chapter and most other chapters in this book can be enhanced by the tools described in the following sections.

Resources and Links

We recommend the following major resources and links:

- The Data Warehousing Institute (tdwi.org)
- Data Science Central (datasciencecentral.com)

- DSS Resources (dssresources.com)
- Microsoft Enterprise Consortium (enterprise.waltoncollege.uark.edu/mec.asp)

Vendors, Products, and Demos

Most vendors provide software demos of their products and applications. Information about products, architecture, and software is available at dssresources.com.

Periodicals

We recommend the following periodicals:

- *Decision Support Systems* (www.journals.elsevier.com/decision-support-systems)
- *CIO Insight* (cioinsight.com)

The Teradata University Network Connection

This book is tightly connected with the free resources provided by TUN (see teradata universitynetwork.com). The TUN portal is divided into two major parts: one for students and one for faculty. This book is connected to the TUN portal via a special section at the end of each chapter. That section includes appropriate links for the specific chapter, pointing to relevant resources. In addition, we provide hands-on exercises, using software and other material (e.g., cases) available at TUN.

The Book's Web Site

This book's Web site, pearsonhighered.com/sharda, contains supplemental textual material organized as Web chapters that correspond to the printed book's chapters. The topics of these chapters are listed in the online chapter table of contents.[1]

---

[1]As this book went to press, we verified that all cited Web sites were active and valid. However, URLs are dynamic. Web sites to which we refer in the text sometimes change or are discontinued because companies change names, are bought or sold, merge, or fail. Sometimes Web sites are down for maintenance, repair, or redesign. Many organizations have dropped the initial "www" designation for their sites, but some still use it. If you have a problem connecting to a Web site that we mention, please be patient and simply run a Web search to try to identify the possible new site. Most times, you can quickly find the new site through one of the popular search engines. We apologize in advance for this inconvenience.

Chapter Highlights

- The business environment is becoming more complex and is rapidly changing, making decision making more difficult.
- Businesses must respond and adapt to the changing environment rapidly by making faster and better decisions.
- The time frame for making decisions is shrinking, whereas the global nature of decision making is expanding, necessitating the development and use of computerized DSSs.
- DSSs use data, models, and sometimes knowledge management to find solutions for semistructured and some unstructured problems.
- BI methods utilize a central repository called a DW that enables efficient data mining, OLAP, BPM, and data visualization.
- BI architecture includes a DW, business analytics tools used by end users, and a user interface (such as a dashboard).
- Many organizations employ descriptive analytics to replace their traditional flat reporting with interactive reporting that provides insights, trends, and patterns in the transactional data.

- Predictive analytics enable organizations to establish predictive rules that drive the business outcomes through historical data analysis of the existing behavior of the customers.
- Prescriptive analytics help in building models that involve forecasting and optimization techniques based on the principles of OR and management science to help organizations to make better decisions.
- Big Data analytics focuses on unstructured, large data sets that may also include vastly different types of data for analysis.
- Analytics as a field is also known by industry-specific application names, such as sports analytics. It is also known by other related names such as data science or network science.
- Healthcare and retail chains are two areas where analytics applications abound, with much more to come.
- The analytics ecosystem can be first viewed as a collection of providers, users, and facilitators. It can be broken into 11 clusters.

Key Terms

analytics	dashboard	descriptive (or reporting) analytics	online transaction processing (OLTP)
analytics ecosystem	data mining	intelligent agents	predictive analytics
Big data analytics	decision or normative analytics	online analytical processing (OLAP)	prescriptive analytics
business intelligence (BI)			Web services

Questions for Discussion

1. Survey the literature from the past 6 months to find one application each for DSS, BI, and analytics. Summarize the applications on one page, and submit it with the exact sources.
2. Distinguish BI from DSS.
3. Compare and contrast predictive analytics with prescriptive and descriptive analytics. Use examples.
4. Discuss the major issues in implementing BI.

Exercises

Teradata University Network and Other Hands-On Exercises

1. Go to teradatauniversitynetwork.com. Using the site password your instructor provides, register for the site if you have not already previously registered. Log on and learn the content of the site. You will receive assignments related to this site. Prepare a list of 20 items on the site that you think could be beneficial to you.

2. Go to the TUN site. Explore the Sports Analytics page, and summarize at least two applications of analytics in any sport of your choice.

3. Enter the TUN site, and select "Cases, Projects, and Assignments." Then select the case study "Harrah's High Payoff from Customer Information." Answer the following questions about this case:
   a. What information does the data mining generate?
   b. How is this information helpful to management in decision making? (Be specific.)
   c. List the types of data that are mined.
   d. Is this a DSS or BI application? Why?

4. Go to teradatauniversitynetwork.com and find the paper titled "Data Warehousing Supports Corporate Strategy at First American Corporation" (by Watson, Wixom, and Goodhue). Read the paper, and answer the following questions:
   a. What were the drivers for the DW/BI project in the company?
   b. What strategic advantages were realized?
   c. What operational and tactical advantages were achieved?
   d. What were the critical success factors for the implementation?

5. Go to http://analytics-magazine.org/issues/digital-editions and find the January/February 2012 edition titled "Special Issue: The Future of Healthcare." Read the article "Predictive Analytics—Saving Lives and Lowering Medical Bills." Answer the following questions:
   a. What problem is being addressed by applying predictive analytics?
   b. What is the FICO Medication Adherence Score?
   c. How is a prediction model trained to predict the FICO Medication Adherence Score HoH? Did the prediction model classify the FICO Medication Adherence Score?
   d. Zoom in on Figure 4, and explain what kind of technique is applied on the generated results.
   e. List some of the actionable decisions that were based on the prediction results.

6. Go to http://analytics-magazine.org/issues/digital-editions, and find the January/February 2013 edition titled "Work Social." Read the article "Big Data, Analytics and Elections," and answer the following questions:
   a. What kinds of Big Data were analyzed in the article Coo? Comment on some of the sources of Big Data.
   b. Explain the term *integrated system*. What is the other technical term that suits an *integrated system*?
   c. What kinds of data analysis techniques are employed in the project? Comment on some initiatives that resulted from data analysis.
   d. What are the different prediction problems answered by the models?
   e. List some of the actionable decisions taken that were based on the prediction results.
   f. Identify two applications of Big Data analytics that are not listed in the article.

7. Search the Internet for material regarding the work of managers and the role analytics plays. What kinds of references to consulting firms, academic departments, and programs do you find? What major areas are represented? Select five sites that cover one area, and report your findings.

8. Explore the public areas of dssresources.com. Prepare a list of its major available resources. You might want to refer to this site as you work through the book.

9. Go to microstrategy.com. Find information on the five styles of BI. Prepare a summary table for each style.

10. Go to oracle.com, and click the Hyperion link under Applications. Determine what the company's major products are. Relate these to the support technologies cited in this chapter.

11. Go to the TUN questions site. Look for BSI videos. Review the video of the "Case of Retail Tweeters." Prepare a one-page summary of the problem, proposed solution, and the reported results. You can also find associated slides on slideshare.net.

12. Review the Analytics Ecosystem section. Identify at least two additional companies in at least five of the industry clusters noted in the discussion.

13. The discussion for the analytics ecosystem also included several typical job titles for graduates of analytics and data science programs. Research Web sites such datasciencecentral.com and tdwi.org to locate at least three additional similar job titles that you may find interesting for your career.

References

Capcredit.com. (2015). "How Much Do Americans Spend on Sports Each Year?" capcredit.com/how-much-americans-spend-on-sports-each-year/ (accessed July 2016).

CDC.gov. (2015, September 21). "Important Facts about Falls." cdc.gov/homeandrecreationalsafety/falls/adultfalls.html (accessed July 2016).

CenterPointEnergy.com. "Company Overview." centerpoint energy.com/en-us/Corp/Pages/Company-overview .aspx (accessed June 2016).

Chiguluri, V., Guthikonda, K., Slabaugh, S., Havens, E., Peña, J., & Cordier, T. (2015, June). *Relationship between diabetes complications and health related quality of life among an elderly population in the United States.* Poster presentation at the American Diabetes Association 75th Annual Scientific Sessions. Boston, MA.

Cordier, T., Slabaugh, L., Haugh, G., Gopal, V., Cusano, D., Andrews, G., & Renda, A. (2015, September). *Quality of life changes with progressing congestive heart failure.* Poster presentation at the 19th Annual Scientific Meeting of the Heart Failure Society of America, Washington, DC.

Davenport, T., & SAS Institute Inc. (2014, February). Analytics in sports: The new science of winning. sas.com/content/dam/SAS/en_us/doc/whitepaper2/iia-analytics-in-sports-106993.pdf (accessed July 2016).

Davenport, T. H., & Patil, D. J. (2012). Data scientist. *Harvard Business Review, 90,* 70–76.

Dundas.com. "How Siemens Drastically Reduced Cost With Managed Bi Applications." dundas.com/resource/get casestudy?caseStudyName=09-03-2016-Siemens%2FDundas-BI-Siemens-Case-Study.pdf (accessed July 2016).

Emc.com. (n.d.). "Data science revealed: A data-driven glimpse into the burgeoning new field". emc.com/collateral/about/news/emc-data-science-study-wp.pdf (accessed July 2016).

Gartner, Inc. (2004). *Using business intelligence to gain a competitive edge. A special report.*

Gates, S., Smith, L. A., Fisher, J. D., et al. (2008). Systematic review of accuracy of screening instruments for predicting fall risk among independently living older adults. *Journal of Rehabilitation Research and Development, 45*(8), 1105–1116.

Gill, T. M., Murphy, T. E., Gahbauer, E. A., et al. (2013). Association of injurious falls with disability outcomes and nursing home admissions in community living older persons. *American Journal of Epidemiology, 178*(3), 418–425.

Gorry, G. A., & Scott-Morton, M. S. (1971). A framework for management information systems. *Sloan Management Review, 13*(1), 55–70.

Keen, P. G. W., & M. S. Scott-Morton. (1978). *Decision support systems: An organizational perspective.* Reading, MA: Addison-Wesley.

Havens, E., Peña, J., Slabaugh, S., Cordier, T., Renda, A., & Gopal, V. (2015, October). Exploring the relationship between health-related quality of life and health conditions, costs, resource utilization, and quality measures. Podium presentation at the ISOQOL 22nd Annual Conference, Vancouver, Canada.

Havens, E., Slabaugh, L., Peña, J., Haugh, G., & Gopal, V. (2015, February). *Are there differences in Healthy Days based on compliance to preventive health screening measures?* Poster presentation at Preventive Medicine 2015, Atlanta, GA.

Humana. *2016 progress report.* populationhealth. humana.com/wp-content/uploads/2016/05/BoldGoal2016ProgressReport_1.pdf (accessed July 2016).

INFORMS. *Analytics section overview.* informs.org/Community/Analytics (accessed July 2016).

NCAA, National Center for Catastrophic Sports Injury Research Report. NCAA Sport Injury fact sheets are produced by the Datalys Center for Sports Injury Research and Prevention in collaboration with the National Collegiate Athletic Association, and STOP Sports Injuries. *Women's soccer injuries.* ncaa.org/sites/default/files/NCAA_W_Soccer_Injuries_WEB.pdf (accessed July 2016).

Pajouh Foad, M., Xing, D., Hariharan, S., Zhou, Y., Balasundaram, B., Liu, T., & Sharda, R. (2013). Available-to-promise in practice: An application of analytics in the specialty steel bar products industry. *Interfaces, 43*(6), 503–517. dx.doi.org/10.1287/inte.2013.0693 (accessed July 2016).

Price Waterhouse Coopers Report. (2011, December). *Changing the game: Outlook for the global sports market to 2015.* pwc.com/gx/en/hospitality-leisure/pdf/changing-the-game-outlook-for-the-global-sports-market-to-2015.pdf (accessed July 2016).

Sap.com. (2013, October). A "Smart" Approach to Big Data in the Energy Industry. sap.com/bin/sapcom/cs_cz/downloadasset.2013-10-oct-09-20.a-smart-approach-to-big-data-in-the-energy-industry-pdf.html (accessed June 2016).

Sharda, R., Asamoah, D., & Ponna, N. (2013). Research and pedagogy in business analytics: Opportunities and illustrative examples. *Journal of Computing and Information Technology, 21*(3), 171–182.

Siemens.com. *About Siemens.* siemens.com/about/en/ (accessed July 2016).

Silvaris.com. *Silvaris overview.* silvaris.com/About/ (accessed July 2016).

Simon, H. (1977). *The New Science of Management Decision.* Englewood Cliffs, NJ: Prentice Hall.

Tableau.com. *Silvaris augments proprietary technology platform with Tableau's real-time reporting capabilities.* tableau.com/sites/default/files/case-studies/silvaris-business-dashboards_0.pdf (accessed July 2016).

TeradataUniversityNetwork.com. (2015, Fall). *BSI: Sports analytics—Precision football* (video). teradatauniversitynetwork.com/About-Us/Whats-New/BSI-Sports-Analytics-Precision-Football/ (accessed July 2016).

Terry, D. (2011), "Sabre Streamlines Decision Making," http://www.teradatamagazine.com/v11n04/Features/Sabre-Streamlines-Decision-Making/ (Accessed July 2016).

Turck, Matt, "Is Big Data Still a Thing? (The 2016 Big Data Landscape)." http://mattturck.com/2016/02/01/big-data-landscape/ (accessed August 2016)

Watson, H. (2005, Winter). Sorting out what's new in decision support. *Business Intelligence Journal.*

Wikipedia.org. *On-base percentage.* en.wikipedia.org /wiki/On_base_percentage (accessed January 2013).

Wikipedia.org. *Sabermetrics.* en.wikipedia.org/wiki /Sabermetrics (accessed January 2013).

Wikipedia.org. *SIEMENS.* en.wikipedia.org/wiki/Siemens (accessed July 2016).

Wintergreen Research Press Release (PR Newswire). (2015, June 25). *Sports analytics market worth $4.7 billion by 2021.* prnewswire.com/news-releases/sports-analytics-market-worth-47-billion-by-2021-509869871.html (accessed July 2016).

YouTube.com. (2013, December 17). *CenterPoint energy talks real time big data analytics.* youtube.com/watch ?v=s7CzeSlIEfI (accessed June 2016).

Descriptive Analytics I: Nature of Data, Statistical Modeling, and Visualization

I n the age of Big Data and business analytics in which we are living, the importance of data is undeniable. The newly coined phrases like "data is the oil," "data is the new bacon," "data is the new currency," and "data is the king" are further stressing the renewed importance of data. But what type of data are we talking about? Obviously, not just any data. The "garbage in garbage out—GIGO" concept/principle applies to today's "Big Data" phenomenon more so than any data definition that we have had in the past. To live up to its promise, its value proposition, and its ability to turn into insight, data has to be carefully created/identified, collected, integrated, cleaned, transformed, and properly contextualized for use in accurate and timely decision making.

Data is the main theme of this chapter. Accordingly, the chapter starts with a description of the nature of data: what it is, what different types and forms it can come in, and how it can be preprocessed and made ready for analytics. The first few sections of the chapter are dedicated to a deep yet necessary understanding and processing of data. The next few sections describe the statistical methods used to prepare data as input to produce both descriptive and inferential measures. Following the statistics sections are sections on reporting and visualization. A report is a communication artifact prepared with the specific intention of converting data into information and knowledge and relaying that information in an easily understandable/digestible format. Nowadays, these reports are more visually oriented, often using colors and graphical icons that collectively look like a dashboard to enhance the information content. Therefore, the latter part of the chapter is dedicated to subsections that present the design, implementation, and best practices for information visualization, storytelling, and information dashboards.

2.1 Opening Vignette: SiriusXM Attracts and Engages a New Generation of Radio Consumers with Data-Driven Marketing   54

2.2 The Nature of Data   57

2.3 A Simple Taxonomy of Data   61

2.4 The Art and Science of Data Preprocessing   65

2.5 Statistical Modeling for Business Analytics   74

2.6 Regression Modeling for Inferential Statistics   86

2.7 Business Reporting   98

2.8 Data Visualization   101

2.9 Different Types of Charts and Graphs   106

2.10 The Emergence of Visual Analytics   110

2.11 Information Dashboards   117

2.1 OPENING VIGNETTE: SiriusXM Attracts and Engages a New Generation of Radio Consumers with Data-Driven Marketing

SiriusXM Radio is a satellite radio powerhouse, the largest radio company in the world with $3.8 billion in annual revenues and a wide range of hugely popular music, sports, news, talk, and entertainment stations. The company, which began broadcasting in 2001 with 50,000 subscribers, grew to 18.8 million subscribers in 2009, and today has nearly 29 million.

Much of SiriusXM's growth to date is rooted in creative arrangements with automobile manufacturers; today, nearly 70% of new cars are SiriusXM-enabled. Yet the company's reach has extended far beyond car radios in the United States to a worldwide presence on the Internet, on smartphones and through other services and distribution channels, including SONOS, JetBlue, and Dish.

Business Challenge

Despite these remarkable successes, over the past few years changing customer demographics, changing technology, and a changing competitive landscape have posed a new series of business challenges and opportunities for SiriusXM. Here are some notable ones:

- As its market penetration among new cars increased, the demographics of the buyers changed, skewing younger, with less discretionary income. How could SiriusXM reach this new demographic?
- As new cars became used cars and changed hands, how could SiriusXM identify, engage, and convert second owners to paying customers?
- With its acquisition of the connected vehicle business from Agero—the leading provider of telematics in the U.S. car market—SiriusXM gained the ability to deliver its service via both satellite and wireless networks. How could it successfully use this acquisition to capture new revenue streams?

Proposed Solution: Shifting the Vision toward Data-Driven Marketing

SiriusXM recognized that to address these challenges it would need to become a high-performance, data-driven marketing organization. The company began making that shift by establishing three fundamental tenets.

First, personalized interactions—not mass marketing—would rule the day. The company quickly understood that to conduct more personalized marketing, it would have to draw on past history and interactions, as well as on a keen understanding of the consumer's place in the subscription life cycle.

Second, to gain that understanding, information technology (IT) and its external technology partners would need the ability to deliver integrated data, advanced analytics, integrated marketing platforms, and multichannel delivery systems.

And third, the company could not achieve its business goals without an integrated and consistent point of view across the company. Most important, the technology and business sides of SiriusXM would have to become true partners to best address the challenges involved in becoming a high-performance marketing organization that draws on data-driven insights to speak directly with consumers in strikingly relevant ways.

Those data-driven insights, for example, would enable the company to differentiate between consumers, owners, drivers, listeners, and account holders. The insights would help SiriusXM understand what other vehicles and services are part of each household—and to create new opportunities for engagement. In addition, by constructing a coherent and reliable 360-degree view of all its consumers, SiriusXM could ensure that all messaging in all campaigns and interactions would be tailored, relevant, and consistent across all channels. The important bonus is that more tailored and effective marketing is typically more cost-efficient.

Implementation: Creating and Following the Path to High-Performance Marketing

At the time of its decision to become a high-performance marketing company, SiriusXM was working with a third-party marketing platform that did not have the capacity to support SiriusXM's ambitions. The company then made an important, forward-thinking decision to bring its marketing capabilities in-house—and then carefully plotted out what it would need to do to make the transition successfully.

1. Improve data cleanliness through improved master data management and governance. Although the company was understandably impatient to put ideas into action, data hygiene was a necessary first step to creating a reliable window into consumer behavior.
2. Bring marketing analytics in-house and expand the data warehouse to enable scale and fully support integrated marketing analytics.
3. Develop new segmentation and scoring models to run in-database, eliminating latency and data duplication.
4. Extend the integrated data warehouse to include marketing data and scoring, leveraging in-database analytics.
5. Adopt a marketing platform for campaign development.
6. Bring all that capability together to deliver real-time offer management across all marketing channels: call center, mobile, Web, and in-app.

Completing those steps meant finding the right technology partner. SiriusXM chose Teradata because its strengths were a strong match for the project and company. Teradata offered the ability to:

• Consolidate data sources with an integrated data warehouse (IDW), advanced analytics, and powerful marketing applications.

- Solve data latency issues.
- Significantly reduce data movement across multiple databases and applications.
- Seamlessly interact with applications and modules for all of the marketing areas.
- Scale and perform at very high levels for running campaigns and analytics in-database.
- Conduct real-time communications with customers.
- Provide operational support, either via the cloud or on-premise.

This partnership has enabled SiriusXM to move smoothly and swiftly along its road map, and the company is now in the midst of a transformational, 5-year process. After establishing its strong data governance process, SiriusXM began by implementing its Integrated Data Warehouse, which allowed the company to quickly and reliably operationalize insights throughout the organization.

Next, the company implemented Customer Interaction Manager—part of the Teradata Integrated Marketing Cloud, which enables real-time, dialog-based customer interaction across the full spectrum of digital and traditional communication channels. And, SiriusXM will incorporate the Teradata Digital Messaging Center.

Together, the suite of capabilities will allow SiriusXM to handle direct communications across multiple channels. This evolution will enable real-time offers, marketing messages and recommendations based on previous behavior.

In addition to streamlining how they execute and optimize outbound marketing activities, SiriusXM is also taking control of their internal marketing operations with the implementation of Marketing Resource Management, also part of the Teradata Integrated Marketing Cloud. The solution will allow SiriusXM to streamline workflow, optimize marketing resources, and drive efficiency through every penny of their marketing budget.

Results: Reaping the Benefits

As the company continues its evolution into a high-performance marketing organization, already SiriusXM is benefiting from its thoughtfully executed strategy. Household-level consumer insights and a complete view of marketing touch strategy with each consumer enable SiriusXM to create more targeted offers at the household, consumer, and device levels. By bringing the data and marketing analytics capabilities in-house, SiriusXM achieved the following:

- Campaign results in near real-time rather than 4 days, resulting in massive reductions in cycle times for campaigns and the analysts that support them.
- Closed-loop visibility allowing the analysts to support multistage dialogs and in-campaign modifications to increase campaign effectiveness.
- Real-time modeling and scoring to increase marketing intelligence and sharpen campaign offers and responses at the speed of their business.

Finally, SiriusXM's experience has reinforced the idea that high-performance marketing is a constantly evolving concept. The company has implemented both processes and the technology that give it the capacity for continued and flexible growth.

QUESTIONS FOR THE OPENING VIGNETTE

1. What does SiriusXM do? In what type of market does it conduct its business?
2. What were the challenges? Comment on both technology and data-related challenges.
3. What were the proposed solutions?
4. How did they implement the proposed solutions? Did they face any implementation challenges?

5. What were the results and benefits? Were they worth the effort/investment?

6. Can you think of other companies facing similar challenges that can potentially benefit from similar data-driven marketing solutions?

What We Can Learn from This Vignette

Striving to thrive in a fast-changing competitive industry, SiriusXM realized the need for a new and improved marketing infrastructure (one that relies on data and analytics) to effectively communicate the value proposition to its existing and potential customers. As is the case in any industry, in entertainment, success or mere survival depends on intelligently sensing the changing trends (likes and dislikes) and putting together the right messages and policies to win new customers while retaining the existing ones. The key is to create and manage successful marketing campaigns that resonate with the target population of customers and have a close feedback loop to adjust and modify the message to optimize the outcome. At the end, it was all about the precision in the way that they conducted business: being proactive about the changing nature of the clientele, creating and transmitting the right products and services in a timely manner using a fact-based/data-driven holistic marketing strategy. Source identification, source creation, access and collection, integration, cleaning, transformation, storage, and processing of relevant data played a critical role in SiriusXM's success in designing and implementing a marketing analytics strategy, as is the case in any analytically savvy successful company nowadays, regardless of the industry in which they are participating.

Sources: Quinn, C. (2016). Data-driven marketing at SiriusXM. Teradata Articles & News. at http://bigdata .teradata.com/US/Articles-News/Data-Driven-Marketing-At-SiriusXM/ (accessed August 2016); Teradata customer success story. SiriusXM attracts and engages a new generation of radio consumers. http://assets.teradata.com/ resourceCenter/downloads/CaseStudies/EB8597.pdf?processed=1.

2.2   The Nature of Data

Data is the main ingredient for any BI, data science, and business analytics initiative. In fact, it can be viewed as the raw material for what these popular decision technologies produce—information, insight, and **knowledge**. Without data none of these technologies could exist and be popularized—although, traditionally we have built analytics models using expert knowledge and experience coupled with very little or no data at all; however, those were the old days, and now data is of the essence. Once perceived as a big challenge to collect, store, and manage, data nowadays is widely considered among the most valuable assets of an organization, with the potential to create invaluable insight to better understand customers, competitors, and the business processes.

Data can be small or it can be very large. It can be structured (nicely organized for computers to process), or it can be unstructured (e.g., text that is created for humans and hence not readily understandable/consumable by computers). It can come in smaller batches continuously or it can pour in all at once as a large batch. These are some of the characteristics that define the inherent nature of today's data, which we often call Big Data. Even though these characteristics of data make it more challenging to process and consume, it also makes it more valuable because it enriches the data beyond its conventional limits, allowing for the discovery of new and novel knowledge. Traditional ways to manually collect data (either via surveys or via human-entered business transactions) mostly left their places to modern-day data collection mechanisms that use Internet and/or sensor/RFID-based computerized networks. These automated data collection systems are not only enabling us to collect more volumes of data but also enhancing the **data quality** and integrity. Figure 2.1 illustrates a typical analytics continuum—data to analytics to actionable information.

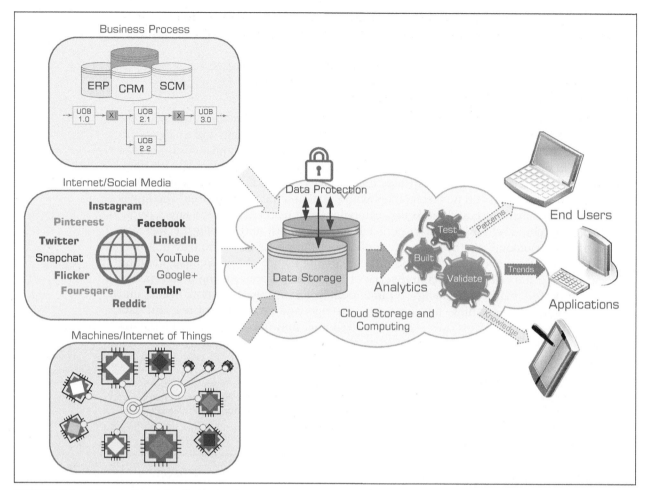

FIGURE 2.1 A Data to Knowledge Continuum.

Although its value proposition is undeniable, to live up its promise, the data has to comply with some basic usability and quality metrics. Not all data is useful for all tasks, obviously. That is, data has to match with (have the coverage of the specifics for) the task for which it is intended to be used. Even for a specific task, the relevant data on hand needs to comply with the quality and quantity requirements. Essentially, data has to be analytics ready. So what does it mean to make data analytics ready? In addition to its relevancy to the problem at hand and the quality/quantity requirements, it also has to have a certain data structure in place with key fields/variables with properly normalized values. Furthermore, there must be an organization-wide agreed-on definition for common variables and subject matters (sometimes also called master data management), such as how you define a customer (what characteristics of customers are used to produce a holistic enough representation to analytics) and where in the business process the customer-related information is captured, validated, stored, and updated.

Sometimes the representation of the data may depend on the type of analytics being employed. Predictive algorithms generally require a flat file with a target variable, so making data **analytics ready** for prediction means that data sets must be transformed into a flat-file format and made ready for ingestion into those predictive algorithms. It is also imperative to match the data to the needs and wants of a specific predictive algorithm and/or a software tool—for instance, neural network algorithms require all input variables to be numerically represented (even the nominal variables need to be converted into pseudo binary numeric variables) and decision tree algorithms do not require such numerical transformation, easily and natively handling a mix of nominal and numeric variables.

Analytics projects that overlook data-related tasks (some of the most critical steps) often end up with the wrong answer for the right problem, and these unintentionally created, seemingly good, answers may lead to inaccurate and untimely decisions. Following are some of the characteristics (metrics) that define the readiness level of data for an analytics study (Delen, 2015; Kock, McQueen, & Corner, 1997).

- **Data source reliability** refers to the originality and appropriateness of the storage medium where the data is obtained—answering the question of "Do we have the right confidence and belief in this data source?" If it all possible, one should always look for the original source/creator of the data to eliminate/mitigate the possibilities of data misrepresentation and data transformation caused by the mishandling of the data as it moved from the source to destination through one or more steps and stops along the way. Every move of the data creates a chance to unintentionally drop or reformat data items, which limits the integrity and perhaps true accuracy of the data set.

- **Data content accuracy** means that data are correct and are a good match for the analytics problem—answering the question of "Do we have the right data for the job?" The data should represent what was intended or defined by the original source of the data. For example, the customer's contact information recorded in a record within a database should be the same as what the patient said it was. Data accuracy will be covered in more detail in the following subsection.

- **Data accessibility** means that the data are easily and readily obtainable—answering the question of "Can we easily get to the data when we need to?" Access to data may be tricky, especially if the data is stored in more than one location and storage medium and need to be merged/transformed while accessing and obtaining it. As the traditional relational database management systems leave their place (or coexist with) a new generation of data storage mediums like data lakes and Hadoop infrastructure, the importance/criticality of data accessibility is also increasing.

- **Data security and data privacy** means that the data is secured to only allow those people who have the authority and the need to access it and to prevent anyone else from reaching it. Increasing popularity in educational degrees and certificate programs for Information Assurance is an evidence to the criticality and the increasing urgency of this data quality metric. Any organization that maintains health records for individual patients must have systems in place that not only safeguard the data from unauthorized access (which is mandated by federal laws like Health Insurance Portability and Accountability Act [HIPPA]) but also accurately identifies each patient to allow proper and timely access to records by authorized users (Annas, 2003).

- **Data richness** means that all the required data elements are included in the data set. In essence, richness (or comprehensiveness) means that the available variables portray a rich enough dimensionality of the underlying subject matter for an accurate and worthy analytics study. It also means that the information content is complete (or near complete) to build a predictive and/or prescriptive analytics model.

- **Data consistency** means that the data are accurately collected and combined/merged. Consistent data represent the dimensional information (variables of interest) coming from potentially disparate sources but pertaining to the same subject. If the data integration/merging is not done properly, some of the variables of different subjects may find themselves in the same record—having two different patient records mixed up—for instance, it may happen while merging the demographic and clinical test result data records.

- **Data currency/data timeliness**   means that the data should be up-to-date (or as recent/new as it needs to be) for a given analytics model. It also means that the data is recorded at or near the time of the event or observation so that the time-delay-related misrepresentation (incorrectly remembering and encoding) of the data is prevented. Because accurate analytics rely on accurate and timely data, an essential characteristic of analytics-ready data is the timeliness of the creation and access to data elements.

- **Data granularity**   requires that the variables and data values be defined at the lowest (or as low as required) level of detail for the intended use of the data. If the data is aggregated, it may not contain the level of detail needed for an analytics algorithm to learn how to discern different records/cases from one another. For example, in a medical setting, numerical values for laboratory results should be recorded to the appropriate decimal place as required for the meaningful interpretation of test results and proper use of those values within an analytics algorithm. Similarly, in the collection of demographic data, data elements should be defined at a granular level to determine the differences in outcomes of care among various subpopulations. One thing to remember is that the data that is aggregated cannot be disaggregated (without access to the original source), but it can easily be aggregated from its granular representation.

- **Data validity**   is the term used to describe a match/mismatch between the actual and expected data values of a given variable. As part of data definition, the acceptable values or value ranges for each data element must be defined. For example, a valid data definition related to gender would include three values: male, female, and unknown.

- **Data relevancy**   means that the variables in the data set are all relevant to the study being conducted. Relevancy is not a dichotomous measure (whether a variable is relevant or not); rather, it has a spectrum of relevancy from least relevant to most relevant. Based on the analytics algorithms being used, one may choose to include only the most relevant information (i.e., variables) or if the algorithm is capable enough to sort them out, may choose to include all the relevant ones, regardless of their relevancy level. One thing that analytics studies should avoid is to include totally irrelevant data into the model building, as this may contaminate the information for the algorithm, resulting in inaccurate and misleading results.

Although these are perhaps the most prevailing metrics to keep up with, the true data quality and excellent analytics readiness for a specific application domain would require different levels of emphasis paid on these metric dimensions and perhaps add more specific ones to this collection. The following section will dive into the nature of data from a taxonomical perspective to list and define different data types as they relate to different analytics projects.

SECTION 2.2 REVIEW QUESTIONS

1. How do you describe the importance of data in analytics? Can we think of analytics without data?
2. Considering the new and broad definition of business analytics, what are the main inputs and outputs to the analytics continuum?
3. Where does the data for business analytics come from?
4. In your opinion, what are the top three data-related challenges for better analytics?
5. What are the most common metrics that make for analytics-ready data?

2.3   A Simple Taxonomy of Data

Data (**datum** in singular form) refers to a collection of facts usually obtained as the result of experiments, observations, transactions, or experiences. Data may consist of numbers, letters, words, images, voice recordings, and so on, as measurements of a set of variables (characteristics of the subject or event that we are interested in studying). Data are often viewed as the lowest level of abstraction from which information and then knowledge is derived.

At the highest level of abstraction, one can classify data as structured and unstructured (or semistructured). **Unstructured data**/semistructured data is composed of any combination of textual, imagery, voice, and Web content. Unstructured/semistructured data will be covered in more detail in the text mining and Web mining chapter. **Structured data** is what data mining algorithms use and can be classified as categorical or numeric. The categorical data can be subdivided into nominal or ordinal data, whereas numeric data can be subdivided into intervals or ratios. Figure 2.2 shows a simple **data taxonomy**.

- **Categorical data**   represent the labels of multiple classes used to divide a variable into specific groups. Examples of categorical variables include race, sex, age group, and educational level. Although the latter two variables may also be considered in a numerical manner by using exact values for age and highest grade completed, it is often more informative to categorize such variables into a relatively small number of ordered classes. The categorical data may also be called discrete data, implying that it represents a finite number of values with no continuum between them. Even if the values used for the categorical (or discrete) variables are numeric, these numbers are nothing more than symbols and do not imply the possibility of calculating fractional values.
- **Nominal data**   contain measurements of simple codes assigned to objects as labels, which are not measurements. For example, the variable *marital status* can be generally categorized as (1) single, (2) married, and (3) divorced. Nominal data can be represented with binomial values having two possible values (e.g., yes/no, true/false, good/bad), or multinomial values having three or more possible values (e.g., brown/green/blue, white/black/Latino/Asian, single/married/divorced).

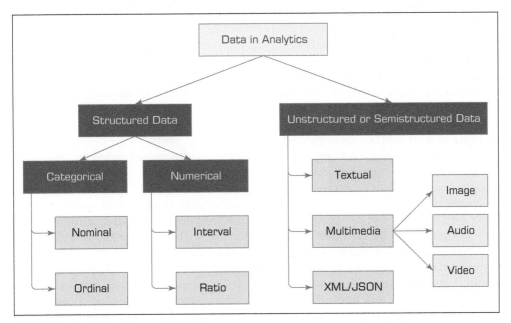

FIGURE 2.2   A Simple Taxonomy of Data.

- **Ordinal data**   contain codes assigned to objects or events as labels that also represent the rank order among them. For example, the variable *credit score* can be generally categorized as (1) low, (2) medium, or (3) high. Similar ordered relationships can be seen in variables such as age group (i.e., child, young, middle-aged, elderly) and educational level (i.e., high school, college, graduate school). Some predictive analytic algorithms, such as *ordinal multiple logistic regression*, take into account this additional rank-order information to build a better classification model.

- **Numeric data**   represent the numeric values of specific variables. Examples of numerically valued variables include age, number of children, total household income (in U.S. dollars), travel distance (in miles), and temperature (in Fahrenheit degrees). Numeric values representing a variable can be integer (taking only whole numbers) or real (taking also the fractional number). The numeric data may also be called continuous data, implying that the variable contains continuous measures on a specific scale that allows insertion of interim values. Unlike a discrete variable, which represents finite, countable data, a continuous variable represents scalable measurements, and it is possible for the data to contain an infinite number of fractional values.

- **Interval data**   are variables that can be measured on interval scales. A common example of interval scale measurement is temperature on the Celsius scale. In this particular scale, the unit of measurement is 1/100 of the difference between the melting temperature and the boiling temperature of water in atmospheric pressure; that is, there is not an absolute zero value.

- **Ratio data**   include measurement variables commonly found in the physical sciences and engineering. Mass, length, time, plane angle, energy, and electric charge are examples of physical measures that are ratio scales. The scale type takes its name from the fact that measurement is the estimation of the ratio between a magnitude of a continuous quantity and a unit magnitude of the same kind. Informally, the distinguishing feature of a ratio scale is the possession of a nonarbitrary zero value. For example, the Kelvin temperature scale has a nonarbitrary zero point of absolute zero, which is equal to –273.15 degrees Celsius. This zero point is nonarbitrary because the particles that comprise matter at this temperature have zero kinetic energy.

Other data types, including textual, spatial, imagery, video, and voice, need to be converted into some form of categorical or numeric representation before they can be processed by analytics methods (data mining algorithms; Delen, 2015). Data can also be classified as static or dynamic (i.e., temporal or time series).

Some predictive analytics (i.e., data mining) methods and machine-learning algorithms are very selective about the type of data that they can handle. Providing them with incompatible data types may lead to incorrect models or (more often) halt the model development process. For example, some data mining methods need all the variables (both input as well as output) represented as numerically valued variables (e.g., neural networks, support vector machines, logistic regression). The nominal or ordinal variables are converted into numeric representations using some type of *1-of-N* pseudo variables (e.g., a categorical variable with three unique values can be transformed into three pseudo variables with binary values—1 or 0). Because this process may increase the number of variables, one should be cautious about the effect of such representations, especially for the categorical variables that have large numbers of unique values.

Similarly, some predictive analytics methods, such as ID3 (a classic decision tree algorithm) and rough sets (a relatively new rule induction algorithm), need all the variables represented as categorically valued variables. Early versions of these methods required the user to discretize numeric variables into categorical representations before they could be processed by the algorithm. The good news is that most implementations of these algorithms in widely available software tools accept a mix of numeric and nominal variables and internally make the necessary conversions before processing the data.

Data comes in many different variable types and representation schemas. Business analytics tools are continuously improving in their ability to help data scientists in the daunting task of data transformation and data representation so that the data requirements of specific predictive models and algorithms can be properly executed. Application Case 2.1 shows a business scenario in which a data-rich medical device research and development company streamlined their analytics practices to have easy access to both the data and the analyses they need to continue the traditions of innovation and quality at the highest levels.

Application Case 2.1

Medical Device Company Ensures Product Quality While Saving Money

Few technologies are advancing faster than those in the medical field—so having the right advanced analytics software can be a game changer. Instrumentation Laboratory is a leader in the development, manufacturing, and distribution of medical devices and related technologies, including technology that is revolutionizing whole blood and hemostasis testing. To help ensure its continued growth and success, the company relies on data analytics and Dell Statistica.

Problem

As a market leader in diagnostic instruments for critical care and hemostasis, Instrumentation Laboratory must take advantage of rapidly evolving technologies while maintaining both quality and efficiency in its product development, manufacturing, and distribution processes. In particular, the company needed to enable its research and development (R&D) scientists and engineers to easily access and analyze the wealth of test data it collects, as well as efficiently monitor its manufacturing processes and supply chains.

"Like many companies, we were data-rich but analysis-poor," explains John Young, Business Analyst for Instrumentation Laboratory. "It's no longer viable to have R&D analysts running off to IT every time they need access to test data and then doing one-off analyses in Minitab. They need to be able to access data quickly and perform complex analyses consistently and accurately."

Implementing sophisticated analytics was especially critical for Instrumentation Laboratory because of the volume and complexity of its products. For example, every year, the company manufactures

hundreds of thousands of cartridges containing a card with a variety of sensors that measure the electrical signals of the blood being tested.

"Those sensors are affected by a wide range of factors, from environmental changes like heat and humidity to inconsistencies in materials from suppliers, so we're constantly monitoring their performance," says Young. "We collect millions of records of data, most of which is stored in SQL Server databases. We needed an analytics platform that would enable our R&D teams to quickly access that data and troubleshoot any problems. Plus, because there are so many factors in play, we also needed a platform that could intelligently monitor the test data and alert us to emerging issues automatically."

Solution

Instrumentation Laboratory began looking for an analytics solution to meet its needs. The company quickly eliminated most tools on the market because they failed to deliver the statistical functionality and level of trust required for the healthcare environment. That left only two contenders: another analytics solution and Dell Statistica. For Instrumentation Laboratory, the clear winner was Statistica.

"Choosing Statistica was an easy decision," recalls Young. "With Statistica, I was able to quickly build a wide range of analysis configurations on top of our data for use by analysts enterprise-wide. Now, when they want to understand specific things, they can simply run a canned analysis from that central store instead of having to ask IT for access to the data or remember how to do a particular test."

(Continued)

Application Case 2.1 (Continued)

Moreover, Statistica was far easier to deploy and use than legacy analytics solutions. "To implement and maintain other analytics solutions, you need to know analytics solutions programming," Young notes. "But with Statistica, I can connect to our data, create an analysis and publish it within an hour—even though I'm not a great programmer."

Finally, in addition to its advanced functionality and ease of use, Statistica delivered world-class support and an attractive price point. "The people who helped us implement Statistica were simply awesome," says Young. "And the price was far below what another analytics solution was quoting."

Results

With Statistica in place, analysts across the enterprise now have easy access to both the data and the analyses they need to continue the twin traditions of innovation and quality at Instrumentation Laboratory. In fact, Statistica's quick, effective analysis and automated alerting is saving the company hundreds of thousands of dollars.

"During cartridge manufacturing, we occasionally experience problems, such as an inaccuracy in a chemical formulation that goes on one of the sensors," Young notes. "Scrapping a single batch of cards would cost us hundreds of thousands of dollars. Statistica helps us quickly figure out what went wrong and fix it so we can avoid those costs. For example, we can marry the test data with electronic device history record data from our SAP environment and perform all sorts of correlations to determine which particular changes—such as changes in temperature and humidity—might be driving a particular issue."

Manual quality checks are, of course, valuable, but Statistica runs a variety of analyses automatically for the company as well, helping to ensure that nothing is missed and issues are identified quickly. "Many analysis configurations are scheduled to run periodically to check different things," Young says. "If there is an issue, the system automatically emails the appropriate people or logs the violations to a database."

Some of the major benefits of advanced data analytics with Dell Statistica included the following:

- *Regulatory compliance.* In addition to saving Instrumentation Laboratory money, Statistica also helps ensure the company's processes comply with Food and Drug Administration (FDA) regulations for quality and consistency. "Because we manufacture medical devices, we're regulated by the FDA," explains Young. "Statistica helps us perform the statistical validations required by the FDA—for example, we can easily demonstrate that two batches of product made using different chemicals are statistically the same."

- *Ensuring consistency.* Creating standardized analysis configurations in Statistica that can be used across the enterprise helps ensure consistency and quality at Instrumentation Laboratory. "You get different results depending on the way you go about analyzing your data. For example, different scientists might use different trims on the data, or not trim it at all—so they would all get different results," explains Young. "With Statistica, we can ensure that all the scientists across the enterprise are performing the analyses in the same way, so we get consistent results."

- *Supply chain monitoring.* Instrumentation Laboratory manufactures not just the card with the sensors but the whole medical instrument, and therefore it relies on suppliers to provide parts. To further ensure quality, the company is planning to extend its use of Statistica to supply chain monitoring.

- *Saving time.* In addition to saving money and improving regulatory compliance for Instrumentation Laboratory, Statistica is also saving the company's engineers and scientists valuable time, enabling them to focus more on innovation and less on routine matters. "Statistica's proactive alerting saves engineers a lot of time because they don't have to remember to check various factors, such as glucose slope, all the time. Just that one test would take half a day," notes Young. "With Statistica monitoring our test data, our engineers can focus on other matters, knowing they will get an email if and when a factor like glucose slope becomes an issue."

Future Possibilities

Instrumentation Laboratory is excited about the opportunities made possible by the visibility Statistica advanced analytics software has provided into its data stores. "Using Statistica, you can discover all sorts of insights about your data that you might not otherwise be able to find," says Young. "There might be hidden pockets of money out there that you're just not seeing because you're not analyzing your data to the extent you could. Using the tool, we've discovered some interesting things in our data that have saved us a tremendous amount of money, and we look forward to finding even more."

QUESTIONS FOR DISCUSSION

1. What were the main challenges for the medical device company? Were they market or technology driven? Explain.

2. What was the proposed solution?

3. What were the results? What do you think was the real return on investment (ROI)?

Source: Dell customer case study. Medical device company ensures product quality while saving hundreds of thousands of dollars. https://software.dell.com/documents/instrumentation-laboratory-medical-device-companyensures-product-quality-while-saving-hundreds-ofthousands-of-dollars-case-study-80048.pdf (accessed August 2016). Used by Permission from Dell.

SECTION 2.3 REVIEW QUESTIONS

1. What is data? How does data differ from information and knowledge?
2. What are the main categories of data? What types of data can we use for BI and analytics?
3. Can we use the same data representation for all analytics models? Why, or why not?
4. What is a *1-of-N* data representation? Why and where is it used in analytics?

2.4 The Art and Science of Data Preprocessing

Data in its original form (i.e., the real-world data) is not usually ready to be used in analytics tasks. It is often dirty, misaligned, overly complex, and inaccurate. A tedious and time-demanding process (so-called **data preprocessing**) is necessary to convert the raw real-world data into a well-refined form for analytics algorithms (Kotsiantis, Kanellopoulos, & Pintelas, 2006). Many analytics professionals would testify that the time spent on data preprocessing (which is perhaps the least enjoyable phase in the whole process) is significantly longer than the time spent on the rest of the analytics tasks (the fun of analytics model building and assessment). Figure 2.3 shows the main steps in the data preprocessing endeavor.

In the first phase of data preprocessing, the relevant data is collected from the identified sources, the necessary records and variables are selected (based on an intimate understanding of the data, the unnecessary information is filtered out), and the records coming from multiple data sources are integrated/merged (again, using the intimate understanding of the data, the synonyms and homonyms are able to be handled properly).

In the second phase of data preprocessing, the data is cleaned (this step is also known as data scrubbing). Data in its original/raw/real-world form is usually dirty (Hernández & Stolfo, 1998; Kim et al., 2003). In this step, the values in the data set are identified and dealt with. In some cases, missing values are an anomaly in the data set, in which case they need to be imputed (filled with a most probable value) or ignored; in other cases, the missing values are a natural part of the data set (e.g., the *household income* field is often left unanswered by people who are in the top income tier). In this step, the analyst should also identify noisy values in the data (i.e., the outliers) and smooth them out.

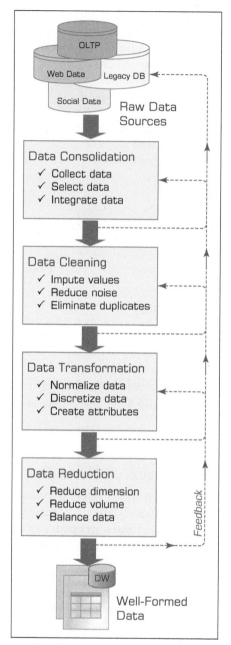

FIGURE 2.3   Data Preprocessing Steps.

In addition, inconsistencies (unusual values within a variable) in the data should be handled using domain knowledge and/or expert opinion.

In the third phase of data preprocessing, the data is transformed for better processing. For instance, in many cases the data is normalized between a certain minimum and maximum for all variables to mitigate the potential bias of one variable (having large numeric values, such as for household income) dominating other variables (such as *number of dependents* or *years in service,* which may potentially be more important) having smaller values. Another transformation that takes place is discretization and/or aggregation. In some cases, the numeric variables are converted to categorical values (e.g., low, medium, high); in other cases, a nominal variable's unique value range is reduced to a smaller set using concept hierarchies (e.g., as opposed to using the individual states with 50 different values, one may choose to use several regions for a variable that shows location) to have a data set that is more amenable to computer processing. Still, in other cases one might choose to create new variables based on the existing ones to magnify the information found in a collection of variables in the data set. For instance, in an organ transplantation data set one might choose to use a single variable showing the blood-type match (1: match, 0: no-match) as opposed to separate multinominal values for the blood type of both the donor and the recipient. Such simplification may increase the information content while reducing the complexity of the relationships in the data.

The final phase of data preprocessing is data reduction. Even though data scientists (i.e., analytics professionals) like to have large data sets, too much data may also be a problem. In the simplest sense, one can visualize the data commonly used in predictive analytics projects as a flat file consisting of two dimensions: variables (the number of columns) and cases/records (the number of rows). In some cases (e.g., image processing and genome projects with complex microarray data), the number of variables can be rather large, and the analyst must reduce the number down to a manageable size. Because the variables are treated as different dimensions that describe the phenomenon from different perspectives, in predictive analytics and data mining this process is commonly called **dimensional reduction** (or **variable selection**). Even though there is not a single best way to accomplish this task, one can use the findings from previously published literature; consult domain experts; run appropriate statistical tests (e.g., principal component analysis or independent component analysis); and, more preferably, use a combination of these techniques to successfully reduce the dimensions in the data into a more manageable and most relevant subset.

With respect to the other dimension (i.e., the number of cases), some data sets may include millions or billions of records. Even though computing power is increasing exponentially, processing such a large number of records may not be practical or feasible. In such cases, one may need to sample a subset of the data for analysis. The underlying assumption of sampling is that the subset of the data will contain all relevant patterns of the complete data set. In a homogeneous data set, such an assumption may hold well, but real-world data is hardly ever homogeneous. The analyst should be extremely careful in selecting a subset of the data that reflects the essence of the complete data set and is not specific to a subgroup or subcategory. The data is usually sorted on some variable, and taking a section of the data from the top or bottom may lead to a biased data set on specific values of the indexed variable; therefore, always try to randomly select the records on the sample set. For skewed data, straightforward random sampling may not be sufficient, and stratified sampling (a proportional representation of different subgroups in the data is represented in the sample data set) may be required. Speaking of skewed data: It is a good practice to balance the highly skewed data by either oversampling the less represented or undersampling the more represented classes. Research has shown that balanced data sets tend to produce better prediction models than unbalanced ones (Thammasiri et al., 2014).

The essence of data preprocessing is summarized in Table 2.1, which maps the main phases (along with their problem descriptions) to a representative list of tasks and algorithms.

It is almost impossible to underestimate the value proposition of data preprocessing. It is one of those time-demanding activities where investment of time and effort pays off without a perceivable limit for diminishing returns. That is, the more resources you invest in it, the more you will gain at the end. Application Case 2.2 illustrates an interesting study where raw, readily available academic data within an educational organization is used to develop predictive models to better understand attrition and improve freshmen

TABLE 2.1 A Summary of Data Preprocessing Tasks and Potential Methods

Main Task	Subtasks	Popular Methods
Data consolidation	Access and collect the data	SQL queries, software agents, Web services.
	Select and filter the data	Domain expertise, SQL queries, statistical tests.
	Integrate and unify the data	SQL queries, domain expertise, ontology-driven data mapping.
Data cleaning	Handle missing values in the data	Fill in missing values (imputations) with most appropriate values (mean, median, min/max, mode, etc.); recode the missing values with a constant such as "ML"; remove the record of the missing value; do nothing.
	Identify and reduce noise in the data	Identify the outliers in data with simple statistical techniques (such as averages and standard deviations) or with cluster analysis; once identified, either remove the outliers or smooth them by using binning, regression, or simple averages.
	Find and eliminate erroneous data	Identify the erroneous values in data (other than outliers), such as odd values, inconsistent class labels, odd distributions; once identified, use domain expertise to correct the values or remove the records holding the erroneous values.
Data transformation	Normalize the data	Reduce the range of values in each numerically valued variable to a standard range (e.g., 0 to 1 or −1 to +1) by using a variety of normalization or scaling techniques.
	Discretize or aggregate the data	If needed, convert the numeric variables into discrete representations using range- or frequency-based binning techniques; for categorical variables, reduce the number of values by applying proper concept hierarchies.
	Construct new attributes	Derive new and more informative variables from the existing ones using a wide range of mathematical functions (as simple as addition and multiplication or as complex as a hybrid combination of log transformations).
Data reduction	Reduce number of attributes	Principal component analysis, independent component analysis, chi-square testing, correlation analysis, and decision tree induction.
	Reduce number of records	Random sampling, stratified sampling, expert-knowledge-driven purposeful sampling.
	Balance skewed data	Oversample the less represented or undersample the more represented classes.

Application Case 2.2

Improving Student Retention with Data-Driven Analytics

Student attrition has become one of the most challenging problems for decision makers in academic institutions. Despite all the programs and services that are put in place to help retain students, according to the U.S. Department of Education, Center for Educational Statistics (nces.ed.gov), only about half of those who enter higher education actually earn a bachelor's degree. Enrollment management and the retention of students has become a top priority for administrators of colleges and universities in the United States and other countries around the world. High dropout of students usually results in overall financial loss, lower graduation rates, and inferior school reputation in the eyes of all stakeholders. The legislators and policy makers who oversee higher education and allocate funds, the parents who pay for their children's education to prepare them for a better future, and the students who make college choices look for evidence of institutional quality and reputation to guide their decision-making processes.

Proposed Solution

To improve student retention, one should try to understand the nontrivial reasons behind the attrition. To be successful, one should also be able to accurately identify those students that are at risk of dropping out. So far, the vast majority of student attrition research has been devoted to understanding this complex, yet crucial, social phenomenon. Even though these qualitative, behavioral, and survey-based studies revealed invaluable insight by developing and testing a wide range of theories, they do not provide the much-needed instruments to accurately predict (and potentially improve) student attrition. The project summarized in this case study proposed a quantitative research approach where the historical institutional data from student databases could be used to develop models that are capable of predicting as well as explaining the institution-specific nature of the attrition problem. The proposed analytics approach is shown in Figure 2.4.

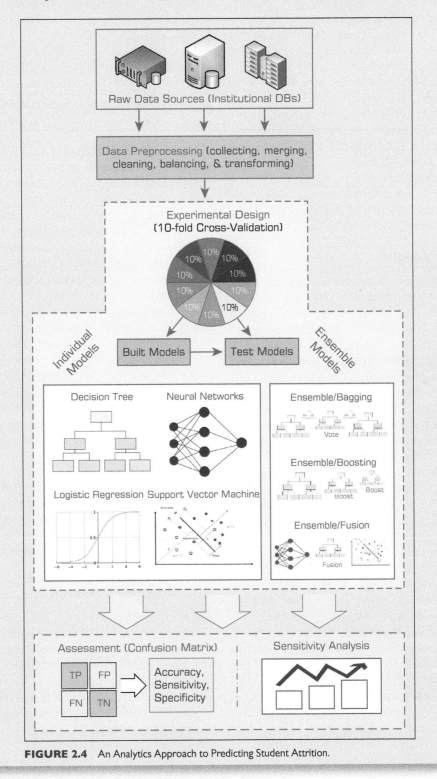

FIGURE 2.4 An Analytics Approach to Predicting Student Attrition.

(*Continued*)

Application Case 2.2 (Continued)

Although the concept is relatively new to higher education, for more than a decade now, similar problems in the field of marketing management have been studied using predictive data analytics techniques under the name of "churn analysis," where the purpose has been to identify among the current customers to answer the question, "Who among our current customers are more likely to stop buying our products or services?" so that some kind of mediation or intervention process can be executed to retain them. Retaining existing customers is crucial because as we all know, and as the related research has shown time and time again, acquiring a new customer costs on an order of magnitude more effort, time, and money than trying to keep the one that you already have.

Data Is of the Essence

The data for this research project came from a single institution (a comprehensive public university located in the Midwest region of the United States) with an average enrollment of 23,000 students, of which roughly 80% are the residents of the same state and roughly 19% of the students are listed under some minority classification. There is no significant difference between the two genders in the enrollment numbers. The average freshman student retention rate for the institution was about 80%, and the average 6-year graduation rate was about 60%.

The study used 5 years of institutional data, which entailed to 16,000+ students enrolled as freshmen, consolidated from various and diverse university student databases. The data contained variables related to students' academic, financial, and demographic characteristics. After merging and converting the multidimensional student data into a single flat file (a file with columns representing the variables and rows representing the student records), the resultant file was assessed and preprocessed to identify and remedy anomalies and unusable values. As an example, the study removed all international student records from the data set because they did not contain information about some of the most reputed predictors (e.g., high school GPA, SAT scores). In the data transformation phase, some of the variables were aggregated (e.g., "Major" and "Concentration" variables aggregated to binary variables MajorDeclared and ConcentrationSpecified) for

better interpretation for the predictive modeling. In addition, some of the variables were used to derive new variables (e.g., Earned/Registered ratio and YearsAfterHighSchool).

$$\text{Earned/Registered} = \text{EarnedHours/RegisteredHours}$$

$$\text{YearsAfterHighSchool} = \text{FreshmenEnrollmentYear} - \text{HighSchoolGraduationYear}$$

The *Earned/Registered* ratio was created to have a better representation of the students' resiliency and determination in their first semester of the freshman year. Intuitively, one would expect greater values for this variable to have a positive impact on retention/persistence. The *YearsAfterHighSchool* was created to measure the impact of the time taken between high school graduation and initial college enrollment. Intuitively, one would expect this variable to be a contributor to the prediction of attrition. These aggregations and derived variables are determined based on a number of experiments conducted for a number of logical hypotheses. The ones that made more common sense and the ones that led to better prediction accuracy were kept in the final variable set. Reflecting the true nature of the subpopulation (i.e., the freshmen students), the dependent variable (i.e., "Second Fall Registered") contained many more *yes* records (~80%) than *no* records (~20%; see Figure 2.5).

Research shows that having such an imbalanced data has a negative impact on model performance. Therefore, the study experimented with the options of using and comparing the results of the same type of models built with the original imbalanced data (biased for the *yes* records) and the well-balanced data.

Modeling and Assessment

The study employed four popular classification methods (i.e., artificial neural networks, decision trees, support vector machines, and logistic regression) along with three model ensemble techniques (i.e., bagging, busting, and information fusion). The results obtained from all model types were then compared to each other using regular classification model assessment methods (e.g., overall predictive accuracy, sensitivity, specificity) on the holdout samples.

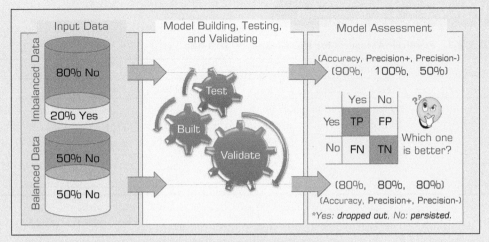

FIGURE 2.5 A Graphical Depiction of the Class Imbalance Problem.

In machine-learning algorithms (some of which will be covered in Chapter 4), sensitivity analysis is a method for identifying the "cause-and-effect" relationship between the inputs and outputs of a given prediction model. The fundamental idea behind sensitivity analysis is that it measures the importance of predictor variables based on the change in modeling performance that occurs if a predictor variable is not included in the model. This modeling and experimentation practice is also called a leave-one-out assessment. Hence, the measure of sensitivity of a specific predictor variable is the ratio of the error of the trained model without the predictor variable to the error of the model that includes this predictor variable. The more sensitive the network is to a particular variable, the greater the performance decrease would be in the absence of that variable, and therefore the greater the ratio of importance. In addition to the predictive power of the models, the study also conducted sensitivity analyses to determine the relative importance of the input variables.

Results

In the first set of experiments, the study used the original imbalanced data set. Based on the 10-fold cross-validation assessment results, the support vector machines produced the best accuracy with an overall prediction rate of 87.23%, the decision tree came out as the runner-up with an overall prediction rate of 87.16%, followed by artificial neural networks and logistic regression with overall prediction rates of 86.45% and 86.12%, respectively (see Table 2.2). A careful examination of these results reveals that the predictions accuracy for the "Yes" class is significantly higher than the prediction accuracy of the "No" class. In fact, all four model types predicted the students who are likely to return for the second year with better than 90% accuracy, but they did poorly on predicting the students who are likely to drop out after the freshman year with less than 50% accuracy. Because the prediction of the "No" class is the main purpose of this study, less than 50% accuracy for this class was deemed not acceptable. Such a difference

TABLE 2.2 Prediction Results for the Original/Unbalanced Dataset

	ANN(MLP)		DT(C5)		SVM		LR	
	No	Yes	No	Yes	No	Yes	No	Yes
No	1494	384	1518	304	1478	255	1438	376
Yes	1596	11142	1572	11222	1612	11271	1652	11150
SUM	3090	11526	3090	11526	3090	11526	3090	11526
Per-Class Accuracy	48.35%	96.67%	49.13%	97.36%	47.83%	97.79%	46.54%	96.74%
Overall Accuracy	86.45%		87.16%		87.23%		86.12%	

(*Continued*)

Application Case 2.2 (Continued)

TABLE 2.3 Prediction Results for the Balanced Data Set

Confusion Matrix	ANN(MLP)		DT(C5)		SVM		LR	
	No	Yes	No	Yes	No	Yes	No	Yes
No	2309	464	2311	417	2313	386	2125	626
Yes	781	2626	779	2673	777	2704	965	2464
SUM	3090	3090	3090	3090	3090	3090	3090	3090
Per-class Accuracy	74.72%	84.98%	74.79%	86.50%	74.85%	87.51%	68.77%	79.74%
Overall Accuracy	79.85%		80.65%		81.18%		74.26%	

in prediction accuracy of the two classes can (and should) be attributed to the imbalanced nature of the training data set (i.e., ~80% "Yes" and ~20% "No" samples).

The next round of experiments used a well-balanced data set where the two classes are represented nearly equally in counts. In realizing this approach, the study took all the samples from the minority class (i.e., the "No" class herein) and randomly selected an equal number of samples from the majority class (i.e., the "Yes" class herein) and repeated this process for 10 times to reduce potential bias of random sampling. Each of these sampling processes resulted in a data set of 7,000+ records, of which both class labels ("Yes" and "No") were equally represented. Again, using a 10-fold cross-validation methodology, the study developed and tested prediction models for all four model types. The results of these experiments are shown in Table 2.3. Based on the holdout sample results, support vector machines once again generated the best overall prediction accuracy with 81.18%, followed by decision trees, artificial neural networks, and logistic regression with an overall prediction accuracy of 80.65%, 79.85%, and 74.26%. As can be seen in the per-class accuracy figures, the prediction models did significantly better on predicting the "No" class with the well-balanced data than they did with the unbalanced data. Overall, the three machine-learning techniques performed significantly better than their statistical counterpart, logistic regression.

Next, another set of experiments were conducted to assess the predictive ability of the three ensemble models. Based on the 10-fold cross-validation methodology, the information fusion–type ensemble model produced the best results with an overall prediction rate of 82.10%, followed by the bagging-type ensembles and boosting-type ensembles with overall prediction rates of 81.80% and 80.21%, respectively (see Table 2.4). Even though the prediction results are slightly better than the individual models, ensembles are known to produce more robust prediction systems compared to a single-best prediction model (more on this can be found in Chapter 4).

In addition to assessing the prediction accuracy for each model type, a sensitivity analysis was also conducted using the developed prediction models to identify the relative importance of the independent variables (i.e., the predictors). In realizing the

TABLE 2.4 Prediction Results for the Three Ensemble Models

	Boosting (Boosted Trees)		Bagging (Random Forest)		Information Fusion (Weighted Average)	
	No	Yes	No	Yes	No	Yes
No	2242	375	2327	362	2335	351
Yes	848	2715	763	2728	755	2739
SUM	3090	3090	3090	3090	3090	3090
Per-Class Accuracy	72.56%	87.86%	75.31%	88.28%	75.57%	88.64%
Overall Accuracy	80.21%		81.80%		82.10%	

overall sensitivity analysis results, each of the four individual model types generated its own sensitivity measures ranking all the independent variables in a prioritized list. As expected, each model type generated slightly different sensitivity rankings of the independent variables. After collecting all four sets of sensitivity numbers, the sensitivity numbers are normalized and aggregated and plotted in a horizontal bar chart (see Figure 2.6).

Conclusions

The study showed that, given sufficient data with the proper variables, data mining methods are capable of predicting freshmen student attrition with approximately 80% accuracy. Results also showed that, regardless of the prediction model employed, the balanced data set (compared to unbalanced/original data set) produced better prediction

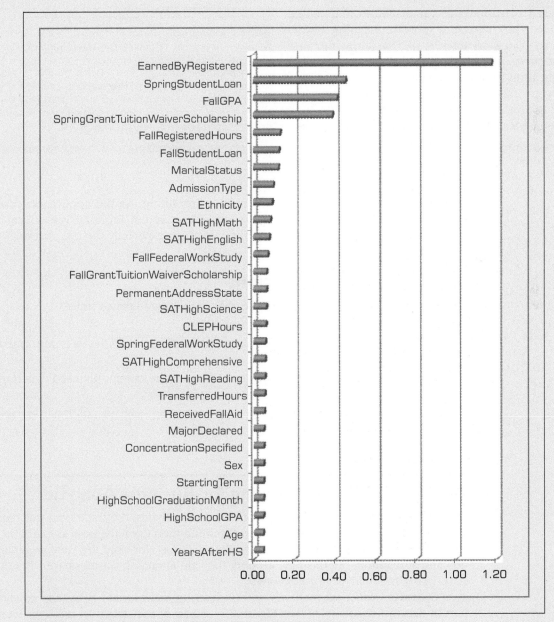

FIGURE 2.6 Sensitivity-Analysis-Based Variable Importance Results.

(Continued)

Application Case 2.2 (Continued)

models for identifying the students who are likely to drop out of the college prior to their sophomore year. Among the four individual prediction models used in this study, support vector machines performed the best, followed by decision trees, neural networks, and logistic regression. From the usability standpoint, despite the fact that support vector machines showed better prediction results, one might choose to use decision trees because compared to support vector machines and neural networks, they portray a more transparent model structure. Decision trees explicitly show the reasoning process of different predictions, providing a justification for a specific outcome, whereas support vector machines and artificial neural networks are mathematical models that do not provide such a transparent view of "how they do what they do."

QUESTIONS FOR DISCUSSION

1. What is student attrition, and why is it an important problem in higher education?
2. What were the traditional methods to deal with the attrition problem?
3. List and discuss the data-related challenges within context of this case study.
4. What was the proposed solution? And, what were the results?

Sources: Thammasiri, D., Delen, D., Meesad, P., & Kasap N. (2014). A critical assessment of imbalanced class distribution problem: The case of predicting freshmen student attrition. *Expert Systems with Applications, 41*(2), 321–330; Delen, D. (2011). Predicting student attrition with data mining methods. *Journal of College Student Retention, 13*(1), 17–35; Delen, D. (2010). A comparative analysis of machine learning techniques for student retention management. *Decision Support Systems, 49*(4), 498–506.

student retention in a large higher education institution. As the application case clearly states, each and every data preprocessing task described in Table 2.1 was critical to a successful execution of the underlying analytics project, especially the task that related to the balancing of the data set.

SECTION 2.4 REVIEW QUESTIONS

1. Why is the original/raw data not readily usable by analytics tasks?
2. What are the main data preprocessing steps?
3. What does it mean to clean/scrub the data? What activities are performed in this phase?
4. Why do we need data transformation? What are the commonly used data transformation tasks?
5. Data reduction can be applied to rows (sampling) and/or columns (variable selection). Which is more challenging?

2.5 Statistical Modeling for Business Analytics

Because of the increasing popularity of business analytics, the traditional statistical methods and underlying techniques are also regaining their attractiveness as enabling tools to support evidence-based managerial decision making. Not only are they regaining attention and admiration, but this time around, they are attracting business users in addition to statisticians and analytics professionals.

Statistics (statistical methods and underlying techniques) is usually considered as part of descriptive analytics (see Figure 2.7). Some of the statistical methods can also be considered as part of predictive analytics such as discriminant analysis, multiple regression, logistic regression, and k-means clustering. As shown in Figure 2.7, descriptive

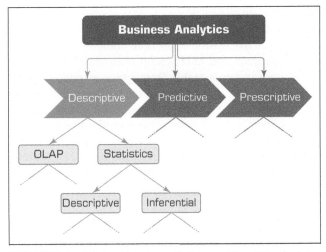

FIGURE 2.7   Relationship between Statistics and Descriptive Analytics.

analytics has two main branches: statistics and **online analytics processing (OLAP)**. OLAP is the term used for analyzing, characterizing, and summarizing structured data stored in organizational databases (often stored in a data warehouse or in a data mart—details of data warehousing will be covered in Chapter 3) using cubes (i.e., multidimensional data structures that are created to extract a subset of data values to answer a specific business question). The OLAP branch of descriptive analytics has also been called Business Intelligence. Statistics, on the other hand, helps to characterize the data either one variable at a time or multivariables all together, using either descriptive or inferential methods.

Statistics—a collection of mathematical techniques to characterize and interpret data—has been around for a very long time. Many methods and techniques have been developed to address the needs of the end users and the unique characteristics of the data being analyzed. Generally speaking, at the highest level, statistical methods can be classified as either descriptive or inferential. The main difference between descriptive and inferential statistics is the data used in these methods—whereas **descriptive statistics** is all about describing the sample data on hand, and **inferential statistics** is about drawing inferences or conclusions about the characteristics of the population. In this section we will briefly describe descriptive statistics (because of the fact that it lays the foundation for, and is the integral part of, descriptive analytics), and in the following section we will cover regression (both linear and logistic regression) as part of inferential statistics.

Descriptive Statistics for Descriptive Analytics

Descriptive statistics, as the name implies, describes the basic characteristics of the data at hand, often one variable at a time. Using formulas and numerical aggregations, descriptive statistics summarizes the data in such a way that often meaningful and easily understandable patterns emerge from the study. Although it is very useful in data analytics and very popular among the statistical methods, descriptive statistics does not allow making conclusions (or inferences) beyond the sample of the data being analyzed. That is, it is simply a nice way to characterize and describe the data on hand, without making conclusions (inferences or extrapolations) regarding the population of related hypotheses we might have in mind.

In business analytics, descriptive statistics plays a critical role—it allows us to understand and explain/present our data in a meaningful manner using aggregated numbers, data tables, or charts/graphs. In essence, descriptive statistics helps us convert our numbers and symbols into meaningful representations for anyone to understand and use. Such an understanding not only helps business users in their decision-making processes, but also helps analytics professionals and data scientists to characterize and validate the data for other more sophisticated analytics tasks. Descriptive statistics allows analysts to identify data concertation, unusually large or small values (i.e., outliers), and unexpectedly distributed data values for numeric variables. Therefore, the methods in descriptive statistics can be classified as either measures for central tendency or measures of dispersion. In the following section we will use a simple description and mathematical formulation/representation of these measures. In mathematical representation, we will use $x_1, x_2, \ldots, x_n$ to represent individual values (observations) of the variable (measure) that we are interested in characterizing.

Measures of Centrality Tendency (May Also Be Called Measures of Location or Centrality)

Measures of centrality are the mathematical methods by which we estimate or describe central positioning of a given variable of interest. A measure of central tendency is a single numerical value that aims to describe a set of data by simply identifying or estimating the central position within the data. The mean (often called the arithmetic mean or the simple average) is the most commonly used measure of central tendency. In addition to mean, you could also see median or mode being used to describe the centrality of a given variable. Although, the mean, median, and mode are all valid measures of central tendency, under different circumstances, one of these measures of centrality becomes more appropriate than the others. What follows are short descriptions of these measures, including how to calculate them mathematically and pointers on the circumstances in which they are the most appropriate measure to use.

Arithmetic Mean

The **arithmetic mean** (or simply *mean* or *average*) is the sum of all the values/observations divided by the number of observations in the data set. It is by far the most popular and most commonly used measure of central tendency. It is used with continuous or discrete numeric data. For a given variable x, if we happen to have n values/observations $(x_1, x_2, \ldots, x_n)$, we can write the arithmetic mean of the data sample ($\bar{x}$, pronounced as x-bar) as follows:

$$\bar{x} = \frac{x_1 + x_2 + \cdots + x_n}{n}$$

or

$$\bar{x} = \frac{\sum_{i=1}^{n} x_i}{n}$$

The mean has several unique characteristics. For instance, the sum of the absolute deviations (differences between the mean and the observations) above the mean are the same as the sum of the deviations below the mean, balancing the values on either side of it. That said, it does not suggest, however, that half the observations are above and the other half are below the mean (a common misconception among those who do not know basic statistics). Also, the mean is unique for every data set and is meaningful and calculable for both interval- and ratio-type numeric data. One major downside is that the mean can be affected by outliers (observations that are considerably larger or smaller than the rest of the data points). Outliers can pull the mean toward their direction and, hence, bias the centrality representation. Therefore, if there are outliers or if the data is erratically dispersed and skewed, one should either avoid using mean as the measure of centrality or augment it with other central tendency measures, such as median and mode.

Median

The **median** is the measure of center value in a given data set. It is the number in the middle of a given set of data that has been arranged/sorted in order of magnitude (either ascending or descending). If the number of observation is an odd number, identifying the median is very easy—just sort the observations based on their values and pick the value right in the middle. If the number of observations is an even number, then identify the two middle values, and then take the simple average of these two values. The median is meaningful and calculable for ratio, interval, and ordinal data types. Once determined, half the data points in the data are above and the other half are below the median. In contrary to the mean, the median is not affected by outliers or skewed data.

Mode

The **mode** is the observation that occurs most frequently (the most frequent value in our data set). On a histogram it represents the highest bar in a bar chart, and hence, it may be considered as being the most popular option/value. The mode is most useful for data sets that contain a relatively small number of unique values. That is, it may be useless if the data have too many unique values (as is the case in many engineering measurements that capture high precision with a large number of decimal places), rendering each value having either one or a very small number representing its frequency. Although it is a useful measure (especially for nominal data), mode is not a very good representation of centrality, and therefore, it should not be used as the only measure of central tendency for a given data set.

In summary, which central tendency measure is the best? Although there is not a clear answer to this question, here are a few hints—use the mean when the data is not prone to outliers and there is no significant level of skewness; use the median when the data has outliers and/or it is ordinal in nature; use the mode when the data is nominal. Perhaps the best practice is to use all three together so that the central tendency of the data set can be captured and represented from three perspectives. Mostly because "average" is a very familiar and highly used concept to everyone in regular daily activities, managers (as well as some scientists and journalists) often use the centrality measures (especially mean) inappropriately when other statistical information should be considered along with the centrality. It is a better practice to present descriptive statistics as a package—a combination of centrality and dispersion measures—as opposed to a single measure like mean.

Measures of Dispersion (May Also Be Called Measures of Spread or Decentrality)

Measures of **dispersion** are the mathematical methods used to estimate or describe the degree of variation in a given variable of interest. They are a representation of the numerical spread (compactness or lack thereof) of a given data set. To describe this dispersion, a number of statistical measures are developed; the most notable ones are range, variance, and standard deviation (and also quartiles and absolute deviation). One of the main reasons why the measures of dispersion/spread of data values are important is the fact that it gives us a framework within which we can judge the central tendency—gives us the indication of how well the mean (or other centrality measures) represents the sample data. If the dispersion of values in the data set is large, the mean is not deemed to be a very good representation of the data. This is because a large dispersion measure indicates large differences between individual scores. Also, in research, it is often perceived as a positive sign to see a small variation within each data sample, as it may indicate homogeneity, similarity, and robustness within the collected data.

Range

The **range** is perhaps the simplest measure of dispersion. It is the difference between the largest and the smallest values in a given data set (i.e., variables). So we calculate range by simply identifying the smallest value in the data set (minimum), identifying the largest value in the data set (maximum), and calculating the difference between them (range = maximum − minimum).

Variance

A more comprehensive and sophisticated measure of dispersion is the **variance**. It is a method used to calculate the deviation of all data points in a given data set from the mean. The larger the variance, the more the data are spread out from the mean and the more variability one can observe in the data sample. To prevent the offsetting of negative and positive differences, the variance takes into account the square of the distances from the mean. The formula for a data sample can be written as

$$s^2 = \frac{\sum_{i=1}^{n}(x_i - \bar{x})^2}{n - 1}$$

where n is the number of samples, $\bar{x}$ is the mean of the sample and x_i is the ith value in the data set. The larger values of variance indicate more dispersion, whereas smaller values indicate compression in the overall data set. Because the differences are squared, larger deviations from the mean contribute significantly to the value of variance. Again, because the differences are squared, the numbers that represent deviation/variance become somewhat meaningless (as opposed to a dollar difference, herein you are given a squared dollar difference). Therefore, instead of variance, in many business applications we use a more meaningful dispersion measure, called standard deviation.

Standard Deviation

The **standard deviation** is also a measure of the spread of values within a set of data. The standard deviation is calculated by simply taking the square root of the variations. The following formula shows the calculation of standard deviation from a given sample of data points.

$$s = \sqrt{\frac{\sum_{i=1}^{n}(x_i - \bar{x})^2}{n - 1}}$$

Mean Absolute Deviation

In addition to variance and standard deviation, sometimes we also use **mean absolute deviation** to measure dispersion in a data set. It is a simpler way to calculate the overall deviation from the mean. Specifically, it is calculated by measuring the absolute values of the differences between each data point and the mean and summing them. It provides a measure of spread without being specific about the data point being lower or higher than the mean. The following formula shows the calculation of the mean absolute deviation:

$$MAD = \frac{\sum_{i=1}^{n}|x_i - \bar{x}|}{n}$$

Quartiles and Interquartile Range

Quartiles help us identify spread within a subset of the data. A **quartile** is a quarter of the number of data points given in a data set. Quartiles are determined by first sorting the data and then splitting the sorted data into four disjoint smaller data sets. Quartiles are a useful measure of dispersion because they are much less affected by outliers or a skewness in the data set than the equivalent measures in the whole data set. Quartiles are often reported along with the median as the best choice of measure of dispersion and central tendency, respectively, when dealing with skewed and/or data with outliers. A common way of expressing quartiles is as an interquartile range, which describes the difference between the third quartile (Q3) and the first quartile (Q1), telling us about the range of the middle half of the scores in the distribution. The quartile-driven descriptive measures (both centrality and dispersion) are best explained with a popular plot called a box plot (or box-and-whiskers plot).

Box-and-Whiskers Plot

The **box-and-whiskers plot** (or simply a **box plot**) is a graphical illustration of several descriptive statistics about a given data set. They can be either horizontal or vertical, but vertical is the most common representation, especially in modern-day analytics software products. It is known to be first created and presented by John W. Tukey in 1969. Box plot is often used to illustrate both centrality and dispersion of a given data set (i.e., the distribution of the sample data) in an easy-to-understand graphical notation. Figure 2.8 shows a couple of box plots side by side, sharing the same y-axis. As shown therein, a single

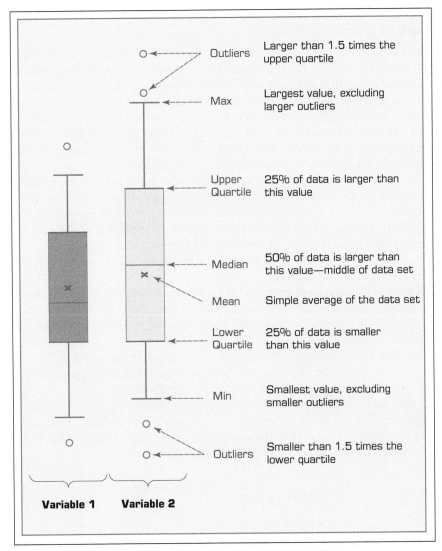

FIGURE 2.8 Understanding the Specifics about Box-and-Whiskers Plots.

chart can have one or more box plots for visual comparison purposes. In such cases, the y-axis would be the common measure of magnitude (the numerical value of the variable), with the x-axis showing different classes/subsets such as different time dimensions (e.g., descriptive statistics for annual Medicare expenses in 2015 versus 2016) or different categories (e.g., descriptive statistics for marketing expenses versus total sales).

Although, historically speaking, the box plot was not used widely and often enough (especially in areas outside of statistics), with the emerging popularity of business analytics, it is gaining fame in less-technical areas of the business world. Its information richness and ease of understanding are largely to credit for its recent popularity.

The box plot shows the **centrality** (median and sometimes also mean) as well as the dispersion (the density of the data within the middle half—drawn as a box between the first and third quartile), the minimum and maximum ranges (shown as extended lines from the box, looking like whiskers, that are calculated as 1.5 times the upper or lower end of the quartile box) along with the outliers that are larger than the limits of the whiskers. A box plot also shows whether the data is symmetrically distributed with respect to the mean or it sways one way or another. The relative position of the median versus mean and the lengths of the whiskers on both side of the box give a good indication of the potential skewness in the data.

The Shape of a Distribution

Although not as common as the centrality and dispersion, the shape of the data distribution is also a useful measure for the descriptive statistics. Before delving into the shape of the distribution we first need to define the distribution itself. Simply put, distribution is the frequency of data points counted and plotted over a small number of class labels or numerical ranges (i.e., bins). In a graphical illustration of distribution, the y-axis shows the frequency (count or %), and the x-axis shows the individual classes or bins in a rank-ordered fashion. A very well-known distribution is called normal distribution, which is perfectly symmetric on both sides of the mean and has numerous well-founded mathematical properties that make it a very useful tool for research and practice. As the dispersion of a data set increases, so does the standard deviation, and the shape of the distribution looks wider. A graphic illustration of the relationship between dispersion and distribution shape (in the context of normal distribution) is shown in Figure 2.9.

There are two commonly used measures to calculate the shape characteristics of a distribution: skewness and kurtosis. A histogram (frequency plot) is often used to visually illustrate both skewness and kurtosis.

Skewness is a measure of asymmetry (sway) in a distribution of the data that portrays a unimodal structure—only one peak exists in the distribution of the data. Because normal distribution is a perfectly symmetric unimodal distribution, it does not have skewness, that is, its skewness measure (i.e., the value of the coefficient of skewness) is equal to zero. The skewness measure/value can be either positive or negative. If the distribution sways left (i.e., tail is on the right side and the mean is smaller than median), then it produces a positive skewness measure, and if the distribution sways right (i.e., the tail is on the left side and the mean is larger than median), then it produces a negative skewness measure. In Figure 2.9, (c) represents a positively skewed distribution, whereas (d) represents a negatively skewed distribution. In the same figure, both (a) and (b) represent perfect symmetry and hence zero measure for skewness.

$$Skewness = S = \frac{\sum_{i=1}^{n}(x_i - \overline{x})^3}{(n - 1)s^3}$$

where s is the standard deviation and n is the number of samples.

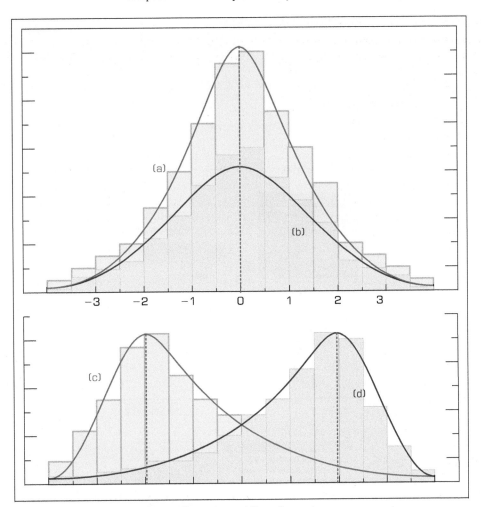

FIGURE 2.9 Relationship between Dispersion and Shape Properties.

Kurtosis is another measure to use in characterizing the shape of a unimodal distribution. As opposed to the sway in shape, kurtosis is more interested in characterizing the peak/tall/skinny nature of the distribution. Specifically, kurtosis measures the degree to which a distribution is more or less peaked than a normal distribution. Whereas a positive kurtosis indicates a relatively peaked/tall distribution, a negative kurtosis indicates a relatively flat/short distribution. As a reference point, a normal distribution has a kurtosis of 3. The formula for kurtosis can be written as

$$Kurtosis = K = \frac{\sum_{i=1}^{n}(x_i - \bar{x})^4}{ns^4} - 3$$

Descriptive statistics (as well as inferential statistics) can easily be calculated using commercially viable statistical software packages (e.g., SAS, SPSS, Minitab, JMP, Statistica) or free/open source tools (e.g., R). Perhaps the most convenient way to calculate descriptive and some of the inferential statistics is to use Excel. Technology Insights 2.1 describes in detail how to use Microsoft Excel to calculate descriptive statistics.

TECHNOLOGY INSIGHTS 2.1
How to Calculate Descriptive Statistics in Microsoft Excel

Excel, arguably the most popular data analysis tool in the world, can easily be used for descriptive statistics. Although, the base configuration of Excel does not seem to have the statistics function readily available for end users, those functions come with the installation and can be activated (turned on) with only a few mouse clicks. Figure 2.10 shows how these statistics functions (as part of the Analysis ToolPak) can be activated in Microsoft Excel 2016.

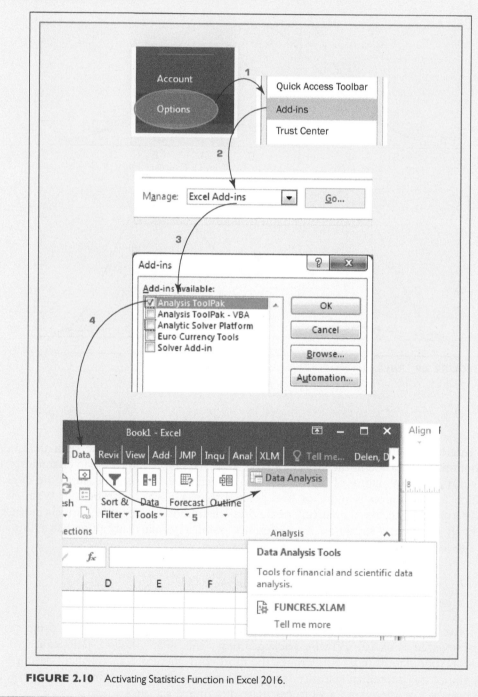

FIGURE 2.10 Activating Statistics Function in Excel 2016.

Once activated, the *Analysis ToolPak* will appear in the *Data* menu option under the name of *Data Analysis*. When you click on Data Analysis in the Analysis group under the Data tab in the Excel menu bar, you will see Descriptive Statistics as one of the options within the list of data analysis tools (see Figure 2.11, steps [1, 2]); click on OK, and the Descriptive Statistics dialog box will appear (see middle of Figure 2.11). In this dialog box you need to enter the range of the data, which can be one or more numerical columns, along with the preference check boxes, and click OK (see Figure 2.11, steps [3, 4]). If the selection includes more than one numeric column, the tool treats each column as a separate data set and provides descriptive statistics for each column separately.

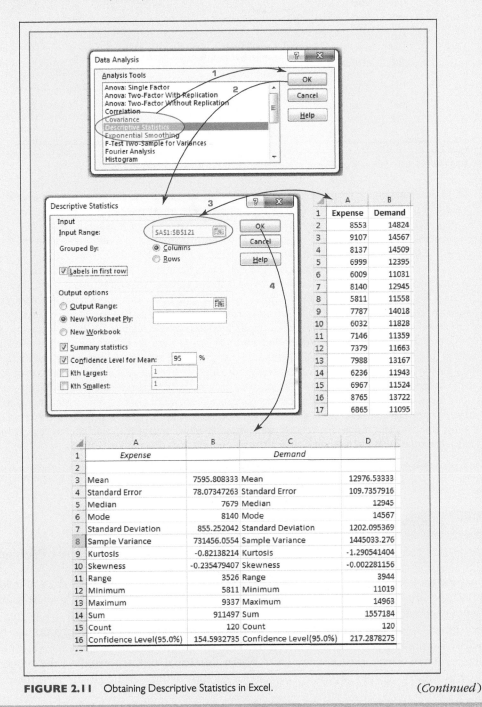

FIGURE 2.11 Obtaining Descriptive Statistics in Excel.   (*Continued*)

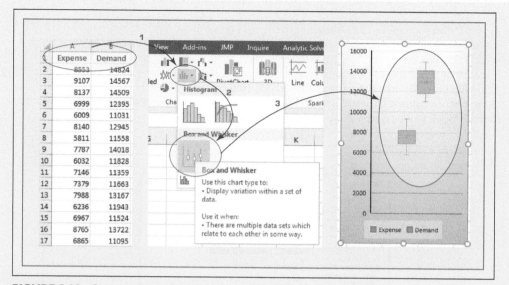

FIGURE 2.12 Creating a Box-and-Whiskers Plot in Excel 2016.

As a simple example, we selected two columns (labeled as Expense and Demand) and executed the Descriptive Statistics option. The bottom section of Figure 2.11 shows the output created by Excel. As can be seen, Excel produced all the descriptive statistics that are covered in the previous section and added a few more to the list. In Excel 2016, it is also very easy (a few mouse clicks) to create a box-and-whiskers plot. Figure 2.12 shows the simple three-step process of creating a box-and-whiskers plot in Excel.

Although this is a very useful tool in Excel, one should be aware of an important point related to the results generated by Analysis ToolPak, which have a different behavior than other ordinary Excel functions: Although Excel functions dynamically change as the underlying data in the spreadsheet are changed, the results generated by the Analysis ToolPak do not. For example, if you change the values in either or both of these columns, the Descriptive Statistics results produced by the Analysis ToolPak will stay the same. However, the same is not true for ordinary Excel functions. If you were to calculate the mean value of a given column (using "=AVERAGE(A1:A121)"), and then change the values within the data range, the mean value would automatically change. In summary, the results produced by Analysis ToolPak do not have a dynamic link to the underlying data, and if the data changes, the analysis needs to be redone using the dialog box.

Successful applications of data analytics cover a wide range of business and organizational settings, addressing the problems once thought unsolvable. Application Case 2.3 is an excellent illustration of those success stories where a small municipality administration adopts a data analytics approach to intelligently detect and solve problems by continuously analyzing demand and consumption patterns.

Application Case 2.3

Town of Cary Uses Analytics to Analyze Data from Sensors, Assess Demand, and Detect Problems

A leaky faucet. A malfunctioning dishwasher. A cracked sprinkler head. These are more than just a headache for a home owner or business to fix. They can be costly, unpredictable, and, unfortunately, hard to pinpoint. Through a combination of wireless water meters and a data-analytics-driven, customer-accessible portal, the Town of Cary, North Carolina,

is making it much easier to find and fix water loss issues. In the process, the town has gained a big-picture view of water usage critical to planning future water plant expansions and promoting targeted conservation efforts.

When the Town of Cary installed the wireless meters for 60,000 customers in 2010, it knew the new technology wouldn't just save money by eliminating manual monthly readings; the town also realized it would get more accurate and timely information about water consumption. The Aquastar wireless system reads meters once an hour—that's 8,760 data points per customer each year instead of 12 monthly readings. The data had tremendous potential, if it could be easily consumed.

"Monthly readings are like having a gallon of water's worth of data. Hourly meter readings are more like an Olympic-size pool of data," says Karen Mills, Finance Director for the Town of Cary. "SAS helps us manage the volume of that data nicely." In fact, the solution enables the town to analyze a half-billion data points on water usage and make them available, and easily consumable, to all customers.

The ability to visually look at data by household or commercial customer, by the hour, has led to some very practical applications:

- The town can notify customers of potential leaks within days.
- Customers can set alerts that notify them within hours if there is a spike in water usage.
- Customers can track their water usage online, helping them to be more proactive in conserving water.

Through the online portal, one business in the Town of Cary saw a spike in water consumption on weekends, when employees are away. This seemed odd, and the unusual reading helped the company learn that a commercial dishwasher was malfunctioning, running continuously over weekends. Without the wireless water-meter data and the customer-accessible portal, this problem could have gone unnoticed, continuing to waste water and money.

The town has a much more accurate picture of daily water usage per person, critical for planning future water plant expansions. Perhaps the most interesting perk is that the town was able to verify a hunch that has far-reaching cost ramifications: Cary residents are very economical in their use of water. "We calculate that with modern high-efficiency appliances, indoor water use could be as low as 35 gallons per person per day. Cary residents average 45 gallons, which is still phenomenally low," explains

town Water Resource Manager Leila Goodwin. Why is this important? The town was spending money to encourage water efficiency—rebates on low-flow toilets or discounts on rain barrels. Now it can take a more targeted approach, helping specific consumers understand and manage both their indoor and outdoor water use.

SAS was critical not just for enabling residents to understand their water use, but also in working behind the scenes to link two disparate databases. "We have a billing database and the meter-reading database. We needed to bring that together and make it presentable," Mills says.

The town estimates that by just removing the need for manual readings, the Aquastar system will save more than $10 million above the cost of the project. But the analytics component could provide even bigger savings. Already, both the town and individual citizens have saved money by catching water leaks early. As the Town of Cary continues to plan its future infrastructure needs, having accurate information on water usage will help it invest in the right amount of infrastructure at the right time. In addition, understanding water usage will help the town if it experiences something detrimental like a drought.

"We went through a drought in 2007," says Goodwin. "If we go through another, we have a plan in place to use Aquastar data to see exactly how much water we are using on a day-by-day basis and communicate with customers. We can show 'here's what's happening, and here is how much you can use because our supply is low.' Hopefully, we'll never have to use it, but we're prepared."

QUESTIONS FOR DISCUSSION

1. What were the challenges the Town of Cary was facing?
2. What was the proposed solution?
3. What were the results?
4. What other problems and data analytics solutions do you foresee for towns like Cary?

Source: "Municipality puts wireless water meter-reading data to work (SAS® Analytics) - The Town of Cary, North Carolina uses SAS Analytics to analyze data from wireless water meters, assess demand, detect problems and engage customers." Copyright © 2016 SAS Institute Inc., Cary, NC, USA. Reprinted with permission. All rights reserved.

SECTION 2.5 REVIEW QUESTIONS

1. What is the relationship between statistics and business analytics?
2. What are the main differences between descriptive and inferential statistics?
3. List and briefly define the central tendency measures of descriptive statistics.
4. List and briefly define the dispersion measures of descriptive statistics.
5. What is a box-and-whiskers plot? What types of statistical information does it represent?
6. What are the two most commonly used shape characteristics to describe a data distribution?

2.6   Regression Modeling for Inferential Statistics

Regression, especially linear regression, is perhaps the most widely known and used analytics technique in statistics. Historically speaking, the roots of regression date back to the 1920s and 1930s, to the earlier work on inherited characteristics of sweet peas by Sir Francis Galton and subsequently by Karl Pearson. Since then regression has become the statistical technique for characterization of relationships between explanatory (input) variable(s) and response (output) variable(s).

As popular as it is, essentially, regression is a relatively simple statistical technique to model the dependence of a variable (response or output variable) on one (or more) explanatory (input) variables. Once identified, this relationship between the variables can be formally represented as a linear/additive function/equation. As is the case with many other modeling techniques, regression aims to capture the functional relationship between and among the characteristics of the real world and describe this relationship with a mathematical model, which may then be used to discover and understand the complexities of reality—explore and explain relationships or forecast future occurrences.

Regression can be used for one of two purposes: hypothesis testing—investigating potential relationships between different variables, and prediction/forecasting—estimating values of a response variables based on one or more explanatory variables. These two uses are not mutually exclusive. The explanatory power of regression is also the foundation of its prediction ability. In hypothesis testing (theory building), regression analysis can reveal the existence/strength and the directions of relationships between a number of explanatory variables (often represented with x_i) and the response variable (often represented with y). In prediction, regression identifies additive mathematical relationships (in the form of an equation) between one or more explanatory variables and a response variable. Once determined, this equation can be used to forecast the values of the response variable for a given set of values of the explanatory variables.

CORRELATION VERSUS REGRESSION   Because regression analysis originated from correlation studies, and because both methods attempt to describe the association between two (or more) variables, these two terms are often confused by professionals and even by scientists. **Correlation** makes no a priori assumption of whether one variable is dependent on the other(s) and is not concerned with the relationship between variables; instead it gives an estimate on the degree of association between the variables. On the other hand, regression attempts to describe the dependence of a response variable on one (or more) explanatory variables where it implicitly assumes that there is a one-way causal effect from the explanatory variable(s) to the response variable, regardless of whether the path of effect is direct or indirect. Also, although correlation is interested in the low-level relationships between two variables, regression is concerned with the relationships between all explanatory variables and the response variable.

SIMPLE VERSUS MULTIPLE REGRESSION If the regression equation is built between one response variable and one explanatory variable, then it is called simple regression. For instance, the regression equation built to predict/explain the relationship between a height of a person (explanatory variable) and the weight of a person (response variable) is a good example of simple regression. Multiple regression is the extension of simple regression where the explanatory variables are more than one. For instance, in the previous example, if we were to include not only the height of the person but also other personal characteristics (e.g., BMI, gender, ethnicity) to predict the weight of a person, then we would be performing multiple regression analysis. In both cases, the relationship between the response variable and the explanatory variable(s) are linear and additive in nature. If the relationships are not linear, then we may want to use one of many other nonlinear regression methods to better capture the relationships between the input and output variables.

How Do We Develop the Linear Regression Model?

To understand the relationship between two variables, the simplest thing that one can do is to draw a scatter plot, where the y-axis represents the values of the response variable and the x-axis represents the values of the explanatory variable (see Figure 2.13). A scatter catter plot would show the changes in the response variable as a function of the changes in the explanatory variable. In the case shown in Figure 2.13, there seems to be a positive relationship between the two; as the explanatory variable values increase, so does the response variable.

Simple regression analysis aims to find a mathematical representation of this relationship. In reality, it tries to find the signature of a straight line passing through right between the plotted dots (representing the observation/historical data) in such a way that it minimizes the distance between the dots and the line (the predicted values on the

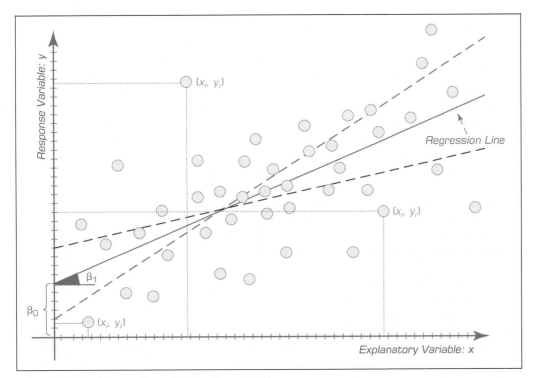

FIGURE 2.13 A Scatter Plot and a Linear Regression Line.

theoretical regression line). Even though there are several methods/algorithms proposed to identify the regression line, the one that is most commonly used is called the **ordinary least squares (OLS)** method. The OLS method aims to minimize the sum of squared residuals (squared vertical distances between the observation and the regression point) and leads to a mathematical expression for the estimated value of the regression line (which are known as β parameters). For simple **linear regression**, the aforementioned relationship between the response variable (y) and the explanatory variable(s) (x) can be shown as a simple equation as follows:

$$y = \beta_0 + \beta_1 x$$

In this equation, β_0 is called the intercept, and β_1 is called the slope. Once OLS determines the values of these two coefficients, the simple equation can be used to forecast the values of y for given values of x. The sign and the value of β_1 also reveal the direction and the strengths of relationship between the two variables.

If the model is of a multiple linear regression type, then there would be more coefficients to be determined, one for each additional explanatory variable. As the following formula shows, the additional explanatory variable would be multiplied with the new β_i coefficients and summed together to establish a linear additive representation of the response variable.

$$y = \beta_0 + \beta_1 x_1 + \beta_2 x_2 + \beta_3 x_3 + \ldots + \beta_n x_n$$

How Do We Know If the Model Is Good Enough?

Because of a variety of reasons, sometimes models as representations of the reality do not prove to be good. Regardless of the number of explanatory variables included, there is always a possibility of not having a good model, and therefore the linear regression model needs to be assessed for its fit (the degree at which it represents the response variable). In the simplest sense, a well-fitting regression model results in predicted values close to the observed data values. For the numerical assessment, three statistical measures are often used in evaluating the fit of a regression model. R^2 (R-squared), the overall F-test, and the root mean square error (RMSE). All three of these measures are based on the sums of the square errors (how far the data are from the mean and how far the data are from the model's predicted values). Different combinations of these two values provide different information about how the regression model compares to the mean model.

Of the three, R^2 has the most useful and understandable meaning because of its intuitive scale. The value of R^2 ranges from zero to one (corresponding to the amount of variability explained in percentage) with zero indicating that the relationship and the prediction power of the proposed model is not good, and one indicating that the proposed model is a perfect fit that produces exact predictions (which is almost never the case). The good R^2 values would usually come close to one, and the closeness is a matter of the phenomenon being modeled—whereas an R^2 value of 0.3 for a linear regression model in social sciences can be considered good enough, an R^2 value of 0.7 in engineering may be considered as not a good-enough fit. The improvement in the regression model can be achieved by adding mode explanatory variables, taking some of the variables out of the model, or using different data transformation techniques, which would result in comparative increases in an R^2 value. Figure 2.14 shows the process flow of developing regression models. As can be seen in the process flow, the model development task is followed by the model assessment task, where not only is the fit of the model assessed, but because of restrictive assumptions with which the linear models have to comply, also the validity of the model needs to be put under the microscope.

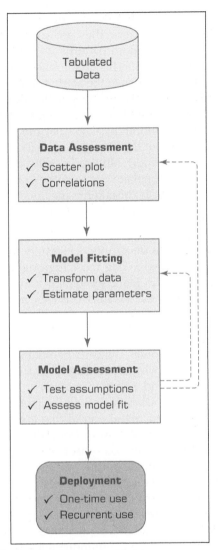

FIGURE 2.14   A Process Flow for Developing Regression Models.

What Are the Most Important Assumptions in Linear Regression?

Even though they are still the choice of many for data analyses (both for explanatory as well as for predictive modeling purposes), linear regression models suffer from several highly restrictive assumptions. The validity of the linear model built depends on its ability to comply with these assumptions. Here are the most commonly pronounced assumptions:

1. **Linearity.** This assumption states that the relationship between the response variable and the explanatory variables are linear. That is, the expected value of the response variable is a straight-line function of each explanatory variable, while holding all other explanatory variables fixed. Also, the slope of the line does not depend on the values of the other variables. It also implies that the effects of different explanatory variables on the expected value of the response variable are additive in nature.

2. **Independence**   (of errors). This assumption states that the errors of the response variable are uncorrelated with each other. This independence of the errors is weaker than actual statistical independence, which is a stronger condition and is often not needed for linear regression analysis.

3. **Normality** (of errors). This assumption states that the errors of the response variable are normally distributed. That is, they are supposed to be totally random and should not represent any nonrandom patterns.

4. **Constant variance** (of errors). This assumption, also called homoscedasticity, states that the response variables have the same variance in their error, regardless of the values of the explanatory variables. In practice this assumption is invalid if the response variable varies over a wide enough range/scale.

5. **Multicollinearity.** This assumption states that the explanatory variables are not correlated (i.e., do not replicate the same but provide a different perspective of the information needed for the model). Multicollinearity can be triggered by having two or more perfectly correlated explanatory variables presented to the model (e.g., if the same explanatory variable is mistakenly included in the model twice, one with a slight transformation of the same variable). A correlation-based data assessment usually catches this error.

There are statistical techniques developed to identify the violation of these assumptions and techniques to mitigate them. The most important part for a modeler is to be aware of their existence and to put in place the means to assess the models to make sure that the models are compliant with the assumptions they are built on.

Logistic Regression

Logistic regression is a very popular, statistically sound, probability-based classification algorithm that employs supervised **learning**. It was developed in the 1940s as a complement to linear regression and linear discriminant analysis methods. It has been used extensively in numerous disciplines, including the medical and social sciences fields. Logistic regression is similar to linear regression in that it also aims to regress to a mathematical function that explains the relationship between the response variable and the explanatory variables using a sample of past observations (training data). It differs from linear regression with one major point: its output (response variable) is a class as opposed to a numerical variable. That is, whereas linear regression is used to estimate a continuous numerical variable, logistic regression is used to classify a categorical variable. Even though the original form of logistic regression was developed for a binary output variable (e.g., 1/0, yes/no, pass/fail, accept/reject), the present-day modified version is capable of predicting multiclass output variables (i.e., multinomial logistic regression). If there is only one predictor variable and one predicted variable, the method is called simple logistic regression (similar to calling linear regression models with only one independent variable as simple linear regression).

In predictive analytics, logistic regression models are used to develop probabilistic models between one or more explanatory/predictor variables (which may be a mix of both continuous and categorical in nature) and a class/response variable (which may be binomial/binary or multinomial/multiclass). Unlike ordinary linear regression, logistic regression is used for predicting categorical (often binary) outcomes of the response variable—treating the response variable as the outcome of a Bernoulli trial. Therefore, logistic regression takes the natural logarithm of the odds of the response variable to create a continuous criterion as a transformed version of the response variable. Thus the logit transformation is referred to as the link function in logistic regression—even though the response variable in logistic regression is categorical or binomial, the logit is the continuous criterion on which linear regression is conducted. Figure 2.15 shows a logistic regression function where the odds are represented in the x-axis (a linear function of the independent variables), whereas the probabilistic outcome is shown in the y-axis (i.e., response variable values change between 0 and 1).

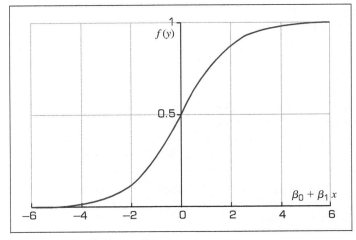

FIGURE 2.15   The Logistic Function.

The logistic function, $f(y)$ in Figure 2.15, is the core of logistic regression, which can only take values between 0 and 1. The following equation is a simple mathematical representation of this function:

$$f(y) = \frac{1}{1 + e^{-(\beta_0 + \beta_1 x)}}$$

The logistic regression coefficients (the βs) are usually estimated using the maximum likelihood estimation method. Unlike linear regression with normally distributed residuals, it is not possible to find a closed-form expression for the coefficient values that maximizes the likelihood function, so an iterative process must be used instead. This process begins with a tentative starting solution, then revises the parameters slightly to see if the solution can be improved and repeats this iterative revision until no improvement can be achieved or are very minimal, at which point the process is said to have completed/converged.

Sports analytics—use of data and statistical/analytics techniques to better manage sports teams/organizations—has been gaining tremendous popularity. Use of data-driven analytics techniques have become mainstream for not only professional teams but also college and amateur sports. Application Case 2.4 is an example of how existing and readily available public data sources can be used to predict college football bowl game outcomes using both classification and regression-type prediction models.

Application Case 2.4

Predicting NCAA Bowl Game Outcomes

Predicting the outcome of a college football game (or any sports game, for that matter) is an interesting and challenging problem. Therefore, challenge-seeking researchers from both academics and industry have spent a great deal of effort on forecasting the outcome of sporting events. Large quantities of historic data exist in different media outlets (often publicly available) regarding the structure and outcomes of sporting events in the form of a variety of numerically or symbolically represented factors that are assumed to contribute to those outcomes.

The end-of-season bowl games are very important to colleges both financially (bringing in millions of dollars of additional revenue) as well

(Continued)

Application Case 2.4 (Continued)

as reputational—for recruiting quality students and highly regarded high school athletes for their athletic programs (Freeman & Brewer, 2016). Teams that are selected to compete in a given bowl game split a purse, the size of which depends on the specific bowl (some bowls are more prestigious and have higher payouts for the two teams), and therefore securing an invitation to a bowl game is the main goal of any division I-A college football program. The decision makers of the bowl games are given the authority to select and invite bowl-eligible (a team that has six wins against its Division I-A opponents in that season) successful teams (as per the ratings and rankings) that will play in an exciting and competitive game, attract fans of both schools, and keep the remaining fans tuned in via a variety of media outlets for advertising.

In a recent data mining study, Delen, Cogdell, and Kasap (2012) used 8 years of bowl game data along with three popular data mining techniques (decision trees, neural networks, and support vector machines) to predict both the classification-type outcome of a game (win versus loss) as well as the regression-type outcome (projected point difference between the scores of the two opponents). What follows is a shorthand description of their study.

Methodology

In this research, Delen and his colleagues followed a popular data mining methodology called CRISP-DM (Cross-Industry Standard Process for Data Mining), which is a six-step process. This popular methodology, which is covered in detail in Chapter 4, provided them with a systematic and structured way to conduct the underlying data mining study and hence improved the likelihood of obtaining accurate and reliable results. To objectively assess the prediction power of the different model types, they used a cross-validation methodology, called k-fold cross-validation. Details on k-fold cross-validation can be found in Chapter 4. Figure 2.16 graphically illustrates the methodology employed by the researchers.

Data Acquisition and Data Preprocessing

The sample data for this study is collected from a variety of sports databases available on the Web, including jhowel.net, ESPN.com, Covers.com, ncaa.org, and rauzulusstreet.com. The data set included 244 bowl games, representing a complete set of eight seasons of college football bowl games played between 2002 and 2009. We also included an out-of-sample data set (2010–2011 bowl games) for

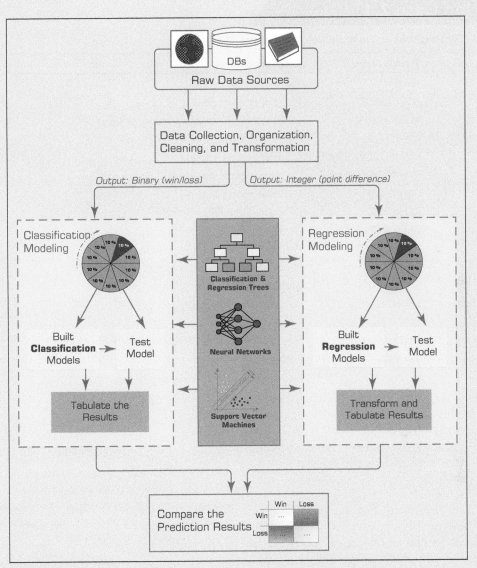

FIGURE 2.16   The Graphical Illustration of the Methodology Employed in the Study.

additional validation purposes. Exercising one of the popular data mining rules-of-thumb, they included as much relevant information into the model as possible. Therefore, after an in-depth variable identification and collection process, they ended up with a data set that included 36 variables, of which the first 6 were the identifying variables (i.e., name and the year of the bowl game, home and away team names and their athletic conferences—see variables 1–6 in Table 2.5), followed by 28 input variables (which included variables delineating a team's seasonal statistics on offense and defense, game outcomes, team composition characteristics, athletic conference

characteristics, and how they fared against the odds—see variables 7–34 in Table 2.5), and finally the last two were the output variables (i.e., ScoreDiff—the score difference between the home team and the away team represented with an integer number, and WinLoss—whether the home team won or lost the bowl game represented with a nominal label).

In the formulation of the data set, each row (a.k.a. tuple, case, sample, example, etc.) represented a bowl game, and each column stood for a variable (i.e., identifier/input or output type). To represent the game-related comparative characteristics of the two opponent teams, in the input variables,

(Continued)

Application Case 2.4 (Continued)

TABLE 2.5   Description of the Variables Used in the Study

No	Cat	Variable Name	Description
1	ID	YEAR	Year of the bowl game
2	ID	BOWLGAME	Name of the bowl game
3	ID	HOMETEAM	Home team (as listed by the bowl organizers)
4	ID	AWAYTEAM	Away team (as listed by the bowl organizers)
5	ID	HOMECONFERENCE	Conference of the home team
6	ID	AWAYCONFERENCE	Conference of the away team
7	I1	DEFPTPGM	Defensive points per game
8	I1	DEFRYDPGM	Defensive rush yards per game
9	I1	DEFYDPGM	Defensive yards per game
10	I1	PPG	Average number of points a given team scored per game
11	I1	PYDPGM	Average total pass yards per game
12	I1	RYDPGM	Team's average total rush yards per game
13	I1	YRDPGM	Average total offensive yards per game
14	I2	HMWIN%	Home winning percentage
15	I2	LAST7	How many games the team won out of their last 7 games
16	I2	MARGOVIC	Average margin of victory
17	I2	NCTW	Nonconference team winning percentage
18	I2	PREVAPP	Did the team appeared in a bowl game previous year
19	I2	RDWIN%	Road winning percentage
20	I2	SEASTW	Winning percentage for the year
21	I2	TOP25	Winning percentage against AP top 25 teams for the year
22	I3	TSOS	Strength of schedule for the year
23	I3	FR%	Percentage of games played by freshmen class players for the year
24	I3	SO%	Percentage of games played by sophomore class players for the year
25	I3	JR%	Percentage of games played by junior class players for the year
26	I3	SR%	Percentage of games played by senior class players for the year
27	I4	SEASOvUn%	Percentage of times a team went over the O/U* in the current season
28	I4	ATSCOV%	Against the spread cover percentage of the team in previous bowl games
39	I4	UNDER%	Percentage of times a team went under in previous bowl games
30	I4	OVER%	Percentage of times a team went over in previous bowl games
31	I4	SEASATS%	Percentage of covering against the spread for the current season
32	I5	CONCH	Did the team win their respective conference championship game
33	I5	CONFSOS	Conference strength of schedule
34	I5	CONFWIN%	Conference winning percentage
35	O1	ScoreDiff°	Score difference (HomeTeamScore − AwayTeamScore)
36	O2	WinLoss°	Whether the home team wins or loses the game

* Over/Under—Whether or not a team will go over or under of the expected score difference.

° Output variables—ScoreDiff for regression models and WinLoss for binary classification models.

I1: Offense/defense; I2: game outcome; I3: team configuration; I4: against the odds; I5: conference stats.

ID: Identifier variables; O1: output variable for regression models; O2: output variable for classification models.

we calculated and used the differences between the measures of the home and away teams. All these variable values are calculated from the home team's perspective. For instance, the variable PPG (average number of points a team scored per game) represents the difference between the home team's PPG and away team's PPG. The output variables represent whether the home team wins or loses the bowl game. That is, if the ScoreDiff variable takes a positive integer number, then the home team is expected to win the game by that margin, otherwise (if the ScoreDiff variable takes a negative integer number) then the home team is expected to lose the game by that margin. In the case of WinLoss, the value of the output variable is a binary label, "Win" or "Loss" indicating the outcome of the game for the home team.

Results and Evaluation

In this study, three popular prediction techniques are used to build models (and to compare them to each other): artificial neural networks, decision trees, and support vector machines. These prediction techniques are selected based on their capability of modeling both classification as well as regression-type prediction problems and their popularity in recently published data mining literature. More details about these popular data mining methods can be found in Chapter 4.

To compare predictive accuracy of all models to one another, the researchers used a stratified k-fold cross-validation methodology. In a stratified version of k-fold cross-validation, the folds are created in a way that they contain approximately the same proportion of predictor labels (i.e., classes)

as the original data set. In this study, the value of k is set to 10 (i.e., the complete set of 244 samples are split into 10 subsets, each having about 25 samples), which is a common practice in predictive data mining applications. A graphical depiction of the 10-fold cross-validations was shown earlier in this chapter. To compare the prediction models that were developed using the aforementioned three data mining techniques, the researchers chose to use three common performance criteria: accuracy, sensitivity, and specificity. The simple formulas for these metrics were also explained earlier in this chapter.

The prediction results of the three modeling techniques are presented in Table 2.6 and Table 2.7. Table 2.6 presents the 10-fold cross-validation results of the classification methodology where the three data mining techniques are formulated to have a binary-nominal output variable (i.e., WinLoss). Table 2.7 presents the 10-fold cross-validation results of the regression-based classification methodology, where the three data mining techniques are formulated to have a numerical output variable (i.e., ScoreDiff). In the regression-based classification prediction, the numerical output of the models is converted to a classification type by labeling the positive WinLoss numbers with a "Win" and negative WinLoss numbers with a "Loss," and then tabulating them in the confusion matrixes. Using the confusion matrices, the overall prediction accuracy, sensitivity, and specificity of each model type are calculated and presented in these two tables. As the results indicate, the classification-type prediction methods performed better than regression-based classification-type prediction methodology. Among the three data mining

TABLE 2.6 Prediction Results for the Direct Classification Methodology

Prediction Method (Classification[*])		Confusion Matrix		Accuracy** (in %)	Sensitivity (in %)	Specificity (in %)
		Win	Loss			
ANN (MLP)	Win	92	42	75.00	68.66	82.73
	Loss	19	91			
SVM (RBF)	Win	105	29	79.51	78.36	80.91
	Loss	21	89			
DT (C&RT)	Win	113	21	**86.48**	84.33	89.09
	Loss	12	98			

[*]The output variable is a binary categorical variable (Win or Loss); differences were sig (** $p < 0.01$).   (Continued)

Application Case 2.4 (Continued)

TABLE 2.7   Prediction Results for the Regression-Based Classification Methodology

Prediction Method (Regression-Based*)		Confusion Matrix		Accuracy**	Sensitivity	Specificity
		Win	Loss			
ANN (MLP)	Win	94	40	72.54	70.15	75.45
	Loss	27	83			
SVM (RBF)	Win	100	34	74.59	74.63	74.55
	Loss	28	82			
DT (C&RT)	Win	106	28	77.87	76.36	79.10
	Loss	26	84			

*The output variable is a numerical/integer variable (point-diff); differences were sig (** $p < 0.01$).

technologies, classification and regression trees produced better prediction accuracy in both prediction methodologies. Overall, classification and regression tree classification models produced a 10-fold cross-validation accuracy of 86.48%, followed by support vector machines (with a 10-fold cross-validation accuracy of 79.51%) and neural networks (with a 10-fold cross-validation accuracy of 75.00%). Using a t-test, researchers found that these accuracy values were significantly different at 0.05 alpha level, that is, the decision tree is a significantly better predictor of this domain than the neural network and support vector machine, and the support vector machine is a significantly better predictor than neural networks.

The results of the study showed that the classification-type models predict the game outcomes better than regression-based classification models. Even though these results are specific to the application domain and the data used in this study, and therefore should not be generalized beyond the scope of the study, they are exciting because decision trees are not only the best predictors but also the best

in understanding and deployment, compared to the other two machine-learning techniques employed in this study. More details about this study can be found in Delen et al. (2012).

QUESTIONS FOR DISCUSSION

1. What are the foreseeable challenges in predicting sporting event outcomes (e.g., college bowl games)?

2. How did the researchers formulate/design the prediction problem (i.e., what were the inputs and output, and what was the representation of a single sample—row of data)?

3. How successful were the prediction results? What else can they do to improve the accuracy?

Sources: Delen, D., Cogdell, D., & Kasap, N. (2012). A comparative analysis of data mining methods in predicting NCAA bowl outcomes. *International Journal of Forecasting, 28,* 543–552; Freeman, K. M., & Brewer, R. M. (2016). The politics of American college football. *Journal of Applied Business and Economics, 18*(2), 97–101.

Time Series Forecasting

Sometimes the variable that we are interested in (i.e., the response variable) may not have distinctly identifiable explanatory variables, or there may be too many of them in a highly complex relationship. In such cases, if the data is available in a desired format, a prediction model, the so-called time series, can be developed. A time series is a sequence of data points of the variable of interest, measured and represented at successive points in time spaced at uniform time intervals. Examples of time series include monthly rain volumes in a geographic area, the daily closing value of the stock market indexes, daily sales totals for

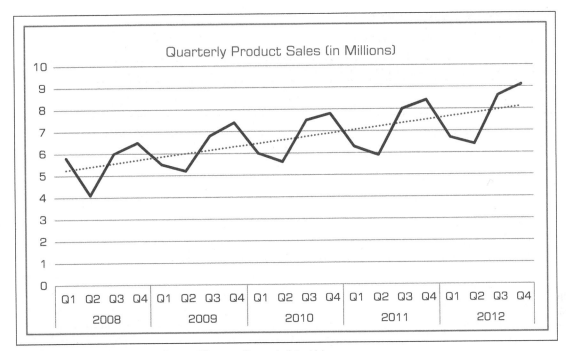

FIGURE 2.17 A Sample Time Series of Data on Quarterly Sales Volumes.

a grocery store. Often, time series are visualized using a line chart. Figure 2.17 shows an example time series of sales volumes for the years 2008 through 2012 in a quarterly basis.

Time series forecasting is the use of mathematical modeling to predict future values of the variable of interest based on previously observed values. The time series plots/charts look and feel very similar to simple linear regression in that as was the case in simple linear regression, in time series there are two variables: the response variable and the time variable presented in a scatter plot. Beyond this look similarity, there is hardly any other commonality between the two. Although regression analysis is often employed in testing theories to see if current values of one or more explanatory variables explain (and hence predict) the response variable, the time series models are focused on extrapolating on their time-varying behavior to estimate the future values.

Time series forecasting assumes all the explanatory variables are aggregated and consumed in the response variable's time-variant behavior. Therefore, capturing of the time-variant behavior is the way to predict the future values of the response variable. To do that the pattern is analyzed and decomposed into its main components: random variations, time trends, and seasonal cycles. The time series example shown in Figure 2.17 illustrates all these distinct patterns.

The techniques used to develop time series forecasts range from very simple (the naïve forecast that suggests today's forecast is the same as yesterday's actual) to very complex like ARIMA (a method that combines autoregressive and moving average patterns in data). Most popular techniques are perhaps the averaging methods that include simple average, moving average, weighted moving average, and exponential smoothing. Many of these techniques also have advanced versions where seasonality and trend can also be taken into account for better and more accurate forecasting. The accuracy of a method is usually assessed by computing its error (calculated deviation between actuals and forecasts for the past observations) via mean absolute error (MAE), mean squared error (MSE), or mean absolute percent error (MAPE). Even though they all use the same core error measure, these three assessment methods emphasize different aspects of the error, some panelizing larger errors more so than the others.

SECTION 2.6 REVIEW QUESTIONS

1. What is regression, and what statistical purpose does it serve?
2. What are the commonalities and differences between regression and correlation?
3. What is OLS? How does OLS determine the linear regression line?
4. List and describe the main steps to follow in developing a linear repression model.
5. What are the most commonly pronounced assumptions for linear regression?
6. What is logistics regression? How does it differ from linear regression?
7. What is time series? What are the main forecasting techniques for time series data?

2.7   Business Reporting

Decision makers are in need of information to make accurate and timely decisions. Information is essentially the contextualization of data. In addition to statistical means that were explained in the previous section, information (descriptive analytics) can also be obtained using online analytics processing [OLTP] systems (see the simple taxonomy of descriptive analytics in Figure 2.7). The information is usually provided to the decision makers in the form of a written report (digital or on paper), although it can also be provided orally. Simply put, a **report** is any communication artifact prepared with the specific intention of conveying information in a digestible form to whoever needs it, whenever and wherever they may need it. It is usually a document that contains information (usually driven from data) organized in a narrative, graphic, and/or tabular form, prepared periodically (recurring) or on an as-needed (ad hoc) basis, referring to specific time periods, events, occurrences, or subjects. Business reports can fulfill many different (but often related) functions. Here are a few of the most prevailing ones:

- To ensure that all departments are functioning properly
- To provide information
- To provide the results of an analysis
- To persuade others to act
- To create an organizational memory (as part of a knowledge management system)

Business reporting (also called OLAP or BI) is an essential part of the larger drive toward improved, evidence-based, optimal managerial decision making. The foundation of these **business reports** is various sources of data coming from both inside and outside the organization (online transaction processing [OLTP] systems). Creation of these reports involves ETL (extract, transform, and load) procedures in coordination with a data warehouse and then using one or more reporting tools (see Chapter 3 for a detailed description of these concepts).

Due to the rapid expansion of information technology coupled with the need for improved competitiveness in business, there has been an increase in the use of computing power to produce unified reports that join different views of the enterprise in one place. Usually, this reporting process involves querying structured data sources, most of which were created using different logical data models and data dictionaries, to produce a human-readable, easily digestible report. These types of business reports allow managers and coworkers to stay informed and involved, review options and alternatives, and make informed decisions. Figure 2.18 shows the continuous cycle of data acquisition → information generation → decision making → business process management. Perhaps the most critical task in this cyclical process is the reporting (i.e., information generation)—converting data from different sources into actionable information.

Key to any successful report are clarity, brevity, completeness, and correctness. The nature of the report and the level of importance of these success factors change significantly

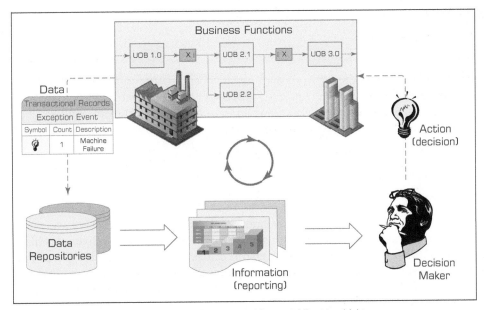

FIGURE 2.18 The Role of Information Reporting in Managerial Decision Making.

based on for whom the report is created. Most of the research in effective reporting is dedicated to internal reports that inform stakeholders and decision makers within the organization. There are also external reports between businesses and the government (e.g., for tax purposes or for regular filings to the Securities and Exchange Commission). Even though there are a wide variety of business reports, the ones that are often used for managerial purposes can be grouped into three major categories (Hill, 2016).

METRIC MANAGEMENT REPORTS   In many organizations, business performance is managed through outcome-oriented metrics. For external groups, these are service-level agreements. For internal management, they are **key performance indicators (KPIs)**. Typically, there are enterprise-wide agreed targets to be tracked against over a period of time. They may be used as part of other management strategies such as Six Sigma or Total Quality Management.

DASHBOARD-TYPE REPORTS   A popular idea in business reporting in recent years has been to present a range of different performance indicators on one page, like a dashboard in a car. Typically, dashboard vendors would provide a set of predefined reports with static elements and fixed structure, but also allow for customization of the dashboard widgets, views, and set targets for various metrics. It's common to have color-coded traffic lights defined for performance (red, orange, green) to draw management's attention to particular areas. A more detailed description of dashboards can be found in later part of this chapter.

BALANCED SCORECARD–TYPE REPORTS   This is a method developed by Kaplan and Norton that attempts to present an integrated view of success in an organization. In addition to financial performance, balanced scorecard–type reports also include customer, business process, and learning and growth perspectives. More details on balanced scorecards are provided later in this chapter.

Application Case 2.5 is an example to illustrate the power and the utility of automated report generation for a large (and, at a time of natural crisis, somewhat chaotic) organization like FEMA.

Application Case 2.5

Flood of Paper Ends at FEMA

Staff at the Federal Emergency Management Agency (FEMA), a U.S. federal agency that coordinates disaster response when the president declares a national disaster, always got two floods at once. First, water covered the land. Next, a flood of paper, required to administer the National Flood Insurance Program (NFIP) covered their desks—pallets and pallets of green-striped reports poured off a mainframe printer and into their offices. Individual reports were sometimes 18 inches thick, with a nugget of information about insurance claims, premiums, or payments buried in them somewhere.

Bill Barton and Mike Miles don't claim to be able to do anything about the weather, but the project manager and computer scientist, respectively, from Computer Sciences Corporation (CSC) have used WebFOCUS software from Information Builders to turn back the flood of paper generated by the NFIP. The program allows the government to work together with national insurance companies to collect flood insurance premiums and pay claims for flooding in communities that adopt flood control measures. As a result of CSC's work, FEMA staff no longer leaf through paper reports to find the data they need. Instead, they browse insurance data posted on NFIP's BureauNet intranet site, select just the information they want to see, and get an on-screen report or download the data as a spreadsheet. And that is only the start of the savings that WebFOCUS has provided. The number of times that NFIP staff asks CSC for special reports has dropped in half because NFIP staff can generate many of the special reports they need without calling on a programmer to develop them. Then there is the cost of creating BureauNet in the first place. Barton estimates that using conventional Web and database software to export data from FEMA's mainframe, store it in a new database, and link that to a Web server would have cost about 100 times as much—more than $500,000—and taken

about 2 years to complete, compared with the few months Miles spent on the WebFOCUS solution.

When Tropical Storm Allison, a huge slug of sodden, swirling cloud, moved out of the Gulf of Mexico onto the Texas and Louisiana coastline in June 2001, it killed 34 people, most from drowning; damaged or destroyed 16,000 homes and businesses; and displaced more than 10,000 families. President George W. Bush declared 28 Texas counties disaster areas, and FEMA moved in to help. This was the first serious test for BureauNet, and it delivered. This first comprehensive use of BureauNet resulted in FEMA field staff readily accessing what they needed when they needed it and asking for many new types of reports. Fortunately, Miles and WebFOCUS were up to the task. In some cases, Barton says, "FEMA would ask for a new type of report one day, and Miles would have it on BureauNet the next day, thanks to the speed with which he could create new reports in WebFOCUS."

The sudden demand on the system had little impact on its performance, noted Barton. "It handled the demand just fine," he says. "We had no problems with it at all. And it made a huge difference to FEMA and the job they had to do. They had never had that level of access before, never had been able to just click on their desktop and generate such detailed and specific reports."

QUESTIONS FOR DISCUSSION

1. What is FEMA, and what does it do?
2. What are the main challenges that FEMA faces?
3. How did FEMA improve its inefficient reporting practices?

Source: Information Builders success story. Useful information flows at disaster response agency. informationbuilders.com/applications/fema (accessed May 2016); and fema.gov.

SECTION 2.7 REVIEW QUESTIONS

1. What is a report? What are reports used for?
2. What is a business report? What are the main characteristics of a good business report?
3. Describe the cyclic process of management, and comment on the role of business reports.
4. List and describe the three major categories of business reports.
5. What are the main components of a business reporting system?

2.8   Data Visualization

Data visualization (or more appropriately, information visualization) has been defined as "the use of visual representations to explore, make sense of, and communicate data" (Few, 2007). Although the name that is commonly used is *data visualization*, usually what is meant by this is information visualization. Because information is the aggregation, summarization, and contextualization of data (raw facts), what is portrayed in visualizations is the information and not the data. However, because the two terms *data visualization* and *information visualization* are used interchangeably and synonymously, in this chapter we will follow suit.

Data visualization is closely related to the fields of information graphics, information visualization, scientific visualization, and statistical graphics. Until recently, the major forms of data visualization available in both BI applications have included charts and graphs, as well as the other types of visual elements used to create scorecards and dashboards.

To better understand the current and future trends in the field of data visualization, it helps to begin with some historical context.

A Brief History of Data Visualization

Despite the fact that predecessors to data visualization date back to the second century AD, most developments have occurred in the last two and a half centuries, predominantly during the last 30 years (Few, 2007). Although visualization has not been widely recognized as a discipline until fairly recently, today's most popular visual forms date back a few centuries. Geographical exploration, mathematics, and popularized history spurred the creation of early maps, graphs, and timelines as far back as the 1600s, but William Playfair is widely credited as the inventor of the modern chart, having created the first widely distributed line and bar charts in his *Commercial and Political Atlas of 1786* and what is generally considered to be the first time series portraying line charts in his *Statistical Breviary*, published in 1801 (see Figure 2.19).

Perhaps the most notable innovator of information graphics during this period was Charles Joseph Minard, who graphically portrayed the losses suffered by Napoleon's army in the Russian campaign of 1812 (see Figure 2.20). Beginning at the Polish–Russian border, the thick band shows the size of the army at each position. The path of Napoleon's retreat from Moscow in the bitterly cold winter is depicted by the dark lower band, which is tied to temperature and time scales. Popular visualization expert, author, and critic Edward Tufte says that this "may well be the best statistical graphic ever drawn." In this graphic Minard managed to simultaneously represent several data dimensions (the size of the army, direction of movement, geographic locations, outside temperature, etc.) in an artistic and informative manner. Many more excellent visualizations were created in the 1800s, and most of them are chronicled on Tufte's Web site (edwardtufte.com) and his visualization books.

The 1900s saw the rise of a more formal, empirical attitude toward visualization, which tended to focus on aspects such as color, value scales, and labeling. In the mid-1900s, cartographer and theorist Jacques Bertin published his *Semiologie Graphique*, which some say serves as the theoretical foundation of modern information visualization. Although most of his patterns are either outdated by more recent research or completely inapplicable to digital media, many are still very relevant.

In the 2000s, the Internet emerged as a new medium for visualization and brought with it a whole lot of new tricks and capabilities. Not only has the worldwide, digital distribution of both data and visualization made them more accessible to a broader audience (raising visual literacy along the way), but it has also spurred the design of new forms that incorporate interaction, animation, and graphics-rendering technology unique to screen

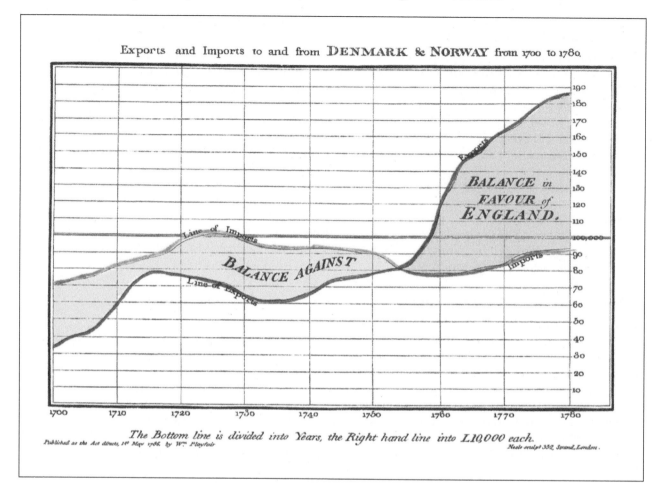

FIGURE 2.19 The First Time Series Line Chart Created by William Playfair in 1801.

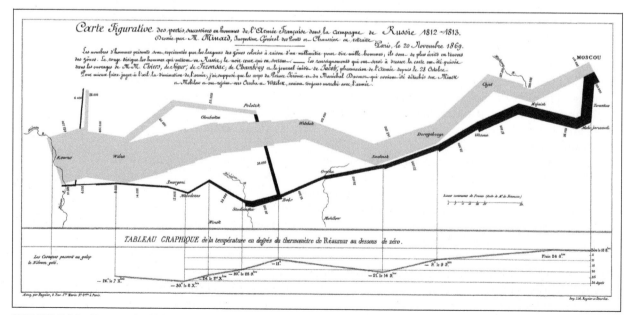

FIGURE 2.20 Decimation of Napoleon's Army during the 1812 Russian Campaign.

media, and real-time data feeds to create immersive environments for communicating and consuming data.

Companies and individuals are, seemingly all of a sudden, interested in data; that interest has in turn sparked a need for visual tools that help them understand it. Cheap hardware sensors and do-it-yourself frameworks for building your own system are driving down the costs of collecting and processing data. Countless other applications, software tools, and low-level code libraries are springing up to help people collect, organize, manipulate, visualize, and understand data from practically any source. The Internet has also served as a fantastic distribution channel for visualizations; a diverse community of designers, programmers, cartographers, tinkerers, and data wonks has assembled to disseminate all sorts of new ideas and tools for working with data in both visual and nonvisual forms.

Google Maps has also single-handedly democratized both the interface conventions (click to pan, double-click to zoom) and the technology (256-pixel square map tiles with predictable file names) for displaying interactive geography online, to the extent that most people just know what to do when they're presented with a map online. Flash has served well as a cross-browser platform on which to design and develop rich, beautiful Internet applications incorporating interactive data visualization and maps; now, new browser-native technologies such as canvas and SVG (sometimes collectively included under the umbrella of HTML5) are emerging to challenge Flash's supremacy and extend the reach of dynamic visualization interfaces to mobile devices.

The future of data/information visualization is very hard to predict. We can only extrapolate from what has already been invented: more three-dimensional visualization, more immersive experience with multidimensional data in a virtual reality environment, and holographic visualization of information. There is a pretty good chance that we will see something that we have never seen in the information visualization realm invented before the end of this decade. Application Case 2.6 shows how visual analytics/reporting tools like Tableau can help facilitate effective and efficient decision making through information/insight creation and sharing.

Application Case 2.6

Macfarlan Smith Improves Operational Performance Insight with Tableau Online

Background

Macfarlan Smith has earned its place in medical history. The company held a royal appointment to provide medicine to Her Majesty Queen Victoria and supplied groundbreaking obstetrician Sir James Simpson with chloroform for his experiments in pain relief during labor and delivery. Today, Macfarlan Smith is a subsidiary of the Fine Chemical and Catalysts division of Johnson Matthey plc. The pharmaceutical manufacturer is the world's leading manufacturer of opiate narcotics such as codeine and morphine.

Every day, Macfarlan Smith is making decisions based on its data. They collect and analyze manufacturing operational data, for example, to allow them to meet continuous improvement goals. Sales, marketing and finance rely on data to identify new pharmaceutical business opportunities, grow revenues and satisfy customer needs. Additionally, the company's manufacturing facility in Edinburgh needs to monitor, trend and report quality data to assure the identity, quality, and purity of its pharmaceutical ingredients for customers and regulatory authorities

(Continued)

such as the U.S. Food and Drug Administration (FDA) and others as part of Good Manufacturing Practice (cGMP).

Challenges: Multiple Sources of Truth and Slow, Onerous Reporting Processes

The process of gathering that data, making decisions and reporting was not easy though. The data was scattered across the business: including in the company's bespoke enterprise resource planning (ERP) platform, inside legacy departmental databases such as SQL, Access databases, and standalone spreadsheets. When that data was needed for decision making, excessive time and resources were devoted to extracting the data, integrating it and presenting it in a spreadsheet or other presentation outlet.

Data quality was another concern. Because teams relied on their own individual sources of data, there were multiple versions of the truth and conflicts between the data. And it was sometimes hard to tell which version of the data was correct and which wasn't.

It didn't stop there. Even once the data had been gathered and presented, it was slow and difficult to make changes 'on the fly.' In fact, whenever a member of the Macfarlan Smith team wanted to perform trend or other analysis, the changes to the data needed to be approved. The end result being that the data was frequently out of date by the time it was used for decision making.

Liam Mills, Head of Continuous Improvement at Macfarlan Smith highlights a typical reporting scenario:

"One of our main reporting processes is the 'Corrective Action and Preventive Action', or CAPA, which is an analysis of Macfarlan Smith's manufacturing processes taken to eliminate causes of nonconformities or other undesirable situations. Hundreds of hours every month were devoted to pulling data together for CAPA—and it took days to produce each report. Trend analysis was tricky too, because the data was static. In other reporting scenarios, we often had to wait for spreadsheet pivot table analysis; which was then presented on a graph, printed out, and pinned to a wall for everyone to review."

Slow, labor-intensive reporting processes, different versions of the truth, and static data were all catalysts for change. "Many people were frustrated because they believed they didn't have a complete picture of the business," says Mills. "We were having more and more discussions about issues we faced—when we should have been talking about business intelligence reporting."

Solution: Interactive Data Visualizations

One of the Macfarlan Smith team had previous experience of using Tableau and recommended Mills explore the solution further. A free trial of Tableau Online quickly convinced Mills that the hosted interactive data visualization solution could conquer the data battles they were facing.

"I was won over almost immediately," he says. "The ease of use, the functionality and the breadth of data visualizations are all very impressive. And of course being a software-as-a-service (SaaS)-based solution, there's no technology infrastructure investment, we can be live almost immediately, and we have the flexibility to add users whenever we need."

One of the key questions that needed to be answered concerned the security of the online data. "Our parent company Johnson Matthey has a cloud-first strategy, but has to be certain that any hosted solution is completely secure. Tableau Online features like single sign-on and allowing only authorized users to interact with the data provide that watertight security and confidence."

The other security question that Macfarlan Smith and Johnson Matthey wanted answered was: Where is the data physically stored? Mills again: "We are satisfied Tableau Online meets our criteria for data security and privacy. The data and workbooks are all hosted in Tableau's new Dublin data center, so it never leaves Europe."

Following a six-week trial, the Tableau sales manager worked with Mills and his team to build a business case for Tableau Online. The management team approved it almost straight away and a pilot program involving 10 users began. The pilot involved a manufacturing quality improvement initiative: looking at deviations from the norm, such as when a heating device used in the opiate narcotics manufacturing process exceeds a temperature threshold. From this, a 'quality operations' dashboard was created to track and measure deviations and put in place measures to improve operational quality and performance.

"That dashboard immediately signaled where deviations might be. We weren't ploughing through rows of data—we reached answers straight away," says Mills.

Throughout this initial trial and pilot, the team used Tableau training aids, such as the free training videos, product walkthroughs and live online training. They also participated in a two-day 'fundamentals training' event in London. According to Mills, "The training was expert, precise and pitched just at the right level. It demonstrated to everyone just how intuitive Tableau Online is. We can visualize 10 years' worth of data in just a few clicks." The company now has five Tableau Desktop users, and up to 200 Tableau Online licensed users.

Mills and his team particularly like the Tableau Union feature in Version 9.3, which allows them to piece together data that's been split into little files. "It's sometimes hard to bring together the data we use for analysis. The Union feature lets us work with data spread across multiple tabs or files, reducing the time we spend on prepping the data," he says.

Results: Cloud Analytics Transform Decision Making and Reporting

By standardizing on Tableau Online, Macfarlan Smith has transformed the speed and accuracy of its decision making and business reporting. This includes:

- New interactive dashboards can be produced within one hour. Previously, it used to take days to integrate and present data in a static spreadsheet.
- The CAPA manufacturing process report, which used to absorb hundreds of man-hours

every month and days to produce, can now be produced in minutes—with insights shared in the cloud.
- Reports can be changed and interrogated 'on the fly' quickly and easily, without technical intervention. Macfarlan Smith has the flexibility to publish dashboards with Tableau Desktop and share them with colleagues, partners or customers.
- The company has one, single, trusted version of the truth.
- Macfarlan Smith is now having discussions about its data—not about the issues surrounding data integration and data quality.
- New users can be brought online almost instantly—and there's no technical infrastructure to manage.

Following this initial success, Macfarlan Smith is now extending Tableau Online out to financial reporting, supply chain analytics and sales forecasting. Mills concludes, "Our business strategy is now based on data-driven decisions, not opinions. The interactive visualizations enable us to spot trends instantly, identify process improvements and take business intelligence to the next level. I'll define my career by Tableau."

QUESTIONS FOR DISCUSSION

1. What were the data and reporting related challenges Macfarlan Smith facing?
2. What was the solution and the obtained results/benefits?

Source: Tableau Customer Case Study, "Macfarlan Smith improves operational performance insight with Tableau Online," http://www.tableau.com/stories/customer/macfarlan-smith-improves-operational-performance-insight-tableau-online (accessed October 2016).

SECTION 2.8 REVIEW QUESTIONS

1. What is data visualization? Why is it needed?
2. What are the historical roots of data visualization?
3. Carefully analyze Charles Joseph Minard's graphical portrayal of Napoleon's march. Identify and comment on all the information dimensions captured in this ancient diagram.
4. Who is Edward Tufte? Why do you think we should know about his work?
5. What do you think is the "next big thing" in data visualization?

2.9 Different Types of Charts and Graphs

Often end users of business analytics systems are not sure what type of chart or graph to use for a specific purpose. Some charts or graphs are better at answering certain types of questions. Some look better than others. Some are simple; some are rather complex and crowded. What follows is a short description of the types of charts and/or graphs commonly found in most business analytics tools and what types of questions they are better at answering/analyzing. This material is compiled from several published articles and other literature (Abela, 2008; Hardin et al., 2012; SAS, 2014).

Basic Charts and Graphs

What follows are the basic charts and graphs that are commonly used for information visualization.

LINE CHART   Line charts are perhaps the most frequently used graphical visuals for time series data. Line charts (or a line graphs) show the relationship between two variables; they are most often used to track changes or trends over time (having one of the variables set to time on the *x*-axis). Line charts sequentially connect individual data points to help infer changing trends over a period of time. Line charts are often used to show time-dependent changes in the values of some measure, such as changes on a specific stock price over a 5-year period or changes on the number of daily customer service calls over a month.

BAR CHART   Bar charts are among the most basic visuals used for data representation. Bar charts are effective when you have nominal data or numerical data that splits nicely into different categories so you can quickly see comparative results and trends within your data. Bar charts are often used to compare data across multiple categories such as percent of advertising spending by departments or by product categories. Bar charts can be vertically or horizontally oriented. They can also be stacked on top of each other to show multiple dimensions in a single chart.

PIE CHART   Pie charts are visually appealing, as the name implies, pie-looking charts. Because they are so visually attractive, they are often incorrectly used. Pie charts should only be used to illustrate relative proportions of a specific measure. For instance, they can be used to show the relative percentage of an advertising budget spent on different product lines, or they can show relative proportions of majors declared by college students in their sophomore year. If the number of categories to show is more than just a few (say more than four), one should seriously consider using a bar chart instead of a pie chart.

SCATTER PLOT   Scatter plots are often used to explore the relationship between two or three variables (in 2-D or 2-D visuals). Because they are visual exploration tools, having more than three variables, translating them into more than three dimensions is not easily achievable. Scatter plots are an effective way to explore the existence of trends, concentrations, and outliers. For instance, in a two-variable (two-axis) graph, a scatter plot can be used to illustrate the corelationship between age and weight of heart disease patients or it can illustrate the relationship between the number of customer care representatives and the number of open customer service claims. Often, a trend line is superimposed on a two-dimensional scatter plot to illustrate the nature of the relationship.

BUBBLE CHART **Bubble charts** are often enhanced versions of scatter plots. Bubble charts, though, are not a new visualization type; instead, they should be viewed as a technique to enrich data illustrated in scatter plots (or even geographic maps). By varying the size and/or color of the circles, one can add additional data dimensions, offering more enriched meaning about the data. For instance, a bubble chart can be used to show a competitive view of college-level class attendance by major and by time of the day, or it can be used to show profit margin by product type and by geographic region.

Specialized Charts and Graphs

The graphs and charts that we review in this section are either derived from the basic charts as special cases or they are relatively new and are specific to a problem type and/ or an application area.

HISTOGRAM Graphically speaking, a **histogram** looks just like a bar chart. The difference between histograms and generic bar charts is the information that is portrayed. Histograms are used to show the frequency distribution of a variable or several variables. In a histogram, the x-axis is often used to show the categories or ranges, and the y-axis is used to show the measures/values/frequencies. Histograms show the distributional shape of the data. That way, one can visually examine if the data is normally or exponentially distributed. For instance, one can use a histogram to illustrate the exam performance of a class, where distribution of the grades as well as comparative analysis of individual results can be shown, or one can use a histogram to show age distribution of the customer base.

GANTT CHART Gantt charts are a special case of horizontal bar charts that are used to portray project timelines, project tasks/activity durations, and overlap among the tasks/ activities. By showing start and end dates/times of tasks/activities and the overlapping relationships, Gantt charts provide an invaluable aid for management and control of projects. For instance, Gantt charts are often used to show project timelines, task overlaps, relative task completions (a partial bar illustrating the completion percentage inside a bar that shows the actual task duration), resources assigned to each task, milestones, and deliverables.

PERT CHART PERT charts (also called network diagrams) are developed primarily to simplify the planning and scheduling of large and complex projects. They show precedence relationships among the project activities/tasks. A PERT chart is composed of nodes (represented as circles or rectangles) and edges (represented with directed arrows). Based on the selected PERT chart convention, either nodes or the edges may be used to represent the project activities/tasks (activity-on-node versus activity-on-arrow representation schema).

GEOGRAPHIC MAP When the data set includes any kind of location data (e.g., physical addresses, postal codes, state names or abbreviations, country names, latitude/longitude, or some type of custom geographic encoding), it is better and more informative to see the data on a map. Maps usually are used in conjunction with other charts and graphs, as opposed to by themselves. For instance, one can use maps to show distribution of customer service requests by product type (depicted in pie charts) by geographic locations. Often a large variety of information (e.g., age distribution, income distribution, education, economic growth, or population changes) can be portrayed in a geographic map to help decide where to open a new restaurant or a new service station. These types of systems are often called geographic information systems (GIS).

BULLET   Bullet graphs are often used to show progress toward a goal. A bullet graph is essentially a variation of a bar chart. Often they are used in place of gauges, meters, and thermometers in a dashboard to more intuitively convey the meaning within a much smaller space. Bullet graphs compare a primary measure (e.g., year-to-date revenue) to one or more other measures (e.g., annual revenue target) and present this in the context of defined performance metrics (e.g., sales quotas). A bullet graph can intuitively illustrate how the primary measure is performing against overall goals (e.g., how close a sales representative is to achieving his/her annual quota).

HEAT MAP   Heat maps are great visuals to illustrate the comparison of continuous values across two categories using color. The goal is to help the user quickly see where the intersection of the categories is strongest and weakest in terms of numerical values of the measure being analyzed. For instance, one can use heat maps to show segmentation analysis of target markets where the measure (color gradient would be the purchase amount) and the dimensions would be age and income distribution.

HIGHLIGHT TABLE   Highlight tables are intended to take heat maps one step further. In addition to showing how data intersects by using color, highlight tables add a number on top to provide additional detail. That is, they are two-dimensional tables with cells populated with numerical values and gradients of colors. For instance, one can show sales representatives' performance by product type and by sales volume.

TREE MAP   Tree maps display hierarchical (tree-structured) data as a set of nested rectangles. Each branch of the tree is given a rectangle, which is then tiled with smaller rectangles representing subbranches. A leaf node's rectangle has an area proportional to a specified dimension on the data. Often the leaf nodes are colored to show a separate dimension of the data. When the color and size dimensions are correlated in some way with the tree structure, one can often easily see patterns that would be difficult to spot in other ways, such as if a certain color is particularly relevant. A second advantage of tree maps is that, by construction, they make efficient use of space. As a result, they can legibly display thousands of items on the screen simultaneously.

Which Chart or Graph Should You Use?

Which chart or graph that we explained in the previous section is the best? The answer is rather easy: there is not one best chart or graph, because if there was we would not have these many chart and graph types. They all have somewhat different data representation "skills." Therefore, the right question should be, "Which chart or graph is the best for a given task?" The capabilities of the charts given in the previous section can help in selecting and using the right chart/graph for a specific task, but it still is not easy to sort out. Several different chart/graph types can be used for the same visualization task. One rule of thumb is to select and use the simplest one from the alternatives to make it easy for the intended audience to understand and digest.

Although there is not a widely accepted, all-encompassing chart selection algorithm or chart/graph taxonomy, Figure 2.21 presents a rather comprehensive and highly logical organization of chart/graph types in a taxonomy-like structure (the original version was published in Abela 2008). The taxonomic structure is organized around the questions of "What would you like to show in your chart or graph?" That is, what the purpose of the chart or graph will be. At that level, the taxonomy divides the purpose into four different types—relationship, comparison, distribution, and composition—and further divides the branches into subcategories based on the number of variables involved and time dependency of the visualization.

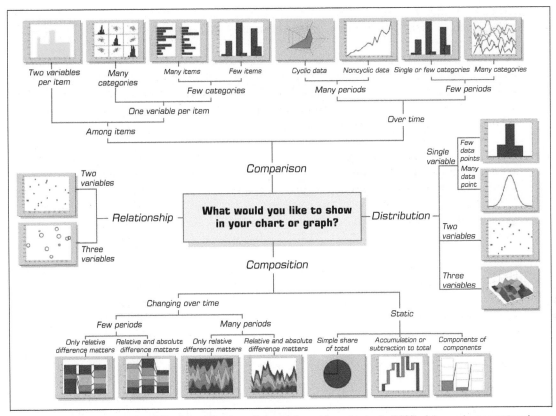

FIGURE 2.21 A Taxonomy of Charts and Graphs. *Source:* Adapted from Abela, A. (2008). Advanced presentations by design: Creating communication that drives action. New York: Wiley.

Even though these charts and graphs cover a major part of what is commonly used in information visualization, they by no means cover it all. Nowadays, one can find many other specialized graphs and charts that serve a specific purpose. Furthermore, the current trend is to combine/hybridize and animate these charts for better-looking and more intuitive visualization of today's complex and volatile data sources. For instance, the interactive, animated, bubble charts available at the Gapminder Web site (gapminder.org) provide an intriguing way of exploring world health, wealth, and population data from a multidimensional perspective. Figure 2.22 depicts the sorts of displays available at the site. In this graph, population size, life expectancy, and per capita income at the continent level are shown; also given is a time-varying animation that shows how these variables change over time.

SECTION 2.9 REVIEW QUESTIONS

1. Why do you think there are many different types of charts and graphs?
2. What are the main differences among line, bar, and pie charts? When should you use one over the others?
3. Why would you use a geographic map? What other types of charts can be combined with a geographic map?
4. Find and explain the role of two types of charts that are not covered in this section.

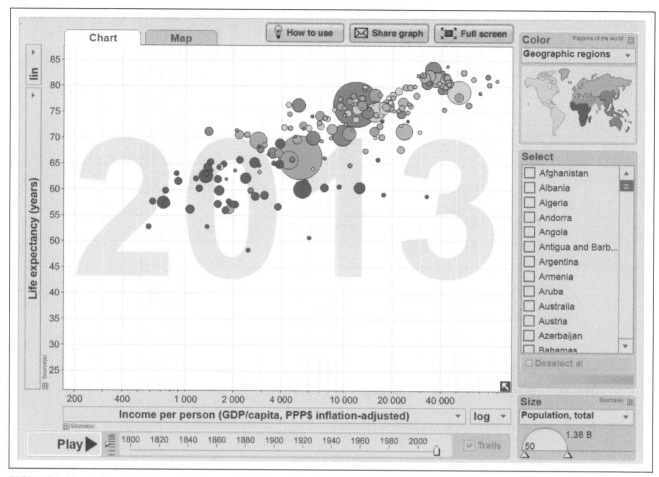

FIGURE 2.22 A Gapminder Chart That Shows the Wealth and Health of Nations. *Source:* gapminder.org.

2.10 The Emergence of Visual Analytics

As Seth Grimes (2009a,b) has noted, there is a "growing palate" of data visualization techniques and tools that enable the users of business analytics and BI systems to better "communicate relationships, add historical context, uncover hidden correlations, and tell persuasive stories that clarify and call to action." The latest Magic Quadrant on Business Intelligence and Analytics Platforms released by Gartner in February 2016 further emphasizes the importance of data visualization in BI and analytics. As the chart shows, all the solution providers in the *Leaders* and *Visionary* quadrants are either relatively recently founded information visualization companies (e.g., Tableau Software, QlikTech) or well-established large analytics companies (e.g., Microsoft, SAS, IBM, SAP, MicroStrategy, Alteryx) that are increasingly focusing their efforts on information visualization and visual analytics. More details on Gartner's latest Magic Quadrant are given in Technology Insights 2.2.

In BI and analytics, the key challenges for visualization have revolved around the intuitive representation of large, complex data sets with multiple dimensions and measures. For the most part, the typical charts, graphs, and other visual elements used in these applications usually involve two dimensions, sometimes three, and fairly small subsets of data sets. In contrast, the data in these systems reside in a data warehouse. At a minimum,

TECHNOLOGY INSIGHTS 2.2
Gartner Magic Quadrant for Business Intelligence and Analytics Platforms

Gartner, Inc., the creator of Magic Quadrants, is the leading information technology research and advisory company publically traded in the United States with over $2 billion annual revenues in 2015. Founded in 1979, Gartner has 7,600 associates, including 1,600 research analysts and consultants, and numerous clients in 90 countries.

Magic Quadrant is a research method designed and implemented by Gartner to monitor and evaluate the progress and positions of companies in a specific, technology-based market. By applying a graphical treatment and a uniform set of evaluation criteria, Magic Quadrant helps users to understand how technology providers are positioned within a market.

Gartner changed the name of this Magic Quadrant from "Business Intelligence Platforms" to "Business Intelligence and Analytics Platforms" to emphasize the growing importance of analytics capabilities to the information systems that organizations are now building. Gartner defines the BI and analytics platform market as a software platform that delivers 15 capabilities across three categories: integration, information delivery, and analysis. These capabilities enable organizations to build precise systems of classification and measurement to support decision making and improve performance.

Figure 2.23 illustrates the latest Magic Quadrant for Business Intelligence and Analytics Platforms. Magic Quadrant places providers in four groups (niche players, challengers, visionaries, and leaders) along two dimensions: completeness of vision (x-axis) and ability to execute (y-axis). As the quadrant clearly shows, most of the well-known BI/BA providers are positioned in the "leaders" category while many of the lesser known, relatively new, emerging providers are positioned in the "niche players" category.

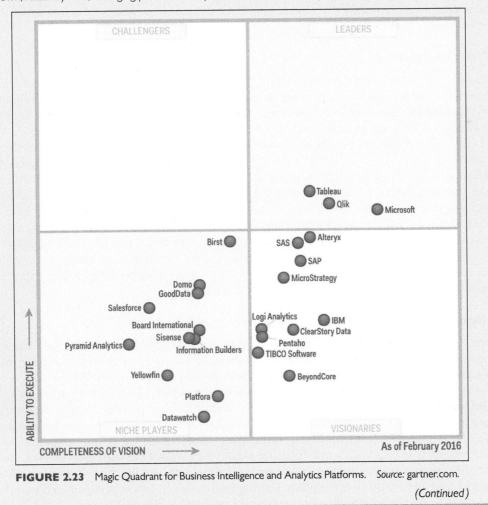

FIGURE 2.23   Magic Quadrant for Business Intelligence and Analytics Platforms.   *Source:* gartner.com.

(Continued)

The BI and analytics platform market's multiyear shift from IT-led enterprise reporting to business-led self-service analytics seem to have passed the tipping point. Most new buying is of modern, business-user-centric visual analytics platforms forcing a new market perspective, significantly reordering the vendor landscape. Most of the activity in the BI and analytics platform market is from organizations that are trying to mature their visualization capabilities and to move from descriptive to predictive and prescriptive analytics echelons. The vendors in the market have overwhelmingly concentrated on meeting this user demand. If there were a single market theme in 2015, it would be that data discovery/visualization became a mainstream architecture. While data discovery/visualization vendors such as Tableau, Qlik, and Microsoft are solidifying their position in the *Leaders* quadrant, others (both emerging and large, well-established tool/solution providers) are trying to move out of *Visionaries* into the *Leaders* quadrant.

This emphasis on data discovery/visualization from most of the leaders and visionaries in the market—which are now promoting tools with business-user-friendly data integration, coupled with embedded storage and computing layers and unfettered drilling—continue to accelerate the trend toward decentralization and user empowerment of BI and analytics and greatly enables organizations' ability to perform diagnostic analytics.

Source: Gartner Magic Quadrant, released on February 4, 2016, gartner.com (accessed August 2016).

these warehouses involve a range of dimensions (e.g., product, location, organizational structure, time), a range of measures, and millions of cells of data. In an effort to address these challenges, a number of researchers have developed a variety of new visualization techniques.

Visual Analytics

Visual analytics is a recently coined term that is often used loosely to mean nothing more than information visualization. What is meant by **visual analytics** is the combination of visualization and predictive analytics. Whereas information visualization is aimed at answering, "What happened?" and "What is happening?" and is closely associated with BI (routine reports, scorecards, and dashboards), visual analytics is aimed at answering, "Why is it happening?" "What is more likely to happen?" and is usually associated with business analytics (forecasting, segmentation, correlation analysis). Many of the information visualization vendors are adding the capabilities to call themselves visual analytics solution providers. One of the top, long-time analytics solution providers, SAS Institute, is approaching it from another direction. They are embedding their analytics capabilities into a high-performance data visualization environment that they call visual analytics.

Visual or not visual, automated or manual, online or paper based, business reporting is not much different than telling a story. Technology Insights 2.3 provides a different, unorthodox viewpoint to better business reporting.

High-Powered Visual Analytics Environments

Due to the increasing demand for visual analytics coupled with fast-growing data volumes, there is an exponential movement toward investing in highly efficient visualization systems. With their latest move into visual analytics, the statistical software giant SAS Institute is now among those who are leading this wave. Their new product, SAS Visual Analytics, is a very **high-performance computing**, in-memory solution for exploring massive amounts of data in a very short time (almost instantaneously). It empowers users to spot patterns, identify opportunities for further analysis, and convey visual results via Web reports or a mobile platform such as tablets and smartphones. Figure 2.25 shows the high-level architecture of the SAS Visual Analytics platform. On one end of the architecture, there is a universal data builder and administrator capabilities, leading into explorer, report designer, and mobile BI modules, collectively providing an end-to-end visual analytics solution.

TECHNOLOGY INSIGHTS 2.3
Telling Great Stories with Data and Visualization

Everyone who has data to analyze has stories to tell, whether it's diagnosing the reasons for manufacturing defects, selling a new idea in a way that captures the imagination of your target audience, or informing colleagues about a particular customer service improvement program. And when it's telling the story behind a big strategic choice so that you and your senior management team can make a solid decision, providing a fact-based story can be especially challenging. In all cases, it's a big job. You want to be interesting and memorable; you know you need to keep it simple for your busy executives and colleagues. Yet you also know you have to be factual, detail oriented, and data driven, especially in today's metric-centric world.

It's tempting to present just the data and facts, but when colleagues and senior management are overwhelmed by data and facts without context, you lose. We have all experienced presentations with large slide decks, only to find that the audience is so overwhelmed with data that they don't know what to think, or they are so completely tuned out that they take away only a fraction of the key points.

Start engaging your executive team and explaining your strategies and results more powerfully by approaching your assignment as a story. You will need the "what" of your story (the facts and data) but you also need the "Who?" "How?" "Why?" and the often-missed "So what?" It's these story elements that will make your data relevant and tangible for your audience. Creating a good story can aid you and senior management in focusing on what is important.

Why Story?

Stories bring life to data and facts. They can help you make sense and order out of a disparate collection of facts. They make it easier to remember key points and can paint a vivid picture of what the future can look like. Stories also create interactivity—people put themselves into stories and can relate to the situation.

Cultures have long used **storytelling** to pass on knowledge and content. In some cultures, storytelling is critical to their identity. For example, in New Zealand, some of the Maori people tattoo their faces with mokus. A moku is a facial tattoo containing a story about ancestors—the family tribe. A man may have a tattoo design on his face that shows features of a hammerhead to highlight unique qualities about his lineage. The design he chooses signifies what is part of his "true self" and his ancestral home.

Likewise, when we are trying to understand a story, the storyteller navigates to finding the "true north." If senior management is looking to discuss how they will respond to a competitive change, a good story can make sense and order out of a lot of noise. For example, you may have facts and data from two studies, one including results from an advertising study and one from a product satisfaction study. Developing a story for what you measured across both studies can help people see the whole where there were disparate parts. For rallying your distributors around a new product, you can employ a story to give vision to what the future can look like. Most important, storytelling is interactive—typically the presenter uses words and pictures that audience members can put themselves into. As a result, they become more engaged and better understand the information.

So What Is a Good Story?

Most people can easily rattle off their favorite film or book. Or they remember a funny story that a colleague recently shared. Why do people remember these stories? Because they contain certain characteristics. First, a good story has great characters. In some cases, the reader or viewer has a vicarious experience where they become involved with the character. The character then has to be faced with a challenge that is difficult but believable. There must be hurdles that the character overcomes. And finally, the outcome or prognosis is clear by the end of the story. The situation may not be resolved—but the story has a clear endpoint.

Think of Your Analysis as a Story—Use a Story Structure

When crafting a data-rich story, the first objective is to find the story. Who are the characters? What is the drama or challenge? What hurdles have to be overcome? And at the end of your story, what do you want your audience to do as a result?

Once you know the core story, craft your other story elements: define your characters, understand the challenge, identify the hurdles, and crystallize the outcome or decision question. Make sure you are clear

(Continued)

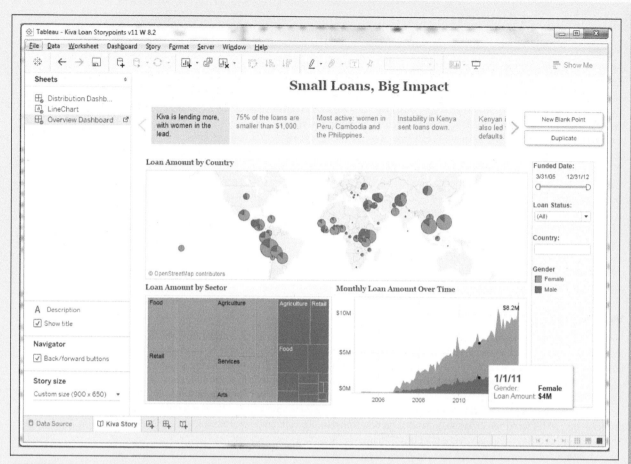

FIGURE 2.24 A Storyline Visualization in Tableau Software.

with what you want people to do as a result. This will shape how your audience will recall your story. With the story elements in place, write out the storyboard, which represents the structure and form of your story. Although it's tempting to skip this step, it is better first to understand the story you are telling and then to focus on the presentation structure and form. Once the storyboard is in place, the other elements will fall into place. The storyboard will help you to think about the best analogies or metaphors, to clearly set up challenge or opportunity, and to finally see the flow and transitions needed. The storyboard also helps you focus on key visuals (graphs, charts, and graphics) that you need your executives to recall. Figure 2.24 shows a storyline for the impact of small loans in a worldwide view within the Tableau visual analytics environment.

In summary, don't be afraid to use data to tell great stories. Being factual, detail oriented, and data driven is critical in today's metric-centric world, but it does not have to mean being boring and lengthy. In fact, by finding the real stories in your data and following the best practices, you can get people to focus on your message—and thus on what's important. Here are those best practices:

1. Think of your analysis as a story—use a story structure.
2. Be authentic—your story will flow.
3. Be visual—think of yourself as a film editor.
4. Make it easy for your audience and you.
5. Invite and direct discussion.

Source: Fink, E., & Moore, S. J. (2012). Five best practices for telling great stories with data. White paper by Tableau Software, Inc., www.tableau.com/whitepapers/telling-data-stories (accessed May 2016).

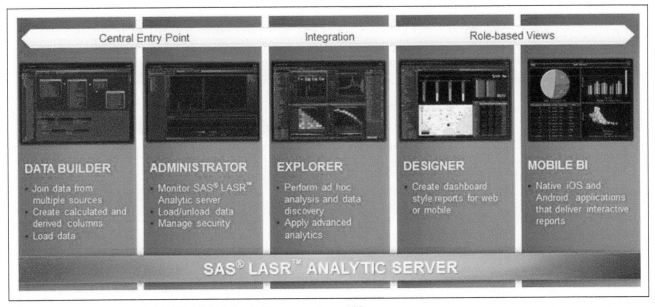

FIGURE 2.25   An Overview of SAS Visual Analytics Architecture.   *Source:* SAS.com.

Some of the key benefits proposed by SAS analytics are the following:

- Empowers all users with data exploration techniques and approachable analytics to drive improved decision making. SAS Visual Analytics enables different types of users to conduct fast, thorough explorations on all available data. Sampling to reduce the data is not required and not preferred.

- Easy-to-use, interactive Web interfaces broaden the audience for analytics, enabling everyone to glean new insights. Users can look at more options, make more precise decisions, and drive success even faster than before.

- Answer complex questions faster, enhancing the contributions from your analytic talent. SAS Visual Analytics augments the data discovery and exploration process by providing extremely fast results to enable better, more focused analysis. Analytically savvy users can identify areas of opportunity or concern from vast amounts of data so further investigation can take place quickly.

- Improves information sharing and collaboration. Large numbers of users, including those with limited analytical skills, can quickly view and interact with reports and charts via the Web, Adobe PDF files, and iPad mobile devices, while IT maintains control of the underlying data and security. SAS Visual Analytics provides the right information to the right person at the right time to improve productivity and organizational knowledge.

- Liberates IT by giving users a new way to access the information they need. Frees IT from the constant barrage of demands from users who need access to different amounts of data, different data views, ad hoc reports, and one-off requests for information. SAS Visual Analytics enables IT to easily load and prepare data for multiple users. Once data is loaded and available, users can dynamically explore data, create reports, and share information on their own.

- Provides room to grow at a self-determined pace. SAS Visual Analytics provides the option of using commodity hardware or database appliances from EMC Greenplum and Teradata. It is designed from the ground up for performance optimization and scalability to meet the needs of any size organization.

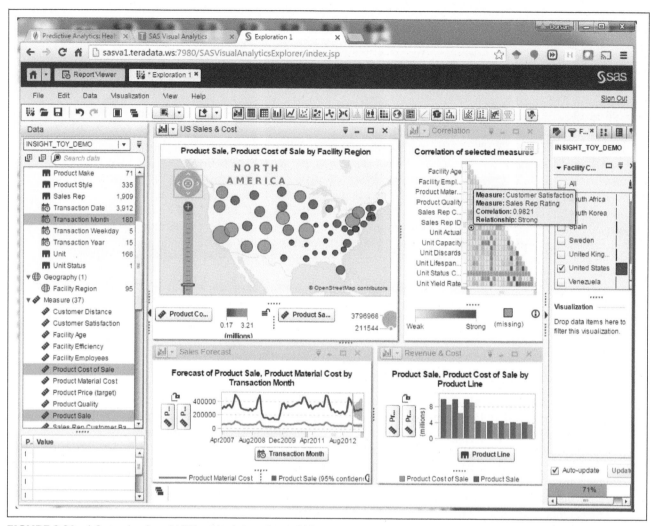

FIGURE 2.26   A Screenshot from SAS Visual Analytics.   *Source:* SAS.com.

Figure 2.26 shows a screenshot of an SAS Analytics platform where time series fore-casting and confidence interval around the forecast are depicted.

SECTION 2.10 REVIEW QUESTIONS

1. What are the main reasons for the recent emergence of visual analytics?
2. Look at Gartner's Magic Quadrant for Business Intelligence and Analytics Platforms. What do you see? Discuss and justify your observations.
3. What is the difference between information visualization and visual analytics?
4. Why should storytelling be a part of your reporting and data visualization?
5. What is a high-powered visual analytics environment? Why do we need it?

2.11 Information Dashboards

Information dashboards are common components of most, if not all, BI or business analytics platforms, business performance management systems, and performance measurement software suites. **Dashboards** provide visual displays of important information that is consolidated and arranged on a single screen so that information can be digested at a single glance and easily drilled in and further explored. A typical dashboard is shown in Figure 2.27. This particular executive dashboard displays a variety of KPIs for a hypothetical software company called Sonatica (selling audio tools). This executive dashboard shows a high-level view of the different functional groups surrounding the products, starting from a general overview to the marketing efforts, sales, finance, and support departments. All of this is intended to give executive decision makers a quick and accurate idea of what is going on within the organization. On the left side of the dashboard, we can see (in a time series fashion) the quarterly changes in revenues, expenses, and margins, as well as the comparison of those figures to previous years' monthly numbers. On the upper-right side we see two dials with color-coded regions showing the amount of

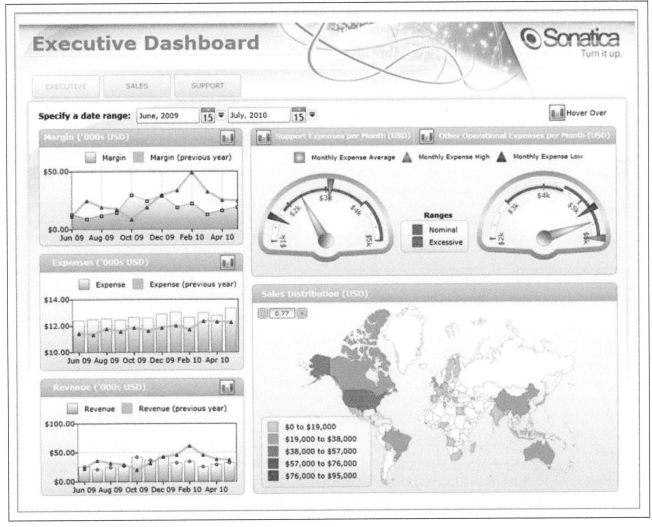

FIGURE 2.27 A Sample Executive Dashboard.   *Source:* dundas.com.

monthly expenses for support services (dial on the left) and the amount of other expenses (dial on the right). As the color coding indicates, although the monthly support expenses are well within the normal ranges, the other expenses are in the red region, indicating excessive values. The geographic map on the bottom right shows the distribution of sales at the country level throughout the world. Behind these graphical icons there are variety of mathematical functions aggregating numerous data points to their highest level of meaningful figures. By clicking on these graphical icons, the consumer of this information can drill down to more granular levels of information and data.

Dashboards are used in a wide variety of businesses for a wide variety of reasons. For instance, in Application Case 2.7, you will find the summary of a successful implementation of information dashboards by the Dallas Cowboys football team.

Application Case 2.7

Dallas Cowboys Score Big with Tableau and Teknion

Founded in 1960, the Dallas Cowboys are a professional American football team headquartered in Irving, Texas. The team has a large national following, which is perhaps best represented by their NFL record for number of consecutive games at sold-out stadiums.

Challenge

Bill Priakos, Chief Operating Officer (COO) of the Dallas Cowboys Merchandising Division, and his team needed more visibility into their data so they could run it more profitably. Microsoft was selected as the baseline platform for this upgrade as well as a number of other sales, logistics, and e-commerce (per MW) applications. The Cowboys expected that this new information architecture would provide the needed analytics and reporting. Unfortunately, this was not the case, and the search began for a robust dashboarding, analytics, and reporting tool to fill this gap.

Solution and Results

Tableau and Teknion together provided real-time reporting and dashboard capabilities that exceeded the Cowboys' requirements. Systematically and methodically the Teknion team worked side by side with data owners and data users within the Dallas Cowboys to deliver all required functionality, on time and under budget. "Early in the process, we were able to get a clear understanding of what it would take to run a more profitable operation for the Cowboys," said Teknion Vice President Bill Luisi. "This process step is a key step in Teknion's approach with any client, and it always pays huge

dividends as the implementation plan progresses." Added Luisi, "Of course, Tableau worked very closely with us and the Cowboys during the entire project. Together, we made sure that the Cowboys could achieve their reporting and analytical goals in record time."

Now, for the first time, the Dallas Cowboys are able to monitor their complete merchandising activities from manufacture to end customer and not only see what is happening across the life cycle, but also drill down even further into why it is happening.

Today, this BI solution is used to report and analyze the business activities of the Merchandising Division, which is responsible for all of the Dallas Cowboys' brand sales. Industry estimates say that the Cowboys generate 20% of all NFL merchandise sales, which reflects the fact that they are the most recognized sports franchise in the world.

According to Eric Lai, a *ComputerWorld* reporter, Tony Romo and the rest of the Dallas Cowboys may have been only average on the football field in the last few years, but off the field, especially in the merchandising arena, they remain America's team.

QUESTIONS FOR DISCUSSION

1. How did the Dallas Cowboys use information visualization?

2. What were the challenge, the proposed solution, and the obtained results?

Sources: Lai, E. (2009, October 8). BI visualization tool helps Dallas Cowboys sell more Tony Romo jerseys. *ComputerWorld;* Tableau case study. tableausoftware.com/learn/stories/ tableau-and-teknion-exceed-cowboys-requirements (accessed July 2016).

Dashboard Design

Dashboards are not a new concept. Their roots can be traced at least to the executive information system of the 1980s. Today, dashboards are ubiquitous. For example, a few years back, Forrester Research estimated that over 40% of the largest 2,000 companies in the world used the technology (Ante & McGregor, 2006). Since then, one can safely assume that this number has gone up quite significantly. In fact, nowadays it would be rather unusual to see a large company using a BI system that does not employ some sort of performance dashboards. The Dashboard Spy Web site (dashboardspy.com/about) provides further evidence of their ubiquity. The site contains descriptions and screenshots of thousands of BI dashboards, scorecards, and BI interfaces used by businesses of all sizes and industries, nonprofits, and government agencies.

According to Eckerson (2006), a well-known expert on BI in general and dashboards in particular, the most distinctive feature of a dashboard is its three layers of information:

1. *Monitoring:*   Graphical, abstracted data to monitor key performance metrics.
2. *Analysis:*   Summarized dimensional data to analyze the root cause of problems.
3. *Management:*   Detailed operational data that identify what actions to take to resolve a problem.

Because of these layers, dashboards pack a lot of information into a single screen. According to Few (2005), "The fundamental challenge of dashboard design is to display all the required information on a single screen, clearly and without distraction, in a manner that can be assimilated quickly." To speed assimilation of the numbers, the numbers need to be placed in context. This can be done by comparing the numbers of interest to other baseline or target numbers, by indicating whether the numbers are good or bad, by denoting whether a trend is better or worse, and by using specialized display widgets or components to set the comparative and evaluative context. Some of the common comparisons that are typically made in BI systems include comparisons against past values, forecasted values, targeted values, benchmark or average values, multiple instances of the same measure, and the values of other measures (e.g., revenues versus costs).

Even with comparative measures, it is important to specifically point out whether a particular number is good or bad and whether it is trending in the right direction. Without these types of evaluative designations, it can be time consuming to determine the status of a particular number or result. Typically, either specialized visual objects (e.g., traffic lights, dials, and gauges) or visual attributes (e.g., color coding) are used to set the evaluative context. An interactive dashboard-driven reporting data exploration solution built by an energy company is featured in Application Case 2.8.

Application Case 2.8

Visual Analytics Helps Energy Supplier Make Better Connections

Energy markets all around the world are going through a significant change and transformation, creating ample opportunities along with significant challenges. As is the case in any industry, opportunities are attracting more players in the marketplace, increasing the competition, and reducing the tolerances for less-than-optimal business decision making. Success requires creating and disseminating accurate and timely information to whomever and whenever it is needed. For instance, if you need to easily track marketing budgets, balance employee workloads, and target customers with tailored marketing messages, you would need three different reporting solutions. Electrabel GDF SUEZ is doing all of that for its marketing and sales business unit with SAS® Visual Analytics platform.

(Continued)

Application Case 2.8 (Continued)

The one-solution approach is a great time-saver for marketing professionals in an industry that is undergoing tremendous change. "It is a huge challenge to stabilize our market position in the energy market. That includes volume, prices, and margins for both retail and business customers," notes Danny Noppe, Reporting Architecture and Development Manager in the Electrabel Marketing and Sales business unit. The company is the largest supplier of electricity in Belgium and the largest producer of electricity for Belgium and the Netherlands. Noppe says it is critical that Electrabel increase the efficiency of its customer communications as it explores new digital channels and develops new energy-related services.

"The better we know the customer, the better our likelihood of success," he says. "That is why we combine information from various sources—phone traffic with the customer, online questions, text messages, and mail campaigns. This enhanced knowledge of our customer and prospect base will be an additional advantage within our competitive market."

One Version of the Truth

Electrabel was using various platforms and tools for reporting purposes. This sometimes led to ambiguity in the reported figures. The utility also had performance issues in processing large data volumes. SAS Visual Analytics with in-memory technology removes the ambiguity and the performance issues. "We have the autonomy and flexibility to respond to the need for customer insight and data visualization internally," Noppe says. "After all, fast reporting is an essential requirement for action-oriented departments such as sales and marketing."

Working More Efficiently at a Lower Cost

SAS Visual Analytics automates the process of updating information in reports. Instead of building a report that is out of date by the time it is completed, the data is refreshed for all the reports once a week and is available on dashboards. In deploying the solution, Electrabel chose a phased approach starting with simple reports and moving on to more complex ones. The first report took a few weeks

to build, and the rest came quickly. The successes include the following:

- Data that took 2 days to prepare now takes only 2 hours.
- Clear graphic insight into the invoicing and composition of invoices for B2B customers.
- A workload management report by the operational teams. Managers can evaluate team workloads on a weekly or long-term basis and can make adjustments accordingly.

"We have significantly improved our efficiency and can deliver quality data and reports more frequently, and at a significantly lower cost," says Noppe. And if the company needs to combine data from multiple sources, the process is equally easy. "Building visual reports, based on these data marts, can be achieved in a few days, or even a few hours."

Noppe says the company plans to continue broadening its insight into the digital behavior of its customers, combining data from Web analytics, e-mail, and social media with data from back-end systems. "Eventually, we want to replace all labor-intensive reporting with SAS Visual Analytics," he says, adding that the flexibility of SAS Visual Analytics is critical for his department. "This will give us more time to tackle other challenges. We also want to make this tool available on our mobile devices. This will allow our account managers to use up-to-date, insightful, and adaptable reports when visiting customers. "We've got a future-oriented reporting platform to do all we need."

QUESTIONS FOR DISCUSSION

1. Why do you think energy supply companies are among the prime users of information visualization tools?
2. How did Electrabel use information visualization for the single version of the truth?
3. What were their challenges, the proposed solution, and the obtained results?

What to Look for in a Dashboard

Although performance dashboards and other information visualization frameworks differ, they all do share some common design characteristics. First, they all fit within the larger BI and/or performance measurement system. This means that their underlying architecture is the BI or performance management architecture of the larger system. Second, all well-designed dashboard and other information visualizations possess the following characteristics (Novell, 2009):

- They use visual components (e.g., charts, performance bars, sparklines, gauges, meters, stoplights) to highlight, at a glance, the data and exceptions that require action.
- They are transparent to the user, meaning that they require minimal training and are extremely easy to use.
- They combine data from a variety of systems into a single, summarized, unified view of the business.
- They enable drill-down or drill-through to underlying data sources or reports, providing more detail about the underlying comparative and evaluative context.
- They present a dynamic, real-world view with timely data refreshes, enabling the end user to stay up to date with any recent changes in the business.
- They require little, if any, customized coding to implement, deploy, and maintain.

Best Practices in Dashboard Design

The real estate saying "location, location, location" makes it obvious that the most important attribute for a piece of real estate property is where it is located. For dashboards, it is "data, data, data." An often overlooked aspect, data is one of the most important things to consider in designing dashboards (Carotenuto, 2007). Even if a dashboard's appearance looks professional, is aesthetically pleasing, and includes graphs and tables created according to accepted visual design standards, it is also important to ask about the data: Is it reliable? Is it timely? Is any data missing? Is it consistent across all dashboards? Here are some of the experience-driven best practices in dashboard design (Radha, 2008).

Benchmark Key Performance Indicators with Industry Standards

Many customers, at some point in time, want to know if the metrics they are measuring are the right metrics to monitor. Sometimes customers have found that the metrics they are tracking are not the right ones to track. Doing a gap assessment with industry benchmarks aligns you with industry best practices.

Wrap the Dashboard Metrics with Contextual Metadata

Often when a report or a visual dashboard/scorecard is presented to business users, questions remain unanswered. The following are some examples:

- Where did you source this data from?
- While loading the data warehouse, what percentage of the data got rejected/encountered data quality problems?
- Is the dashboard presenting "fresh" information or "stale" information?
- When was the data warehouse last refreshed?
- When is it going to be refreshed next?
- Were any high-value transactions that would skew the overall trends rejected as a part of the loading process?

Validate the Dashboard Design by a Usability Specialist

In most dashboard environments, the dashboard is designed by a tool specialist without giving consideration to usability principles. Even though it's a well-engineered data warehouse that can perform well, many business users do not use the dashboard, as it is perceived as not being user friendly, leading to poor adoption of the infrastructure and change management issues. Up-front validation of the dashboard design by a usability specialist can mitigate this risk.

Prioritize and Rank Alerts/Exceptions Streamed to the Dashboard

Because there are tons of raw data, it is important to have a mechanism by which important exceptions/behaviors are proactively pushed to the information consumers. A business rule can be codified, which detects the alert pattern of interest. It can be coded into a program, using database-stored procedures, which can crawl through the fact tables and detect patterns that need immediate attention. This way, information finds the business user as opposed to the business user polling the fact tables for the occurrence of critical patterns.

Enrich the Dashboard with Business-User Comments

When the same dashboard information is presented to multiple business users, a small text box can be provided that can capture the comments from an end-user's perspective. This can often be tagged to the dashboard to put the information in context, adding perspective to the structured KPIs being rendered.

Present Information in Three Different Levels

Information can be presented in three layers depending on the granularity of the information: the visual dashboard level, the static report level, and the self-service cube level. When a user navigates the dashboard, a simple set of 8 to 12 KPIs can be presented, which would give a sense of what is going well and what is not.

Pick the Right Visual Construct Using Dashboard Design Principles

In presenting information in a dashboard, some information is presented best with bar charts, some with time series line graphs, and when presenting correlations, a scatter plot is useful. Sometimes merely rendering it as simple tables is effective. Once the dashboard design principles are explicitly documented, all the developers working on the front end can adhere to the same principles while rendering the reports and dashboard.

Provide for Guided Analytics

In a typical organization, business users can be at various levels of analytical maturity. The capability of the dashboard can be used to guide the "average" business user to access the same navigational path as that of an analytically savvy business user.

SECTION 2.11 REVIEW QUESTIONS

1. What is an information dashboard? Why are they so popular?
2. What are the graphical widgets commonly used in dashboards? Why?
3. List and describe the three layers of information portrayed on dashboards.
4. What are the common characteristics of dashboards and other information visuals?
5. What are the best practices in dashboard design?

Chapter Highlights

- Data has become one of the most valuable assets of today's organizations.
- Data is the main ingredient for any BI, data science, and business analytics initiative.
- Although its value proposition is undeniable, to live up its promise, the data has to comply with some basic usability and quality metrics.
- *Data* (datum in singular form) refers to a collection of facts usually obtained as the result of experiments, observations, transactions, or experiences.
- At the highest level of abstraction, data can be classified as structured and unstructured.
- Data in its original/raw form is not usually ready to be useful in analytics tasks.
- Data preprocessing is a tedious, time-demanding, yet crucial task in business analytics.
- Statistics is a collection of mathematical techniques to characterize and interpret data.
- Statistical methods can be classified as either descriptive or inferential.
- Statistics in general, and descriptive statistics in particular, is a critical part of BI and business analytics.
- Descriptive statistics methods can be used to measure central tendency, dispersion, or the shape of a given data set.
- Regression, especially linear regression, is perhaps the most widely known and used analytics technique in statistics.
- Linear regression and logistic regression are the two major regression types in statistics.
- Logistics regression is a probability-based classification algorithm.

- Time series is a sequence of data points of a variable, measured and recorded at successive points in time spaced at uniform time intervals.
- A report is any communication artifact prepared with the specific intention of conveying information in a presentable form.
- A business report is a written document that contains information regarding business matters.
- The key to any successful business report is clarity, brevity, completeness, and correctness.
- Data visualization is the use of visual representations to explore, make sense of, and communicate data.
- Perhaps the most notable information graphic of the past was developed by Charles J. Minard, who graphically portrayed the losses suffered by Napoleon's army in the Russian campaign of 1812.
- Basic chart types include line, bar, and pie chart.
- Specialized charts are often derived from the basic charts as exceptional cases.
- Data visualization techniques and tools make the users of business analytics and BI systems better information consumers.
- Visual analytics is the combination of visualization and predictive analytics.
- Increasing demand for visual analytics coupled with fast-growing data volumes led to exponential growth in highly efficient visualization systems investment.
- Dashboards provide visual displays of important information that is consolidated and arranged on a single screen so that information can be digested at a single glance and easily drilled in and further explored.

Key Terms

analytics ready	data visualization	linear regression	ratio data
arithmetic mean	datum	logistic regression	regression
box-and-whiskers plot	descriptive statistics	mean absolute deviation	report
box plot	dimensional reduction	median	scatter plot
bubble chart	dispersion	mode	skewness
business report	high-performance	nominal data	standard deviation
categorical data	computing	online analytics	statistics
centrality	histogram	processing (OLAP)	storytelling
correlation	inferential statistics	ordinal data	structured data
dashboards	key performance	ordinary least squares	time series forecasting
data preprocessing	indicator (KPI)	(OLS)	unstructured data
data quality	knowledge	pie chart	variable selection
data security	kurtosis	quartile	variance
data taxonomy	learning	range	visual analytics

Questions for Discussion

1. How do you describe the importance of data in analytics? Can we think of analytics without data? Explain.
2. Considering the new and broad definition of business analytics, what are the main inputs and outputs to the analytics continuum?
3. Where does the data for business analytics come from? What are the sources and the nature of that incoming data?
4. What are the most common metrics that make for analytics-ready data?
5. What are the main categories of data? What types of data can we use for BI and analytics?
6. Can we use the same data representation for all analytics models (i.e., do different analytics models require different data representation schema)? Why, or why not?
7. Why is the original/raw data not readily usable by analytics tasks?
8. What are the main data preprocessing steps? List and explain their importance in analytics.
9. What does it mean to clean/scrub the data? What activities are performed in this phase?
10. Data reduction can be applied to rows (sampling) and/or columns (variable selection). Which is more challenging? Explain.
11. What is the relationship between statistics and business analytics (consider the placement of statistics in a business analytics taxonomy)?
12. What are the main differences between descriptive and inferential statistics?
13. What is a box-and-whiskers plot? What types of statistical information does it represent?
14. What are the two most commonly used shape characteristics to describe a data distribution?
15. List and briefly define the central tendency measures of descriptive statistics?
16. What are the commonalities and differences between regression and correlation?
17. List and describe the main steps to follow in developing a linear regression model.
18. What are the most commonly pronounced assumptions for linear regression? What is crucial to the regression models against these assumptions?
19. What are the commonalities and differences between linear regression and logistic regression?
20. What is time series? What are the main forecasting techniques for time series data?
21. What is a business report? Why is it needed?
22. What are the best practices in business reporting? How can we make our reports stand out?
23. Describe the cyclic process of management, and comment on the role of business reports.
24. List and describe the three major categories of business reports.
25. Why has information visualization become a centerpiece in BI and business analytics? Is there a difference between information visualization and visual analytics?
26. What are the main types of charts/graphs? Why are there so many of them?
27. How do you determine the right chart for the job? Explain and defend your reasoning.
28. What is the difference between information visualization and visual analytics?
29. Why should storytelling be a part of your reporting and data visualization?
30. What is an information dashboard? What do they present?
31. What are the best practices in designing highly informative dashboards?
32. Do you think information/performance dashboards are here to stay? Or are they about to be outdated? What do you think will be the next big wave in BI and business analytics in terms of data/information visualization?

Exercises

Teradata University and Other Hands-on Exercises

1. Download the "Voting Behavior" data and the brief data description from the book's Web site. This is a data set manually compiled from counties all around the United States. The data is partially processed, that is, some derived variables are created. Your task is to thoroughly preprocess the data by identifying the error and anomalies and proposing remedies and solutions. At the end you should have an analytics-ready version of this data. Once the preprocessing is completed, pull this data into Tableau (or into some other data visualization software tool) to extract useful visual information from it. To do so, conceptualize relevant questions and hypotheses (come up with at least three of them) and create proper visualizations that address those questions of "tests" of those hypotheses.

2. Download Tableau (at tableau.com, following academic free software download instructions on their site). Using the Visualization_MFG_Sample data set (available as an Excel file on this book's Web site) answer the following questions:
   a. What is the relationship between gross box office revenue and other movie-related parameters given in the data set?

b. How does this relationship vary across different years? Prepare a professional-looking written report that is enhanced with screenshots of your graphic findings.

3. Go to teradatauniversitynetwork.com. Look for an article that deals with the nature of data, management of data, and/or governance of data as it relates to BI and analytics, and critically analyze the content of the article.

4. Go to UCI data repository (archive.ics.uci.edu/ml/datasets.html), and identify a large data set that contains both numeric and nominal values. Using Microsoft Excel, or any other statistical software:
   a. Calculate and interpret central tendency measures for each and every variable.
   b. Calculate and interpret the dispersion/spread measures for each and every variable.

5. Go to UCI data repository (archive.ics.uci.edu/ml/datasets.html), and identify two data sets, one for estimation/regression and one for classification. Using Microsoft Excel, or any other statistical software:
   a. Develop and interpret a linear regression model.
   b. Develop and interpret a logistic regression model.

6. Go to KDnuggest.com, and become familiar with the range of analytics resources available on this portal. Then, identify an article, a white paper, or an interview script that deals with the nature of data, management of data, and/or governance of data as it relates to BI and business analytics, and critically analyze the content of the article.

7. Go to Stephen Few's blog, "The Perceptual Edge" (perceptualedge.com). Go to the section of "Examples." In this section, he provides critiques of various dashboard examples. Read a handful of these examples. Now go to dundas.com. Select the "Gallery" section of the site. Once there, click the "Digital Dashboard" selection. You will be shown a variety of different dashboard demos. Run a couple of the demos.
   a. What sorts of information and metrics are shown on the demos? What sorts of actions can you take?
   b. Using some of the basic concepts from Few's critiques, describe some of the good design points and bad design points of the demos.

8. Download an information visualization tool, such as Tableau, QlikView, or Spotfire. If your school does not have an educational agreement with these companies, then a trial version would be sufficient for this exercise. Use your own data (if you have any) or use one of the data sets that comes with the tool (they usually have one or more data sets for demonstration purposes). Study the data, come up with a couple of business problems, and use data visualization to analyze, visualize, and potentially solve those problems.

9. Go to teradatauniversitynetwork.com. Find the "Tableau Software Project." Read the description, execute the tasks, and answer the questions.

10. Go to teradatauniversitynetwork.com. Find the assignments for SAS Visual Analytics. Using the information and step-by-step instructions provided in the assignment, execute the analysis on the SAS Visual Analytics tool (which is a Web-enabled system that does not require any local installation). Answer the questions posed in the assignment.

11. Find at least two articles (one journal article and one white paper) that talk about storytelling, especially within the context of analytics (i.e., data-driven storytelling). Read and critically analyze the article and paper, and write a report to reflect your understanding and opinions about the importance of storytelling in BI and business analytics.

12. Go to Data.gov—a U.S. government–sponsored data portal that has a very large number of data sets on a wide variety of topics ranging from healthcare to education, climate to public safety. Pick a topic that you are most passionate about. Go through the topic-specific information and explanation provided on the site. Explore the possibilities of downloading the data, and use your favorite data visualization tool to create your own meaningful information and visualizations.

Team Assignments and Role-Playing Projects

1. Analytics starts with data. Identifying, accessing, obtaining, and processing of relevant data are the most essential tasks in any analytics study. As a team, you are tasked to find a large enough real-world data (either from your own organization, which is the most preferred, or from the Internet that can start with a simple search, or from the data links posted on KDnuggets.com), one that has tens of thousands of rows and more than 20 variables to go through and document a thorough data preprocessing project. In your processing of the data, identify anomalies and discrepancies using descriptive statistics methods and measures, and make the data analytics ready. List and justify your preprocessing steps and decisions in a comprehensive report.

2. Go to a well-known information dashboard provider Web site (dundas.com, idashboards.com, enterprise-dashboard.com). These sites provide a number of examples of executive dashboards. As a team, select a particular industry (e.g., healthcare, banking, airline). Locate a handful of example dashboards for that industry. Describe the types of metrics found on the dashboards. What types of displays are used to provide the information? Using what you know about dashboard design, provide a paper prototype of a dashboard for this information.

3. Go to teradatauniversitynetwork.com. From there, go to University of Arkansas data sources. Choose one of the large data sets, and download a large number of records (this may require you to write an SQL statement that creates the variables that you want to include in the data set). Come up with at least 10 questions that can be addressed with information visualization. Using your favorite data visualization tool (e.g., Tableau), analyze the data, and prepare a detailed report that includes screenshots and other visuals.

References

Abela, A. (2008). *Advanced presentations by design: Creating communication that drives action*. New York: Wiley.

Annas, G. J. (2003). HIPAA regulations—A new era of medical-record privacy? *New England Journal of Medicine, 348*(15), 1486–1490.

Ante, S. E., & McGregor, J. (2006). Giving the boss the big picture: A dashboard pulls up everything the CEO needs to run the show. *Business Week*, 43–51.

Carotenuto, D. (2007). Business intelligence best practices for dashboard design. WebFOCUS white paper. www .datawarehouse.inf.br/papers/information_builders_ dashboard_best_practices.pdf (accessed August 2016).

Dell customer case study. Medical device company ensures product quality while saving hundreds of thousands of dollars. https://software.dell.com/documents/instrumen-tation-laboratory-medical-device-companyensures-prod-uct-quality-while-saving-hundreds-ofthousands-of-dollars-case-study-80048.pdf (accessed August 2016).

Delen, D. (2010). A comparative analysis of machine learning techniques for student retention management. *Decision Support Systems, 49*(4), 498–506.

Delen, D. (2011). Predicting student attrition with data mining methods. *Journal of College Student Retention 13*(1), 17–35.

Delen, D., Cogdell, D., & Kasap, N. (2012). A comparative analysis of data mining methods in predicting NCAA bowl outcomes. *International Journal of Forecasting, 28*, 543–552.

Delen, D. (2015). *Real-world data mining: Applied business analytics and decision making*. Upper Saddle River, NJ: Financial Times Press (A Pearson Company).

Eckerson, W. (2006). *Performance dashboards*. New York: Wiley.

Few, S. (2005, Winter). Dashboard design: Beyond meters, gauges, and traffic lights. *Business Intelligence Journal, 10*(1).

Few, S. (2007). Data visualization: Past, present and future. perceptualedge.com/articles/Whitepapers/Data _Visualization.pdf (accessed July 2016).

Fink, E., & Moore, S. J. (2012). Five best practices for telling great stories with data. White paper by Tableau Software, Inc., www.tableau.com/whitepapers/telling-data-stories (accessed May 2016).

Freeman, K. M., & Brewer, R. M. (2016). The politics of American college football. *Journal of Applied Business and Economics, 18*(2), 97–101.

Gartner Magic Quadrant, released on February 4, 2016, gartner.com (accessed August 2016).

Grimes, S. (2009a, May 2). Seeing connections: Visualizations makes sense of data. *Intelligent Enterprise*. i.cmpnet. com/intelligententerprise/next-era-business-intelli-gence/Intelligent_Enterprise_Next_Era_BI_Visualization .pdf (accessed January 2010).

Grimes, S. (2009b). Text analytics 2009: User perspectives on solutions and providers. Alta Plana. altaplana.com/ TextAnalyticsPerspectives2009.pdf (accessed July, 2016).

Hardin, M., Hom, D., Perez, R., & Williams, L. (2012). Which chart or graph is right for you? Tableau Software: Tell Impactful Stories with Data‼. Tableau Software. http:// www.tableau.com/sites/default/files/media/which _chart_v6_final_0.pdf (accessed August 2016).

Hernández, M. A., & Stolfo, S. J. (1998, January). Real-world data is dirty: Data cleansing and the merge/purge prob-lem. *Data Mining and Knowledge Discovery, 2*(1), 9–37.

Hill, G. (2016). A Guide to enterprise reporting. ghill .customer.netspace.net.au/reporting/definition.html (accessed July 2016).

Kim, W., Choi, B. J., Hong, E. K., Kim, S. K., & Lee, D. (2003). A taxonomy of dirty data. *Data Mining and Knowledge Discovery, 7*(1), 81–99.

Kock, N. F., McQueen, R. J., & Corner, J. L. (1997). The nature of data, information and knowledge exchanges in busi-ness processes: Implications for process improvement and organizational learning. *The Learning Organization, 4*(2), 70–80.

Kotsiantis, S. B., Kanellopoulos, D., & Pintelas, P. E. (2006). Data preprocessing for supervised leaning. *International Journal of Computer Science, 1*(2), 111–117.

Lai, E. (2009, October 8). BI visualization tool helps Dallas Cowboys sell more Tony Romo jerseys. *ComputerWorld*.

Quinn, C. (2016). Data-driven marketing at SiriusXM. Teradata Articles & News. at http://bigdata.teradata.com/ US/Articles-News/Data-Driven-Marketing-At-SiriusXM/ (accessed August 2016); Teradata customer success story. SiriusXM attracts and engages a new generation of radio consumers. http://assets.teradata.com/resourceCenter/ downloads/CaseStudies/EB8597.pdf?processed=1.

Novell. (2009, April). Executive dashboards elements of success. Novell white paper. www.novell.com/docrep/ documents/3rkw3etfc3/Executive%20Dashboards_ Elements_of_Success_White_Paper_en.pdf (accessed June 2016).

Radha, R. (2008). Eight best practices in dashboard design. *Information Management*. www.information-manage-ment.com/news/columns/-10001129-1.html (accessed July 2016).

SAS. (2014). Data visualization techniques: From basics to Big Data. http://www.sas.com/content/dam/SAS/en_us/doc/ whitepaper1/data-visualization-techniques-106006.pdf (accessed July 2016).

Thammasiri, D., Delen, D., Meesad, P., & Kasap N. (2014). A critical assessment of imbalanced class distribution prob-lem: The case of predicting freshmen student attrition. *Expert Systems with Applications, 41*(2), 321–330.

CHAPTER 3

Descriptive Analytics II: Business Intelligence and Data Warehousing

The concept of data warehousing has been around since the late 1980s. This chapter provides the foundation for an important type of database, called a *data warehouse*, which is primarily used for decision support and provides the informational foundation for improved analytical capabilities. We discuss data warehousing concepts and, relatedly, business performance management in the following sections.

3.1 Opening Vignette: Targeting Tax Fraud with Business Intelligence and Data Warehousing   128
3.2 Business Intelligence and Data Warehousing   130
3.3 Data Warehousing Process   137
3.4 Data Warehousing Architectures   139
3.5 Data Integration and the Extraction, Transformation, and Load (ETL) Processes   145
3.6 Data Warehouse Development   150
3.7 Data Warehousing Implementation Issues   160
3.8 Data Warehouse Administration, Security Issues, and Future Trends   164
3.9 Business Performance Management   170

3.10 Performance Measurement   175

3.11 Balanced Scorecards   177

3.12 Six Sigma as a Performance Measurement System   179

3.1 OPENING VIGNETTE: Targeting Tax Fraud with Business Intelligence and Data Warehousing

Governments have to work hard to keep tax fraud from taking a significant bite from their revenues. In 2013, the Internal Revenue Service (IRS) successfully foiled attempts, which were based on stolen identities, to cheat the federal government out of $24.2 billion in tax refunds. However, that same year the IRS paid out $5.8 billion on claims it only later identified as fraud.

States also lose money when fraudsters use stolen Social Security numbers, W-2 forms, and other personal information to file false refund claims. This kind of crime has increased in recent years at an alarming rate. "Virtually all Americans have heard of identity theft, but very few are aware of this explosive increase in tax return fraud," says Maryland Comptroller Peter Franchot. "This is an alarming problem, affecting every state. It is, literally, systematic burglary of the taxpayer's money."

In Maryland, the people charged with rooting out false refund claims are members of the Questionable Return Detection Team (QRDT). Like their counterparts in many other states, these experts use software to identify suspicious returns. They then investigate the returns to pinpoint which ones are fraudulent.

Challenge

In the past, Maryland used metrics that examined tax returns one by one. If a return displayed specific traits—for instance, a certain ratio of wages earned to wages withheld—the software suspended that return for further investigation. Members of the QRDT then researched each suspended return—for example, by comparing its wage and withholding information with figures from a W-2 form submitted by an employer. The process was labor intensive and inefficient. Of the approximately 2.8 million tax returns Maryland received each year, the QRDT suspended about 110,000. But most of those turned out to be legitimate returns. "Only about 10% were found to be fraudulent," says Andy Schaufele, director of the Bureau of Revenue Estimates for the Maryland Comptroller.

In a typical year, that process saved Maryland from mailing out $5 million to $10 million in fraudulent refunds. Although that's a success, it's only a modest one, considering the resources tied up in the process and the inconvenience to honest taxpayers whose returns were flagged for investigation. "The thought that we were holding up 90,000 to 100,000 tax refunds was tough to stomach," Schaufele says. "We wanted to get those refunds to the taxpayers faster, since many people count on that money as part of their income."

Solution

Maryland needed a more effective process. It also needed new strategies for staying ahead of fraudsters. "All the states, as well as the IRS, were using the same metrics we were using," Schaufele says. "I don't think it was hard for criminals to figure out what our defenses were." Fortunately, Maryland had recently gained a powerful new weapon against tax fraud. In 2010, the Maryland Comptroller of the Treasury worked with Teradata of Dayton, Ohio, to implement a data warehouse designed to support a variety of compliance initiatives.

As officials discussed which initiatives to launch, one idea rose to the top. "We determined that we should prioritize our efforts to go after refund fraud," says Sharonne Bonardi, Maryland's deputy comptroller. So the state started working with Teradata and with ASR Analytics of Potomac, Maryland, to develop a better process for isolating fraudulent tax returns (Temple-West, 2013).

"The first step was to analyze our data and learn what we knew about fraud," Schaufele says. Among other discoveries, the analysis showed that when multiple returns were suspended—even for completely different reasons—they often had traits in common. The state built a database of traits that characterize fraudulent returns and traits that characterize honest ones. "We worked with ASR to put that information together and develop linear regressions," Schaufele says. "Instead of looking at one-off metrics, we began to bring many of those metrics together." The result was a far more nuanced portrait of the typical fraudulent return.

Instead of flagging returns one by one, the new system identifies groups of returns that look suspicious for similar reasons. That strategy speeds up investigations. The analytics system also assigns a score to each return, based on how likely it is to be fraudulent. It then produces a prioritized list to direct the QRDT's workflow. "We're first working on the returns that are more likely not to be fraudulent, so we can get them out of the queue," Schaufele says. The more suspicious-looking returns go back for further review.

Results

"With these analytics models, we're able to reduce false positives, so that we don't overburden the taxpayers who have accurately reported their information to the state," Bonardi says. Once investigators remove their returns from the queue, those taxpayers can get their refunds.

Thanks to the new technology, QRDT expects to suspend only 40,000 to 50,000 tax returns, compared with 110,000 in past years. "Of those we've worked so far, we're getting an accuracy rate of about 65%," says Schaufele. That's a big improvement over the historical 10% success rate. "Once the returns are identified which may be fraudulent, the team of expert examiners can then carefully review them, one at a time, to eliminate returns that are found to be legitimate," Maryland Comptroller Franchot says. "The entire operation is getting better and stronger all the time."

As of late March, advanced analytics had helped the QRDT recover approximately $10 million in the current filing season. Schaufele says, "Under the old system, that number would have been about $3 million at this point." Not only does the new technology help the QRDT work faster and more efficiently, but it also helps the team handle a heavier and more complex workload. As tax criminals have ramped up their efforts, the QRDT has had to deploy new strategies against them. For example, in 2015 the team received some 10,000 notifications from taxpayers whose identifications had been stolen. "So we have a new workflow: We look up their Social Security numbers and try to find any incidences of fraud that might have been perpetrated with them," says Schaufele. "That's a new level of effort that this group is now completing without additional resources."

To stay ahead of more sophisticated tax schemes, investigators now not only examine current W-2 forms, but also compare them with the same taxpayers' forms from prior years, looking for inconsistencies. "The investigations are becoming more complex and taking longer," Schaufele says. "If we hadn't winnowed down the universe for review, we would have had some real problems pursuing them."

QUESTIONS FOR THE OPENING VIGNETTE

1. Why is it important for IRS and for U.S. state governments to use data warehousing and business intelligence (BI) tools in managing state revenues?
2. What were the challenges the state of Maryland was facing with regard to tax fraud?
3. What was the solution they adopted? Do you agree with their approach? Why?
4. What were the results that they obtained? Did the investment in BI and data warehousing pay off?
5. What other problems and challenges do you think federal and state governments are having that can benefit from BI and data warehousing?

What We Can Learn from This Vignette

The opening vignette illustrates the value of BI, decision support systems, and data warehousing in management of government revenues. With their data warehouse implementation, the State of Maryland was able to leverage its data assets to make more accurate and timely decisions on identifying fraudulent tax returns. Consolidating and processing a wide variety of data sources within a unified data warehouse enabled Maryland to automate the identification of tax fraud signals/rules/traits from historic facts as opposed to merely relying on traditional ways where they have been implementing intuition-based filtering rules. By using data warehousing and BI, Maryland managed to significantly reduce the false positive rate (and by doing so ease the pain on the part of taxpayers) and improved the prediction accuracy rate from 10% to 65% (more than a sixfold improvement in accurate identification of fraudulent tax returns). The key lesson here is that a properly designed and implemented data warehouse combined with BI tools and techniques can and will result in significant improvement (both on accuracy and on timeliness) resulting in benefits (both financial and nonfinancial) for any organization, including state governments like Maryland.

Sources: Teradata case study. (2016). Targeting tax fraud with advanced analytics. http://assets.teradata.com/resourceCenter/downloads/CaseStudies/EB7183_GT16_CASE_STUDY_Teradata_V.PDF (accessed June 2016); Temple-West, P. (2013, November 7). Tax refund ID theft is growing "epidemic": U.S. IRS watchdog. Reuters. http://www.reuters.com/article/us-usa-tax-refund-idUSBRE9A61HB20131107 (accessed July 2016).

3.2 Business Intelligence and Data Warehousing

Business intelligence (BI), as a term to describe evidence/fact-based managerial decision making, has been around for more than 20 years. With the emergence of business analytics as a new buzzword to describe pretty much the same managerial phenomenon, the popularity of BI as a term has gone down. As opposed to being an all-encompassing term, nowadays BI is used to describe the early stages of business analytics (i.e., descriptive analytics).

Figure 3.1 (a simplified version of which was shown and described in Chapter 1 to describe business analytics taxonomy) illustrates the relationship between BI and business analytics from a conceptual perspective. As shown therein, BI is the descriptive analytics portion of the business analytics continuum, the maturity of which leads to advanced analytics—a combination of predictive and prescriptive analytics.

Descriptive analytics (i.e., BI) is the entry level in the business analytics taxonomy. It is often called business reporting because of the fact that most of the analytics activities at this level deal with creating reports to summarize business activities to answer questions such as "What happened?" and "What is happening?" The spectrum of these reports

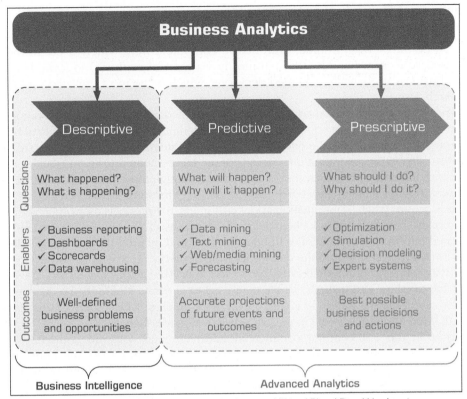

FIGURE 3.1   Relationship between Business Analytics and BI, and BI and Data Warehousing.

includes static snapshots of business transactions delivered to knowledge workers (i.e., decision makers) on a fixed schedule (e.g., daily, weekly, quarterly); ad hoc reporting where the decision maker is given the capability of creating his or her own specific report (using an intuitive drag-and-drop graphical user interface) to address a specific or unique decision situation; and dynamic views of key business performance indicators (often captured and presented within a business performance management system) delivered to managers and executives in an easily digestible form (e.g., dashboard-looking graphical interfaces) on a continuous manner.

Generally speaking, and as depicted in Figure 3.1, BI systems rely on a data warehouse as the information source for creating insight and supporting managerial decisions. A multitude of organizational and external data is captured, transformed, and stored in a data warehouse to support timely and accurate decisions through enriched business insight. This chapter aims to cover the concepts, methods, and tools related to data warehousing and business performance management.

What Is a Data Warehouse?

In simple terms, a **data warehouse (DW)** is a pool of data produced to support decision making; it is also a repository of current and historical data of potential interest to managers throughout the organization. Data are usually structured to be available in a form ready for analytical processing activities (i.e., online analytical processing [OLAP], data mining, querying, reporting, and other decision support applications). A data warehouse is a subject-oriented, integrated, time-variant, nonvolatile collection of data in support of management's decision-making process.

A Historical Perspective to Data Warehousing

Even though *data warehousing* is a relatively new term in information technology (IT), its roots can be traced back in time, even before computers were widely used. In the early 1900s, people were using data (though mostly via manual methods) to formulate trends to help business users make informed decisions, which is the most prevailing purpose of data warehousing.

The motivations that led to the development of data warehousing technologies go back to the 1970s, when the computing world was dominated by mainframes. Real business data-processing applications, the ones run on the corporate mainframes, had complicated file structures using early-generation databases (not the table-oriented relational databases most applications use today) in which they stored data. Although these applications did a decent job of performing routine transactional data-processing functions, the data created as a result of these functions (such as information about customers, the products they ordered, and how much money they spent) was locked away in the depths of the files and databases. When aggregated information such as sales trends by region and by product type was needed, one had to formally request it from the data-processing department, where it was put on a waiting list with a couple of hundred other report requests (Hammergren & Simon, 2009). Even though the need for information and the data used to generate it existed, the database technology was not there to satisfy it. Figure 3.2 shows a timeline where some of the significant events that led to the development of data warehousing are shown.

Later in the last century, commercial hardware and software companies began to emerge with solutions to this problem. Between 1976 and 1979, the concept for a new company, Teradata, grew out of research at the California Institute of Technology (Caltech), driven from discussions with Citibank's advanced technology group. Founders worked to design a database management system for parallel processing with multiple microprocessors, targeted specifically for decision support. Teradata was incorporated on July 13, 1979, and started in a garage in Brentwood, California. The name *Teradata* was chosen to symbolize the ability to manage terabytes (trillions of bytes) of data.

The 1980s were the decade of personal computers and minicomputers. Before anyone knew it, real computer applications were no longer only on mainframes; they were all over the place—everywhere you looked in an organization. That led to a portentous problem called *islands of data*. The solution to this problem led to a new type of software, called a *distributed database management system*, which would magically pull the

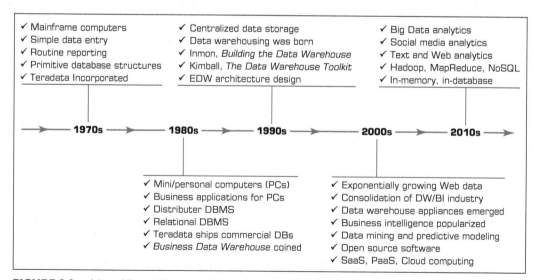

FIGURE 3.2   A List of Events That Led to Data Warehousing Development.

requested data from databases across the organization, bring all the data back to the same place, and then consolidate it, sort it, and do whatever else was necessary to answer the user's question. Although the concept was a good one and early results from research were promising, the results were plain and simple: They just didn't work efficiently in the real world, and the islands-of-data problem still existed.

Meanwhile, Teradata began shipping commercial products to solve this problem. Wells Fargo Bank received the first Teradata test system in 1983, a parallel RDBMS (relational database management system) for decision support—the world's first. By 1984, Teradata released a production version of their product, and in 1986, *Fortune* magazine named Teradata "Product of the Year." Teradata, still in existence today, built the first data warehousing appliance—a combination of hardware and software to solve the data warehousing needs of many. Other companies began to formulate their strategies, as well.

During the 1980s, several other events occurred, collectively making it the decade of data warehousing innovation. For instance, Ralph Kimball founded Red Brick Systems in 1986. Red Brick began to emerge as a visionary software company by discussing how to improve data access; in 1988, Barry Devlin and Paul Murphy of IBM Ireland introduced the term *business data warehouse* as a key component of business information systems.

In the 1990s, a new approach to solving the islands-of-data problem surfaced. If the 1980s approach of reaching out and accessing data directly from the files and databases didn't work, the 1990s philosophy involved going back to the 1970s, in which data from those places was copied to another location—only doing it right this time; hence, data warehousing was born. In 1993, Bill Inmon wrote the seminal book, *Building the Data Warehouse*. Many people recognize Inmon as the father of data warehousing. Additional publications emerged, including the 1996 book by Ralph Kimball, *The Data Warehouse Toolkit*, which discussed general-purpose dimensional design techniques to improve the data architecture for query-centered decision support systems.

In the 2000s, in the world of data warehousing, both popularity and the amount of data continued to grow. The vendor community and options began to consolidate. In 2006, Microsoft acquired ProClarity, jumping into the data warehousing market. In 2007, Oracle purchased Hyperion, SAP acquired Business Objects, and IBM merged with Cognos. The data warehousing leaders of the 1990s have been swallowed by some of the largest providers of information system solutions in the world. During this time, other innovations emerged, including data warehouse appliances from vendors such as Netezza (acquired by IBM), Greenplum (acquired by EMC), DATAllegro (acquired by Microsoft), and performance management appliances that enabled real-time performance monitoring. These innovative solutions provided cost savings because they were plug-compatible to legacy data warehouse solutions.

Since 2010, the big buzz has been *Big Data*. Many believe that Big Data is going to make an impact on data warehousing as we know it. Either they will find a way to coexist (which seems to be the most likely case, at least for several years) or Big Data (and the technologies that come with it) will make traditional data warehousing obsolete. The technologies that came with Big Data include Hadoop, MapReduce, NoSQL, and Hive. Maybe we will see a new term coined in the world of data that combines the needs and capabilities of traditional data warehousing and the Big Data phenomenon.

Characteristics of Data Warehousing

A common way to introduce data warehousing is to refer to its fundamental characteristics (see Inmon, 2005):

- *Subject oriented.*   Data are organized by detailed subject, such as sales, products, or customers, containing only information relevant for decision support. Subject orientation enables users to determine not only how their business is performing, but also why. A data warehouse differs from an operational database in that most operational databases have a product orientation and are tuned to handle transactions that update the database. Subject orientation provides a more comprehensive view of the organization.

- *Integrated.* Integration is closely related to subject orientation. Data warehouses must place data from different sources into a consistent format. To do so, they must deal with naming conflicts and discrepancies among units of measure. A data warehouse is presumed to be totally integrated.
- *Time variant (time series).* A warehouse maintains historical data. The data do not necessarily provide current status (except in real-time systems). They detect trends, deviations, and long-term relationships for forecasting and comparisons, leading to decision making. Every data warehouse has a temporal quality. Time is the one important dimension that all data warehouses must support. Data for analysis from multiple sources contain multiple time points (e.g., daily, weekly, monthly views).
- *Nonvolatile.* After data are entered into a data warehouse, users cannot change or update the data. Obsolete data are discarded, and changes are recorded as new data.

These characteristics enable data warehouses to be tuned almost exclusively for data access. Some additional characteristics may include the following:

- *Web based.* Data warehouses are typically designed to provide an efficient computing environment for Web-based applications.
- *Relational/multidimensional.* A data warehouse uses either a relational structure or a multidimensional structure. A recent survey on multidimensional structures can be found in Romero and Abelló (2009).
- *Client/server.* A data warehouse uses the client/server architecture to provide easy access for end users.
- *Real time.* Newer data warehouses provide real-time, or active, data-access and analysis capabilities (see Basu, 2003; Bonde & Kuckuk, 2004).
- *Include metadata.* A data warehouse contains metadata (data about data) about how the data are organized and how to effectively use them.

Whereas a data warehouse is a repository of data, data warehousing is literally the entire process (see Watson, 2002). Data warehousing is a discipline that results in applications that provide decision support capability, allows ready access to business information, and creates business insight. The three main types of data warehouses are data marts (DMs), operational data stores (ODS), and enterprise data warehouses (EDW). In addition to discussing these three types of warehouses next, we also discuss metadata.

Data Marts

Whereas a data warehouse combines databases across an entire enterprise, a **data mart (DM)** is usually smaller and focuses on a particular subject or department. A DM is a subset of a data warehouse, typically consisting of a single subject area (e.g., marketing, operations). A DM can be either dependent or independent. A **dependent data mart** is a subset that is created directly from the data warehouse. It has the advantages of using a consistent data model and providing quality data. Dependent DMs support the concept of a single enterprise-wide data model, but the data warehouse must be constructed first. A dependent DM ensures that the end user is viewing the same version of the data that is accessed by all other data warehouse users. The high cost of data warehouses limits their use to large companies. As an alternative, many firms use a lower-cost, scaled-down version of a data warehouse referred to as an *independent DM*. An **independent data mart** is a small warehouse designed for a strategic business unit or a department, but its source is not an EDW.

Operational Data Stores

An **operational data store (ODS)** provides a fairly recent form of customer information file. This type of database is often used as an interim staging area for a data warehouse. Unlike the static contents of a data warehouse, the contents of an ODS are updated throughout the course of business operations. An ODS is used for short-term decisions involving mission-critical applications rather than for the medium- and long-term decisions associated with an EDW. An ODS is similar to short-term memory in that it stores only very recent information. In comparison, a data warehouse is like long-term memory because it stores permanent information. An ODS consolidates data from multiple source systems and provides a near–real-time, integrated view of volatile, current data. The exchange, transfer, and load (ETL) processes (discussed later in this chapter) for an ODS are identical to those for a data warehouse. Finally, **oper marts** (see Imhoff, 2001) are created when operational data needs to be analyzed multidimensionally. The data for an oper mart come from an ODS.

Enterprise Data Warehouses (EDW)

An **enterprise data warehouse (EDW)** is a large-scale data warehouse that is used across the enterprise for decision support. The large-scale nature of an EDW provides integration of data from many sources into a standard format for effective BI and decision support applications. EDWs are used to provide data for many types of decision support systems (DSS), including customer relationship management (CRM), supply chain management (SCM), business performance management (BPM), business activity monitoring, product life cycle management, revenue management, and sometimes even knowledge management systems. Application Case 3.1 shows the variety of benefits that telecommunication companies leverage from implementing data warehouse–driven analytics solutions.

Metadata

Metadata are data about data (e.g., see Sen, 2004; Zhao, 2005). Metadata describe the structure of and some meaning about data, thereby contributing to their effective or ineffective use. Mehra (2005) indicated that few organizations really understand metadata, and fewer understand how to design and implement a metadata strategy. Metadata are generally defined in terms of usage as technical or business metadata. Patterns are another way to view metadata. According to the pattern view, we can differentiate between syntactic metadata (i.e., data describing the syntax of data), structural metadata (i.e., data describing the structure of the data), and semantic metadata (i.e., data describing the meaning of the data in a specific domain).

Application Case 3.1

A Better Data Plan: Well-Established TELCOs Leverage Data Warehousing and Analytics to Stay on Top in a Competitive Industry

Mobile service providers (i.e., Telecommunication Companies, or TELCOs in short) that helped trigger the explosive growth of the industry in the mid- to late-1990s have long reaped the benefits of being first to market. But to stay competitive, these companies must continuously refine everything from customer service to plan pricing. In fact, veteran carriers face many of the same challenges that up-and-coming carriers do: retaining customers, decreasing costs, fine-tuning pricing models, improving customer satisfaction, acquiring new customers, and understanding the role of social media in customer loyalty.

(Continued)

Highly targeted data analytics play an ever-more-critical role in helping carriers secure or improve their standing in an increasingly competitive marketplace. Here's how some of the world's leading providers are creating a strong future based on solid business and customer intelligence.

Customer Retention

It's no secret that the speed and success with which a provider handles service requests directly affects customer satisfaction and, in turn, the propensity to churn. But getting down to which factors have the greatest impact is a challenge.

"If we could trace the steps involved with each process, we could understand points of failure and acceleration," notes Roxanne Garcia, Manager of the Commercial Operations Center for Telefónica de Argentina. "We could measure workflows both within and across functions, anticipate rather than react to performance indicators, and improve the overall satisfaction with onboarding new customers."

The company's solution was its traceability project, which began with 10 dashboards in 2009. It has since realized $2.4 million in annualized revenues and cost savings, shortened customer provisioning times, and reduced customer defections by 30%.

Cost Reduction

Staying ahead of the game in any industry depends, in large part, on keeping costs in line. For France's Bouygues Telecom, cost reduction came in the form of automation. Aladin, the company's Teradata-based marketing operations management system, automates marketing/communications collateral production. It delivered more than $1 million in savings in a single year while tripling their e-mail campaign and content production.

"The goal is to be more productive and responsive, to simplify teamwork, [and] to standardize and protect our expertise," notes Catherine Corrado, the company's Project Lead and Retail Communications Manager. "[Aladin lets] team members focus on value-added work by reducing low-value tasks. The end result is more quality and more creative [output]."

An unintended but very welcome benefit of Aladin is that other departments have been inspired to begin deploying similar projects for everything from call center support to product/offer launch processes.

Customer Acquisition

With market penetration near or above 100% in many countries, thanks to consumers who own multiple devices, the issue of new customer acquisition is no small challenge. Pakistan's largest carrier, Mobilink, also faces the difficulty of operating in a market where 98% of users have a prepaid plan that requires regular purchases of additional minutes.

"Topping up, in particular, keeps the revenues strong and is critical to our company's growth," says Umer Afzal, Senior Manager, BI. "Previously we lacked the ability to enhance this aspect of incremental growth. Our sales information model gave us that ability because it helped the distribution team plan sales tactics based on smarter data-driven strategies that keep our suppliers [of SIM cards, scratch cards, and electronic top-up capability] fully stocked."

As a result, Mobilink has not only grown subscriber recharges by 2% but also expanded new customer acquisition by 4% and improved the profitability of those sales by 4%.

Social Networking

The expanding use of social networks is changing how many organizations approach everything from customer service to sales and marketing. More carriers are turning their attention to social networks to better understand and influence customer behavior.

Mobilink has initiated a social network analysis project that will enable the company to explore the concept of viral marketing and identify key influencers who can act as brand ambassadors to cross-sell products. Velcom is looking for similar key influencers as well as low-value customers whose social value can be leveraged to improve existing relationships. Meanwhile, Swisscom is looking to combine the social network aspect of customer behavior with the rest of its analysis over the next several months.

Rise to the Challenge

Although each market presents its own unique challenges, most mobile carriers spend a great deal of time and resources creating, deploying, and refining plans to address each of the challenges outlined here. The good news is that just as the industry and mobile technology have expanded and improved over the years, so also have the data analytics solutions that have been created to meet these challenges head on.

Sound data analysis uses existing customer, business, and market intelligence to predict and influence future behaviors and outcomes. The end result is a smarter, more agile, and more successful approach to gaining market share and improving profitability.

QUESTIONS FOR DISCUSSION

1. What are the main challenges for TELCOs?
2. How can data warehousing and data analytics help TELCOs in overcoming their challenges?
3. Why do you think TELCOs are well suited to take full advantage of data analytics?

Source: Marble, C. (2013). A better data plan: Well-established TELCOs leverage analytics to stay on top in a competitive industry. *Teradata Magazine.* http://www.teradatamagazine. com/v13n01/Features/A-Better-Data-Plan (accessed June 2016).

SECTION 3.2 REVIEW QUESTIONS

1. What is a data warehouse?
2. How does a data warehouse differ from a transactional database?
3. What is an ODS?
4. Differentiate among a DM, an ODS, and an EDW.
5. What is metadata? Explain the importance of metadata.

3.3   Data Warehousing Process

Organizations, private and public, continuously collect data, information, and knowledge at an increasingly accelerated rate and store them in computerized systems. Maintaining and using these data and information becomes extremely complex, especially as scalability issues arise. In addition, the number of users needing to access the information continues to increase as a result of improved reliability and availability of network access, especially the Internet. Working with multiple databases, either integrated in a data warehouse or not, has become an extremely difficult task requiring considerable expertise, but it can provide immense benefits far exceeding its cost. As an illustrative example, Figure 3.3 shows business benefits of the EDW built by Teradata for a major automobile manufacturer.

Many organizations need to create data warehouses—massive data stores of time series data for decision support. Data are imported from various external and internal resources and are cleansed and organized in a manner consistent with the organization's needs. After the data are populated in the data warehouse, DMs can be loaded for a specific area or department. Alternatively, DMs can be created first, as needed, and then integrated into an EDW. Often, though, DMs are not developed, but data are simply loaded onto PCs or left in their original state for direct manipulation using BI tools.

In Figure 3.4, we show the data warehouse concept. The following are the major components of the data warehousing process:

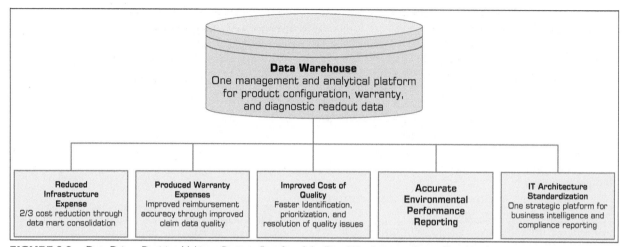

FIGURE 3.3 Data-Driven Decision Making—Business Benefits of the Data Warehouse. *Source:* Teradata Corp.

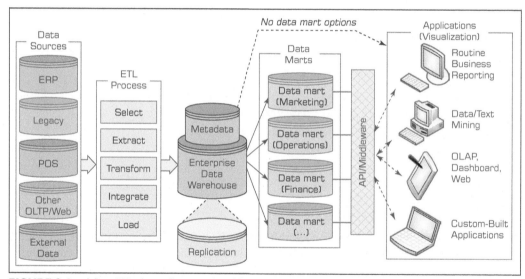

FIGURE 3.4 A Data Warehouse Framework and Views.

- ***Data sources.*** Data are sourced from multiple independent operational "legacy" systems and possibly from external data providers (such as the U.S. Census). Data may also come from an OLTP or enterprise resource planning (ERP) system. Web data in the form of Web logs may also feed to a data warehouse.
- ***Data extraction and transformation.*** Data are extracted and properly transformed using custom-written or commercial software called ETL.
- ***Data loading.*** Data are loaded into a staging area, where they are transformed and cleansed. The data are then ready to load into the data warehouse and/or DMs.
- ***Comprehensive database.*** Essentially, this is the EDW to support all decision analysis by providing relevant summarized and detailed information originating from many different sources.

- *Metadata.* Metadata are maintained so that they can be assessed by IT personnel and users. Metadata include software programs about data and rules for organizing data summaries that are easy to index and search, especially with Web tools.
- *Middleware tools.* Middleware tools enable access to the data warehouse. Power users such as analysts may write their own SQL queries. Others may employ a managed query environment, such as Business Objects, to access data. There are many front-end applications that business users can use to interact with data stored in the data repositories, including data mining, OLAP, reporting tools, and data visualization tools.

SECTION 3.3 REVIEW QUESTIONS

1. Describe the data warehousing process.
2. Describe the major components of a data warehouse.
3. Identify and discuss the role of middleware tools.

3.4 Data Warehousing Architectures

Several basic information system architectures can be used for data warehousing. Generally speaking, these architectures are commonly called client/server or n-tier architectures, of which two-tier and three-tier architectures are the most common (see Figures 3.5 and 3.6), but sometimes there is simply one tier. These types of multitiered architectures are known to be capable of serving the needs of large-scale, performance-demanding information systems such as data warehouses. Referring to the use of n-tiered architectures for data warehousing, Hoffer, Prescott, and McFadden (2007) distinguished among these architectures by dividing the data warehouse into three parts:

1. The data warehouse itself, which contains the data and associated software
2. Data acquisition (back-end) software, which extracts data from legacy systems and external sources, consolidates and summarizes them, and loads them into the data warehouse
3. Client (front-end) software, which allows users to access and analyze data from the warehouse (a DSS/BI/business analytics [BA] engine)

In a three-tier architecture, operational systems contain the data and the software for data acquisition in one tier (i.e., the server), the data warehouse is another tier, and the third tier includes the DSS/BI/BA engine (i.e., the application server) and the client (see

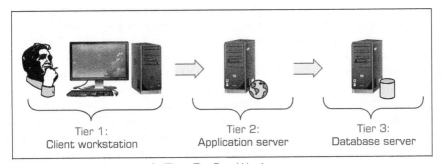

Tier 1:
Client workstation

Tier 2:
Application server

Tier 3:
Database server

FIGURE 3.5   Architecture of a Three-Tier Data Warehouse.

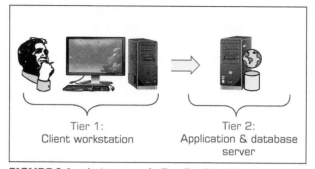

FIGURE 3.6 Architecture of a Two-Tier Data Warehouse.

Figure 3.5). Data from the warehouse are processed twice and deposited in an additional multidimensional database, organized for easy multidimensional analysis and presentation, or replicated in DMs. The advantage of the three-tier architecture is its separation of the functions of the data warehouse, which eliminates resource constraints and makes it possible to easily create DMs.

In a two-tier architecture, the DSS engine physically runs on the same hardware platform as the data warehouse (see Figure 3.6). Therefore, it is more economical than the three-tier structure. The two-tier architecture can have performance problems for large data warehouses that work with data-intensive applications for decision support.

Much of the common wisdom assumes an absolutist approach, maintaining that one solution is better than the other, despite the organization's circumstances and unique needs. To further complicate these architectural decisions, many consultants and software vendors focus on one portion of the architecture, therefore limiting their capacity and motivation to assist an organization through the options based on its needs. But these aspects are being questioned and analyzed. For example, Ball (2005) provided decision criteria for organizations that plan to implement a BI application and have already determined their need for multidimensional DMs but need help determining the appropriate tiered architecture. His criteria revolve around forecasting needs for space and speed of access (see Ball, 2005, for details).

Data warehousing and the Internet are two key technologies that offer important solutions for managing corporate data. The integration of these two technologies produces Web-based data warehousing. In Figure 3.7, we show the architecture of Web-based data warehousing. The architecture is three tiered and includes the PC client, Web server, and application server. On the client side, the user needs an Internet connection and a Web browser (preferably Java enabled) through the familiar graphical user interface (GUI). The Internet/intranet/extranet is the communication medium between client and servers. On the server side, a Web server is used to manage the inflow and outflow of information between client and server. It is backed by both a data warehouse and an application server. Web-based data warehousing offers several compelling advantages, including ease of access, platform independence, and lower cost.

Web architectures for data warehousing are similar in structure to other data warehousing architectures, requiring a design choice for housing the Web data warehouse with the transaction server or as a separate server(s). Page-loading speed is an important consideration in designing Web-based applications; therefore, server capacity must be planned carefully.

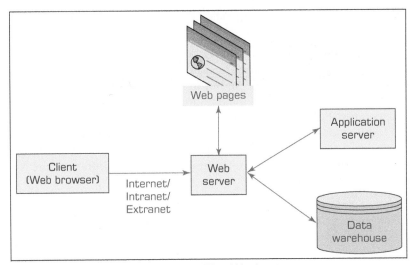

FIGURE 3.7   Architecture of Web-Based Data Warehousing.

Several issues must be considered when deciding which architecture to use. Among them are the following:

- *Which database management system (DBMS) should be used?*   Most data warehouses are built using RDBMS. Oracle (Oracle Corporation, oracle.com), SQL Server (Microsoft Corporation, microsoft.com/sql), and DB2 (IBM Corporation, http://www-01.ibm.com/software/data/db2) are the ones most commonly used. Each of these products supports both client/server and Web-based architectures.

- *Will parallel processing and/or partitioning be used?*   Parallel processing enables multiple central processing units (CPUs) to process data warehouse query requests simultaneously and provides scalability. Data warehouse designers need to decide whether the database tables will be partitioned (i.e., split into smaller tables) for access efficiency and what the criteria will be. This is an important consideration that is necessitated by the large amounts of data contained in a typical data warehouse. A recent survey on parallel and distributed data warehouses can be found in Furtado (2009). Teradata (teradata.com) has successfully adopted and is often commended on its novel implementation of this approach.

- *Will data migration tools be used to load the data warehouse?*   Moving data from an existing system into a data warehouse is a tedious and laborious task. Depending on the diversity and the location of the data assets, migration may be a relatively simple procedure or (on the contrary) a months-long project. The results of a thorough assessment of the existing data assets should be used to determine whether to use migration tools, and if so, what capabilities to seek in those commercial tools.

- *What tools will be used to support data retrieval and analysis?*   Often it is necessary to use specialized tools to periodically locate, access, analyze, extract, transform, and load necessary data into a data warehouse. A decision has to be made on (1) developing the migration tools in-house, (2) purchasing them from a third-party provider, or (3) using the ones provided with the data warehouse system. Overly complex, real-time migrations warrant specialized third-party ETL tools.

Alternative Data Warehousing Architectures

At the highest level, data warehouse architecture design viewpoints can be categorized into enterprise-wide data warehouse (EDW) design and DM design (Golfarelli & Rizzi, 2009). In Figure 3.8a–e, we show some alternatives to the basic architectural design types that are neither pure EDW nor pure DM, but in between or beyond the traditional architectural structures. Notable new ones include hub-and-spoke and federated architectures. The five architectures shown in Figure 3.8a–e, are proposed by Ariyachandra and Watson (2005, 2006a,b). Previously, in an extensive study, Sen and Sinha (2005) identified 15 different data warehousing methodologies. The sources of these methodologies are classified into three broad categories: core-technology vendors, infrastructure vendors, and information-modeling companies.

a. *Independent data marts.* This is arguably the simplest and the least costly architecture alternative. The DMs are developed to operate independent of each other to serve the needs of individual organizational units. Because of their independence, they may have inconsistent data definitions and different dimensions and measures, making it difficult to analyze data across the DMs (i.e., it is difficult, if not impossible, to get to the "one version of the truth").

b. *Data mart bus architecture.* This architecture is a viable alternative to the independent DMs where the individual marts are linked to each other via some kind of middleware. Because the data are linked among the individual marts, there is a better chance of maintaining data consistency across the enterprise (at least at the metadata level). Even though it allows for complex data queries across DMs, the performance of these types of analysis may not be at a satisfactory level.

c. *Hub-and-spoke architecture.* This is perhaps the most famous data warehousing architecture today. Here the attention is focused on building a scalable and maintainable infrastructure (often developed in an iterative way, subject area by subject area) that includes a centralized data warehouse and several dependent DMs (each for an organizational unit). This architecture allows for easy customization of user interfaces and reports. On the negative side, this architecture lacks the holistic enterprise view and may lead to data redundancy and data latency.

d. *Centralized data warehouse.* The centralized data warehouse architecture is similar to the hub-and-spoke architecture except that there are no dependent DMs; instead, there is a gigantic EDW that serves the needs of all organizational units. This centralized approach provides users with access to all data in the data warehouse instead of limiting them to DMs. In addition, it reduces the amount of data the technical team has to transfer or change, therefore simplifying data management and administration. If designed and implemented properly, this architecture provides a timely and holistic view of the enterprise to whoever, whenever, and wherever they may be within the organization.

e. *Federated data warehouse.* The federated approach is a concession to the natural forces that undermine the best plans for developing a perfect system. It uses all possible means to integrate analytical resources from multiple sources to meet changing needs or business conditions. Essentially, the federated approach involves integrating disparate systems. In a federated architecture, existing decision support structures are left in place, and data are accessed from those sources as needed. The federated approach is supported by middleware vendors that propose distributed query and join capabilities. These eXtensible Markup Language (XML)–based tools offer users a global view of distributed data sources, including data warehouses, DMs, Web sites, documents, and operational systems. When users choose query objects from this view and press the submit button, the tool automatically queries the distributed sources, joins the results, and presents them to the user. Because of

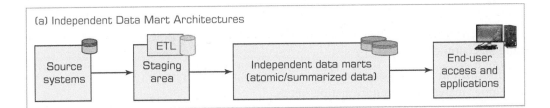

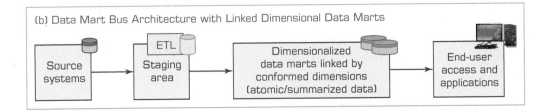

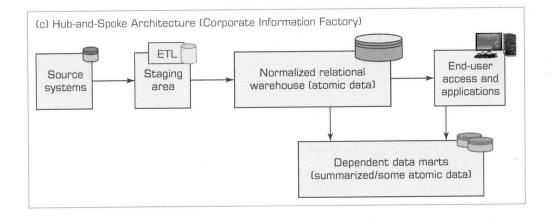

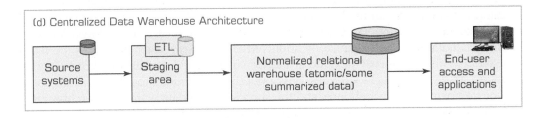

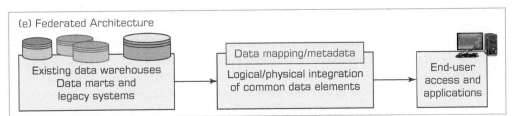

FIGURE 3.8   Alternative Data Warehouse Architectures.   *Source:* Adapted from Ariyachandra, T., & Watson, H. (2006b). Which data warehouse architecture is most successful? *Business Intelligence Journal, 11*(1), 4–6.

performance and data quality issues, most experts agree that federated approaches work well to supplement data warehouses, not replace them (see Eckerson, 2005).

Ariyachandra and Watson (2005) identified 10 factors that potentially affect the architecture selection decision:

1. Information interdependence between organizational units
2. Upper management's information needs
3. Urgency of need for a data warehouse
4. Nature of end-user tasks
5. Constraints on resources
6. Strategic view of the data warehouse prior to implementation
7. Compatibility with existing systems
8. Perceived ability of the in-house IT staff
9. Technical issues
10. Social/political factors

These factors are similar to many success factors described in the literature for information system projects and DSS and BI projects. Technical issues, beyond providing technology that is feasibly ready for use, is important, but often not as important as behavioral issues, such as meeting upper management's information needs and user involvement in the development process (a social/political factor). Each data warehousing architecture has specific applications for which it is most (and least) effective and thus provides maximal benefits to the organization. However, overall, the DM structure seems to be the least effective in practice. See Ariyachandra and Watson (2006a) for some additional details.

Which Architecture Is the Best?

Ever since data warehousing became a critical part of modern enterprises, the question of which data warehouse architecture is the best has been a topic of regular discussion. The two gurus of the data warehousing field, Bill Inmon and Ralph Kimball, are at the heart of this discussion. Inmon advocates the hub-and-spoke architecture (e.g., the Corporate Information Factory), whereas Kimball promotes the DM bus architecture with conformed dimensions. Other architectures are possible, but these two options are fundamentally different approaches, and each has strong advocates. To shed light on this controversial question, Ariyachandra and Watson (2006b) conducted an empirical study. To collect the data, they used a Web-based survey targeted at individuals involved in data warehouse implementations. Their survey included questions about the respondent, the respondent's company, the company's data warehouse, and the success of the data warehouse architecture.

In total, 454 respondents provided usable information. Surveyed companies ranged from small (less than $10 million in revenue) to large (in excess of $10 billion). Most of the companies were located in the United States (60%) and represented a variety of industries, with the financial services industry (15%) providing the most responses. The predominant architecture was the hub-and-spoke architecture (39%), followed by the bus architecture (26%), the centralized architecture (17%), independent DMs (12%), and the federated architecture (4%). The most common platform for hosting the data warehouses was Oracle (41%), followed by Microsoft (19%) and IBM (18%). The average (mean) gross revenue varied from $3.7 billion for independent DMs to $6 billion for the federated architecture.

They used four measures to assess the success of the architectures: (1) information quality, (2) system quality, (3) individual impacts, and (4) organizational impacts. The questions used a 7-point scale, with the higher score indicating a more successful architecture. Table 3.1 shows the average scores for the measures across the architectures.

TABLE 3.1	Average Assessment Scores for the Success of the Architectures				
	Independent DMs	Bus Architecture	Hub-and-Spoke Architecture	Centralized Architecture (No Dependent DMs)	Federated Architecture
Information Quality	4.42	5.16	5.35	5.23	4.73
System Quality	4.59	5.60	5.56	5.41	4.69
Individual Impacts	5.08	5.80	5.62	5.64	5.15
Organizational Impacts	4.66	5.34	5.24	5.30	4.77

As the results of the study indicate, independent DMs scored the lowest on all measures. This finding confirms the conventional wisdom that independent DMs are a poor architectural solution. Next lowest on all measures was the federated architecture. Firms sometimes have disparate decision-support platforms resulting from mergers and acquisitions, and they may choose a federated approach, at least in the short term. The findings suggest that the federated architecture is not an optimal long-term solution. What is interesting, however, is the similarity of the averages for the bus, hub-and-spoke, and centralized architectures. The differences are sufficiently small that no claims can be made for a particular architecture's superiority over the others, at least based on a simple comparison of these success measures.

They also collected data on the domain (e.g., varying from a subunit to company-wide) and the size (i.e., amount of data stored) of the warehouses. They found that the hub-and-spoke architecture is typically used with more enterprise-wide implementations and larger warehouses. They also investigated the cost and time required to implement the different architectures. Overall, the hub-and-spoke architecture was the most expensive and time-consuming to implement.

SECTION 3.4 REVIEW QUESTIONS

1. What are the key similarities and differences between a two-tiered architecture and a three-tiered architecture?
2. How has the Web influenced data warehouse design?
3. List the alternative data warehousing architectures discussed in this section.
4. What issues should be considered when deciding which architecture to use in developing a data warehouse? List the 10 most important factors.
5. Which data warehousing architecture is the best? Why?

3.5 Data Integration and the Extraction, Transformation, and Load (ETL) Processes

Global competitive pressures, demand for return on investment (ROI), management and investor inquiry, and government regulations are forcing business managers to rethink how they integrate and manage their businesses. A decision maker typically needs access to multiple sources of data that must be integrated. Before data warehouses, DMs, and BI software, providing access to data sources was a major, laborious process. Even with modern Web-based data management tools, recognizing what data to access and providing them to the decision maker is a nontrivial task that requires database specialists. As data warehouses grow in size, the issues of integrating data grow as well.

The business analysis needs continue to evolve. Mergers and acquisitions, regulatory requirements, and the introduction of new channels can drive changes in BI requirements. In addition to historical, cleansed, consolidated, and point-in-time data, business users increasingly demand access to real-time, unstructured, and/or remote data. And everything must be integrated with the contents of an existing data warehouse. Moreover, access via PDAs and through speech recognition and synthesis is becoming more commonplace, further complicating integration issues (Edwards, 2003). Many integration projects involve enterprise-wide systems. Orovic (2003) provided a checklist of what works and what does not work when attempting such a project. Properly integrating data from various databases and other disparate sources is difficult. When it is not done properly, though, it can lead to disaster in enterprise-wide systems such as CRM, ERP, and supply-chain projects (Nash, 2002).

Data Integration

Data integration comprises three major processes that, when correctly implemented, permit data to be accessed and made accessible to an array of ETL and analysis tools and the data warehousing environment: data access (i.e., the ability to access and extract data from any data source), data federation (i.e., the integration of business views across multiple data stores), and change capture (based on the identification, capture, and delivery of the changes made to enterprise data sources). See Application Case 3.2 for an example of how BP Lubricant benefits from implementing a data warehouse that integrates data from many sources. Some vendors, such as SAS Institute, Inc., have developed strong data integration tools. The SAS enterprise data integration server includes customer data integration tools that improve data quality in the integration process. The Oracle Business Intelligence Suite assists in integrating data as well.

Application Case 3.2

BP Lubricants Achieves BIGS Success

BP Lubricants established the BIGS program following recent merger activity to deliver globally consistent and transparent management information. As well as timely BI, BIGS provides detailed, consistent views of performance across functions such as finance, marketing, sales, and supply and logistics.

BP is one of the world's largest oil and petrochemicals groups. Part of the BP plc group, BP Lubricants is an established leader in the global automotive lubricants market. Perhaps best known for its Castrol brand of oils, the business operates in over 100 countries and employs 10,000 people. Strategically, BP Lubricants is concentrating on further improving its customer focus and increasing its effectiveness in automotive markets. Following recent merger activity, the company is undergoing a transformation to become more effective and agile and to seize opportunities for rapid growth.

Challenge

Following recent merger activity, BP Lubricants wanted to improve the consistency, transparency, and accessibility of management information and BI. To do so, it needed to integrate data held in disparate source systems, without the delay of introducing a standardized ERP system.

Solution

BP Lubricants implemented the pilot for its Business Intelligence and Global Standards (BIGS) program, a strategic initiative for management information and BI. At the heart of BIGS is Kalido, an adaptive EDW solution for preparing, implementing, operating, and managing data warehouses.

Kalido's federated EDW solution supported the pilot program's complex data integration and diverse reporting requirements. To adapt to the program's evolving reporting requirements, the software also enabled the underlying information architecture to be easily modified at high speed while preserving all information. The system integrates and stores information from multiple source systems to provide consolidated views for:

- *Marketing* Customer proceeds and margins for market segments with drill-down to invoice-level detail
- *Sales* Invoice reporting augmented with both detailed tariff costs and actual payments
- *Finance* Globally standard profit and loss, balance sheet, and cash flow statements—with audit ability; customer debt management supply and logistics; consolidated view of order and movement processing across multiple ERP platforms

Benefits

By improving the visibility of consistent, timely data, BIGS provides the information needed to assist the business in identifying a multitude of business opportunities to maximize margins and/or manage associated costs. Typical responses to the benefits of consistent data resulting from the BIGS pilot include the following:

- Improved consistency and transparency of business data
- Easier, faster, and more flexible reporting
- Accommodation of both global and local standards
- Fast, cost-effective, and flexible implementation cycle
- Minimal disruption of existing business processes and the day-to-day business
- Identification of data quality issues and encourages their resolution
- Improved ability to respond intelligently to new business opportunities

QUESTIONS FOR DISCUSSION

1. What is BIGS?
2. What were the challenges, the proposed solution, and the obtained results with BIGS?

Sources: Kalido. BP Lubricants. http://kalido.com/download/BP-Lubricants.pdf (accessed July 2016); BP Lubricants, www.bp.com/en/global/corporate/about-bp/bp-at-a-glance.html (accessed July 2016).

A major purpose of a data warehouse is to integrate data from multiple systems. Various integration technologies enable data and metadata integration:

- Enterprise application integration (EAI)
- Service-oriented architecture (SOA)
- Enterprise information integration (EII)
- Extraction, transformation, and load (ETL)

Enterprise application integration (EAI) provides a vehicle for pushing data from source systems into the data warehouse. It involves integrating application functionality and is focused on sharing functionality (rather than data) across systems, thereby enabling flexibility and reuse. Traditionally, EAI solutions have focused on enabling application reuse at the application programming interface level. Recently, EAI is accomplished by using SOA coarse-grained services (a collection of business processes or functions) that are well defined and documented. Using Web services is a specialized way of implementing an SOA. EAI can be used to facilitate data acquisition directly into a near–real-time data warehouse or to deliver decisions to the OLTP systems. There are many different approaches to and tools for EAI implementation.

Enterprise information integration (EII) is an evolving tool space that promises real-time data integration from a variety of sources, such as relational databases, Web services, and multidimensional databases. It is a mechanism for pulling data from source systems to satisfy a request for information. EII tools use predefined metadata to populate views that make integrated data appear relational to end users. XML may be the most important aspect of EII because XML allows data to be tagged either at creation time or later. These tags can be extended and modified to accommodate almost any area of knowledge (see Kay, 2005).

Physical data integration has conventionally been the main mechanism for creating an integrated view with data warehouses and DMs. With the advent of EII tools (see Kay, 2005), new virtual data integration patterns are feasible. Manglik and Mehra (2005) discussed the benefits and constraints of new data integration patterns that can expand traditional physical methodologies to present a comprehensive view for the enterprise.

We next turn to the approach for loading data into the warehouse: ETL.

Extraction, Transformation, and Load

At the heart of the technical side of the data warehousing process is **extraction, transformation, and load (ETL)**. ETL technologies, which have existed for some time, are instrumental in the process and use of data warehouses. The ETL process is an integral component in any data-centric project. IT managers are often faced with challenges because the ETL process typically consumes 70% of the time in a data-centric project.

The ETL process consists of extraction (i.e., reading data from one or more databases), transformation (i.e., converting the extracted data from its previous form into the form in which it needs to be so that it can be placed into a data warehouse or simply another database), and load (i.e., putting the data into the data warehouse). Transformation occurs by using rules or lookup tables or by combining the data with other data. The three database functions are integrated into one tool to pull data out of one or more databases and place them into another, consolidated database or a data warehouse.

ETL tools also transport data between sources and targets, document how data elements (e.g., metadata) change as they move between source and target, exchange metadata with other applications as needed, and administer all runtime processes and operations (e.g., scheduling, error management, audit logs, statistics). ETL is extremely important for data integration as well as for data warehousing. The purpose of the ETL process is to load the warehouse with integrated and cleansed data. The data used in ETL processes can come from any source: a mainframe application, an ERP application, a CRM tool, a flat file, an Excel spreadsheet, or even a message queue. In Figure 3.9, we outline the ETL process.

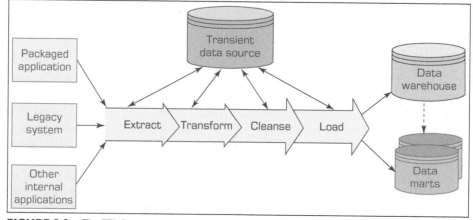

FIGURE 3.9 The ETL Process.

The process of migrating data to a data warehouse involves the extraction of data from all relevant sources. Data sources may consist of files extracted from OLTP databases, spreadsheets, personal databases (e.g., Microsoft Access), or external files. Typically, all the input files are written to a set of staging tables, which are designed to facilitate the load process. A data warehouse contains numerous business rules that define such things as how the data will be used, summarization rules, standardization of encoded attributes, and calculation rules. Any data quality issues pertaining to the source files need to be corrected before the data are loaded into the data warehouse. One of the benefits of a well-designed data warehouse is that these rules can be stored in a metadata repository and applied to the data warehouse centrally. This differs from an OLTP approach, which typically has data and business rules scattered throughout the system. The process of loading data into a data warehouse can be performed either through data transformation tools that provide a GUI to aid in the development and maintenance of business rules or through more traditional methods, such as developing programs or utilities to load the data warehouse, using programming languages such as PL/SQL, C++, Java, or .NET Framework languages. This decision is not easy for organizations. Several issues affect whether an organization will purchase data transformation tools or build the transformation process itself:

- Data transformation tools are expensive.
- Data transformation tools may have a long learning curve.
- It is difficult to measure how the IT organization is doing until it has learned to use the data transformation tools.

In the long run, a transformation-tool approach should simplify the maintenance of an organization's data warehouse. Transformation tools can also be effective in detecting and scrubbing (i.e., removing any anomalies in the data). OLAP and data mining tools rely on how well the data are transformed.

As an example of effective ETL, Motorola, Inc., uses ETL to feed its data warehouses. Motorola collects information from 30 different procurement systems and sends them to its global SCM data warehouse for analysis of aggregate company spending (see Songini, 2004).

Solomon (2005) classified ETL technologies into four categories: sophisticated, enabler, simple, and rudimentary. It is generally acknowledged that tools in the sophisticated category will result in the ETL process being better documented and more accurately managed as the data warehouse project evolves.

Even though it is possible for programmers to develop software for ETL, it is simpler to use an existing ETL tool. The following are some of the important criteria in selecting an ETL tool (see Brown, 2004):

- Ability to read from and write to an unlimited number of data source architectures
- Automatic capturing and delivery of metadata
- A history of conforming to open standards
- An easy-to-use interface for the developer and the functional user

Performing extensive ETL may be a sign of poorly managed data and a fundamental lack of a coherent data management strategy. Karacsony (2006) indicated that there is a direct correlation between the extent of redundant data and the number of ETL processes. When data are managed correctly as an enterprise asset, ETL efforts are significantly reduced, and redundant data are completely eliminated. This leads to huge savings in maintenance and greater efficiency in new development while also improving data quality. Poorly designed ETL processes are costly to maintain, change, and update. Consequently, it is crucial to make the proper choices in terms of the technology and tools to use for developing and maintaining the ETL process.

A number of packaged ETL tools are available. Database vendors currently offer ETL capabilities that both enhance and compete with independent ETL tools. SAS acknowledges the importance of data quality and offers the industry's first fully integrated solution that merges ETL and data quality to transform data into strategic valuable assets. Other ETL software providers include Microsoft, Oracle, IBM, Informatica, Embarcadero, and Tibco. For additional information on ETL, see Golfarelli and Rizzi (2009), Karacsony (2006), and Songini (2004).

SECTION 3.5 REVIEW QUESTIONS

1. Describe data integration.
2. Describe the three steps of the ETL process.
3. Why is the ETL process so important for data warehousing efforts?

3.6 Data Warehouse Development

A data warehousing project is a major undertaking for any organization and is more complicated than a simple mainframe selection and implementation project because it comprises and influences many departments and many input and output interfaces and it can be part of a CRM business strategy. A data warehouse provides several benefits that can be classified as direct and indirect. Direct benefits include the following:

- End users can perform extensive analysis in numerous ways.
- A consolidated view of corporate data (i.e., a single version of the truth) is possible.
- Better and more timely information is possible. A data warehouse permits information processing to be relieved from costly operational systems onto low-cost servers; therefore, many more end-user information requests can be processed more quickly.
- Enhanced system performance can result. A data warehouse frees production processing because some operational system reporting requirements are moved to DSS.
- Data access is simplified.

Indirect benefits result from end users using these direct benefits. On the whole, these benefits enhance business knowledge, present a competitive advantage, improve customer service and satisfaction, facilitate decision making, and help in reforming business processes; therefore, they are the strongest contributions to competitive advantage (Parzinger & Frolick, 2001). For a detailed discussion of how organizations can obtain exceptional levels of payoffs, see Watson, Goodhue, and Wixom (2002). Given the potential benefits that a data warehouse can provide and the substantial investments in time and money that such a project requires, it is critical that an organization structure its data warehouse project to maximize the chances of success. In addition, the organization must, obviously, take costs into consideration. Kelly (2001) described an ROI approach that considers benefits in the categories of keepers (i.e., money saved by improving traditional decision support functions), gatherers (i.e., money saved due to automated collection and dissemination of information), and users (i.e., money saved or gained from decisions made using the data warehouse). Costs include those related to hardware, software, network bandwidth, internal development, internal support, training, and external consulting. The net present value is calculated over the expected life of the data warehouse. Because the benefits are broken down approximately as 20% for keepers, 30% for gatherers, and 50% for users, Kelly indicated that users should be involved in the development process, a success factor typically mentioned as critical for systems that imply change in an organization.

Application Case 3.3 provides an example of a data warehouse that was developed and delivered an intense competitive advantage for a Dutch retail company. Combining Teradata data warehousing and analytics capabilities with an SAP enterprise information infrastructure led to tremendous success in the marketplace.

Application Case 3.3

Use of Teradata Analytics for SAP Solutions Accelerates Big Data Delivery

The company being profiled within this case study is a privately held Dutch retailer with 2,800 stores across several European countries. This retailer has 15 different brands that include products from toys to cookware, each brand having its own infrastructure. Each business entity is managed independently as one of 15 individual companies in the way they develop their processes, maintain their legacy systems, and make business decisions across finance, IT, supply chain, and general operations.

Background

Meeting the needs of a constantly evolving competitive environment requires global business visibility, which is a challenge for this large retailer with 15 independent brands to manage. To gain better visibility, increase business efficiencies, and lower costs, the retailer decided to develop a corporate strategy to manage data in a centralized system using a single IT department. Data centralization means that all brands will be managed within a single data warehouse and implemented brand by brand to take into account individual business processes and needs. A big challenge for this large retailer is that several systems have to be integrated, including their (15) SAP ERPs, warehouse management systems, point-of-sale (POS) systems, and materials master data.

With a focus on maintaining business agility for sales and margin analysis, the retailer's goal was to provide access to the transactional level of data originating from the roughly 50 SAP tables within each ERP system. The move to a centralized approach was especially exacerbated by the complexity and nuances across the 15 ERP instances. Work was estimated at 400 days of effort per source system to bring this data into their central warehouse. Consequently, they needed a way to justify their expenditure, develop an ongoing value proposition of their data warehouse approach, and develop a way to expedite this process.

Product Acquisition Story

On the business side, the focus is on creating a centralized analytic platform with access to a global view of transactional data. Due to the seasonal nature of retail, being able to leverage multiple years of data is important to help identify seasonal trends, create forecasts, and develop pricing and promotions. The goal is to improve visibility and provide freedom of analytics across their supply chain, materials, sales, and marketing to help this organization become more efficient in the way it does business. Consequently, the retailer selected the Teradata Database because it could handle both the transactional analytics in addition to providing advanced analytics capabilities. Their goal was to support operational analytics and flexibility by loading data without developing DMs or other logical models in advance of users asking business questions. This approach enables them to save data centrally within a Teradata Database while providing future flexibility related to data access, reports, and analytics for all of the brands.

Underestimating the complexities of SAP ERP, the company spent the first 6 months cutting their teeth on a customer homegrown SAP integration. After 6 months with little to show, they recognized the risks and stopped the project to investigate if there were better approaches to this problem. They first met with a major SAP SI, who provided a 400-day integration estimate to load data from just the first SAP ERP system. This would not provide value fast enough, so the retailer escalated the issue and investigated a new Teradata solution used to automate the data acquisition processes when using SAP ERP. Teradata Analytics for SAP Solutions was selected because it was specifically designed to address the challenges associated with bringing data in from SAP ERP to the Teradata Database. The solution also delivers an automated approach to integrating SAP ERP data into the data warehouse and enabled them to load the data required for the first

(Continued)

Application Case 3.3 (Continued)

brand in just 5 days instead of the estimated 400. The retailer spent an additional 45 days adding 25 custom (Z) tables and preparing the data for consumption. This accelerated the integration of SAP data by 800%, thereby saving 350 days of work.

Challenges

Combining a full ERP consolidation project across several legacy systems creates a project with many complexities. Although Teradata Analytics for SAP Solutions provided automation for the SAP-related data management portion of the project, the retailer still encountered technical challenges due to the fact that its data warehousing initiative was combined with a broader integration project. Their approach was to standardize the tools and develop a framework with the first couple of brands that could be applied to the incremental rollout to the rest of the organization.

First, they needed to standardize on an ETL tool and develop a new methodology and way of leveraging ETL. They used the ETL tool as an Extract Load Transform (ELT) tool to maintain the integrity of the granular transactional data. The retailer ended up choosing Informatica® as the ETL standard and its ETL environment by using the ELT tool as just a data mover and job scheduler.

Second, in addition to storing the atomic transactional data, the retailer was able to leverage the Teradata platform to perform all of its business transformations in-database when moving data into the reporting environment. This approach allowed them to keep a copy of the granular transactions, leverage the out-of-the box integrations provided within the Analytics for SAP Solutions to add context to the SAP data, and harness the database power to apply other transformations and analytics.

Third, high data quality was imperative for them. They wanted to ensure that data could be accessed and managed in a consistent way. Material numbers highlight the importance of data governance to this retailer. Material numbers are structured differently across multiple systems and historically would have been reconciled during the load/model process. In this new architecture, they were able to easily overcome this challenge by creating unique material views in the data warehouse to harmonize the material numbers for reporting.

Finally, they required an agile way to deliver data and analytics for both reports and ad hoc analytical access, which could also meet the diverse requirements of the brands. By taking advantage of Teradata partnerships with solution providers such as MicroStrategy®, the retailer was able to access the granular data stored in the data warehouse while using the BI tools to apply the relevant algorithms and leverage the flexibility designed into the data warehouse solution.

The development of the data warehouse as a centralized data access hub was challenging at first due to the requirement to develop a new framework and the overall learning curve because of the change in approach to data warehouse design. Luckily, once this framework was developed, integration using Teradata Analytics for SAP Solutions was simple and repeatable. According to the architect at the European retailer, "Teradata Analytics for SAP is a fast and flexible integrated solution, offering lower project risk, faster development, an integrated semantic model, and direct access to detailed data."

Lessons Learned

Overall, the retailer's goal is to provide a repeatable implementation strategy across their brands to enable better business decisions, improve business efficiencies, and lower operating costs through IT centralization. Although they are still in the early phases of the project, they have already learned from the implementation of integrating their first brand into the Teradata data warehouse. Due to the retailer's use of Teradata Analytics for SAP Solutions, they were able to accelerate the time to value and simplify integration activities. In addition, they were able to develop some of the following takeaways to apply to the integration of their subsequent brands and to similar projects.

- Take the time for due diligence and learn what technologies/solutions exist to support implementations. In this case, the retailer was able to take advantage of Teradata Analytics for SAP Solutions, decreasing time to value and enabling it to focus on analytics as opposed to integration.
- Develop a framework to enable repeatable processes that can address the complexities of

the vast amount of data and custom needs of the business.

- Keep the system design as simple as possible to ensure technology and business adoption.
- Make sure to align technical decisions with the overall vision of enabling business agility.
- Develop a standard data governance approach to ensure data integrity that extends beyond the implementation process so that business and technical users understand how they can apply data for reports and analytics.
- Identify latency requirements to ensure that solutions—both data warehouse and integration approach—support needs. This meant ensuring that the Teradata SAP Solution also supported their operational needs.

These lessons learned apply to the broader implementation and use of Teradata Analytics for SAP. The retailer was committed to centralizing their infrastructure and managing their brands more

effectively. Consequently, they were able to take advantage of a way to automate the process and lessen time to value because of the ability to leverage a targeted solution to tie their ERP solutions to their analytics.

QUESTIONS FOR DISCUSSION

1. What were the challenges faced by the large Dutch retailer?
2. What was the proposed multivendor solution? What were the implementation challenges?
3. What were the lessons learned?

Source: Teradata case study. (2015). 800 percent: Use of Teradata® Analytics for SAP® Solutions accelerates Big Data delivery. assets.teradata.com/resourceCenter/downloads/CaseStudies/EB8559_TAS_Case_Study.pdf?processed=1 (accessed July 2016); Enterprise Management, Teradata-SAP Solution to Big Data analytics. www.enterprisemanagement.com/research/asset.php/3047/800-Percent:-Use-of-Teradata-Analytics-for-SAP-Solutions-Accelerates-Big-Data-Delivery (accessed July 2016).

Clearly defining the business objective, gathering project support from management end users, setting reasonable time frames and budgets, and managing expectations are critical to a successful data warehousing project. A data warehousing strategy is a blueprint for the successful introduction of the data warehouse. The strategy should describe where the company wants to go, why it wants to go there, and what it will do when it gets there. It needs to take into consideration the organization's vision, structure, and culture. See Matney (2003) for the steps that can help in developing a flexible and efficient support strategy. When the plan and support for a data warehouse are established, the organization needs to examine data warehouse vendors. (See Table 3.2 for a sample list of vendors; also see The Data Warehousing Institute [twdi.org] and Information Builders [informationbuilders.com].) Many vendors provide software demos of their data warehousing and BI products.

Data Warehouse Development Approaches

Many organizations need to create the data warehouses used for decision support. Two competing approaches are employed. The first approach is that of Bill Inmon, who is often called "the father of data warehousing." Inmon supports a top-down development approach that adapts traditional relational database tools to the development needs of an enterprise-wide data warehouse, also known as the EDW approach. The second approach is that of Ralph Kimball, who proposed a bottom-up approach that employs dimensional modeling, also known as the DM approach.

Knowing how these two models are alike and how they differ helps us understand the basic data warehouse concepts (e.g., see Breslin, 2004). Table 3.3 compares the two approaches. We describe these approaches in detail next.

TABLE 3.2	Sample List of Data Warehousing Vendors
Vendor	Product Offerings
Business Objects (businessobjects.com)	A comprehensive set of BI and data visualization software (now owned by SAP)
Computer Associates (cai.com)	Comprehensive set of data warehouse (DW) tools and products
DataMirror (datamirror.com)	DW administration, management, and performance products
Data Advantage Group (dataadvantagegroup.com)	Metadata software
Dell (dell.com)	DW servers
Embarcadero Technologies (embarcadero.com)	DW administration, management, and performance products
Greenplum (greenplum.com)	Data warehousing and data appliance solution provider (now owned by EMC)
Harte-Hanks (harte-hanks.com)	Customer relationship management (CRM) products and services
HP (hp.com)	DW servers
Hummingbird Ltd. (hummingbird.com)	DW engines and exploration warehouses
Hyperion Solutions (hyperion.com)	Comprehensive set of DW tools, products, and applications
IBM InfoSphere (www-01.ibm.com/software/data/infosphere)	Data integration, DW, master data management, Big Data products
Informatica (informatica.com)	DW administration, management, and performance products
Microsoft (microsoft.com)	DW tools and products
Netezza	DW software and hardware (DW appliance) provider (now owned by IBM)
Oracle (including PeopleSoft and Siebel; oracle.com)	DW, ERP, and CRM tools, products, and applications
SAS Institute (sas.com)	DW tools, products, and applications
Siemens (siemens.com)	DW servers
Sybase (sybase.com)	Comprehensive set of DW tools and applications
Teradata (teradata.com)	DW tools, DW appliances, DW consultancy, and applications

THE INMON MODEL: THE EDW APPROACH Inmon's approach emphasizes top-down development, employing established database development methodologies and tools, such as entity-relationship diagrams (ERD) and an adjustment of the spiral development approach. The EDW approach does not preclude the creation of DMs. The EDW is the ideal in this approach because it provides a consistent and comprehensive view of the enterprise. Murtaza (1998) presented a framework for developing EDW.

THE KIMBALL MODEL: THE DATA MART APPROACH Kimball's DM strategy is a "plan big, build small" approach. A DM is a subject-oriented or department-oriented data warehouse. It is a scaled-down version of a data warehouse that focuses on the requests of a specific department, such as marketing or sales. This model applies dimensional data modeling, which starts with tables. Kimball advocated a development methodology that

TABLE 3.3   Contrasts between the DM and EDW Development Approaches

Effort	DM Approach	EDW Approach
Scope	One subject area	Several subject areas
Development time	Months	Years
Development cost	$10,000 to $100,000+	$1,000,000+
Development difficulty	Low to medium	High
Data prerequisite for sharing	Common (within business area)	Common (across enterprise)
Sources	Only some operational and external systems	Many operational and external systems
Size	Megabytes to several gigabytes	Gigabytes to petabytes
Time horizon	Near-current and historical data	Historical data
Data transformations	Low to medium	High
Update frequency	Hourly, daily, weekly	Weekly, monthly
Technology		
Hardware	Workstations and departmental servers	Enterprise servers and mainframe computers
Operating system	Windows and Linux	Unix, Z/OS, OS/390
Databases	Workgroup or standard database servers	Enterprise database servers
Usage		
Number of simultaneous users	10s	100s to 1,000s
User types	Business area analysts and managers	Enterprise analysts and senior executives
Business spotlight	Optimizing activities within the business area	Cross-functional optimization and decision making

Sources: Adapted from Van den Hoven, J. (2003). Data marts: Plan big, build small. In *IS Management Handbook,* 8th ed., Boca Raton, FL: CRC Press; Ariyachandra, T., & Watson, H. (2006b). <per Ref List> Which data warehouse architecture is most successful? *Business Intelligence Journal, 11*(1), 4–6.

entails a bottom-up approach, which in the case of data warehouses means building one DM at a time.

WHICH MODEL IS BEST?   There is no one-size-fits-all strategy to data warehousing. An enterprise's data warehousing strategy can evolve from a simple DM to a complex data warehouse in response to user demands, the enterprise's business requirements, and the enterprise's maturity in managing its data resources. For many enterprises, a DM is frequently a convenient first step to acquiring experience in constructing and managing a data warehouse while presenting business users with the benefits of better access to their data; in addition, a DM commonly indicates the business value of data warehousing. Ultimately, engineering an EDW that consolidates old DMs and data warehouses is the ideal solution (see Application Case 3.4). However, the development of individual DMs can often provide many benefits along the way toward developing an EDW, especially if the organization is unable or unwilling to invest in a large-scale project. DMs can also demonstrate feasibility and success in providing benefits. This could potentially lead to an investment in an EDW. Table 3.4 summarizes the most essential characteristic differences between the two models.

TABLE 3.4   Essential Differences between Inmon's and Kimball's Approaches

Characteristic	Inmon	Kimball
Methodology and Architecture		
Overall approach	Top-down	Bottom-up
Architecture structure	Enterprise-wide (atomic) data warehouse "feeds" departmental databases	DMs model a single business process, and enterprise consistency is achieved through a data bus and conformed dimensions
Complexity of the method	Quite complex	Fairly simple
Comparison with established development methodologies	Derived from the spiral methodology	Four-step process; a departure from RDBMS methods
Discussion of physical design	Fairly thorough	Fairly light
Data Modeling		
Data orientation	Subject or data driven	Process oriented
Tools	Traditional (entity-relationship diagrams [ERD], data flow diagrams [DFD])	Dimensional modeling; a departure from relational modeling
End-user accessibility	Low	High
Philosophy		
Primary audience	IT professionals	End users
Place in the organization	Integral part of the corporate information factory	Transformer and retainer of operational data
Objective	Deliver a sound technical solution based on proven database methods and technologies	Deliver a solution that makes it easy for end users to directly query the data and still get reasonable response times

Sources: Adapted from Breslin, M. (2004, Winter). Data warehousing battle of the giants: Comparing the basics of Kimball and Inmon models. *Business Intelligence Journal, 9*(1), 6–20; Ariyachandra, T., & Watson, H. (2006b). Which data warehouse architecture is most successful? *Business Intelligence Journal, 11*(1).

Additional Data Warehouse Development Considerations

Some organizations want to completely outsource their data warehousing efforts. They simply do not want to deal with software and hardware acquisitions, and they do not want to manage their information systems. One alternative is to use hosted data warehouses. In this scenario, another firm—ideally, one that has a lot of experience and expertise—develops and maintains the data warehouse. However, there are security and privacy concerns with this approach. See Technology Insights 3.1 for some details.

Representation of Data in Data Warehouse

A typical data warehouse structure is shown in Figure 3.4. Many variations of data warehouse architecture are possible (see Figure 3.8). No matter what the architecture was, the design of data representation in the data warehouse has always been based on the concept of dimensional modeling. **Dimensional modeling** is a retrieval-based system that supports high-volume query access. Representation and storage of data in a data warehouse should be designed in such a way that not only accommodates but also boosts the processing of complex multidimensional queries. Often, the star schema and the snowflake schema are the means by which dimensional modeling is implemented in data warehouses.

TECHNOLOGY INSIGHTS 3.1
Hosted Data Warehouses

A hosted data warehouse has nearly the same, if not more, functionality as an on-site data warehouse, but it does not consume computer resources on client premises. A hosted data warehouse offers the benefits of BI minus the cost of computer upgrades, network upgrades, software licenses, in-house development, and in-house support and maintenance.

A hosted data warehouse offers the following benefits:

- Requires minimal investment in infrastructure
- Frees up capacity on in-house systems
- Frees up cash flow
- Makes powerful solutions affordable
- Enables powerful solutions that provide for growth
- Offers better-quality equipment and software
- Provides faster connections
- Enables users to access data from remote locations
- Allows a company to focus on core business
- Meets storage needs for large volumes of data

Despite its benefits, a hosted data warehouse is not necessarily a good fit for every organization. Large companies with revenue upwards of $500 million could lose money if they already have underused internal infrastructure and IT staff. Furthermore, companies that see the paradigm shift of outsourcing applications as loss of control of their data are not likely to use a BI service provider. Finally, the most significant and common argument against implementing a hosted data warehouse is that it may be unwise to outsource sensitive applications for reasons of security and privacy.

Sources: Compiled from Thornton, M., & Lampa, M. (2002). Hosted data warehouse. *Journal of Data Warehousing, 7*(2), 27–34; Thornton, M. (2002, March 18). What about security? The most common, but unwarranted, objection to hosted data warehouses. *DM Review, 12*(3), 30–43.

The **star schema** (sometimes referenced as star join schema) is the most commonly used and the simplest style of dimensional modeling. A star schema contains a central fact table surrounded by and connected to several **dimension tables** (Adamson, 2009). The fact table contains a large number of rows that correspond to observed facts and external links (i.e., foreign keys). A fact table contains the descriptive attributes needed to perform decision analysis and query reporting, and foreign keys are used to link to dimension tables. The decision analysis attributes consist of performance measures, operational metrics, aggregated measures (e.g., sales volumes, customer retention rates, profit margins, production costs, scrap rate), and all the other metrics needed to analyze the organization's performance. In other words, the fact table primarily addresses what the data warehouse supports for decision analysis.

Surrounding the central fact tables (and linked via foreign keys) are dimension tables. The dimension tables contain classification and aggregation information about the central fact rows. Dimension tables contain attributes that describe the data contained within the fact table; they address how data will be analyzed and summarized. Dimension tables have a one-to-many relationship with rows in the central fact table. In querying, the dimensions are used to slice and dice the numerical values in the fact table to address the requirements of an ad hoc information need. The star schema is designed to provide fast query-response time, simplicity, and ease of maintenance for read-only database

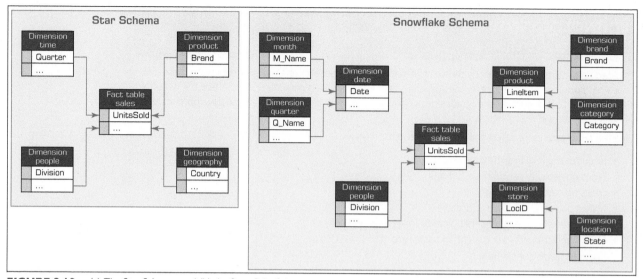

FIGURE 3.10   (a) The Star Schema, and (b) the Snowflake Schema.

structures. A simple star schema is shown in Figure 3.10a. The star schema is considered a special case of the snowflake schema.

The **snowflake schema** is a logical arrangement of tables in a multidimensional database in such a way that the entity-relationship diagram resembles a snowflake in shape. Closely related to the star schema, the snowflake schema is represented by centralized fact tables (usually only one), which are connected to multiple dimensions. In the snowflake schema, however, dimensions are normalized into multiple related tables, whereas the star schema's dimensions are denormalized, with each dimension being represented by a single table. A simple snowflake schema is shown in Figure 3.10b.

Analysis of Data in Data Warehouse

Once the data is properly stored in a data warehouse, it can be used in various ways to support organizational decision making. OLAP is arguably the most commonly used data analysis technique in data warehouses, and it has been growing in popularity due to the exponential increase in data volumes and the recognition of the business value of data-driven analytics. Simply, OLAP is an approach to quickly answer ad hoc questions by executing multidimensional analytical queries against organizational data repositories (i.e., data warehouses, DMs).

OLAP versus OLTP

OLTP (online transaction processing system) is a term used for a transaction system that is primarily responsible for capturing and storing data related to day-to-day business functions such as ERP, CRM, SCM, POS, and so forth. An OLTP system addresses a critical business need, automating daily business transactions, and running real-time reports and routine analysis. But these systems are not designed for ad hoc analysis and complex queries that deal with a number of data items. OLAP, on the other hand, is designed to address this need by providing ad hoc analysis of organizational data much more effectively and efficiently. OLAP and OLTP rely heavily on each other: OLAP uses the data captured by OLTP, and OLTP automates the business processes that are managed

TABLE 3.5   A Comparison between OLTP and OLAP

Criteria	OLTP	OLAP
Purpose	To carry out day-to-day business functions	To support decision making and provide answers to business and management queries
Data source	Transaction database (a normalized data repository primarily focused on efficiency and consistency)	Data warehouse or DM (a nonnormalized data repository primarily focused on accuracy and completeness)
Reporting	Routine, periodic, narrowly focused reports	Ad hoc, multidimensional, broadly focused reports and queries
Resource requirements	Ordinary relational databases	Multiprocessor, large-capacity, specialized databases
Execution speed	Fast (recording of business transactions and routine reports)	Slow (resource intensive, complex, large-scale queries)

by decisions supported by OLAP. Table 3.5 provides a multicriteria comparison between OLTP and OLAP.

OLAP Operations

The main operational structure in OLAP is based on a concept called cube. A **cube** in OLAP is a multidimensional data structure (actual or virtual) that allows fast analysis of data. It can also be defined as the capability of efficiently manipulating and analyzing data from multiple perspectives. The arrangement of data into cubes aims to overcome a limitation of relational databases: Relational databases are not well suited for near instantaneous analysis of large amounts of data. Instead, they are better suited for manipulating records (adding, deleting, and updating data) that represent a series of transactions. Although many report-writing tools exist for relational databases, these tools are slow when a multidimensional query that encompasses many database tables needs to be executed.

Using OLAP, an analyst can navigate through the database and screen for a particular subset of the data (and its progression over time) by changing the data's orientations and defining analytical calculations. These types of user-initiated navigation of data through the specification of slices (via rotations) and **drill down**/up (via aggregation and disaggregation) is sometimes called "slice and dice." Commonly used OLAP operations include slice and dice, drill down, roll-up, and pivot.

- *Slice.*   A slice is a subset of a multidimensional array (usually a two-dimensional representation) corresponding to a single value set for one (or more) of the dimensions not in the subset. A simple slicing operation on a three-dimensional cube is shown in Figure 3.11.
- *Dice.*   The dice operation is a slice on more than two dimensions of a data cube.
- *Drill Down/Up.*   Drilling down or up is a specific OLAP technique whereby the user navigates among levels of data ranging from the most summarized (up) to the most detailed (down).
- *Roll-up.*   A roll-up involves computing all the data relationships for one or more dimensions. To do this, a computational relationship or formula might be defined.
- *Pivot.*   This is used to change the dimensional orientation of a report or ad hoc query-page display.

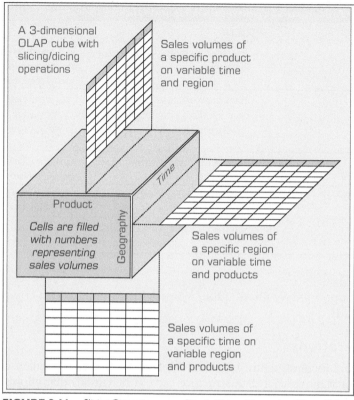

FIGURE 3.11   Slicing Operations on a Simple Three-Dimensional Data Cube.

SECTION 3.6 REVIEW QUESTIONS

1. List the benefits of data warehouses.

2. List several criteria for selecting a data warehouse vendor, and describe why they are important.

3. What is OLAP, and how does it differ from OLTP?

4. What is a cube? What do drill down, roll-up, slice, and dice mean?

3.7 Data Warehousing Implementation Issues

Implementing a data warehouse is generally a massive effort that must be planned and executed according to established methods. However, the project life cycle has many facets, and no single person can be an expert in each area. Here we discuss specific ideas and issues as they relate to data warehousing.

People want to know how successful their BI and data warehousing initiatives are in comparison to those of other companies. Ariyachandra and Watson (2006a) proposed some benchmarks for BI and data warehousing success. Watson, Gerard, Gonzalez, Haywood, and Fenton (1999) researched data warehouse failures. Their results showed that people define a "failure" in different ways, and this was confirmed by Ariyachandra and Watson (2006a). The Data Warehousing Institute (tdwi.org) has developed a data warehousing maturity model that an enterprise can apply to benchmark its evolution. The model offers a fast means to gauge where the organization's data warehousing initiative is now and where it needs to go next. The maturity model consists of six stages: prenatal, infant, child, teenager, adult, and sage. Business value rises as the data warehouse progresses through each succeeding stage. The stages are identified by a number of characteristics, including scope, analytic structure, executive perceptions, types of analytics, stewardship, funding, technology platform, change management, and administration. See Eckerson, Hackathorn, McGivern, Twogood, and Watson (2009) and Eckerson (2003) for more details.

Data warehouse projects have many risks. Most of them are also found in other IT projects, but data warehousing risks are more serious because data warehouses are expensive, time-and-resource demanding, large-scale projects. Each risk should be assessed at the inception of the project. When developing a successful data warehouse, it is important to carefully consider various risks and avoid the following issues:

- *Starting with the wrong sponsorship chain.*   You need an executive sponsor who has influence over the necessary resources to support and invest in the data warehouse. You also need an executive project driver, someone who has earned the respect of other executives, has a healthy skepticism about technology, and is decisive but flexible. You also need an IS/IT manager to head up the project.
- *Setting expectations that you cannot meet.*   You do not want to frustrate executives at the moment of truth. Every data warehousing project has two phases: Phase 1 is the selling phase, in which you internally market the project by selling the benefits to those who have access to needed resources. Phase 2 is the struggle to meet the expectations described in Phase 1. For a mere $1 to $7 million, hopefully, you can deliver.
- *Engaging in politically naive behavior.*   Do not simply state that a data warehouse will help managers make better decisions. This may imply that you feel they have been making bad decisions until now. Sell the idea that they will be able to get the information they need to help in decision making.
- *Loading the warehouse with information just because it is available.*   Do not let the data warehouse become a data landfill. This would unnecessarily slow down the use of the system. There is a trend toward real-time computing and analysis. Data warehouses must be shut down to load data in a timely way.
- *Believing that data warehousing database design is the same as transactional database design.*   In general, it is not. The goal of data warehousing is to access aggregates rather than a single or a few records, as in transaction-processing systems. Content is also different, as is evident in how data are organized. DBMS tend to be nonredundant, normalized, and relational, whereas data warehouses are redundant, not normalized, and multidimensional.
- *Choosing a data warehouse manager who is technology oriented rather than user oriented.*   One key to data warehouse success is to understand that the users must get what they need, not advanced technology for technology's sake.
- *Focusing on traditional internal record-oriented data and ignoring the value of external data and of text, images, and, perhaps, sound and video.*   Data come in many formats and must be made accessible to the right people at the right time and in the right format. They must be cataloged properly.
- *Delivering data with overlapping and confusing definitions.*   Data cleansing is a critical aspect of data warehousing. It includes reconciling conflicting data definitions and formats organization-wide. Politically, this may be difficult because it involves change, typically at the executive level.
- *Believing promises of performance, capacity, and scalability.*   Data warehouses generally require more capacity and speed than is originally budgeted for. Plan ahead to scale up.
- *Believing that your problems are over when the data warehouse is up and running.*   DSS/BI projects tend to evolve continually. Each deployment is an

iteration of the prototyping process. There will always be a need to add more and different data sets to the data warehouse, as well as additional analytic tools for existing and additional groups of decision makers. High energy and annual budgets must be planned for because success breeds success. Data warehousing is a continuous process.

- *Focusing on ad hoc data mining and periodic reporting instead of alerts.* The natural progression of information in a data warehouse is (1) extract the data from legacy systems, cleanse them, and feed them to the warehouse; (2) support ad hoc reporting until you learn what people want; and (3) convert the ad hoc reports into regularly scheduled reports. This process of learning what people want in order to provide it seems natural, but it is not optimal or even practical. Managers are busy and need time to read reports. Alert systems are better than periodic reporting systems and can make a data warehouse mission critical. Alert systems monitor the data flowing into the warehouse and inform all key people who have a need to know as soon as a critical event occurs.

In many organizations, a data warehouse will be successful only if there is strong senior management support for its development and if there is a project champion who is high up in the organizational chart. Although this would likely be true for any large-scale IT project, it is especially important for a data warehouse realization. The successful implementation of a data warehouse results in the establishment of an architectural framework that may allow for decision analysis throughout an organization and in some cases also provides comprehensive SCM by granting access to information on an organization's customers and suppliers. The implementation of Web-based data warehouses (sometimes called *Webhousing*) has facilitated ease of access to vast amounts of data, but it is difficult to determine the hard benefits associated with a data warehouse. Hard benefits are defined as benefits to an organization that can be expressed in monetary terms. Many organizations have limited IT resources and must prioritize projects. Management support and a strong project champion can help ensure that a data warehouse project will receive the resources necessary for successful implementation. Data warehouse resources can be significantly costly, in some cases requiring high-end processors and large increases in direct-access storage devices. Web-based data warehouses may also have special security requirements to ensure that only authorized users have access to the data.

User participation in the development of data and access modeling is a critical success factor in data warehouse development. During data modeling, expertise is required to determine what data are needed, define business rules associated with the data, and decide what aggregations and other calculations may be necessary. Access modeling is needed to determine how data are to be retrieved from a data warehouse, and it assists in the physical definition of the warehouse by helping to define which data require indexing. It may also indicate whether dependent DMs are needed to facilitate information retrieval. Team skills are needed to develop and implement a data warehouse, including in-depth knowledge of the database technology and development tools used. Source systems and development technology, as mentioned previously, reference the many inputs and the processes used to load and maintain a data warehouse.

Application Case 3.4 presents an excellent example of a large-scale implementation of an integrated data warehouse by a state government.

Massive Data Warehouses and Scalability

In addition to flexibility, a data warehouse needs to support scalability. The main issues pertaining to scalability are the amount of data in the warehouse, how quickly the warehouse is expected to grow, the number of concurrent users, and the complexity of user queries. A data warehouse must scale both horizontally and vertically. The warehouse will

Application Case 3.4

EDW Helps Connect State Agencies in Michigan

Through customer service, resource optimization, and the innovative use of information and technology, the Michigan Department of Technology, Management and Budget (DTMB) impacts every area of government. Nearly 10,000 users in 5 major departments, 20 agencies, and more than 100 bureaus rely on the EDW to do their jobs more effectively and better serve Michigan residents. The EDW achieves $1 million per business day in financial benefits.

The EDW helped Michigan achieve $200 million in annual financial benefits within the Department of Community Health alone, plus another $75 million per year within the Department of Human Services (DHS). These savings include program integrity benefits, cost avoidance due to improved outcomes, sanction avoidance, operational efficiencies, and the recovery of inappropriate payments within its Medicaid program.

The Michigan DHS data warehouse (DW) provides unique and innovative information critical to the efficient operation of the agency from both a strategic and tactical level. Over the last 10 years, the DW has yielded a 15:1 cost-effectiveness ratio. Consolidated information from the DW now contributes to nearly every function of DHS, including accurate delivery of and accounting for benefits

delivered to almost 2.5 million DHS public assistance clients.

Michigan has been ambitious in its attempts to solve real-life problems through the innovative sharing and comprehensive analyses of data. Its approach to BI/DW has always been "enterprise" (statewide) in nature, rather than having separate BI/DW platforms for each business area or state agency. By removing barriers to sharing enterprise data across business units, Michigan has leveraged massive amounts of data to create innovative approaches to the use of BI/DW, delivering efficient, reliable enterprise solutions using multiple channels.

QUESTIONS FOR DISCUSSION

1. Why would a state invest in a large and expensive IT infrastructure (such as an EDW)?
2. What is the size and complexity of the EDW used by state agencies in Michigan?
3. What were the challenges, the proposed solution, and the obtained results of the EDW?

Sources: Compiled from TDWI Best Practices Awards 2012 Winner, Enterprise Data Warehousing, Government and Non-Profit Category. Michigan Departments of Technology, Management & Budget (DTMB), Community Health (DCH), and Human Services (DHS). *TDWI What Works, 34,* 22; michigan.michigan.gov.

grow as a function of data growth and the need to expand the warehouse to support new business functionality. Data growth may be a result of the addition of current cycle data (e.g., this month's results) and/or historical data.

Hicks (2001) described huge databases and data warehouses. Walmart is continually increasing the size of its massive data warehouse. Walmart is believed to use a warehouse with hundreds of terabytes of data to study sales trends, track inventory, and perform other tasks. IBM recently publicized its 50-terabyte warehouse benchmark (IBM, 2009). The U.S. Department of Defense is using a 5-petabyte data warehouse and repository to hold medical records for 9 million military personnel. Because of the storage required to archive its news footage, CNN also has a petabyte-sized data warehouse.

Given that the size of data warehouses is expanding at an exponential rate, scalability is an important issue. Good scalability means that queries and other data-access functions will grow (ideally) linearly with the size of the warehouse. See Rosenberg (2006) for approaches to improve query performance. In practice, specialized methods have been developed to create scalable data warehouses. Scalability is difficult when managing hundreds of terabytes or more. Terabytes of data have considerable inertia, occupy a lot of physical space, and require powerful computers. Some firms use parallel processing, and others use clever indexing and search schemes to manage their data. Some spread their data across different physical data stores. As more data warehouses approach the petabyte size, better and better solutions to scalability continue to be developed.

Hall (2002) also addressed scalability issues. AT&T is an industry leader in deploying and using massive data warehouses. With its 26-terabyte data warehouse, AT&T can detect fraudulent use of calling cards and investigate calls related to kidnappings and other crimes. It also used the capacity to compute millions of call-in votes from TV viewers selecting the next American Idol. For a sample of successful data warehousing implementations, see Edwards (2003). Jukic and Lang (2004) examined the trends and specific issues related to the use of offshore resources in the development and support of data warehousing and BI applications. Davison (2003) indicated that IT-related offshore outsourcing had been growing at 20 to 25% per year. When considering offshoring data warehousing projects, careful consideration must be given to culture and security (for details, see Jukic & Lang, 2004).

SECTION 3.7 REVIEW QUESTIONS

1. What are the major DW implementation tasks that can be performed in parallel?
2. List and discuss the most pronounced DW implementation guidelines.
3. When developing a successful data warehouse, what are the most important risks and issues to consider and potentially avoid?
4. What is scalability? How does it apply to DW?

3.8 Data Warehouse Administration, Security Issues, and Future Trends

Data warehouses provide a distinct competitive edge to enterprises that effectively create and use them. Due to its huge size and its intrinsic nature, a data warehouse requires especially strong monitoring to sustain satisfactory efficiency and productivity. The successful administration and management of a data warehouse entails skills and proficiency that go past what is required of a traditional database administrator (DBA). A **data warehouse administrator (DWA)** should be familiar with high-performance software, hardware, and networking technologies. He or she should also possess solid business insight. Because data warehouses feed BI systems and DSS that help managers with their decision-making activities, the DWA should be familiar with the decision-making processes to suitably design and maintain the data warehouse structure. It is particularly significant for a DWA to keep the existing requirements and capabilities of the data warehouse stable while simultaneously providing flexibility for rapid improvements. Finally, a DWA must possess excellent communication skills. See Benander, Benander, Fadlalla, and James (2000) for a description of the key differences between a DBA and a DWA.

Security and privacy of information are main and significant concerns for a data warehouse professional. The U.S. government has passed regulations (e.g., the Gramm-Leach-Bliley privacy and safeguards rules, the Health Insurance Portability and Accountability Act of 1996 [HIPAA]), instituting obligatory requirements in the management of customer information. Hence, companies must create security procedures that are effective yet flexible to conform to numerous privacy regulations. According to Elson and LeClerc (2005), effective security in a data warehouse should focus on four main areas:

1. Establishing effective corporate and security policies and procedures. An effective security policy should start at the top, with executive management, and should be communicated to all individuals within the organization.
2. Implementing logical security procedures and techniques to restrict access. This includes user authentication, access controls, and encryption technology.
3. Limiting physical access to the data center environment.
4. Establishing an effective internal control review process with an emphasis on security and privacy.

In the near term, data warehousing developments will be determined by noticeable factors (e.g., data volumes, increased intolerance for latency, the diversity and complexity of data types) and less noticeable factors (e.g., unmet end-user requirements for dashboards, balanced scorecards, master data management, information quality). Given these drivers, Moseley (2009) and Agosta (2006) suggested that data warehousing trends will lean toward simplicity, value, and performance.

The Future of Data Warehousing

The field of data warehousing has been a vibrant area in IT in the last couple of decades, and the evidence in the BI/BA and Big Data world shows that the importance of the field will only get even more interesting. Following are some of the recently popularized concepts and technologies that will play a significant role in defining the future of data warehousing.

Sourcing (mechanisms for acquisition of data from diverse and dispersed sources):

- *Web, social media, and Big Data.* The recent upsurge in the use of the Web for personal as well as business purposes coupled with the tremendous interest in social media creates opportunities for analysts to tap into very rich data sources. Because of the sheer volume, velocity, and variety of the data, a new term, "Big Data," has been coined to name the phenomenon. Taking advantage of Big Data requires development of new and dramatically improved BI/BA technologies, which will result in a revolutionized data warehousing world.
- *Open source software.* Use of open source software tools is increasing at an unprecedented level in warehousing, BI, and data integration. There are good reasons for the upswing of open source software used in data warehousing (Russom, 2009): (1) the recession has driven up interest in low-cost open source software, (2) open source tools are coming into a new level of maturity, and (3) open source software augments traditional enterprise software without replacing it.
- *SaaS (software as a service), "The Extended ASP Model."* SaaS is a creative way of deploying information systems applications where the provider licenses its applications to customers for use as a service on demand (usually over the Internet). SaaS software vendors may host the application on their own servers or upload the application to the consumer site. In essence, SaaS is the new and improved version of the ASP model. For data warehouse customers, finding SaaS-based software applications and resources that meet specific needs and requirements can be challenging. As these software offerings become more agile, the appeal and the actual use of SaaS as the choice of data warehousing platform will also increase.
- *Cloud computing.* Cloud computing is perhaps the newest and the most innovative platform choice to come along in years. Numerous hardware and software resources are pooled and virtualized, so that they can be freely allocated to applications and software platforms as resources are needed. This enables information systems applications to dynamically scale up as workloads increase. Although cloud computing and similar virtualization techniques are fairly well established for operational

applications today, they are just now starting to be used as data warehouse platforms of choice. The dynamic allocation of a cloud is particularly useful when the data volume of the warehouse varies unpredictably, making capacity planning difficult.

- **Data lakes.** With the emergence of Big Data, there came a new data platform: data lake, which is a large storage location that can hold vast quantities of data (mostly unstructured) in its native/raw format for future/potential analytics consumption. Traditionally speaking, whereas a data warehouse stores structured data, a data lake stores all kinds of data. While they are both data storage mechanisms, a data warehouse is all about structured/tabular data and a data lake is about all types of data. Although much has been said and written about the relationship between the two (some of which suggests that data lake is the future name of data warehouses), as it stands, a data lake is not a replacement for a data warehouse; rather, they are complementary to one another. Technology Insight 3.2 digs deeper into explaining data lakes and their role in the worlds of data warehousing and business analytics.

TECHNOLOGY INSIGHT 3.2
Data Lakes

With the emergence of Big Data phenomenon, a new term, "data lake," has been coined. Many believe that a data lake is just the reincarnation of the good old data warehouse. The underlying assumption suggests that in the age of Big Data, the old way of data storage is not suitable (or sufficient) and therefore a new way of data storage/management is needed, which is paving the way for data lakes. Although most believe that a data lake is the way to go and are ready to jump in, others are standing back and being more cautious (and perhaps skeptical of its viability), calling it a swamp. So, what really is a data lake? Simply put, a data lake is a large storage location that can hold huge quantities of data (structured, unstructured, or semistructured) in its native/raw format for a potential future use. Whereas a data warehouse stores structured data in related tables, files, or folders, a data lake uses a loosely defined (i.e., unstructured) architecture to store all kinds of data. The main commonality between a data lake and data warehouse is that they are both data storage mechanisms, and conversely, the main difference is that one is all about structured/tabular data and the other is about all kinds of data (i.e., Big Data).

Although the definition of data lake changes among data scientists, the most commonly used definition of it comes from James Dixon, the founder and CTO of Pentaho, who has also been credited with coming up with the term itself. This is how he describes a data lake (Dixon, 2010):

> If you think of a data mart as a store of bottled water—cleansed and packaged and structured for easy consumption—the data lake is a large body of water in a more natural state. The contents of the data lake stream in from a source to fill the lake, and various users of the lake can come to examine, dive in, or take samples.

Perhaps the best way to characterize a data lake is to compare it to a data warehouse in a multidimensional table. Table 3.6 is a summary table (followed by brief descriptions) of the most commonly used dimensions to compare a data lake to a data warehouse (Dull, 2016; Campbell, 2015).

Data. A data warehouse only stores data that has been modeled/aggregated/structured, whereas a data lake stores all kinds of data—structured, semistructured, and unstructured—in its native/raw format.

Processing. Before loading data into a data warehouse, we first need to give it some shape and structure—that is, we need to model it into a star or snowflake schema, which is called schema-on-write. With a data lake, we just load in the raw data, as-is, and then when we are ready to use the data, we give it a shape or structure, which is called schema-on-read. These are two very different processing approaches.

Retrieval speed. For more than two decades, many algorithms have been developed to improve the speed at which the data is retrieved from large and feature-rich data warehouses. Such techniques included triggers, columnar data representation, in-database processing. As of now, the retrieval of data (which can be in any form or fashion—including unstructured text) is a time-demanding activity.

TABLE 3.6 A Simple Comparison between a Data Warehouse and a Data Lake

Dimension	Data Warehouse	Data Lake
The nature of data	Structured, processed	Any data in raw/native format
Processing	Schema-on-write (SQL)	Schema-on-read (NoSQL)
Retrieval speed	Very fast	Slow
Cost	Expensive for large data volumes	Designed for low-cost storage
Agility	Less agile, fixed configuration	Highly agile, flexible configuration
Novelty/newness	Not new/matured	Very new/maturing
Security	Well-secured	Not yet well-secured
Users	Business professionals	Data scientists

Storage.   One of the primary features of Big Data technologies like Hadoop is that the cost of storing data is relatively low as compared to the data warehouse. There are two key reasons for this: First, Hadoop is open source software, so the licensing and community support is free. And second, Hadoop is designed to be installed on low-cost commodity hardware.

Agility.   A data warehouse is a highly structured repository, by definition. It's not technically hard to change the structure, but it can be very time consuming given all the business processes that are tied to it. A data lake, on the other hand, lacks the structure of a data warehouse—which gives developers and data scientists the ability to easily configure and reconfigure their models, queries, and apps on-the-fly.

Novelty/newness.   The technologies underlying data warehousing have been around for a long time. Most of the innovations have been accomplished in the last 20–30 years. Therefore, there is very little, if any, newness coming out of data warehousing (with the exclusion of the technologies to leverage and use Big Data within a data warehouse). On the other hand, data lakes are new and are going through a novelty/innovation phase to become a mainstream data storage technology.

Security.   Because data warehouse technologies have been around for decades the ability to secure data in a data warehouse is much more mature than securing data in a data lake. It should be noted, however, that there is a significant effort being placed on security right now in the Big Data industry. It is not a question of if, but when, the security of the data lakes will meet the needs and wants of the analytics professionals and other end users.

Users.   For a long time, the motto in the analytic world has been "Business intelligence and analytics for everyone!" We have built the data warehouse and invited "everyone" to come, but have they come? On average, only 20–25% of them have. Is it the same cry for the data lake? Will we build the data lake and invite everyone to come? Maybe in the future. For now, a data lake, at this point in its maturity, is best suited for the data scientists.

In summary, a data lake and a data warehouse are not the same. Also, the data lake is not Data Warehouse 2.0 (as suggested by some) or a replacement for the data warehouse. They both are needed and therefore optimized for different data mediums and different tasks/purposes. That is, they need to coexist in the analytics world (at least for a while—until data lakes mature to a level to accomplish what nowadays data warehouses are good for). The goal is to design and properly use each for what they were intended to do—use the best option for the job, which may turn out to be a hybrid of data warehouse and data lake storage mediums.

Sources: Campbell, C. (2015). Top five differences between data lakes and data warehouses. www.blue-granite.com/blog/bid/402596/Top-Five-Differences-between-Data-Lakes-and-Data-Warehouses (accessed July 2016); Woods, D. (2011, July). Big Data requires a big, new architecture. *Forbes.*www.forbes.com/sites/ciocentral/2011/07/21/big-data-requires-a-big-new-architecture/#598623291d75 (accessed August 2016); Dixon, J. (2010). Pentaho, Hadoop, and data lakes. James Dixon's Blog.https://jamesdixon.wordpress.com/2010/10/14/pentaho-hadoop-and-data-lakes/ (accessed August 2016); Dull, T. (2016). Data lake vs data warehouse: Key differences. KDnuggets.com. http://www.kdnuggets.com/2015/09/data-lake-vs-data-warehouse-key-differences.html (accessed August 2016).

Infrastructure (architectural—hardware and software—enhancements):

- *Columnar (a new way to store and access data in the database).* A column-oriented database management system (also commonly called a *columnar database*) is a system that stores data tables as sections of columns of data rather than as rows of data (which is the way most RDBMS do it). That is, these columnar databases store data by columns instead of rows (all values of a single column are stored consecutively on disk memory). Such a structure gives a much finer grain of control to the RDBMS. It can access only the columns required for the query as opposed to being forced to access all columns of the row. It performs significantly better for queries that need a small percentage of the columns in the tables they are in, but performs significantly worse when you need most of the columns due to the overhead in attaching all of the columns together to form the result sets. Comparisons between row-oriented and column-oriented data layouts are typically concerned with the efficiency of hard disk access for a given workload (which happens to be one of the most time-consuming operations in a computer). Based on the task at hand, one may have significant advantages over the other. Column-oriented organizations are more efficient when (1) an aggregate needs to be computed over many rows but only for a notably smaller subset of all columns of data, because reading that smaller subset of data can be faster than reading all data; and (2) new values of a column are supplied for all rows at once because that column data can be written efficiently and replace old column data without touching any other columns for the rows. Row-oriented organizations are more efficient when (1) many columns of a single row are required at the same time, and when row size is relatively small, as the entire row can be retrieved with a single-disk seek; and (2) writing a new row if all of the column data is supplied at the same time, as the entire row can be written with a single disk seek. In addition, because the data stored in a column is of uniform type, it lends itself better for compression. That is, significant storage size optimization is available in column-oriented data that is not available in row-oriented data. Such optimal compression of data reduces storage size, making it more economically justifiable to pursue in-memory or solid-state storage alternatives.
- *Real-time data warehousing.* **Real-time data warehousing** (**RDW**) implies that the refresh cycle of an existing data warehouse to update the data is more frequent (almost at the same time as the data becomes available at operational databases). These RDW systems can achieve near real-time updates of data, where the data latency typically is in the range from minutes to hours. As the latency gets smaller, the cost of data updates seems to be increasing exponentially. Future advancements in many technological fronts (ranging from automatic data acquisition to intelligent software agents) are needed to make RDW a reality with an affordable price tag.
- *Data warehouse appliances (all-in-one solutions to DW).* A data warehouse appliance consists of an integrated set of servers, storage, operating system(s), database management systems, and software specifically preinstalled and preoptimized for data warehousing. In practice, data warehouse appliances provide solutions for the mid-warehouse to Big Data warehouse market, offering low-cost performance on data volumes in the terabyte to petabyte range. To improve performance, most data warehouse appliance vendors use massively parallel processing architectures. Even though most database and data warehouse vendors provide appliances nowadays, many believe that Teradata was the first to provide a commercial data warehouse appliance product. What is most currently observed is the emergence of data warehouse bundles where vendors combine their hardware and database software as a data warehouse platform. From a benefits standpoint, data warehouse appliances have significantly low total cost of ownership, which includes initial purchase costs,

ongoing maintenance costs, and the cost of changing capacity as the data grows. The resource cost for monitoring and tuning the data warehouse makes up a large part of the total cost of ownership, often as much as 80%. DW appliances reduce administration for day-to-day operations, setup, and integration. Because data warehouse appliances provide a single-vendor solution, they tend to better optimize the hardware and software within the appliance. Such a unified integration maximizes the chances of successful integration and testing of the DBMS, storage, and operating system by avoiding some of the compatibility issues that arise from multivendor solutions. A data warehouse appliance also provides a single point of contact for problem resolution and a much simpler upgrade path for both software and hardware.

- *Data management technologies and practices.* Some of the most pressing needs for a next-generation data warehouse platform involve technologies and practices that we generally don't think of as part of the platform. In particular, many users need to update the data management tools that process data for use through the data warehousing. The future holds strong growth for master data management (MDM). This relatively new, but extremely important, concept is gaining popularity for many reasons, including the following: (1) tighter integration with operational systems demands MDM; (2) most data warehouses still lack MDM and data quality functions; and (3) regulatory and financial reports must be perfectly clean and accurate.

- *In-database processing technology (putting the algorithms where the data is).* In-database processing (also called *in-database analytics*) refers to the integration of the algorithmic extent of data analytics into data warehousing. By doing so, the data and the analytics that work off the data live within the same environment. Having the two in close proximity increases the efficiency of the computationally intensive analytics procedures. Today, many large database-driven decision support systems, such as those used for credit card fraud detection and investment bank risk management, use this technology because it provides significant performance improvements over traditional methods in a decision environment where time is of the essence. In-database processing is a complex endeavor compared to the traditional way of conducting analytics, where the data is moved out of the database (often in a flat-file format that consists of rows and columns) into a separate analytics environment (such as SAS Enterprise Modeler, Statistica Data Miner, or IBM SPSS Modeler) for processing. In-database processing makes more sense for high-throughput, real-time application environments, including fraud detection, credit scoring, risk management, transaction processing, pricing and margin analysis, usage-based micro-segmenting, behavioral ad targeting, and recommendation engines, such as those used by customer service organizations to determine next-best actions. In-database processing is performed and promoted as a feature by many of the major data warehousing vendors, including Teradata (integrating SAS analytics capabilities into the data warehouse appliances), IBM Netezza, EMC Greenplum, and Sybase, among others.

- *In-memory storage technology (moving the data in the memory for faster processing).* Conventional database systems, such as RDBMS, typically use physical hard drives to store data for an extended period of time. When a data-related process is requested by an application, the database management system loads the data (or parts of the data) into the main memory, processes it, and responds back to the application. Although data (or parts of the data) are cached temporarily in the main memory in a database management system, the primary storage location remains a magnetic hard disk. In contrast, an in-memory database system keeps the data permanently in the main memory. When a data-related process is requested by an application, the database management system directly accesses the data, which is already in the main memory, processes it, and responds back to the requesting application. This direct access to data in main memory makes the processing of data orders of magnitude faster than the traditional method. So the main benefit of in-memory technology (may be the only benefit of it) is the incredible speed at which it accesses the data. The disadvantages include the cost of paying for a very large main memory (even though it is getting cheaper, it still costs a great deal to have a large enough main memory to hold all of a company's data) and the need for sophisticated data recovery strategies (because main memory is volatile and can be wiped out accidentally).

- *New database management systems.* A data warehouse platform consists of several basic components, of which the most critical is the database management system (DBMS). This is only natural, given the fact that the DBMS is the component of the platform where the most work must be done to implement a data model and optimize it for query performance. Therefore, the DBMS is where many next-generation innovations are expected to happen.
- *Advanced analytics.* There are different analytic methods users can choose as they move beyond basic OLAP-based methods and into advanced analytics. Some users choose advanced analytic methods based on data mining, predictive analytics, statistics, artificial intelligence, and so on. Still, the majority of users seem to be choosing SQL-based methods. Whether SQL-based or not, advanced analytics seem to be among the most important promises of next-generation data warehousing.

The future of data warehousing seems to be full of promises and significant challenges. As the world of business becomes more global and complex, the need for BI and data warehousing tools will also become more prominent. The fast-improving IT tools and techniques seem to be moving in the right direction to address the needs of the future BI systems.

SECTION 3.8 REVIEW QUESTIONS

1. What steps can an organization take to ensure the security and confidentiality of customer data in its data warehouse?
2. What skills should a DWA possess? Why?
3. What recent technologies may shape the future of data warehousing? Why?

3.9 Business Performance Management

Many data warehouse implementations end up with the development of a BPM system. In the business and trade literature, BPM has a number of names, including corporate performance management (CPM), enterprise performance management (EPM), and strategic enterprise management (SEM). CPM was coined by the market analyst firm Gartner (gartner.com). EPM is a term associated with Oracle's (oracle.com) offering by the same name. SEM is the term that SAP (sap.com) uses. In this chapter, BPM is preferred over the other terms because it is the earliest, the most generally used, and the one that does not closely tie to a single solution provider. The term **business performance management (BPM)** refers to the business processes, methodologies, metrics, and technologies used by enterprises to measure, monitor, and manage business performance. It encompasses three key components (Colbert, 2009):

1. A set of integrated, closed-loop management and analytic processes (supported by technology) that addresses financial as well as operational activities

2. Tools for businesses to define strategic goals and then measure and manage performance against those goals

3. A core set of processes, including financial and operational planning, consolidation and reporting, modeling, analysis, and monitoring of key performance indicators (KPIs), linked to organizational strategy

Closed-Loop BPM Cycle

Maybe the most significant differentiator of BPM from any other BI tools and practices is its strategy focus. BPM encompasses a closed-loop set of processes that link strategy to execution to optimize business performance (see Figure 3.12). The loop implies that optimum performance is achieved by setting goals and objectives (i.e., strategize), establishing initiatives and plans to achieve those goals (i.e., plan), monitoring actual performance against the goals and objectives (i.e., monitor), and taking corrective action (i.e., act and adjust). The continuous and repetitive nature of the cycle implies that the completion of an iteration leads to a new and improved one (supporting continued process improvement efforts). In the following section these four processes are described.

1. ***Strategize: Where do we want to go?***   Strategy, in general terms, is a high-level plan of action, encompassing a long period of time (often several years) to achieve a defined goal. It is especially necessary in a situation where there are numerous constraints (driven by market conditions, resource availabilities, and legal/political alterations) to deal with on the way to achieving the goal. In a business setting, strategy is the art and the science of crafting decisions that help businesses achieve their goals. More specifically, it is the process of identifying and stating the organization's mission, vision, and objectives, and developing plans (at different levels of granularity—strategic, tactical, and operational) to achieve these objectives.

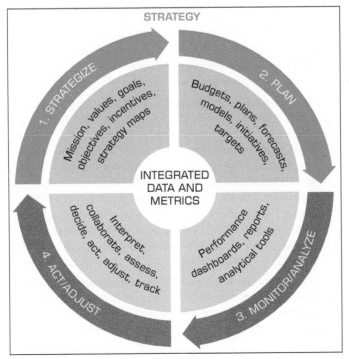

FIGURE 3.12   Closed-Loop BPM Cycle.

Business strategies are normally planned and created by a team of corporate executives (often led by the CEO), approved and authorized by the board of directors, and then implemented by the company's management team under the supervision of the senior executives. Business strategy provides an overall direction to the enterprise and is the first and foremost important process in the BPM methodology.

2. ***Plan: How do we get there?*** When operational managers know and understand the *what* (i.e., the organizational objectives and goals), they will be able to come up with the *how* (i.e., detailed operational and financial plans). Operational and financial plans answer two questions: What tactics and initiatives will be pursued to meet the performance targets established by the strategic plan? What are the expected financial results of executing the tactics?

An **operational plan** translates an organization's strategic objectives and goals into a set of well-defined tactics and initiatives, resource requirements, and expected results for some future time period, usually, but not always, a year. In essence, an operational plan is like a project plan that is designed to ensure that an organization's strategy is realized. Most operational plans encompass a portfolio of tactics and initiatives. The key to successful operational planning is integration. Strategy drives tactics, and tactics drive results. Basically, the tactics and initiatives defined in an operational plan need to be directly linked to key objectives and targets in the strategic plan. If there is no linkage between an individual tactic and one or more strategic objectives or targets, management should question whether the tactic and its associated initiatives are really needed at all. The BPM methodologies discussed later in this chapter are designed to ensure that these linkages exist.

The financial planning and budgeting process has a logical structure that typically starts with those tactics that generate some form of revenue or income. In organizations that sell goods or services, the ability to generate revenue is based on either the ability to directly produce goods and services or acquire the right amount of goods and services to sell. After a revenue figure has been established, the associated costs of delivering that level of revenue can be generated. Quite often, this entails input from several departments or tactics. This means the process has to be collaborative and that dependencies between functions need to be clearly communicated and understood. In addition to the collaborative input, the organization also needs to add various overhead costs, as well as the costs of the capital required. This information, once consolidated, shows the cost by tactic as well as the cash and funding requirements to put the plan into operation.

3. ***Monitor/Analyze: How are we doing?*** When the operational and financial plans are under way, it is imperative that the performance of the organization be monitored. A comprehensive framework for monitoring performance should address two key issues: what to monitor and how to monitor. Because it is impossible to look at everything, an organization needs to focus on monitoring specific issues. After the organization has identified the indicators or measures to look at, it needs to develop a strategy for monitoring those factors and responding effectively. These measures are most often called key performance indicators (or KPIs in short). An overview of the process of determining KPIs is given later in this chapter. A related topic to the selection of the optimal set of KPIs is the balance scorecard method, which will also be covered in detail later in this chapter.

4. ***Act and Adjust: What do we need to do differently?*** Whether a company is interested in growing its business or simply improving its operations, virtually all strategies depend on new projects—creating new products, entering new markets, acquiring new customers or businesses, or streamlining some processes. Most companies approach these new projects with a spirit of optimism rather than objectivity, ignoring the fact that most new projects and ventures fail. What is the chance

of failure? Obviously, it depends on the type of project (Slywotzky & Weber, 2007). Hollywood movies have around a 60% chance of failure. The same is true for mergers and acquisitions. Large IT projects fail at the rate of 70%. For new food products, the failure rate is 80%. For new pharmaceutical products, it is even higher, around 90%. Overall, the rate of failure for most new projects or ventures runs between 60 and 80%. Given these numbers, the answer to the question of "What do we need to do differently?" becomes a vital issue.

Application Case 3.5 shows how a large nonprofit organization achieved extraordinary results by transforming and modernizing their BI infrastructure with modern-day data warehousing appliances.

Application Case 3.5

AARP Transforms Its BI Infrastructure and Achieves a 347% ROI in Three Years

AARP, Inc., formerly the American Association of Retired Persons, is a U.S.-based membership and interest group, founded in 1958 by Ethel Percy Andrus, PhD, a retired educator from California, and Leonard Davis, founder of Colonial Penn Group of insurance companies. As described in their Web site (aarp.org), AARP is a nonprofit, nonpartisan, social welfare organization with a membership of nearly 38 million that helps people turn their goals and dreams into real possibilities, strengthens communities, and fights for the issues that matter most to families—such as healthcare, employment and income security, and protection from financial abuse.

A Growing Demand for BI

In 2002, the organization first launched a BI initiative that would centralize information (AARP has offices in all 50 states as well as the District of Columbia) and empower its staff with current, relevant, accurate, and flexible analytics to:

- Match services and product offerings to membership base and expectations.
- Improve member profitability, retention, and acquisition.
- Protect AARP brand image by managing relationships with third-party service providers.

This insight helped fuel AARP's success and, with this success, came larger data volumes and an increased demand for new analytics.

By 2009, the BI team faced a new challenge. Its data warehouse—based on an SQL relational database from Oracle—could no longer keep up with the demand. The team experienced more than 30 systems failures that year. This was both unacceptable and costly.

System performance was a key concern as well. As the data volumes grew, daily loads into the warehouse couldn't be completed until 3:00 P.M.—which affected how long staff had to wait for reports. "Our analysts would run a report, then go for coffee or for lunch, and, maybe if they were lucky, by 5:00 P.M. they would get the response," says Bruni, Practice Director, Business Intelligence, AARP. "It was unacceptable. The system was so busy writing the new daily data that it didn't give any importance to the read operations performed by users."

Analysts also couldn't create ad hoc queries without IT intervention. When IT received a request for a new type of report, the BI team would have to optimize the queries and send a report sample back to the requestors for review. The process, from start to finish, could take weeks to months. Finally, with more than 36 terabytes of data in the data warehouse, staff found it impossible to back up the system each night. Backups were limited to a few critical tables, making it difficult for staff to create an effective disaster recovery plan.

According to Bruni, if left unsolved, these challenges could have affected AARP's work. "Analytics provide key metrics that are critical to evaluate how well our membership and social goals are being attained," says Bruni. "It is essential to enabling continuous improvement and decision making to support member needs."

(Continued)

Application Case 3.5 (Continued)

Creating an Agile BI Environment

As Bruni's team looked to modernize the BI environment, they evaluated two options—upgrading the existing environment or moving to a single data warehouse appliance. "We found the cost of each option comparable, but only the appliance provided us a paradigm shift in terms of the performance we needed," says Bruni. "Among the different partners we looked at, the IBM Netezza data warehouse appliance provided the safest bet because it didn't require the data model fine-tuning that other data warehouses do. We were also able to try the solution before we bought it to see whether it really could do everything we needed. Most vendors do not provide this type of 'try-before-you-buy' option."

In building the new environment, the organization adopted a "Scrum" development model, usually used by software developers, to provide a framework that shortens development cycles and speeds time to market for BI requests. "Using Scrum in data warehousing is kind of unheard of," says Bruni. "But the basic premise it provides is an agile, iterative process that enables us to rapidly transform our users' analytic needs into operating reports that show meaningful data."

Within 9 months from the acquisition of its new platform, the team had converted all the scripts and procedures from Oracle Database into the IBM® Netezza® data warehouse appliance. Core accounts and membership data (which resides on an IBM DB2® for z/OS® database running on an IBM System z® server), financial and human resource data from other smaller databases, and campaign analysis and segmentation data from third-party data sources are now loaded in the IBM Netezza data warehouse appliance nightly and accessible via the organization's BI tools without interruption.

Running Complex Queries at Lightning Speed

In terms of performance (which was the BI team's most pressing concern), daily data loads are now completed before 8:00 A.M.—a 1,400% improvement—and reports that previously took minutes to run are completed in seconds—a 1,700% improvement. The solution also helped compress the data size from 36 terabytes to just 1.5 terabytes, enabling staff to easily back up the data warehouse in only 30 minutes.

Equally important, the nearly 220 human resources, finance, marketing, and campaign staff members that use the system can now conduct what Bruni refers to as "train-of-thought analysis"— creating ad hoc reports to test theories regarding membership needs. "The IBM Netezza data warehouse appliance is like driving a Ferrari," says Bruni. "We have opened a whole new realm of possibilities to our internal customers, who are actually able to create reports on-the-fly and get the results back in a matter of seconds. In the first few months of operation, we saw a huge spike in the number of reports being created—nearly three times the number that we had previously supported. With the deep dive they can conduct now, we've seen a steady growth in member renewals, acquisitions and engagement."

Achieving Rapid ROI

The new platform has also enabled the organization to redeploy IT support staff from the BI group to other areas. Previously, the team needed one full-time database administrator (DBA) along with part-time support from the organization's storage area network (SAN) and midrange service teams. "It's amazing," says Bruni. "We no longer need IT support. The IBM Netezza data warehouse appliance is shipped already optimized. Give it power, give it network, and you're done. It doesn't need anything else."

These improvements have enabled the organization to realize a 9% return on investment in the first year, with an anticipated 274% ROI by the second year, and a 347% investment by the third year. "Our initial analysis projected a positive ROI already in the first year—which is very unusual for infrastructure upgrades given all costs are incurrent in the first year," says Bruni. "Our actual ROI post-implementation was even higher as we completed the swap three months ahead of schedule."

Expanding the Influence of BI

By modernizing its infrastructure, Bruni's team has elevated the value and perception of BI in the organization. "After we moved to IBM Netezza, the word spread that we were doing things right and that leveraging us as an internal service was really smart," says Bruni. "We've gained new mission-critical areas, such as the social-impact area which supports our Drive to End Hunger and Create the Good campaigns, based on the fact that we have such a robust infrastructure and that we changed our approach to business. We can develop in a more agile way from a development standpoint. From a program management standpoint, it shrinks our release cycles from months, which is typical with traditional data warehouse infrastructures, to just weeks."

QUESTIONS FOR DISCUSSION
1. What were the challenges AARP was facing?
2. What was the approach for a potential solution?
3. What were the results obtained in the short term, and what were the future plans?

Source: IBM customer success story. (2011). AARP transforms its business intelligence infrastructure—Achieving a 347% ROI in three years from BI modernization effort. http://www-03.ibm.com/software/businesscasestudies/us/en/corp?synkey=A735189Y23828M82 (accessed June 2016).

SECTION 3.9 REVIEW QUESTIONS

1. What is business performance management? How does it relate to BI?
2. What are the three key components of a BPM system?
3. List and briefly describe the four phases of the BPM cycle.
4. Why is strategy the most important part of a BPM implementation?

3.10 Performance Measurement

Underlying BPM is a performance measurement system. According to Simons (2002), **performance measurement systems**:

> Assist managers in tracking the implementations of business strategy by comparing actual results against strategic goals and objectives. A performance measurement system typically comprises systematic methods of setting business goals together with periodic feedback reports that indicate progress against goals. (p. 108)

All measurement is about comparisons. Raw numbers are rarely of value. If you were told that a salesperson completed 50% of the deals he or she was working on within a month, that would have little meaning. Now, suppose you were told that the same salesperson had a monthly close rate of 30% last year. Obviously, the trend is good. What if you were also told that the average close rate for all salespeople at the company was 80%? Obviously, that particular salesperson needs to pick up the pace. As Simons's definition suggests, in performance measurement, the key comparisons revolve around strategies, goals, and objectives. Operational metrics that are used to measure performance are usually called key performance indicators (KPIs).

Key Performance Indicator (KPI)

There is a difference between a "run of the mill" metric and a "strategically aligned" metric. The term **key performance indicator (KPI)** is often used to denote the latter. A KPI represents a strategic objective and measures performance against a goal. According to Eckerson (2009), KPIs are multidimensional. Loosely translated, this means that KPIs have a variety of distinguishing features, including

- *Strategy.* KPIs embody a strategic objective.
- *Targets.* KPIs measure performance against specific targets. Targets are defined in strategy, planning, or budget sessions and can take different forms (e.g., achievement targets, reduction targets, absolute targets).

- *Ranges.*   Targets have performance ranges (e.g., above, on, or below target).
- *Encodings.*   Ranges are encoded in software, enabling the visual display of performance (e.g., green, yellow, red). Encodings can be based on percentages or more complex rules.
- *Time frames.*   Targets are assigned time frames by which they must be accomplished. A time frame is often divided into smaller intervals to provide performance mileposts.
- *Benchmarks.*   Targets are measured against a baseline or benchmark. The previous year's results often serve as a benchmark, but arbitrary numbers or external benchmarks may also be used.

A distinction is sometimes made between KPIs that are "outcomes" and those that are "drivers." Outcome KPIs—sometimes known as *lagging indicators*—measure the output of past activity (e.g., revenues). They are often financial in nature, but not always. Driver KPIs—sometimes known as *leading indicators* or *value drivers*—measure activities that have a significant impact on outcome KPIs (e.g., sales leads).

In some circles, driver KPIs are sometimes called *operational KPIs*, which is a bit of an oxymoron (Hatch, 2008). Most organizations collect a wide range of operational metrics. As the name implies, these metrics deal with the operational activities and performance of a company. The following list of examples illustrates the variety of operational areas covered by these metrics:

- *Customer performance.*   Metrics for customer satisfaction, speed and accuracy of issue resolution, and customer retention.
- *Service performance.*   Metrics for service-call resolution rates, service renewal rates, service level agreements, delivery performance, and return rates.
- *Sales operations.*   New pipeline accounts, sales meetings secured, conversion of inquiries to leads, and average call closure time.
- *Sales plan/forecast.*   Metrics for price-to-purchase accuracy, purchase order-to-fulfillment ratio, quantity earned, forecast-to-plan ratio, and total closed contracts.

Whether an operational metric is strategic or not depends on the company and its use of the measure. In many instances, these metrics represent critical drivers of strategic outcomes. For instance, Hatch (2008) recalls the case of a midtier wine distributor that was being squeezed upstream by the consolidation of suppliers and downstream by the consolidation of retailers. In response, it decided to focus on four operational measures: on-hand/on-time inventory availability, outstanding "open" order value, net-new accounts, and promotion costs and return on marketing investment. The net result of its efforts was a 12% increase in revenues in 1 year. Obviously, these operational metrics were key drivers. However, as described in the following section, in many cases, companies simply measure what is convenient with minimal consideration of why the data are being collected. The result is a significant waste of time, effort, and money.

Performance Measurement System

There is a difference between a performance measurement system and a performance management system. The latter encompasses the former. That is, any performance management system has a performance measurement system but not the other way around. If you were to ask, most companies today would claim that they have a performance measurement system but not necessarily a performance management system, even though a performance measurement system has very little, if any, use without the overarching structure of the performance management system.

The most popular performance measurement systems in use are some variant of Kaplan and Norton's balanced scorecard (BSC). Various surveys and benchmarking studies indicate that anywhere from 50 to over 90% of all companies have implemented some form of a BSC at one time or another. Although there seems to be some confusion about what constitutes "balance," there is no doubt about the originators of the BSC, Kaplan and Norton (1996): "Central to the BSC methodology is a holistic vision of a measurement system tied to the strategic direction of the organization. It is based on a four-perspective view of the world, with financial measures supported by customer, internal, and learning and growth metrics."

SECTION 3.10 REVIEW QUESTIONS

1. What is a performance management system? Why do we need one?
2. What are the distinguishing features of KPIs?
3. List and briefly define the four most commonly cited operational areas for KPIs.
4. What is a performance measurement system? How does it work?

3.11　Balanced Scorecards

Probably the best-known and most widely used performance management system is the balanced scorecard (BSC). Kaplan and Norton first articulated this methodology in their *Harvard Business Review* article, "The Balanced Scorecard: Measures That Drive Performance," which appeared in 1992. A few years later, in 1996, these same authors produced a groundbreaking book—*The Balanced Scorecard: Translating Strategy into Action*—that documented how companies were using the BSC to not only supplement their financial measures with nonfinancial measures, but also to communicate and implement their strategies. Over the past few years, BSC has become a generic term that is used to represent virtually every type of scorecard application and implementation, regardless of whether it is balanced or strategic. In response to this bastardization of the term, Kaplan and Norton released a new book in 2000, *The Strategy-Focused Organization: How Balanced Scorecard Companies Thrive in the New Business Environment*. This book was designed to reemphasize the strategic nature of the BSC methodology. This was followed a few years later, in 2004, by *Strategy Maps: Converting Intangible Assets into Tangible Outcomes*, which describes a detailed process for linking strategic objectives to operational tactics and initiatives. Finally, their latest book, *The Execution Premium*, published in 2008, focuses on the strategy gap—linking strategy formulation and planning with operational execution.

The Four Perspectives

The balanced scorecard suggests that we view the organization from four perspectives—customer, financial, internal business processes, and learning and growth—and to develop objectives, measures, targets, and initiatives relative to each of these perspectives. Figure 3.13 shows these four objectives and their interrelationship with the organization's vision and strategy.

THE CUSTOMER PERSPECTIVE Recent management philosophies have shown an increasing realization of the importance of customer focus and customer satisfaction in any business. These are leading indicators: If customers are not satisfied, they will eventually find other suppliers that will meet their needs. Poor performance from this perspective is thus a leading indicator of future decline, even though the current financial picture may look good. In developing metrics for satisfaction, customers should be analyzed in

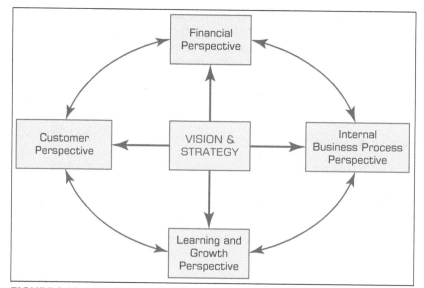

FIGURE 3.13 Four Perspectives in Balanced Scorecard Methodology.

terms of kinds of customers and the kinds of processes for which we are providing a product or service to those customer groups.

THE FINANCIAL PERSPECTIVE Kaplan and Norton do not disregard the traditional need for financial data. Timely and accurate funding data will always be a priority, and managers will do whatever is necessary to provide it. In fact, often there is more than enough handling and processing of financial data. With the implementation of a corporate database, it is hoped that more of the processing can be centralized and automated. But the point is that the current emphasis on financials leads to the "unbalanced" situation with regard to other perspectives. There is perhaps a need to include additional financial-related data, such as risk assessment and cost–benefit data, in this category.

THE LEARNING AND GROWTH PERSPECTIVE This perspective aims to answer the question of "to achieve our vision, how will we sustain our ability to change and improve?" It includes employee training, knowledge management, and corporate cultural character-istics related to both individual and corporate-level improvement. In the current climate of rapid technological change, it is becoming necessary for knowledge workers to be in a continuous learning and growing mode. Metrics can be put in place to guide managers in focusing training funds where they can help the most. In any case, learning and growth constitute the essential foundation for success of any knowledge-worker organization. Kaplan and Norton emphasize that "learning" is more than "training"; it also includes things like mentors and tutors within the organization, as well as ease of communication among workers that allows them to readily get help on a problem when it is needed.

THE INTERNAL BUSINESS PROCESS PERSPECTIVE This perspective focuses on the importance of business processes. Metrics based on this perspective allow the manag-ers to know how well their internal business processes and functions are running and whether the outcomes of these processes (i.e., products and services) meet and exceed the customer requirements (the mission).

The Meaning of Balance in BSC

From a high-level viewpoint, the **balanced scorecard (BSC)** is both a performance measurement and a management methodology that helps translate an organization's financial, customer, internal process, and learning and growth objectives and targets into a set of actionable initiatives. As a measurement methodology, BSC is designed to overcome the limitations of systems that are financially focused. It does this by translating an organization's vision and strategy into a set of interrelated financial and nonfinancial objectives, measures, targets, and initiatives. The nonfinancial objectives fall into one of three perspectives:

- *Customer.* This objective defines how the organization should appear to its customers if it is to accomplish its vision.
- *Internal business process.* This objective specifies the processes the organization must excel at to satisfy its shareholders and customers.
- *Learning and growth.* This objective indicates how an organization can improve its ability to change and improve in order to achieve its vision.

Basically, nonfinancial objectives form a simple causal chain with "learning and growth" driving "internal business process" change, which produces "customer" outcomes that are responsible for reaching a company's "financial" objectives. In BSC, the term *balance* arises because the combined set of measures is supposed to encompass indicators that are

- Financial and nonfinancial
- Leading and lagging
- Internal and external
- Quantitative and qualitative
- Short term and long term

SECTION 3.11 REVIEW QUESTIONS

1. What is a balanced scorecard (BSC)? Where did it come from?
2. What are the four perspectives that BSC suggests to view organizational performance?
3. Why do we need to define separate objectives, measures, targets, and initiatives for each of these four BSC perspectives?
4. What is the meaning of and motivation for *balance* in BSC?
5. What are the differences and commonalities between dashboards and scorecards?

3.12 Six Sigma as a Performance Measurement System

Since its inception in the mid-1980s, Six Sigma has enjoyed widespread adoption by companies throughout the world. For the most part, it has not been used as a performance measurement and management methodology. Instead, most companies use it as a process improvement methodology that enables them to scrutinize their processes, pinpoint problems, and apply remedies. In recent years, some companies, such as Motorola, have recognized the value of using Six Sigma for strategic purposes. In these instances, Six Sigma provides the means to measure and monitor key processes related to a company's profitability and to accelerate improvement in overall business performance. Because of its focus on business processes, Six Sigma also provides a straightforward way to address performance problems after they are identified or detected.

Sigma, σ, is a letter in the Greek alphabet that statisticians use to measure the variability in a process. In the quality arena, *variability* is synonymous with the number of defects. Generally, companies have accepted a great deal of variability in their business processes. In numeric terms, the norm has been 6,200 to 67,000 defects per million opportunities (DPMO). For instance, if an insurance company handles 1 million claims, then under normal operating procedures 6,200 to 67,000 of those claims would be defective (e.g., mishandled, have errors in the forms). This level of variability represents a three- to four-sigma level of performance. To achieve a Six Sigma level of performance, the company would have to reduce the number of defects to no more than 3.4 DPMO. Therefore, **Six Sigma** is a performance management methodology aimed at reducing the number of defects in a business process to as close to zero DPMO as possible.

The DMAIC Performance Model

Six Sigma rests on a simple performance improvement model known as DMAIC. Like BPM, **DMAIC** is a closed-loop business improvement model, and it encompasses the steps of defining, measuring, analyzing, improving, and controlling a process. The steps can be described as follows:

1. *Define.* Define the goals, objectives, and boundaries of the improvement activity. At the top level, the goals are the strategic objectives of the company. At lower levels—department or project levels—the goals are focused on specific operational processes.
2. *Measure.* Measure the existing system. Establish quantitative measures that will yield statistically valid data. The data can be used to monitor progress toward the goals defined in the previous step.
3. *Analyze.* Analyze the system to identify ways to eliminate the gap between the current performance of the system or process and the desired goal.
4. *Improve.* Initiate actions to eliminate the gap by finding ways to do things better, cheaper, or faster. Use project management and other planning tools to implement the new approach.
5. *Control.* Institutionalize the improved system by modifying compensation and incentive systems, policies, procedures, manufacturing resource planning, budgets, operation instructions, or other management systems.

For new processes, the model that is used is called *DMADV* (define, measure, analyze, design, and verify). Traditionally, DMAIC and DMADV have been used primarily with operational issues. However, nothing precludes the application of these methodologies to strategic issues such as company profitability. In recent years, there has been a focus on combining the Six Sigma methodology with other successful methodologies. For instance, the methodology known as *Lean Manufacturing*, *Lean Production*, or simply as *Lean* has been combined with Six Sigma to improve its impact in performance management.

Balanced Scorecard versus Six Sigma

Although many have combined Six Sigma and balanced scorecards for a more holistic solution, some focused on favoring one versus the other. Gupta (2006), in his book titled *Six Sigma Business Scorecard*, provides a good summary of the differences between the balanced scorecard and Six Sigma methodologies (see Table 3.7). In a nutshell, the main difference is that BSC is focused on improving overall strategy, whereas Six Sigma is focused on improving processes.

TABLE 3.7 Comparison of the Balanced Scorecard and Six Sigma

Balanced Scorecard	Six Sigma
Strategic management system	Performance measurement system
Relates to the longer-term view of the business	Provides snapshot of business's performance and identifies measures that drive performance toward profitability
Designed to develop a balanced set of measures	Designed to identify a set of measurements that impact profitability
Identifies measurements around vision and values	Establishes accountability for leadership for wellness and profitability
Critical management processes are to clarify vision/strategy, communicate, plan, set targets, align strategic initiatives, and enhance feedback	Includes all business processes—management and operational
Balances customer and internal operations without a clearly defined leadership role	Balances management and employees' roles; balances costs and revenue of heavy processes
Emphasizes targets for each measurement	Emphasizes aggressive rate of improvement for each measurement, irrespective of target
Emphasizes learning of executives based on feedback	Emphasizes learning and innovation at all levels based on process feedback; enlists all employees' participation
Focuses on growth	Focuses on maximizing profitability
Heavy on strategic content	Heavy on execution for profitability
Management system consisting of measures	Measurement system based on process management

Source: Gupta, P. (2006). *Six Sigma business scorecard,* 2nd ed. New York: McGraw-Hill Professional.

Effective Performance Measurement

A number of books provide recipes for determining whether a collection of performance measures is good or bad. Among the basic ingredients of a good collection are the following:

- Measures should focus on key factors.
- Measures should be a mix of past, present, and future.
- Measures should balance the needs of shareholders, employees, partners, suppliers, and other stakeholders.
- Measures should start at the top and flow down to the bottom.
- Measures need to have targets that are based on research and reality rather than arbitrary.

As the section on KPIs notes, although all of these characteristics are important, the real key to an effective performance measurement system is to have a good strategy. Measures need to be derived from the corporate and business unit strategies and from an analysis of the key business processes required to achieve those strategies. Of course, this is easier said than done. If it were simple, most organizations would already have effective performance measurement systems in place, but they do not.

Application Case 3.6, which describes the Web-based KPI scorecard system at Expedia.com, offers insights into the difficulties of defining both outcome and driver KPIs and the importance of aligning departmental KPIs to overall company objectives.

Application Case 3.6

Expedia.com's Customer Satisfaction Scorecard

Expedia, Inc., is the parent company to some of the world's leading travel companies, providing travel products and services to leisure and corporate travelers in the United States and around the world. It owns and operates a diversified portfolio of well-recognized brands, including Expedia.com, Hotels .com, Hotwire.com, TripAdvisor, Egencia, Classic Vacations, and a range of other domestic and international businesses. The company's travel offerings consist of airline flights, hotel stays, car rentals, destination services, cruises, and package travel provided by various airlines, lodging properties, car rental companies, destination service providers, cruise lines, and other travel product and service companies on a stand-alone and package basis. It also facilitates the booking of hotel rooms, airline seats, car rentals, and destination services from its travel suppliers. It acts as an agent in the transaction, passing reservations booked by its travelers to the relevant airline, hotel, car rental company, or cruise line. Together, these popular brands and innovative businesses make Expedia the largest online travel agency in the world, the third-largest travel company in the United States, and the fourth-largest travel company in the world. Its mission is to become the largest and most profitable seller of travel in the world, by helping everyone everywhere plan and purchase everything in travel.

Problem

Customer satisfaction is key to Expedia's overall mission, strategy, and success. Because Expedia.com is an online business, the customer's shopping experience is critical to Expedia's revenues. The online shopping experience can make or break an online business. It is also important that the customer's shopping experience is mirrored by a good trip experience. Because the customer experience is critical, all customer issues need to be tracked, monitored, and resolved as quickly as possible. Unfortunately, a few years back, Expedia lacked visibility into the "voice of the customer." It had no uniform way of measuring satisfaction, of analyzing the drivers of satisfaction, or of determining the impact of satisfaction on the company's profitability or overall business objectives.

Solution

Expedia's problem was not lack of data. The customer satisfaction group at Expedia knew that it had lots of data. In all, there were 20 disparate databases with 20 different owners. Originally, the group charged one of its business analysts with the task of pulling together and aggregating the data from these various sources into a number of key measures for satisfaction. The business analyst spent 2 to 3 weeks every month pulling and aggregating the data, leaving virtually no time for analysis. Eventually, the group realized that it wasn't enough to aggregate the data. The data needed to be viewed in the context of strategic goals, and individuals had to take ownership of the results.

To tackle the problem, the group decided it needed a refined vision. It began with a detailed analysis of the fundamental drivers of the department's performance and the link between this performance and Expedia's overall goals. Next, the group converted these drivers and links into a scorecard. This process involved three steps:

1. *Deciding how to measure satisfaction.* This required the group to determine which measures in the 20 databases would be useful for demonstrating a customer's level of satisfaction. This became the basis for the scorecards and KPIs.

2. *Setting the right performance targets.* This required the group to determine whether KPI targets had short-term or long-term payoffs. Just because a customer was satisfied with his or her online experience did not mean that the customer was satisfied with the vendor providing the travel service.

3. *Putting data into context.* The group had to tie the data to ongoing customer satisfaction projects.

The various real-time data sources are fed into a main database (called the Decision Support Factory). In the case of the customer satisfaction group, these include customer surveys, CRM systems, interactive voice response systems, and other customer-service systems. The data in the DSS Factory are loaded on a daily basis into several DMs and multidimensional cubes. Users can access the data in a variety of ways that are relevant to their particular business needs.

Benefits

Ultimately, the customer satisfaction group came up with 10 to 12 objectives that linked directly to Expedia's corporate initiatives. These objectives were, in turn, linked to more than 200 KPIs within the customer satisfaction group. KPI owners can build, manage, and consume their own scorecards, and managers and executives have a transparent view of how well actions are aligning with the strategy. The scorecard also provides the customer satisfaction group with the ability to drill down into the data underlying any of the trends or patterns observed. In the past, all of this would have taken weeks or months to do, if it was done at all. With the scorecard, the Customer Service group can immediately see how well it is doing with respect to the KPIs, which, in turn, are reflected in the group's objectives and the company's objectives.

As an added benefit, the data in the system support not only the customer satisfaction group, but also other business units in the company. For example, a frontline manager can analyze airline expenditures on a market-by-market basis to evaluate negotiated contract performance or determine the savings potential for consolidating spending with a single carrier. A travel manager can leverage the BI to discover areas with high volumes of unused tickets or offline bookings and devise strategies to adjust behavior and increase overall savings.

QUESTIONS FOR DISCUSSION

1. Who are the customers for Expedia.com? Why is customer satisfaction a very important part of their business?
2. How did Expedia.com improve customer satisfaction with scorecards?
3. What were the challenges, the proposed solution, and the obtained results?

Sources: Based on Microsoft. (2005). Expedia: Scorecard solution helps online travel company measure the road to greatness. download.microsoft.com/documents/customerevidence/22483_ Expedia_Case_Study.doc (accessed June 2016); Editor's note. (2004). Expedia incorporates customer satisfaction feedback and employee input to enhance service and support. Quirk's Marketing Research Media. http://www.quirks.com/articles/ a2004/20041001.aspx (accessed July 2016).

SECTION 3.12 REVIEW QUESTIONS

1. What is Six Sigma? How is it used as a performance measurement system?
2. What is DMAIC? List and briefly describe the steps involved in DMAIC.
3. Compare BSC and Six Sigma as two competing performance measurement systems.
4. What are the ingredients for an effective performance management system?

Chapter Highlights

- A data warehouse is a specially constructed data repository where data are organized so that they can be easily accessed by end users for several applications.
- DMs contain data on one topic (e.g., marketing). A DM can be a replication of a subset of data in the data warehouse. DMs are a less-expensive solution that can be replaced by or can supplement a data warehouse. DMs can be independent of or dependent on a data warehouse.
- An ODS is a type of customer-information-file database that is often used as a staging area for a data warehouse.
- Data integration comprises three major processes: data access, data federation, and change capture. When these three processes are correctly

implemented, data can be accessed and made accessible to an array of ETL and analysis tools and data warehousing environments.

• ETL technologies pull data from many sources, cleanse them, and load them into a data warehouse. ETL is an integral process in any data-centric project.

• Real-time or active data warehousing supplements and expands traditional data warehousing, moving into the realm of operational and tactical decision making by loading data in real time and providing data to users for active decision making.

• The security and privacy of data and information are critical issues for a data warehouse professional.

Key Terms

balanced scorecard (BSC)

business performance management (BPM)

cube

data integration

data mart (DM)

data warehouse (DW)

data warehouse administrator (DWA)

dependent data mart

dimension table

dimensional modeling

DMAIC

drill down

enterprise application integration (EAI)

enterprise data warehouse (EDW)

enterprise information integration (EII)

extraction, transformation, and load (ETL)

independent data mart

key performance indicator (KPI)

metadata

OLTP

oper mart

operational data store (ODS)

operational plan

performance measurement systems

real-time data warehousing (RDW)

Six Sigma

snowflake schema

star schema

Questions for Discussion

1. Compare data integration and ETL. How are they related?

2. What is a data warehouse, and what are its benefits? Why is Web accessibility important with a data warehouse?

3. A DM can replace a data warehouse or complement it. Compare and discuss these options.

4. Discuss the major drivers and benefits of data warehousing to end users.

5. List the differences and/or similarities between the roles of a database administrator and a data warehouse administrator.

6. Describe how data integration can lead to higher levels of data quality.

7. Compare the Kimball and Inmon approaches toward data warehouse development. Identify when each one is most effective.

8. Discuss security concerns involved in building a data warehouse.

9. Investigate current data warehouse development implementation through offshoring. Write a report about it. In class, debate the issue in terms of the benefits and costs, as well as social factors.

10. SAP uses the term *strategic enterprise management* (SEM), Cognos uses the term *corporate performance management* (CPM), and Hyperion uses the term *business performance management* (BPM). Are they referring

to the same basic ideas? Provide evidence to support your answer.

11. BPM encompasses five basic processes: strategize, plan, monitor, act, and adjust. Select one of these processes, and discuss the types of software tools and applications that are available to support it. Figure 3.10 provides some hints. Also, refer to Bain & Company's list of management tools for assistance (bain.com/management_tools/home.asp).

12. Select a public company of interest. Using the company's 2016 annual report, create three strategic financial objectives for 2017. For each objective, specify a strategic goal or target. The goals should be consistent with the company's 2016 financial performance.

13. Distinguish between performance management and performance measurement.

14. Create a strategy for a hypothetical company, using the four perspectives of the BSC. Express the strategy as a series of strategic objectives. Produce a strategy map depicting the linkages among the objectives.

15. Compare and contrast the DMAIC model with the closed-loop processes of BPM.

16. Select two companies that you are familiar with. What terms do they use to describe their BPM initiatives and software suites? Compare and contrast their offerings in terms of BPM applications and functionality.

Exercises

Teradata University and Other Hands-On Exercises

1. Consider the case of developing a data warehouse for Coca-Cola Japan available at the DSS Resources Web site, http://dssresources.com/cases/coca-colajapan. Read the case, and answer the nine questions for further analysis and discussion.

2. Read the Ball (2005) article and rank-order the criteria (ideally for a real organization). In a report, explain how important each criterion is and why.

3. Explain when you should implement a two- or three-tiered architecture when considering developing a data warehouse.

4. Read the full Continental Airlines case (a hugely popular data warehousing success story) at teradatauniversitynetwork.com, and answer the questions.

5. At teradatauniversitynetwork.com, read and answer the questions to the case, "Harrah's High Payoff from Customer Information." Relate Harrah's results to how airlines and other casinos use their customer data.

6. At teradatauniversitynetwork.com, read and answer the questions of the assignment "Data Warehousing Failures." Because eight cases are described in that assignment, the class may be divided into eight groups, with one case assigned per group. In addition, read Ariyachandra and Watson (2006a), and for each case identify how the failure occurred as related to not focusing on one or more of the reference's success factor(s).

7. At teradatauniversitynetwork.com, read and answer the questions with the assignment "Ad-Vent Technology: Using the MicroStrategy Sales Analytic Model." The MicroStrategy software is accessible from the TUN site. Also, you might want to use Barbara Wixom's PowerPoint presentation about the MicroStrategy software ("Demo Slides for MicroStrategy Tutorial Script"), which is also available at the TUN site.

8. At teradatauniversitynetwork.com, watch the Web seminars titled "Real-Time Data Warehousing: The Next Generation of Decision Support Data Management" and "Building the Real-Time Enterprise." Read the article "Teradata's Real-Time Enterprise Reference Architecture: A Blueprint for the Future of IT," also available at this site. Describe how real-time concepts and technologies work and how they can be used to extend existing data warehousing and BI architectures to support day-to-day decision making. Write a report indicating how RDW is specifically providing competitive advantage for organizations. Describe in detail the difficulties in such implementations and operations, and describe how they are being addressed in practice.

9. At teradatauniversitynetwork.com, watch the Web seminars "Data Integration Renaissance: New Drivers and Emerging Approaches," "In Search of a Single Version of the Truth: Strategies for Consolidating Analytic Silos," and "Data Integration: Using ETL, EAI, and EII Tools to Create an Integrated Enterprise." Also read the "Data Integration" research report. Compare and contrast the presentations. What is the most important issue described in these seminars? What is the best way to handle the strategies and challenges of consolidating DMs and spreadsheets into a unified data warehousing architecture? Perform a Web search to identify the latest developments in the field. Compare the presentation to the material in the text and the new material that you found.

10. Consider the future of data warehousing. Perform a Web search on this topic. Also, read these two articles: Agosta, L. (2006, March 31). Data warehousing in a flat world: Trends for 2006. *DM Direct Newsletter*; and Geiger, J. G. (2005, November). CIFe: Evolving with the times. *DM Review*, 38–41. Compare and contrast your findings.

11. Access teradatauniversitynetwork.com. Identify the latest articles, research reports, and cases on data warehousing. Describe recent developments in the field. Include in your report how data warehousing is used in BI and DSS.

12. Go to YouTube.com, and search for "Teradata BSI Cases," where BSI stands for "Business Solutions Inc." Select three interesting data warehousing cases, watch them carefully, and write a report to discuss your findings about the business problems and proposed investigative solutions.

13. Go to teradatauniversitynetwork.com. Select the "Articles" content type. Browse down the list of articles, and locate one titled "Business/Corporate Performance Management: Changing Vendor Landscape and New Market Targets." Based on the article, answer the following questions:
    a. What is the basic focus of the article?
    b. What are the major "takeaways" from the article?
    c. In the article, which organizational function or role is most intimately involved in CPM?
    d. Which applications are covered by CPM?
    e. How are these applications similar to or different from the applications covered by Gartner's CPM?
    f. What is GRC, and what is its link to corporate performance?
    g. What are some of the major acquisitions that have occurred in the CPM marketplace over the last couple of years?
    h. Select two of the companies discussed by the article (not SAP, Oracle, or IBM). What are the CPM strategies of each of the companies? What do the authors think about these strategies?

14. Go to teradatauniversitynetwork.com. Select the "Case Studies" content type. Browse down the list of cases, and locate the one titled "Real-Time Dashboards at Western Digital." Based on the article, answer the following questions:

a. What is VIS?

b. In what ways is the architecture of VIS similar to or different from the architecture of BPM?

c. What are the similarities and differences between the closed-loop processes of BPM and the processes in the OODA (observe, orient, decide, act) decision cycle?

d. What types of dashboards are in the system? Are they operational or tactical, or are they actually scorecards? Explain.

e. What are the basic benefits provided by Western Digital's VIS and dashboards?

f. What sorts of advice can you provide to a company that is getting ready to create its own VIS and dashboards?

Team Assignments and Role-Playing Projects

1. Kathryn Avery has been a DBA with a nationwide retail chain (Big Chain) for the past 6 years. She has recently been asked to lead the development of Big Chain's first data warehouse. The project has the sponsorship of senior management and the CIO. The rationale for developing the data warehouse is to advance the reporting systems, particularly in sales and marketing and, in the longer term, to improve Big Chain's CRM. Kathryn has been to a Data Warehousing Institute conference and has been doing some reading, but she is still mystified about development methodologies. She knows there are two groups—EDW (Inmon) and architected DMs (Kimball)—that have equally robust features.

Initially, she believed that the two methodologies were extremely dissimilar, but as she has examined them more carefully, she isn't so certain. Kathryn has a number of questions that she would like answered:

a. What are the real differences between the methodologies?

b. What factors are important in selecting a particular methodology?

c. What should be her next steps in thinking about a methodology?

Help Kathryn answer these questions. (This exercise was adapted from Duncan, K., Reeves, L., & Griffin, J. (2003, Fall). BI experts' perspective. *Business Intelligence Journal, 8*(4), 14–19.)

2. Jeet Kumar is the administrator of data warehousing at a big regional bank. He was appointed 5 years ago to implement a data warehouse to support the bank's CRM business strategy. Using the data warehouse, the bank has been successful in integrating customer information, understanding customer profitability, attracting customers, enhancing customer relationships, and retaining customers.

Over the years, the bank's data warehouse has moved closer to real time by moving to more frequent refreshes of the data warehouse. Now, the bank wants to implement customer self-service and call center applications that require even fresher data than is currently available in the warehouse.

Jeet wants some support in considering the possibilities for presenting fresher data. One alternative is to entirely commit to implementing RDW. His ETL vendor is prepared to assist him make this change. Nevertheless, Jeet has been informed about EAI and EII technologies and wonders how they might fit into his plans.

In particular, he has the following questions:

a. What exactly are EAI and EII technologies?

b. How are EAI and EII related to ETL?

c. How are EAI and EII related to RDW?

d. Are EAI and EII required, complementary, or alternatives to RDW?

Help Jeet answer these questions. (This exercise was adapted from Brobst, S., Levy, E., & Muzilla, C. (2005, Spring). Enterprise application integration and enterprise information integration. *Business Intelligence Journal, 10*(2), 27–33.)

3. Interview administrators in your college or executives in your organization to determine how data warehousing could assist them in their work. Write a proposal describing your findings. Include cost estimates and benefits in your report.

4. Go through the list of data warehousing risks described in this chapter and find two examples of each in practice.

5. Access teradata.com and read the white papers "Measuring Data Warehouse ROI" and "Realizing ROI: Projecting and Harvesting the Business Value of an Enterprise Data Warehouse." Also, watch the Web-based course "The ROI Factor: How Leading Practitioners Deal with the Tough Issue of Measuring DW ROI." Describe the most important issues described in them. Compare these issues to the success factors described in Ariyachandra and Watson (2006a).

6. Read the article by Liddell Avery, K., & Watson, H. J. (2004, Fall). Training data warehouse end-users. *Business Intelligence Journal, 9*(4), 40–51 (which is available at teradatauniversitynetwork.com). Consider the different classes of end users, describe their difficulties, and discuss the benefits of appropriate training for each group. Have each member of the group take on one of the roles, and have a discussion about how an appropriate type of data warehousing training would be good for each of you.

7. Virtually every BPM/CPM vendor provides case studies on their Web sites. As a team, select two of these vendors (you can get their names from the Gartner or AMR lists). Select two case studies from each of these sites. For each, summarize the problem the customer was trying to address, the applications or solutions implemented, and the benefits the customer received from the system.

Internet Exercises

1. Search the Internet to find information about data warehousing. Identify some newsgroups that have an interest in this concept. Explore ABI/INFORM in your library, e-library, and Google for recent articles on the topic. Begin with tdwi.org, technologyevaluation.com, and the major vendors: teradata.com, sas.com, oracle.com, and ncr.com. Also check cio.com, dmreview.com, dssre sources.com, and db2mag.com.

2. Survey some ETL tools and vendors. Start with fairisaac .com and egain.com. Also consult dmreview.com (now called informationbuilders.com).

3. Contact some data warehouse vendors and obtain information about their products. Give special attention to vendors that provide tools for multiple purposes, such as Cognos, Software A&G, SAS Institute, and Oracle. Free online demos are available from some of these vendors. Download a demo or two and try them. Write a report describing your experience.

4. Explore teradata.com for developments and success stories about data warehousing. Write a report about what you have discovered.

5. Explore teradata.com for white papers and Web-based courses on data warehousing. Read the former and watch the latter. (Divide the class so that all the sources are covered.) Write a report about what you have discovered.

6. Find recent cases of successful data warehousing applications. Go to data warehouse vendors' sites and look for cases or success stories. Select one, and write a brief summary to present to your class.

References

Adamson, C. (2009). *The star schema handbook: The complete reference to dimensional data warehouse design.* Hoboken, NJ: Wiley.

Agosta, L. (2006, January). The data strategy adviser: The year ahead—Data warehousing trends 2006. *DM Review, 16*(1).

Ariyachandra, T., & Watson, H. (2005). Key factors in selecting a data warehouse architecture. *Business Intelligence Journal, 10*(3).

Ariyachandra, T., & Watson, H. (2006a, January). Benchmarks for BI and data warehousing success. *DM Review, 16*(1).

Ariyachandra, T., & Watson, H. (2006b). Which data warehouse architecture is most successful? *Business Intelligence Journal, 11*(1).

Ball, S. K. (2005, November 14). Do you need a data warehouse layer in your business intelligence architecture? information-management.com/infodirect/20050916/1036931-1 .html (accessed June 2016).

Basu, R. (2003, November). Challenges of real-time data warehousing. *DM Review.* http://www.information-management.com/specialreports/20031111/7684-1.html (accessed September 2016).

Benander, A., Benander, B., Fadlalla, A., & James, G. (2000, Winter). Data warehouse administration and management. *Information Systems Management, 17*(1).

Bonde, A., & Kuckuk, M. (2004, April). Real world business intelligence: The implementation perspective. *DM Review, 14*(4).

Breslin, M. (2004, Winter). Data warehousing battle of the giants: Comparing the basics of Kimball and Inmon models. *Business Intelligence Journal, 9*(1), 6–20.

Brobst, S., Levy, & Muzilla. (2005, Spring). Enterprise application integration and enterprise information integration. *Business Intelligence Journal, 10*(3).

Brown, M. (2004, May 9–12). 8 characteristics of a successful data warehouse. *Proceedings of the 29th Annual SAS Users Group International Conference* (SUGI 29). Montreal, Canada.

Colbert, J. (2009). Performance management in turbulent times. BeyeNETWORK. http://www.b-eye-network .com/view/10717, (accessed September 2016).

Davison, D. (2003, November 14). Top 10 risks of offshore outsourcing. Stamford, CT META Group research report, now Gartner, Inc.

Dull, T. (2015). Data lake vs data warehouse: Key differences. KDnuggets.com. http://www.kdnuggets.com/2015/09/datalake-vs-data-warehouse-key-differences.html (accessed August 2016).

Eckerson, W. (2003, Fall). The evolution of ETL. *Business Intelligence Journal, 8*(4).

Eckerson, W. (2005, April 1). Data warehouse builders advocate for different architectures. *Application Development Trends.* https://adtmag.com/articles/2005/04/01/data-warehouse-builders-advocate-for-different-architectures .aspx (accessed September 2016).

Eckerson, W. (2009, January). Performance management strategies: How to create and deploy effective metrics. *TDWI Best Practices Report* (accessed January 2016). https:// tdwi.org/research/2009/01/bpr-1q-performance-management-strategies.aspx (accessed August 2016)

Eckerson, W., Hackathorn, R., McGivern, M., Twogood, C., & Watson, G. (2009). Data warehousing appliances. *Business Intelligence Journal, 14*(1), 40–48.

Edwards, M. (2003, Fall). 2003 Best Practices Awards winners: Innovators in business intelligence and data warehousing. *Business Intelligence Journal, 8*(4).

Elson, R., & LeClerc, R. (2005). Security and privacy concerns in the data warehouse environment. *Business Intelligence Journal, 10*(3).

Furtado, P. (2009). A survey of parallel and distributed data warehouses. *International Journal of Data Warehousing and Mining, 5*(2), 57–78.

Golfarelli, M., & Rizzi, S. (2009). *Data warehouse design: Modern principles and methodologies.* San Francisco: McGraw-Hill Osborne Media.

Gupta, P. (2006). *Six Sigma business scorecard,* 2nd ed. New York: McGraw-Hill Professional.

Hall, M. (2002, April 15). Seeding for data growth. *Computerworld, 36*(16).

Hammergren, T. C., & Simon, A. R. (2009). *Data warehousing for dummies,* 2nd ed. Hoboken, NJ: Wiley.

Hatch, D. (2008, January). Operational BI: Getting "real time" about performance. *Intelligent Enterprise* (accessed March 2016). http://www.intelligententerprise.com/showArticle .jhtml?articleID=205920233 (accessed July 2016)

Hicks, M. (2001, November 26). Getting pricing just right. *eWeek, 18*(46).

Hoffer, J. A., Prescott, M. B., & McFadden, F. R. (2007). *Modern database management,* 8th ed. Upper Saddle River, NJ: Prentice Hall.

IBM. (2009). *50 Tb data warehouse benchmark on IBM System Z.* Armonk, NY: IBM Redbooks.

Imhoff, C. (2001, May). Power up your enterprise portal. *E-Business Advise.*

Inmon, W. H. (2005). *Building the data warehouse,* 4th ed. New York: Wiley.

Jukic, N., & Lang, C. (2004, Summer). Using offshore resources to develop and support data warehousing applications. *Business Intelligence Journal, 9*(3).

Kalido. BP Lubricants achieves BIGS success. kalido. com/collateral/Documents/English-US/CS-BP%20BIGS .pdf (accessed August 2015).

Kalido. BP Lubricants achieves BIGS, key IT solutions. keyitsolutions.com/asp/rptdetails/report/95/cat/1175 (accessed August 2015).

Kaplan, R., & Norton, D. (1996). *The balanced scorecard: Translating strategy into action.* Boston, MA: Harvard University Press.

Kaplan, R. S., & Norton, D. P. (2005). The balanced scorecard: measures that drive performance. Harvard business review, 83(7), 172.

Karacsony, K. (2006, January). ETL is a symptom of the problem, not the solution. *DM Review, 16*(1).

Kay, R. (2005, September 19). EII. *Computerworld, 39*(38).

Kelly, C. (2001, June 14). Calculating data warehousing ROI. SearchSQLServer.com.

Manglik, A., & Mehra, V. (2005, Winter). Extending enterprise BI capabilities: New patterns for data integration." *Business Intelligence Journal, 10*(1).

Matney, D. (2003, Spring). End-user support strategy. *Business Intelligence Journal, 8*(3).

Mehra, V. (2005, Summer). Building a metadata-driven enterprise: A holistic approach. *Business Intelligence Journal, 10*(3).

Moseley, M. (2009). Eliminating data warehouse pressures with master data services and SOA. *Business Intelligence Journal, 14*(2), 33–43.

Murtaza, A. (1998, Fall). A framework for developing enterprise data warehouses. *Information Systems Management, 15*(4).

Nash, K. S. (2002, July). Chemical reaction. *Baseline.* Issue 8, 27–36.

Orovic, V. (2003, June). To do & not to do. *eAI Journal.* pp. 37–43.

Parzinger, M. J., & Frolick, M. N. (2001, July). Creating competitive advantage through data warehousing. *Information Strategy, 17*(4).

Romero, O., & Abelló, A. (2009). A survey of multidimensional modeling methodologies. *International Journal of Data Warehousing and Mining, 5*(2), 1–24.

Rosenberg, A. (2006, Quarter 1). Improving query performance in data warehouses. *Business Intelligence Journal, 11*(1).

Russom, P. (2009). *Next generation data warehouse platforms.* TDWI best practices report. tdwi.org/research/reportseries/reports.aspx?pid=842 (accessed January 2016).

Sen, A. (2004, April). Metadata management: Past, present and future. *Decision Support Systems, 37*(1).

Sen, A., & Sinha, P. (2005). A comparison of data warehousing methodologies. *Communications of the ACM, 48*(3).

Simons, R. (2002). *Performance measurement and control systems for implementing strategy.* Upper Saddle River, NJ: Prentice Hall.

Slywotzky, A. J., & Weber, K. (2007). *The Upside: The 7 strategies for turning big threats into growth breakthroughs.* Crown Business.

Solomon, M. (2005, Winter). Ensuring a successful data warehouse initiative. *Information Systems Management Journal.* 22(1), 26–36.

Songini, M. L. (2004, February 2). ETL quickstudy. *Computerworld, 38*(5).

Thornton, M. (2002, March 18). What about security? The most common, but unwarranted, objection to hosted data warehouses. *DM Review, 12*(3), 30–43.

Thornton, M., & Lampa, M. (2002). Hosted data warehouse. *Journal of Data Warehousing, 7*(2), 27–34.

Van den Hoven, J. (1998). Data marts: Plan big, build small. *Information Systems Management, 15*(1).

Watson, H. J. (2002). Recent developments in data warehousing. *Communications of the ACM, 8*(1).

Watson, H. J., Goodhue, D. L., & Wixom, B. H. (2002). The benefits of data warehousing: Why some organizations realize exceptional payoffs. *Information & Management, 39.*

Watson, H., Gerard, J., Gonzalez, L., Haywood, M., & Fenton, D. (1999). Data warehouse failures: Case studies and findings. *Journal of Data Warehousing, 4*(1).

Zhao, X. (2005, October 7). Meta data management maturity model. *DM Direct Newsletter.*

Predictive Analytics I: Data Mining Process, Methods, and Algorithms

Generally speaking, data mining is a way to develop intelligence (i.e., actionable information or knowledge) from data that an organization collects, organizes, and stores. A wide range of data mining techniques are being used by organizations to gain a better understanding of their customers and their operations and to solve complex organizational problems. In this chapter, we study data mining as an enabling technology for business analytics and predictive analytics, learn about the standard processes of conducting data mining projects, understand and build expertise in the use of major data mining techniques, develop awareness of the existing software tools, and explore privacy issues, common myths, and pitfalls that are often associated with data mining.

4.1 Opening Vignette: Miami-Dade Police Department Is Using Predictive Analytics to Foresee and Fight Crime 190
4.2 Data Mining Concepts and Applications 193
4.3 Data Mining Applications 203
4.4 Data Mining Process 206
4.5 Data Mining Methods 215
4.6 Data Mining Software Tools 231
4.7 Data Mining Privacy Issues, Myths, and Blunders 237

4.1 OPENING VIGNETTE: Miami-Dade Police Department Is Using Predictive Analytics to Foresee and Fight Crime

Predictive analytics and data mining have become an integral part of many law enforcement agencies including the Miami-Dade Police Department, whose mission is not only to protect the safety of Florida's largest county with 2.5 million citizens (making it the seventh largest in the United States), but also to provide a safe and inviting climate for the millions of tourists that come from around the world to enjoy the county's natural beauty, warm climate, and stunning beaches. With tourists spending nearly US$20 billion every year and generating nearly a third of Florida's sales taxes, it's hard to overstate the importance of tourism to the region's economy. So although few of the county's police officers would likely list economic development in their job description, nearly all grasp the vital link between safe streets and the region's tourist-driven prosperity.

That connection is paramount for Lieutenant Arnold Palmer, currently supervising the Robbery Investigations Section, and a former supervisor of the department's Robbery Intervention Detail. This specialized team of detectives is focused on intensely policing the county's robbery hot spots and worst repeat offenders. He and the team occupy modest offices on the second floor of a modern-looking concrete building, set back from a palm-lined street on the western edge of Miami. In his 10 years in the unit, out of 23 in total on the force, Palmer has seen a lot of changes. It's not just in policing practices, like the way his team used to mark street crime hot spots with colored pushpins on a map.

Policing with Less

Palmer and the team have also seen the impact of a growing population, shifting demographics, and a changing economy on the streets they patrol. Like any good police force, they've continually adapted their methods and practices to meet a policing challenge that has grown in scope and complexity. But like nearly all branches of the county's government, intensifying budget pressures have placed the department in a squeeze between rising demands and shrinking resources.

Palmer, who sees detectives as front-line fighters against a rising tide of street crime and the looming prospect of ever-tightening resources, put it this way: "Our basic challenge was how to cut street crime even as tighter resources have reduced the number of cops on the street." Over the years, the team had been open to trying new tools, the most notable of which was a program called "analysis-driven enforcement" that used crime history data as the basis for positioning teams of detectives. "We've evolved a lot since then in our ability to predict where robberies are likely to occur, both through the use of analysis and our own collective experience."

New Thinking on Cold Cases

The more confounding challenge for Palmer and his team of investigators, one shared with the police of all major urban areas, is in closing the hardest cases, where leads, witnesses, video—any facts or evidence that can help solve a case—are lacking. It's not surprising, explains Palmer, because "the standard practices we used to generate leads, like talking to informants or to the community or to patrol officers, haven't changed much, if at all," says Palmer. "That kind of an approach works okay, but it relies a lot on the experience our detectives carry in their head. When the detectives retire or move on, that experience goes with them."

Palmer's conundrum was that turnover, due to the retirement of many of his most experienced detectives, was on an upward trend. True, he saw the infusion of young blood as an inherently good thing, especially given their greater comfort with the new types of information—from e-mails, social media, and traffic cameras, to name a few—that his team had access to. But as Palmer recounts, the problem came when the handful of new detectives coming into the unit turned to look for guidance from the senior officers "and it's just not there. We knew at that point we needed a different way to fill the experience gap going forward."

His ad hoc efforts to come up with a solution led to blue-sky speculation. What if new detectives on the squad could pose the same questions to a computer database as they would to a veteran detective? That speculation planted a seed in Palmer's mind that wouldn't go away.

The Big Picture Starts Small

What was taking shape within the robbery unit demonstrated how big ideas can come from small places. But more important, it showed that for these ideas to reach fruition, the "right" conditions need to be in alignment at the right time. On a leadership level, that means a driving figure in the organization who knows what it takes to nurture top-down support as well as crucial bottom-up buy-in from the ranks, while at the same time keeping the department's information technology (IT) personnel on the same page. That person was Palmer. At the organizational level, the robbery unit served as a particularly good launching point for lead modeling because of the prevalence of repeat offenders among perpetrators. Ultimately, the department's ability to unleash the broader transformative potential of lead modeling would hinge in large part on the team's ability to deliver results on a smaller scale.

When early tests and demos proved encouraging—with the model yielding accurate results when the details of solved cases were fed into it—the team started gaining attention. The initiative received a critical boost when the robbery bureau's unit major and captain voiced their support for the direction of the project, telling Palmer that "if you can make this work, run with it." But more important than the encouragement, Palmer explains, was their willingness to advocate for the project among the department's higher-ups. "I can't get it off the ground if the brass doesn't buy in," says Palmer. "So their support was crucial."

Success Brings Credibility

Having been appointed the official liaison between IT and the robbery unit, Palmer set out to strengthen the case for the lead-modeling tool—now officially called Blue PALMS, for Predictive Analytics Lead Modeling Software—by building up a series of successes. His constituency was not only the department brass, but also the detectives whose support would be critical to its successful adoption as a robbery-solving tool. In his attempts to introduce Blue PALMS, resistance was predictably stronger among veteran detectives, who saw no reason to give up their long-standing practices. Palmer knew that dictates or coercion wouldn't win their hearts and minds. He would need to build a beachhead of credibility.

Palmer found that opportunity in one of his best and most experienced detectives. Early in a robbery investigation, the detective indicated to Palmer that he had a strong hunch who the perpetrator was and wanted, in essence, to test the Blue PALMS system. So at the detective's request, the department analyst fed key details of the crime into the system, including the modus operandi, or MO. The system's statistical models compared these details to a database of historical data, looking for important correlations and similarities in the crime's signature. The report that came out of the process included a list of 20 suspects ranked in order of match strength, or likelihood. When the analyst handed the detective the report, his "hunch" suspect was listed in the top five. Soon after his arrest, he confessed, and Palmer had gained a solid convert.

Though it was a useful exercise, Palmer realized that the true test wasn't in confirming hunches but in breaking cases that had come to a dead end. Such was the situation in a carjacking that had, in Palmer's words, "no witnesses, no video and no crime scene—nothing to go on." When the senior detective on the stalled case went on leave after three months, the junior detective to whom it was assigned requested a Blue PALMS report. Shown photographs of the top people on the suspect list, the victim made a positive identification of the suspect leading to the successful conclusion of the case. That suspect was number one on the list.

Just the Facts

The success that Blue PALMS continues to build has been a major factor in Palmer's success in getting his detectives on board. But if there's a part of his message that resonates even more with his detectives, it's the fact that Blue PALMS is designed not to change the basics of policing practices, but to enhance them by giving them a second chance of cracking the case. "Police work is at the core about human relations—about talking to witnesses, to victims, to the community—and we're not out to change that," says Palmer. "Our aim is to give investigators factual insights from information we already have that might make a difference, so even if we're successful 5% of the time, we're going to take a lot of offenders off the street."

The growing list of cold cases solved has helped Palmer in his efforts to reinforce the merits of Blue PALMS. But, in showing where his loyalty lies, he sees the detectives who've closed these cold cases—not the program—as most deserving of the spotlight, and that approach has gone over well. At his chief's request, Palmer is beginning to use his liaison role as a platform for reaching out to other areas in the Miami-Dade Police Department.

Safer Streets for a Smarter City

When he speaks of the impact of tourism, a thread that runs through Miami-Dade's Smarter Cities vision, Palmer sees Blue PALMS as an important tool to protect one of the county's greatest assets. "The threat to tourism posed by rising street crime was a big reason the unit was established," says Palmer. "The fact that we're able to use analytics and intelligence to help us close more cases and keep more criminals off the street is good news for our citizens and our tourist industry."

QUESTIONS FOR THE OPENING VIGNETTE

1. Why do law enforcement agencies and departments like Miami-Dade Police Department embrace advanced analytics and data mining?
2. What are the top challenges for law enforcement agencies and departments like Miami-Dade Police Department? Can you think of other challenges (not mentioned in this case) that can benefit from data mining?
3. What are the sources of data that law enforcement agencies and departments like Miami-Dade Police Department use for their predictive modeling and data mining projects?
4. What type of analytics do law enforcement agencies and departments like Miami-Dade Police Department use to fight crime?
5. What does "the big picture starts small" mean in this case? Explain.

What We Can Learn from This Vignette

The law enforcement agencies and departments are under tremendous pressure to carry out their mission of safeguarding people with limited resources. The environment within which they perform their duties is becoming increasingly more challenging so that they have to constantly adopt and perhaps stay a few steps ahead to prevent the likelihood of catastrophes. Understanding the changing nature of crime and criminals is an ongoing challenge. In the midst of these challenges, what works in favor of these agencies is the availability of the data and analytics technologies to better analyze past occurrences and to foresee future events. Data has become available more than it has in the past. Applying advanced analytics and data mining tools (i.e., knowledge discovery techniques) to these large and rich data sources provides them with the insight that they need to better prepare and act on their duties. Therefore, law enforcement agencies are becoming one of the leading users of the new face of analytics. Data mining is a prime candidate for better understanding and management of these mission critical tasks with a high level of accuracy and timeliness. The study described in the opening vignette clearly illustrates the power of analytics and data mining to create a holistic view of the world of crime and criminals for better and faster reaction and management. In this chapter, you will see a wide variety of data mining applications solving complex problems in a variety of industries and organizational settings where the data is used to discover actionable insight to improve mission readiness, operational efficiency, and competitive advantage.

Sources: Miami-Dade Police Department: Predictive modeling pinpoints likely suspects based on common crime signatures of previous crimes, IBM Customer Case Studies, www-03.ibm.com/software/businesscasestudies/om/en/corp?synkey=C894638H25952N07; Law Enforcement Analytics: Intelligence-Led and Predictive Policing by Information Builder www.informationbuilders.com/solutions/gov-lea.

4.2 Data Mining Concepts and Applications

Data mining, a new and exciting technology of only a few years ago, has become a common practice for a vast majority of organizations. In an interview with *Computerworld* magazine in January 1999, Dr. Arno Penzias (Nobel laureate and former chief scientist of Bell Labs) identified data mining from organizational databases as a key application for corporations of the near future. In response to *Computerworld*'s age-old question of "What will be the killer applications in the corporation?" Dr. Penzias replied: "Data mining." He then added, "Data mining will become much more important and companies will throw away nothing about their customers because it will be so valuable. If you're not doing this, you're out of business." Similarly, in an article in *Harvard Business Review,* Thomas Davenport (2006) argued that the latest strategic weapon for companies is analytical decision making, providing examples of companies such as Amazon.com, Capital One, Marriott International, and others that have used analytics to better understand their customers and optimize their extended supply chains to maximize their returns on investment while providing the best customer service. This level of success is highly dependent on a company understanding its customers, vendors, business processes, and the extended supply chain very well.

A large portion of "understanding the customer" can come from analyzing the vast amount of data that a company collects. The cost of storing and processing data has decreased dramatically in the recent past, and, as a result, the amount of data stored in electronic form has grown at an explosive rate. With the creation of large databases, the possibility of analyzing the data stored in them has emerged. The term *data mining* was originally used to describe the process through which previously unknown patterns in data were discovered. This definition has since been stretched beyond those limits by some software vendors to include most forms of data analysis in order to increase sales with the popularity of the data mining label. In this chapter, we accept the original definition of data mining.

Although the term *data mining* is relatively new, the ideas behind it are not. Many of the techniques used in data mining have their roots in traditional statistical analysis and artificial intelligence work done since the early part of the 1980s. Why, then, has it suddenly gained the attention of the business world? Following are some of most pronounced reasons:

- More intense competition at the global scale driven by customers' ever-changing needs and wants in an increasingly saturated marketplace.
- General recognition of the untapped value hidden in large data sources.
- Consolidation and integration of database records, which enables a single view of customers, vendors, transactions, and so on.
- Consolidation of databases and other data repositories into a single location in the form of a data warehouse.
- The exponential increase in data processing and storage technologies.
- Significant reduction in the cost of hardware and software for data storage and processing.
- Movement toward the demassification (conversion of information resources into nonphysical form) of business practices.

Data generated by the Internet is increasing rapidly in both volume and complexity. Large amounts of genomic data are being generated and accumulated all over the world. Disciplines such as astronomy and nuclear physics create huge quantities of data on a regular basis. Medical and pharmaceutical researchers constantly generate and store data that can then be used in data mining applications to identify better ways to accurately diagnose and treat illnesses and to discover new and improved drugs.

On the commercial side, perhaps the most common use of data mining has been in the finance, retail, and healthcare sectors. Data mining is used to detect and reduce fraudulent activities, especially in insurance claims and credit card use (Chan et al., 1999); to identify customer buying patterns (Hoffman, 1999); to reclaim profitable customers (Hoffman, 1998); to identify trading rules from historical data; and to aid in increased profitability using market-basket analysis. Data mining is already widely used to better target clients, and with the widespread development of e-commerce, this can only become more imperative with time. See Application Case 4.1 for information on how Infinity P&C has used predictive analytics and data mining to improve customer service, combat fraud, and increase profit.

Application Case 4.1

Visa Is Enhancing the Customer Experience While Reducing Fraud with Predictive Analytics and Data Mining

When card issuers first started using automated business rules software to counter debit and credit card fraud, the limits on that technology were quickly evident: Customers reported frustrating payment rejections on dream vacations or critical business trips. Visa works with its clients to improve customer experience by providing cutting-edge fraud risk tools and consulting services that make its strategies more effective. Through this approach, Visa enhances customer experience and minimizes invalid transaction declines.

The company's global network connects thousands of financial institutions with millions of merchants and cardholders every day. It has been a pioneer in cashless payments for more than 50 years. By using

SAS® Analytics, Visa is supporting financial institutions to reduce fraud without upsetting customers with unnecessary payment rejections. Whenever it processes a transaction, Visa analyzes up to 500 unique variables in real time to assess the risk of that transaction. Using vast data sets, including global fraud hot spots and transactional patterns, the company can more accurately assess whether you're buying escargot in Paris, or someone who stole your credit card is.

"What that means is that if you are likely to travel we know it, and we tell your financial institution so you're not declined at the point of sale," says Nathan Falkenborg, Head of Visa Performance Solutions for North Asia. "We also will assist your bank in developing the right strategies for using the Visa tools and scoring systems," he adds. Visa estimates that Big Data analytics works; state-of-the-art models and scoring systems have the potential to prevent an incremental $2 billion of fraudulent payment volume annually.

A globally recognized name, Visa facilitates electronic funds transfer through branded products that are issued by its thousands of financial institution partners. The company processed 64.9 billion transactions in 2014, and $4.7 trillion in purchases were made with a Visa card in that same year.

It has the computing capability to process 56,000 transaction messages per second, which is greater than four times the actual peak transaction rate to date. Visa doesn't just process and compute—it is continually using analytics to share strategic and operational insights with its partner financial institutions and assist them in improving performance. This business goal is supported by a robust data management system. Visa also assists its clients in improving performance by developing and delivering deep analytical insight.

"We understand patterns of behavior by performing clustering and segmentation at a granular level, and we provide this insight to our financial institution partners," says Falkenborg. "It's an effective way to help our clients communicate better and deepen their understanding of the customer."

As an example of marketing support, Visa has assisted clients globally in identifying segments of customers that should be offered a different Visa product. "Understanding the customer lifecycle is incredibly important, and Visa provides information to clients that help them take action and offer the right product to the right customer before a value proposition becomes stale," says Falkenborg.

How Can Using In-Memory Analytics Make a Difference?

In a recent proof-of-concept, Visa used a high-performance solution from SAS that relies on in-memory computing to power statistical and machine-learning algorithms and then present the information visually. In-memory analytics reduces the need to move data and perform more model iterations, making it much faster and accurate.

Falkenborg describes the solution as like having the information memorized, versus having to get up and go to a filing cabinet to retrieve it. "In-memory analytics is just taking your brain and making it bigger. Everything is instantly accessible."

Ultimately, solid analytics helps the company do more than just process payments. "We can deepen the client conversation and serve our clients even better with our incredible big data set and expertise in mining transaction data," says Falkenborg. "We use our consulting and analytics capabilities to assist our clients in tackling business challenges and protect the payment ecosystem. And that's what we do with high-performance analytics."

"The challenge that we have, as with any company managing and using massive data sets, is how we use all necessary information to solve a business challenge—whether that is improving our fraud models, or assisting a client to more effectively communicate with its customers," elaborates Falkenborg. "In-memory analytics enables us to be more nimble; with a 100× analytical system processing speed improvement, our data and decision scientists can iterate much faster."

Fast and accurate predictive analytics allows Visa to better serve clients with tailored consulting services, helping them succeed in today's fast-changing payments industry.

Questions for Discussion

1. What challenges were Visa and the rest of the credit card industry facing?
2. How did Visa improve customer service while also improving retention of fraud?
3. What is in-memory analytics, and why was it necessary?

Definitions, Characteristics, and Benefits

Simply defined, **data mining** is a term used to describe discovering or "mining" knowledge from large amounts of data. When considered by analogy, one can easily realize that the term *data mining* is a misnomer; that is, mining of gold from within rocks or dirt is referred to as "gold" mining rather than "rock" or "dirt" mining. Therefore, data mining perhaps should have been named "knowledge mining" or "knowledge discovery." Despite the mismatch between the term and its meaning, *data mining* has become the choice of the community. Many other names that are associated with data mining include *knowledge extraction, pattern analysis, data archaeology, information harvesting, pattern searching,* and *data dredging.*

Technically speaking, data mining is a process that uses statistical, mathematical, and artificial intelligence techniques to extract and identify useful information and subsequent knowledge (or patterns) from large sets of data. These patterns can be in the form of business rules, affinities, correlations, trends, or prediction models (see Nemati and Barko, 2001). Most literature defines data mining as "the nontrivial process of identifying valid, novel, potentially useful, and ultimately understandable patterns in data stored in structured databases," where the data are organized in records structured by categorical, ordinal, and continuous variables (Fayyad et al., 1996, pp. 40–41). In this definition, the meanings of the key term are as follows:

- *Process* implies that data mining comprises many iterative steps.
- *Nontrivial* means that some experimentation-type search or inference is involved; that is, it is not as straightforward as a computation of predefined quantities.
- *Valid* means that the discovered patterns should hold true on new data with a sufficient degree of certainty.
- *Novel* means that the patterns are not previously known to the user within the context of the system being analyzed.
- *Potentially useful* means that the discovered patterns should lead to some benefit to the user or task.
- *Ultimately understandable* means that the pattern should make business sense that leads to the user saying, "Mmm! It makes sense; why didn't I think of that," if not immediately, at least after some postprocessing.

Data mining is not a new discipline, but rather a new definition for the use of many disciplines. Data mining is tightly positioned at the intersection of many disciplines, including statistics, artificial intelligence, machine learning, management science, information systems (IS), and databases (see Figure 4.1). Using advances in all of these disciplines, data mining strives to make progress in extracting useful information and knowledge from large databases. It is an emerging field that has attracted much attention in a very short time.

The following are the major characteristics and objectives of data mining:

- Data are often buried deep within very large databases, which sometimes contain data from several years. In many cases, the data are cleansed and consolidated into a data warehouse. Data may be presented in a variety of formats (see Chapter 2 for a brief taxonomy of data).
- The data mining environment is usually a client/server architecture or a Web-based IS architecture.
- Sophisticated new tools, including advanced visualization tools, help to remove the information ore buried in corporate files or archival public records. Finding it involves massaging and synchronizing the data to get the right results. Cutting-edge data miners are also exploring the usefulness of soft data (i.e., unstructured text stored in such places as Lotus Notes databases, text files on the Internet, or enterprise-wide intranets).

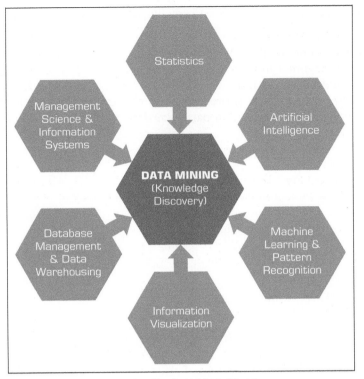

FIGURE 4.1   Data Mining Is a Blend of Multiple Disciplines.

- The miner is often an end user, empowered by data drills and other powerful query tools to ask ad hoc questions and obtain answers quickly, with little or no programming skill.
- Striking it rich often involves finding an unexpected result and requires end users to think creatively throughout the process, including the interpretation of the findings.
- Data mining tools are readily combined with spreadsheets and other software development tools. Thus, the mined data can be analyzed and deployed quickly and easily.
- Because of the large amounts of data and massive search efforts, it is sometimes necessary to use parallel processing for data mining.

A company that effectively leverages data mining tools and technologies can acquire and maintain a strategic competitive advantage. Data mining offers organizations an indispensable decision-enhancing environment to exploit new opportunities by transforming data into a strategic weapon. See Nemati and Barko (2001) for a more detailed discussion on the strategic benefits of data mining.

How Data Mining Works

Using existing and relevant data obtained from within and outside the organization, data mining builds models to discover patterns among the attributes presented in the data set. Models are the mathematical representations (simple linear relationships/affinities and/or complex and highly nonlinear relationships) that identify the patterns among the attributes of the things (e.g., customers, events) described within the data set. Some of these patterns are explanatory (explaining the interrelationships and affinities among the attributes), whereas others are predictive (foretelling future values of certain attributes). In general, data mining seeks to identify four major types of patterns:

1. *Associations* find the commonly co-occurring groupings of things, such as beer and diapers going together in market-basket analysis.
2. *Predictions* tell the nature of future occurrences of certain events based on what has happened in the past, such as predicting the winner of the Super Bowl or forecasting the absolute temperature of a particular day.

Application Case 4.2

Dell Is Staying Agile and Effective with Analytics in the 21st Century

The digital revolution is changing how people shop. Studies show that even commercial customers spend more of their buyer journey researching solutions online before they engage a vendor. To compete, companies like Dell are transforming sales and marketing models to support these new requirements. However, doing so effectively requires a Big Data solution that can analyze corporate databases along with unstructured information from sources such as clickstreams and social media.

Dell has evolved into a technology leader by using efficient, data-driven processes. For decades, employees could get measurable results by using enterprise applications to support insight and facilitate processes such as customer relationship management (CRM), sales, and accounting. When Dell recognized that customers were spending dramatically more time researching products online before contacting a sales representative, it wanted to update marketing models accordingly so that it could deliver the new types of personalized services and the support that customers expected. To make such changes, however, marketing employees needed more data about customers' online behavior. Staff also needed an easier way to condense insight from numerous business intelligence (BI) tools and data sources. Drew Miller, Executive Director, Marketing Analytics and Insights at Dell, says, "There are petabytes of available information about customers' online and offline shopping habits. We just needed to give marketing employees an easy-to-use solution

that could assimilate all of it, pinpoint patterns and make recommendations about marketing spend and activities."

Setting Up an Agile Team to Boost Return on Investment (ROI) with BI and Analytics

To improve its global BI and analytics strategy and communications, Dell established an IT task force. Executives created a flexible governance model for the team so that it can rapidly respond to employees' evolving BI and analytics requirements and deliver rapid ROI. For example, in addition to having the freedom to collaborate with internal business groups, the task force is empowered to modify business and IT processes using agile and innovative strategies. The team must dedicate more than 50% of its efforts identifying and implementing quick-win BI and analytics projects that are typically too small for the "A" priority list of Dell's IT department. And the team must also spend at least 30% of its time evangelizing within internal business groups to raise awareness about BI's transformative capabilities—as well as opportunities for collaboration.

One of the task force's first projects was a new BI and analytics solution called the Marketing Analytics Workbench. Its initial application was focused on a select set of use cases around online and offline commercial customer engagements. This effort was cofunded by Dell's IT and marketing organizations. "There was a desire to expand the usage of this solution to support many more sales and marketing activities as soon as possible. However, we knew we could build a more effective solution if we scaled it out via iterative quick sprint efforts," says Fadi Taffal, Director, Enterprise IT at Dell.

One Massive Data Mart Facilitates a Single Source of Truth

Working closely with marketing, task force engineers use lean software development strategies and numerous technologies to create a highly scalable data mart. The overall solution utilizes multiple technologies and tools to enable different types of data storage, manipulation, and automation activities. For example, engineers store unstructured data from digital/social media sources on servers running Apache Hadoop. They use the Teradata Aster platform to then integrate and explore large amounts of customer data from other sources in near real time. For various data transformation and automation needs, the solution includes the use of Dell's Toad software suite, specifically Toad Data Point and Toad Intelligence Central, and Dell Statistica. Toad Data Point provides a business-friendly interface for data manipulation and automation, which is a critical gap in the ecosystem. For advanced analytical models, the system uses Dell Statistica, which provides data preparation, predictive analytics, data mining and machine learning, statistics, text analytics, visualization and reporting, and model deployment and monitoring. Engineers also utilize this solution to develop analytical models that can sift through all of the disparate data and provide an accurate picture of customers' shopping behavior. Tools provide suggestions for improving service, as well as ROI metrics for multivehicle strategies that include Web site marketing, phone calls, and site visits.

Within several months, employees were using the initial Marketing Analytics Workbench. The task force plans to expand the solution's capabilities so it can analyze data from more sources, provide additional visualizations, and measure the returns of other channel activities such as tweets, texts, e-mail messages, and social media posts.

Saves More Than $2.5 Million in Operational Costs

With its new solution, Dell has already eliminated several third-party BI applications. "Although we're just in the initial phases of rolling out our Marketing Analytics Workbench, we've saved approximately $2.5 million in vendor outsourcing costs," says Chaitanya Laxminarayana, Marketing Program Manager at Dell. "Plus, employees gain faster and more detailed insights." As Dell scales the Marketing Analytics Workbench, it will phase out additional third-party BI applications, further reducing costs and boosting efficiency.

Facilitates $5.3 Million in Revenue

Marketing employees now have the insight they need to identify emerging trends in customer engagements—and update models accordingly. "We've already realized $5.3 million in incremental revenue by initiating more personalized marketing programs and uncovering new opportunities with our big data Marketing Analytics Workbench," says Laxman Srigiri, Director, Marketing Analytics at Dell. "Additionally, we have programs on track to scale this impact many times over in the next three years."

For example, employees can now see a timeline of a customer's online and offline interactions with Dell, including purchases, the specific Dell Web site pages the customer visited, and the files they downloaded. Plus, employees receive database suggestions for when and how to contact a customer, as well as the URLs of specific pages they should read to learn more about the technologies a customer is researching. Srigiri says, "It was imperative that we understand changing requirements so we could stay agile. Now that we have that insight, we can quickly develop more effective marketing models that deliver the personalized information and support customers expect."

QUESTIONS FOR DISCUSSION

1. What was the challenge Dell was facing that led to their analytics journey?
2. What solution did Dell develop and implement? What were the results?
3. As an analytics company itself, Dell has used its service offerings for its own business. Do you think it is easier or harder for a company to taste its own medicine? Explain.

Source: Dell: Staying agile and effective in the 21st century. Dell Case Study, software.dell.com/casestudy/dell-staying -agile-and-effective-in-the-21st-century881389. Used by permission from Dell.

3. *Clusters* identify natural groupings of things based on their known characteristics, such as assigning customers in different segments based on their demographics and past purchase behaviors.

4. *Sequential relationships* discover time-ordered events, such as predicting that an existing banking customer who already has a checking account will open a savings account followed by an investment account within a year.

These types of patterns have been *manually* extracted from data by humans for centuries, but the increasing volume of data in modern times has created a need for more automatic approaches. As data sets have grown in size and complexity, direct manual data analysis has increasingly been augmented with indirect, automatic data processing tools that use sophisticated methodologies, methods, and algorithms. The manifestation of such evolution of automated and semiautomated means of processing large data sets is now commonly referred to as *data mining*.

Generally speaking, data mining tasks can be classified into three main categories: prediction, association, and clustering. Based on the way in which the patterns are extracted from the historical data, the learning algorithms of data mining methods can be classified as either supervised or unsupervised. With supervised learning algorithms, the training data includes both the descriptive attributes (i.e., independent variables or decision variables) as well as the class attribute (i.e., output variable or result variable). In contrast, with unsupervised learning the training data includes only the descriptive attributes. Figure 4.2 shows a simple taxonomy for data mining tasks, along with the learning methods and popular algorithms for each of the data mining tasks.

PREDICTION   **Prediction** is commonly referred to as the act of telling about the future. It differs from simple guessing by taking into account the experiences, opinions, and other relevant information in conducting the task of foretelling. A term that is commonly associated with prediction is *forecasting*. Even though many believe that these two terms are synonymous, there is a subtle but critical difference between the two. Whereas prediction is largely experience and opinion based, forecasting is data and model based. That is, in order of increasing reliability, one might list the relevant terms as *guessing, predicting,* and *forecasting*, respectively. In data mining terminology, *prediction* and *forecasting* are used synonymously, and the term *prediction* is used as the common representation of the act. Depending on the nature of what is being predicted, prediction can be named more specifically as classification (where the predicted thing, such as tomorrow's forecast, is a class label such as "rainy" or "sunny") or regression (where the predicted thing, such as tomorrow's temperature, is a real number, such as "65°F").

CLASSIFICATION   **Classification**, or supervised induction, is perhaps the most common of all data mining tasks. The objective of classification is to analyze the historical data stored in a database and automatically generate a model that can predict future behavior. This induced model consists of generalizations over the records of a training data set, which help distinguish predefined classes. The hope is that the model can then be used to predict the classes of other unclassified records and, more important, to accurately predict actual future events.

Common classification tools include neural networks and decision trees (from machine learning), logistic regression and discriminant analysis (from traditional statistics), and emerging tools such as rough sets, support vector machines (SVMs), and genetic algorithms. Statistics-based classification techniques (e.g., logistic regression and discriminant analysis) have received their share of criticism—that they make unrealistic assumptions about the data, such as independence and normality—which limit their use in classification-type data mining projects.

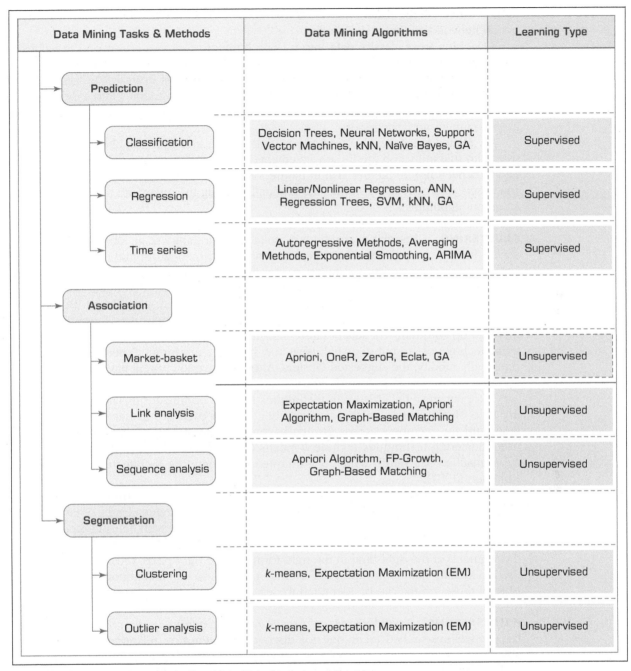

Data Mining Tasks & Methods	Data Mining Algorithms	Learning Type
Prediction		
Classification	Decision Trees, Neural Networks, Support Vector Machines, kNN, Naïve Bayes, GA	Supervised
Regression	Linear/Nonlinear Regression, ANN, Regression Trees, SVM, kNN, GA	Supervised
Time series	Autoregressive Methods, Averaging Methods, Exponential Smoothing, ARIMA	Supervised
Association		
Market-basket	Apriori, OneR, ZeroR, Eclat, GA	Unsupervised
Link analysis	Expectation Maximization, Apriori Algorithm, Graph-Based Matching	Unsupervised
Sequence analysis	Apriori Algorithm, FP-Growth, Graph-Based Matching	Unsupervised
Segmentation		
Clustering	k-means, Expectation Maximization (EM)	Unsupervised
Outlier analysis	k-means, Expectation Maximization (EM)	Unsupervised

FIGURE 4.2 A Simple Taxonomy for Data Mining Tasks, Methods, and Algorithms.

Neural networks involve the development of mathematical structures (somewhat resembling the biological neural networks in the human brain) that have the capability to learn from past experiences presented in the form of well-structured data sets. They tend to be more effective when the number of variables involved is rather large and the relationships among them are complex and imprecise. Neural networks have disadvantages as well as advantages. For example, it is usually very difficult to provide a good rationale for the predictions made by a neural network. Also, neural networks tend to need considerable training. Unfortunately, the time needed for training tends to increase exponentially as the volume of data increases, and in general, neural networks cannot be trained on very large databases. These and other factors have limited the applicability of neural networks in data-rich domains.

Decision trees classify data into a finite number of classes based on the values of the input variables. Decision trees are essentially a hierarchy of if-then statements and are thus significantly faster than neural networks. They are most appropriate for **categorical** and **interval data**. Therefore, incorporating continuous variables into a decision tree framework requires *discretization*; that is, converting continuous valued numerical variables to ranges and categories.

A related category of classification tools is rule induction. Unlike with a decision tree, with rule induction the if-then statements are induced from the training data directly, and they need not be hierarchical in nature. Other, more recent techniques such as SVM, rough sets, and genetic algorithms are gradually finding their way into the arsenal of classification algorithms.

CLUSTERING **Clustering** partitions a collection of things (e.g., objects, events, presented in a structured data set) into segments (or natural groupings) whose members share similar characteristics. Unlike in classification, in clustering the class labels are unknown. As the selected algorithm goes through the data set, identifying the commonalities of things based on their characteristics, the clusters are established. Because the clusters are determined using a heuristic-type algorithm, and because different algorithms may end up with different sets of clusters for the same data set, before the results of clustering techniques are put to actual use it may be necessary for an expert to interpret, and potentially modify, the suggested clusters. After reasonable clusters have been identified, they can be used to classify and interpret new data.

Not surprisingly, clustering techniques include optimization. The goal of clustering is to create groups so that the members within each group have maximum similarity and the members across groups have minimum similarity. The most commonly used clustering techniques include *k*-means (from statistics) and self-organizing maps (from machine learning), which is a unique neural network architecture developed by Kohonen (1982).

Firms often effectively use their data mining systems to perform market segmentation with cluster analysis. Cluster analysis is a means of identifying classes of items so that items in a cluster have more in common with each other than with items in other clusters. It can be used in segmenting customers and directing appropriate marketing products to the segments at the right time in the right format at the right price. Cluster analysis is also used to identify natural groupings of events or objects so that a common set of characteristics of these groups can be identified to describe them.

ASSOCIATIONS **Associations**, or *association rule learning in data mining*, is a popular and well-researched technique for discovering interesting relationships among variables in large databases. Thanks to automated data-gathering technologies such as bar code scanners, the use of association rules for discovering regularities among products in large-scale transactions recorded by point-of-sale systems in supermarkets has become a common knowledge discovery task in the retail industry. In the context of the retail industry, association rule mining is often called *market-basket analysis*.

Two commonly used derivatives of association rule mining are **link analysis** and **sequence mining**. With link analysis, the linkage among many objects of interest is discovered automatically, such as the link between Web pages and referential relationships among groups of academic publication authors. With sequence mining, relationships are examined in terms of their order of occurrence to identify associations over time. Algorithms used in association rule mining include the popular Apriori (where frequent itemsets are identified) and FP-Growth, OneR, ZeroR, and Eclat.

VISUALIZATION AND TIME-SERIES FORECASTING Two techniques often associated with data mining are *visualization* and *time-series forecasting*. Visualization can be used in conjunction with other data mining techniques to gain a clearer understanding of underlying relationships. As the importance of visualization has increased in recent years, a new term, *visual analytics*, has emerged. The idea is to combine analytics and visualization in a single environment for easier and faster knowledge creation. Visual analytics is covered in detail in Chapter 3. In time-series forecasting, the data consists of values of the same variable that is captured and stored over time in regular intervals. These data are then used to develop forecasting models to extrapolate the future values of the same variable.

Data Mining versus Statistics

Data mining and statistics have a lot in common. They both look for relationships within data. Most people call statistics the "foundation of data mining." The main difference between the two is that statistics starts with a well-defined proposition and hypothesis, whereas data mining starts with a loosely defined discovery statement. Statistics collects sample data (i.e., primary data) to test the hypothesis, whereas data mining and analytics use all the existing data (i.e., often observational, secondary data) to discover novel patterns and relationships. Another difference comes from the size of data that they use. Data mining looks for data sets that are as "big" as possible, whereas statistics looks for the right size of data (if the data is larger than what is needed/required for the statistical analysis, a sample of the data is used). The meaning of "large data" is rather different between statistics and data mining. A few hundred to a thousand data points are large enough to a statistician, but several million to a few billion data points are considered large for data mining studies.

SECTION 4.2 REVIEW QUESTIONS

1. Define *data mining*. Why are there many different names and definitions for data mining?
2. What recent factors have increased the popularity of data mining?
3. Is data mining a new discipline? Explain.
4. What are some major data mining methods and algorithms?
5. What are the key differences between the major data mining tasks?

4.3 Data Mining Applications

Data mining has become a popular tool in addressing many complex businesses problems and opportunities. It has been proven to be very successful and helpful in many areas, some of which are shown by the following representative examples. The goal of many of these business data mining applications is to solve a pressing problem or to explore an emerging business opportunity to create a sustainable competitive advantage.

- **Customer relationship management.** Customer relationship management (CRM) is the extension of traditional marketing. The goal of CRM is to create one-on-one relationships with customers by developing an intimate understanding of their needs and wants. As businesses build relationships with their customers over time through a variety of interactions (e.g., product inquiries, sales, service requests, warranty calls, product reviews, social media connections), they accumulate tremendous amounts of data. When combined with demographic and socioeconomic attributes, this information-rich data can be used to (1) identify most likely responders/buyers of new products/services (i.e., customer profiling); (2) understand the root causes of customer attrition to improve customer retention (i.e., churn analysis); (3) discover time-variant associations between products and services to maximize sales and customer value; and (4) identify the most profitable customers and their preferential needs to strengthen relationships and to maximize sales.

- **Banking.** Data mining can help banks with the following: (1) automating the loan application process by accurately predicting the most probable defaulters, (2) detecting fraudulent credit card and online banking transactions, (3) identifying ways to maximize customer value by selling them products and services that they are most likely to buy, and (4) optimizing the cash return by accurately forecasting the cash flow on banking entities (e.g., ATM machines, banking branches).

- **Retailing and logistics.** In the retailing industry, data mining can be used to (1) predict accurate sales volumes at specific retail locations to determine correct inventory levels; (2) identify sales relationships between different products (with market-basket analysis) to improve the store layout and optimize sales promotions; (3) forecast consumption levels of different product types (based on seasonal and environmental conditions) to optimize logistics and, hence, maximize sales; and (4) discover interesting patterns in the movement of products (especially for the products that have a limited shelf life because they are prone to expiration, perishability, and contamination) in a supply chain by analyzing sensory and radio-frequency identification (RFID) data.

- **Manufacturing and production.** Manufacturers can use data mining to (1) predict machinery failures before they occur through the use of sensory data (enabling what is called *condition-based maintenance*); (2) identify anomalies and commonalities in production systems to optimize manufacturing capacity; and (3) discover novel patterns to identify and improve product quality.

- **Brokerage and securities trading.** Brokers and traders use data mining to (1) predict when and how much certain bond prices will change; (2) forecast the range and direction of stock fluctuations; (3) assess the effect of particular issues and events on overall market movements; and (4) identify and prevent fraudulent activities in securities trading.

- **Insurance.** The insurance industry uses data mining techniques to (1) forecast claim amounts for property and medical coverage costs for better business planning, (2) determine optimal rate plans based on the analysis of claims and customer data, (3) predict which customers are more likely to buy new policies with special features, and (4) identify and prevent incorrect claim payments and fraudulent activities.

- **Computer hardware and software.** Data mining can be used to (1) predict disk drive failures well before they actually occur, (2) identify and filter unwanted Web content and e-mail messages, (3) detect and prevent computer network security breaches and (4) identify potentially unsecure software products.

- **Government and defense.** Data mining also has a number of military applications. It can be used to (1) forecast the cost of moving military personnel and equipment; (2) predict an adversary's moves and, hence, develop more successful strategies for military engagements; (3) predict resource consumption for better planning and budgeting; and (4) identify classes of unique experiences, strategies, and lessons learned from military operations for better knowledge sharing throughout the organization.

- **Travel industry (airlines, hotels/resorts, rental car companies).** Data mining has a variety of uses in the travel industry. It is successfully used to (1) predict sales of different services (seat types in airplanes, room types in hotels/resorts, car types in rental car companies) in order to optimally price services to maximize revenues as a function of time-varying transactions (commonly referred to as *yield management*);

(2) forecast demand at different locations to better allocate limited organizational resources; (3) identify the most profitable customers and provide them with personalized services to maintain their repeat business; and (4) retain valuable employees by identifying and acting on the root causes for attrition.

- **Healthcare.** Data mining has a number of healthcare applications. It can be used to (1) identify people without health insurance and the factors underlying this undesired phenomenon, (2) identify novel cost–benefit relationships between different treatments to develop more effective strategies, (3) forecast the level and the time of demand at different service locations to optimally allocate organizational resources, and (4) understand the underlying reasons for customer and employee attrition.

- **Medicine.** Use of data mining in medicine should be viewed as an invaluable complement to traditional medical research, which is mainly clinical and biological in nature. Data mining analyses can (1) identify novel patterns to improve survivability of patients with cancer, (2) predict success rates of organ transplantation patients to develop better organ donor matching policies, (3) identify the functions of different genes in the human chromosome (known as genomics), and (4) discover the relationships between symptoms and illnesses (as well as illnesses and successful treatments) to help medical professionals make informed and correct decisions in a timely manner.

- **Entertainment industry.** Data mining is successfully used by the entertainment industry to (1) analyze viewer data to decide what programs to show during prime time and how to maximize returns by knowing where to insert advertisements, (2) predict the financial success of movies before they are produced to make investment decisions and to optimize the returns, (3) forecast the demand at different locations and different times to better schedule entertainment events and to optimally allocate resources, and (4) develop optimal pricing policies to maximize revenues.

- **Homeland security and law enforcement.** Data mining has a number of homeland security and law enforcement applications. Data mining is often used to (1) identify patterns of terrorist behaviors (see Application Case 4.3 for an example of the use of data mining to track funding of terrorists' activities); (2) discover crime patterns (e.g., locations, timings, criminal behaviors, and other related attributes) to help solve criminal cases in a timely manner; (3) predict and eliminate potential biological and chemical attacks to the nation's critical infrastructure by analyzing special-purpose sensory data; and (4) identify and stop malicious attacks on critical information infrastructures (often called *information warfare*).

Application Case 4.3

Predictive Analytic and Data Mining Help Stop Terrorist Funding

The terrorist attack on the World Trade Center on September 11, 2001, underlined the importance of open-source intelligence. The USA PATRIOT Act and the creation of the U.S. Department of Homeland Security heralded the potential application of information technology and data mining techniques to detect money laundering and other forms of terrorist financing. Law enforcement agencies had been focusing on money laundering activities via normal transactions through banks and other financial service organizations.

Law enforcement agencies are now focusing on international trade pricing as a terrorism funding tool. International trade has been used by money launderers to move money silently out of a country without attracting government attention. This transfer is achieved by overvaluing imports and undervaluing exports. For example, a domestic importer and foreign exporter could form a partnership and overvalue imports, thereby transferring money from the home country, resulting in crimes related

(Continued)

Application Case 4.3 (Continued)

to customs fraud, income tax evasion, and money laundering. The foreign exporter could be a member of a terrorist organization.

Data mining techniques focus on analysis of data on import and export transactions from the U.S. Department of Commerce and commerce-related entities. Import prices that exceed the upper quartile import prices and export prices that are lower than the lower quartile export prices are tracked. The focus is on abnormal transfer prices between corporations that may result in shifting taxable income and taxes out of the United States. An observed price deviation may be related to income tax avoidance/evasion, money laundering, or terrorist financing. The observed price deviation may also be due to an error in the U.S. trade database.

Data mining will result in efficient evaluation of data, which, in turn, will aid in the fight against

terrorism. The application of information technology and data mining techniques to financial transactions can contribute to better intelligence information.

QUESTIONS FOR DISCUSSION

1. How can data mining be used to fight terrorism? Comment on what else can be done beyond what is covered in this short application case.

2. Do you think data mining, although essential for fighting terrorist cells, also jeopardizes individuals' rights of privacy?

Sources: Zdanowic, J. S. (2004, May). Detecting money laundering and terrorist financing via data mining. *Communications of the ACM, 47*(5), 53; Bolton, R. J. (2002, January). Statistical fraud detection: A review. *Statistical Science, 17*(3), 235.

- **Sports.** Data mining was used to improve the performance of National Basketball Association (NBA) teams in the United States. Major League Baseball teams are into predictive analytics and data mining to optimally utilize their limited resources for a winning season (see Moneyball article in Chapter 1). In fact, most, if not all, professional sports nowadays employ data crunchers and use data mining to increase their chances of winning. Data mining applications are not limited to professional sports. In a 2012 article, Delen, Cogdell, and Kasap (2012) developed data mining models to predict National Collegiate Athletic Association (NCAA) Bowl Game outcomes using a wide range of variables about the two opposing teams' previous games statistics (more details about this case study are provided in Chapter 2). Wright (2012) used a variety of predictors for examination of the NCAA men's basketball championship bracket (a.k.a. March Madness).

SECTION 4.3 REVIEW QUESTIONS

1. What are the major application areas for data mining?
2. Identify at least five specific applications of data mining and list five common characteristics of these applications.
3. What do you think is the most prominent application area for data mining? Why?
4. Can you think of other application areas for data mining not discussed in this section? Explain.

4.4 Data Mining Process

To systematically carry out data mining projects, a general process is usually followed. Based on best practices, data mining researchers and practitioners have proposed several processes (workflows or simple step-by-step approaches) to maximize the chances of success in conducting data mining projects. These efforts have led to several standardized processes, some of which (a few of the most popular ones) are described in this section.

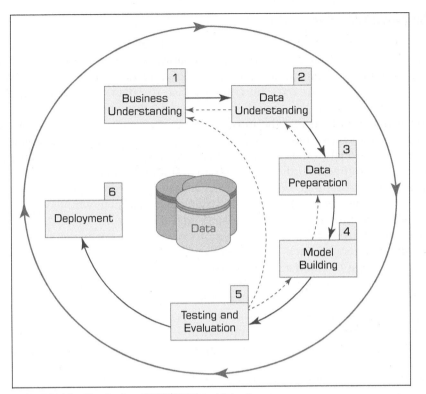

FIGURE 4.3   The Six-Step CRISP-DM Data Mining Process.

One such standardized process, arguably the most popular one, Cross-Industry Standard Process for Data Mining—**CRISP-DM**—was proposed in the mid-1990s by a European consortium of companies to serve as a nonproprietary standard methodology for data mining (CRISP-DM, 2013). Figure 4.3 illustrates this proposed process, which is a sequence of six steps that starts with a good understanding of the business and the need for the data mining project (i.e., the application domain) and ends with the deployment of the solution that satisfies the specific business need. Even though these steps are sequential in nature, there is usually a great deal of backtracking. Because the data mining is driven by experience and experimentation, depending on the problem situation and the knowledge/ experience of the analyst, the whole process can be very iterative (i.e., one should expect to go back and forth through the steps quite a few times) and time-consuming. Because later steps are built on the outcomes of the former ones, one should pay extra attention to the earlier steps in order not to put the whole study on an incorrect path from the onset.

Step 1: Business Understanding

The key element of any data mining study is to know what the study is for. Answering such a question begins with a thorough understanding of the managerial need for new knowledge and an explicit specification of the business objective regarding the study to be conducted. Specific goals such as "What are the common characteristics of the customers we have lost to our competitors recently?" or "What are typical profiles of our customers, and how much value does each of them provide to us?" are needed. Then a project plan for finding such knowledge is developed that specifies the people responsible for collecting the data, analyzing the data, and reporting the findings. At this early stage, a budget to support the study should also be established, at least at a high level with rough numbers.

Step 2: Data Understanding

A data mining study is specific to addressing a well-defined business task, and different business tasks require different sets of data. Following the business understanding, the main activity of the data mining process is to identify the relevant data from many available databases. Some key points must be considered in the data identification and selection phase. First and foremost, the analyst should be clear and concise about the description of the data mining task so that the most relevant data can be identified. For example, a retail data mining project may seek to identify spending behaviors of female shoppers who purchase seasonal clothes based on their demographics, credit card transactions, and socioeconomic attributes. Furthermore, the analyst should build an intimate understanding of the data sources (e.g., where the relevant data are stored and in what form; what the process of collecting the data is—automated versus manual; who the collectors of the data are and how often the data are updated) and the variables (e.g., What are the most relevant variables? Are there any synonymous and/or homonymous variables? Are the variables independent of each other—do they stand as a complete information source without overlapping or conflicting information?).

To better understand the data, the analyst often uses a variety of statistical and graphical techniques, such as simple statistical summaries of each variable (e.g., for numeric variables the average, minimum/maximum, median, and standard deviation are among the calculated measures, whereas for categorical variables the mode and frequency tables are calculated), correlation analysis, scatterplots, histograms, and box plots. A careful identification and selection of data sources and the most relevant variables can make it easier for data mining algorithms to quickly discover useful knowledge patterns.

Data sources for data selection can vary. Traditionally, data sources for business applications include demographic data (such as income, education, number of households, and age), sociographic data (such as hobby, club membership, and entertainment), transactional data (sales record, credit card spending, issued checks), and so on. Nowadays, data sources also use external (open or commercial) data repositories, social media, and machine-generated data.

Data can be categorized as quantitative and qualitative. Quantitative data is measured using numeric values, or **numeric data**. It can be discrete (such as integers) or continuous (such as real numbers). Qualitative data, also known as categorical data, contains both nominal and ordinal data. **Nominal data** has finite nonordered values (e.g., gender data, which has two values: male and female). **Ordinal data** has finite ordered values. For example, customer credit ratings are considered ordinal data because the ratings can be excellent, fair, and bad. A simple taxonomy of data (i.e., the nature of data) is provided in Chapter 2.

Quantitative data can be readily represented by some sort of probability distribution. A probability distribution describes how the data is dispersed and shaped. For instance, normally distributed data is symmetric and is commonly referred to as being a bell-shaped curve. Qualitative data may be coded to numbers and then described by frequency distributions. Once the relevant data are selected according to the data mining business objective, data preprocessing should be pursued.

Step 3: Data Preparation

The purpose of data preparation (more commonly called *data preprocessing*) is to take the data identified in the previous step and prepare it for analysis by data mining methods. Compared to the other steps in CRISP-DM, data preprocessing consumes the most time and effort; most believe that this step accounts for roughly 80% of the total time spent on a data mining project. The reason for such an enormous effort spent on this step is the fact that real-world data is generally incomplete (lacking attribute values, lacking certain attributes of interest, or containing only aggregate data), noisy (containing errors or outliers), and inconsistent (containing discrepancies in codes or names). The nature of the data and the issues related to preprocessing of data for analytics are explained in detail in Chapter 2.

Step 4: Model Building

In this step, various modeling techniques are selected and applied to an already prepared data set to address the specific business need. The model-building step also encompasses the assessment and comparative analysis of the various models built. Because there is not a universally known *best* method or algorithm for a data mining task, one should use a variety of viable model types along with a well-defined experimentation and assessment strategy to identify the "best" method for a given purpose. Even for a single method or algorithm, a number of parameters need to be calibrated to obtain optimal results. Some methods may have specific requirements in the way that the data is to be formatted; thus, stepping back to the data preparation step is often necessary. Application Case 4.4 presents a research study where a number of model types are developed and compared to each other.

Application Case 4.4

Data Mining Helps in Cancer Research

According to the American Cancer Society, half of all men and one-third of all women in the United States will develop cancer during their lifetimes; approximately 1.5 million new cancer cases were expected to be diagnosed in 2013. Cancer is the second-most-common cause of death in the United States and in the world, exceeded only by cardiovascular disease. This year, over 500,000 Americans are expected to die of cancer—more than 1,300 people a day—accounting for nearly one of every four deaths.

Cancer is a group of diseases generally characterized by uncontrolled growth and spread of abnormal cells. If the growth and/or spread are not controlled, it can result in death. Even though the exact reasons are not known, cancer is believed to be caused by both external factors (e.g., tobacco, infectious organisms, chemicals, and radiation) and internal factors (e.g., inherited mutations, hormones, immune conditions, and mutations that occur from metabolism). These causal factors may act together or in sequence to initiate or promote carcinogenesis. Cancer is treated with surgery, radiation, chemotherapy, hormone therapy, biological therapy, and targeted therapy. Survival statistics vary greatly by cancer type and stage at diagnosis.

The 5-year relative survival rate for all cancers is improving, and decline in cancer mortality had reached 20% in 2013, translating into the avoidance of about 1.2 million deaths from cancer since 1991. That's more than 400 lives saved per day! The improvement in survival reflects progress in diagnosing certain cancers at an earlier stage and improvements in treatment. Further improvements are needed to prevent and treat cancer.

Even though cancer research has traditionally been clinical and biological in nature, in recent years data-driven analytic studies have become a common complement. In medical domains where data- and analytics-driven research have been applied successfully, novel research directions have been identified to further advance the clinical and biological studies. Using various types of data, including molecular, clinical, literature-based, and clinical trial data, along with suitable data mining tools and techniques, researchers have been able to identify novel patterns, paving the road toward a cancer-free society.

In one study, Delen (2009) used three popular data mining techniques (decision trees, artificial neural networks, and SVMs) in conjunction with logistic regression to develop prediction models for prostate cancer survivability. The data set contained around 120,000 records and 77 variables. A *k*-fold cross-validation methodology was used in model building, evaluation, and comparison. The results showed

(Continued)

Application Case 4.4 (Continued)

that support vector models are the most accurate predictor (with a test set accuracy of 92.85%) for this domain, followed by artificial neural networks and decision trees. Furthermore, using a sensitivity–analysis-based evaluation method, the study also revealed novel patterns related to prognostic factors of prostate cancer.

In a related study, Delen, Walker, and Kadam (2005) used two data mining algorithms (artificial neural networks and decision trees) and logistic regression to develop prediction models for breast cancer survival using a large data set (more than 200,000 cases). Using a 10-fold cross-validation method to measure the unbiased estimate of the prediction models for performance comparison purposes, the results indicated that the decision tree (C5 algorithm) was the best predictor, with 93.6% accuracy on the holdout sample (which was the best prediction accuracy reported in the literature), followed by artificial neural networks, with 91.2% accuracy, and logistic regression, with 89.2% accuracy. Further analysis of prediction models revealed prioritized importance of the prognostic factors, which can then be used as a basis for further clinical and biological research studies.

In the most recent study, Zolbanin, Delen, and Zadeh (2015) studied the impact of comorbidity in cancer survivability. Although prior research has shown that diagnostic and treatment recommendations might be altered based on the severity of comorbidities, chronic diseases are still being investigated in isolation from one another in most cases. To illustrate the significance of concurrent chronic diseases in the course of treatment, their study used the Surveillance, Epidemiology, and End Results (SEER) Program's cancer data to create two comorbid data sets: one for breast and female genital cancers and another for prostate and urinal cancers. Several popular machine-learning techniques are then applied to the resultant data sets to build predictive models (see Figure 4.4). Comparison of the results has shown that having more information about comorbid conditions of patients can improve models' predictive power, which in turn can help

practitioners make better diagnostic and treatment decisions. Therefore, the study suggested that proper identification, recording, and use of patients' comorbidity status can potentially lower treatment costs and ease the healthcare-related economic challenges.

These examples (among many others in the medical literature) show that advanced data mining techniques can be used to develop models that possess a high degree of predictive as well as explanatory power. Although data mining methods are capable of extracting patterns and relationships hidden deep in large and complex medical databases, without the cooperation and feedback from the medical experts, their results are not of much use. The patterns found via data mining methods should be evaluated by medical professionals who have years of experience in the problem domain to decide whether they are logical, actionable, and novel enough to warrant new research directions. In short, data mining is not meant to replace medical professionals and researchers, but to complement their invaluable efforts to provide data-driven new research directions and to ultimately save more human lives.

QUESTIONS FOR DISCUSSION

1. How can data mining be used for ultimately curing illnesses like cancer?
2. What do you think are the promises and major challenges for data miners in contributing to medical and biological research endeavors?

Sources: Zolbanin, H. M., Delen, D., & Zadeh, A. H. (2015). Predicting overall survivability in comorbidity of cancers: A data mining approach. *Decision Support Systems, 74,* 150–161; Delen, D. (2009). Analysis of cancer data: A data mining approach. *Expert Systems, 26*(1), 100–112; Thongkam, J., Xu, G., Zhang, Y., & Huang, F. (2009). Toward breast cancer survivability prediction models through improving training space. *Expert Systems with Applications, 36*(10), 12200–12209; Delen, D., Walker, G., & Kadam, A. (2005). Predicting breast cancer survivability: A comparison of three data mining methods. *Artificial Intelligence in Medicine, 34*(2), 113–127.

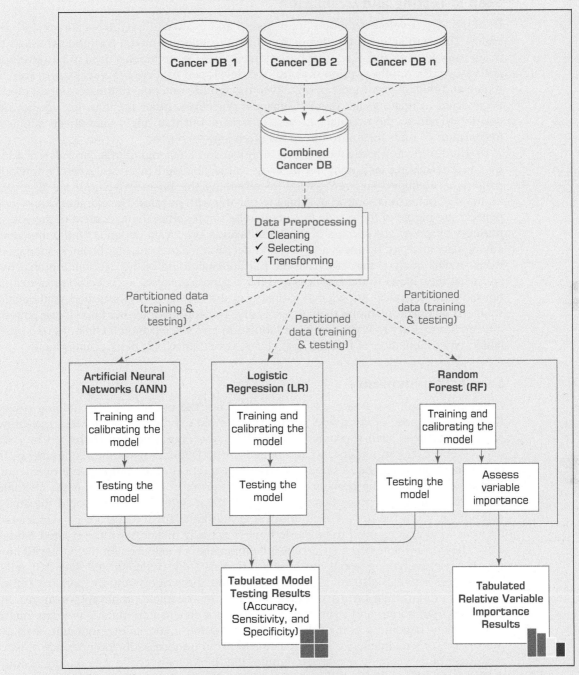

FIGURE 4.4 A Data Mining Methodology for Investigation of Comorbidity in Cancer Survivability.

Depending on the business need, the data mining task can be of a prediction (either classification or regression), an association, or a clustering type. Each of these data mining tasks can use a variety of data mining methods and algorithms. Some of these data mining methods were explained earlier in this chapter, and some of the most popular algorithms, including decision trees for classification, *k*-means for clustering, and the Apriori algorithm for association rule mining, are described later in this chapter.

Step 5: Testing and Evaluation

In step 5, the developed models are assessed and evaluated for their accuracy and generality. This step assesses the degree to which the selected model (or models) meets the business objectives and, if so, to what extent (i.e., Do more models need to be developed and assessed?). Another option is to test the developed model(s) in a real-world scenario if time and budget constraints permit. Even though the outcome of the developed models is expected to relate to the original business objectives, other findings that are not necessarily related to the original business objectives but that might also unveil additional information or hints for future directions often are discovered.

The testing and evaluation step is a critical and challenging task. No value is added by the data mining task until the business value obtained from discovered knowledge patterns is identified and recognized. Determining the business value from discovered knowledge patterns is somewhat similar to playing with puzzles. The extracted knowledge patterns are pieces of the puzzle that need to be put together in the context of the specific business purpose. The success of this identification operation depends on the interaction among data analysts, business analysts, and decision makers (such as business managers). Because data analysts may not have the full understanding of the data mining objectives and what they mean to the business and the business analysts, and decision makers may not have the technical knowledge to interpret the results of sophisticated mathematical solutions, interaction among them is necessary. To properly interpret knowledge patterns, it is often necessary to use a variety of tabulation and visualization techniques (e.g., pivot tables, cross-tabulation of findings, pie charts, histograms, box plots, scatterplots).

Step 6: Deployment

Development and assessment of the models is not the end of the data mining project. Even if the purpose of the model is to have a simple exploration of the data, the knowledge gained from such exploration will need to be organized and presented in a way that the end user can understand and benefit from. Depending on the requirements, the deployment phase can be as simple as generating a report or as complex as implementing a repeatable data mining process across the enterprise. In many cases, it is the customer, not the data analyst, who carries out the deployment steps. However, even if the analyst will not carry out the deployment effort, it is important for the customer to understand up front what actions need to be carried out to actually make use of the created models.

The deployment step may also include maintenance activities for the deployed models. Because everything about the business is constantly changing, the data that reflect the business activities also are changing. Over time, the models (and the patterns embedded within them) built on the old data may become obsolete, irrelevant, or misleading. Therefore, monitoring and maintenance of the models are important if the data mining results are to become a part of the day-to-day business and its environment. A careful preparation of a maintenance strategy helps to avoid unnecessarily long periods of incorrect usage of data mining results. To monitor the deployment of the data mining result(s), the project needs a detailed plan on the monitoring process, which may not be a trivial task for complex data mining models.

Other Data Mining Standardized Processes and Methodologies

To be applied successfully, a data mining study must be viewed as a process that follows a standardized methodology rather than as a set of automated software tools and techniques. In addition to CRISP-DM, there is another well-known methodology developed by the SAS Institute, called SEMMA (2009). The acronym **SEMMA** stands for "sample, explore, modify, model, and assess."

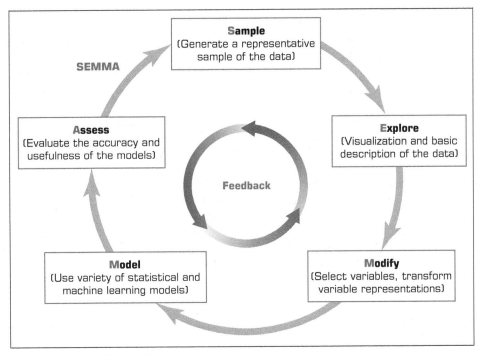

FIGURE 4.5 SEMMA Data Mining Process.

Beginning with a statistically representative sample of the data, SEMMA makes it easy to apply exploratory statistical and visualization techniques, select and transform the most significant predictive variables, model the variables to predict outcomes, and confirm a model's accuracy. A pictorial representation of SEMMA is given in Figure 4.5.

By assessing the outcome of each stage in the SEMMA process, the model developer can determine how to model new questions raised by the previous results and thus proceed back to the exploration phase for additional refinement of the data; that is, as with CRISP-DM, SEMMA is driven by a highly iterative experimentation cycle. The main difference between CRISP-DM and SEMMA is that CRISP-DM takes a more comprehensive approach—including understanding of the business and the relevant data—to data mining projects, whereas SEMMA implicitly assumes that the data mining project's goals and objectives along with the appropriate data sources have been identified and understood.

Some practitioners commonly use the term **knowledge discovery in databases (KDD)** as a synonym for data mining. Fayyad et al. (1996) defined *knowledge discovery in databases* as a process of using data mining methods to find useful information and patterns in the data, as opposed to data mining, which involves using algorithms to identify patterns in data derived through the KDD process (see Figure 4.6). KDD is a comprehensive process that encompasses data mining. The input to the KDD process consists of organizational data. The enterprise data warehouse enables KDD to be implemented efficiently because it provides a single source for data to be mined. Dunham (2003) summarized the KDD process as consisting of the following steps: data selection, data preprocessing, data transformation, data mining, and interpretation/evaluation.

Figure 4.7 shows the polling results for the question, "What main methodology are you using for data mining?" (conducted by kdnuggets.com in August 2007).

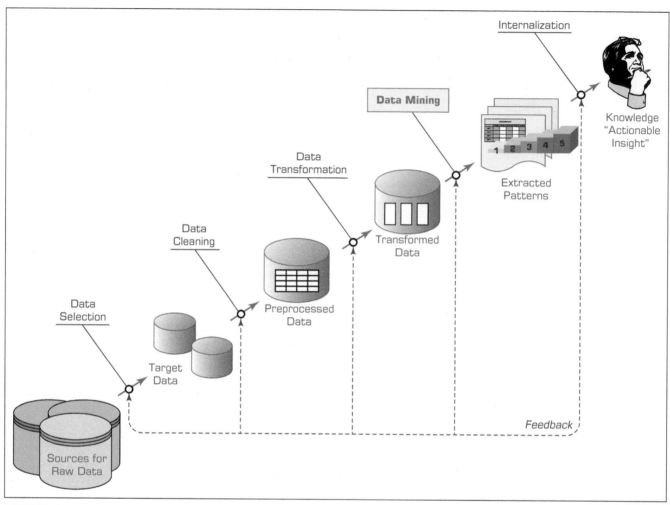

FIGURE 4.6 KDD (Knowledge Discovery in Databases) Process.

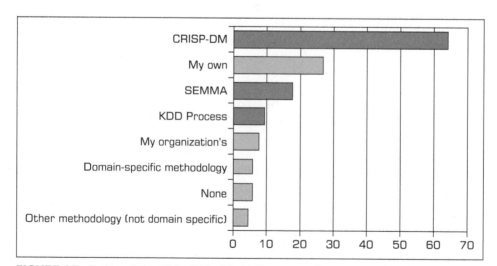

FIGURE 4.7 Ranking of Data Mining Methodologies/Processes. *Source:* Used with permission from KDnuggets.com.

SECTION 4.4 REVIEW QUESTIONS

1. What are the major data mining processes?

2. Why do you think the early phases (understanding of the business and understanding of the data) take the longest in data mining projects?

3. List and briefly define the phases in the CRISP-DM process.

4. What are the main data preprocessing steps? Briefly describe each step, and provide relevant examples.

5. How does CRISP-DM differ from SEMMA?

4.5　Data Mining Methods

A variety of methods are available for performing data mining studies, including classification, regression, clustering, and association. Most data mining software tools employ more than one technique (or algorithm) for each of these methods. This section describes the most popular data mining methods and explains their representative techniques.

Classification

Classification is perhaps the most frequently used data mining method for real-world problems. As a popular member of the machine-learning family of techniques, classification learns patterns from past data (a set of information—traits, variables, features—on characteristics of the previously labeled items, objects, or events) to place new instances (with unknown labels) into their respective groups or classes. For example, one could use classification to predict whether the weather on a particular day will be "sunny," "rainy," or "cloudy." Popular classification tasks include credit approval (i.e., good or bad credit risk), store location (e.g., good, moderate, bad), target marketing (e.g., likely customer, no hope), fraud detection (i.e., yes/no), and telecommunication (e.g., likely to turn to another phone company, yes/no). If what is being predicted is a class label (e.g., "sunny," "rainy," or "cloudy"), the prediction problem is called a classification, whereas if it is a numeric value (e.g., temperature, such as 68°F), the prediction problem is called a **regression**.

Even though clustering (another popular data mining method) can also be used to determine groups (or class memberships) of things, there is a significant difference between the two. Classification learns the function between the characteristics of things (i.e., independent variables) and their membership (i.e., output variable) through a supervised learning process where both types (input and output) of variables are presented to the algorithm; in clustering, the membership of the objects is learned through an unsupervised learning process where only the input variables are presented to the algorithm. Unlike classification, clustering does not have a supervising (or controlling) mechanism that enforces the learning process; instead, clustering algorithms use one or more heuristics (e.g., multidimensional distance measure) to discover natural groupings of objects.

The most common two-step methodology of classification-type prediction involves model development/training and model testing/deployment. In the model development phase, a collection of input data, including the actual class labels, is used. After a model has been trained, the model is tested against the holdout sample for accuracy assessment and eventually deployed for actual use where it is to predict classes of new data instances (where the class label is unknown). Several factors are considered in assessing the model, including the following.

- **Predictive accuracy.**　The model's ability to correctly predict the class label of new or previously unseen data. Prediction accuracy is the most commonly used assessment factor for classification models. To compute this measure, actual class labels

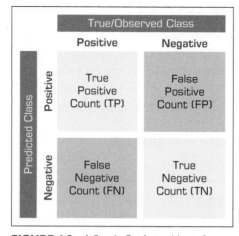

FIGURE 4.8 A Simple Confusion Matrix for Tabulation of Two-Class Classification Results.

of a test data set are matched against the class labels predicted by the model. The accuracy can then be computed as the *accuracy rate*, which is the percentage of test data set samples correctly classified by the model (more on this topic is provided later in the chapter).

- **Speed.** The computational costs involved in generating and using the model, where faster is deemed to be better.
- **Robustness.** The model's ability to make reasonably accurate predictions, given noisy data or data with missing and erroneous values.
- **Scalability.** The ability to construct a prediction model efficiently given a rather large amount of data.
- **Interpretability.** The level of understanding and insight provided by the model (e.g., how and/or what the model concludes on certain predictions).

Estimating the True Accuracy of Classification Models

In classification problems, the primary source for accuracy estimation is the *confusion matrix* (also called a *classification matrix* or a *contingency table*). Figure 4.8 shows a confusion matrix for a two-class classification problem. The numbers along the diagonal from the upper left to the lower right represent correct decisions, and the numbers outside this diagonal represent the errors.

Table 4.1 provides equations for common accuracy metrics for classification models.

When the classification problem is not binary, the confusion matrix gets bigger (a square matrix with the size of the unique number of class labels), and accuracy metrics become limited to *per class accuracy rates* and the *overall classifier accuracy*.

$$(\textit{True Classification Rate})_i = \frac{(\textit{True Classification})}{\sum_{i=1}^{n}(\textit{False Classification})}$$

$$(\textit{Overall Classifier Accuracy})_i = \frac{\sum_{i=1}^{n}(\textit{True Classification})_i}{\textit{Total Number of Cases}}$$

TABLE 4.1 Common Accuracy Metrics for Classification Models	
Metric	Description
$Accuracy = \dfrac{TP + TN}{TP + TN + FP + FN}$	The ratio of correctly classified instances (positives and negative) divided by the total numbers of instances
$True\ Positive\ Rate = \dfrac{TP}{TP + FN}$	(a.k.a. Sensitivity) The ratio of correctly classified positives divided by the total positive count (i.e., hit rate or recall)
$True\ Negative\ Rate = \dfrac{TN}{TN + FP}$	(a.k.a. Specificity) The ratio of correctly classified negatives divided by the total negative count (i.e., false alarm rate)
$Precision = \dfrac{TP}{TP + FP}$	The ratio of correctly classified positives divided by the sum of correctly classified positives and incorrectly classified positives
$Recall = \dfrac{TP}{TP + FN}$	Ratio of correctly classified positives divided by the sum of correctly classified positives and incorrectly classified negatives

Estimating the accuracy of a classification model (or classifier) induced by a supervised learning algorithm is important for the following two reasons: First, it can be used to estimate its future prediction accuracy, which could imply the level of confidence one should have in the classifier's output in the prediction system. Second, it can be used for choosing a classifier from a given set (identifying the "best" classification model among the many trained). The following are among the most popular estimation methodologies used for classification-type data mining models.

SIMPLE SPLIT The **simple split** (or holdout or test sample estimation) partitions the data into two mutually exclusive subsets called a *training set* and a *test set* (or *holdout set*). It is common to designate two-thirds of the data as the training set and the remaining one-third as the test set. The training set is used by the inducer (model builder), and the built classifier is then tested on the test set. An exception to this rule occurs when the classifier is an artificial neural network. In this case, the data is partitioned into three mutually exclusive subsets: training, validation, and testing. The validation set is used during model building to prevent overfitting. Figure 4.9 shows the simple split methodology.

The main criticism of this method is that it makes the assumption that the data in the two subsets are of the same kind (i.e., have the exact same properties). Because this

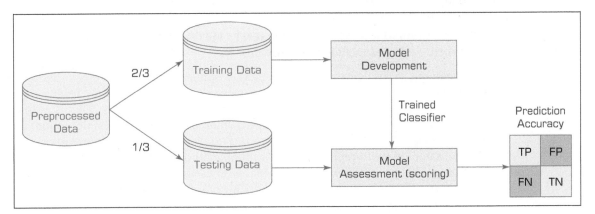

FIGURE 4.9 Simple Random Data Splitting.

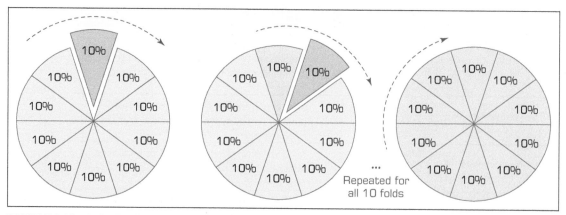

FIGURE 4.10 A Graphical Depiction of *k*-Fold Cross-Validation.

is a simple random partitioning, in most realistic data sets where the data are skewed on the classification variable, such an assumption may not hold true. To improve this situation, stratified sampling is suggested, where the strata become the output variable. Even though this is an improvement over the simple split, it still has a bias associated from the single random partitioning.

K-FOLD CROSS-VALIDATION To minimize the bias associated with the random sampling of the training and holdout data samples in comparing the predictive accuracy of two or more methods, one can use a methodology called **k-fold cross-validation**. In *k*-fold cross-validation, also called *rotation estimation*, the complete data set is randomly split into *k* mutually exclusive subsets of approximately equal size. The classification model is trained and tested *k* times. Each time it is trained on all but one fold and then tested on the remaining single fold. The cross-validation estimate of the overall accuracy of a model is calculated by simply averaging the *k* individual accuracy measures, as shown in the following equation:

$$CVA = \frac{1}{k}\sum_{i=1}^{k}A_i$$

where *CVA* stands for cross-validation accuracy, *k* is the number of folds used, and *A* is the accuracy measure (e.g., hit rate, sensitivity, specificity) of each fold. Figure 4.10 shows a graphical illustration of *k*-fold cross-validation where *k* is set to 10.

ADDITIONAL CLASSIFICATION ASSESSMENT METHODOLOGIES Other popular assessment methodologies include the following:

- *Leave-one-out.* The leave-one-out method is similar to the *k*-fold cross-validation where the *k* takes the value of 1; that is, every data point is used for testing once on as many models developed as there are number of data points. This is a time-consuming methodology, but sometimes for small data sets it is a viable option.
- *Bootstrapping.* With **bootstrapping**, a fixed number of instances from the original data are sampled (with replacement) for training, and the rest of the data set is used for testing. This process is repeated as many times as desired.
- *Jackknifing.* Though similar to the leave-one-out methodology, with jackknifing the accuracy is calculated by leaving one sample out at each iteration of the estimation process.

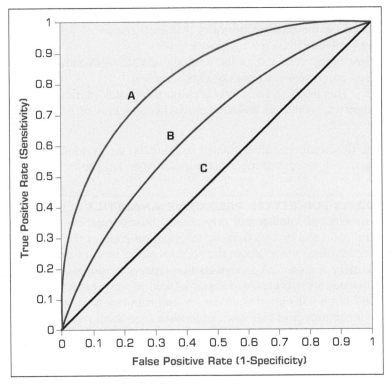

FIGURE 4.11 A Sample ROC Curve.

- *Area under the ROC curve.* The **area under the ROC curve** is a graphical assessment technique where the true positive rate is plotted on the *y*-axis and the false positive rate is plotted on the *x*-axis. The area under the ROC curve determines the accuracy measure of a classifier: A value of 1 indicates a perfect classifier, whereas 0.5 indicates no better than random chance; in reality, the values would range between the two extreme cases. For example in Figure 4.11, *A* has a better classification performance than *B*, whereas *C* is not any better than the random chance of flipping a coin.

CLASSIFICATION TECHNIQUES A number of techniques (or algorithms) are used for classification modeling, including the following:

- *Decision tree analysis.* Decision tree analysis (a machine-learning technique) is arguably the most popular classification technique in the data mining arena. A detailed description of this technique is given in the following section.
- *Statistical analysis.* Statistical techniques were the primary classification algorithm for many years until the emergence of machine-learning techniques. Statistical classification techniques include logistic regression and discriminant analysis, both of which make the assumptions that the relationships between the input and output variables are linear in nature, the data is normally distributed, and the variables are not correlated and are independent of each other. The questionable nature of these assumptions has led to the shift toward machine-learning techniques.
- *Neural networks.* These are among the most popular machine-learning techniques that can be used for classification-type problems.
- *Case-based reasoning.* This approach uses historical cases to recognize commonalities to assign a new case into the most probable category.

- *Bayesian classifiers.* This approach uses probability theory to build classification models based on the past occurrences that are capable of placing a new instance into a most probable class (or category).
- *Genetic algorithms.* The use of the analogy of natural evolution to build directed-search-based mechanisms to classify data samples.
- *Rough sets.* This method takes into account the partial membership of class labels to predefined categories in building models (collection of rules) for classification problems.

A complete description of all of these classification techniques is beyond the scope of this book; thus, only several of the most popular ones are presented here.

ENSEMBLE MODELS FOR BETTER PREDICTIVE ANALYTICS Creating ensembles is essentially the process of intelligently combining the information (forecasts or predictions) created and provided by two or more information sources (i.e., prediction models). While there is an ongoing debate about the sophistication level of the ensemble methods to be employed, there is a general consensus that ensemble models produce more robust and reliable information for business decisions (Seni & Elder, 2010). That is, combining forecasts can (and often will) improve accuracy and robustness of information outcomes, while reducing uncertainty and bias associated with individual models.

As we all know, in data mining and prediction modeling there is not a universally accepted "best model" that works for any problem. The best model depends on the scenario being analyzed and the data set being used; and can only be obtained through an extensive trial-and-error experimentation (and only happens if time and resources permit). Just as there is not a single best model, there is also not a single best implementation of different model types—for instance decision trees, neural networks, and support vector machines have different architectures and parameter sets that need to be "optimized" for the best possible results. Data scientists are developing new ways to improve the accuracy and efficiency of today's prediction models. One proven way to do so has been combining the outputs of prediction models into a single composite score, which is a model ensemble. Ensembles have been the winners of many data mining and prediction modeling competitions in recent years (see kaggle.org for a list of recent predictive analytics competitions and winners).

Ensemble models can be categorized as either homogeneous or heterogamous (Abbott 2014, p. 307). As the name implies, homogeneous model ensembles combine the outcomes of two or more of the same type of models such as decision trees. In fact, a vast majority of homogeneous model ensembles are developed using a combination of decision tree structures. The two common categories of decision tree ensembles are bagging and boosting. A well-recognized and hugely successful example of bagging-type decision tree ensembles is called Random Forest—as opposed to building a large tree, Random Forest develops a forest of many small trees. And a good example of boosting-type decision tree ensembles is called AdaBoosting (a short name for "Adaptive Boosting")—an algorithm that changes the weight (i.e., the importance or contribution) assigned to each data sample in each iteration in the learning process based on the misclassification outcomes; so that the accuracy of the classifier/predictor will be optimized for all class labels.

Heterogeneous model ensembles, again as the name implies, combines the outcomes of two or more different types of models such as decision trees, artificial neural networks, logistic regression, and support vector machines. One of the key success factors in ensemble modeling is to use models that are fundamentally different than one another, ones that look at the data from a different perspective. Because of the way it combines the outcomes of different models of different model types, heterogeneous model ensembles

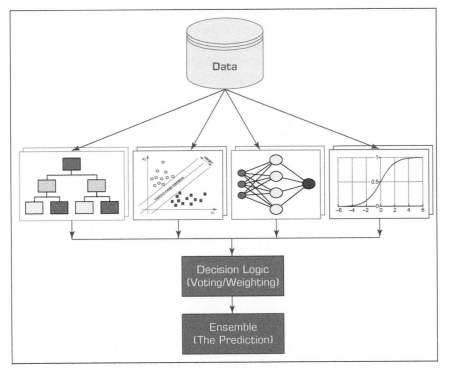

FIGURE 4.12   Graphical Illustration of a Heterogeneous Ensemble.

are also called information fusion models (Delen & Sharda, 2010). In the process of combining the outcomes of multiple models, either a simple voting (each model contributes equally, one vote) or a weighted combination of voting (each model is contributing based on its prediction accuracy—more accurate models are having higher weight value) can be used. Regardless of the combination method, ensembles have been shown to be an invaluable addition to any data mining and predictive modeling project. Although ensemble modeling improves accuracy and robustness, on the negative side, it also increases the model complexity, and hence the lack of interpretability (i.e., transparency). Figure 4.12 graphically illustrates a heterogeneous model ensemble process.

DECISION TREES   Before describing the details of **decision trees**, we need to discuss some simple terminology. First, decision trees include many input variables that may have an impact on the classification of different patterns. These input variables are usually called *attributes*. For example, if we were to build a model to classify loan risks on the basis of just two characteristics—income and a credit rating—these two characteristics would be the attributes, and the resulting output would be the *class label* (e.g., low, medium, or high risk). Second, a tree consists of branches and nodes. A *branch* represents the outcome of a test to classify a pattern (on the basis of a test) using one of the attributes. A *leaf node* at the end represents the final class choice for a pattern (a chain of branches from the root node to the leaf node, which can be represented as a complex if-then statement).

The basic idea behind a decision tree is that it recursively divides a training set until each division consists entirely or primarily of examples from one class. Each nonleaf node of the tree contains a *split point*, which is a test on one or more attributes and determines how the data are to be divided further. Decision tree algorithms, in general, build an initial tree from the training data such that each leaf node is pure, and they then prune the tree to increase its generalization, and hence, the prediction accuracy on test data.

In the growth phase, the tree is built by recursively dividing the data until each division is either pure (i.e., contains members of the same class) or relatively small. The basic idea is to ask questions whose answers would provide the most information, similar to what we may do when playing the game "Twenty Questions."

The split used to partition the data depends on the type of the attribute used in the split. For a continuous attribute A, splits are of the form value(A) < x, where x is some "optimal" split value of A. For example, the split based on income could be "Income < 50,000." For the categorical attribute A, splits are of the form value(A) belongs to x, where x is a subset of A. As an example, the split could be on the basis of gender: "Male versus Female."

A general algorithm for building a decision tree is as follows:

1. Create a root node and assign all of the training data to it.
2. Select the *best* splitting attribute.
3. Add a branch to the root node for each value of the split. Split the data into mutually exclusive (nonoverlapping) subsets along the lines of the specific split and move to the branches.
4. Repeat steps 2 and 3 for each and every leaf node until the stopping criteria is reached (e.g., the node is dominated by a single class label).

Many different algorithms have been proposed for creating decision trees. These algorithms differ primarily in terms of the way in which they determine the splitting attribute (and its split values), the order of splitting the attributes (splitting the same attribute only once or many times), the number of splits at each node (binary versus ternary), the stopping criteria, and the pruning of the tree (pre- versus postpruning). Some of the most well-known algorithms are ID3 (followed by C4.5 and C5 as the improved versions of ID3) from machine learning, classification and regression trees (CART) from statistics, and the chi-squared automatic interaction detector (CHAID) from pattern recognition.

When building a decision tree, the goal at each node is to determine the attribute and the split point of that attribute that best divides the training records to purify the class representation at that node. To evaluate the goodness of the split, some splitting indices have been proposed. Two of the most common ones are the Gini index and information gain. The Gini index is used in CART and SPRINT (Scalable PaRallelizable INduction of Decision Trees) algorithms. Versions of information gain are used in ID3 (and its newer versions, C4.5 and C5).

The **Gini index** has been used in economics to measure the diversity of a population. The same concept can be used to determine the purity of a specific class as a result of a decision to branch along a particular attribute or variable. The best split is the one that increases the purity of the sets resulting from a proposed split. Let us briefly look into a simple calculation of the Gini index.

If a data set S contains examples from n classes, the Gini index is defined as

$$gini(S) = 1 - \sum_{j=1}^{n} p_j^2$$

where p_j is a relative frequency of class j in S. If a data set S is split into two subsets, S_1 and S_2, with sizes N_1 and N_2, respectively, the Gini index of the split data contains examples from n classes, and the Gini index is defined as

$$gini_{split}(S) = \frac{N_1}{N} gini(S_1) + \frac{N_2}{N} gini(S_2)$$

The attribute/split combination that provides the smallest $gini_{split}(S)$ is chosen to split the node. In such a determination, one should enumerate all possible splitting points for each attribute.

Information gain is the splitting mechanism used in ID3, which is perhaps the most widely known decision tree algorithm. It was developed by Ross Quinlan in 1986, and since then he has evolved this algorithm into the C4.5 and C5 algorithms. The basic idea behind ID3 (and its variants) is to use a concept called *entropy* in place of the Gini index. **Entropy** measures the extent of uncertainty or randomness in a data set. If all the data in a subset belong to just one class, there is no uncertainty or randomness in that data set, so the entropy is zero. The objective of this approach is to build subtrees so that the entropy of each final subset is zero (or close to zero). Let us also look at the calculation of the information gain.

Assume that there are two classes, P (positive) and N (negative). Let the set of examples S contain p counts of class P and n counts of class N. The amount of information needed to decide if an arbitrary example in S belongs to P or N is defined as

$$I(p, n) = -\frac{p}{p + n}\log_2\frac{p}{p + n} - \frac{n}{p + n}\log_2\frac{n}{p + n}$$

Assume that using attribute A, the set S will be partitioned into sets $\{S_1, S_2,..., S_v\}$. If S_i contains p_i examples of P and n_i examples of N, the entropy, or the expected information needed to classify objects in all subtrees, S_p, is

$$E(A) = \sum_{i=1}^{n}\frac{p_i + n_i}{p + n}I(p_i,n_i)$$

Then, the information that would be gained by branching on attribute A would be

$$Gain(A) = I(p,n) - E(A)$$

These calculations are repeated for each and every attribute, and the one with the highest information gain is selected as the splitting attribute. The basic ideas behind these splitting indices are rather similar to each other, but the specific algorithmic details vary. A detailed definition of the ID3 algorithm and its splitting mechanism can be found in Quinlan (1986).

Application Case 4.5 illustrates how significant the gains may be if the right data mining techniques are used for a well-defined business problem.

Application Case 4.5

Influence Health Uses Advanced Predictive Analytics to Focus on the Factors That Really Influence People's Healthcare Decisions

Influence Health provides the healthcare industry's only integrated digital consumer engagement and activation platform. The Influence Health platform enables providers, employers, and payers to positively influence consumer decision making and health behaviors well beyond the physical care setting through personalized and interactive multichannel engagement. Since 1996, the Birmingham, Alabama-based company has helped more than 1,100 provider organizations influence consumers in a way that is transformative to financial and quality outcomes.

Healthcare is a personal business. Each patient's needs are different and require an individual response. On the other hand—as the cost of providing healthcare services continues to rise—hospitals

(Continued)

Application Case 4.5 (Continued)

and health systems increasingly need to harness economies of scale by catering to larger and larger populations. The challenge then becomes providing a personalized approach while operating on a large scale. Influence Health specializes in helping its healthcare sector clients solve this challenge by getting to know their existing and potential patients better and targeting each individual with the right health services at the right time. Advanced predictive analytics technology from IBM allows Influence Health to help its clients discover the factors that have the most influence on patients' healthcare decisions. By assessing the propensity of hundreds of millions of prospects to require specific healthcare services, Influence Health is able to boost revenues and response rates for healthcare campaigns, improving outcomes for its clients and their patients alike.

Targeting the Savvy Consumer

Today's healthcare industry is becoming more competitive than ever before. If the utilization of an organization's services drops, so do its profits. Rather than simply seeking out the nearest hospital or clinic, consumers are now more likely to make positive choices between healthcare providers. Paralleling efforts common in other industries, healthcare organizations must make more effort to market themselves effectively to both existing and potential patients, building long-term engagement and loyalty.

The keys to successful healthcare marketing are timeliness and relevance. If you can predict what kind of health services an individual prospect might need, you can engage and influence them much more effectively for wellness care.

Venky Ravirala, Chief Analytics Officer at Influence Health, explains, "Healthcare organizations risk losing people's attention if they bombard them with irrelevant messaging. We help our clients avoid this risk by using analytics to segment their existing and potential prospects and market to them in a much more personal and relevant way."

Faster and More Flexible Analytics

As its client base has expanded, the total volume of data in Influence Health's analytics systems has grown to include over 195 million patient records,

with a detailed disease encounter history for several million patients. Ravirala comments: "With so much data to analyze, our existing method of scoring data was becoming too complex and time-consuming. We wanted to be able to extract insights at greater speed and accuracy."

By leveraging predictive analytics software from IBM, Influence Health is now able to develop models that calculate how likely each patient is to require particular services and express this likelihood as a percentage score. Micro-segmentation and numerous disease-specific models draw on demographic, socioeconomic, geographical, behavioral, disease history, and census data and examine different aspects of each patient's predicted healthcare needs.

"The IBM solution allows us to combine all these models using an ensemble technique, which helps to overcome the limitations of individual models and provide more accurate results," comments Ravirala. "It gives us the flexibility to apply multiple techniques to solve a problem and arrive at the best solution. It also automates much of the analytics process, enabling us to respond to clients' requests faster than before, and often give them a much deeper level of insight into their patient population."

For example, Influence Health decided to find out how disease prevalence and risk vary between different cohorts within the general population. By using very sophisticated cluster analysis techniques, the team was able to discover new comorbidity patterns that improve risk predictability for over 100 common diseases by up to 800%.

This helps to reliably differentiate between high-risk and very high-risk patients—making it easier to target campaigns at the patients and prospects who need them most. With insights like these in hand, Influence Health is able to use its healthcare marketing expertise to advise its clients on how best to allocate marketing resources.

"Our clients make significant budgeting decisions based on the guidance we give them," states Ravirala. "We help them maximize the impact of one-off campaigns—such as health insurance marketplace campaigns when Obamacare began—as well as their long-term strategic plans and ongoing marketing communications."

Reaching the Right Audience

By enabling its clients to target their marketing activities more effectively, Influence Health is helping to drive greater revenue and enhance population health. "Working with us, clients have been able to achieve return on investment of up to 12 to 1 through better targeted marketing," elaborates Ravirala. "And it's not just about revenues: by ensuring that vital healthcare information gets sent to the people who need it, we are helping our clients improve general health levels in the communities they serve."

Influence Health continues to refine its modeling techniques, gaining an ever-deeper understanding of the critical attributes that influence healthcare decisions. With a flexible analytics toolset at its fingertips, the company is well equipped to keep improving its service to clients. Ravirala concludes, "In the future, we want to take our understanding of patient and prospect data to the next level, identifying patterns in behavior and incorporating analysis with machine learning libraries. IBM SPSS has already given us the ability to apply and combine multiple models without writing a single line of code. We're eager to further leverage this IBM solution as we expand our healthcare analytics to support clinical outcomes and population health management services."

"We are achieving analytics on an unprecedented scale. Today, we can analyze 195 million records with 35 different models in less than two days—a task which was simply not possible for us in the past," says Venky Ravirala, Chief Analytics Officer at Influence Health.

QUESTIONS FOR DISCUSSION

1. What did Influence Health do?
2. What were the challenges, the proposed solutions, and the obtained results?
3. How can data mining help companies in the healthcare industry (in ways other than the ones mentioned in this case)?

Source: Influence Health: Focusing on the factors that really influence people's healthcare decisions. IBM Case Study, www.presidion.com/case-study-influence-health.

Cluster Analysis for Data Mining

Cluster analysis is an essential data mining method for classifying items, events, or concepts into common groupings called *clusters*. The method is commonly used in biology, medicine, genetics, social network analysis, anthropology, archaeology, astronomy, character recognition, and even in management information systems (MIS) development. As data mining has increased in popularity, the underlying techniques have been applied to business, especially to marketing. Cluster analysis has been used extensively for fraud detection (both credit card and e-commerce fraud) and market segmentation of customers in contemporary CRM systems. More applications in business continue to be developed as the strength of cluster analysis is recognized and used.

Cluster analysis is an exploratory data analysis tool for solving classification problems. The objective is to sort cases (e.g., people, things, events) into groups, or clusters, so that the degree of association is strong among members of the same cluster and weak among members of different clusters. Each cluster describes the class to which its members belong. An obvious one-dimensional example of cluster analysis is to establish score ranges into which to assign class grades for a college class. This is similar to the cluster analysis problem that the U.S. Treasury faced when establishing new tax brackets in the 1980s. A fictional example of clustering occurs in J. K. Rowling's *Harry Potter* books. The Sorting Hat determines to which House (e.g., dormitory) to assign first-year students at the Hogwarts School. Another example involves determining how to seat guests at a wedding. As far as data mining goes, the importance of cluster analysis is that it may reveal associations and structures in data that were not previously apparent but are sensible and useful once found.

Cluster analysis results may be used to:

- Identify a classification scheme (e.g., types of customers)
- Suggest statistical models to describe populations
- Indicate rules for assigning new cases to classes for identification, targeting, and diagnostic purposes
- Provide measures of definition, size, and change in what were previously broad concepts
- Find typical cases to label and represent classes
- Decrease the size and complexity of the problem space for other data mining methods
- Identify outliers in a specific domain (e.g., rare-event detection)

DETERMINING THE OPTIMAL NUMBER OF CLUSTERS Clustering algorithms usually require one to specify the number of clusters to find. If this number is not known from prior knowledge, it should be chosen in some way. Unfortunately, there is not an optimal way of calculating what this number is supposed to be. Therefore, several different heuristic methods have been proposed. The following are among the most commonly referenced ones:

- Look at the percentage of variance explained as a function of the number of clusters; that is, choose a number of clusters so that adding another cluster would not give much better modeling of the data. Specifically, if one graphs the percentage of variance explained by the clusters, there is a point at which the marginal gain will drop (giving an angle in the graph), indicating the number of clusters to be chosen.
- Set the number of clusters to $(n/2)^{1/2}$, where n is the number of data points.
- Use the Akaike information criterion (AIC), which is a measure of the goodness of fit (based on the concept of entropy) to determine the number of clusters.
- Use Bayesian information criterion, which is a model-selection criterion (based on maximum likelihood estimation) to determine the number of clusters.

ANALYSIS METHODS Cluster analysis may be based on one or more of the following general methods:

- Statistical methods (including both hierarchical and nonhierarchical), such as k-means or k-modes
- Neural networks (with the architecture called self-organizing map)
- Fuzzy logic (e.g., fuzzy c-means algorithm)
- Genetic algorithms

Each of these methods generally works with one of two general method classes:

- *Divisive.* With divisive classes, all items start in one cluster and are broken apart.
- *Agglomerative.* With agglomerative classes, all items start in individual clusters, and the clusters are joined together.

Most cluster analysis methods involve the use of a **distance measure** to calculate the closeness between pairs of items. Popular distance measures include Euclidian distance (the ordinary distance between two points that one would measure with a ruler) and Manhattan distance (also called the rectilinear distance, or taxicab distance, between two points). Often, they are based on true distances that are measured, but this need not be so, as is typically the case in IS development. Weighted averages may be used to establish these distances. For example, in an IS development project, individual modules of the system may be related by the similarity between their inputs, outputs, processes, and

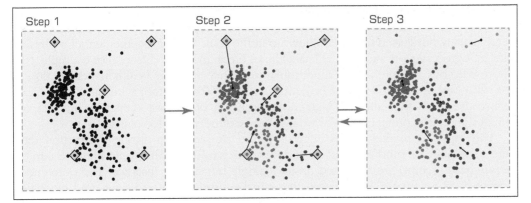

FIGURE 4.13 A Graphical Illustration of the Steps in the *k*-Means Algorithm.

the specific data used. These factors are then aggregated, pairwise by item, into a single distance measure.

K-MEANS CLUSTERING ALGORITHM The *k*-means algorithm (where *k* stands for the predetermined number of clusters) is arguably the most referenced clustering algorithm. It has its roots in traditional statistical analysis. As the name implies, the algorithm assigns each data point (customer, event, object, etc.) to the cluster whose center (also called the *centroid*) is the nearest. The center is calculated as the average of all the points in the cluster; that is, its coordinates are the arithmetic mean for each dimension separately over all the points in the cluster. The algorithm steps are listed below and shown graphically in Figure 4.13:

> **Initialization step:** Choose the number of clusters (i.e., the value of *k*).
>
> **Step 1:** Randomly generate *k* random points as initial cluster centers.
>
> **Step 2:** Assign each point to the nearest cluster center.
>
> **Step 3:** Recompute the new cluster centers.
>
> **Repetition step:** Repeat steps 2 and 3 until some convergence criterion is met (usually that the assignment of points to clusters becomes stable).

Association Rule Mining

Association rule mining (also known as affinity analysis or market-basket analysis) is a popular data mining method that is commonly used as an example to explain what data mining is and what it can do to a technologically less-savvy audience. Most of you might have heard the famous (or infamous, depending on how you look at it) relationship discovered between the sales of beer and diapers at grocery stores. As the story goes, a large supermarket chain (maybe Walmart, maybe not; there is no consensus on which supermarket chain it was) did an analysis of customers' buying habits and found a statistically significant correlation between purchases of beer and purchases of diapers. It was theorized that the reason for this was that fathers (presumably young men) were stopping off at the supermarket to buy diapers for their babies (especially on Thursdays), and because they could no longer go down to the sports bar as often, would buy beer as well. As a result of this finding, the supermarket chain is alleged to have placed the diapers next to the beer, resulting in increased sales of both.

In essence, association rule mining aims to find interesting relationships (affinities) between variables (items) in large databases. Because of its successful application to retail business problems, it is commonly called *market-basket analysis*. The main idea in market-basket analysis is to identify strong relationships among different products (or services) that are usually purchased together (show up in the same basket together, either a physical basket at a grocery store or a virtual basket at an e-commerce Web site). For example, 65% of those who buy comprehensive automobile insurance also buy health insurance; 80% of those who buy books online also buy music online; 60% of those who have high blood pressure and are overweight have high cholesterol; 70% of the customers who buy a laptop computer and virus protection software also buy extended service plans.

The input to market-basket analysis is the simple point-of-sale transaction data, where a number of products and/or services purchased together (just like the content of a purchase receipt) are tabulated under a single transaction instance. The outcome of the analysis is invaluable information that can be used to better understand customer-purchase behavior to maximize the profit from business transactions. A business can take advantage of such knowledge by (1) putting the items next to each other to make it more convenient for the customers to pick them up together and not forget to buy one when buying the others (increasing sales volume); (2) promoting the items as a package (do not put one on sale if the other(s) are on sale); and (3) placing them apart from each other so that the customer has to walk the aisles to search for it, and by doing so potentially seeing and buying other items.

Applications of market-basket analysis include cross-marketing, cross-selling, store design, catalog design, e-commerce site design, optimization of online advertising, product pricing, and sales/promotion configuration. In essence, market-basket analysis helps businesses infer customer needs and preferences from their purchase patterns. Outside the business realm, association rules are successfully used to discover relationships between symptoms and illnesses, diagnosis and patient characteristics and treatments (which can be used in a medical decision support system), and genes and their functions (which can be used in genomics projects), among others. Here are a few common areas and uses for association rule mining:

- *Sales transactions:* Combinations of retail products purchased together can be used to improve product placement on the sales floor (placing products that go together in close proximity) and promotional pricing of products (not having promotions on both products that are often purchased together).
- *Credit card transactions:* Items purchased with a credit card provide insight into other products the customer is likely to purchase or fraudulent use of credit card numbers.
- *Banking services:* The sequential patterns of services used by customers (checking account followed by savings account) can be used to identify other services they may be interested in (investment account).
- *Insurance service products:* Bundles of insurance products bought by customers (car insurance followed by home insurance) can be used to propose additional insurance products (life insurance), or unusual combinations of insurance claims can be a sign of fraud.
- *Telecommunication services:* Commonly purchased groups of options (e.g., call waiting, caller ID, three-way calling) help better structure product bundles to maximize revenue; the same is also applicable to multichannel telecom providers with phone, television, and Internet service offerings.
- *Medical records:* Certain combinations of conditions can indicate increased risk of various complications; or, certain treatment procedures at certain medical facilities can be tied to certain types of infections.

A good question to ask with respect to the patterns/relationships that association rule mining can discover is "Are all association rules interesting and useful?" To answer such a question, association rule mining uses two common metrics: **support**, and **confidence** and **lift**. Before defining these terms, let's get a little technical by showing what an association rule looks like:

$X \Rightarrow Y$ [$Supp$(%), $Conf$(%)]

{Laptop Computer, Antivirus Software} $\Rightarrow$ {Extended Service Plan}[30%, 70%]

Here, X (products and/or service; called the *left-hand side, LHS,* or the antecedent) is associated with Y (products and/or service; called the *right-hand side, RHS,* or consequent). S is the support, and C is the confidence for this particular rule. Here are the simple formulas for *Supp, Conf,* and *Lift*.

$$Support = Supp(X \Rightarrow Y) = \frac{number\ of\ baskets\ that\ contains\ both\ X\ and\ Y}{total\ number\ of\ baskets}$$

$$Confidence = Conf(X \Rightarrow Y) = \frac{Supp(X \Rightarrow Y)}{Supp(X)}$$

$$Lift(X \Rightarrow Y) = \frac{Conf(X \Rightarrow Y)}{Expected\ Conf(X \Rightarrow Y)} = \frac{\frac{S(X \Rightarrow Y)}{S(X)}}{\frac{S(X) * S(Y)}{S(X)}} = \frac{S(X \Rightarrow Y)}{S(X) * S(Y)}$$

The support (S) of a collection of products is the measure of how often these products and/or services (i.e., LHS + RHS = Laptop Computer, Antivirus Software, and Extended Service Plan) appear together in the same transaction; that is, the proportion of transactions in the data set that contain all of the products and/or services mentioned in a specific rule. In this example, 30% of all transactions in the hypothetical store database had all three products present in a single sales ticket. The confidence of a rule is the measure of how often the products and/or services on the RHS (consequent) go together with the products and/or services on the LHS (antecedent), that is, the proportion of transactions that include LHS while also including the RHS. In other words, it is the conditional probability of finding the RHS of the rule present in transactions where the LHS of the rule already exists. The lift value of an association rule is the ratio of the confidence of the rule and the expected confidence of the rule. The expected confidence of a rule is defined as the product of the support values of the LHS and the RHS divided by the support of the LHS.

Several algorithms are available for discovering association rules. Some well-known algorithms include Apriori, Eclat, and FP-Growth. These algorithms only do half the job, which is to identify the frequent itemsets in the database. Once the frequent itemsets are identified, they need to be converted into rules with antecedent and consequent parts. Determination of the rules from frequent itemsets is a straightforward matching process, but the process may be time consuming with large transaction databases. Even though there can be many items on each section of the rule, in practice the consequent part usually contains a single item. In the following section, one of the most popular algorithms for identification of frequent itemsets is explained.

APRIORI ALGORITHM The **Apriori algorithm** is the most commonly used algorithm to discover association rules. Given a set of itemsets (e.g., sets of retail transactions, each listing individual items purchased), the algorithm attempts to find subsets that are common to at least a minimum number of the itemsets (i.e., complies with a minimum support). Apriori uses a bottom-up approach, where frequent subsets are extended one item at a time (a method known as *candidate generation*, whereby the size of frequent

Raw Transaction Data		One-Item Itemsets		Two-Item Itemsets		Three-Item Itemsets	
Transaction No	SKUs (Item No)	Itemset (SKUs)	Support	Itemset (SKUs)	Support	Itemset (SKUs)	Support
1001234	1, 2, 3, 4	1	3	1, 2	3	1, 2, 4	3
1001235	2, 3, 4	2	6	1, 3	2	2, 3, 4	3
1001236	2, 3	3	4	1, 4	3		
1001237	1, 2, 4	4	5	2, 3	4		
1001238	1, 2, 3, 4			2, 4	5		
1001239	2, 4			3, 4	3		

FIGURE 4.14   Identification of Frequent Itemsets in the Apriori Algorithm.

subsets increases from one-item subsets to two-item subsets, then three-item subsets, etc.), and groups of candidates at each level are tested against the data for minimum support. The algorithm terminates when no further successful extensions are found.

As an illustrative example, consider the following. A grocery store tracks sales transactions by SKU (stock keeping unit) and thus knows which items are typically purchased together. The database of transactions, along with the subsequent steps in identifying the frequent itemsets, is shown in Figure 4.14. Each SKU in the transaction database corresponds to a product, such as "1 = butter," "2 = bread," "3 = water," and so on. The first step in Apriori is to count up the frequencies (i.e., the supports) of each item (one-item itemsets). For this overly simplified example, let us set the minimum support to 3 (or 50%, meaning an itemset is considered to be a frequent itemset if it shows up in at least 3 out of 6 transactions in the database). Because all the one-item itemsets have at least 3 in the support column, they are all considered frequent itemsets. However, had any of the one-item itemsets not been frequent, they would not have been included as a possible member of possible two-item pairs. In this way, Apriori *prunes* the tree of all possible itemsets. As Figure 4.14 shows, using one-item itemsets, all possible two-item itemsets are generated and the transaction database is used to calculate their support values. Because the two-item itemset {1, 3} has a support less than 3, it should not be included in the frequent itemsets that will be used to generate the next-level itemsets (three-item itemsets). The algorithm seems deceivingly simple, but only for small data sets. In much larger data sets, especially those with huge amounts of items present in low quantities and small amounts of items present in big quantities, the search and calculation become a computationally intensive process.

SECTION 4.5 REVIEW QUESTIONS

1. Identify at least three of the main data mining methods.
2. Give examples of situations in which classification would be an appropriate data mining technique. Give examples of situations in which regression would be an appropriate data mining technique.
3. List and briefly define at least two classification techniques.
4. What are some of the criteria for comparing and selecting the best classification technique?
5. Briefly describe the general algorithm used in decision trees.
6. Define *Gini index*. What does it measure?
7. What is an ensemble model in data mining? What are the pros and cons of ensemble models?

8. Give examples of situations in which cluster analysis would be an appropriate data mining technique.

9. What is the major difference between cluster analysis and classification?

10. What are some of the methods for cluster analysis?

11. Give examples of situations in which association would be an appropriate data mining technique.

4.6 Data Mining Software Tools

Many software vendors provide powerful data mining tools. Examples of these vendors include IBM (IBM SPSS Modeler, formerly known as SPSS PASW Modeler and Clementine), SAS (Enterprise Miner), Dell (Statistica, formerly known as StatSoft Statistica Data Miner), SAP (Infinite Insight, formerly known as KXEN Infinite Insight), Salford Systems (CART, MARS, TreeNet, RandomForest), Angoss (KnowledgeSTUDIO, KnowledgeSEEKER), and Megaputer (PolyAnalyst). Noticeably but not surprisingly, the most popular data mining tools are developed by the well-established statistical software companies (SAS, SPSS, and StatSoft)—largely because statistics is the foundation of data mining, and these companies have the means to cost-effectively develop them into full-scale data mining systems. Most of the business intelligence tool vendors (e.g., IBM Cognos, Oracle Hyperion, SAP Business Objects, Tableau, Tibco, Qlik, MicroStrategy, Teradata, and Microsoft) also have some level of data mining capabilities integrated into their software offerings. These BI tools are still primarily focused on multidimensional modeling and data visualization and are not considered to be direct competitors of the data mining tool vendors.

In addition to these commercial tools, several open-source and/or free data mining software tools are available online. Traditionally, especially in educational circles, the most popular free and open-source data mining tool is **Weka**, which was developed by a number of researchers from the University of Waikato in New Zealand (the tool can be downloaded from cs.waikato.ac.nz/ml/weka). Weka includes a large number of algorithms for different data mining tasks and has an intuitive user interface. Recently, a number of free open-source, highly capable data mining tools emerged: leading the pack are **KNIME** (knime.org) and **RapidMiner** (rapidminer.com). Their graphically enhanced user interfaces, employment of a rather large number of algorithms, and incorporation of a variety of data visualization features set them apart from the rest of the free tools. These two free software tools are also platform agnostic (i.e., can natively run on both Windows and Mac operating systems). With a recent change in their offerings, RapidMiner has created a scaled-down version of their analytics tool for free (i.e., community edition) while making the full commercial product. Therefore, once listed under the free/open-source tools category, RapidMiner nowadays is often listed under commercial tools. The main difference between commercial tools, such as SAS Enterprise Miner, IBM SPSS Modeler, and Statistica, and free tools, such as Weka, RapidMiner (community edition), and KNIME, is the computational efficiency. The same data mining task involving a rather large and feature-rich data set may take a whole lot longer to complete with the free software tools, and for some algorithms the job may not even complete (i.e., crashing due to the inefficient use of computer memory). Table 4.2 lists a few of the major products and their Web sites.

A suite of business intelligence and analytics capabilities that has become increasingly more popular for data mining studies is **Microsoft's SQL Server** (it has been including increasingly more analytics capabilities, such as BI and predictive modeling modules, starting with the SQL Server 2012 version), where data and the models are stored in the same relational database environment, making model management a considerably easier task. The **Microsoft Enterprise Consortium** serves as the worldwide source for access to Microsoft's SQL Server software suite for academic purposes—teaching and research. The

TABLE 4.2   Selected Data Mining Software

Product Name	Web Site (URL)
IBM SPSS Modeler	www-01.ibm.com/software/analytics/spss/products/modeler/
IBM Watson Analytics	ibm.com/analytics/watson-analytics/
SAS Enterprise Miner	sas.com/en_id/software/analytics/enterprise-miner.html
Dell Statistica	statsoft.com/products/statistica/product-index
PolyAnalyst	megaputer.com/site/polyanalyst.php
CART, RandomForest	salford-systems.com
Insightful Miner	solutionmetrics.com.au/products/iminer/default.html
XLMiner	solver.com/xlminer-data-mining
SAP InfiniteInsight (KXEN)	help.sap.com/ii
GhostMiner	fqs.pl/ghostminer
SQL Server Data Mining	msdn.microsoft.com/en-us/library/bb510516.aspx
Knowledge Miner	knowledgeminer.com
Teradata Warehouse Miner	teradata.com/products-and-services/ teradata-warehouse-miner/
Oracle Data Mining (ODM)	oracle.com/technetwork/database/options/odm/
FICO Decision Management	fico.com/en/analytics/decision-management-suite/
Orange Data Mining Tool	orange.biolab.si/
Zementis Predictive Analytics	zementis.com

consortium has been established to enable universities around the world to access enterprise technology without having to maintain the necessary hardware and software on their own campus. The consortium provides a wide range of business intelligence development tools (e.g., data mining, cube building, business reporting) as well as a number of large, realistic data sets from Sam's Club, Dillard's, and Tyson Foods. The Microsoft Enterprise Consortium is free of charge and can only be used for academic purposes. The Sam M. Walton College of Business at the University of Arkansas hosts the enterprise system and allows consortium members and their students to access these resources using a simple remote desktop connection. The details about becoming a part of the consortium along with easy-to-follow tutorials and examples can be found at walton.uark.edu/enterprise/.

In May 2016, KDnuggets.com conducted the 13th Annual Software Poll on the following question: "What software you used for Analytics, Data Mining, Data Science, Machine Learning projects in the past 12 months?" The poll has received remarkable participation from analytics and data science community and vendors, attracting 2,895 voters, who chose from a record number of 102 different tools. Here are some of the interesting findings that came out of the poll:

- R remains the leading tool, with 49% shares (up from 46.9% in 2015), but Python usage grew faster and it almost caught up to R with 45.8% shares (up from 30.3%).
- RapidMiner remains the most popular general platform for data mining/data science, with about 33% shares. Notable tools with the most growth in popularity include Dato, Dataiku, MLlib, H2O, Amazon Machine Learning, scikit-learn, and IBM Watson.
- The increased choice of tools is reflected in wider usage. The average number of tools used was 6.0 (versus 4.8 in May 2015).
- The usage of Hadoop/Big Data tools grew to 39%, up from 29% in 2015 (and 17% in 2014), driven by Apache Spark, MLlib (Spark Machine Learning Library), and H2O.
- The participation by region was: US/Canada (40%), Europe (39%), Asia (9.4%), Latin America (5.8%), Africa/MidEast (2.9%), and Australia/NZ (2.2%).

- This year, 86% of voters used commercial software, and 75% used free software. About 25% used only commercial software, and 13% used only open-source/free software. A majority of 61% used both free and commercial software, similar to 64% in 2015.
- The usage of Hadoop/Big Data tools grew to 39%, up from 29% in 2015 and 17% in 2014, driven mainly by big growth in Apache Spark, MLlib (Spark Machine Learning Library), and H2O, which we included among Big Data tools.
- For the second year KDnuggets.com's poll included Deep Learning tools. This year, 18% of voters used Deep Learning tools, doubling the 9% in 2015—Google Tensorflow jumped to first place, displacing last year's leader, Theano/Pylearn2 ecosystem.
- In the programming languages category, Python, Java, Unix tools, and Scala grew in popularity, while C/C++, Perl, Julia, F#, Clojure, and Lisp declined.

To reduce bias through multiple voting, in this poll KDnuggets.com used e-mail verification and, by doing so, aimed to make results more representative of the reality in the analytics world. The results for the top 40 software tools (as per total number of votes received) are shown in Figure 4.15. The horizontal bar chart also makes a differentiation among free/open-source, commercial, and Big Data/Hadoop tools using a color-coding schema.

Application Case 4.6

Data Mining Goes to Hollywood: Predicting Financial Success of Movies

Application Case 4.6 is about a research study where a number of software tools and data mining techniques are used to build data mining models to predict financial success (box-office receipts) of Hollywood movies while they are nothing more than ideas.

Predicting box-office receipts (i.e., financial success) of a particular motion picture is an interesting and challenging problem. According to some domain experts, the movie industry is the "land of hunches and wild guesses" due to the difficulty associated with forecasting product demand, making the movie business in Hollywood a risky endeavor. In support of such observations, Jack Valenti (the longtime president and CEO of the Motion Picture Association of America) once mentioned that "… no one can tell you how a movie is going to do in the marketplace … not until the film opens in darkened theatre and sparks fly up between the screen and the audience." Entertainment industry trade journals and magazines have been full of examples, statements, and experiences that support such a claim.

Like many other researchers who have attempted to shed light on this challenging real-world problem, Ramesh Sharda and Dursun Delen have been exploring the use of data mining to predict the financial performance of a motion picture at the box office before it even enters production (while the movie is nothing more than a conceptual idea). In their highly publicized prediction models, they convert the forecasting (or regression) problem into a classification problem; that is, rather than forecasting the point estimate of box-office receipts, they classify a movie based on its box-office receipts in one of nine categories, ranging from "flop" to "blockbuster," making the problem a multinomial classification problem. Table 4.3 illustrates the definition of the nine classes in terms of the range of box-office receipts.

TABLE 4.3 Movie Classification Based on Receipts

Class No.	1	2	3	4	5	6	7	8	9
Range (in millions of dollars)	> 1 (Flop)	> 1 < 6 10	> 10 < 20	> 20 < 6 40	> 40 < 6 65	> 65 < 6 100	> 100 < 6 150	> 150 < 6 200	> 200 (Blockbuster)

(Continued)

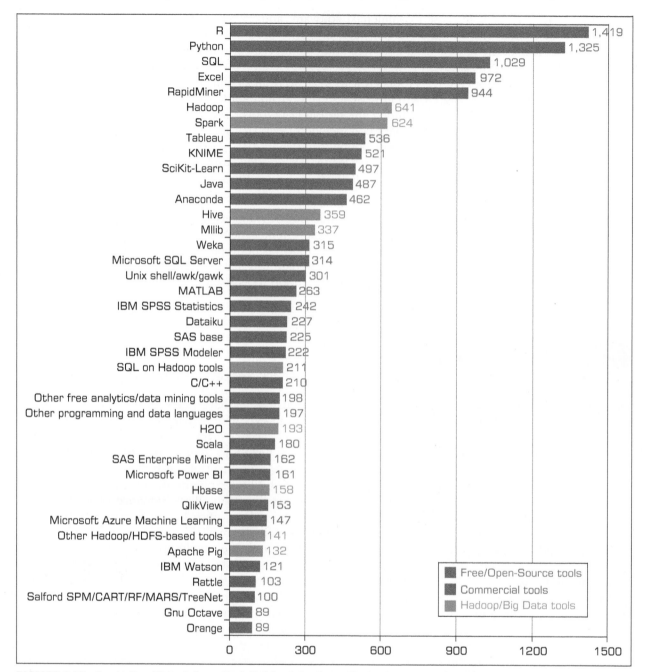

FIGURE 4.15 Popular Data Mining Software Tools (Poll Results). *Source:* Used with permission from KDnuggets.com.

Application Case 4.6 (Continued)

Data

Data was collected from a variety of movie-related databases (e.g., ShowBiz, IMDb, IMSDb, AllMovie, BoxofficeMojo, etc.) and consolidated into a single data set. The data set for the most recently developed models contained 2,632 movies released between 1998 and 2006. A summary of the independent variables along with their specifications is provided in

TABLE 4.4   Summary of Independent Variables

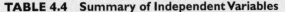

Independent Variable	Number of Values	Possible Values
MPAA Rating	5	G, PG, PG-13, R, NR
Competition	3	High, Medium, Low
Star value	3	High, Medium, Low
Genre	10	Sci-Fi, Historic Epic Drama, Modern Drama, Politically Related, Thriller, Horror, Comedy, Cartoon, Action, Documentary
Special effects	3	High, Medium, Low
Sequel	2	Yes, No
Number of screens	1	A positive integer between 1 and 3876

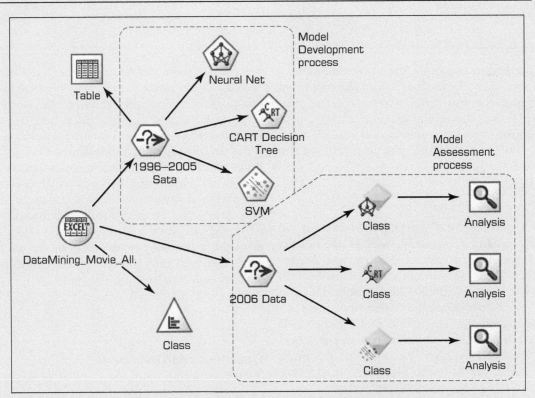

FIGURE 4.16   Process Flow Screenshot for the Box-Office Prediction System.   *Source:* Used with permission from IBM SPSS.

Table 4.4. For more descriptive details and justification for inclusion of these independent variables, the reader is referred to Sharda and Delen (2006).

Methodology

Using a variety of data mining methods, including neural networks, decision trees, SVMs, and three types of ensembles, Sharda and Delen developed the prediction models. The data from 1998 to 2005 were used as training data to build the prediction models, and the data from 2006 was used as the test data to assess and compare the models' prediction accuracy. Figure 4.16 shows a screenshot of IBM SPSS Modeler (formerly Clementine data mining tool) depicting the process map employed

(Continued)

Application Case 4.6 (Continued)

TABLE 4.5 Tabulated Prediction Results for Individual and Ensemble Models

| | Prediction Models | | | | | |
| | Individual Models | | | Ensemble Models | | |
Performance Measure	SVM	ANN	CART	Random Forest	Boosted Tree	Fusion (Average)
Count (Bingo)	192	182	140	189	187	**194**
Count (1-Away)	104	120	126	121	104	**120**
Accuracy (% Bingo)	55.49%	52.60%	40.46%	54.62%	54.05%	**56.07%**
Accuracy (% 1-Away)	85.55%	87.28%	76.88%	89.60%	84.10%	**90.75%**
Standard deviation	0.93	0.87	1.05	0.76	0.84	**0.63**

for the prediction problem. The upper-left side of the process map shows the model development process, and the lower-right corner of the process map shows the model assessment (i.e., testing or scoring) process (more details on IBM SPSS Modeler tool and its usage can be found on the book's Web site).

Results

Table 4.5 provides the prediction results of all three data mining methods as well as the results of the three different ensembles. The first performance measure is the percent correct classification rate, which is called *Bingo*. Also reported in the table is the *1-Away* correct classification rate (i.e., within one category). The results indicate that SVM performed the best among the individual prediction models, followed by ANN; the worst of the three was the CART decision tree algorithm. In general, the ensemble models performed better than the individual prediction models, of which the fusion algorithm performed the best. What is probably more important to decision makers, and standing out in the results table, is the significantly low standard deviation obtained from the ensembles compared to the individual models.

Conclusion

The researchers claim that these prediction results are better than any reported in the published literature for this problem domain. Beyond the attractive accuracy of their prediction results of the box-office receipts, these models could also be used to further analyze (and potentially optimize) the decision variables to maximize the financial return. Specifically, the parameters used for modeling could be altered using the already trained prediction models to better understand the impact of different parameters on the end results. During this process, which is commonly referred to as *sensitivity analysis*, the decision maker of a given entertainment firm could find out, with a fairly high accuracy level, how much value a specific actor (or a specific release date, or the addition of more technical effects, etc.) brings to the financial success of a film, making the underlying system an invaluable decision aid.

QUESTIONS FOR DISCUSSION

1. Why is it important for many Hollywood professionals to predict the financial success of movies?
2. How can data mining be used for predicting financial success of movies before the start of their production process?
3. How do you think Hollywood did, and perhaps still is performing, this task without the help of data mining tools and techniques?

Sources: Sharda, R., & Delen, D. (2006). Predicting box-office success of motion pictures with neural networks. *Expert Systems with Applications, 30*, 243–254; Delen, D., Sharda, R., & Kumar, P. (2007). Movie forecast Guru: A Web-based DSS for Hollywood managers. *Decision Support Systems, 43*(4), 1151–1170.

SECTION 4.6 REVIEW QUESTIONS

1. What are the most popular commercial data mining tools?
2. Why do you think the most popular tools are developed by statistics-based companies?
3. What are the most popular free data mining tools? Why are they gaining overwhelming popularity (especially R)?
4. What are the main differences between commercial and free data mining software tools?
5. What would be your top five selection criteria for a data mining tool? Explain.

4.7 Data Mining Privacy Issues, Myths, and Blunders

Data that is collected, stored, and analyzed in data mining often contains information about real people. Such information may include identification data (name, address, Social Security number, driver's license number, employee number, etc.), demographic data (e.g., age, sex, ethnicity, marital status, number of children), financial data (e.g., salary, gross family income, checking or savings account balance, home ownership, mortgage or loan account specifics, credit card limits and balances, investment account specifics), purchase history (i.e., what is bought from where and when—either from vendor's transaction records or from credit card transaction specifics), and other personal data (e.g., anniversary, pregnancy, illness, loss in the family, bankruptcy filings). Most of these data can be accessed through some third-party data providers. The main question here is the privacy of the person to whom the data belongs. To maintain the privacy and protection of individuals' rights, data mining professionals have ethical (and often legal) obligations. One way to accomplish this is the process of de-identification of the customer records prior to applying data mining applications, so that the records cannot be traced to an individual. Many publicly available data sources (e.g., CDC data, SEER data, UNOS data) are already de-identified. Prior to accessing these data sources, users are often asked to consent that, under no circumstances, will they try to identify the individuals behind those figures.

There have been a number of instances in the recent past where the companies shared their customer data with others without seeking the explicit consent of their customers. For instance, as most of you might recall, in 2003, JetBlue Airlines provided more than a million passenger records of their customers to Torch Concepts, a U.S. government contractor. Torch then subsequently augmented the passenger data with additional information such as family sizes and Social Security numbers—information purchased from a data broker called Acxiom. The consolidated personal database was intended to be used for a data mining project to develop potential terrorist profiles. All of this was done without notification or consent of passengers. When news of the activities got out, however, dozens of privacy lawsuits were filed against JetBlue, Torch, and Acxiom, and several U.S. senators called for an investigation into the incident (Wald, 2004). Similar, but not as dramatic, privacy-related news came out in the recent past about the popular social network companies, which allegedly were selling customer-specific data to other companies for personalized target marketing.

There was another peculiar story about privacy concerns that made it to the headlines in 2012. In this instance, the company did not even use any private and/or personal data. Legally speaking, there was no violation of any laws. It was about Target and is summarized in Application Case 4.7.

Application Case 4.7

Predicting Customer Buying Patterns—The Target Story

In early 2012, an infamous story appeared concerning Target's practice of predictive analytics. The story was about a teenage girl who was being sent advertising flyers and coupons by Target for the kinds of things that a new mother-to-be would buy from a store like Target. The story goes like this: An angry man went into a Target outside of Minneapolis, demanding to talk to a manager: "My daughter got this in the mail!" he said. "She's still in high school, and you're sending her coupons for baby clothes and cribs? Are you trying to encourage her to get pregnant?" The manager didn't have any idea what the man was talking about. He looked at the mailer. Sure enough, it was addressed to the man's daughter and contained advertisements for maternity clothing, nursery furniture, and pictures of smiling infants. The manager apologized and then called a few days later to apologize again. On the phone, though, the father was somewhat abashed. "I had a talk with my daughter," he said. "It turns out there's been some activities in my house I haven't been completely aware of. She's due in August. I owe you an apology."

As it turns out, Target figured out a teen girl was pregnant before her father did! Here is how they did it. Target assigns every customer a Guest ID number (tied to their credit card, name, or e-mail address) that becomes a placeholder that keeps a history of everything they have bought. Target augments this data with any demographic information that they had collected from them or bought from other information sources. Using this information, Target looked at historical buying data for all the females who had signed up for Target baby registries in the past. They analyzed the data from all directions, and soon enough some useful patterns emerged. For example, lotions and special vitamins were among the products with interesting purchase patterns. Lots of people buy lotion, but what they noticed was that women on the baby registry were buying larger quantities of unscented lotion around the beginning of their second trimester. Another analyst noted that

sometime in the first 20 weeks, pregnant women loaded up on supplements like calcium, magnesium, and zinc. Many shoppers purchase soap and cotton balls, but when someone suddenly starts buying lots of scent-free soap and extra-large bags of cotton balls, in addition to hand sanitizers and washcloths, it signals that they could be getting close to their delivery date. In the end, they were able to identify about 25 products that, when analyzed together, allowed them to assign each shopper a "pregnancy prediction" score. More important, they could also estimate a woman's due date to within a small window, so Target could send coupons timed to very specific stages of her pregnancy.

If you look at this practice from a legal perspective, you would conclude that Target did not use any information that violates customer privacy; rather, they used transactional data that almost every other retail chain is collecting and storing (and perhaps analyzing) about their customers. What was disturbing in this scenario was perhaps the targeted concept: pregnancy. There are certain events or concepts that should be off limits or treated extremely cautiously, such as terminal disease, divorce, and bankruptcy.

QUESTIONS FOR DISCUSSION

1. What do you think about data mining and its implication for privacy? What is the threshold between discovery of knowledge and infringement of privacy?

2. Did Target go too far? Did it do anything illegal? What do you think Target should have done? What do you think Target should do next (quit these types of practices)?

Sources: Hill, K. (2012, February 16). How Target figured out a teen girl was pregnant before her father did. *Forbes*; Nolan, R. (2012, February 21). Behind the cover story: How much does Target know? NYTimes.com.

Data Mining Myths and Blunders

Data mining is a powerful analytical tool that enables business executives to advance from describing the nature of the past (looking at a rearview mirror) to predicting the future (looking ahead) to better manage their business operations (making accurate and

TABLE 4.6	Data Mining Myths
Myth	**Reality**
Data mining provides instant, crystal-ball-like predictions.	Data mining is a multistep process that requires deliberate, proactive design and use.
Data mining is not yet viable for mainstream business applications.	The current state of the art is ready to go for almost any business type and/or size.
Data mining requires a separate, dedicated database.	Because of the advances in database technology, a dedicated database is not required.
Only those with advanced degrees can do data mining.	Newer Web-based tools enable managers of all educational levels to do data mining.
Data mining is only for large firms that have lots of customer data.	If the data accurately reflect the business or its customers, any company can use data mining.

timely decisions). Data mining helps marketers find patterns that unlock the mysteries of customer behavior. The results of data mining can be used to increase revenue and reduce cost by identifying fraud and discovering business opportunities, offering a whole new realm of competitive advantage. As an evolving and maturing field, data mining is often associated with a number of myths, including those listed in Table 4.6 (Delen, 2014; Zaima, 2003).

Data mining visionaries have gained enormous competitive advantage by understanding that these myths are just that: myths.

Although the value proposition and therefore the necessity of it is obvious to anyone, those who carry out data mining projects (from novice to seasoned data scientist) sometimes make mistakes that result in projects with less-than-desirable outcomes. The following 16 data mining mistakes (also called blunders, pitfalls, or bloopers) are often made in practice (Nesbit et al., 2009 Shultz, 2004; Skalak, 2001), and data scientists should be aware of them, and to the extent that is possible, do their best to avoid them:

1. Selecting the wrong problem for data mining. Not every business problem can be solved with data mining (i.e., the magic bullet syndrome). When there is no representative data (large and feature rich), there cannot be a practicable data mining project.

2. Ignoring what your sponsor thinks data mining is and what it really can and cannot do. Expectation management is the key for successful data mining projects.

3. Beginning without the end in mind. Although data mining is a process of knowledge discovery, one should have a goal/objective (a stated business problem) in mind to succeed. Because, as the saying goes, "if you don't know where you are going, you will never get there."

4. Define the project around a foundation that your data can't support. Data mining is all about data; that is, the biggest constraint that you have in a data mining project is the richness of the data. Knowing what the limitations of data are help you craft feasible projects that deliver results and meet expectations.

5. Leaving insufficient time for data preparation. It takes more effort than is generally understood. The common knowledge suggests that up to a third of the total project time is spent on data acquisition, understanding, and preparation tasks. To succeed, avoid proceeding into modeling until after your data is properly processed (aggregated, cleaned, and transformed).

6. Looking only at aggregated results and not at individual records. Data mining is at its best when the data is at a granular representation. Try to avoid

unnecessarily aggregating and overly simplifying data to help data mining algorithms—they don't really need your help; they are more than capable of figuring it out themselves.

7. Being sloppy about keeping track of the data mining procedure and results. Because it is a discovery process that involves many iterations and experimentations, it is highly likely to lose track of the findings. Success requires a systematic and orderly planning, execution, and tracking/recording of all data mining tasks.

8. Using data from the future to predict the future. Because of the lack of description and understanding of the data, oftentimes analysts include variables that are unknown at the time when the prediction is supposed to be made. By doing so, their prediction models produce unbelievable accurate results (a phenomenon that is often called "fool's gold"). If your prediction results are too good to be true, they usually are; in that case, the first thing that you need to look for is the incorrect use of a variable from the future.

9. Ignoring suspicious findings and quickly moving on. The unexpected findings are often the indicators of real novelties in data mining projects. Proper investigation of such oddities can lead to surprisingly pleasing discoveries.

10. Starting with a high-profile complex project that will make you a superstar. Data mining projects often fail if they are not thought out carefully from start to end. Success often comes with a systematic and orderly progression of projects from smaller/simpler to larger/complex ones. The goal should be to show incremental and continuous value added, as opposed to taking on a large project that will consume resources without producing any valuable outcomes.

11. Running data mining algorithms repeatedly and blindly. Although today's data mining tools are capable of consuming data and setting algorithmic parameters to produce results, one should know how to transform the data and set the proper parameter values to obtain the best possible results. Each algorithm has its own unique way of processing data, and knowing that is necessary to get the most out of each model type.

12. Ignore the subject matter experts. Understanding the problem domain and the related data requires a highly involved collaboration between the data mining and the domain experts. Working together helps the data mining expert to go beyond the syntactic representation and also obtain semantic nature (i.e., the true meaning of the variables) of the data.

13. Believing everything you are told about the data. Although it is necessary to talk to domain experts to better understand the data and the business problem, the data scientist should not take anything for granted. Validation and verification through a critical analysis is the key to intimate understanding and processing of the data.

14. Assuming that the keepers of the data will be fully on board with cooperation. Many data mining projects fail because the data mining expert did not know/understand the organizational politics. One of the biggest obstacles in data mining projects can be the people who own and control the data. Understanding and managing the politics is a key to identify, access, and properly understand the data to produce a successful data mining project.

15. Measuring your results differently from the way your sponsor measures them. The results should talk/appeal to the end user (manager/decision maker) who will be using them. Therefore, producing the results in a measure and format that appeals to the end user tremendously increases the likelihood of true understanding and proper use of the data mining outcomes.

16. If you build it, they will come: don't worry about how to serve it up. Usually, data mining experts think they are done once they build models that meet and hopefully

exceed the needs/wants/expectations of the end user (i.e., the customer). Without a proper deployment, the value deliverance of data mining outcomes is rather limited. Therefore, deployment is a necessary last step in the data mining process where models are integrated into the organizational decision support infrastructure for enablement of better and faster decision making.

SECTION 4.7 REVIEW QUESTIONS

1. What are the privacy issues in data mining?
2. How do you think the discussion between privacy and data mining will progress? Why?
3. What are the most common myths about data mining?
4. What do you think are the reasons for these myths about data mining?
5. What are the most common data mining mistakes/blunders? How can they be alleviated or completely eliminated?

Chapter Highlights

- Data mining is the process of discovering new knowledge from databases.
- Data mining can use simple flat files as data sources or it can be performed on data in data warehouses.
- There are many alternative names and definitions for data mining.
- Data mining is at the intersection of many disciplines, including statistics, artificial intelligence, and mathematical modeling.
- Companies use data mining to better understand their customers and optimize their operations.
- Data mining applications can be found in virtually every area of business and government, including healthcare, finance, marketing, and homeland security.
- Three broad categories of data mining tasks are prediction (classification or regression), clustering, and association.
- Similar to other IS initiatives, a data mining project must follow a systematic project management process to be successful.
- Several data mining processes have been proposed: CRISP-DM, SEMMA, KDD, and so on.
- CRISP-DM provides a systematic and orderly way to conduct data mining projects.

- The earlier steps in data mining projects (i.e., understanding the domain and the relevant data) consume most of the total project time (often more than 80% of the total time).
- Data preprocessing is essential to any successful data mining study. Good data leads to good information; good information leads to good decisions.
- Data preprocessing includes four main steps: data consolidation, data cleaning, data transformation, and data reduction.
- Classification methods learn from previous examples containing inputs and the resulting class labels, and once properly trained they are able to classify future cases.
- Clustering partitions pattern records into natural segments or clusters. Each segment's members share similar characteristics.
- A number of different algorithms are commonly used for classification. Commercial implementations include ID3, C4.5, C5, CART, CHAID, and SPRINT.
- Decision trees partition data by branching along different attributes so that each leaf node has all the patterns of one class.
- The Gini index and information gain (entropy) are two popular ways to determine branching choices in a decision tree.

- The Gini index measures the purity of a sample. If everything in a sample belongs to one class, the Gini index value is zero.
- Several assessment techniques can measure the prediction accuracy of classification models, including simple split, *k*-fold cross-validation, bootstrapping, and area under the ROC curve.
- Cluster algorithms are used when the data records do not have predefined class identifiers (i.e., it is not known to what class a particular record belongs).
- Cluster algorithms compute measures of similarity in order to group similar cases into clusters.
- The most commonly used similarity measure in cluster analysis is a distance measure.
- The most commonly used clustering algorithms are *k*-means and self-organizing maps.

- Association rule mining is used to discover two or more items (or events or concepts) that go together.
- Association rule mining is commonly referred to as market-basket analysis.
- The most commonly used association algorithm is Apriori, whereby frequent itemsets are identified through a bottom-up approach.
- Association rules are assessed based on their support and confidence measures.
- Many commercial and free data mining tools are available.
- The most popular commercial data mining tools are SPSS PASW and SAS Enterprise Miner.
- The most popular free data mining tools are Weka and RapidMiner.

Key Terms

Apriori algorithm	decision tree	knowledge discovery in	prediction
area under the ROC curve	distance measure	databases (KDD)	RapidMiner
association	ensemble	lift	regression
bootstrapping	entropy	link analysis	SEMMA
categorical data	Gini index	Microsoft Enterprise	sequence mining
classification	information gain	Consortium	simple split
clustering	interval data	Microsoft SQL Server	support
confidence	*k*-fold cross-validation	nominal data	Weka
CRISP-DM	KNIME	numeric data	
data mining		ordinal data	

Questions for Discussion

1. Define *data mining*. Why are there many names and definitions for data mining?
2. What are the main reasons for the recent popularity of data mining?
3. Discuss what an organization should consider before making a decision to purchase data mining software.
4. Distinguish data mining from other analytical tools and techniques.
5. Discuss the main data mining methods. What are the fundamental differences among them?
6. What are the main data mining application areas? Discuss the commonalities of these areas that make them a prospect for data mining studies.
7. Why do we need a standardized data mining process? What are the most commonly used data mining processes?
8. Discuss the differences between the two most commonly used data mining processes.
9. Are data mining processes a mere sequential set of activities? Explain.
10. Why do we need data preprocessing? What are the main tasks and relevant techniques used in data preprocessing?
11. Discuss the reasoning behind the assessment of classification models.
12. What is the main difference between classification and clustering? Explain using concrete examples.
13. Moving beyond the chapter discussion, where else can association be used?
14. What are the privacy issues with data mining? Do you think they are substantiated?
15. What are the most common myths and mistakes about data mining?

Exercises

Teradata University Network (TUN) and Other Hands-On Exercises

1. Visit teradatauniversitynetwork.com. Identify case studies and white papers about data mining. Describe recent developments in the field of data mining and predictive modeling.
2. Go to teradatauniversitynetwork.com. Locate Web seminars related to data mining. In particular, locate a seminar given by C. Imhoff and T. Zouqes. Watch the Web seminar. Then answer the following questions:
   a. What are some of the interesting applications of data mining?
   b. What types of payoffs and costs can organizations expect from data mining initiatives?
3. For this exercise, your goal is to build a model to identify inputs or predictors that differentiate risky customers from others (based on patterns pertaining to previous customers) and then use those inputs to predict new risky customers. This sample case is typical for this domain.

   The sample data to be used in this exercise are in Online File W4.1 in the file CreditRisk.xlsx. The data set has 425 cases and 15 variables pertaining to past and current customers who have borrowed from a bank for various reasons. The data set contains customer-related information such as financial standing, reason for the loan, employment, demographic information, and the outcome or dependent variable for credit standing, classifying each case as good or bad, based on the institution's past experience.

   Take 400 of the cases as training cases and set aside the other 25 for testing. Build a decision tree model to learn the characteristics of the problem. Test its performance on the other 25 cases. Report on your model's learning and testing performance. Prepare a report that identifies the decision tree model and training parameters, as well as the resulting performance on the test set. Use any decision tree software. (This exercise is courtesy of StatSoft, Inc., based on a German data set from ftp.ics.uc,i.edu/pub/machine-learning-databases/statlog/german renamed CreditRisk and altered.)
4. For this exercise, you will replicate (on a smaller scale) the box-office prediction modeling explained in Application Case 4.6. Download the training data set from Online File W4.2, MovieTrain.xlsx, which is in Microsoft Excel format. Use the data description given in Application Case 4.6 to understand the domain and the problem you are trying to solve. Pick and choose your independent variables. Develop at least three classification models (e.g., decision tree, logistic regression, neural networks). Compare the accuracy results using 10-fold cross-validation and percentage split techniques, use confusion matrices, and comment on the outcome. Test the models you have developed on the test set (see Online File W4.3, MovieTest.xlsx). Analyze the results with different models, and come up with the best classification model, supporting it with your results.
5. This exercise is aimed at introducing you to association rule mining. The Excel data set baskets1ntrans.xlsx has around 2,800 observations/records of supermarket trans products data. Each record contains the customer's ID and Products that they have purchased. Use this data set to understand the relationships among products (i.e., which products are purchased together). Look for interesting relationships and add screenshots of any subtle association patterns that you might: find. More specifically, answer the following questions.
   - Which association rules do you think are most important?
   - Based on some of the association rules you found, make at least three business recommendations that might be beneficial to the company. These recommendations up-selling may include ideas about shelf organization, upselling, or cross-selling products. (Bonus points will be given to new/innovative ideas.)
   - What are the Support, Confidence, and Lift values for the following rule?

     Wine, Canned Veg → Frozen Meal
6. In this assignment you will use a free/open-source data mining tool, KNIME (knime.org) to build predictive models for a relatively small Customer Churn Analysis data set. You are to analyze the given data set (about the customer retention/attrition behavior for 1,000 customers) to develop and compare at least three prediction (i.e., classification) models. For example, you can include decision trees, neural networks, SVM, k nearest neighbor, and/or logistic regression models in your comparison. Here are the specifics for this assignment:

   - Install and use the KNIME software tool from (knime.org).
     - You can also use MS Excel to preprocess the data (if you need to/want to).
   - Download CustomerChurnData.csv data file from the book's Web site.
     - The data is given in CSV (Comma Separated Value) format. This format is the most common flat-file format that many software tools can easily open/handle (including KNIME and MS Excel).
   - Present your results in a well-organized professional document.
     - Include a cover page (with proper information about you and the assignment).
     - Make sure to nicely integrate figures (graphs, charts, tables, screenshots) within your textual description

in a professional manner. The report should have six main sections (resembling CRISP-DM phases).

- Try not to exceed 15 pages in total, including the cover (use 12-point Times New Roman fonts, and 1.5-line spacing).

Team Assignments and Role-Playing Projects

1. Examine how new data capture devices such as RFID tags help organizations accurately identify and segment their customers for activities such as targeted marketing. Many of these applications involve data mining. Scan the literature and the Web and then propose five potential new data mining applications that can use the data created with RFID technology. What issues could arise if a country's laws required such devices to be embedded in everyone's body for a national identification system?

2. Interview administrators in your college or executives in your organization to determine how data mining, data warehousing, OLAP, and visualization tools could assist them in their work. Write a proposal describing your findings. Include cost estimates and benefits in your report.

3. A very good repository of data that has been used to test the performance of many data mining algorithms is available at ics.uci.edu/~mlearn/MLRepository.html. Some of the data sets are meant to test the limits of current machine-learning algorithms and to compare their performance with new approaches to learning. However, some of the smaller data sets can be useful for exploring the functionality of any data mining software, such as RapidMiner or KNIME. Download at least one data set from this repository (e.g., Credit Screening Databases, Housing Database) and apply decision tree or clustering methods, as appropriate. Prepare a report based on your results. (Some of these exercises, especially the ones that involve large/challenging data/problem may be used as semester-long term projects.)

4. Large and feature-rich data sets are made available by the U.S. government or its subsidiaries on the Internet. For instance, see a large collection of government data sets (data.gov), the Centers for Disease Control and Prevention data sets (www.cdc.gov/DataStatistics), Surveillance, Cancer.org's Epidemiology and End Results data sets (http://seer.cancer.gov/data), and the Department of Transportation's Fatality Analysis Reporting System crash data sets (www.nhtsa.gov/FARS). These data sets are not preprocessed for data mining, which makes them a great resource to experience the complete data mining process. Another rich source for a collection of analytics data sets is listed on KDnuggets.com (kdnuggets.com/datasets/index.html).

5. Consider the following data set, which includes three attributes and a classification for admission decisions into an MBA program:

GMAT	GPA	Quantitative GMAT Score (percentile)	Decision
650	2.75	35	No
580	3.50	70	No
600	3.50	75	Yes
450	2.95	80	No
700	3.25	90	Yes
590	3.50	80	Yes
400	3.85	45	No
640	3.50	75	Yes
540	3.00	60	?
690	2.85	80	?
490	4.00	65	?

a. Using the data shown, develop your own manual expert rules for decision making.

b. Use the Gini index to build a decision tree. You can use manual calculations or a spreadsheet to perform the basic calculations.

c. Use an automated decision tree software program to build a tree for the same data.

Internet Exercises

1. Visit the AI Exploratorium at cs.ualberta.ca/~aixplore. Click the Decision Tree link. Read the narrative on basketball game statistics. Examine the data, and then build a decision tree. Report your impressions of the accuracy of this decision tree. Also, explore the effects of different algorithms.

2. Survey some data mining tools and vendors. Start with fico.com and egain.com. Consult dmreview.com, and identify some data mining products and service providers that are not mentioned in this chapter.

3. Find recent cases of successful data mining applications. Visit the Web sites of some data mining vendors, and look for cases or success stories. Prepare a report summarizing five new case studies.

4. Go to vendor Web sites (especially those of SAS, SPSS, Cognos, Teradata, StatSoft, and Fair Isaac) and look at success stories for BI (OLAP and data mining) tools. What do the various success stories have in common? How do they differ?

5. Go to statsoft.com (now a Dell company). Download at least three white papers on applications. Which of these applications may have used the data/text/Web mining techniques discussed in this chapter?

6. Go to sas.com. Download at least three white papers on applications. Which of these applications may have used the data/text/Web mining techniques discussed in this chapter?

7. Go to spss.com (an IBM company). Download at least three white papers on applications. Which of these applications may have used the data/text/Web mining techniques discussed in this chapter?

8. Go to teradata.com. Download at least three white papers on applications. Which of these applications may have used the data/text/Web mining techniques discussed in this chapter?

9. Go to fico.com. Download at least three white papers on applications. Which of these applications may have used the data/text/Web mining techniques discussed in this chapter?

10. Go to salfordsystems.com. Download at least three white papers on applications. Which of these applications may have used the data/text/Web mining techniques discussed in this chapter?

11. Go to rulequest.com. Download at least three white papers on applications. Which of these applications may have used the data/text/Web mining techniques discussed in this chapter?

12. Go to kdnuggets.com. Explore the sections on applications as well as software. Find names of at least three additional packages for data mining and text mining.

References

Abbott, D. (2014). *Applied predictive analytics: Principles and techniques for the professional data analyst.* John Wiley & Sons.

Anthes, G. H. (1999). "The next decade: interview with Arno A. Penzias," *Computerworld, 33*(1), pp. 3–4.

Chan, P. K., Phan, W., Prodromidis, A., & Stolfo, S. (1999). Distributed data mining in credit card fraud detection. *IEEE Intelligent Systems, 14*(6), 67–74.

CRISP-DM. (2013). Cross-Industry Standard Process for Data Mining (CRISP-DM). http://crisp-dm.orgwww .the-modeling-agency.com/crisp-dm.pdf (accessed February 2, 2013).

Davenport, T. H. (2006, January). Competing on analytics. *Harvard Business Review,* 99–107.

Delen, D. (2009). Analysis of cancer data: A data mining approach. *Expert Systems, 26*(1), 100–112.

Delen, D. (2014). *Real-world data mining: Applied business analytics and decision making.* Upper Saddle River, NJ: Pearson.

Delen, D., Cogdell, D., & Kasap, N. (2012). A comparative analysis of data mining methods in predicting NCAA Bowl outcomes. *International Journal of Forecasting, 28,* 543–552.

Delen, D., & Sharda, R. (2010). Predicting the financial success of Hollywood movies using an information fusion approach. *Industrial Engineering Journal, 21*(1), 30–37.

Delen, D., Sharda, R., & Kumar, P. (2007). Movie forecast Guru: A Web-based DSS for Hollywood managers. *Decision Support Systems, 43*(4), 1151–1170.

Delen, D., Walker, G., & Kadam, A. (2005). Predicting breast cancer survivability: A comparison of three data mining methods. *Artificial Intelligence in Medicine, 34*(2), 113–127.

Dunham, M. (2003). *Data mining: Introductory and advanced topics.* Upper Saddle River, NJ: Prentice Hall.

Fayyad, U., Piatetsky-Shapiro, G., & Smyth, P. (1996). From knowledge discovery in databases. *AI Magazine, 17*(3), 37–54.

Hoffman, T. (1998, December 7). Banks turn to IT to reclaim most profitable customers. *Computerworld.*

Hoffman, T. (1999, April 19). Insurers mine for age-appropriate offering. *Computerworld.*

Kohonen, T. (1982). Self-organized formation of topologically correct feature maps. *Biological Cybernetics, 43*(1), 59–69.

Nemati, H. R., & Barko, C. D. (2001). Issues in organizational data mining: A survey of current practices. *Journal of Data Warehousing, 6*(1), 25–36.

Nisbet, R., Miner, G., & Elder IV, J. (2009). "Top 10 Data Mining Mistakes" in the Handbook of statistical analysis and data mining applications. pp. 733–754. Academic Press.

Quinlan, J. R. (1986). Induction of decision trees. *Machine Learning, 1,* 81–106.

SEMMA. (2009). SAS's data mining process: Sample, explore, modify, model, assess. sas.com/offices/europe/ uk/technologies/analytics/datamining/miner/semma .html (accessed August 2009).

Seni, G., & Elder, J. F. (2010). Ensemble methods in data mining: Improving accuracy through combining predictions. Synthesis Lectures on Data Mining and Knowledge Discovery, *2*(1), 1–126.

Sharda, R., & Delen, D. (2006). Predicting box-office success of motion pictures with neural networks. *Expert Systems with Applications, 30,* 243–254.

Shultz, R. (2004, December 7). Live from NCDM: Tales of database buffoonery. directmag.com/news/ncdm-12-07-04/index.html (accessed April 2009).

Skalak, D. (2001). Data mining blunders exposed! *DB2 Magazine, 6*(2), 10–13.

Thongkam, J., Xu, G., Zhang, Y., & Huang, F. (2009). Toward breast cancer survivability prediction models through improving training space. *Expert Systems with Applications, 36*(10), 12200–12209.

Wald, M. L. (2004, February 21). U.S. calls release of JetBlue data improper. *The New York Times.*

Wright, C. (2012). *Statistical predictors of March Madness: An examination of the NCAA Men's Basketball Championship.* http://economics-files.pomona.edu/GarySmith/Econ190/ Wright%20March%20Madness%20Final%20Paper.pdf (accessed February 2, 2013).

Zaima, A. (2003). The five myths of data mining. *What Works: Best practices in business intelligence and data warehousing,* Vol. 15. Chatsworth, CA: The Data Warehousing Institute, pp. 42–43.

Zolbanin, H. M., Delen, D., & Zadeh, A. H. (2015). Predicting overall survivability in comorbidity of cancers: A data mining approach. *Decision Support Systems, 74,* 150–161.

CHAPTER 5

Predictive Analytics II: Text, Web, and Social Media Analytics

LEARNING OBJECTIVES

- Describe text analytics and understand the need for text mining
- Differentiate among text analytics, text mining, and data mining
- Understand the different application areas for text mining
- Know the process of carrying out a text mining project
- Appreciate the different methods to introduce structure to text-based data
- Describe sentiment analysis
- Develop familiarity with popular applications of sentiment analysis
- Learn the common methods for sentiment analysis
- Become familiar with speech analytics as it relates to sentiment analysis

This chapter provides a comprehensive overview of text analytics/mining and Web analytics/mining along with their popular application areas such as search engines, sentiment analysis, and social network/media analytics. As we have been witnessing in the recent years, the unstructured data generated over the *Internet of Things* (Web, sensor networks, radio-frequency identification [RFID]-enabled supply chain systems, surveillance networks, etc.) is increasing at an exponential pace, and there is no indication of it slowing down. This changing nature of data is forcing organizations to make text and Web analytics a critical part of their business intelligence/analytics infrastructure.

5.1 Opening Vignette: Machine versus Men on *Jeopardy!*: The Story of Watson   248
5.2 Text Analytics and Text Mining Overview   251
5.3 Natural Language Processing (NLP)   255
5.4 Text Mining Applications   261
5.5 Text Mining Process   268
5.6 Sentiment Analysis   276
5.7 Web Mining Overview   287

5.8 Search Engines 291

5.9 Web Usage Mining (Web Analytics) 298

5.10 Social Analytics 304

5.1   OPENING VIGNETTE: Machine versus Men on *Jeopardy!*: The Story of Watson

Can a machine beat the best of man in what man is supposed to be the best at? Evidently, yes, and the machine's name is Watson. Watson is an extraordinary computer system (a novel combination of advanced hardware and software) designed to answer questions posed in natural human language. It was developed in 2010 by an IBM Research team as part of a DeepQA project and was named after IBM's first president, Thomas J. Watson.

Background

Roughly 3 years ago, IBM Research was looking for a major research challenge to rival the scientific and popular interest of Deep Blue, the computer chess-playing champion, which would also have clear relevance to IBM business interests. The goal was to advance computer science by exploring new ways for computer technology to affect science, business, and society. Accordingly, IBM Research undertook a challenge to build a computer system that could compete at the human champion level in real time on the American TV quiz show *Jeopardy!* The extent of the challenge included fielding a real-time automatic contestant on the show, capable of listening, understanding, and responding—not merely a laboratory exercise.

Competing against the Best

In 2011, as a test of its abilities, Watson competed on the quiz show *Jeopardy!*, which was the first ever human-versus-machine matchup for the show. In a two-game, combined-point match (broadcast in three *Jeopardy!* episodes during February 14–16), Watson beat Brad Rutter, the biggest all-time money winner on *Jeopardy!*, and Ken Jennings, the record holder for the longest championship streak (75 days). In these episodes, Watson consistently outperformed its human opponents on the game's signaling device, but had trouble responding to a few categories, notably those having short clues containing only a few words. Watson had access to 200 million pages of structured and unstructured content consuming 4 terabytes of disk storage. During the game Watson was not connected to the Internet.

Meeting the *Jeopardy!* Challenge required advancing and incorporating a variety of QA technologies (text mining and natural language processing), including parsing, question classification, question decomposition, automatic source acquisition and evaluation, entity and relation detection, logical form generation, and knowledge representation and reasoning. Winning at *Jeopardy!* required accurately computing confidence in your answers. The questions and content are ambiguous and noisy, and none of the individual algorithms are perfect. Therefore, each component must produce a confidence in its output, and individual component confidences must be combined to compute the overall confidence of the final answer. The final confidence is used to determine whether the computer system should risk choosing to answer at all. In *Jeopardy!* parlance, this confidence is used to determine whether the computer will "ring in" or "buzz in" for a question. The confidence must be computed during the time the question is read and before the opportunity to buzz in. This is roughly between 1 and 6 seconds with an average around 3 seconds.

How Does Watson Do It?

The system behind Watson, which is called DeepQA, is a massively parallel, text mining–focused, probabilistic evidence-based computational architecture. For the *Jeopardy!* Challenge, Watson used more than 100 different techniques for analyzing natural language, identifying sources, finding and generating hypotheses, finding and scoring evidence, and merging and ranking hypotheses. What is far more important than any particular technique that they used was how they combine them in DeepQA such that overlapping approaches can bring their strengths to bear and contribute to improvements in accuracy, confidence, and speed.

DeepQA is an architecture with an accompanying methodology, which is not specific to the *Jeopardy!* Challenge. The overarching principles in DeepQA are massive parallelism, many experts, pervasive confidence estimation, and integration of the latest and greatest in text analytics.

- **Massive parallelism:** Exploitsts massive parallelism in the consideration of multiple interpretations and hypotheses.
- **Many experts:** Facilitate the integration, application, and contextual evaluation of a wide range of loosely coupled probabilistic question and content analytics.
- **Pervasive confidence estimation:** No component commits to an answer; all components produce features and associated confidences, scoring different question and content interpretations. An underlying confidence-processing substrate learns how to stack and combine the scores.
- **Integrate shallow and deep knowledge:** Balance the use of strict semantics and shallow semantics, leveraging many loosely formed ontologies.

Figure 5.1 illustrates the DeepQA architecture at a very high level. More technical details about the various architectural components and their specific roles and capabilities can be found in Ferrucci et al. (2010).

Conclusion

The *Jeopardy!* challenge helped IBM address requirements that led to the design of the DeepQA architecture and the implementation of Watson. After 3 years of intense research and development by a core team of about 20 researchers, Watson is performing at human expert levels in terms of precision, confidence, and speed at the *Jeopardy!* quiz show.

IBM claims to have developed many computational and linguistic algorithms to address different kinds of issues and requirements in QA. Even though the internals of these algorithms are not known, it is imperative that they made the most out of text analytics and text mining. Now IBM is working on a version of Watson to take on surmountable problems in healthcare and medicine (Feldman et al., 2012).

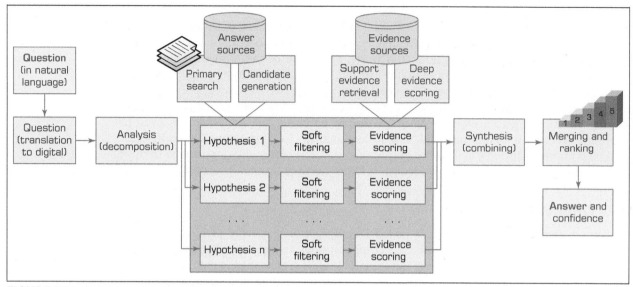

FIGURE 5.1 A High-Level Depiction of DeepQA Architecture.

QUESTIONS FOR THE OPENING VIGNETTE

1. What is Watson? What is special about it?
2. What technologies were used in building Watson (both hardware and software)?
3. What are the innovative characteristics of DeepQA architecture that made Watson superior?
4. Why did IBM spend all that time and money to build Watson? Where is the return on investment (ROI)?

What We Can Learn from This Vignette

It is safe to say that computer technology, both on the hardware and software fronts, is advancing faster than anything else in the last 50-plus years. Things that were too big, too complex, impossible to solve are now well within the reach of information technology. One of the enabling technologies is perhaps text analytics/text mining. We created databases to structure the data so that it can be processed by computers. Text, on the other hand, has always been meant for humans to process. Can machines do the things that require human creativity and intelligence, and were not originally designed for machines? Evidently, yes! Watson is a great example of the distance that we have traveled in addressing the impossible. Computers are now intelligent enough to take on men at what we think men are the best at. Understanding the question that was posed in spoken human language, processing and digesting it, searching for an answer, and replying within a few seconds was something that we could not have imagined possible before Watson actually did it. In this chapter, you will learn the tools and techniques embedded in Watson and many other smart machines to create miracles in tackling problems that were once believed impossible to solve.

Sources: Ferrucci, D., Brown, E., Chu-Carroll, J., Fan, J., Gondek, D., Kalyanpur, A. A., . . . Welty, C. (2010). Building Watson: An overview of the DeepQA Project. *AI Magazine, 31*(3); DeepQA. DeepQA Project: FAQ, IBM Corporation (2011). research.ibm.com/deepqa/faq.shtml (accessed January 2013); Feldman, S., Hanover, J., Burghard, C., & Schubmehl, D. (2012). Unlocking the power of unstructured data. IBM white paper. www-01.ibm .com/software/ebusiness/jstart/downloads/unlockingUnstructuredData.pdf (accessed February 2013).

5.2 Text Analytics and Text Mining Overview

The information age that we are living in is characterized by the rapid growth in the amount of data and information collected, stored, and made available in electronic format. A vast majority of business data are stored in text documents that are virtually unstructured. According to a study by Merrill Lynch and Gartner, 85% of all corporate data is captured and stored in some sort of unstructured form (McKnight, 2005). The same study also stated that this unstructured data is doubling in size every 18 months. Because knowledge is power in today's business world, and knowledge is derived from data and information, businesses that effectively and efficiently tap into their text data sources will have the necessary knowledge to make better decisions, leading to a competitive advantage over those businesses that lag behind. This is where the need for text analytics and text mining fits into the big picture of today's businesses.

Even though the overarching goal for both text analytics and text mining is to turn unstructured textual data into actionable information through the application of natural language processing (NLP) and analytics, their definitions are somewhat different, at least to some experts in the field. According to them, text analytics is a broader concept that includes information retrieval (e.g., searching and identifying relevant documents for a given set of key terms), as well as information extraction, data mining, and Web mining, whereas text mining is primarily focused on discovering new and useful knowledge from the textual data sources. Figure 5.2 illustrates the relationships between text analytics and text mining along with other related application areas. The bottom of Figure 5.2 lists the main disciplines (the foundation of the house) that play a critical role in the development

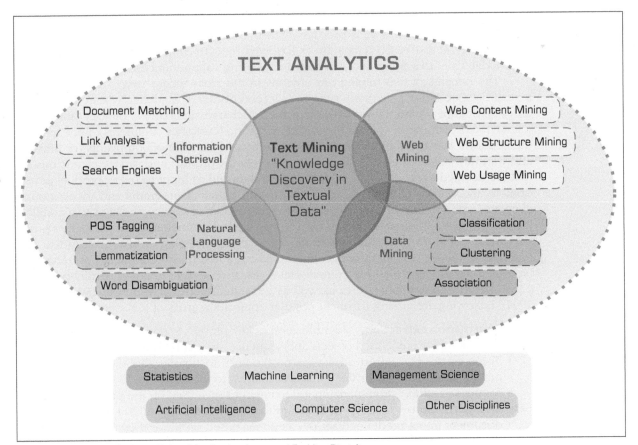

FIGURE 5.2 Text Analytics, Related Application Areas, and Enabling Disciplines.

of these increasingly more popular application areas. Based on this definition of text analytics and text mining, one could simply formulate the difference between the two as follows:

Text Analytics = Information Retrieval + Information Extraction + Data Mining + Web Mining,

or simply

Text Analytics = Information Retrieval + Text Mining

Compared to text mining, *text analytics* is a relatively new term. With the recent emphasis on *analytics*, as has been the case in many other related technical application areas (e.g., consumer analytics, completive analytics, visual analytics, social analytics), the field of text has also wanted to get on the analytics bandwagon. Although the term *text analytics* is more commonly used in a business application context, text mining is frequently used in academic research circles. Even though they may be defined somewhat differently at times, text analytics and text mining are usually used synonymously, and we (authors of this book) concur with this.

Text mining (also known as *text data mining* or *knowledge discovery in textual databases*) is the semiautomated process of extracting patterns (useful information and knowledge) from large amounts of unstructured data sources. Remember that data mining is the process of identifying valid, novel, potentially useful, and ultimately understandable patterns in data stored in structured databases, where the data are organized in records structured by categorical, ordinal, or continuous variables. Text mining is the same as data mining in that it has the same purpose and uses the same processes, but with text mining the input to the process is a collection of unstructured (or less structured) data files such as Word documents, PDF files, text excerpts, XML files, and so on. In essence, text mining can be thought of as a process (with two main steps) that starts with imposing structure on the text-based data sources followed by extracting relevant information and knowledge from this structured text-based data using data mining techniques and tools.

The benefits of text mining are obvious in the areas where very large amounts of textual data are being generated, such as law (court orders), academic research (research articles), finance (quarterly reports), medicine (discharge summaries), biology (molecular interactions), technology (patent files), and marketing (customer comments). For example, the free-form text-based interactions with customers in the form of complaints (or praises) and warranty claims can be used to objectively identify product and service characteristics that are deemed to be less than perfect and can be used as input to better product development and service allocations. Likewise, market outreach programs and focus groups generate large amounts of data. By not restricting product or service feedback to a codified form, customers can present, in their own words, what they think about a company's products and services. Another area where the automated processing of unstructured text has had a lot of impact is in electronic communications and e-mail. Text mining not only can be used to classify and filter junk e-mail, but it can also be used to automatically prioritize e-mail based on importance level as well as generate automatic responses (Weng & Liu, 2004). Following are among the most popular application areas of text mining:

- **Information extraction.** Identification of key phrases and relationships within text by looking for predefined objects and sequences in text by way of pattern matching.
- **Topic tracking.** Based on a user profile and documents that a user views, text mining can predict other documents of interest to the user.
- **Summarization.** Summarizing a document to save time on the part of the reader.
- **Categorization.** Identifying the main themes of a document and then placing the document into a predefined set of categories based on those themes.

- **Clustering.** Grouping similar documents without having a predefined set of categories.
- **Concept linking.** Connects related documents by identifying their shared concepts and, by doing so, helps users find information that they perhaps would not have found using traditional search methods.
- **Question answering.** Finding the best answer to a given question through knowledge-driven pattern matching.

See Technology Insights 5.1 for explanations of some of the terms and concepts used in text mining. Application Case 5.1 describes the use of text mining in the insurance industry.

TECHNOLOGY INSIGHTS 5.1
Text Mining Terminology

The following list describes some commonly used text mining terms:

- ***Unstructured data (versus structured data).*** Structured data has a predetermined format. It is usually organized into records with simple data values (categorical, ordinal, and continuous variables) and stored in databases. In contrast, **unstructured data** does not have a predetermined format and is stored in the form of textual documents. In essence, the structured data is for the computers to process while the unstructured data is for humans to process and understand.
- ***Corpus.*** In linguistics, a **corpus** (plural *corpora*) is a large and structured set of texts (now usually stored and processed electronically) prepared for the purpose of conducting knowledge discovery.
- ***Terms.*** A *term* is a single word or multiword phrase extracted directly from the corpus of a specific domain by means of NLP methods.
- ***Concepts.*** *Concepts* are features generated from a collection of documents by means of manual, statistical, rule-based, or hybrid categorization methodology. Compared to terms, concepts are the result of higher level abstraction.
- ***Stemming.*** **Stemming** is the process of reducing inflected words to their stem (or base or root) form. For instance, *stemmer, stemming, stemmed* are all based on the root *stem*.
- ***Stop words.*** **Stop words** (or *noise words*) are words that are filtered out prior to or after processing of natural language data (i.e., text). Even though there is no universally accepted list of stop words, most NLP tools use a list that includes articles (*a, am, the, of*, etc.), auxiliary verbs (*is, are, was, were*, etc.), and context-specific words that are deemed not to have differentiating value.
- ***Synonyms and polysemes.*** Synonyms are syntactically different words (i.e., spelled differently) with identical or at least similar meanings (e.g., *movie, film*, and *motion picture*). In contrast, **polysemes**, which are also called *homonyms*, are syntactically identical words (i.e., spelled exactly the same) with different meanings (e.g., *bow* can mean "to bend forward," "the front of the ship," "the weapon that shoots arrows," or "a kind of tied ribbon").
- ***Tokenizing.*** A *token* is a categorized block of text in a sentence. The block of text corresponding to the token is categorized according to the function it performs. This assignment of meaning to blocks of text is known as **tokenizing**. A token can look like anything; it just needs to be a useful part of the structured text.
- ***Term dictionary.*** A collection of terms specific to a narrow field that can be used to restrict the extracted terms within a corpus.
- ***Word frequency.*** The number of times a word is found in a specific document.
- ***Part-of-speech tagging.*** The process of marking up the words in a text as corresponding to a particular part of speech (such as nouns, verbs, adjectives, adverbs, etc.) based on a word's definition and the context in which it is used.
- ***Morphology.*** A branch of the field of linguistics and a part of NLP that studies the internal structure of words (patterns of word formation within a language or across languages).

- **Term-by-document matrix (occurrence matrix).** A common representation schema of the frequency-based relationship between the terms and documents in tabular format where terms are listed in columns, documents are listed in rows, and the frequency between the terms and documents is listed in cells as integer values.
- **Singular value decomposition (latent semantic indexing).** A dimensionality reduction method used to transform the term-by-document matrix to a manageable size by generating an intermediate representation of the frequencies using a matrix manipulation method similar to principal component analysis.

Application Case 5.1

Insurance Group Strengthens Risk Management with Text Mining Solution

When asked for the biggest challenge facing the Czech automobile insurance industry, Peter Jedlička, PhD, doesn't hesitate. "Bodily injury claims are growing disproportionately compared with vehicle damage claims," says Jedlička, team leader of actuarial services for the Czech Insurers' Bureau (CIB). CIB is a professional organization of insurance companies in the Czech Republic that handles uninsured, international, and untraced claims for what's known as motor third-party liability. "Bodily injury damages now represent about 45% of the claims made against our members, and that proportion will continue to increase because of recent legislative changes."

One of the difficulties that bodily injury claims pose for insurers is that the extent of an injury is not always predictable in the immediate aftermath of a vehicle accident. Injuries that were not at first obvious may become acute later, and apparently minor injuries can turn into chronic conditions. The earlier that insurance companies can accurately estimate their liability for medical damages, the more precisely they can manage their risk and consolidate their resources. However, because the needed information is contained in unstructured documents such as accident reports and witness statements, it is extremely time consuming for individual employees to perform the needed analysis.

To expand and automate the analysis of unstructured accident reports, witness statements, and claim narratives, CIB deployed a data analysis solution based on Dell Statistica Data Miner and the Statistica Text Miner extension. Statistica Data Miner offers a set of intuitive, user-friendly tools that are accessible even to nonanalysts.

The solution reads and writes data from virtually all standard file formats and offers strong, sophisticated data cleaning tools. It also supports even novice users with query wizards, called Data Mining Recipes, that help them arrive at the answers they need more quickly.

With the Statistica Text Miner extension, users have access to extraction and selection tools that can be used to index, classify, and cluster information from large collections of unstructured text data, such as the narratives of insurance claims. In addition to using the Statistica solution to make predictions about future medical damage claims, CIB can also use it to find patterns that indicate attempted fraud or to identify needed road safety improvements.

Improves Accuracy of Liability Estimates

Jedlička expects the Statistica solution to greatly improve the ability of CIB to predict the total medical claims that might arise from a given accident. "The Statistica solution's data mining and text mining capabilities are already helping us expose additional risk characteristics, thus making it possible to predict serious medical claims in earlier stages of the investigation," he says. "With the Statistica solution, we can make much more accurate estimates of total damages and plan accordingly."

Expands Service Offerings to Members

Jedlička is also pleased that the Statistica solution helps CIB offer additional services to its member companies. "We are in a data-driven business," he says. "With Statistica, we can provide our members with detailed analyses of claims and market trends. Statistica also helps us provide even stronger recommendations concerning claims reserves."

Intuitive for Business Users

The intuitive Statistica tools are accessible by even nontechnical users. "The outputs of our Statistica analyses are easy to understand for business users," says Jedlička. "Our business users also find that the analysis results are in line with their own experience and recommendations, so they readily see the value in the Statistica solution."

Questions for Discussion

1. How can text analytics and mining be used to keep up with changing business needs of insurance companies?
2. What were the challenges, the proposed solution, and the obtained results?
3. Can you think of other uses of text analytics and text mining for insurance companies?

Sources: Dell Statistica Case Study. Insurance group strengthens risk management with text mining solution. https://software.dell .com/casestudy/czech-insurers-bureau-insurance-group-strengthens-risk-management-with875134/ (accessed June 2016). Used by permission from Dell.

SECTION 5.2 REVIEW QUESTIONS

1. What is text analytics? How does it differ from text mining?
2. What is text mining? How does it differ from data mining?
3. Why is the popularity of text mining as an analytics tool increasing?
4. What are some of the most popular application areas of text mining?

5.3 Natural Language Processing (NLP)

Some of the early text mining applications used a simplified representation called *bag-of-words* when introducing structure to a collection of text-based documents to classify them into two or more predetermined classes or to cluster them into natural groupings. In the bag-of-words model, text, such as a sentence, paragraph, or complete document, is represented as a collection of words, disregarding the grammar or the order in which the words appear. The bag-of-words model is still used in some simple document classification tools. For instance, in spam filtering an e-mail message can be modeled as an unordered collection of words (a bag-of-words) that is compared against two different predetermined bags. One bag is filled with words found in spam messages and the other is filled with words found in legitimate e-mails. Although some of the words are likely to be found in both bags, the "spam" bag will contain spam-related words such as *stock*, *Viagra*, and *buy* much more frequently than the legitimate bag, which will contain more words related to the user's friends or workplace. The level of match between a specific e-mail's bag-of-words and the two bags containing the descriptors determines the membership of the e-mail as either spam or legitimate.

Naturally, we (humans) do not use words without some order or structure. We use words in sentences, which have semantic as well as syntactic structure. Thus, automated techniques (such as text mining) need to look for ways to go beyond the bag-of-words interpretation and incorporate more and more semantic structure into their operations. The current trend in text mining is toward including many of the advanced features that can be obtained using NLP.

It has been shown that the bag-of-words method may not produce good enough information content for text mining tasks (e.g., classification, clustering, association). A good example of this can be found in evidence-based medicine. A critical component of evidence-based medicine is incorporating the best available research findings into the clinical decision-making process, which involves appraisal of the information collected from the printed media for validity and relevance. Several researchers from the University of Maryland developed evidence assessment models using a bag-of-words method (Lin & Demner-Fushman, 2005). They employed popular machine-learning methods along with more than half a million research articles collected from MEDLINE (Medical Literature Analysis and Retrieval System Online). In their models, they represented each abstract as a bag-of-words, where each stemmed term represented a feature. Despite using popular classification methods with proven experimental design methodologies, their prediction results were not much better than simple guessing, which may indicate that the bag-of-words is not generating a good enough representation of the research articles in this domain; hence, more advanced techniques such as NLP are needed.

Natural language processing (NLP) is an important component of text mining and is a subfield of artificial intelligence and computational linguistics. It studies the problem of "understanding" the natural human language, with the view of converting depictions of human language (such as textual documents) into more formal representations (in the form of numeric and symbolic data) that are easier for computer programs to manipulate. The goal of NLP is to move beyond syntax-driven text manipulation (which is often called "word counting") to a true understanding and processing of natural language that considers grammatical and semantic constraints as well as the context.

The definition and scope of the word *understanding* is one of the major discussion topics in NLP. Considering that the natural human language is vague and that a true understanding of meaning requires extensive knowledge of a topic (beyond what is in the words, sentences, and paragraphs), will computers ever be able to understand natural language the same way and with the same accuracy that humans do? Probably not! NLP has come a long way from the days of simple word counting, but it has an even longer way to go to really understanding natural human language. The following are just a few of the challenges commonly associated with the implementation of NLP:

- **Part-of-speech tagging.** It is difficult to mark up terms in a text as corresponding to a particular part of speech (such as nouns, verbs, adjectives, or adverbs) because the part of speech depends not only on the definition of the term but also on the context within which it is used.
- **Text segmentation.** Some written languages, such as Chinese, Japanese, and Thai, do not have single-word boundaries. In these instances, the text-parsing task requires the identification of word boundaries, which is often a difficult task. Similar challenges in speech segmentation emerge when analyzing spoken language because sounds representing successive letters and words blend into each other.
- **Word sense disambiguation.** Many words have more than one meaning. Selecting the meaning that makes the most sense can only be accomplished by taking into account the context within which the word is used.
- **Syntactic ambiguity.** The grammar for natural languages is ambiguous; that is, multiple possible sentence structures often need to be considered. Choosing the most appropriate structure usually requires a fusion of semantic and contextual information.
- **Imperfect or irregular input.** Foreign or regional accents and vocal impediments in speech and typographical or grammatical errors in texts make the processing of the language an even more difficult task.
- **Speech acts.** A sentence can often be considered an action by the speaker. The sentence structure alone may not contain enough information to define this action. For example, "Can you pass the class?" requests a simple yes/no answer, whereas "Can you pass the salt?" is a request for a physical action to be performed.

It is a long-standing dream of the artificial intelligence community to have algorithms that are capable of automatically reading and obtaining knowledge from text. By applying a learning algorithm to parsed text, researchers from Stanford University's NLP lab have developed methods that can automatically identify the concepts and relationships between those concepts in the text. By applying a unique procedure to large amounts of text, their algorithms automatically acquire hundreds of thousands of items of world knowledge and use them to produce significantly enhanced repositories for WordNet. **WordNet** is a laboriously hand-coded database of English words, their definitions, sets of synonyms, and various semantic relations between synonym sets. It is a major resource for NLP applications, but it has proven to be very expensive to build and maintain manually. By automatically inducing knowledge into WordNet, the potential exists to make WordNet an even greater and more comprehensive resource for NLP at a fraction of the cost. One prominent area where the benefits of NLP and WordNet are already being harvested is in customer relationship management (CRM). Broadly speaking, the goal of CRM is to maximize customer value by better understanding and effectively responding to their actual and perceived needs. An important area of CRM, where NLP is making a significant impact, is sentiment analysis. **Sentiment analysis** is a technique used to detect favorable and unfavorable opinions toward specific products and services using a large number of textual data sources (customer feedback in the form of Web postings). A detailed coverage of sentiment analysis and WordNet is given in Section 5.6.

Analytics in general and text analytics and text mining in specific can be used in the broadcasting industry. Application Case 5.2 provides an example where a wide range of analytics capabilities are used to capture new viewers, predict ratings, and add business value to a broadcasting company.

Application Case 5.2

AMC Networks Is Using Analytics to Capture New Viewers, Predict Ratings, and Add Value for Advertisers in a Multichannel World

Over the past 10 years, the cable television sector in the United States has enjoyed a period of growth that has enabled unprecedented creativity in the creation of high-quality content. AMC Networks has been at the forefront of this new golden age of television, producing a string of successful, critically acclaimed shows such as *Breaking Bad*, *Mad Men*, and *The Walking Dead*.

Dedicated to producing quality programming and movie content for more than 30 years, AMC Networks Inc. owns and operates several of the most popular and award-winning brands in cable television, producing and delivering distinctive, compelling, and culturally relevant content that engages audiences across multiple platforms.

Getting Ahead of the Game

Despite its success, the company has no plans to rest on its laurels. As Vitaly Tsivin, SVP Business Intelligence, explains: "We have no interest in standing still. Although a large percentage of our business is still linear cable TV, we need to appeal to a new generation of millennials who consume content in very different ways.

"TV has evolved into a multichannel, multistream business, and cable networks need to get smarter about how they market to and connect with audiences across all of those streams. Relying on traditional ratings data and third-party analytics providers is going to be a losing strategy: you need to take ownership of your data, and use it to get a richer picture of who your viewers are, what they want, and how you can keep their attention in an increasingly crowded entertainment marketplace."

Zoning in on the Viewer

The challenge is that there is just so much information available—hundreds of billions of rows of data from industry data providers such as Nielsen and comScore, from channels such as AMC's TV Everywhere live Web streaming and video on-demand service,

(Continued)

Application Case 5.2 (Continued)

from retail partners such as iTunes and Amazon, and from third-party online video services such as Netflix and Hulu.

"We can't rely on high-level summaries; we need to be able to analyze both structured and unstructured data, minute-by-minute and viewer-by-viewer," says Vitaly Tsivin. "We need to know who's watching and why—and we need to know it quickly so that we can decide, for example, whether to run an ad or a promo in a particular slot during tomorrow night's episode of *Mad Men*."

AMC decided it needed to develop an industry-leading analytics capability in-house—and focused on delivering this capability as quickly as possible. Instead of conducting a prolonged and expensive vendor and product selection process, AMC decided to leverage its existing relationship with IBM as its trusted strategic technology partner. The time and money traditionally spent on procurement were instead invested in realizing the solution—accelerating AMC's progress on its analytics roadmap by at least 6 months.

Empowering the Research Department

In the past, AMC's research team spent a large portion of its time processing data. Today, thanks to its new analytics tools, it is able to focus most of its energy on gaining actionable insights.

"By investing in big data analytics technology from IBM, we've been able to increase the pace and detail of our research an order of magnitude," says Vitaly Tsivin. "Analyses that used to take days and weeks are now possible in minutes, or even seconds.

"Bringing analytics in-house will provide major ongoing cost-savings. Instead of paying hundreds of thousands of dollars to external vendors when we

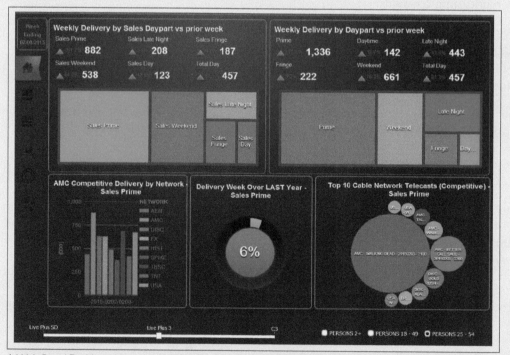

A Web-Based Dashboard Used by AMC Networks.   *Source:* AMC Networks.

need some analysis done, we can do it ourselves—more quickly, more accurately, and much more cost-effectively. We're expecting to see a rapid return on investment.

"As more sources of potential insight become available and analytics becomes more strategic to the business, an in-house approach is really the only viable way forward for any network that truly wants to gain competitive advantage from its data."

Driving Decisions with Data

Many of the results delivered by this new analytics capability demonstrate a real transformation in the way AMC operates. For example, the company's business intelligence department has been able to create sophisticated statistical models that help the company refine its marketing strategies and make smarter decisions about how intensively it should promote each show.

	Instrumented	AMC combines ratings data with viewer information from a wide range of digital channels: its own video on-demand and live-streaming services, retailers, and online TV services.
	Interconnected	A powerful and comprehensive big data and analytics engine centralizes the data and makes it available to a range of descriptive and predictive analytics tools for accelerated modeling, reporting, and analysis.
	Intelligent	AMC can predict which shows will be successful, how it should schedule them, what promos it should create, and to whom it should market them—helping to win new audience share in an increasingly competitive market.

With deeper insight into viewership, AMC's direct marketing campaigns are also much more successful. In one recent example, intelligent segmentation and lookalike modeling helped the company target new and existing viewers so effectively that AMC video on-demand transactions were higher than would be expected otherwise.

This newfound ability to reach out to new viewers based on their individual needs and preferences is not just valuable for AMC—it also has huge potential value for the company's advertising partners. AMC is currently working on providing access to its rich data sets and analytics tools as a service for advertisers, helping them fine-tune their campaigns to appeal to ever-larger audiences across both linear and digital channels.

Vitaly Tsivin concludes: "Now that we can really harness the value of big data, we can build a much more attractive proposition for both consumers and advertisers—creating even better content, marketing it more effectively, and helping it reach a wider audience by taking full advantage of our multichannel capabilities."

(Continued)

Application Case 5.2 (Continued)

Questions for Discussion

1. What are the common challenges broadcasting companies are facing nowadays? How can analytics help to alleviate these challenges?

2. How did AMC leverage analytics to enhance their business performance?

3. What were the types of text analytics and text mini solutions developed by AMC networks? Can you think of other potential uses of text mining applications in the broadcasting industry?

Sources: IBM Customer Case Study. Using analytics to capture new viewers, predict ratings and add value for advertisers in a multichannel world. http://www-03.ibm.com/software/businesscasestudies/us/en/corp?synkey=A023603A76220M60 (accessed July 2016); www.ibm.com; www.amcnetworks .com.

NLP has successfully been applied to a variety of domains for a wide range of tasks via computer programs to automatically process natural human language that previously could only be done by humans. Following are among the most popular of these tasks:

- **Question answering.** The task of automatically answering a question posed in natural language; that is, producing a human language answer when given a human language question. To find the answer to a question, the computer program may use either a prestructured database or a collection of natural language documents (a text corpus such as the World Wide Web).
- **Automatic summarization.** The creation of a shortened version of a textual document by a computer program that contains the most important points of the original document.
- **Natural language generation.** Systems convert information from computer databases into readable human language.
- **Natural language understanding.** Systems convert samples of human language into more formal representations that are easier for computer programs to manipulate.
- **Machine translation.** The automatic translation of one human language to another.
- **Foreign language reading.** A computer program that assists a nonnative language speaker to read a foreign language with correct pronunciation and accents on different parts of the words.
- **Foreign language writing.** A computer program that assists a nonnative language user in writing in a foreign language.
- **Speech recognition.** Converts spoken words to machine-readable input. Given a sound clip of a person speaking, the system produces a text dictation.
- **Text-to-speech.** Also called *speech synthesis*, a computer program automatically converts normal language text into human speech.
- **Text proofing.** A computer program reads a proof copy of a text to detect and correct any errors.
- **Optical character recognition.** The automatic translation of images of handwritten, typewritten, or printed text (usually captured by a scanner) into machine-editable textual documents.

The success and popularity of text mining depends greatly on advancements in NLP in both generation as well as understanding of human languages. NLP enables the extraction of features from unstructured text so that a wide variety of data mining techniques can be used to extract knowledge (novel and useful patterns and relationships) from it. In that sense, simply put, text mining is a combination of NLP and data mining.

SECTION 5.3 REVIEW QUESTIONS

1. What is NLP?
2. How does NLP relate to text mining?
3. What are some of the benefits and challenges of NLP?
4. What are the most common tasks addressed by NLP?

5.4 Text Mining Applications

As the amount of unstructured data collected by organizations increases, so does the value proposition and popularity of text mining tools. Many organizations are now realizing the importance of extracting knowledge from their document-based data repositories through the use of text mining tools. Following is only a small subset of the exemplary application categories of text mining.

Marketing Applications

Text mining can be used to increase cross-selling and up-selling by analyzing the unstructured data generated by call centers. Text generated by call center notes as well as transcriptions of voice conversations with customers can be analyzed by text mining algorithms to extract novel, actionable information about customers' perceptions toward a company's products and services. In addition, blogs, user reviews of products at independent Web sites, and discussion board postings are a gold mine of customer sentiments. This rich collection of information, once properly analyzed, can be used to increase satisfaction and the overall lifetime value of the customer (Coussement & Van den Poel, 2008).

Text mining has become invaluable for CRM. Companies can use text mining to analyze rich sets of unstructured text data, combined with the relevant structured data extracted from organizational databases, to predict customer perceptions and subsequent purchasing behavior. Coussement and Van den Poel (2009) successfully applied text mining to significantly improve the ability of a model to predict customer churn (i.e., customer attrition) so that those customers identified as most likely to leave a company are accurately identified for retention tactics.

Ghani et al. (2006) used text mining to develop a system capable of inferring implicit and explicit attributes of products to enhance retailers' ability to analyze product databases. Treating products as sets of attribute–value pairs rather than as atomic entities can potentially boost the effectiveness of many business applications, including demand forecasting, assortment optimization, product recommendations, assortment comparison across retailers and manufacturers, and product supplier selection. The proposed system allows a business to represent its products in terms of attributes and attribute values without much manual effort. The system learns these attributes by applying supervised and semisupervised learning techniques to product descriptions found on retailers' Web sites.

Security Applications

One of the largest and most prominent text mining applications in the security domain is probably the highly classified ECHELON surveillance system. As rumor has it, ECHELON is assumed to be capable of identifying the content of telephone calls, faxes, e-mails, and other types of data, intercepting information sent via satellites, public-switched telephone networks, and microwave links.

In 2007, EUROPOL developed an integrated system capable of accessing, storing, and analyzing vast amounts of structured and unstructured data sources to track transnational organized crime. Called the Overall Analysis System for Intelligence Support (OASIS), this system aims to integrate the most advanced data and text mining technologies available in today's market. The system has enabled EUROPOL to make significant progress in supporting its law enforcement objectives at the international level (EUROPOL, 2007).

The U.S. Federal Bureau of Investigation (FBI) and the Central Intelligence Agency (CIA), under the direction of the Department for Homeland Security, are jointly developing a supercomputer data and text mining system. The system is expected to create a gigantic data warehouse along with a variety of data and text mining modules to meet the knowledge-discovery needs of federal, state, and local law enforcement agencies. Prior to this project, the FBI and CIA each had its own separate database, with little or no interconnection.

Another security-related application of text mining is in the area of **deception detection**. Applying text mining to a large set of real-world criminal (person-of-interest) statements, Fuller, Biros, and Delen (2008) developed prediction models to differentiate deceptive statements from truthful ones. Using a rich set of cues extracted from the textual statements, the model predicted the holdout samples with 70% accuracy, which is believed to be a significant success considering that the cues are extracted only from textual statements (no verbal or visual cues are present). Furthermore, compared to other deception-detection techniques, such as polygraph, this method is nonintrusive and widely applicable to not only textual data, but also (potentially) to transcriptions of voice recordings. A more detailed description of text-based deception detection is provided in Application Case 5.3.

Application Case 5.3

Mining for Lies

Driven by advancements in Web-based information technologies and increasing globalization, computer-mediated communication continues to filter into everyday life, bringing with it new venues for deception. The volume of text-based chat, instant messaging, text messaging, and text generated by online communities of practice is increasing rapidly. Even e-mail continues to grow in use. With the massive growth of text-based communication, the potential for people to deceive others through computer-mediated communication has also grown, and such deception can have disastrous results.

Unfortunately, in general, humans tend to perform poorly at deception-detection tasks. This phenomenon is exacerbated in text-based communications. A large part of the research on deception detection (also known as *credibility assessment*) has involved face-to-face meetings and interviews. Yet, with the growth of text-based communication, text-based deception-detection techniques are essential.

Techniques for successfully detecting deception—that is, lies—have wide applicability. Law enforcement can use decision support tools and techniques to investigate crimes, conduct security screening in airports, and monitor communications of suspected terrorists. Human resources professionals might use deception-detection tools to screen applicants. These tools and techniques also have the potential to screen e-mails to uncover fraud or other wrongdoings committed by corporate officers. Although some people believe that they can readily identify those who are not being truthful, a summary of deception research showed that, on average, people are only 54% accurate in making veracity determinations (Bond & DePaulo, 2006). This figure may actually be worse when humans try to detect deception in text.

Using a combination of text mining and data mining techniques, Fuller et al. (2008) analyzed person-of-interest statements completed by people involved in crimes on military bases. In these statements, suspects and witnesses are required to write their recollection of the event in their own words. Military law enforcement personnel searched archival data for statements that they could conclusively identify as being truthful or deceptive. These decisions were made on the basis of corroborating evidence and case resolution. Once labeled as truthful or deceptive, the law enforcement personnel removed identifying information and gave the statements to the research team. In total, 371 usable statements were received for analysis. The text-based deception-detection method used by Fuller et al. (2008) was based on a process known as *message feature mining*, which relies on elements of data and text mining techniques. A simplified depiction of the process is provided in Figure 5.3.

First, the researchers prepared the data for processing. The original handwritten statements had to be transcribed into a word processing file. Second, features (i.e., cues) were identified. The researchers identified 31 features representing categories or types of language that are relatively independent of the text content and that can be readily analyzed by automated means. For example, first-person pronouns such as *I* or *me* can be identified without analysis of the surrounding text. Table 5.1 lists the categories and an example list of features used in this study.

The features were extracted from the textual statements and input into a flat file for further processing. Using several feature-selection methods along with 10-fold cross-validation, the researchers compared the prediction accuracy of three popular data mining methods. Their results indicated that neural network models performed the best, with 73.46% prediction accuracy on test data samples; decision trees performed second best, with 71.60% accuracy; and logistic regression was last, with 65.28% accuracy.

The results indicate that automated text-based deception detection has the potential to aid those who must try to detect lies in text and can be successfully applied to real-world data. The accuracy of these techniques exceeded the accuracy of most other deception-detection techniques, even though it was limited to textual cues.

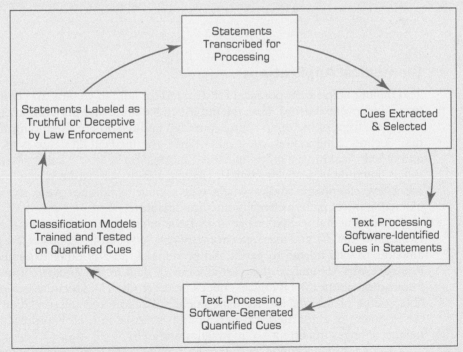

FIGURE 5.3   Text-Based Deception-Detection Process.   *Source:* Fuller, C. M., Biros, D., & Delen, D. (2008, January). Exploration of feature selection and advanced classification models for high-stakes deception detection. *Proceedings of the 41st Annual Hawaii International Conference on System Sciences (HICSS)*, Big Island, HI: IEEE Press, 80–99.

(Continued)

Application Case 5.3 (Continued)

TABLE 5.1 Categories and Examples of Linguistic Features Used in Deception Detection

Number	Construct (Category)	Example Cues
1	Quantity	Verb count, noun-phrase count, etc.
2	Complexity	Average number of clauses, average sentence length, etc.
3	Uncertainty	Modifiers, modal verbs, etc.
4	Nonimmediacy	Passive voice, objectification, etc.
5	Expressivity	Emotiveness
6	Diversity	Lexical diversity, redundancy, etc.
7	Informality	Typographical error ratio
8	Specificity	Spatiotemporal information, perceptual information, etc.
9	Affect	Positive affect, negative affect, etc.

Questions for Discussion

1. Why is it difficult to detect deception?
2. How can text/data mining be used to detect deception in text?
3. What do you think are the main challenges for such an automated system?

Sources: Fuller, C. M., Biros, D., & Delen, D. (2008). Exploration of feature selection and advanced classification models for high-stakes deception detection. *Proceedings of the 41st Annual Hawaii International Conference on System Sciences (HICSS),* Big Island, HI: IEEE Press, 80–99; Bond C. F., & DePaulo, B. M. (2006). Accuracy of deception judgments. *Personality and Social Psychology Reports, 10*(3), 214–234.

Biomedical Applications

Text mining holds great potential for the medical field in general and biomedicine in particular for several reasons. First, the published literature and publication outlets (especially with the advent of the open-source journals) in the field are expanding at an exponential rate. Second, compared to most other fields, the medical literature is more standardized and orderly, making it a more "minable" information source. Finally, the terminology used in this literature is relatively constant, having a fairly standardized ontology. What follows are a few exemplary studies where text mining techniques were successfully used in extracting novel patterns from biomedical literature.

Experimental techniques such as DNA microarray analysis, serial analysis of gene expression (SAGE), and mass spectrometry proteomics, among others, are generating large amounts of data related to genes and proteins. As in any other experimental approach, it is necessary to analyze this vast amount of data in the context of previously known information about the biological entities under study. The literature is a particularly valuable source of information for experiment validation and interpretation. Therefore, the development of automated text mining tools to assist in such interpretation is one of the main challenges in current bioinformatics research.

Knowing the location of a protein within a cell can help to elucidate its role in biological processes and to determine its potential as a drug target. Numerous location-prediction systems are described in the literature; some focus on specific organisms, whereas others attempt to analyze a wide range of organisms. Shatkay et al. (2007)

proposed a comprehensive system that uses several types of sequence- and text-based features to predict the location of proteins. The main novelty of their system lies in the way in which it selects its text sources and features and integrates them with sequence-based features. They tested the system on previously used data sets and on new data sets devised specifically to test its predictive power. The results showed that their system consistently beat previously reported results.

Chun et al. (2006) described a system that extracts disease–gene relationships from literature accessed via MEDLINE. They constructed a dictionary for disease and gene names from six public databases and extracted relation candidates by dictionary matching. Because dictionary matching-produces a large number of false positives, they developed a method of machine-learning–based named entity recognition (NER) to filter out false recognitions of disease/gene names. They found that the success of relation extraction is heavily dependent on the performance of NER filtering and that the filtering improved the precision of relation extraction by 26.7%, at the cost of a small reduction in recall.

Figure 5.4 shows a simplified depiction of a multilevel text analysis process for discovering gene–protein relationships (or protein–protein interactions) in the biomedical literature (Nakov et al., 2005). As can be seen in this simplified example that uses a simple sentence from biomedical text, first (at the bottom three levels) the text is tokenized using **part-of-speech tagging** and shallow-parsing. The tokenized terms (words) are then matched (and interpreted) against the hierarchical representation of the domain ontology to derive the gene–protein relationship. Application of this method (and/or some variation of it) to the biomedical literature offers great potential to decode the complexities in the Human Genome Project.

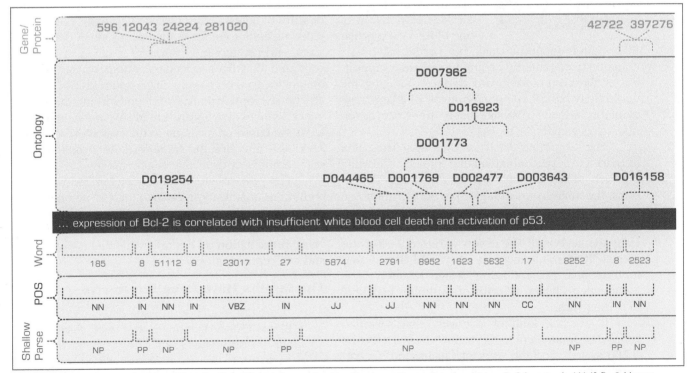

FIGURE 5.4 Multilevel Analysis of Text for Gene/Protein Interaction Identification. *Source:* Based on Nakov, P., Schwartz, A., Wolf, B., & Hearst, M. A. (2005). Supporting annotation layers for natural language processing. *Proceedings of the Association for Computational Linguistics (ACL),* Interactive Poster and Demonstration Sessions, Ann Arbor, MI. Association for Computational Linguistics, 65–68.

Academic Applications

The issue of text mining is of great importance to publishers who hold large databases of information requiring indexing for better retrieval. This is particularly true in scientific disciplines, in which highly specific information is often contained within written text. Initiatives have been launched, such as *Nature*'s proposal for an Open Text Mining Interface and the National Institutes of Health's common Journal Publishing Document Type Definition, which would provide semantic cues to machines to answer specific queries contained within text without removing publisher barriers to public access.

Academic institutions have also launched text mining initiatives. For example, the National Centre for Text Mining, a collaborative effort between the Universities of Manchester and Liverpool, provides customized tools, research facilities, and advice on text mining to the academic community. With an initial focus on text mining in the biological and biomedical sciences, research has since expanded into the social sciences. In the United States, the School of Information at the University of California, Berkeley, is developing a program called BioText to assist bioscience researchers in text mining and analysis.

As described in this section, text mining has a wide variety of applications in a number of different disciplines. See Application Case 5.4 for an example of how a leading computing product manufacturer uses text mining to better understand their current and potential customers' needs and wants related to product quality and product design.

Application Case 5.4

Bringing the Customer into the Quality Equation: Lenovo Uses Analytics to Rethink Its Redesign

Lenovo was near final design on an update to the keyboard layout of one of its most popular PCs when it spotted a small, but significant, online community of gamers who are passionately supportive of the current keyboard design. Changing the design may have led to a mass revolt of a large segment of Lenovo's customer base—freelance developers and gamers.

The Corporate Analytics unit was using SAS as part of a perceptual quality project. Crawling the Web, sifting through text data for Lenovo mentions, the analysis unearthed a previously unknown forum, where an existing customer had written a glowing six-page review of the current design, especially the keyboard. The review attracted 2,000 comments! "It wasn't something we would have found in traditional preproduction design reviews," says Mohammed Chaara, Director of Customer Insight & VOC Analytics.

It was the kind of discovery that solidified Lenovo's commitment to the Lenovo Early Detection (LED) system, and the work of Chaara and his corporate analytics team.

Lenovo, the largest global manufacturer of PCs and tablets, didn't set out to gauge sentiment around obscure bloggers or discover new forums. The company wanted to inform quality, product development, and product innovation by studying data—its own and that from outside the four walls. "We're mainly focused on supply chain optimization, cross-sell/up-sell opportunities and pricing and packaging of services. Any improvements we make in these areas are based on listening to the customer," Chaara says. SAS provides the framework to "manage the crazy amount of data" that is generated.

The project's success has traveled like wildfire within the organization. Lenovo initially planned on about 15 users, but word of mouth has led to 300 users signing up to log in to the LED dashboard for a visual presentation on customer sentiment, warranty, and call center analysis.

The Results Have Been Impressive

- Over 50% reduction in issue detection time.
- 10 to 15% reduction in warranty costs from out-of-norm defects.
- 30 to 50% reduction in general information calls to the contact center.

Looking at the Big Picture

Traditional methods of gauging sentiment and understanding quality have built-in weaknesses and time lags:

- Customer surveys only surface information from customers who are willing to fill them out.
- Warranty information often comes in months after delivery of the new product.
- It can be difficult to decipher myriad causes of customer discontent and product issues.

In addition, Lenovo sells its product packaged with software it doesn't produce, and customers use a variety of accessories (docking stations and mouse devices) that might or might not be Lenovo products. To compound the issue, the company operates in 165 countries and supports more than 30 languages, so the manual methods to evaluate the commentary were inconsistent, took too much time, and couldn't scale to the volumes of feedback it was seeing in social media. The sentiment analysis needed to be able to sense nuances within the native languages. (For example, Australians describe things differently than Americans.)

The analysis-driven discovery of an issue with docking stations provided the second big win for Lenovo's LED initiative. Customers were calling tech support to say they were having issues with the screen, or the machine shutting down abruptly, or the battery wasn't charging. Similar accounts were turning up on social media posts. Sometimes, though not always, the customer mentioned docking. It wasn't until Lenovo used SAS to analyze the combination of call center notes and social media posts that the word *docking* was connected to the problem, helping quality engineers figure out the root cause and issue a software update.

"We were able to pick up that feedback within weeks. It used to take 60 to 90 days because we had to wait for the reports to come back from the field," Chaara says. Now it takes just 15 to 30 days. That reduction in detection time has driven a 10 to 15% reduction in warranty costs for those issues. As warranty claims cost the company about $1.2 billion yearly, this is a significant savings.

Although the call center information was crucial, the social media component was what sealed the deal. "With Twitter and Facebook, people described what they were doing at that minute, "I docked the machine and X happened.' It's raw, unbiased and so powerful," Chaara says.

An unforeseen insight was found when analyzing what customers were saying as they got their PCs up and running. Lenovo realized its documentation to explain its products, warranties, and the like was unclear. "There is a cost to every call center call. With the improved documentation, we've seen a 30 to 50% reduction in calls coming in for general information," Chaara said.

Winning Praise beyond the Frontlines

The project has been so successful that Chaara demoed it for the CEO. The goal is to configure a dashboard view for the C-suite. "That's the level of thinking from our senior executives. They believe in this," Chaara says. In addition, Chaara's group will be formally measuring the success of the effort and expanding it to measure issues like customer experience when buying a Lenovo product.

"The application of analytics has ultimately led us to a more holistic understanding of the concept of quality. Quality isn't just a PC working correctly. It's people knowing how to use it, getting quick and accurate help from the company, getting the non-Lenovo components to work well with the hardware, and understanding what the customers like about the existing product—rather than just redesigning it because product designers think it's the right thing to do. "SAS has allowed us to get a definition of quality from the view of the customer," Chaara says.

Questions for Discussion

1. How did Lenovo use text analytics and text mining to improve quality and design of their products and ultimately improve customer satisfaction?
2. What were the challenges, the proposed solution, and the obtained results?

Source: "Bringing the customer into the quality equation (SAS® Visual Analytics, SAS® Contextual Analysis, SAS® Sentiment Analysis, SAS® Text Miner) - Sentiment analysis and advanced analytics help Lenovo better identify quality issues and customer desires." Copyright © 2016 SAS Institute Inc., Cary, NC, USA. Reprinted with permission. All rights reserved.

SECTION 5.4 REVIEW QUESTIONS

1. List and briefly discuss some of the text mining applications in marketing.

2. How can text mining be used in security and counterterrorism?

3. What are some promising text mining applications in biomedicine?

5.5 Text Mining Process

To be successful, text mining studies should follow a sound methodology based on best practices. A standardized process model is needed similar to Cross-Industry Standard Process for Data Mining (CRISP-DM), which is the industry standard for data mining projects (see Chapter 4). Even though most parts of CRISP-DM are also applicable to text mining projects, a specific process model for text mining would include much more elaborate data preprocessing activities. Figure 5.5 depicts a high-level context diagram of a typical text mining process (Delen & Crossland, 2008). This context diagram presents the scope of the process, emphasizing its interfaces with the larger environment. In essence, it draws boundaries around the specific process to explicitly identify what is included in (and excluded from) the text mining process.

As the context diagram indicates, the input (inward connection to the left edge of the box) into the text-based knowledge-discovery process is the unstructured as well as structured data collected, stored, and made available to the process. The output (outward extension from the right edge of the box) of the process is the context-specific knowledge that can be used for decision making. The controls, also called the *constraints* (inward connection to the top edge of the box), of the process include software and hardware limitations, privacy issues, and the difficulties related to processing of the text that is presented in the form of natural language. The mechanisms (inward connection to the bottom edge of the box) of the process include proper techniques, software tools, and domain expertise. The primary purpose of text mining (within the context of knowledge discovery) is to process unstructured (textual) data (along with structured data, if relevant to the problem being addressed and available) to extract meaningful and actionable patterns for better decision making.

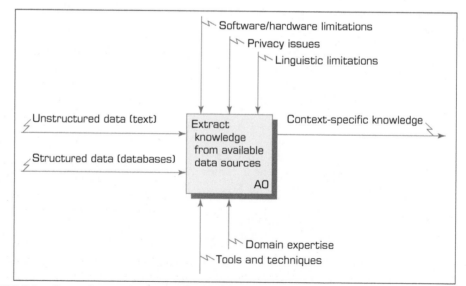

FIGURE 5.5 Context Diagram for the Text Mining Process.

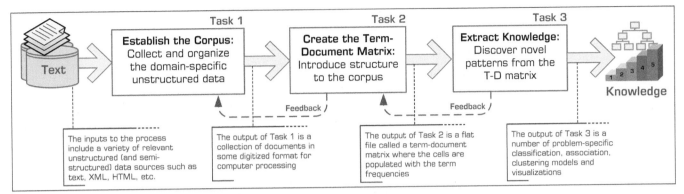

FIGURE 5.6 The Three-Step/Task Text Mining Process.

At a very high level, the text mining process can be broken down into three consecutive tasks, each of which has specific inputs to generate certain outputs (see Figure 5.6). If, for some reason, the output of a task is not that which is expected, a backward redirection to the previous task execution is necessary.

Task 1: Establish the Corpus

The main purpose of the first task activity is to collect all the documents related to the context (domain of interest) being studied. This collection may include textual documents, XML files, e-mails, Web pages, and short notes. In addition to the readily available textual data, voice recordings may also be transcribed using speech-recognition algorithms and made a part of the text collection.

Once collected, the text documents are transformed and organized in a manner such that they are all in the same representational form (e.g., ASCII text files) for computer processing. The organization of the documents can be as simple as a collection of digitized text excerpts stored in a file folder or it can be a list of links to a collection of Web pages in a specific domain. Many commercially available text mining software tools could accept these as input and convert them into a flat file for processing. Alternatively, the flat file can be prepared outside the text mining software and then presented as the input to the text mining application.

Task 2: Create the Term–Document Matrix

In this task, the digitized and organized documents (the corpus) are used to create the **term–document matrix (TDM)**. In the TDM, rows represent the documents and columns represent the terms. The relationships between the terms and documents are characterized by indices (i.e., a relational measure that can be as simple as the number of occurrences of the term in respective documents). Figure 5.7 is a typical example of a TDM.

The goal is to convert the list of organized documents (the corpus) into a TDM where the cells are filled with the most appropriate indices. The assumption is that the essence of a document can be represented with a list and frequency of the terms used in that document. However, are all terms important when characterizing documents? Obviously, the answer is "no." Some terms, such as articles, auxiliary verbs, and terms used in almost all the documents in the corpus, have no differentiating power and, therefore, should be excluded from the indexing process. This list of terms, commonly called *stop terms* or *stop words*, is specific to the domain of study and should be identified by the domain experts. On the other hand, one might choose a set of predetermined terms under which the documents are to be indexed (this list of terms is conveniently called *include terms* or *dictionary*). In addition, synonyms (pairs of terms that are to be treated the same) and specific phrases (e.g., "Eiffel Tower") can also be provided so that the index entries are more accurate.

Terms / Documents	Investment Risk	Project Management	Software Engineering	Development	SAP	...
Document 1	1			1		
Document 2		1				
Document 3			3		1	
Document 4		1				
Document 5			2	1		
Document 6	1			1		
...						

FIGURE 5.7 A Simple Term–Document Matrix.

Another filtration that should take place to accurately create the indices is *stemming*, which refers to the reduction of words to their roots so that, for example, different grammatical forms or declinations of a verb are identified and indexed as the same word. For example, stemming will ensure that *modeling* and *modeled* will be recognized as the word *model*.

The first generation of the TDM includes all the unique terms identified in the corpus (as its columns), excluding the ones in the stop term list; all the documents (as its rows); and the occurrence count of each term for each document (as its cell values). If, as is commonly the case, the corpus includes a rather large number of documents, then there is a very good chance that the TDM will have a very large number of terms. Processing such a large matrix might be time-consuming and, more important, might lead to extraction of inaccurate patterns. At this point, one has to decide the following: (1) What is the best representation of the indices? and (2) How can we reduce the dimensionality of this matrix to a manageable size?

REPRESENTING THE INDICES   Once the input documents are indexed and the initial word frequencies (by document) computed, a number of additional transformations can be performed to summarize and aggregate the extracted information. The raw term frequencies generally reflect on how salient or important a word is in each document. Specifically, words that occur with greater frequency in a document are better descriptors of the contents of that document. However, it is not reasonable to assume that the word counts themselves are proportional to their importance as descriptors of the documents. For example, if a word occurs one time in document *A*, but three times in document *B*, then it is not necessarily reasonable to conclude that this word is three times as important a descriptor of document *B* as compared to document *A*. To have a more consistent TDM for further analysis, these raw indices need to be normalized. As opposed to showing the actual frequency counts, the numerical representation between terms and documents can be normalized using a number of alternative methods, such as log frequencies, binary frequencies, and inverse document frequencies, among others.

REDUCING THE DIMENSIONALITY OF THE MATRIX   Because the TDM is often very large and rather sparse (most of the cells filled with zeros), another important question is, "How do we reduce the dimensionality of this matrix to a manageable size?" Several options are available for managing the matrix size.

- A domain expert goes through the list of terms and eliminates those that do not make much sense for the context of the study (this is a manual, labor-intensive process).
- Eliminate terms with very few occurrences in very few documents.
- Transform the matrix using SVD.

Singular value decomposition (SVD), which is closely related to principal components analysis, reduces the overall dimensionality of the input matrix (number of input documents by number of extracted terms) to a lower-dimensional space, where each consecutive dimension represents the largest degree of variability (between words and documents) possible (Manning & Schutze, 1999). Ideally, the analyst might identify the two or three most salient dimensions that account for most of the variability (differences) between the words and documents, thus identifying the latent semantic space that organizes the words and documents in the analysis. Once such dimensions are identified, the underlying "meaning" of what is contained (discussed or described) in the documents has been extracted.

Task 3: Extract the Knowledge

Using the well-structured TDM, and potentially augmented with other structured data elements, novel patterns are extracted in the context of the specific problem being addressed. The main categories of knowledge extraction methods are classification, clustering, association, and trend analysis. A short description of these methods follows.

CLASSIFICATION Arguably the most common knowledge-discovery topic in analyzing complex data sources is the **classification** (or categorization) of certain objects. The task is to classify a given data instance into a predetermined set of categories (or classes). As it applies to the domain of text mining, the task is known as *text categorization*, where for a given set of categories (subjects, topics, or concepts) and a collection of text documents the goal is to find the correct topic (subject or concept) for each document using models developed with a training data set that includes both the documents and actual document categories. Today, automated text classification is applied in a variety of contexts, including automatic or semiautomatic (interactive) indexing of text, spam filtering, Web page categorization under hierarchical catalogs, automatic generation of metadata, detection of genre, and many others.

The two main approaches to text classification are knowledge engineering and machine learning (Feldman & Sanger, 2007). With the knowledge-engineering approach, an expert's knowledge about the categories is encoded into the system either declaratively or in the form of procedural classification rules. With the machine-learning approach, a general inductive process builds a classifier by learning from a set of reclassified examples. As the number of documents increases at an exponential rate and as knowledge experts become harder to come by, the popularity trend between the two is shifting toward the machine-learning approach.

CLUSTERING **Clustering** is an unsupervised process whereby objects are classified into "natural" groups called *clusters*. Compared to categorization, where a collection of preclassified training examples is used to develop a model based on the descriptive features of the classes to classify a new unlabeled example, in clustering the problem is to group an unlabeled collection of objects (e.g., documents, customer comments, Web pages) into meaningful clusters without any prior knowledge.

Clustering is useful in a wide range of applications, from document retrieval to enabling better Web content searches. In fact, one of the prominent applications of clustering is the analysis and navigation of very large text collections, such as Web pages. The basic underlying assumption is that relevant documents tend to be more similar to each other than to irrelevant ones. If this assumption holds, the clustering of documents based on the similarity of their content improves search effectiveness (Feldman & Sanger, 2007):

- **Improved search recall.** Clustering, because it is based on overall similarity as opposed to the presence of a single term, can improve the recall of a query-based search in such a way that when a query matches a document its whole cluster is returned.
- **Improved search precision.** Clustering can also improve search precision. As the number of documents in a collection grows, it becomes difficult to browse through the list of matched documents. Clustering can help by grouping the documents into a number of much smaller groups of related documents, ordering them by relevance and returning only the documents from the most relevant group (or groups).

The two most popular clustering methods are scatter/gather clustering and query-specific clustering:

- **Scatter/gather.** This document browsing method uses clustering to enhance the efficiency of human browsing of documents when a specific search query cannot be formulated. In a sense, the method dynamically generates a table of contents for the collection and adapts and modifies it in response to the user selection.
- **Query-specific clustering.** This method employs a hierarchical clustering approach where the most relevant documents to the posed query appear in small tight clusters that are nested in larger clusters containing less-similar documents, creating a spectrum of relevance levels among the documents. This method performs consistently well for document collections of realistically large sizes.

ASSOCIATION A formal definition and detailed description of **association** was provided in the chapter on data mining (Chapter 4). Associations or association rule learning in data mining is a popular and well-researched technique for discovering interesting relationships among variables in large databases. The main idea in generating association rules (or solving market-basket problems) is to identify the frequent sets that go together.

In text mining, associations specifically refer to the direct relationships between concepts (terms) or sets of concepts. The concept set association rule $A + C$ relating two frequent concept sets A and C can be quantified by the two basic measures of support and confidence. In this case, confidence is the percentage of documents that include all the concepts in C within the same subset of those documents that include all the concepts in A. Support is the percentage (or number) of documents that include all the concepts in A and C. For instance, in a document collection the concept "Software Implementation Failure" may appear most often in association with "Enterprise Resource Planning" and "Customer Relationship Management" with significant support (4%) and confidence (55%), meaning that 4% of the documents had all three concepts represented together in the same document, and of the documents that included "Software Implementation Failure," 55% of them also included "Enterprise Resource Planning" and "Customer Relationship Management."

Text mining with association rules was used to analyze published literature (news and academic articles posted on the Web) to chart the outbreak and progress of the bird flu (Mahgoub et al., 2008). The idea was to automatically identify the association among the geographic areas, spreading across species, and countermeasures (treatments).

TREND ANALYSIS Recent methods of trend analysis in text mining have been based on the notion that the various types of concept distributions are functions of document collections; that is, different collections lead to different concept distributions for the same set of concepts. It is, therefore, possible to compare two distributions that are otherwise identical except that they are from different subcollections. One notable direction of this type of analysis is having two collections from the same source (such as from the same set of academic journals) but from different points in time. Delen and Crossland (2008) applied **trend analysis** to a large number of academic articles (published in the three highest-rated academic journals) to identify the evolution of key concepts in the field of information systems.

As described in this section, a number of methods are available for text mining. Application Case 5.5 describes the use of a number of different techniques in analyzing a large set of literature.

Application Case 5.5

Research Literature Survey with Text Mining

Researchers conducting searches and reviews of relevant literature face an increasingly complex and voluminous task. In extending the body of relevant knowledge, it has always been important to work hard to gather, organize, analyze, and assimilate existing information from the literature, particularly from one's home discipline. With the increasing abundance of potentially significant research being reported in related fields, and even in what are traditionally deemed to be nonrelated fields of study, the researcher's task is ever more daunting, if a thorough job is desired.

In new streams of research, the researcher's task may be even more tedious and complex. Trying to ferret out relevant work that others have reported may be difficult, at best, and perhaps even near impossible if traditional, largely manual reviews of published literature are required. Even with a legion of dedicated graduate students or helpful colleagues, trying to cover all potentially relevant published work is problematic.

Many scholarly conferences take place every year. In addition to extending the body of knowledge of the current focus of a conference, organizers often desire to offer additional minitracks and workshops. In many cases, these additional events are intended to introduce the attendees to significant streams of research in related fields of study and to try to identify the "next big thing" in terms of research interests and focus. Identifying reasonable candidate topics for such minitracks and workshops is often subjective rather than derived objectively from the existing and emerging research.

In a recent study, Delen and Crossland (2008) proposed a method to greatly assist and enhance the efforts of the researchers by enabling a semi-automated analysis of large volumes of published literature through the application of text mining. Using standard digital libraries and online publication search engines, the authors downloaded and collected all the available articles for the three major journals in the field of management information systems: *MIS Quarterly* (MISQ), *Information Systems Research* (ISR), and the *Journal of Management Information Systems* (JMIS). To maintain the same time interval for all three journals (for potential comparative longitudinal studies), the journal with the most recent starting date for its digital publication availability was used as the start time for this study (i.e., JMIS articles have been digitally available since 1994). For each article, they extracted the title, abstract, author list, published keywords, volume, issue number, and year of publication. They then loaded all the article data into a simple database file. Also included in the combined data set was a field that designated the journal type of each article for likely discriminatory analysis. Editorial notes, research notes, and executive overviews were omitted from the collection. Table 5.2 shows how the data was presented in a tabular format.

In the analysis phase, they chose to use only the abstract of an article as the source of information extraction. They chose not to include the keywords listed with the publications for two main reasons: (1) under normal circumstances, the abstract would already include the listed keywords, and therefore inclusion of the listed keywords for the analysis would mean repeating the same information and potentially giving them unmerited weight; and (2) the listed keywords may be terms that authors would like their article to be associated with (as opposed to what is really contained in the article), therefore

(Continued)

Application Case 5.5 (Continued)

TABLE 5.2 **Tabular Representation of the Fields Included in the Combined Data Set**

	A	B	C	D
	A1		f_x	ID
1	ID	YEAR	JOURNAL	ABSTRACT
2	PID001	2005	MISQ	The need for continual value innovation is driving supply chains to evolve from
3	PID002	1999	ISR	Although much contemporary thought considers advanced information techno
4	PID003	2001	JMIS	When producers of goods (or services) are confronted by a situation in which
5	PID004	1995	ISR	Preservation of organizational memory becomes increasingly important to org
6	PID005	1994	ISR	The research reported here is an adaptation of a model developed to measure
7	PID006	1995	MISQ	This study evaluates the extent to which the added value to customers from a
8	PID007	2003	MISQ	This paper reports the results(-) of a field-study of six medical project teams t
9	PID008	1999	JMIS	Researchers and managers are beginning to realize that the full advantages o
10	PID009	2000	JMIS	The Internet commerce technologies have significantly reduced sellers' costs
11	PID010	1997	ISR	Adaptive Structuration Theory (AST) is rapidly becoming an influential theoret
12	PID011	1995	JMIS	Research shows that group support systems (GSS) have dramatically increa
13	PID012	2000	MISQ	Increasingly, business leaders are demanding that IT play the role of a busine
14	PID013	2001	ISR	Alignment between business strategy and IS strategy is widely believed to im
15	PID014	1999	JMIS	A framework is outlined that includes the planning of and setting goals for IT,
16	PID015	1999	JMIS	The continuously growing importance of information technology (IT) requires c
17	PID016	1994	MISQ	Identifying the best way to organize the IS functions within an interprise has b
18	PID017	1996	ISR	Reasons for the mixed reactions to todays electronic off-exchange trading sy
19	PID018	1996	JMIS	The performance impacts of information technology investments in organizati
20	PID019	1997	JMIS	Anonymity is a fundamental concept in group support systems (GSS) resear
21	PID020	2002	ISR	Although electronic commerce (EC) has created new opportunities for busine
22	PID021	2005	JMIS	Understanding the successful adoption of information technology is largely ba
23	PID022	2005	MISQ	Enterprise resource planning (ERP) systems and other complex information s
24	PID023	1994	JMIS	Model management systems support modelers in various phases of the mode
25	PID024	1995	ISR	While computer training is widely recognized as an essential contributor to th

potentially introducing unquantifiable bias to the analysis of the content.

The first exploratory study was to look at the longitudinal perspective of the three journals (i.e., evolution of research topics over time). In order to conduct a longitudinal study, they divided the 12-year period (from 1994 to 2005) into four 3-year periods for each of the three journals. This framework led to 12 text mining experiments with 12 mutually exclusive data sets. At this point, for each of the 12 data sets they used text mining to extract the most descriptive terms from these collections of articles represented by their abstracts. The results were tabulated and examined for time-varying changes in the terms published in these three journals.

As a second exploration, using the complete data set (including all three journals and all four periods), they conducted a clustering analysis. Clustering is arguably the most commonly used text mining technique. Clustering was used in this study to identify the natural groupings of the articles (by putting them into separate clusters) and then to list the most descriptive terms that characterized those clusters. They used SVD to reduce the dimensionality of the term-by-document matrix and then an expectation-maximization algorithm to create the clusters. They conducted several experiments to identify the *optimal* number of clusters, which turned out to be nine. After the construction of the nine clusters, they analyzed the content of those clusters from two perspectives: (1) representation of the journal type (see Figure 5.8a) and (2) representation of time (Figure 5.8b). The idea was to explore the potential differences and/or commonalities among the three journals and potential changes in the emphasis on those clusters; that is, to answer questions such as "Are there clusters that represent different research themes specific to a single journal?" and "Is there a time-varying characterization of those clusters?" They discovered and discussed several interesting patterns using tabular and graphical representation of their findings (for further information see Delen & Crossland, 2008).

Questions for Discussion

1. How can text mining be used to ease the insurmountable task of literature review?

2. What are the common outcomes of a text mining project on a specific collection of journal articles? Can you think of other potential outcomes not mentioned in this case?

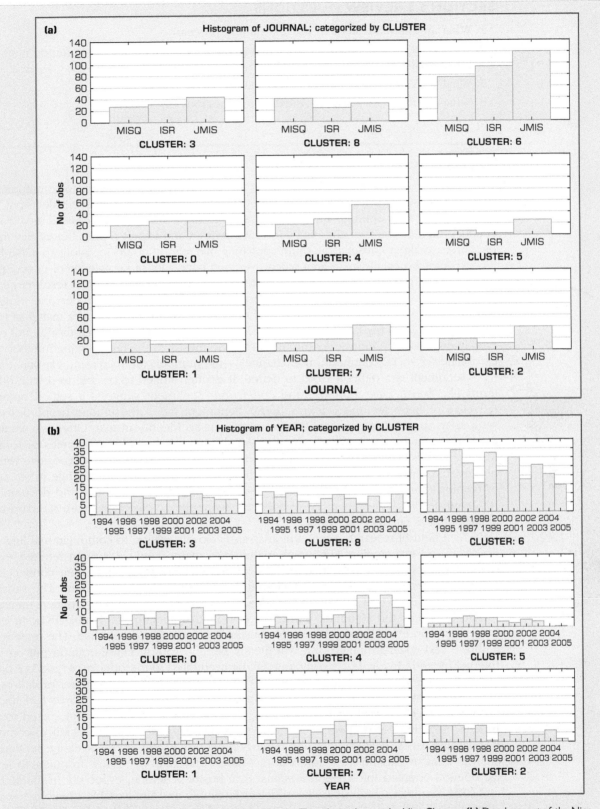

FIGURE 5.8 **(a)** Distribution of the Number of Articles for the Three Journals over the Nine Clusters; **(b)** Development of the Nine Clusters over the Years *Source:* Delen, D., & Crossland, M. (2008). Seeding the survey and analysis of research literature with text mining. *Expert Systems with Applications, 34*(3), 1707–1720.

SECTION 5.5 REVIEW QUESTIONS

1. What are the main steps in the text mining process?
2. What is the reason for normalizing word frequencies? What are the common methods for normalizing word frequencies?
3. What is SVD? How is it used in text mining?
4. What are the main knowledge extraction methods from corpus?

5.6 Sentiment Analysis

We humans are social beings. We are adept at utilizing a variety of means to communicate. We often consult financial discussion forums before making an investment decision; ask our friends for their opinions on a newly opened restaurant or a newly released movie; and conduct Internet searches and read consumer reviews and expert reports before making a big purchase like a house, a car, or an appliance. We rely on others' opinions to make better decisions, especially in an area where we don't have a lot of knowledge or experience. Thanks to the growing availability and popularity of opinion-rich Internet resources such as social media outlets (e.g., Twitter, Facebook), online review sites, and personal blogs, it is now easier than ever to find opinions of others (thousands of them, as a matter of fact) on everything from the latest gadgets to political and public figures. Even though not everybody expresses opinions over the Internet—due mostly to the fast-growing number and capabilities of social communication channels—the numbers are increasing exponentially.

Sentiment is a difficult word to define. It is often linked to or confused with other terms like *belief, view, opinion,* and *conviction.* Sentiment suggests a settled opinion reflective of one's feelings (Mejova, 2009). Sentiment has some unique properties that set it apart from other concepts that we may want to identify in text. Often we want to categorize text by topic, which may involve dealing with whole taxonomies of topics. Sentiment classification, on the other hand, usually deals with two classes (positive versus negative), a range of polarity (e.g., star ratings for movies), or even a range in strength of opinion (Pang & Lee, 2008). These classes span many topics, users, and documents. Although dealing with only a few classes may seem like an easier task than standard text analysis, this is far from the truth.

As a field of research, sentiment analysis is closely related to computational linguistics, NLP, and text mining. Sentiment analysis has many names. It's often referred to as opinion mining, subjectivity analysis, and appraisal extraction, with some connections to affective computing (computer recognition and expression of emotion). The sudden upsurge of interest and activity in the area of sentiment analysis (i.e., opinion mining), which deals with the automatic extraction of opinions, feelings, and subjectivity in text, is creating opportunities and threats for businesses and individuals alike. The ones who embrace and take advantage of it will greatly benefit from it. Every opinion put on the Internet by an individual or a company will be accredited to the originator (good or bad) and will be retrieved and mined by others (often automatically by computer programs).

Sentiment analysis is trying to answer the question "What do people feel about a certain topic?" by digging into opinions of many using a variety of automated tools. Bringing together researchers and practitioners in business, computer science, computational linguistics, data mining, text mining, psychology, and even sociology, sentiment analysis aims to expand the traditional fact-based text analysis to new frontiers, to realize opinion-oriented information systems. In a business setting, especially in marketing and CRM, sentiment analysis seeks to detect favorable and unfavorable opinions toward specific products and/or services using large numbers of textual data sources (customer feedback in the form of Web postings, tweets, blogs, etc.).

Sentiment that appears in text comes in two flavors: explicit, where the subjective sentence directly expresses an opinion ("It's a wonderful day"), and implicit, where the text implies an opinion ("The handle breaks too easily"). Most of the earlier work done in sentiment analysis focused on the first kind of sentiment because it is easier to analyze. Current trends are to implement analytical methods to consider both implicit and explicit sentiments. Sentiment polarity is a particular feature of text that sentiment analysis primarily focuses on. It is usually dichotomized into two—positive and negative—but polarity can also be thought of as a range. A document containing several opinionated statements will have a mixed polarity overall, which is different from not having a polarity at all (being objective; Mejova, 2009). Timely collection and analysis of textual data, which may be coming from a variety of sources—ranging from customer call center transcripts to social media postings—is a crucial part of the capabilities of proactive and customer-focused companies, nowadays. These real-time analyses of textual data are often visualized in easy-to-understand dashboards. Application Case 5.6 provides a customer success story, where a collection of analytics solutions is collectively used to enhance viewers' experience at the Wimbledon tennis tournament.

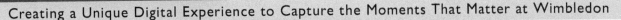

Application Case 5.6

Creating a Unique Digital Experience to Capture the Moments That Matter at Wimbledon

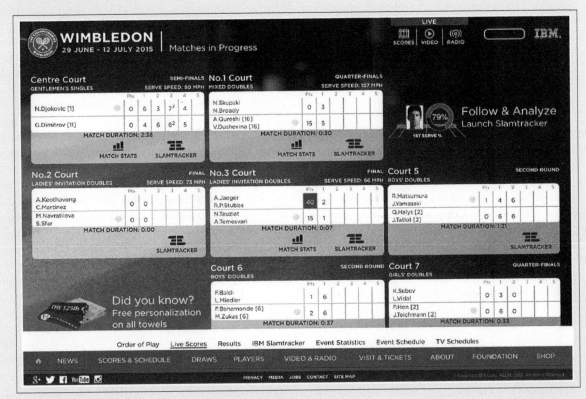

Known to millions of fans simply as "Wimbledon," The Championships is the oldest of tennis' four Grand Slams, and one of the world's highest-profile sporting events. Organized by the All England Lawn Tennis Club (AELTC) it has been a global sporting and cultural institution since 1877.

Application Case 5.6 (Continued)

The Champion of Championships

The organizers of The Championships, Wimbledon, the AELTC, have a simple objective: every year, they want to host the best tennis championships in the world—in every way, and by every metric.

The motivation behind this commitment is not simply pride; it also has a commercial basis. Wimbledon's brand is built on its premier status: this is what attracts both fans and partners. The world's best media organizations and greatest corporations—IBM included—want to be associated with Wimbledon precisely because of its reputation for excellence.

For this reason, maintaining the prestige of The Championships is one of the AELTC's top priorities, but there are only two ways that the organization can directly control how The Championships are perceived by the rest of the world.

The first, and most important, is to provide an outstanding experience for the players, journalists, and spectators who are lucky enough to visit and watch the tennis courtside. The AELTC has vast experience in this area. Since 1877 it has delivered two weeks of memorable, exciting competition in an idyllic setting: tennis in an English country garden.

The second is The Championships' online presence, which is delivered via the wimbledon.com Website, mobile apps, and social media channels. The constant evolution of these digital platforms is the result of a 26-year partnership between the AELTC and IBM.

Mick Desmond, Commercial and Media Director at the AELTC, explains: "When you watch Wimbledon on TV, you are seeing it through the broadcaster's lens. We do everything we can to help our media partners put on the best possible show, but at the end of the day, their broadcast is their presentation of The Championships.

"Digital is different: it's our platform, where we can speak directly to our fans—so it's vital that we give them the best possible experience. No sporting event or media channel has the right to demand a viewer's attention, so if we want to strengthen our brand, we need people to see our digital experience as the number-one place to follow The Championships online."

To that end, the AELTC set a target of attracting 70 million visits, 20 million unique devices, and 8 million social followers during the two weeks of The Championships 2015. It was up to IBM and AELTC to find a way to deliver.

Delivering a Unique Digital Experience

IBM and the AELTC embarked on a complete redesign of the digital platform, using their intimate knowledge of The Championships' audience to develop an experience tailor-made to attract and retain tennis fans from across the globe.

"We recognized that while mobile is increasingly important, 80% of our visitors are using desktop computers to access our website," says Alexandra Willis, Head of Digital and Content at the AELTC. "Our challenge for 2015 was how to update our digital properties to adapt to a mobile-first world, while still offering the best possible desktop experience. We wanted our new site to take maximum advantage of that large screensize and give desktop users the richest possible experience in terms of high-definition visuals and video content—while also reacting and adapting seamlessly to smaller tablet or mobile formats.

"Second, we placed a major emphasis on putting content in context—integrating articles with relevant photos, videos, stats and snippets of information, and simplifying the navigation so that users could move seamlessly to the content that interests them most."

On the mobile side, the team recognized that the wider availability of high-bandwidth 4G connections meant that the mobile Website would become more popular than ever—and ensured that it would offer easy access to all rich media content. At the same time, The Championships' mobile apps were enhanced with real-time notifications of match scores and events—and could even greet visitors as they passed through stations on the way to the grounds.

The team also built a special set of Websites for the most important tennis fans of all: the players themselves. Using IBM® Bluemix® technology, it built a secure Web application that provided players with a personalized view of their court bookings, transport, and on-court times, as well as helping them review their performance with access to stats on every match they played.

Turning Data into Insight—and Insight into Narrative

To supply its digital platforms with the most compelling possible content, the team took advantage of a unique advantage: its access to real-time, shot-by-shot data on every match played during The Championships. Over the course of the Wimbledon fortnight, 48 courtside experts capture approximately 3.4 million datapoints, tracking the type of shot, the strategies, and the outcome of each and every point.

This data is collected and analyzed in real time to produce statistics for TV commentators and journalists—and also for the digital platform's own editorial team.

"This year IBM gave us an advantage that we had never had before—using data streaming technology to provide our editorial team with real-time insight into significant milestones and breaking news," says Alexandra Willis.

"The system automatically watched the streams of data coming in from all 19 courts, and whenever something significant happened—such as Sam Groth hitting the second-fastest serve in Championships, history—it let us know instantly. Within seconds, we were able to bring that news to our digital audience and share it on social media to drive even more traffic to our site.

"The ability to capture the moments that matter and uncover the compelling narratives within the data, faster than anyone else, was key. If you wanted to experience the emotions of The Championships live, the next best thing to being there in person was to follow the action on wimbledon.com."

Harnessing the Power of Natural Language

Another new capability trialed this year was the use of IBM's NLP technologies to help mine the AELTC's huge library of tennis history for interesting contextual information. The team trained IBM Watson™ Engagement Advisor to digest this rich unstructured data set and use it to answer queries from the press desk.

The same NLP front-end was also connected to a comprehensive structured database of match statistics, dating back to the first Championships

in 1877—providing a one-stop shop for both basic questions and more complex inquiries.

"The Watson trial showed a huge amount of potential. Next year, as part of our annual innovation planning process, we will look at how we can use it more widely—ultimately in pursuit of giving fans more access to this incredibly rich source of tennis knowledge," says Mick Desmond.

Taking to the Cloud

The whole digital environment was hosted by IBM in its Hybrid Cloud. IBM used sophisticated modeling techniques to predict peaks in demand based on the schedule, the popularity of each player, the time of day, and many other factors—enabling it to dynamically allocate cloud resources appropriately to each piece of digital content and ensure a seamless experience for millions of visitors around the world.

In addition to the powerful private cloud platform that has supported The Championships for several years, IBM also used a separate SoftLayer® cloud to host the Wimbledon Social Command Centre and also provide additional incremental capacity to supplement the main cloud environment during times of peak demand.

The elasticity of the cloud environment is key, as The Championships' digital platforms need to be able to scale efficiently by a factor of more than 100 within a matter of days as the interest builds ahead of the first match on Centre Court.

Keeping Wimbledon Safe and Secure

Online security is a key concern nowadays for all organizations. For major sporting events in particular, brand reputation is everything—and while the world is watching, it is particularly important to avoid becoming a high-profile victim of cyber-crime. For these reasons, security has a vital role to play in IBM's partnership with the AELTC.

Over the first five months of 2015, IBM security systems detected a 94% increase in security events on the wimbledon.com infrastructure, compared to the same period in 2014.

As security threats—and in particular distributed denial of service (DDoS) attacks—become ever more prevalent, IBM continually increases its focus on providing industry-leading levels of security for the AELTC's whole digital platform.

(Continued)

Application Case 5.6 (Continued)

A full suite of IBM security products, including IBM QRadar® SIEM and IBM Preventia Intrusion Prevention, enabled this year's Championships to run smoothly and securely and the digital platform to deliver a high-quality user experience at all times.

Capturing Hearts and Minds

The success of the new digital platform for 2015—supported by IBM cloud, analytics, mobile, social, and security technologies—was immediate and complete. Targets for total visits and unique visitors were not only met, but exceeded. Achieving 71 million visits and 542 million page views from 21.1 million unique devices demonstrates the platform's success in attracting a larger audience than ever before and keeping those viewers engaged throughout The Championships.

"Overall, we had 13% more visits from 23% more devices than in 2014, and the growth in the use of wimbledon.com on mobile was even more impressive," says Alexandra Willis. "We saw 125% growth in unique devices on mobile, 98% growth in total visits, and 79% growth in total page views."

Mick Desmond concludes: "The results show that in 2015, we won the battle for fans' hearts and minds. People may have favorite newspapers and sports websites that they visit for 50 weeks of the year—but for two weeks, they came to us instead.

"That's a testament to the sheer quality of the experience we can provide—harnessing our unique advantages to bring them closer to the action than any other media channel. The ability to capture and communicate relevant content in real time helped our fans experience The Championships more vividly than ever before."

Questions for Discussion

1. How did Wimbledon use analytics capabilities to enhance viewers' experience?
2. What were the challenges, the proposed solution, and the obtained results?

Source: IBM Case Study. Creating a unique digital experience to capture the moments that matter. http://www.ibm.com/software/businesscasestudies/us/en/corp?synkey=D140192K15783Q68 (accessed May 2016).

Sentiment Analysis Applications

Compared to traditional sentiment analysis methods, which were survey based or focus group centered, costly, and time consuming (and therefore driven from a small sample of participants), the new face of text analytics–based sentiment analysis is a limit breaker. Current solutions automate very large-scale data collection, filtering, classification, and clustering methods via NLP and data mining technologies that handle both factual and subjective information. Sentiment analysis is perhaps the most popular application of text analytics, tapping into data sources like tweets, Facebook posts, online communities, discussion boards, Web logs, product reviews, call center logs and recordings, product rating sites, chat rooms, price comparison portals, search engine logs, and newsgroups. The following applications of sentiment analysis are meant to illustrate the power and the widespread coverage of this technology.

VOICE OF THE CUSTOMER (VOC) **Voice of the customer** (VOC) is an integral part of analytic CRM and customer experience management systems. As the enabler of VOC, sentiment analysis can access a company's product and service reviews (either continuously or periodically) to better understand and better manage customer complaints and praises. For instance, a motion picture advertising/marketing company may detect negative sentiments toward a movie that is about to open in theatres (based on its trailers) and quickly change the composition of trailers and advertising strategy (on all media outlets) to mitigate the negative impact. Similarly, a software company may detect the negative buzz regarding the bugs found in their newly released product early enough to release patches and quick fixes to alleviate the situation.

Often, the focus of VOC is individual customers, their service- and support-related needs, wants, and issues. VOC draws data from the full set of customer touch points, including e-mails, surveys, call center notes/recordings, and social media postings, and matches customer voices to transactions (inquiries, purchases, returns) and individual customer profiles captured in enterprise operational systems. VOC, mostly driven by sentiment analysis, is a key element of customer experience management initiatives, where the goal is to create an intimate relationship with the customer.

VOICE OF THE MARKET (VOM) VOM is about understanding aggregate opinions and trends. It's about knowing what stakeholders—customers, potential customers, influencers, whoever—are saying about your (and your competitors') products and services. A well-done VOM analysis helps companies with competitive intelligence and product development and positioning.

VOICE OF THE EMPLOYEE (VOE) Traditionally, VOE has been limited to employee satisfaction surveys. Text analytics in general (and sentiment analysis in particular) is a huge enabler of assessing the VOE. Using rich, opinionated textual data is an effective and efficient way to listen to what employees are saying. As we all know, happy employees empower customer experience efforts and improve customer satisfaction.

BRAND MANAGEMENT Brand management focuses on listening to social media where anyone (past/current/prospective customers, industry experts, other authorities) can post opinions that can damage or boost your reputation. A number of relatively newly launched start-up companies offer analytics-driven brand management services for others. Brand management is product and company (rather than customer) focused. It attempts to shape perceptions rather than to manage experiences using sentiment analysis techniques.

FINANCIAL MARKETS Predicting the future values of individual (or a group of) stocks has been an interesting and seemingly unsolvable problem. What makes a stock (or a group of stocks) move up or down is anything but an exact science. Many believe that the stock market is mostly sentiment driven, making it anything but rational (especially for short-term stock movements). Therefore, the use of sentiment analysis in financial markets has gained significant popularity. Automated analysis of market sentiment using social media, news, blogs, and discussion groups seems to be a proper way to compute the market movements. If done correctly, sentiment analysis can identify short-term stock movements based on the buzz in the market, potentially impacting liquidity and trading.

POLITICS As we all know, opinions matter a great deal in politics. Because political discussions are dominated by quotes, sarcasm, and complex references to persons, organizations, and ideas, politics is one of the most difficult, and potentially fruitful, areas for sentiment analysis. By analyzing the sentiment on election forums, one may predict who is more likely to win or lose. Sentiment analysis can help understand what voters are thinking and can clarify a candidate's position on issues. Sentiment analysis can help political organizations, campaigns, and news analysts to better understand which issues and positions matter the most to voters. The technology was successfully applied by both parties to the 2008 and 2012 American presidential election campaigns.

GOVERNMENT INTELLIGENCE Government intelligence is another application that has been used by intelligence agencies. For example, it has been suggested that one could monitor sources for increases in hostile or negative communications. Sentiment analysis can allow the automatic analysis of the opinions that people submit about pending policy or government-regulation proposals. Furthermore, monitoring communications for spikes in negative sentiment may be of use to agencies like Homeland Security.

OTHER INTERESTING AREAS Sentiments of customers can be used to better design e-commerce sites (product suggestions, up-sell/cross-sell advertising), better place advertisements (e.g., placing dynamic advertisements of products and services that consider the sentiment on the page the user is browsing), and manage opinion- or review-oriented search engines (i.e., an opinion-aggregation Web site, an alternative to sites like Epinions, summarizing user reviews). Sentiment analysis can help with e-mail filtration by categorizing and prioritizing incoming e-mails (e.g., it can detect strongly negative or flaming e-mails and forward them to a proper folder), as well as citation analysis, where it can determine whether an author is citing a piece of work as supporting evidence or as research that he or she dismisses.

Sentiment Analysis Process

Because of the complexity of the problem (underlying concepts, expressions in text, context in which the text is expressed, etc.), there is no readily available standardized process to conduct sentiment analysis. However, based on the published work in the field of sensitivity analysis so far (both on research methods and range of applications), a multistep, simple logical process, as given in Figure 5.9, seems to be an appropriate methodology for sentiment analysis. These logical steps are iterative (i.e., feedback, corrections, and iterations are part of the discovery process) and experimental in nature, and once completed and combined, capable of producing desired insight about the opinions in the text collection.

STEP 1: SENTIMENT DETECTION After the retrieval and preparation of the text documents, the first main task in sensitivity analysis is the detection of objectivity. Here the goal is to differentiate between a fact and an opinion, which may be viewed as classification of text as objective or subjective. This may also be characterized as calculation of O–S Polarity (Objectivity–Subjectivity Polarity, which may be represented with a numerical value ranging from 0 to 1). If the objectivity value is close to 1, then there is no opinion to mine (i.e., it is a fact); therefore, the process goes back and grabs the next text data to analyze. Usually opinion detection is based on the examination of adjectives in text. For example, the polarity of "what a wonderful work" can be determined relatively easily by looking at the adjective.

STEP 2: N–P POLARITY CLASSIFICATION The second main task is that of polarity classification. Given an opinionated piece of text, the goal is to classify the opinion as falling under one of two opposing sentiment polarities, or locate its position on the continuum between these two polarities (Pang & Lee, 2008). When viewed as a binary feature, polarity classification is the binary classification task of labeling an opinionated document as expressing either an overall positive or an overall negative opinion (e.g., thumbs up or thumbs down). In addition to the identification of N–P polarity, one should also be interested in identifying the strength of the sentiment (as opposed to just positive, it may be expressed as mildly, moderately, strongly, or very strongly positive). Most of this research was done on product or movie reviews where the definitions of "positive" and "negative" are quite clear. Other tasks, such as classifying news as "good" or "bad," present some difficulty. For instance, an article may contain negative news without explicitly using any subjective words or terms. Furthermore, these classes usually appear intermixed when a document expresses both positive and negative

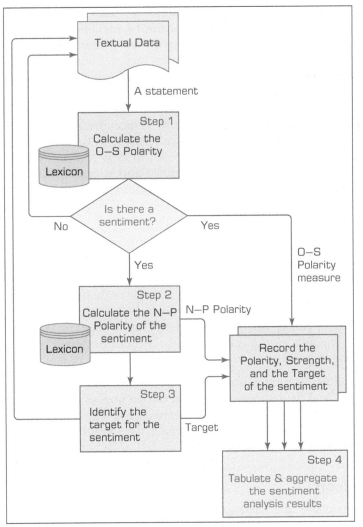

FIGURE 5.9 A Multistep Process to Sentiment Analysis.

sentiments. Then the task can be to identify the main (or dominating) sentiment of the document. Still, for lengthy texts, the tasks of classification may need to be done at several levels: term, phrase, sentence, and perhaps document level. For those, it is common to use the outputs of one level as the inputs for the next higher layer. Several methods used to identify the polarity and strengths of the polarity are explained in the next section.

STEP 3: TARGET IDENTIFICATION The goal of this step is to accurately identify the target of the expressed sentiment (e.g., a person, a product, an event). The difficulty of this task depends largely on the domain of the analysis. Even though it is usually easy to accurately identify the target for product or movie reviews because the review is directly connected to the target, it may be quite challenging in other domains. For instance, lengthy, general-purpose text such as Web pages, news articles, and blogs do not always have a predefined topic that they are assigned to, and often mention many objects, any of which may be deduced as the target. Sometimes there is more than one target in a sentiment sentence, which is the case in comparative texts. A subjective comparative sentence orders objects in order of preferences—for example, "This laptop computer is better than my desktop PC." These sentences can be identified using comparative adjectives and adverbs (more, less, better, longer), superlative adjectives (most, least, best), and other words (such as same, differ, win, prefer). Once the sentences have been retrieved, the objects can be put in an order that is most representative of their merits, as described in the text.

STEP 4: COLLECTION AND AGGREGATION   Once the sentiments of all text data points in the document are identified and calculated, in this step they are aggregated and converted to a single sentiment measure for the whole document. This aggregation may be as simple as summing up the polarities and strengths of all texts, or as complex as using semantic aggregation techniques from NLP to come up with the ultimate sentiment.

Methods for Polarity Identification

As mentioned in the previous section, **polarity identification** can be made at the word, term, sentence, or document level. The most granular level for polarity identification is at the word level. Once the polarity identification is made at the word level, then it can be aggregated to the next higher level, and then the next until the level of aggregation desired from the sentiment analysis is reached. There seem to be two dominant techniques used for identification of polarity at the word/term level, each having its advantages and disadvantages:

1. Using a lexicon as a reference library (developed either manually or automatically, by an individual for a specific task or developed by an institution for general use)
2. Using a collection of training documents as the source of knowledge about the polarity of terms within a specific domain (i.e., inducing predictive models from opinionated textual documents)

Using a Lexicon

A lexicon is essentially the catalog of words, their synonyms, and their meanings for a given language. In addition to lexicons for many other languages, there are several general-purpose lexicons created for English. Often general-purpose lexicons are used to create a variety of special-purpose lexicons for use in sentiment analysis projects. Perhaps the most popular general-purpose lexicon is WordNet, created at Princeton University, which has been extended and used by many researchers and practitioners for sentiment analysis purposes. As described on the WordNet Web site (wordnet.princeton.edu), it is a large lexical database of English, including nouns, verbs, adjectives, and adverbs grouped into sets of cognitive synonyms (i.e., synsets), each expressing a distinct concept. Synsets are interlinked by means of conceptual–semantic and lexical relations.

An interesting extension of WordNet was created by Esuli and Sebastiani (2006) where they added polarity (Positive–Negative; P–N) and objectivity (Subjective–Objective; S–O) labels for each term in the lexicon. To label each term, they classify the synset (a group of synonyms) to which this term belongs using a set of ternary classifiers (a measure that attaches to each object exactly one out of three labels), each of them capable of deciding whether a synset is Positive, or Negative, or Objective. The resulting scores range from 0.0 to 1.0, giving a graded evaluation of opinion-related properties of the terms. These can be summed up visually as in Figure 5.10. The edges of the triangle represent one of the three classifications (positive, negative, and objective). A term can be

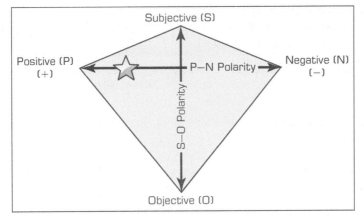

FIGURE 5.10   A Graphical Representation of the P–N Polarity and S–O Polarity Relationship.

located in this space as a point, representing the extent to which it belongs to each of the classifications.

A similar extension methodology is used to create SentiWordNet, a publicly available lexicon specifically developed for opinion mining (sentiment analysis) purposes. **SentiWordNet** assigns to each synset of WordNet three sentiment scores: positivity, negativity, objectivity. More about SentiWordNet can be found at sentiwordnet.isti.cnr.it.

Another extension to WordNet is WordNet-Affect, developed by Strapparava and Valitutti (2004). They label WordNet synsets using affective labels representing different affective categories like emotion, cognitive state, attitude, and feeling. WordNet has been also directly used in sentiment analysis. For example, Kim and Hovy (2004) and Liu, Hu, and Cheng (2005) generate lexicons of positive and negative terms by starting with a small list of "seed" terms of known polarities (e.g., love, like, nice) and then using the antonymy and synonymy properties of terms to group them into either of the polarity categories.

Using a Collection of Training Documents

It is possible to perform sentiment classification using statistical analysis and machine-learning tools that take advantage of the vast resources of labeled (manually by annotators or using a star/point system) documents available. Product review Web sites like Amazon, C-NET, eBay, RottenTomatoes, and the Internet Movie Database have all been extensively used as sources of annotated data. The star (or tomato, as it were) system provides an explicit label of the overall polarity of the review, and it is often taken as a gold standard in algorithm evaluation.

A variety of manually labeled textual data is available through evaluation efforts such as the Text REtrieval Conference, NII Test Collection for IR Systems, and Cross Language Evaluation Forum. The data sets these efforts produce often serve as a standard in the text mining community, including for sentiment analysis researchers. Individual researchers and research groups have also produced many interesting data sets. Technology Insights 5.2 lists some of the most popular ones. Once an already labeled textual data set is obtained, a variety of predictive modeling and other machine-learning algorithms can be used to train sentiment classifiers. Some of the most popular algorithms used for this task include Artificial Neural Networks, Support Vector Machines, *k*-Nearest Neighbor, Naive Bayes, Decision Trees, and expectation maximization-based Clustering.

TECHNOLOGY INSIGHTS 5.2
Large Textual Data Sets for Predictive Text Mining and Sentiment Analysis

Congressional Floor-Debate Transcripts: Published by Thomas, Pang, and Lee (2006); contains political speeches that are labeled to indicate whether the speaker supported or opposed the legislation discussed.

Economining: Published by Stern School at New York University; consists of feedback postings for merchants at Amazon.com.

Cornell Movie-Review Data Sets: Introduced by Pang and Lee (2008); contains 1,000 positive and 1,000 negative automatically derived document-level labels and 5,331 positive and 5,331 negative sentences/snippets.

Stanford—Large Movie Review Data Set: A set of 25,000 highly polar movie reviews for training and 25,000 for testing. There is additional unlabeled data for use as well. Raw text and already processed bag-of-words formats are provided. (See http://ai.stanford.edu/~amaas/data/sentiment.)

MPQA Corpus: Corpus and Opinion Recognition System corpus; contains 535 manually annotated news articles from a variety of news sources containing labels for opinions and private states (beliefs, emotions, speculations, etc.).

Multiple-Aspect Restaurant Reviews: Introduced by Snyder and Barzilay (2007); contains 4,488 reviews with an explicit 1-to-5 rating for five different aspects: food, ambiance, service, value, and overall experience.

Identifying Semantic Orientation of Sentences and Phrases

Once the semantic orientation of individual words has been determined, it is often desirable to extend this to the phrase or sentence the word appears in. The simplest way to accomplish such aggregation is to use some type of averaging for the polarities of words in the phrases or sentences. Though rarely applied, such aggregation can be as complex as using one or more machine-learning techniques to create a predictive relationship between the words (and their polarity values) and phrases or sentences.

Identifying Semantic Orientation of Documents

Even though the vast majority of the work in this area is done in determining semantic orientation of words and phrases/sentences, some tasks like summarization and information retrieval may require semantic labeling of the whole document (Ramage et al., 2009). Similar to the case in aggregating sentiment polarity from word level to phrase or sentence level, aggregation to document level is also accomplished by some type of averaging. Sentiment orientation of the document may not make sense for very large documents; therefore, it is often used on small to medium-sized documents posted on the Internet.

SECTION 5.6 REVIEW QUESTIONS

1. What is sentiment analysis? How does it relate to text mining?
2. What are the most popular application areas for sentiment analysis? Why?
3. What would be the expected benefits and beneficiaries of sentiment analysis in politics?
4. What are the main steps in carrying out sentiment analysis projects?
5. What are the two common methods for polarity identification? Explain.

5.7 Web Mining Overview

The Internet has changed the landscape for conducting business forever. Because of the highly connected, flattened world and broadened competition field, today's companies are increasingly facing greater opportunities (being able to reach customers and markets that they may have never thought possible) and bigger challenges (a globalized and ever-changing competitive marketplace). Ones with the vision and capabilities to deal with such a volatile environment are greatly benefiting from it, whereas others who resist adapting are having a hard time surviving. Having an engaged presence on the Internet is not a choice anymore; it is a business requirement. Customers are expecting companies to offer their products and/or services over the Internet. They are not only buying products and services but also talking about companies and sharing their transactional and usage experiences with others over the Internet.

The growth of the Internet and its enabling technologies has made data creation, data collection, and data/information/opinion exchange easier. Delays in service, manufacturing, shipping, delivery, and customer inquiries are no longer private incidents and are accepted as necessary evils. Now, thanks to social media tools and technologies on the Internet, everybody knows everything. Successful companies are the ones who embrace these Internet technologies and use them for the betterment of their business processes so that they can better communicate with their customers, understand their needs and wants, and serve them thoroughly and expeditiously. Being customer focused and keeping customers happy has never been as important a concept for businesses as they are now, in this age of Internet and social media.

The World Wide Web (or for short, Web) serves as an enormous repository of data and information on virtually everything one can conceive; business, personal, you name it, an abundant amount of it is there. The Web is perhaps the world's largest data and text repository, and the amount of information on the Web is growing rapidly. A lot of interesting information can be found online: whose home page is linked to which other pages, how many people have links to a specific Web page, and how a particular site is organized. In addition, each visitor to a Web site, each search on a search engine, each click on a link, and each transaction on an e-commerce site creates additional data. Although unstructured textual data in the form of Web pages coded in HTML or XML is the dominant content of the Web, the Web infrastructure also contains hyperlink information (connections to other Web pages) and usage information (logs of visitors' interactions with Web sites), all of which provide rich data for knowledge discovery. Analysis of this information can help us make better use of Web sites and also aid us in enhancing relationships and value for the visitors to our own Web sites.

Because of its sheer size and complexity, mining the Web is not an easy undertaking by any means. The Web also poses great challenges for effective and efficient knowledge discovery (Han & Kamber, 2006):

- *The Web is too big for effective data mining.* The Web is so large and growing so rapidly that it is difficult to even quantify its size. Because of the sheer size of the Web, it is not feasible to set up a data warehouse to replicate, store, and integrate all of the data on the Web, making data collection and integration a challenge.
- *The Web is too complex.* The complexity of a Web page is far greater than that of a page in a traditional text document collection. Web pages lack a unified structure. They contain far more authoring style and content variation than any set of books, articles, or other traditional text-based document.
- *The Web is too dynamic.* The Web is a highly dynamic information source. Not only does the Web grow rapidly, but also its content is constantly being updated. Blogs, news stories, stock market results, weather reports, sports scores, prices,

company advertisements, and numerous other types of information are updated regularly on the Web.

- **The Web is not specific to a domain.** The Web serves a broad diversity of communities and connects billions of workstations. Web users have very different backgrounds, interests, and usage purposes. Most users may not have good knowledge of the structure of the information network and may not be aware of the heavy cost of a particular search that they perform.

- **The Web has everything.** Only a small portion of the information on the Web is truly relevant or useful to someone (or some task). It is said that 99% of the information on the Web is useless to 99% of Web users. Although this may not seem obvious, it is true that a particular person is generally interested in only a tiny portion of the Web, whereas the rest of the Web contains information that is uninteresting to the user and may swamp desired results. Finding the portion of the Web that is truly relevant to a person and the task being performed is a prominent issue in Web-related research.

These challenges have prompted many research efforts to enhance the effectiveness and efficiency of discovering and using data assets on the Web. A number of index-based Web search engines constantly search the Web and index Web pages under certain keywords. Using these search engines, an experienced user may be able to locate documents by providing a set of tightly constrained keywords or phrases. However, a simple keyword-based search engine suffers from several deficiencies. First, a topic of any breadth can easily contain hundreds or thousands of documents. This can lead to a large number of document entries returned by the search engine, many of which are marginally relevant to the topic. Second, many documents that are highly relevant to a topic may not contain the exact keywords defining them. As we will cover in more detail later in this chapter, compared to keyword-based Web search, Web mining is a prominent (and more challenging) approach that can be used to substantially enhance the power of Web search engines because Web mining can identify authoritative Web pages, classify Web documents, and resolve many ambiguities and subtleties raised in keyword-based Web search engines.

Web mining (or Web data mining) is the process of discovering intrinsic relationships (i.e., interesting and useful information) from Web data, which are expressed in the form of textual, linkage, or usage information. The term *Web mining* was first used by Etzioni (1996); today, many conferences, journals, and books focus on Web data mining. It is a continually evolving area of technology and business practice. Web mining is essentially the same as data mining that uses data generated over the Web. The goal is to turn vast repositories of business transactions, customer interactions, and Web site usage data into actionable information (i.e., knowledge) to promote better decision making throughout the enterprise. Because of the increased popularity of the term *analytics*, nowadays many have started to refer to Web mining as *Web analytics*. However, these two terms are not the same. Whereas Web analytics is primarily Web site usage data focused, Web mining is inclusive of all data generated via the Internet including transaction, social, and usage data. Where Web analytics aims to describe what has happened on the Web site (employing a predefined, metrics-driven descriptive analytics methodology), Web mining aims to discover previously unknown patterns and relationships (employing a novel predictive or prescriptive analytics methodology). From a big-picture perspective, Web analytics can be considered to be a part of Web mining. Figure 5.11 presents a simple taxonomy of Web mining, where it is divided into three main areas: Web content mining, Web structure mining, and Web usage mining. In the figure, the data sources used in these three main areas are also specified. Although these three areas are shown separately, as you will see in the following section, they are often used collectively and synergistically to address business problems and opportunities.

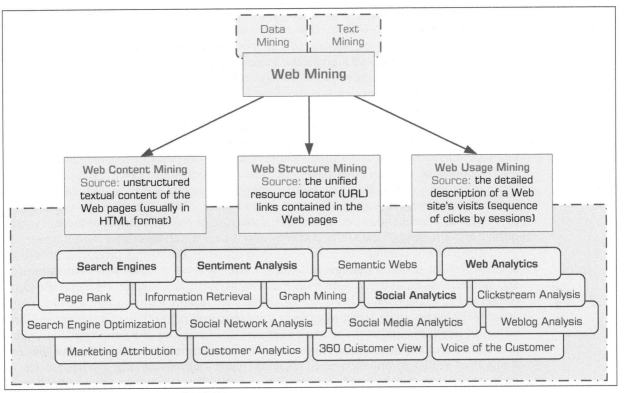

FIGURE 5.11 A Simple Taxonomy of Web Mining.

As Figure 5.11 indicates, Web mining relies heavily on data mining and text mining and their enabling tools and techniques, which we have covered in detail early in this chapter and in the previous chapter (Chapter 4). The figure also indicates that these three generic areas are further extended into several very well-known application areas. Some of these areas were explained in the previous chapters, and some of the others will be covered in detail in this chapter.

Web Content and Web Structure Mining

Web content mining refers to the extraction of useful information from Web pages. The documents may be extracted in some machine-readable format so that automated techniques can extract some information from these Web pages. **Web crawlers** (also called **spiders**) are used to read through the content of a Web site automatically. The information gathered may include document characteristics similar to what is used in text mining, but it may also include additional concepts, such as the document hierarchy. Such an automated (or semiautomated) process of collecting and mining of Web content can be used for competitive intelligence (collecting intelligence about competitors' products, services, and customers). It can also be used for information/news/opinion collection and summarization, sentiment analysis, and automated data collection and structuring for predictive modeling. As an illustrative example to using Web content mining as an automated data collection tool, consider the following. For more than 10 years now, two of the three authors of this book (Drs. Sharda and Delen) have been developing models to predict the financial success of Hollywood movies before their theatrical release. The data that they use for training of the models come from several Web sites, each having a different hierarchical page structure. Collecting a large set of variables on thousands of movies (from the past several years) from these Web sites is a time-demanding, error-prone process. Therefore, they use Web content mining and spiders as an enabling technology to automatically collect, verify, validate (if the specific data item is available on more than one Web site, then the values are validated against each other and anomalies are captured and recorded), and store these values in a relational database. That way, they ensure the quality of the data while saving valuable time (days or weeks) in the process.

In addition to text, Web pages also contain hyperlinks pointing one page to another. Hyperlinks contain a significant amount of hidden human annotation that can potentially help to automatically infer the notion of centrality or *authority*. When a Web page developer includes a link pointing to another Web page, this may be regarded as the developer's endorsement of the other page. The collective endorsement of a given page by different developers on the Web may indicate the importance of the page and may naturally lead to the discovery of authoritative Web pages (Miller, 2005). Therefore, the vast amount of Web linkage information provides a rich collection of information about the relevance, quality, and structure of the Web's contents, and thus is a rich source for Web mining.

Web content mining can also be used to enhance the results produced by search engines. In fact, search is perhaps the most prevailing application of Web content mining and Web structure mining. A search on the Web to obtain information on a specific topic (presented as a collection of keywords or a sentence) usually returns a few relevant, high-quality Web pages and a larger number of unusable Web pages. Use of a relevance index based on keywords and authoritative pages (or some measure of it) improves the search results and ranking of relevant pages. The idea of authority (or **authoritative pages**) stems from earlier information retrieval work using citations among journal articles to evaluate the impact of research papers (Miller, 2005). Though that was the origination of the idea, there are significant differences between the citations in research articles and hyperlinks on Web pages. First, not every hyperlink represents an endorsement (some links are created for navigation purposes and some are for paid advertisements). Although this is true, if the majority of the hyperlinks are of the endorsement type, then the collective opinion will still prevail. Second, for commercial and competitive interests, one authority will rarely have its Web page point to rival authorities in the same domain. For example, Microsoft may prefer not to include links on its Web pages to Apple's Web sites because this may be regarded as an endorsement of its competitor's authority. Third, authoritative pages are seldom particularly descriptive. For example, the main Web page of Yahoo! may not contain the explicit self-description that it is in fact a Web search engine.

The structure of Web hyperlinks has led to another important category of Web pages called a **hub**. A hub is one or more Web pages that provide a collection of links to authoritative pages. Hub pages may not be prominent, and only a few links may point to them; however, they provide links to a collection of prominent sites on a specific topic of interest. A hub could be a list of recommended links on an individual's home page, recommended reference sites on a course Web page, or a professionally assembled resource list on a specific topic. Hub pages play the role of implicitly conferring the authorities on a narrow field. In essence, a close symbiotic relationship exists between good hubs and authoritative pages; a good hub is good because it points to many good authorities, and a good authority is good because it is being pointed to by many good hubs. Such relationships between hubs and authorities make it possible to automatically retrieve high-quality content from the Web.

The most popular publicly known and referenced algorithm used to calculate hubs and authorities is **hyperlink-induced topic search** (**HITS**). It was originally developed by Kleinberg (1999) and has since been improved on by many researchers. HITS is a link-analysis algorithm that rates Web pages using the hyperlink information contained within them. In the context of Web search, the HITS algorithm collects a base document set for a specific query. It then recursively calculates the hub and authority values for each document. To gather the base document set, a root set that matches the query is fetched from a search engine. For each document retrieved, a set of documents that points to the original document and another set of documents that is pointed to by the original document are added to the set as the original document's neighborhood. A recursive process of document identification and link analysis continues until the hub and authority values converge. These values are then used to index and prioritize the document collection generated for a specific query.

Web structure mining is the process of extracting useful information from the links embedded in Web documents. It is used to identify authoritative pages and hubs, which are the cornerstones of the contemporary page-rank algorithms that are central to popular search engines such as Google and Yahoo! Just as links going to a Web page may indicate a site's popularity (or authority), links within the Web page (or the complete Web site) may indicate the depth of coverage of a specific topic. Analysis of links is very important in understanding the interrelationships among large numbers of Web pages, leading to a better understanding of a specific Web community, clan, or clique.

SECTION 5.7 REVIEW QUESTIONS

1. What are some of the main challenges the Web poses for knowledge discovery?
2. What is Web mining? How does it differ from regular data mining or text mining?
3. What are the three main areas of Web mining?
4. What is Web content mining? How can it be used for competitive advantage?
5. What is Web structure mining? How does it differ from Web content mining?

5.8 Search Engines

In this day and age, there is no denying the importance of Internet search engines. As the size and complexity of the World Wide Web increase, finding what you want is becoming a complex and laborious process. People use search engines for a variety of reasons. We use them to learn about a product or service before committing to buy it (including who else is selling it, what the prices are at different locations/sellers, the common issues people are discussing about it, how satisfied previous buyers are, what other products or services might be better, etc.), and to search for places to go, people to meet, things to do. In a sense, search engines have become the centerpiece of most Internet-based transactions and other activities. The incredible success and popularity of Google, the most popular search engine company, is a good testament to this claim. What is somewhat of a mystery to many is how a search engine actually does what it is meant to do. In simplest terms, a **search engine** is a software program that searches for documents (Internet sites or files), based on the keywords (individual words, multiword terms, or a complete sentence) users have provided, that have to do with the subject of their inquiry. Search engines are the workhorses of the Internet, responding to billions of queries in hundreds of different languages every day.

Technically speaking, "search engine" is the popular term for information retrieval systems. Although Web search engines are the most popular, search engines are often used in contexts other than the Web, such as desktop search engines and document search engines. As you will see in this section, many of the concepts and techniques that we have covered in text analytics and text mining early in this chapter also apply here. The overall goal of a search engine is to return one or more documents/pages (if more than one document/page applies, then a ranked-order list is often provided) that best match the user's query. The two metrics that are often used to evaluate search engines are *effectiveness* (or quality—finding the right documents/pages) and *efficiency* (or speed—returning a response quickly). These two metrics tend to work in reverse directions; improving one tends to worsen the other. Often, based on the user expectation, search engines focus on one at the expense of the other. Better search engines are the ones that excel in both at the same time. Because search engines not only search, but in fact find and return documents/pages, perhaps a more appropriate name for them would have been *finding engines*.

Anatomy of a Search Engine

Now let us dissect a search engine and look inside it. At the highest level, a search engine system is composed of two main cycles: a development cycle and a responding cycle (see the structure of a typical Internet search engine in Figure 5.12). While one is interfacing with the World Wide Web, the other is interfacing with the user. One can think of the development cycle as a production process (manufacturing and inventorying documents/pages) and the responding cycle as a retailing process (providing customers/users what they want). In the following section these two cycles are explained in more detail.

1. Development Cycle

The two main components of the development cycle are the Web crawler and document indexer. The purpose of this cycle is to create a huge database of documents/pages organized and indexed based on their content and information value. The reason for developing such a repository of documents/pages is quite obvious: Due to its sheer size and complexity, searching the Web to find pages in response to a user query is not practical (or feasible within a reasonable time frame); therefore, search engines "cache the Web" into their database and use the cached version of the Web for searching and finding. Once created, this database allows search engines to rapidly and accurately respond to user queries.

WEB CRAWLER   A Web crawler (also called a spider or a Web spider) is a piece of software that systematically browses (crawls through) the World Wide Web for the purpose of finding and fetching Web pages. Often Web crawlers copy all the pages they visit for later processing by other functions of a search engine.

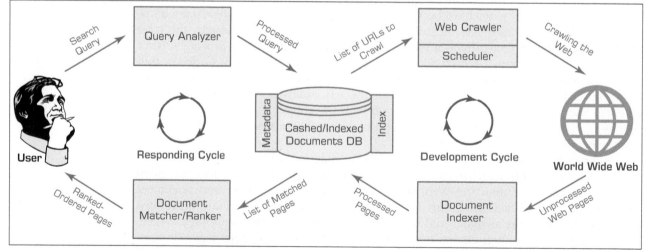

FIGURE 5.12   Structure of a Typical Internet Search Engine.

A Web crawler starts with a list of URLs to visit, which are listed in the scheduler and often are called the *seeds*. These URLs may come from submissions made by Webmasters or, more often, they come from the internal hyperlinks of previously crawled documents/pages. As the crawler visits these URLs, it identifies all the hyperlinks in the page and adds them to the list of URLs to visit (i.e., the scheduler). URLs in the scheduler are recursively visited according to a set of policies determined by the specific search engine. Because there are large volumes of Web pages, the crawler can only download a limited number of them within a given time; therefore, it may need to prioritize its downloads.

DOCUMENT INDEXER   As the documents are found and fetched by the crawler, they are stored in a temporary staging area for the document indexer to grab and process. The document indexer is responsible for processing the documents (Web pages or document files) and placing them into the document database. To convert the documents/pages into the desired, easily searchable format, the document indexer performs the following tasks.

STEP 1: PREPROCESSING THE DOCUMENTS   Because the documents fetched by the crawler may all be in different formats, for the ease of processing them further, in this step they all are converted to some type of standard representation. For instance, different content types (text, hyperlink, image, etc.) may be separated from each other, formatted (if necessary), and stored in a place for further processing.

STEP 2: PARSING THE DOCUMENTS   This step is essentially the application of text mining (i.e., computational linguistic, NLP) tools and techniques to a collection of documents/pages. In this step, first the standardized documents are parsed into components to identify index-worthy words/terms. Then, using a set of rules, the words/terms are indexed. More specifically, using tokenization rules, the words/terms/entities are extracted from the sentences in these documents. Using proper lexicons, the spelling errors and other anomalies in these words/terms are corrected. Not all the terms are discriminators. The nondiscriminating words/terms (also known as stop words) are eliminated from the list of index-worthy words/terms. Because the same word/term can be in many different forms, stemming is applied to reduce the words/terms to their root forms. Again, using lexicons and other language-specific resources (e.g., WordNet), synonyms and homonyms are identified, and the word/term collection is processed before moving into the indexing phase.

STEP 3: CREATING THE TERM-BY-DOCUMENT MATRIX   In this step, the relationships between the words/terms and documents/pages are identified. The weight can be as simple as assigning 1 for presence or 0 for absence of the word/term in the document/page. Usually more sophisticated weight schemas are used. For instance, as opposed to binary, one may choose to assign frequency of occurrence (number of times the same word/term is found in a document) as a weight. As we have seen early in this chapter, text mining research and practice have clearly indicated that the best weighting may come from the use of *term frequency* divided by inverse document frequency (TF/IDF). This algorithm measures the frequency of occurrence of each word/term within a document and then compares that frequency against the frequency of occurrence in the document collection. As we all know, not all high-frequency words/term are good document discriminators, and a good document discriminator in a domain may not be one in another domain. Once the weighing schema is determined, the weights are calculated and the term-by-document index file is created.

2. Response Cycle

The two main components of the responding cycle are the query analyzer and document matcher/ranker.

QUERY ANALYZER The query analyzer is responsible for receiving a search request from the user (via the search engine's Web server interface) and converting it into a standardized data structure, so that it can be easily queried/matched against the entries in the document database. How the query analyzer does what it is supposed to do is quite similar to what the document indexer does (as we have just explained). The query analyzer parses the search string into individual words/terms using a series of tasks that include tokenization, removal of stop words, stemming, and word/term disambiguation (identification of spelling errors, synonyms, and homonyms). The close similarity between the query analyzer and document indexer is not coincidental. In fact, it is quite logical because both are working off the document database; one is putting in documents/pages using a specific index structure, and the other is converting a query string into the same structure so that it can be used to quickly locate most relevant documents/pages.

DOCUMENT MATCHER/RANKER This is where the structured query data is matched against the document database to find the most relevant documents/pages and also rank them in the order of relevance/importance. The proficiency of this step is perhaps the most important component when different search engines are compared to one another. Every search engine has its own (often proprietary) algorithm that it uses to carry out this important step.

The early search engines used a simple keyword match against the document database and returned a list of ordered documents/pages, where the determinant of the order was a function that used the number of words/terms matched between the query and the document along with the weights of those words/terms. The quality and the usefulness of the search results were not all that good. Then, in 1997, the creators of Google came up with a new algorithm, called PageRank. As the name implies, PageRank is an algorithmic way to rank-order documents/pages based on their relevance and value/importance. Even though PageRank is an innovative way to rank documents/pages, it is an augmentation to the process of retrieving relevant documents from the database and ranking them based on the weights of the words/terms. Google does all these collectively and more to come up with the most relevant list of documents/pages for a given search request. Once an ordered list of documents/pages is created, it is pushed back to the user in an easily digestible format. At this point, users may choose to click on any of the documents in the list, and it may not be the one at the top. If they click on a document/page link that is not at the top of the list, then can we assume that the search engine did not do a good job ranking them? Perhaps, yes. Leading search engines like Google monitor the performance of their search results by capturing, recording, and analyzing postdelivery user actions and experiences. These analyses often lead to more and more rules to further refine the ranking of the documents/pages so that the links at the top are more preferable to the end users.

Search Engine Optimization

Search engine optimization (SEO) is the intentional activity of affecting the visibility of an e-commerce site or a Web site in a search engine's natural (unpaid or organic) search results. In general, the higher ranked on the search results page, and the more frequently a site appears in the search results list, the more visitors it will receive from the search engine's users. As an Internet marketing strategy, SEO considers how search engines work, what people search for, the actual search terms or keywords typed into search engines, and which search engines are preferred by their targeted audience. Optimizing a Web site may involve editing its content, HTML, and associated coding to both increase its relevance to specific keywords and to remove barriers to the indexing activities of search engines. Promoting a site to increase the number of backlinks, or inbound links, is another SEO tactic.

In the early days, in order to be indexed, all Webmasters needed to do was to submit the address of a page, or URL, to the various engines, which would then send a "spider" to "crawl" that page, extract links to other pages from it, and return information found on the page to the server for indexing. The process, as explained before, involves a search engine spider downloading a page and storing it on the search engine's own server, where a second program, known as an indexer, extracts various information about the page, such as the words it contains and where these are located, as well as any weight for specific words, and all links the page contains, which are then placed into a scheduler for crawling at a later date. Nowadays, search engines are no longer relying on Webmasters submitting URLs (even though they still can); instead, they are proactively and continuously crawling the Web and finding, fetching, and indexing everything about it.

Being indexed by search engines like Google, Bing, and Yahoo! is not good enough for businesses. Getting ranked on the most widely used search engines (see Technology Insights 5.3 for a list of most widely used search engines) and getting ranked higher than your competitors are what make the difference. A variety of methods can increase the ranking of a Web page within the search results. Cross-linking between pages of the same Web site to provide more links to the most important pages may improve its visibility. Writing content that includes frequently searched keyword phrases, so as to be relevant to a wide variety of search queries, will tend to increase traffic. Updating content to keep search engines crawling back frequently can give additional weight to a site. Adding relevant keywords to a Web page's metadata, including the title tag and metadescription, will tend to improve the relevancy of a site's search listings, thus increasing traffic. URL normalization of Web pages so that they are accessible via multiple URLs and using canonical link elements, and redirects can help make sure links to different versions of the URL all count toward the page's link popularity score.

Methods for Search Engine Optimization

In general, SEO techniques can be classified into two broad categories: techniques that search engines recommend as part of good site design, and those techniques of which search engines do not approve. The search engines attempt to minimize the effect of the latter, which is often called *spamdexing* (also known as *search spam*, *search engine spam*, or *search engine poisoning*). Industry commentators have classified these methods, and the practitioners who employ them, as either white-hat SEO or black-hat SEO (Goodman, 2005). White hats tend to produce results that last a long time, whereas black hats anticipate that their sites may eventually be banned either temporarily or permanently once the search engines discover what they are doing.

An SEO technique is considered white hat if it conforms to the search engine's guidelines and involves no deception. Because search engine guidelines are not written as a series of rules or commandments, this is an important distinction to note. White-hat SEO is not just about following guidelines, but about ensuring that the content a search engine indexes and subsequently ranks is the same content a user will see. White-hat advice is generally summed up as creating content for users, not for search engines, and then making that content easily accessible to the spiders, rather than attempting to trick the algorithm from its intended purpose. White-hat SEO is in many ways similar to Web development that promotes accessibility, although the two are not identical.

TECHNOLOGY INSIGHTS 5.3
Top 15 Most Popular Search Engines (August 2016)

Here are the 15 most popular search engines as derived from eBizMBA Rank (ebizmba.com/articles/search-engines), which is a constantly updated average of each Web site's *Alexa* Global Traffic Rank, and U.S. Traffic Rank from both Compete and Quantcast.

Rank	Name	Estimated Unique Monthly Visitors
1	Google	1,600,000,000
2	Bing	400,000,000
3	Yahoo! Search	300,000,000
4	Ask	245,000,000
5	AOL Search	125,000,000
6	Wow	100,000,000
7	WebCrawler	65,000,000
8	MyWebSearch	60,000,000
9	Infospace	24,000,000
10	Info	13,500,000
11	DuckDuckGo	11,000,000
12	Contenko	10,500,000
13	Dogpile	7,500,000
14	Alhea	4,000,000
15	ixQuick	1,000,000

Black-hat SEO attempts to improve rankings in ways that are not approved by the search engines, or involve deception. One black-hat technique uses text that is hidden, either as text colored similar to the background, in an invisible div tag, or positioned off-screen. Another method gives a different page depending on whether the page is being requested by a human visitor or a search engine, a technique known as *cloaking*. Search engines may penalize sites they discover using black-hat methods, either by reducing their rankings or eliminating their listings from their databases altogether. Such penalties can be applied either automatically by the search engines' algorithms or by a manual site review. One example was the February 2006 Google removal of both BMW Germany and Ricoh Germany for use of unapproved practices (Cutts, 2006). Both companies, however, quickly apologized, fixed their practices, and were restored to Google's list.

For some businesses, SEO may generate a significant return on investment. However, one should keep in mind that search engines are not paid for organic search traffic, their algorithms change constantly, and there are no guarantees of continued referrals. Due to this lack of certainty and stability, a business that relies heavily on search engine traffic can suffer major losses if the search engine decides to change its algorithms and stop sending visitors. According to Google's CEO, Eric Schmidt, in 2010, Google made over 500 algorithm changes—almost 1.5 per day. Because of the difficulty in keeping up with changing search engine rules, companies that rely on search traffic practice one or more of the following: (1) Hire a company that specializes in SEO (there seem to be an abundant number of those nowadays) to continuously improve your site's appeal to changing practices of the search engines; (2) pay the search engine providers to be listed on the paid sponsors' sections; and (3) consider liberating yourself from dependence on search engine traffic.

Either originating from a search engine (organically or otherwise) or coming from other sites and places, what is most important for an e-commerce site is to maximize the likelihood of customer transactions. Having a lot of visitors without sales is not what a typical e-commerce site is built for. Application Case 5.7 is about a large Internet-based shopping mall where detailed analysis of customer behavior (using clickstreams and other data sources) is used to significantly improve the conversion rate.

Application Case 5.7

Understanding Why Customers Abandon Shopping Carts Results in a $10 Million Sales Increase

Lotte.com, the leading Internet shopping mall in Korea with 13 million customers, has developed an integrated Web traffic analysis system using SAS for Customer Experience Analytics. As a result, Lotte.com has been able to improve the online experience for its customers, as well as generate better returns from its marketing campaigns. Now, Lotte.com executives can confirm results anywhere, anytime, as well as make immediate changes.

With almost one million Web site visitors each day, Lotte.com needed to know how many visitors were making purchases and which channels were bringing the most valuable traffic. After reviewing many diverse solutions and approaches, Lotte.com introduced its integrated Web traffic analysis system using the SAS for Customer Experience Analytics solution. This is the first online behavioral analysis system applied in Korea.

With this system, Lotte.com can accurately measure and analyze Web site visitor numbers, page view status of site visitors and purchasers, the popularity of each product category and product, clicking preferences for each page, the effectiveness of campaigns, and much more. This information enables Lotte.com to better understand customers and their behavior online, and conduct sophisticated, cost-effective targeted marketing.

Commenting on the system, Assistant General Manager Jung Hyo-hoon of the Marketing Planning Team for Lotte.com said, "As a result of introducing the SAS system of analysis, many 'new truths' were uncovered around customer behavior, and some of them were 'inconvenient truths.'" He added, "Some site-planning activities that had been undertaken with the expectation of certain results actually had a low reaction from customers, and the site planners had a difficult time recognizing these results."

Benefits

Introducing the SAS for Customer Experience Analytics solution fully transformed the Lotte.com Web site. As a result, Lotte.com has been able to improve the online experience for its customers as well as generate better returns from its marketing campaigns.

Since implementing SAS for Customer Experience Analytics, Lotte.com has seen many benefits.

A Jump in Customer Loyalty

A large amount of sophisticated activity information can be collected under a visitor environment, including quality of traffic. Deputy Assistant General Manager Jung said that "by analyzing actual valid traffic and looking only at one to two pages, we can carry out campaigns to heighten the level of loyalty, and determine a certain range of effect, accordingly." He added, "In addition, it is possible to classify and confirm the order rate for each channel and see which channels have the most visitors."

Optimized Marketing Efficiency Analysis

Rather than just analyzing visitor numbers only, the system is capable of analyzing the conversion rate (shopping cart, immediate purchase, wish list, purchase completion) compared to actual visitors for each campaign type (affiliation or e-mail, banner, keywords, and others), so detailed analysis of channel effectiveness is possible. In addition, it can confirm the most popular search words used by visitors for each campaign type, location, and purchased

(Continued)

Application Case 5.7 (Continued)

products. The page overlay function can measure the number of clicks and number of visitors for each item in a page to measure the value for each location in a page. This capability enables Lotte.com to promptly replace or renew low-traffic items.

Enhanced Customer Satisfaction and Customer Experience Lead to Higher Sales

Lotte.com built a customer behavior analysis database that measures each visitor, what pages are visited, how visitors navigate the site, and what activities are undertaken to enable diverse analysis and improve site efficiency. In addition, the database captures customer demographic information, shopping cart size and conversion rate, number of orders, and number of attempts.

By analyzing which stage of the ordering process deters the most customers and fixing those stages, conversion rates can be increased. Previously, analysis was done only on placed orders. By analyzing the movement pattern of visitors before ordering and at the point where breakaway occurs, customer behavior can be forecast, and sophisticated marketing activities can be undertaken. Through a pattern analysis of visitors, purchases can be more effectively influenced and customer demand can be reflected in real time to ensure quicker responses. Customer satisfaction has also improved as Lotte.com has better insight into each customer's behaviors, needs, and interests.

Evaluating the system, Jung commented, "By finding out how each customer group moves on the basis of the data, it is possible to determine customer service improvements and target marketing subjects, and this has aided the success of a number of campaigns."

However, the most significant benefit of the system is gaining insight into individual customers and various customer groups. By understanding when customers will make purchases and the manner in which they navigate throughout the Web page, targeted channel marketing and better customer experience can now be achieved.

Plus, when SAS for Customer Experience Analytics was implemented by Lotte.com's largest overseas distributor, it resulted in a first-year sales increase of 8 million euros (US$10 million) by identifying the causes of shopping cart abandonment.

Questions for Discussion

1. How did Lotte.com use analytics to improve sales?
2. What were the challenges, the proposed solution, and the obtained results?
3. Do you think e-commerce companies are in better position to leverage benefits of analytics? Why? How?

SECTION 5.8 REVIEW QUESTIONS

1. What is a search engine? Why are they important for today's businesses?
2. What is a Web crawler? What is it used for? How does it work?
3. What is "search engine optimization?" Who benefits from it?
4. What things can help Web pages rank higher in the search engine results?

5.9 Web Usage Mining (Web Analytics)

Web usage mining (also called **Web analytics**) is the extraction of useful information from data generated through Web page visits and transactions. Analysis of the information collected by Web servers can help us better understand user behavior. Analysis of this data is often called **clickstream analysis**. By using the data and text mining techniques, a company might be able to discern interesting patterns from the clickstreams. For example, it might learn that 60% of visitors who searched for "hotels in Maui" had searched earlier

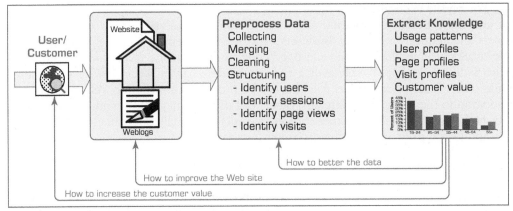

FIGURE 5.13 Extraction of Knowledge from Web Usage Data.

for "airfares to Maui." Such information could be useful in determining where to place online advertisements. Clickstream analysis might also be useful for knowing *when* visitors access a site. For example, if a company knew that 70% of software downloads from its Web site occurred between 7 and 11 P.M., it could plan for better customer support and network bandwidth during those hours. Figure 5.13 shows the process of extracting knowledge from clickstream data and how the generated knowledge is used to improve the process, improve the Web site, and most important, increase the customer value.

Web Analytics Technologies

There are numerous tools and technologies for Web analytics in the marketplace. Because of their power to measure, collect, and analyze Internet data to better understand and optimize Web usage, the popularity of Web analytics tools is increasing. Web analytics holds the promise of revolutionizing how business is done on the Web. Web analytics is not just a tool for measuring Web traffic; it can also be used as a tool for e-business and market research and to assess and improve the effectiveness of e-commerce Web sites. Web analytics applications can also help companies measure the results of traditional print or broadcast advertising campaigns. It can help estimate how traffic to a Web site changes after the launch of a new advertising campaign. Web analytics provides information about the number of visitors to a Web site and the number of page views. It helps gauge traffic and popularity trends, which can be used for market research.

There are two main categories of Web analytics: off-site and on-site. Off-site Web analytics refers to Web measurement and analysis about you and your products that takes place outside your Web site. It includes the measurement of a Web site's potential audience (prospect or opportunity), share of voice (visibility or word-of-mouth), and buzz (comments or opinions) that is happening on the Internet.

What is more mainstream has been on-site Web analytics. Historically, Web analytics has referred to on-site visitor measurement. However, in recent years this has blurred, mainly because vendors are producing tools that span both categories. On-site Web analytics measure visitors' behavior once they are on your Web site. This includes its drivers and conversions—for example, the degree to which different landing pages are associated with online purchases. On-site Web analytics measure the performance of your Web site in a commercial context. The data collected on the Web site is then compared against key performance indicators for performance and used to improve a Web site's or marketing campaign's audience response. Even though Google Analytics is the most widely used on-site Web analytics service, others are provided by Yahoo! and Microsoft, and newer and better tools are emerging constantly that provide additional layers of information.

For on-site Web analytics, there are two technical ways of collecting the data. The first and more traditional method is the server log file analysis, where the Web server records file requests made by browsers. The second method is page tagging, which uses JavaScript embedded in the site page code to make image requests to a third-party analytics-dedicated server whenever a page is rendered by a Web browser (or when a mouse click occurs). Both collect data that can be processed to produce Web traffic reports. In addition to these two main streams, other data sources may also be added to augment Web site behavior data. These other sources may include e-mail, direct mail campaign data, sales and lead history, or social media–originated data.

Web Analytics Metrics

Using a variety of data sources, Web analytics programs provide access to a lot of valuable marketing data, which can be leveraged for better insights to grow your business and better document your return on investment (ROI). The insight and intelligence gained from Web analytics can be used to effectively manage the marketing efforts of an organization and its various products or services. Web analytics programs provide nearly real-time data, which can document your marketing campaign successes or empower you to make timely adjustments to your current marketing strategies.

Whereas Web analytics provides a broad range of metrics, there are four categories of metrics that are generally actionable and can directly impact your business objectives (The Westover Group, 2013). These categories include

- Web site usability: How were they using my Web site?
- Traffic sources: Where did they come from?
- Visitor profiles: What do my visitors look like?
- Conversion statistics: What does it all mean for the business?

Web Site Usability

Beginning with your Web site, let's take a look at how well it works for your visitors. This is where you can learn how "user friendly" it really is or whether or not you are providing the right content.

1. *Page views.* The most basic of measurements, this metric is usually presented as the "average page views per visitor." If people come to your Web site and don't view many pages, then your Web site may have issues with its design or structure. Another explanation for low page views is a disconnect in the marketing messages that brought them to the site and the content that is actually available.

2. *Time on site.* Similar to page views, it's a fundamental measurement of a visitor's interaction with your Web site. Generally, the longer a person spends on your Web site, the better it is. That could mean they're carefully reviewing your content, utilizing interactive components you have available, and building toward an informed decision to buy, respond, or take the next step you've provided. On the contrary, the time on site also needs to be examined against the number of pages viewed to make sure the visitor isn't spending his or her time trying to locate content that should be more readily accessible.

3. *Downloads.* This includes PDFs, videos, and other resources you make available to your visitors. Consider how accessible these items are as well as how well they're promoted. If your Web statistics, for example, reveal that 60% of the individuals who watch a demo video also make a purchase, then you'll want to strategize to increase viewership of that video.

4. ***Click map.*** Most analytics programs can show you the percentage of clicks each item on your Web page received. This includes clickable photos, text links in your copy, downloads, and, of course, any navigation you may have on the page. Are they clicking the most important items?

5. ***Click paths.*** Although an assessment of click paths is more involved, it can quickly reveal where you might be losing visitors in a specific process. A well-designed Web site uses a combination of graphics and information architecture to encourage visitors to follow "predefined" paths through your Web site. These are not rigid pathways but rather intuitive steps that align with the various processes you've built into the Web site. One process might be that of "educating" a visitor who has minimum understanding of your product or service. Another might be a process of "motivating" a returning visitor to consider an upgrade or repurchase. A third process might be structured around items you market online. You'll have as many process pathways in your Web site as you have target audiences, products, and services. Each can be measured through Web analytics to determine how effective it is.

Traffic Sources

Your Web analytics program is an incredible tool for identifying where your Web traffic originates. Basic categories such as search engines, referral Web sites, and visits from bookmarked pages (i.e., direct) are compiled with little involvement by the marketer. With a little effort, however, you can also identify Web traffic that was generated by your various offline or online advertising campaigns.

1. ***Referral Web sites.*** Other Web sites that contain links that send visitors directly to your Web site are considered referral Web sites. Your analytics program will identify each referral site your traffic comes from, and a deeper analysis will help you determine which referrals produce the greatest volume, the highest conversions, the most new visitors, and so on.

2. ***Search engines.*** Data in the search engine category is divided between paid search and organic (or natural) search. You can review the top keywords that generated Web traffic to your site and see if they are representative of your products and services. Depending upon your business, you might want to have hundreds (or thousands) of keywords that draw potential customers. Even the simplest product search can have multiple variations based on how the individual phrases the search query.

3. ***Direct.*** Direct searches are attributed to two sources. An individual who bookmarks one of your Web pages in their favorites and clicks that link will be recorded as a direct search. Another source occurs when someone types your URL directly into their browser. This happens when someone retrieves your URL from a business card, brochure, print ad, radio commercial, and so on. That's why it's a good strategy to use coded URLs.

4. ***Offline campaigns.*** If you utilize advertising options other than Web-based campaigns, your Web analytics program can capture performance data if you include a mechanism for sending them to your Web site. Typically, this is a dedicated URL that you include in your advertisement (i.e., "www.mycompany.com/offer50") that delivers those visitors to a specific landing page. You now have data on how many responded to that ad by visiting your Web site.

5. ***Online campaigns.*** If you are running a banner ad campaign, search engine advertising campaign, or even e-mail campaign, you can measure individual campaign effectiveness by simply using a dedicated URL similar to the offline campaign strategy.

Visitor Profiles

One of the ways you can leverage your Web analytics into a really powerful marketing tool is through segmentation. By blending data from different analytics reports, you'll begin to see a variety of user profiles emerge.

1. **Keywords.** Within your analytics report, you can see what keywords visitors used in search engines to locate your Web site. If you aggregate your keywords by similar attributes, you'll begin to see distinct visitor groups that are using your Web site. For example, the particular search phrase that was used can indicate how well they understand your product or its benefits. If they use words that mirror your own product or service descriptions, then they probably are already aware of your offerings from effective advertisements, brochures, and so on. If the terms are more general in nature, then your visitor is seeking a solution for a problem and has happened upon your Web site. If this second group of searchers is sizable, then you'll want to ensure that your site has a strong education component to convince them they've found their answer and then move them into your sales channel.

2. **Content groupings.** Depending on how you group your content, you may be able to analyze sections of your Web site that correspond with specific products, services, campaigns, and other marketing tactics. If you conduct a lot of trade shows and drive traffic to your Web site for specific product literature, then your Web analytics will highlight the activity in that section.

3. **Geography.** Analytics permits you to see where your traffic geographically originates, including country, state, and city locations. This can be especially useful if you use geo-targeted campaigns or want to measure your visibility across a region.

4. **Time of day.** Web traffic generally has peaks at the beginning of the workday, during lunch, and toward the end of the workday. It's not unusual, however, to find strong Web traffic entering your Web site up until the late evening. You can analyze this data to determine when people browse versus buy and also make decisions on what hours you should offer customer service.

5. **Landing page profiles.** If you structure your various advertising campaigns properly, you can drive each of your targeted groups to a different landing page, which your Web analytics will capture and measure. By combining these numbers with the demographics of your campaign media, you can know what percentage of your visitors fit each demographic.

Conversion Statistics

Each organization will define a "conversion" according to its specific marketing objectives. Some Web analytics programs use the term *goal* to benchmark certain Web site objectives, whether that be a certain number of visitors to a page, a completed registration form, or an online purchase.

1. **New visitors.** If you're working to increase visibility, you'll want to study the trends in your new visitors data. Analytics identifies all visitors as either new or returning.

2. **Returning visitors.** If you're involved in loyalty programs or offer a product that has a long purchase cycle, then your returning visitors data will help you measure progress in this area.

3. **Leads.** Once a form is submitted and a thank-you page is generated, you have created a lead. Web analytics will permit you to calculate a completion rate (or abandonment rate) by dividing the number of completed forms by the number of Web visitors that came to your page. A low completion percentage would indicate a page that needs attention.

4. **Sales/conversions.** Depending on the intent of your Web site, you can define a "sale" by an online purchase, a completed registration, an online submission, or any number of other Web activities. Monitoring these figures will alert you to any changes (or successes!) that occur further upstream.

5. **Abandonment/exit rates.** Just as important as those moving through your Web site are those who began a process and quit or came to your Web site and left after a page or two. In the first case, you'll want to analyze where the visitor terminated the process and whether there are a number of visitors quitting at the same place. Then, investigate the situation for resolution. In the latter case, a high exit rate on a Web site or a specific page generally indicates an issue with expectations. Visitors click to your Web site based on some message contained in an advertisement, a presentation, and so on, and expect some continuity in that message. Make sure you're advertising a message that your Web site can reinforce and deliver.

Within each of these items are metrics that can be established for your specific organization. You can create a weekly dashboard that includes specific numbers or percentages that will indicate where you're succeeding—or highlight a marketing challenge that should be addressed. When these metrics are evaluated consistently and used in conjunction with other available marketing data, they can lead you to a highly quantified marketing program. Figure 5.14 shows a Web analytics dashboard created with freely available Google Analytics tools.

SECTION 5.9 REVIEW QUESTIONS

1. What are the three types of data generated through Web page visits?
2. What is clickstream analysis? What is it used for?
3. What are the main applications of Web mining?
4. What are commonly used Web analytics metrics? What is the importance of metrics?

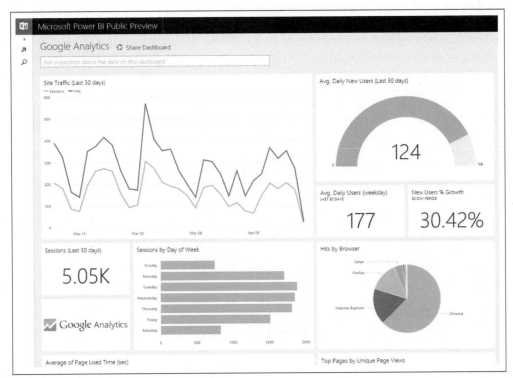

FIGURE 5.14   A Sample Web Analytics Dashboard.

5.10 Social Analytics

Social analytics may mean different things to different people, based on their worldview and field of study. For instance, the dictionary definition of social analytics refers to a philosophical perspective developed by the Danish historian and philosopher Lars-Henrik Schmidt in the 1980s. The theoretical object of the perspective is *socius*, a kind of "commonness" that is neither a universal account nor a communality shared by every member of a body (Schmidt, 1996). Thus, social analytics differs from traditional philosophy as well as sociology. It might be viewed as a perspective that attempts to articulate the contentions between philosophy and sociology.

Our definition of social analytics is somewhat different; as opposed to focusing on the "social" part (as is done in its philosophical definition), we are more interested in the "analytics" part of the term. Gartner (a very well-known global IT consultancy company) defined social analytics as "monitoring, analyzing, measuring and interpreting digital interactions and relationships of people, topics, ideas and content" (gartner.com/it-glossary/social-analytics/). Social analytics include mining the textual content created in social media (e.g., sentiment analysis, NLP) and analyzing socially established networks (e.g., influencer identification, profiling, prediction) for the purpose of gaining insight about existing and potential customers' current and future behaviors, and about the likes and dislikes toward a firm's products and services. Based on this definition and the current practices, social analytics can be classified into two different, but not necessarily mutually exclusive, branches: social network analysis (SNA) and social media analytics.

Social Network Analysis

A **social network** is a social structure composed of individuals/people (or groups of individuals or organizations) linked to one another with some type of connections/relationships. The social network perspective provides a holistic approach to analyzing the structure and dynamics of social entities. The study of these structures uses SNA to identify local and global patterns, locate influential entities, and examine network dynamics. Social networks and the analysis of them is essentially an interdisciplinary field that emerged from social psychology, sociology, statistics, and graph theory. Development and formalization of the mathematical extent of SNA dates back to the 1950s; the development of foundational theories and methods of social networks dates back to the 1980s (Scott & Davis, 2003). SNA is now one of the major paradigms in business analytics, consumer intelligence, and contemporary sociology and is also employed in a number of other social and formal sciences.

A social network is a theoretical construct useful in the social sciences to study relationships between individuals, groups, organizations, or even entire societies (social units). The term is used to describe a social structure determined by such interactions. The ties through which any given social unit connects represent the convergence of the various social contacts of that unit. In general, social networks are self-organizing, emergent, and complex, such that a globally coherent pattern appears from the local interaction of the elements (individuals and groups of individuals) that make up the system.

Following are a few typical social network types that are relevant to business activities.

COMMUNICATION NETWORKS Communication studies are often considered a part of both the social sciences and the humanities, drawing heavily on fields such as sociology, psychology, anthropology, information science, biology, political science, and economics. Many communications concepts describe the transfer of information from one source to another and thus can be represented as a social network. Telecommunication companies are tapping into this rich information source to optimize their business practices and to improve customer relationships.

COMMUNITY NETWORKS Traditionally, community referred to a specific geographic location, and studies of community ties had to do with who talked, associated, traded, and attended social activities with whom. Today, however, there are extended "online" communities developed through social networking tools and telecommunications devices. Such tools and devices continuously generate large amounts of data, which can be used by companies to discover invaluable, actionable information.

CRIMINAL NETWORKS In criminology and urban sociology, much attention has been paid to the social networks among criminal actors. For example, studying gang murders and other illegal activities as a series of exchanges between gangs can lead to better understanding and prevention of such criminal activities. Now that we live in a highly connected world (thanks to the Internet), much of the criminal networks' formations and their activities are being watched/pursued by security agencies using state-of-the-art Internet tools and tactics. Even though the Internet has changed the landscape for criminal networks and law enforcement agencies, the traditional social and philosophical theories still apply to a large extent.

INNOVATION NETWORKS Business studies on diffusion of ideas and innovations in a network environment focus on the spread and use of ideas among the members of the social network. The idea is to understand why some networks are more innovative, and why some communities are early adopters of ideas and innovations (i.e., examining the impact of social network structure on influencing the spread of an innovation and innovative behavior).

Social Network Analysis Metrics

SNA is the systematic examination of social networks. SNA views social relationships in terms of network theory, consisting of nodes (representing individuals or organizations within the network) and ties/connections (which represent relationships between the individuals or organizations, such as friendship, kinship, or organizational position). These networks are often represented using social network diagrams, where nodes are represented as points and ties are represented as lines.

Application Case 5.8 provides an interesting example to multichannel social analytics.

Application Case 5.8

Tito's Vodka Establishes Brand Loyalty with an Authentic Social Strategy

If Tito's Handmade Vodka had to identify a single social media metric that most accurately reflects its mission, it would be engagement. Connecting with vodka lovers in an inclusive, authentic way is something Tito's takes very seriously, and the brand's social strategy reflects that vision.

Founded nearly two decades ago, the brand credits the advent of social media with playing an integral role in engaging fans and raising brand awareness. In an interview with *Entrepreneur*, founder Bert "Tito" Beveridge credited social media for enabling Tito's to compete for shelf space with more established liquor brands. "Social media is a great platform for a word-of-mouth brand, because it's not just about who has the biggest megaphone," Beveridge told *Entrepreneur*.

As Tito's has matured, the social team has remained true to the brand's founding values and

(Continued)

actively uses Twitter and Instagram to have one-on-one conversations and connect with brand enthusiasts. "We never viewed social media as another way to advertise," said Katy Gelhausen, Web & Social Media Coordinator. "We're on social so our customers can talk to us."

To that end, Tito's uses Sprout Social to understand the industry atmosphere, develop a consistent social brand, and create a dialogue with its audience. Recently and as a result, Tito's organically grew its Twitter and Instagram communities by 43.5% and 12.6%, respectively, within 4 months.

Informing a Seasonal, Integrated Marketing Strategy

Tito's quarterly cocktail program is a key part of the brand's integrated marketing strategy. Each quarter, a cocktail recipe is developed and distributed through Tito's online and offline marketing initiatives.

It is important for Tito's to ensure the recipe is aligned with the brand's focus as well as larger industry direction. Therefore, Gelhausen uses Sprout's Brand Keywords to monitor industry trends and cocktail flavor profiles. "Sprout has been a really important tool for social monitoring. The Inbox is a

nice way to keep on top of hashtags and see general trends in one stream," said Gelhausen.

These learnings are presented to Tito's in-house mixology team and used to ensure the same quarterly recipe is communicated to the brand's sales team and across marketing channels. "Whether you're drinking Tito's at a bar, buying it from a liquor store or following us on social media you're getting the same quarterly cocktail," said Gelhausen.

The program ensures that, at every consumer touchpoint, a person is receiving a consistent brand experience—and that consistency is vital. In fact, according to an Infosys study on the omnichannel shopping experience, 34% of consumers attribute cross-channel consistency as a reason they spend more with a brand. Meanwhile, 39% cite inconsistency as a reason enough to spend less.

At Tito's, gathering industry insights starts with social monitoring on Twitter and Instagram through Sprout. But the brand's social strategy doesn't stop there. Staying true to its roots, Tito's uses the platform on a daily basis to authentically connect with customers.

Sprout's Smart Inbox displays Tito's Twitter and Instagram accounts in a single, cohesive feed.

This helps Gelhausen manage inbound messages and quickly identify which require a response.

"Sprout allows us to stay on top of the conversations we're having with our followers. I love how you can easily interact with content from multiple accounts in one place," said Gelhausen.

Spreading the Word on Twitter

Tito's approach to Twitter is simple: engage in personal, one-on-one conversations with fans. Dialogue is a driving force for the brand, and over the course of 4 months, 88% of Tweets sent were replies to inbound messages.

Using Twitter as an open line of communication between Tito's and its fans resulted in a 162.2% increase in engagement and a 43.5% gain in followers. Even more impressively, Tito's ended the quarter with 538,306 organic impressions—an 81% rise. A similar strategy is applied to Instagram, which Tito's uses to strengthen and foster a relationship with fans by publishing photos and videos of new recipe ideas, brand events and initiatives.

Capturing the Party on Instagram

On Instagram, Tito's primarily publishes lifestyle content and encourages followers to incorporate the brand into everyday occasions. Tito's also uses the platform to promote its cause marketing efforts and to tell its brand story. The team finds value in Sprout's Instagram Profiles Report, which helps them identify what media is receiving the most engagement, analyze audience demographics and growth, dive deeper into publishing patterns, and quantify outbound hashtag performance. "Given Instagram's new personalized feed, it's important that we pay attention to what really does resonate," said Gelhausen.

Using the Instagram Profiles Report, Tito's has been able to measure the impact of its Instagram marketing strategy and revise its approach accordingly. By utilizing the network as another way to engage with fans, the brand has steadily grown its organic audience. In 4 months, @TitosVodka saw a 12.6% rise in followers and a 37.1% increase in engagement. On average, each piece of published content gained 534 interactions, and mentions of the brand's hashtag, #titoshandmadevodka, grew by 33%.

Where to from Here?

Social is an ongoing investment in time and attention. Tito's will continue the momentum the brand experienced by segmenting each quarter into its own campaign. "We're always getting smarter with our social strategies and making sure that what we're posting is relevant and resonates," said Gelhausen. Using social to connect with fans in a consistent, genuine, and memorable way will remain a

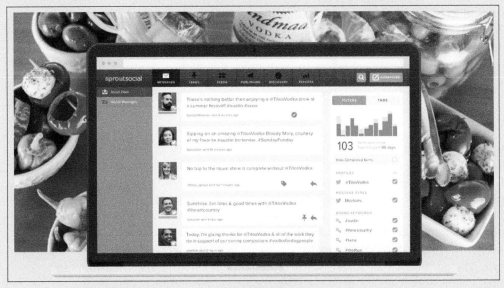

(Continued)

Application Case 5.8 (Continued)

cornerstone of the brand's digital marketing efforts. Using Sprout's suite of social media management tools, Tito's will continue to foster a community of loyalists.

Highlights:

- A **162%** increase in organic engagement on Twitter
- An **81%** increase in organic Twitter impressions
- A **37%** increase in engagement on Instagram

Questions for Discussion

1. How can social media analytics be used in the consumer products industry?
2. What do you think are the key challenges, potential solutions, and probable results in applying social media analytics in consumer products and services firms?

Source: SproutSocial Case Study, "Tito's Vodka Establishes Brand Loyalty with an Authentic Social Strategy. http://sproutsocial.com/insights/case-studies/titos/ (accessed July 2016).

Over the years, various metrics (or measurements) have been developed to analyze social network structures from different perspectives. These metrics are often grouped into three categories: connections, distributions, and segmentation.

Connections

Homophily: The extent to which actors form ties with similar versus dissimilar others. Similarity can be defined by gender, race, age, occupation, educational achievement, status, values, or any other salient characteristic.

Multiplexity: The number of content forms contained in a tie. For example, two people who are friends and also work together would have a multiplexity of two. Multiplexity has been associated with relationship strength.

Mutuality/reciprocity: The extent to which two actors reciprocate each other's friendship or other interaction.

Network closure: A measure of the completeness of relational triads. An individual's assumption of network closure (i.e., that their friends are also friends) is called *transitivity.* Transitivity is an outcome of the individual or situational trait of need for cognitive closure.

Propinquity: The tendency for actors to have more ties with geographically close others.

Distributions

Bridge: An individual whose weak ties fill a structural hole, providing the only link between two individuals or clusters. It also includes the shortest route when a longer one is unfeasible due to a high risk of message distortion or delivery failure.

Centrality: Refers to a group of metrics that aim to quantify the importance or influence (in a variety of senses) of a particular node (or group) within a network. Examples of common methods of measuring centrality include betweenness centrality, closeness centrality, eigenvector centrality, alpha centrality, and degree centrality.

Density: The proportion of direct ties in a network relative to the total number possible.

Distance: The minimum number of ties required to connect two particular actors.

Structural holes: The absence of ties between two parts of a network. Finding and exploiting a structural hole can give an entrepreneur a competitive advantage. This concept was developed by sociologist Ronald Burt and is sometimes referred to as an alternate conception of social capital.

Tie strength: Defined by the linear combination of time, emotional intensity, intimacy, and reciprocity (i.e., mutuality). Strong ties are associated with homophily, propinquity, and transitivity, whereas weak ties are associated with bridges.

Segmentation

Cliques and social circles: Groups are identified as *cliques* if every individual is directly tied to every other individual or *social circles* if there is less stringency of direct contact, which is imprecise, or as structurally cohesive blocks if precision is wanted.

Clustering coefficient: A measure of the likelihood that two members of a node are associates. A higher clustering coefficient indicates a greater *cliquishness*.

Cohesion: The degree to which actors are connected directly to each other by cohesive bonds. Structural cohesion refers to the minimum number of members who, if removed from a group, would disconnect the group.

Social Media Analytics

Social media refers to the enabling technologies of social interactions among people in which they create, share, and exchange information, ideas, and opinions in virtual communities and networks. It is a group of Internet-based software applications that build on the ideological and technological foundations of Web 2.0 and that allow the creation and exchange of user-generated content (Kaplan & Haenlein, 2010). Social media depends on mobile and other Web-based technologies to create highly interactive platforms for individuals and communities to share, co-create, discuss, and modify user-generated content. It introduces substantial changes to communication among organizations, communities, and individuals.

Since their emergence in the early 1990s, Web-based social media technologies have seen a significant improvement in both quality and quantity. These technologies take on many different forms, including online magazines, Internet forums, Web logs, social blogs, microblogging, wikis, social networks, podcasts, pictures, video, and product/service evaluations/ratings. By applying a set of theories in the field of media research (social presence, media richness) and social processes (self-presentation, self-disclosure), Kaplan and Haenlein (2010) created a classification scheme with six different types of social media: collaborative projects (e.g., Wikipedia), blogs and microblogs (e.g., Twitter), content communities (e.g., YouTube), social networking sites (e.g., Facebook), virtual game worlds (e.g., World of Warcraft), and virtual social worlds (e.g. Second Life).

Web-based social media are different from traditional/industrial media, such as newspapers, television, and film, as they are comparatively inexpensive and accessible to enable anyone (even private individuals) to publish or access/consume information. Industrial media generally require significant resources to publish information, as in most cases the articles (or books) go through many revisions before being published (as was the case in the publication of this very book). Here are some of the most prevailing characteristics that help differentiate between social and industrial media (Morgan, Jones, & Hodges, 2010):

Quality: In industrial publishing—mediated by a publisher—the typical range of quality is substantially narrower than in niche, unmediated markets. The main challenge posed by content in social media sites is the fact that the distribution of quality has high variance: from very high-quality items to low-quality, sometimes abusive, content.

Reach: Both industrial and social media technologies provide scale and are capable of reaching a global audience. Industrial media, however, typically use a centralized framework for organization, production, and dissemination, whereas social media are by their very nature more decentralized, less hierarchical, and distinguished by multiple points of production and utility.

Frequency: Compared to industrial media, updating and reposting on social media platforms is easier, faster, and cheaper, and therefore practiced more frequently, resulting in fresher content.

Accessibility: The means of production for industrial media are typically government and/or corporate (privately owned) and are costly, whereas social media tools are generally available to the public at little or no cost.

Usability: Industrial media production typically requires specialized skills and training. Conversely, most social media production requires only modest reinterpretation of existing skills; in theory, anyone with access can operate the means of social media production.

Immediacy: The time lag between communications produced by industrial media can be long (weeks, months, or even years) compared to social media (which can be capable of virtually instantaneous responses).

Updatability: Industrial media, once created, cannot be altered (once a magazine article is printed and distributed, changes cannot be made to that same article), whereas social media can be altered almost instantaneously by comments or editing.

How Do People Use Social Media?

Not only are the numbers on social networking sites growing, but so is the degree to which they are engaged with the channel. Brogan and Bastone (2011) presented research results that stratify users according to how actively they use social media and tracked evolution of these user segments over time. They listed six different engagement levels (Figure 5.15).

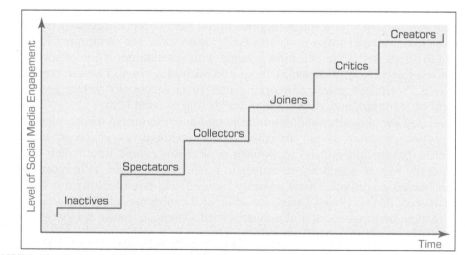

FIGURE 5.15   Evolution of Social Media User Engagement.

According to the research results, the online user community has been steadily migrating upward on this engagement hierarchy. The most notable change is among Inactives. Forty-four percent of the online population fell into this category. Two years later, more than half of those Inactives had jumped into social media in some form or another. "Now roughly 82% of the adult population online is in one of the upper categories," said Bastone. "Social media has truly reached a state of mass adoption."

Social media analytics refers to the systematic and scientific ways to consume the vast amount of content created by Web-based social media outlets, tools, and techniques for the betterment of an organization's competitiveness. Social media analytics is rapidly becoming a new force in organizations around the world, allowing them to reach out to and understand consumers as never before. In many companies, it is becoming the tool for integrated marketing and communications strategies.

The exponential growth of social media outlets, from blogs, Facebook, and Twitter to LinkedIn and YouTube, and analytics tools that tap into these rich data sources offer organizations the chance to join a conversation with millions of customers around the globe every day. This aptitude is why nearly two-thirds of the 2,100 companies who participated in a recent survey by Harvard Business Review Analytic Services said they are either currently using social media channels or have social media plans in the works (*Harvard Business Review*, 2010). But many still say social media is an experiment, as they try to understand how to best use the different channels, gauge their effectiveness, and integrate social media into their strategy.

Measuring the Social Media Impact

For organizations, small or large, there is valuable insight hidden in all the user-generated content on social media sites. But how do you dig it out of dozens of review sites, thousands of blogs, millions of Facebook posts, and billions of tweets? Once you do that, how do you measure the impact of your efforts? These questions can be addressed by the analytics extension of the social media technologies. Once you decide on your goal for social media (what it is that you want to accomplish), there is a multitude of tools to help you get there. These analysis tools usually fall into three broad categories:

- *Descriptive analytics:* Uses simple statistics to identify activity characteristics and trends, such as how many followers you have, how many reviews were generated on Facebook, and which channels are being used most often.
- *Social network analysis:* Follows the links between friends, fans, and followers to identify connections of influence as well as the biggest sources of influence.
- *Advanced analytics:* Includes predictive analytics and text analytics that examine the *content* in online conversations to identify themes, sentiments, and connections that would not be revealed by casual surveillance.

Sophisticated tools and solutions to social media analytics use all three categories of analytics (i.e., descriptive, predictive, and prescriptive) in a somewhat progressive fashion.

Best Practices in Social Media Analytics

As an emerging tool, social media analytics is practiced by companies in a somewhat haphazard fashion. Because there are not well-established methodologies, everybody is trying to create their own by trial and error. What follows are some of the field-tested best practices for social media analytics proposed by Paine and Chaves (2012).

THINK OF MEASUREMENT AS A GUIDANCE SYSTEM, NOT A RATING SYSTEM

Measurements are often used for punishment or rewards; they should not be. They should be about figuring out what the most effective tools and practices are, what needs to be discontinued because it doesn't work, and what needs to be done more because it does work very well. A good analytics system should tell you where you need to focus. Maybe all that emphasis on Facebook doesn't really matter because that is not where your audience is. Maybe they are all on Twitter, or vice versa. According to Paine and Chaves, channel preference won't necessarily be intuitive, "We just worked with a hotel that had virtually no activity on Twitter for one brand but lots of Twitter activity for one of their higher brands." Without an accurate measurement tool, you would not know.

TRACK THE ELUSIVE SENTIMENT Customers want to take what they are hearing and learning from online conversations and act on it. The key is to be precise in extracting and tagging their intentions by measuring their sentiments. As we have seen earlier in this chapter, text analytic tools can categorize online content, uncover linked concepts, and reveal the sentiment in a conversation as "positive," "negative," or "neutral," based on the words people use. Ideally, you would like to be able to attribute sentiment to a specific product, service, and business unit. The more precise you can get in understanding the tone and perception that people express, the more actionable the information becomes, because you are mitigating concerns about mixed polarity. A mixed-polarity phrase, such as "hotel in great location but bathroom was smelly," should not be tagged as "neutral" because you have positives and negatives offsetting each other. To be actionable, these types of phrases are to be treated separately; "bathroom was smelly" is something someone can own and improve on. One can classify and categorize these sentiments, look at trends over time, and see significant differences in the way people speak either positively or negatively about you. Furthermore, you can compare sentiment about your brand to your competitors.

CONTINUOUSLY IMPROVE THE ACCURACY OF TEXT ANALYSIS An industry-specific text analytics package will already know the vocabulary of your business. The system will have linguistic rules built into it, but it learns over time and gets better and better. Much as you would tune a statistical model as you get more data, better parameters, or new techniques to deliver better results, you would do the same thing with the NLP that goes into sentiment analysis. You set up rules, taxonomies, categorization, and meaning of words; watch what the results look like; and then go back and do it again.

LOOK AT THE RIPPLE EFFECT It is one thing to get a great hit on a high-profile site, but that's only the start. There's a difference between a great hit that just sits there and goes away versus a great hit that is tweeted, retweeted, and picked up by influential bloggers. Analysis should show you which social media activities go "viral" and which quickly go dormant—and why.

LOOK BEYOND THE BRAND One of the biggest mistakes people make is to be concerned only about their brand. To successfully analyze and act on social media, you need to understand not just what is being said about your brand, but the broader conversation about the spectrum of issues surrounding your product or service, as well. Customers don't usually care about a firm's message or its brand; they care about themselves. Therefore, you should pay attention to what they are talking about, where they are talking, and where their interests are.

IDENTIFY YOUR MOST POWERFUL INFLUENCERS Organizations struggle to identify who has the most power in shaping public opinion. It turns out, your most important influencers are not necessarily the ones who advocate specifically for your brand; they are the ones who influence the whole realm of conversation about your topic. You need to understand whether they are saying nice things, expressing support, or simply making observations or critiquing. What is the nature of their conversations? How is my brand being positioned relative to the competition in that space?

LOOK CLOSELY AT THE ACCURACY OF YOUR ANALYTIC TOOL   Until recently, computer-based automated tools were not as accurate as humans for sifting through online content. Even now, accuracy varies depending on the media. For product review sites, hotel review sites, and Twitter, it can reach anywhere between 80 and 90% accuracy because the context is more boxed in. When you start looking at blogs and discussion forums, where the conversation is more wide-ranging, the software can deliver 60 to 70% accuracy (Paine & Chaves, 2012). These figures will increase over time because the analytics tools are continually upgraded with new rules and improved algorithms to reflect field experience, new products, changing market conditions, and emerging patterns of speech.

INCORPORATE SOCIAL MEDIA INTELLIGENCE INTO PLANNING   Once you have a big-picture perspective and detailed insight, you can begin to incorporate this information into your planning cycle. But that is easier said than done. A quick audience poll revealed that very few people currently incorporate learning from online conversations into their planning cycles (Paine & Chaves, 2012). One way to achieve this is to find time-linked associations between social media metrics and other business activities or market events. Social media is typically either organically invoked or invoked by something your organization does; therefore, if you see a spike in activity at some point in time, you want to know what was behind that.

SECTION 5.10 REVIEW QUESTIONS

1. What is meant by social analytics? Why is it an important business topic?
2. What is a social network? What is the need for SNA?
3. What is social media? How does it relate to Web 2.0?
4. What is social media analytics? What are the reasons behind its increasing popularity?
5. How can you measure the impact of social media analytics?

Chapter Highlights

- Text mining is the discovery of knowledge from unstructured (mostly text-based) data sources. Given that a great deal of information is in text form, text mining is one of the fastest-growing branches of the business intelligence field.
- Text mining applications are in virtually every area of business and government, including marketing, finance, healthcare, medicine, and homeland security.
- Text mining uses NLP to induce structure into the text collection and then uses data mining algorithms such as classification, clustering, association, and sequence discovery to extract knowledge from it.

- Sentiment can be defined as a settled opinion reflective of one's feelings.
- Sentiment analysis deals with differentiating between two classes, positive and negative.
- As a field of research, sentiment analysis is closely related to computational linguistics, NLP, and text mining.
- Sentiment analysis is trying to answer the question, "What do people feel about a certain topic?" by digging into opinions of many using a variety of automated tools.
- The VOC is an integral part of an analytic CRM and customer experience management systems and is often powered by sentiment analysis.

- The VOM is about understanding aggregate opinions and trends at the market level.
- Polarity identification in sentiment analysis is accomplished either by using a lexicon as a reference library or by using a collection of training documents.
- WordNet is a popular general-purpose lexicon created at Princeton University.
- SentiWordNet is an extension of WordNet to be used for sentiment identification.
- Speech analytics is a growing field of science that allows users to analyze and extract information from both live and recorded conversations.
- Web mining can be defined as the discovery and analysis of interesting and useful information from the Web, about the Web, and usually using Web-based tools.
- Web mining can be viewed as consisting of three areas: Web content mining, Web structure mining, and Web usage mining.
- Web content mining refers to the automatic extraction of useful information from Web pages. It may be used to enhance search results produced by search engines.
- Web structure mining refers to generating interesting information from the links included in Web pages.
- Web structure mining can also be used to identify the members of a specific community and perhaps even the roles of the members in the community.
- Web usage mining refers to developing useful information through analysis of Web server logs, user profiles, and transaction information.

- Text and Web mining are emerging as critical components of the next generation of business intelligence tools to enable organizations to compete successfully.
- A search engine is a software program that searches for documents (Internet sites or files), based on the keywords (individual words, multiword terms, or a complete sentence) users have provided, that have to do with the subject of their inquiry.
- SEO is the intentional activity of affecting the visibility of an e-commerce site or a Web site in a search engine's natural (unpaid or organic) search results.
- VOC is a term usually used to describe the analytic process of capturing a customer's expectations, preferences, and aversions.
- Social analytics is the monitoring, analyzing, measuring, and interpreting of digital interactions and relationships of people, topics, ideas, and content.
- A social network is a social structure composed of individuals/people (or groups of individuals or organizations) linked to one another with some type of connections/relationships.
- Social media analytics refers to the systematic and scientific ways to consume the vast amount of content created by Web-based social media outlets, tools, and techniques for the betterment of an organization's competitiveness.

Key Terms

association
authoritative pages
classification
clickstream analysis
clustering
corpus
deception detection
hubs
hyperlink-induced topic search (HITS)

natural language processing (NLP)
part-of-speech tagging
polarity identification
polyseme
search engine
sentiment analysis
SentiWordNet
singular value decomposition (SVD)

social media analytics
social network
spider
stemming
stop words
term–document matrix (TDM)
text mining
tokenizing
trend analysis

unstructured data
voice of the customer (VOC)
Web analytics
Web content mining
Web crawler
Web mining
Web structure mining
Web usage mining
WordNet

Questions for Discussion

1. Explain the relationship among data mining, text mining, and sentiment analysis.
2. In your own words, define text mining, and discuss its most popular applications.
3. What does it mean to induce structure into the text-based data? Discuss the alternative ways of inducing structure into text-based data.
4. What is the role of NLP in text mining? Discuss the capabilities and limitations of NLP in the context of text mining.
5. List and discuss three prominent application areas for text mining. What is the common theme among the three application areas you chose?
6. What is sentiment analysis? How does it relate to text mining?
7. What are the common challenges that sentiment analysis has to deal with?
8. What are the most popular application areas for sentiment analysis? Why?
9. What are the main steps in carrying out sentiment analysis projects?
10. What are the two common methods for polarity identification? Explain.
11. Discuss the differences and commonalities between text mining and Web mining.
12. In your own words, define Web mining, and discuss its importance.
13. What are the three main areas of Web mining? Discuss the differences and commonalities among these three areas.
14. What is a search engine? Why are they important for businesses?
15. What is SEO? Who benefits from it? How?
16. What is Web analytics? What are the metrics used in Web analytics?
17. Define *social analytics*, *social network*, and *social network analysis*. What are the relationships among them?
18. What is social media analytics? How is it done? Who does it? What comes out of it?

Exercises

Teradata University Network (TUN) and Other Hands-on Exercises

1. Visit teradatauniversitynetwork.com. Identify cases about text mining. Describe recent developments in the field. If you cannot find enough cases at the Teradata University Network Web site, broaden your search to other Web-based resources.
2. Go to teradatauniversitynetwork.com or locate white papers, Web seminars, and other materials related to text mining. Synthesize your findings into a short written report.
3. Go to teradatauniversitynetwork.com and find the case study named "eBay Analytics." Read the case carefully, extend your understanding of the case by searching the Internet for additional information, and answer the case questions.
4. Go to teradatauniversitynetwork.com and find the sentiment analysis case named "How Do We Fix an App Like That?" Read the description, and follow the directions to download the data and the tool to carry out the exercise.
5. Visit teradatauniversitynetwork.com. Identify cases about Web mining. Describe recent developments in the field. If you cannot find enough cases at the Teradata University Network Web site, broaden your search to other Web-based resources.
6. Browse the Web and your library's digital databases to identify articles that make the linkage between text/Web mining and contemporary business intelligence systems.

Team Assignments and Role-Playing Projects

1. Examine how textual data can be captured automatically using Web-based technologies. Once captured, what are the potential patterns that you can extract from these unstructured data sources?
2. Interview administrators in your college or executives in your organization to determine how text mining and Web mining could assist them in their work. Write a proposal describing your findings. Include a preliminary cost–benefit analysis in your report.
3. Go to your library's online resources. Learn how to download attributes of a collection of literature (journal articles) in a specific topic. Download and process the data using a methodology similar to the one explained in Application Case 5.5.
4. Find a readily available sentiment text data set (see Technology Insights 5.3 for a list of popular data sets) and download it into your computer. If you have an analytics tool that is capable of text mining, use that. If not, download RapidMiner (http://rapid-i.com) and install it. Also install the Text Analytics add-on for RapidMiner. Process the downloaded data using your text mining tool (i.e., convert the data into a structured form). Build models and assess the sentiment detection accuracy of several classification models (e.g., support vector machines, decision trees, neural networks, logistic regression). Write a detailed report in which you explain your finings and your experiences.

5. Examine how Web-based data can be captured automatically using the latest technologies. Once captured, what are the potential patterns that you can extract from these content-rich, mostly unstructured data sources?

Internet Exercises

1. Find recent cases of successful text mining and Web mining applications. Try text and Web mining software vendors and consultancy firms and look for cases or success stories. Prepare a report summarizing five new case studies.
2. Go to statsoft.com. Select Downloads, and download at least three white papers on applications. Which of these applications may have used the data/text/Web mining techniques discussed in this chapter?
3. Go to sas.com. Download at least three white papers on applications. Which of these applications may have used the data/text/Web mining techniques discussed in this chapter?
4. Go to ibm.com. Download at least three white papers on applications. Which of these applications may have used the data/text/Web mining techniques discussed in this chapter?
5. Go to teradata.com. Download at least three white papers on applications. Which of these applications may have used the data/text/Web mining techniques discussed in this chapter?
6. Go to clarabridge.com. Download at least three white papers on applications. Which of these applications may have used text mining in a creative way?
7. Go to kdnuggets.com. Explore the sections on applications as well as software. Find names of at least three additional packages for data mining and text mining.
8. Survey some Web mining tools and vendors. Identify some Web mining products and service providers that are not mentioned in this chapter.
9. Go to attensity.com. Download at least three white papers on Web analytics applications. Which of these applications may have used a combination of data/text/Web mining techniques?

References

Bond C. F., & DePaulo, B. M. (2006). Accuracy of deception judgments. *Personality and Social Psychology Reports, 10*(3), 214–234.

Brogan, C., & Bastone, J. (2011). Acting on customer intelligence from social media: The new edge for building customer loyalty and your brand. SAS white paper.

Chun, H. W., Tsuruoka, Y., Kim, J. D., Shiba, R., Nagata, N., & Hishiki, T. (2006). Extraction of gene-disease relations from MEDLINE using domain dictionaries and machine learning. *Proceedings of the 11th Pacific Symposium on Biocomputing,* 4–15.

Coussement, K., & Van Den Poel, D. (2008). Improving customer complaint management by automatic email classification using linguistic style features as predictors. *Decision Support Systems, 44*(4), 870–882.

Coussement, K., & Van Den Poel, D. (2009). Improving customer attrition prediction by integrating emotions from client/company interaction emails and evaluating multiple classifiers. *Expert Systems with Applications, 36*(3), 6127–6134.

Cutts, M. (2006, February 4). Ramping Up on International Webspam. mattcutts.com/blog. mattcutts.com/blog/ramping-up-on-international-webspam (accessed March 2013).

Delen, D., & Crossland, M. (2008). Seeding the survey and analysis of research literature with text mining. *Expert Systems with Applications, 34*(3), 1707–1720.

Esuli, A., & Sebastiani, F. (2006, May). SentiWordNet: A publicly available lexical resource for opinion mining. In *Proceedings of LREC, 6,* 417–422.

Etzioni, O. (1996). The World Wide Web: Quagmire or gold mine? *Communications of the ACM, 39*(11), 65–68.

EUROPOL. (2007). EUROPOL Work Program 2005. statewatch.org/news/2006/apr/europol-work-programme-2005.pdf (accessed October 2008).

Feldman, R., & Sanger, J. (2007). *The text mining handbook: Advanced approaches in analyzing unstructured data.* Boston: ABS Ventures.

Fuller, C. M., Biros, D., & Delen, D. (2008). Exploration of feature selection and advanced classification models for high-stakes deception detection. *Proceedings of the 41st Annual Hawaii International Conference on System Sciences (HICSS),* Big Island, HI: IEEE Press, 80–99.

Ghani, R., Probst, K., Liu, Y., Krema, M., & Fano, A. (2006). Text mining for product attribute extraction. *SIGKDD Explorations, 8*(1), 41–48.

Goodman, A. (2005). Search engine showdown: Black hats versus white hats at SES. SearchEngineWatch. searchenginewatch.com/article/2066090/Search-Engine-Showdown-Black-Hats-vs.-White-Hats-at-SES (accessed February 2013).

Han, J., & Kamber, M. (2006). *Data mining: Concepts and techniques,* 2nd ed. San Francisco: Morgan Kaufmann.

Harvard Business Review. (2010). The new conversation: Taking social media from talk to action. A SAS-Sponsored Research Report by Harvard Business Review Analytic Services. sas.com/resources/whitepaper/wp_23348.pdf (accessed March 2013).

Kaplan, A. M., & Haenlein, M. (2010). Users of the world, unite! The challenges and opportunities of social media. *Business Horizons, 53*(1), 59–68.

Kim, S. M., & Hovy, E. (2004, August). Determining the sentiment of opinions. In *Proceedings of the 20th International*

Conference on Computational Linguistics (p. 1367). Association for Computational Linguistics.

Kleinberg, J. (1999). Authoritative sources in a hyperlinked environment. *Journal of the ACM, 46*(5), 604–632.

Lin, J., & Demner-Fushman, D. (2005). "Bag of words" is not enough for strength of evidence classification. *AMIA Annual Symposium Proceedings,* 1031–1032. pubmedcentral.nih.gov/articlerender.fcgi?artid=1560897.

Liu, B., Hu, M., & Cheng, J. (2005, May). Opinion observer: Analyzing and comparing opinions on the Web. In *Proceedings of the 14th International Conference on World Wide Web* (pp. 342–351). ACM.

Mahgoub, H., Rösner, D., Ismail, N., & Torkey, F. (2008). A text mining technique using association rules extraction. *International Journal of Computational Intelligence, 4*(1), 21–28.

Manning, C. D., & Schutze, H. (1999). *Foundations of statistical natural language processing.* Cambridge, MA: MIT Press.

McKnight, W. (2005, January 1). Text data mining in business intelligence. *Information Management Magazine.* information-management.com/issues/20050101/1016487-1.html (accessed May 22, 2009).

Mejova, Y. (2009). Sentiment analysis: An overview. Comprehensive exam paper. http://www.cs.uiowa.edu/~ymejova/publications/CompsYelenaMejova.pdf (accessed February 2013).

Miller, T. W. (2005). *Data and text mining: A business applications approach.* Upper Saddle River, NJ: Prentice Hall.

Morgan, N., Jones, G., & Hodges, A. (2010). The complete guide to social media from the social media guys. thesocialmediaguys.co.uk/wp-content/uploads/downloads/2011/03/CompleteGuidetoSocialMedia.pdf (accessed February 2013).

Nakov, P., Schwartz, A., Wolf, B., & Hearst, M. A. (2005). Supporting annotation layers for natural language processing. *Proceedings of the ACL,* Interactive Poster and Demonstration Sessions, Ann Arbor, MI. Association for Computational Linguistics, 65–68.

Paine, K. D., & Chaves, M. (2012). Social media metrics. SAS white paper. sas.com/resources/whitepaper/wp_19861.pdf (accessed February 2013).

Pang, B., & Lee, L. (2008). *Opinion mining and sentiment analysis.* Hanover, MA: Now Publishers, available at http://books.google.com.

Ramage, D., Hall, D., Nallapati, R., & Manning, C. D. (2009, August). Labeled LDA: A supervised topic model for credit attribution in multi-labeled corpora. In *Proceedings of the 2009 Conference on Empirical Methods in Natural Language Processing: Volume 1* (pp. 248–256). Association for Computational Linguistics.

Schmidt, L.-H. (1996). Commonness across cultures. In A. N. Balslev (Ed.), *Cross-cultural conversation: Initiation* (pp. 119–132). New York: Oxford University Press.

Scott, W. R., & Davis, G. F. (2003). Networks in and around organizations. In *Organizations and Organizing.* Upper Saddle River: NJ: Pearson Prentice Hall.

Shatkay, H., Höglund, A., Brady, S., Blum, T., Dönnes, P., & Kohlbacher, O. (2007). SherLoc: High-accuracy prediction of protein subcellular localization by integrating text and protein sequence data. *Bioinformatics, 23*(11), 1410–1415.

Snyder, B., & Barzilay, R. (2007, April). Multiple aspect ranking using the good grief algorithm. In *HLT-NAACL* (pp. 300–307).

Strapparava, C., & Valitutti, A. (2004, May). WordNet affect: An affective extension of WordNet. In *LREC* (Vol. 4, pp. 1083–1086).

The Westover Group. (2013). 20 key Web analytics metrics and how to use them. http://www.thewestovergroup.com (accessed February 2013).

Thomas, M., Pang, B., & Lee, L. (2006, July). Get out the vote: Determining support or opposition from Congressional floor-debate transcripts. In *Proceedings of the 2006 Conference on Empirical Methods in Natural Language Processing* (pp. 327–335). Association for Computational Linguistics.

Weng, S. S., & Liu, C. K. (2004). Using text classification and multiple concepts to answer e-mails. *Expert Systems with Applications, 26*(4), 529–543.

CHAPTER 6

Prescriptive Analytics: Optimization and Simulation

LEARNING OBJECTIVES

- Understand the applications of prescriptive analytics techniques in combination with reporting and predictive analytics
- Understand the basic concepts of analytical decision modeling
- Understand the concepts of analytical models for selected decision problems, including linear programming and simulation models for decision support
- Describe how spreadsheets can be used for analytical modeling and solutions

- Explain the basic concepts of optimization and when to use them
- Describe how to structure a linear programming model
- Explain what is meant by sensitivity analysis, what-if analysis, and goal seeking
- Understand the concepts and applications of different types of simulation
- Understand potential applications of discrete event simulation

This chapter, a new addition to this book, extends the analytics applications beyond reporting and predictive analytics. It includes coverage of selected techniques that can be employed in combination with predictive models to help support decision making. We focus on techniques that can be implemented relatively easily using either spreadsheet tools or by using stand-alone software tools. Of course, there is much additional detail to be learned about management science models, but the objective of this chapter is to simply illustrate what is possible and how it has been implemented in real settings.

We present this material with a note of caution: Modeling can be a difficult topic and is as much an art as it is a science. The purpose of this chapter is not necessarily for you to *master the topics* of modeling and analysis. Rather, the material is geared toward *gaining familiarity* with the important concepts as they relate to prescriptive analytics and their use in decision making. It is important to recognize that the modeling we discuss here is only cursorily related to the concepts of data modeling. You should not confuse the two.

We walk through some basic concepts and definitions of decision modeling. We next introduce the idea of modeling directly in spreadsheets. We then discuss the structure and application of two successful time-proven models and methodologies: linear programming and discrete event simulation. As noted earlier, one could take multiple courses just in these two topics, but our goal is to give you a sense of what is possible. This chapter includes the following sections:

6.1 Opening Vignette: School District of Philadelphia Uses Prescriptive Analytics to Find Optimal Solution for Awarding Bus Route Contracts   320

6.2 Model-Based Decision Making   322

6.3 Structure of Mathematical Models for Decision Support   328

6.4 Certainty, Uncertainty, and Risk

6.5 Decision Modeling with Spreadsheets   330

6.6 Mathematical Programming Optimization   331

6.7 Multiple Goals, Sensitivity Analysis, What-If Analysis, and Goal Seeking   336

6.8 Decision Analysis with Decision Tables and Decision Trees   346

6.9 Introduction to Simulation   349

6.10 Visual Interactive Simulation   352

6.1 OPENING VIGNETTE: School District of Philadelphia Uses Prescriptive Analytics to Find Optimal Solution for Awarding Bus Route Contracts

Background

Selecting the best vendors to work with is a laborious yet important task for companies and government organizations. After a vendor submits a proposal for a specific task through a bidding process, the company or organization evaluates the proposal and makes a decision on which vendor is best suited for their needs. Typically, governments are required to use a bidding process to select one or more vendors. The School District of Philadelphia was in search of private bus vendors to outsource some of their bus routes. The district owned a few school buses, but needed more to serve their student population. They wanted to use their own school buses for 30 to 40% of the routes, and outsource the rest of the routes to these private vendors. Charles Lowitz, the fiscal coordinator for the transportation office, was tasked with determining how to maximize the return on investment and refine the way routes were awarded to various vendors.

Historically, the process of deciding which bus vendor contracts to award given the budget and time constraints was laborious as it was done manually by hand. In addition, the different variables and factors that had to be taken into account added to the complexity. The vendors were evaluated based on five variables: cost, capabilities, reliance, financial stability, and business acumen. Each vendor submitted a proposal with a different price for different routes. Some vendors specified a minimum number of routes, and if that minimum wasn't met, their cost would increase. Lowitz needed to figure out how to combine the information from each proposal to determine which bus route to award to which vendor to meet all the route requirements at the least cost for the district.

Solution

Lowitz initially looked for software that he could use in conjunction with his contract model in Excel. He began using the Premium Solver Platform from Frontline Systems, Inc., which allowed him to find the most beneficial vendors for the district from a financial and operational standpoint. He created an optimization model that took into account the aforementioned variables associated with each vendor. The model included binary integer variables (yes/no) for each of the routes to be awarded to the bidders who proposed to serve a specific route at a specific cost. This amounted to about 1,600 yes/no variables. The model also included constraints indicating that each route was to be awarded to one vendor, and of course, each route had to be serviced. Other constraints specified the minimum number of routes a vendor would accept and a few other details. All such constraints can be written as equations and entered in an integer linear programming model. Such models can be formulated and solved through many software tools, but using Microsoft Excel makes it easier to understand the model. Frontline Systems' Solver software is built into Microsoft Excel to solve smaller problems for free. A larger version can be purchased to solve larger and more complex models. That is what Lowitz used.

Benefits

In addition to determining how many of the vendors should be awarded contracts, the model helped develop the size of each of the contracts. The size of the contracts varied from one vendor getting 4 routes to another receiving 97 routes. Ultimately, the School District of Philadelphia was able to create a plan with an optimized number of bus company vendors using Excel instead of a manual handwritten process. By using the Premium Solver Platform analytic tools to create an optimization model with the different variables, the district saved both time and money.

QUESTIONS FOR THE OPENING VIGNETTE

1. What decision was being made in this vignette?
2. What data (descriptive and or predictive) might one need to make the best allocations in this scenario?
3. What other costs or constraints might you have to consider in awarding contracts for such routes?
4. Which other situations might be appropriate for applications of such models?

What Can We Learn from This Opening Vignette?

Most organizations face the problem of making decisions where one has to select from multiple options. Each option has a cost and capability associated with it. The goal of such models is to select the combination of options that meet all the requirements and yet optimizes the costs. Prescriptive analytics particularly apply to the problem of such decisions. And tools such as built-in or Premium Solver for Excel make it easy to apply such techniques.

Source: Adapted with permission from "Optimizing Vendor Contract Awards Gets an A+," http://www.solver .com/news/optimizing-vendor-contract-awards-gets, 2016 (accessed July 2016).

6.2 Model-Based Decision Making

As the preceding vignette indicates, making decisions using some kind of analytical model is what we call prescriptive analytics. In the last several chapters we have learned the value and the process of knowing the history of what has been going on and use that information to also predict what is likely to happen. However, we go through that exercise to determine what we should do next. This might entail deciding which customers are likely to buy from us and making an offer or giving a price point that will maximize the likelihood that they would buy and our profit would be optimized. Conversely, it might involve being able to predict which customer is likely to go somewhere else and making a promotion offer to retain them as a customer and optimize our value. We may need to make decisions on awarding contracts to our vendors to make sure all our needs are covered and the costs are minimized. We could be facing a situation of deciding which prospective customers should receive what promotional campaign material so that our cost of promotion is not outrageous, and we maximize the response rate while managing within a budget. We may be deciding how much to pay for different paid search keywords to maximize the return on investment of our advertising budget. In another setting, we may have to study the history of our customers' arrival patterns and use that information to predict future arrival rates, and apply that to schedule an appropriate number of store employees to maximize customer responses and optimize our labor costs. We could be deciding where to locate our warehouses based on our analysis and prediction of demand for our products and the supply chain costs. We could be setting daily delivery routes on the basis of product volumes to be delivered at various locations and the delivery costs and vehicle availability. One can find hundreds of examples of situations where data-based decisions are valuable. Indeed, the biggest opportunity for the growing analytics profession is the ability to use descriptive and predictive insights to help a decision maker make better decisions. Although there are situations where one can use experience and intuition to make decisions, it is more likely that a decision supported by a model will help a decision maker make better decisions. In addition, it also provides decision makers with justification for what they are recommending. Thus prescriptive analytics has emerged as the next frontier for analytics. It essentially involves using an analytical model to help guide a decision maker in making a decision, or automating the decision process so that a model can make recommendations or decisions. Because the focus of prescriptive analytics is on making recommendations or making decisions, some call this category of analytics decision analytics.

INFORMS publications such as *Interfaces*, *ORMS Today*, and *Analytics* magazine, all include stories that illustrate successful applications of decision models in real settings. This chapter includes many examples of such prescriptive analytic applications. Applying models to real-world situations can save millions of dollars or generate millions of dollars in revenue. Christiansen et al. (2009) describe the applications of such models in shipping company operations using TurboRouter, a decision support system (DSS) for ship routing and scheduling. They claim that over the course of a 3-week period, a company used this model to better utilize its fleet, generating additional profit of $1–2 million in such a short time. We provide another example of a model application in Application Case 6.1.

Prescriptive Analytics Model Examples

Modeling is a key element for prescriptive analytics. In the examples mentioned earlier in the introduction and application cases, one has to employ a mathematical model to be able to recommend a decision for any realistic problem. For example, deciding which customers (among potentially millions) will receive what offer so as to maximize the overall response value but staying within a budget is not something you can do manually. Building a probability-based response maximization model with the budget as a

Application Case 6.1

Optimal Transport for ExxonMobil Downstream through a DSS

ExxonMobil, a petroleum and natural gas company, operates in several countries worldwide. It provides several ranges of petroleum products, including clean fuels, lubricants, and high-value products and feedstock to several customers. This is completed through a complex supply chain between its refineries and customers. One of the main products ExxonMobil transports is vacuum gas oil (VGO). ExxonMobil transports several shiploads of VGO from Europe to the United States. In a year, it is estimated that ExxonMobil transports about 60–70 ships of VGO across the Atlantic Ocean. Hitherto, both ExxonMobil-managed vessels and third-party vessels were scheduled to transport VGO across the Atlantic through a cumbersome manual process. The whole process required the collaboration of several individuals across the supply chain organization. Several customized spreadsheets with special constraints, requirements, and economic trade-offs were used to determine the transportation schedule of the vessels. Some of the constraints included the following:

1. Constantly varying production and demand projections
2. Maximum and minimum inventory constraints
3. A pool of heterogeneous vessels (e.g., ships with varying speed, cargo size)
4. Vessels that load and discharge at multiple ports
5. Both ExxonMobil-managed and third-party supplies and ports
6. Complex transportation cost that includes variable overage and demurrage costs
7. Vessel size and draft limits for different ports

The manual process could not determine the actual routes of vessels, the timing of each vessel, and the quantity of VGO loaded and discharged. In addition, consideration of the production and consumption data at several locations rendered the manual process burdensome and inefficient.

Methodology/Solution

A decision support tool that supported schedulers in planning an optimal schedule for ships to load, transport, and discharge VGO to and from multiple locations was developed. The problem was formulated as a mixed-integer linear programming problem. The solution had to satisfy requirements for routing, transportation, scheduling, and inventory management vis-à-vis varying production and demand profiles. A mathematical programming language, GAMS, was used for the problem formulation, and Microsoft Excel was used as the user interface. When the solver (ILOG CPLEX) is run, an optimal solution is reached at a point when the objective value of the incumbent solution stops improving. This stopping criterion is determined by the user during each program run.

Results/Benefits

It is expected that using the optimization model will lead to reduced shipping costs and less demurrage expenses. These would be achieved because the tool would be able to support higher utilization of ships and help make ship selection (e.g., *Panamax* versus *Aframax*) and design more optimal routing schedules. The researchers intend to further the research by exploring other alternate mathematical methods to solve the scheduling problem. They also intend to give the DSS tool the capability to consider multiple products for a pool of vessels.

QUESTIONS FOR DISCUSSION

1. List three ways in which manual scheduling of ships could result in more operational costs as compared to the tool developed.
2. In what other ways can ExxonMobil leverage the decision support tool developed to expand and optimize their other business operations?
3. What are some strategic decisions that could be made by decision makers using the tool developed?

Source: Adapted from Furman, K. C., Song, J. H., Kocis, G. R., McDonald, M. K., & Warrick, P. H. (2011). Feedstock routing in the ExxonMobil downstream sector. *Interfaces, 41*(2), 149–163.

constraint would give us the information we are seeking. Depending on the problem we are addressing, there are many classes of models, and there are often many specialized techniques for solving each one. We will learn about two different modeling methods in this chapter. Most universities have multiple courses that cover these topics under titles such as Operations Research, Management Science, Decision Support Systems, and Simulation that can help you build more expertise in these topics. Because prescriptive analytics typically involves the application of mathematical models, sometimes the term *data science* is more commonly associated with the application of such mathematical models. Before we learn about mathematical modeling support in prescriptive analytics, let us understand some modeling issues first.

Identification of the Problem and Environmental Analysis

No decision is made in a vacuum. It is important to analyze the scope of the domain and the forces and dynamics of the environment. A decision maker needs to identify the organizational culture and the corporate decision-making processes (e.g., who makes decisions, degree of centralization). It is entirely possible that environmental factors have created the current problem. This can formally be called **environmental scanning and analysis**, which is the monitoring, scanning, and interpretation of collected information. Business intelligence/business analytics (BI/BA) tools can help identify problems by scanning for them. The problem must be understood, and everyone involved should share the same frame of understanding because the problem will ultimately be represented by the model in one form or another. Otherwise, the model will not help the decision maker.

VARIABLE IDENTIFICATION   Identification of a model's variables (e.g., decision, result, uncontrollable) is critical, as are the relationships among the variables. Influence diagrams, which are graphical models of mathematical models, can facilitate the identification process. A more general form of an influence diagram, a cognitive map, can help a decision maker develop a better understanding of a problem, especially of variables and their interactions.

FORECASTING (PREDICTIVE ANALYTICS)   As we have noted previously, an important prerequisite of prescriptive analytics is knowing what has happened and what is likely to happen. This form of predictive analytics is essential for construction and manipulating models because when a decision is implemented, the results usually occur in the future. There is no point in running a what-if (sensitivity) analysis on the past because decisions made then have no impact on the future. Online commerce and communication has created an immense need for **forecasting** and an abundance of available information for performing it. These activities occur quickly, yet information about such purchases is gathered and should be analyzed to produce forecasts. Part of the analysis involves simply predicting demand; however, forecasting models can use product life-cycle needs and information about the marketplace and consumers to analyze the entire situation, ideally leading to additional sales of products and services.

We describe an effective example of such forecasting and its use in decision making at Ingram Micro in Application Case 6.2.

Model Categories

Table 6.1 classifies some decision models into seven groups and lists several representative techniques for each category. Each technique can be applied to either a **static** or a **dynamic model**, which can be constructed under assumed environments of certainty,

Application Case 6.2

Ingram Micro Uses Business Intelligence Applications to Make Pricing Decisions

Ingram Micro is the world's largest two-tier distributor of technology products. In a two-tier distribution system, a company purchases products from manufacturers and sells them to retailers who in turn sell these products to the end users. For example, one can purchase a Microsoft Office 365 package from Ingram rather than purchasing it directly from Microsoft. Ingram has partnerships with Best Buy, Buffalo, Google, Honeywell, Libratone, and Sharper Image. The company delivers its products to 200,000 solution providers across the world and thus has a large volume of transaction data. Ingram wanted to use insights from this data to identify cross-selling opportunities and determine prices to offer to specific customers in conjunction with product bundles. This required setting up a business intelligence center (BIC) to compile and analyze the data. In setting up the BIC, Ingram faced various issues.

1. Ingram faced several issues in their data-capture process such as a lack of loss data, ensuring the accuracy of end-user information, and linking quotes to orders.
2. Ingram faced technical issues in implementing a customer relationship management (CRM) system capable enough to handle its operations around the world.
3. They faced resistance to the idea of demand pricing (determining price based on demand of product).

Methodology/Solution

Ingram explored communicating directly with its customers (resellers) using e-mail and offered them discounts on the purchase of supporting technologies related to the products being ordered. They identified these opportunities through segmented market-basket analysis and developed the following business intelligence applications that helped in determining optimized prices. Ingram developed a new price optimization tool known as IMPRIME, which is capable of setting data-driven prices and providing data-driven negotiation guidance. IMPRIME sets an optimized price for each level of the product hierarchy (i.e., customer level, vendor-customer level, customer-segment level, and vendor-customer segment level). It does so by taking into account the trade-off between the demand signal and pricing at that level.

The company also developed a digital marketing platform known as Intelligence INGRAM. This platform utilizes predictive lead scoring (PLS), which selects end users to target with specific marketing programs. PLS is their system to score predictive leads for companies that have no direct relation with end users. Intelligence INGRAM is used to run white space programs, which encourage a reseller to purchase related products by offering discounts. For example, if a reseller purchases a server from INGRAM, then INGRAM offers a discount on disk storage units as both products are required to work together. Similarly, Intelligence INGRAM is used to run growth incentive campaigns (offering cash rewards to resellers on exceeding quarterly spend goals) and cross-sell campaigns (e-mailing the end users about the products that are related to their recently purchased product).

Results/Benefits

Profit generated by using IMPRIME is measured using a lift measurement methodology. This methodology compares periods before and after changing the prices and compares test groups versus control groups. Lift measurement is done on average daily sales, gross margin, and machine margin. The use of IMPRIME led to a $757 million growth in revenue and a $18.8 million increase in gross profits.

Questions for Discussion

1. What were the main challenges faced by Ingram Micro in developing a BIC?
2. List all the business intelligence solutions developed by Ingram to optimize the prices of their products and to profile their customers.
3. What benefits did Ingram receive after using the newly developed BI applications?

What Can We Learn from This Application Case?

By first building a BIC, a company begins to better understand its product lines, its customers, and

(Continued)

Application Case 6.2 (Continued)

their purchasing patterns. This insight is derived from what we call descriptive and predictive analytics. Further value from this is derived through price optimization, a purview of prescriptive analytics.

Sources: Mookherjee, R., Martineau, J., Xu, L., Gullo, M., Zhou, K., Hazlewood, A., Zhang, X., Griarte, F., & Li, N. (2016). End-to-end predictive analytics and optimization in Ingram Micro's two-tier distribution business. *Interfaces, 46*(1), 49–73; ingrammicrocommerce.com, "CUSTOMERS," https://www.ingrammicrocommerce.com/customers/ (accessed July 2016).

uncertainty, or risk. To expedite model construction, we can use special decision analysis systems that have modeling languages and capabilities embedded in them. These include spreadsheets, data mining systems, online analytic processing (OLAP) systems, and modeling languages that help an analyst build a model. We will introduce one of these systems later in the chapter.

MODEL MANAGEMENT   Models, like data, must be managed to maintain their integrity, and thus their applicability. Such management is done with the aid of model-based management systems, which are analogous to database management systems (DBMS).

KNOWLEDGE-BASED MODELING   DSS uses mostly quantitative models, whereas expert systems use qualitative, knowledge-based models in their applications. Some knowledge is necessary to construct solvable (and therefore usable) models. Many of the predictive analytics techniques, such as classification and clustering, can be used in building knowledge-based models.

TABLE 6.1   Categories of Models

Category	Process and Objective	Representative Techniques
Optimization of problems with few alternatives	Find the best solution from a small number of alternatives	Decision tables, decision trees, analytic hierarchy process
Optimization via algorithm	Find the best solution from a large number of alternatives, using a step-by-step improvement process	Linear and other mathematical programming models, network models
Optimization via an analytic formula	Find the best solution in one step, using a formula	Some inventory models
Simulation	Find a good enough solution or the best among the alternatives checked, using experimentation	Several types of simulation
Heuristics	Find a good enough solution, using rules	Heuristic programming, expert systems
Predictive models	Predict the future for a given scenario	Forecasting models, Markov analysis
Other models	Solve a what-if case, using a formula	Financial modeling, waiting lines

CURRENT TRENDS IN MODELING   One recent trend in modeling involves the development of model libraries and solution technique libraries. Some of these codes can be run directly on the owner's Web server for free, and others can be downloaded and run on a local computer. The availability of these codes means that powerful optimization and simulation packages are available to decision makers who may have only experienced these tools from the perspective of classroom problems. For example, the Mathematics and Computer Science Division at Argonne National Laboratory (Argonne, Illinois) maintains the NEOS Server for Optimization at https://neos-server.org/neos/index.html. You can find links to other sites by clicking the Resources link at informs.org, the Web site of the Institute for Operations Research and the Management Sciences (INFORMS). A wealth of modeling and solution information is available from INFORMS. The Web site for one of INFORMS' publications, *OR/MS Today*, at http://www.orms-today.org/ormsmain.shtml includes links to many categories of modeling software. We will learn about some of these shortly.

There is a clear trend toward developing and using cloud-based tools and software to access and even run software to perform modeling, optimization, simulation, and so on. This has, in many ways, simplified the application of many models to real-world problems. However, to use models and solution techniques effectively, it is necessary to truly gain experience through developing and solving simple ones. This aspect is often overlooked. Organizations that have key analysts who understand how to apply models indeed apply them very effectively. This is most notably occurring in the revenue management area, which has moved from the province of airlines, hotels, and automobile rentals to retail, insurance, entertainment, and many other areas. CRM also uses models, but they are often transparent to the user. With management models, the amount of data and model sizes are quite large, necessitating the use of data warehouses to supply the data and parallel computing hardware to obtain solutions in a reasonable time frame.

There is a continuing trend toward making analytics models completely transparent to the decision maker. For example, **multidimensional analysis (modeling)** involves data analysis in several dimensions. In multidimensional analysis (modeling), data are generally shown in a spreadsheet format, with which most decision makers are familiar. Many decision makers accustomed to slicing and dicing data cubes are now using OLAP systems that access data warehouses. Although these methods may make modeling palatable, they also eliminate many important and applicable model classes from consideration, and they eliminate some important and subtle solution interpretation aspects. Modeling involves much more than data analysis with trend lines and establishing relationships with statistical methods.

There is also a trend to build a model of a model to help in its analysis. An **influence diagram** is a graphical representation of a model; that is, a model of a model. Some influence diagram software packages are capable of generating and solving the resultant model.

SECTION 6.2 REVIEW QUESTIONS

1. List three lessons learned from modeling.

2. List and describe the major issues in modeling.

3. What are the major types of models used in DSS?

4. Why are models not used in industry as frequently as they should or could be?

5. What are the current trends in modeling?

6.3 Structure of Mathematical Models for Decision Support

In the following sections, we present the topics of analytical mathematical models (e.g., mathematical, financial, and engineering). These include the components and the structure of models.

The Components of Decision Support Mathematical Models

All **quantitative models** are typically made up of four basic components (see Figure 6.1): result (or outcome) variables, decision variables, uncontrollable variables (and/or parameters), and intermediate result variables. Mathematical relationships link these components together. In nonquantitative models, the relationships are symbolic or qualitative. The results of decisions are determined based on the decision made (i.e., the values of the decision variables), the factors that cannot be controlled by the decision maker (in the environment), and the relationships among the variables. The modeling process involves identifying the variables and relationships among them. Solving a model determines the values of these and the result variable(s).

RESULT (OUTCOME) VARIABLES Result (outcome) variables reflect the level of effectiveness of a system; that is, they indicate how well the system performs or attains its goal(s). These variables are outputs. Examples of result variables are shown in Table 6.2. Result variables are considered *dependent variables*. Intermediate result variables are sometimes used in modeling to identify intermediate outcomes. In the case of a dependent variable, another event must occur first before the event described by the variable can occur. Result variables depend on the occurrence of the decision variables and the uncontrollable variables.

DECISION VARIABLES Decision variables describe alternative courses of action. The decision maker controls the decision variables. For example, for an investment problem, the amount to invest in bonds is a decision variable. In a scheduling problem, the decision variables are people, times, and schedules. Other examples are listed in Table 6.2.

UNCONTROLLABLE VARIABLES, OR PARAMETERS In any decision-making situation, there are factors that affect the result variables but are not under the control of the decision maker. Either these factors can be fixed, in which case they are called **uncontrollable variables**, or **parameters**, or they can vary, in which case they are called *variables*. Examples of factors are the prime interest rate, a city's building code, tax regulations, and utilities costs. Most of these factors are uncontrollable because they are in and determined

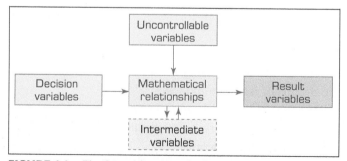

FIGURE 6.1 The General Structure of a Quantitative Model.

TABLE 6.2   Examples of Components of Models

Area	Decision Variables	Result Variables	Uncontrollable Variables and Parameters
Financial investment	Investment alternatives and amounts	Total profit, risk Rate of return on investment (ROI) Earnings per share Liquidity level	Inflation rate Prime rate Competition
Marketing	Advertising budget Where to advertise	Market share Customer satisfaction	Customer's income Competitor's actions
Manufacturing	What and how much to produce Inventory levels Compensation programs	Total cost Quality level Employee satisfaction	Machine capacity Technology Materials prices
Accounting	Use of computers Audit schedule	Data processing cost Error rate	Computer technology Tax rates Legal requirements
Transportation	Shipments schedule Use of smart cards	Total transport cost Payment float time	Delivery distance Regulations
Services	Staffing levels	Customer satisfaction	Demand for services

by elements of the system environment in which the decision maker works. Some of these variables limit the decision maker and therefore form what are called *constraints* of the problem.

INTERMEDIATE RESULT VARIABLES   **Intermediate result variables** reflect intermediate outcomes in mathematical models. For example, in determining machine scheduling, spoilage is an intermediate result variable, and total profit is the result variable (i.e., spoilage is one determinant of total profit). Another example is employee salaries. This constitutes a decision variable for management: It determines employee satisfaction (i.e., intermediate outcome), which, in turn, determines the productivity level (i.e., final result).

The Structure of Mathematical Models

The components of a quantitative model are linked by mathematical (algebraic) expressions—equations or inequalities.

A very simple financial model is

$$P = R - C$$

where P = profit, R = revenue, and C = cost. This equation describes the relationship among the variables. Another well-known financial model is the simple present-value cash flow model, where P = present value, F = a future single payment in dollars, i = interest rate (percentage), and n = number of years. With this model, it is possible to determine the present value of a payment of $100,000 to be made 5 years from today, at a 10% (0.1) interest rate, as follows:

$$P = 100,000/ (1 + 0.1)^5 = 62,092$$

We present more interesting and complex mathematical models in the following sections.

SECTION 6.3 REVIEW QUESTIONS

1. What is a decision variable?

2. List and briefly discuss the major components of a quantitative model.

3. Explain the role of intermediate result variables.

6.4 Certainty, Uncertainty, and Risk[1]

The decision-making process involves evaluating and comparing alternatives. During this process, it is necessary to predict the future outcome of each proposed alternative. Decision situations are often classified on the basis of what the decision maker knows (or believes) about the forecasted results. We customarily classify this knowledge into three categories (see Figure 6.2), ranging from complete knowledge to complete ignorance:

- Certainty
- Uncertainty
- Risk

When we develop models, any of these conditions can occur, and different kinds of models are appropriate for each case. Next, we discuss both the basic definitions of these terms and some important modeling issues for each condition.

Decision Making under Certainty

In decision making under **certainty**, it is *assumed* that complete knowledge is available so that the decision maker knows exactly what the outcome of *each course of action* will be (as in a deterministic environment). It may not be true that the outcomes are 100% known, nor is it necessary to really evaluate *all* the outcomes, but often this assumption simplifies the model and makes it tractable. The decision maker is viewed as a perfect predictor of the future because it is assumed that there is only one outcome for each alternative. For example, the alternative of investing in U.S. Treasury bills is one for which there is

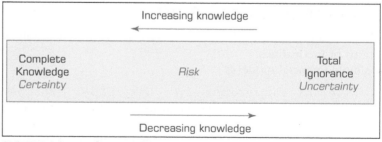

FIGURE 6.2 The Zones of Decision Making.

---

[1] Some parts of the original versions of these sections were adapted from Turban and Meredith (1994).

complete availability of information about the future return on investment if it is held to maturity. A situation involving decision making under certainty occurs most often with structured problems and short time horizons (up to 1 year). Certainty models are relatively easy to develop and solve, and they can yield optimal solutions. Many financial models are constructed under assumed certainty, even though the market is anything but 100% certain.

Decision Making under Uncertainty

In decision making under **uncertainty**, the decision maker considers situations in which several outcomes are possible for each course of action. In contrast to the risk situation, in this case, the decision maker does not know, or cannot estimate, the probability of occurrence of the possible outcomes. Decision making under uncertainty is more difficult than decision making under certainty because there is insufficient information. Modeling of such situations involves assessment of the decision maker's (or the organization's) attitude toward risk.

Managers attempt to avoid uncertainty as much as possible, even to the point of assuming it away. Instead of dealing with uncertainty, they attempt to obtain more information so that the problem can be treated under certainty (because it can be "almost" certain) or under calculated (i.e., assumed) risk. If more information is not available, the problem must be treated under a condition of uncertainty, which is less definitive than the other categories.

Decision Making under Risk (Risk Analysis)

A decision made under **risk**[2] (also known as a *probabilistic* or *stochastic* decision-making situation) is one in which the decision maker must consider several possible outcomes for each alternative, each with a given probability of occurrence. The long-run probabilities that the given outcomes will occur are assumed to be known or can be estimated. Under these assumptions, the decision maker can assess the degree of risk associated with each alternative (called *calculated* risk). Most major business decisions are made under assumed risk. **Risk analysis** (i.e., calculated risk) is a decision-making method that analyzes the risk (based on assumed known probabilities) associated with different alternatives. Risk analysis can be performed by calculating the expected value of each alternative and selecting the one with the best expected value. Application Case 6.3 illustrates one application to reduce uncertainty.

SECTION 6.4 REVIEW QUESTIONS

1. Define what it means to perform decision making under assumed certainty, risk, and uncertainty.
2. How can decision-making problems under assumed certainty be handled?
3. How can decision-making problems under assumed uncertainty be handled?
4. How can decision-making problems under assumed risk be handled?

6.5 Decision Modeling with Spreadsheets

Models can be developed and implemented in a variety of programming languages and systems. We focus primarily on *spreadsheets* (with their add-ins), modeling languages, and transparent data analysis tools. With their strength and flexibility, spreadsheet

---

[2] Our definitions of the terms *risk* and *uncertainty* were formulated by F. H. Knight of the University of Chicago in 1933. Other, comparable definitions also are in use.

Application Case 6.3

American Airlines Uses Should-Cost Modeling to Assess the Uncertainty of Bids for Shipment Routes

American Airlines, Inc. (AA) is one of the world's largest airlines. Its core business is passenger transportation, but it has other vital ancillary functions that include full-truckload (FTL) freight shipment of maintenance equipment and in-flight shipment of passenger service items that could add up to over $1 billion in inventory at any given time. AA receives numerous bids from suppliers in response to requests for quotes (RFQs) for inventories. AA's RFQs could total over 500 in any given year. Bid quotes vary significantly as a result of the large number of bids and resultant complex bidding process. Sometimes, a single contract bid could deviate by about 200%. As a result of the complex process, it is common to either overpay or underpay suppliers for their services. To this end, AA wanted a should-cost model that would streamline and assess bid quotes from suppliers to choose bid quotes that were fair to both them and their suppliers.

Methodology/Solution

To determine fair cost for supplier products and services, three steps were taken:

1. Primary (e.g., interviews) and secondary (e.g., Internet) sources were scouted for base-case and range data that would inform cost variables that affect an FTL bid.
2. Cost variables were chosen so that they were mutually exclusive and collectively exhaustive.
3. The DPL decision analysis software was used to model the uncertainty.

Furthermore, Extended Swanson-Megill approximation was used to model the probability distribution of the most sensitive cost variables used. This was done to account for the high variability in the bids in the initial model.

Results/Benefits

A pilot test was done on an RFQ that attracted bids from six FTL carriers. Out of the six bids presented, five were within three standard deviations from the mean, whereas one was considered an outlier. Subsequently, AA used the should-cost FTL model on more than 20 RFQs to determine what a fair and accurate cost of goods and services should be. It is expected that this model will help in reducing the risk of either overpaying or underpaying its suppliers.

QUESTIONS FOR DISCUSSION

1. Besides reducing the risk of overpaying or underpaying suppliers, what are some other benefits AA would derive from its "should-be" model?
2. Can you think of other domains besides air transportation where such a model could be used?
3. Discuss other possible methods with which AA could have solved its bid overpayment and underpayment problem.

Source: Adapted from Bailey, M. J., Snapp, J., Yetur, S., Stonebraker, J. S., Edwards, S. A., Davis, A., & Cox, R. (2011). Practice summaries: American Airlines uses should-cost modeling to assess the uncertainty of bids for its full-truckload shipment routes. *Interfaces, 41*(2), 194–196.

packages were quickly recognized as easy-to-use implementation software for the development of a wide range of applications in business, engineering, mathematics, and science. Spreadsheets include extensive statistical, forecasting, and other modeling and database management capabilities, functions, and routines. As spreadsheet packages evolved, add-ins were developed for structuring and solving specific model classes. Among the add-in packages, many were developed for DSS development. These DSS-related add-ins include Solver (Frontline Systems Inc., solver.com) and What's*Best!* (a version of Lindo, from Lindo Systems, Inc., lindo.com) for performing linear and nonlinear optimization; Braincel (Jurik Research Software, Inc., jurikres.com) and NeuralTools (Palisade Corp., palisade.com) for artificial neural networks; Evolver (Palisade Corp.) for genetic algorithms; and @RISK (Palisade Corp.) for performing simulation studies. Comparable add-ins are available for free or at a very low cost. (Conduct a Web search to find them; new ones are added to the marketplace on a regular basis.)

The spreadsheet is clearly the most popular *end-user modeling tool* because it incorporates many powerful financial, statistical, mathematical, and other functions. Spreadsheets can perform model solution tasks such as linear programming and regression analysis. The spreadsheet has evolved into an important tool for analysis, planning, and modeling (see Farasyn, Perkoz, & Van de Velde, 2008; Hurley & Balez, 2008; Ovchinnikov & Milner, 2008). Application Cases 6.4 and 6.5 describe interesting applications of spreadsheet-based models in a nonprofit setting.

Application Case 6.4

Pennsylvania Adoption Exchange Uses Spreadsheet Model to Better Match Children with Families

The Pennsylvania Adoption Exchange (PAE) was established in 1979 by the State of Pennsylvania to help county and nonprofit agencies find prospective families for orphan children who had not been adopted due to age or special needs. The PAE keeps detailed records about children and preferences of families who may adopt them. The exchange looks for families for the children across all 67 counties of Pennsylvania.

The Pennsylvania Statewide Adoption and Permanency Network is responsible for finding permanent homes for orphans. If after a few attempts the network fails to place a child with a family, they then get help from the PAE. The PAE uses an automated assessment tool to match children to families. This tool gives matching recommendations by calculating a score between 0 to 100% for a child on 78 pairs of the child's attribute values and family preferences. For some years now, the PAE has struggled to give adoption match recommendations to caseworkers for children. They are finding it difficult to manage a vast database of children collected over time for all 67 counties. The basic search algorithm produced match recommendations that were proving unfruitful for caseworkers. As a result, the number of children who have not been adopted has increased significantly, and there is a growing urgency to find families for these orphans.

Methodology/Solution

The PAE started collecting information about the orphans and families through online surveys that include a new set of questions. These questions collect information about hobbies of the child, child–caseworker preferences for families, and preference of the age range of children by families. The PAE and consultants created a spreadsheet matching tool that included additional features compared to the previously used automated tool. In this model, caseworkers can specify the weight of the attributes for selecting a family for a child. For example, if a family had a narrow set of preferences regarding gender, age, and race, then those factors can receive a higher weight. Also, caseworkers can give preference about the family's county of residence, as community relationship is an important factor for a child. Using this tool, the matching committee can compare a child and family on each attribute, thus making a more accurate match decision between a family and a child.

Results/Benefits

Since the PAE started using the new spreadsheet model for matching a family with a child, they have been able to make better matching decisions. As a

(Continued)

Application Case 6.4 (Continued)

result, the percentage of children getting a permanent home has increased.

This short case is one of the many examples of using spreadsheets as a decision support tool. By creating a simple scoring system for a family's desire and a child's attribute, a better matching system is produced so that fewer rejections are reported on either side.

QUESTIONS FOR DISCUSSION

1. What were the challenges faced by PAE while making adoption matching decisions?
2. What features of the new spreadsheet tool helped PAE solve their issues of matching a family with a child?

Source: Adapted from Slaugh, V. W., Akan, M., Kesten, O., & Unver, M. U. (2016). The Pennsylvania Adoption Exchange improves its matching process. *Interfaces, 46*(2), 133–154.

Application Case 6.5

Metro Meals on Wheels Treasure Valley Uses Excel to Find Optimal Delivery Routes

Meals on Wheels Association of America (now Meals on Wheels America) is a not-for-profit organization that delivers approximately one million meals to homes of older people in need across the United States. Metro Meals on Wheels Treasure Valley is a local branch of Meals on Wheels America operating in Idaho. This branch has a team of volunteer drivers that drive their personal vehicles each day to deliver meals to 800 clients along 21 routes and cover an area of 2,745 square kilometers.

The Meals on Wheels Treasure Valley organization was facing many issues. First, they were looking to minimize the delivery time as the cooked food was temperature sensitive and could perish easily. They wanted to deliver the cooked food within 90 minutes after a driver left for the delivery. Second, the scheduling process was very time consuming. Two employees spent much of their time developing scheduled routes for delivery. A route coordinator determined the stops according to the number of meal recipients for a given day. After determining the stops, the coordinator made a sequence of stops that minimized the travel time of volunteers. This routing schedule was then entered into an online tool to determine turn-by-turn driving instructions for drivers. The whole process of manually deciding routes was taking a lot of extra time. Metro Meals on Wheels wanted a routing tool that could improve their delivery system and generate routing solutions for both one-way and round-trip directions for delivering meals. Those who drive regularly could deliver the warmers or coolers the next day. Others who drive only occasionally would need to come back to the kitchen to drop off the warmers/coolers.

Methodology/Solution

To solve the routing problem, a spreadsheet-based tool was developed. This tool had an interface to easily input information about the recipient such as his/her name, meal requirements, and delivery address. This information needed to be filled in the spreadsheet for each stop in the route. Next, Excel's Visual Basic for Applications functionality was used to access a developer's networking map application programming interface (API) called MapQuest. This API was used to create a travel matrix that calculated time and distance needed for delivery of the meal. This tool gave time and distance information for 5,000 location pairs a day without any cost.

When the program starts, the MapQuest API first validates the entered addresses of meal recipients. Then the program uses the API to retrieve driving distance, estimated driving time, and turn-by-turn instructions for driving between all stops in the route. The tool can then find the optimal route for up to 30 stops within a feasible time limit.

Results/Benefits

As a result of using this tool, the total annual driving distance decreased by 10,000 miles, while travel time was reduced by 530 hours. Metro Meals on Wheels Treasure Valley saved $5,800 in 2015, based on an estimated savings rate of $0.58 per mile (for a mid-size sedan). This tool also reduced the time spent on route planning for meal deliveries. Other benefits included increased volunteer satisfaction and more retention of volunteers.

QUESTIONS FOR DISCUSSION

1. What were the challenges faced by Metro Meals on Wheels Treasure Valley related to meal delivery before adoption of the spreadsheet-based tool?
2. Explain the design of the spreadsheet-based model.
3. What are the intangible benefits of using the Excel-based model to Metro Meals on Wheels?

Source: Adapted from Manikas, A. S., Kroes, J. R., & Gattiker, T. F. (2016). Metro Meals on Wheels Treasure Valley employs a low-cost routing tool to improve deliveries. *Interfaces, 46*(2), 154–167.

Other important spreadsheet features include what-if analysis, goal seeking, data management, and programmability (i.e., macros). With a spreadsheet, it is easy to change a cell's value and immediately see the result. Goal seeking is performed by indicating a target cell, its desired value, and a changing cell. Extensive database management can be performed with small data sets, or parts of a database can be imported for analysis (which is essentially how OLAP works with multidimensional data cubes; in fact, most OLAP systems have the look and feel of advanced spreadsheet software after the data are loaded). Templates, macros, and other tools enhance the productivity of building DSS.

Most spreadsheet packages provide fairly seamless integration because they read and write common file structures and easily interface with databases and other tools. Microsoft Excel is the most popular spreadsheet package. In Figure 6.3, we show a simple loan calculation model in which the boxes on the spreadsheet describe the contents of the cells, which contain formulas. A change in the interest rate in cell E7 is immediately

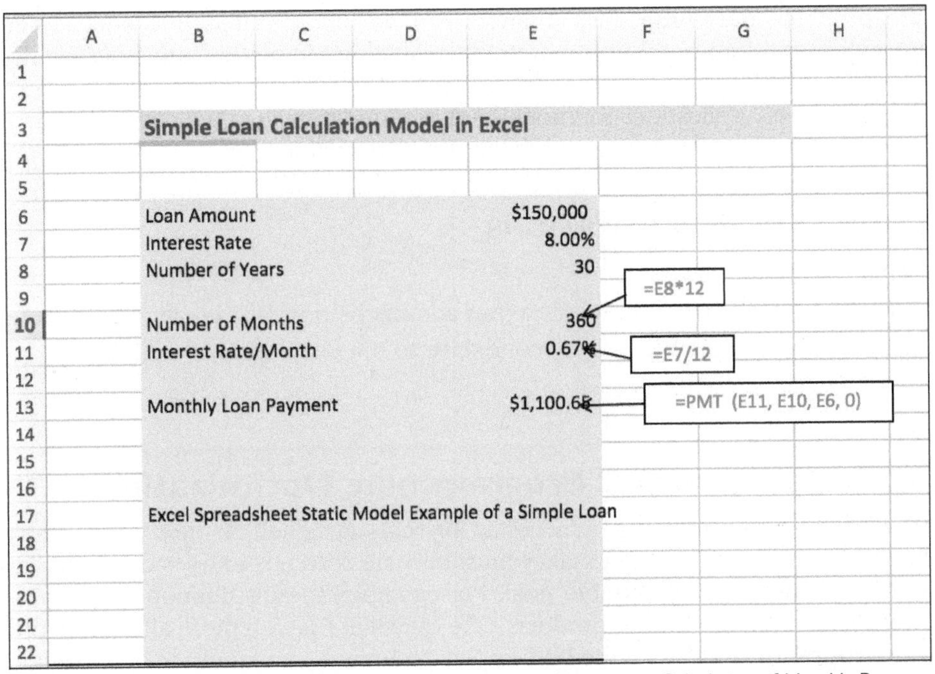

FIGURE 6.3   Excel Spreadsheet Static Model Example of a Simple Loan Calculation of Monthly Payments.

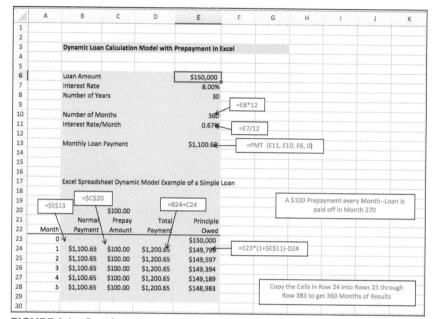

FIGURE 6.4 Excel Spreadsheet Dynamic Model Example of a Simple Loan Calculation of Monthly Payments and the Effects of Prepayment.

reflected in the monthly payment in cell E13. The results can be observed and analyzed immediately. If we require a specific monthly payment, we can use goal seeking to determine an appropriate interest rate or loan amount.

Static or dynamic models can be built in a spreadsheet. For example, the monthly loan calculation spreadsheet shown in Figure 6.3 is static. Although the problem affects the borrower over time, the model indicates a single month's performance, which is replicated. A dynamic model, in contrast, represents behavior over time. The loan calculations in the spreadsheet shown in Figure 6.4 indicate the effect of prepayment on the principal over time. Risk analysis can be incorporated into spreadsheets by using built-in random-number generators to develop simulation models (see the next chapter).

Spreadsheet applications for models are reported regularly. We will learn how to use a spreadsheet-based optimization model in the next section.

SECTION 6.5 REVIEW QUESTIONS

1. What is a spreadsheet?
2. What is a spreadsheet add-in? How can add-ins help in DSS creation and use?
3. Explain why a spreadsheet is so conducive to the development of DSS.

6.6 Mathematical Programming Optimization

Mathematical programming is a family of tools designed to help solve managerial problems in which the decision maker must allocate scarce resources among competing activities to optimize a measurable goal. For example, the distribution of machine time (the resource) among various products (the activities) is a typical allocation problem. **Linear programming (LP)** is the best-known technique in a family of optimization tools called *mathematical programming*; in LP, all relationships among the variables are linear.

It is used extensively in DSS (see Application Case 6.6). LP models have many important applications in practice. These include supply chain management, product mix decisions, routing, and so on. Special forms of the models can be used for specific applications. For example, Application Case 6.6 describes a spreadsheet model that was used to create a schedule for physicians.

Application Case 6.6

Mixed-Integer Programming Model Helps the University of Tennessee Medical Center with Scheduling Physicians

Regional Neonatal Associates is a nine-physician group working for the Neonatal Intensive Care Unit (NICU) at the University of Tennessee Medical Center in Knoxville, Tennessee. The group also serves two local hospitals in the Knoxville area for emergency purposes. For many years, one member of the group would schedule physicians manually. However, as his retirement approached, there was a need for a more automatic system to schedule physicians. The physicians wanted this system to balance their workload, as the previous schedules did not properly balance workload among them. In addition, the schedule needed to ensure there would be 24-7 NICU coverage by the physicians, and if possible, accommodate individual preferences of physicians for shift types. To address this problem, the physicians contacted the faculty of Management Science at the University of Tennessee.

The problem of scheduling physicians to shifts was characterized by constraints based on workload and lifestyle choices. The first step in solving the scheduling issue was to group shifts according to their types (day and night). The next step was determining constraints for the problem. The model needed to cover a nine-week period with nine physicians, with two physicians working weekdays and one physician overnight and on weekends. In addition, one physician had to be assigned exclusively for 24-7 coverage to the two local hospitals. Other obvious constraints also needed to be considered. For example, a day shift could not be assigned to a physician just after a night shift.

Methodology/Solution

The problem was formulated by creating a binary, mixed-integer optimization model. The first model divided workload equally among the nine physicians.

But it could not assign an equal number of day and night shifts among them. This created a question of fair distribution. In addition, the physicians had differing opinions of the assigned workload. Six physicians wanted a schedule in which an equal number of day and night shifts would be assigned to each physician in the nine-week schedule, while the others wanted a schedule based on individual preference of shifts. To satisfy requirements of both groups of physicians, a new model was formed and named the Hybrid Preference Scheduling Model (HPSM). For satisfying the equality requirement of six physicians, the model first calculated one week's workload and divided it for nine weeks for them. This way, the work was divided equally for all six physicians. The workload for the three remaining physicians was distributed in the nine-week schedule according to their preference. The resulting schedule was reviewed by the physicians and they found the schedule more acceptable.

Results/Benefits

The HPSM method accommodated both the equality and individual preference requirements of the physicians. In addition, the schedules from this model provided better rest times for the physicians compared to the previous manual schedules, and vacation requests could also be accommodated in the schedules. The HPSM model can solve similar scheduling problems demanding relative preferences among shift types.

Techniques such as mixed-integer programming models can build optimal schedules and help in operations. These techniques have been used in large organizations for a long time. Now it is possible to implement such prescriptive analytic models in spreadsheets and other easily available software.

Application Case 6.6 (Continued)

Source: Adapted from Bowers, M. R., Noon, C. E., Wu, W., & Bass, J. K. (2016). Neonatal physician scheduling at the University of Tennessee Medical Center. *Interfaces, 46*(2), 168–182.

QUESTIONS FOR DISCUSSION

1. What was the issue faced by the Regional Neonatal Associates group?
2. How did the HPSM model solve all of the physician's requirements?

LP allocation problems usually display the following characteristics:

- A limited quantity of economic resources is available for allocation.
- The resources are used in the production of products or services.
- There are two or more ways in which the resources can be used. Each is called a *solution* or a *program*.
- Each activity (product or service) in which the resources are used yields a return in terms of the stated goal.
- The allocation is usually restricted by several limitations and requirements, called *constraints*.

The LP allocation model is based on the following rational economic assumptions:

- Returns from different allocations can be compared; that is, they can be measured by a common unit (e.g., dollars, utility).
- The return from any allocation is independent of other allocations.
- The total return is the sum of the returns yielded by the different activities.
- All data are known with certainty.
- The resources are to be used in the most economical manner.

Allocation problems typically have a large number of possible solutions. Depending on the underlying assumptions, the number of solutions can be either infinite or finite. Usually, different solutions yield different rewards. Of the available solutions, at least one is the best, in the sense that the degree of goal attainment associated with it is the highest (i.e., the total reward is maximized). This is called an **optimal solution**, and it can be found by using a special algorithm.

Linear Programming Model

Every LP model is composed of *decision variables* (whose values are unknown and are searched for), an *objective function* (a linear mathematical function that relates the decision variables to the goal, measures goal attainment, and is to be optimized), *objective function coefficients* (unit profit or cost coefficients indicating the contribution to the objective of one unit of a decision variable), *constraints* (expressed in the form of linear inequalities or equalities that limit resources and/or requirements; these relate the variables through linear relationships), *capacities* (which describe the upper and sometimes lower limits on the constraints and variables), and *input/output (technology) coefficients* (which indicate resource utilization for a decision variable).

Let us look at an example. MBI Corporation, which manufactures special-purpose computers, needs to make a decision: How many computers should it produce

TECHNOLOGY INSIGHTS 6.1
Linear Programming

LP is perhaps the best-known optimization model. It deals with the optimal allocation of resources among competing activities. The allocation problem is represented by the model described here.

The problem is to find the values of the decision variables X_1, X_2, and so on, such that the value of the result variable Z is maximized, subject to a set of linear constraints that express the technology, market conditions, and other uncontrollable variables. The mathematical relationships are all linear equations and inequalities. Theoretically, any allocation problem of this type has an infinite number of possible solutions. Using special mathematical procedures, the LP approach applies a unique computerized search procedure that finds the best solution(s) in a matter of seconds. Furthermore, the solution approach provides automatic sensitivity analysis.

next month at the Boston plant? MBI is considering two types of computers: the CC-7, which requires 300 days of labor and $10,000 in materials, and the CC-8, which requires 500 days of labor and $15,000 in materials. The profit contribution of each CC-7 is $8,000, whereas that of each CC-8 is $12,000. The plant has a capacity of 200,000 working days per month, and the material budget is $8 million per month. Marketing requires that at least 100 units of the CC-7 and at least 200 units of the CC-8 be produced each month. The problem is to maximize the company's profits by determining how many units of the CC-7 and how many units of the CC-8 should be produced each month. Note that in a real-world environment, it could possibly take months to obtain the data in the problem statement, and while gathering the data the decision maker would no doubt uncover facts about how to structure the model to be solved. Web-based tools for gathering data can help.

Modeling in LP: An Example

A standard LP model can be developed for the MBI Corporation problem just described. As discussed in Technology Insights 6.1, the LP model has three components: decision variables, result variables, and uncontrollable variables (constraints).

The decision variables are as follows:

$$X_1 = \text{units of CC} - 7 \text{ to be produced}$$
$$X_2 = \text{units of CC} - 8 \text{ to be produced}$$

The result variable is as follows:

$$\text{Total profit} = Z$$

The objective is to maximize total profit:

$$Z = 8,000X_1 + 12,000X_2$$

The uncontrollable variables (constraints) are as follows:

$$\text{Labor constraint: } 300X_1 + 500X_2 \leq 200,000 \text{ (in days)}$$

$$\text{Budget constraint: } 10,000X_1 + 15,000X_2 \leq 8,000,000 \text{ (in dollars)}$$
$$\text{Marketing requirement for CC} - 7: X_1 \geq 100 \text{ (in units)}$$
$$\text{Marketing requirement for CC} - 8: X_2 \geq 200 \text{ (in units)}$$

This information is summarized in Figure 6.5.

The model also has a fourth, hidden component. Every LP model has some internal intermediate variables that are not explicitly stated. The labor and budget constraints may each have some slack in them when the left-hand side is strictly less than the right-hand side. This slack is represented internally by slack variables that indicate excess resources available. The marketing requirement constraints may each have some surplus in them when the left-hand side is strictly greater than the right-hand side. This surplus is represented internally by surplus variables indicating that there is some room to adjust the right-hand sides of these constraints. These slack and surplus variables are intermediate. They can be of great value to a decision maker because LP solution methods use them in establishing sensitivity parameters for economic what-if analyses.

The product-mix model has an infinite number of possible solutions. Assuming that a production plan is not restricted to whole numbers—which is a reasonable assumption in a monthly production plan—we want a solution that maximizes total profit: an optimal solution. Fortunately, Excel comes with the add-in Solver, which can readily obtain an optimal (best) solution to this problem. Although the location of Solver add-in has moved from one version of Excel to another, it is still available as a free add-in. Look for it under the Data tab and on the Analysis ribbon. If it is not there, you should be able to enable it by going to Excel's Options Menu and selecting Add-ins.

We enter these data directly into an Excel spreadsheet, activate Solver, and identify the goal (by setting Target Cell equal to Max), decision variables (by setting By Changing Cells), and constraints (by ensuring that Total Consumed elements is less than or equal to Limit for the first two rows and is greater than or equal to Limit for the third and fourth rows). Cells C7 and D7 constitute the decision variable cells. Results in these cells will be filled after running the Solver Add-in. Target Cell is Cell E7, which is also the result variable, representing a product of decision variable cells and their per unit profit coefficients (in Cells C8 and D8). Note that all the numbers have been divided by 1,000 to make it easier to type (except the decision variables). Rows 9–12 describe the constraints of the problem: the constraints on labor capacity, budget, and the desired minimum production of the two products X_1 and X_2. Columns C and D define the coefficients of these constraints. Column E includes the formulae that multiply the decision variables (Cells C7 and D7)

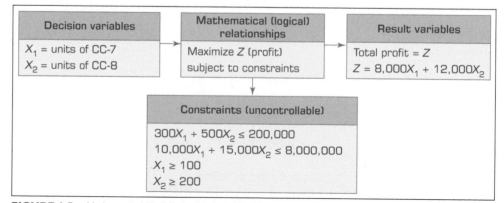

FIGURE 6.5 Mathematical Model of a Product-Mix Example.

with their respective coefficients in each row. Column F defines the right-hand side value of these constraints. Excel's matrix multiplication capabilities (e.g., SUMPRODUCT function) can be used to develop such row and column multiplications easily.

After the model's calculations have been set up in Excel, it is time to invoke the Solver Add-in. Clicking on the Solver Add-in (again under the Analysis group under Data Tab) opens a dialog box (window) that lets you specify the cells or ranges that define the objective function cell, decision/changing variables (cells), and the constraints. Also, in Options, we select the solution method (usually Simplex LP), and then we solve the problem. Next, we select all three reports—Answer, Sensitivity, and Limits—to obtain an optimal solution of $X_1 = 333.33$, $X_2 = 200$, Profit = $5,066,667, as shown in Figure 6.6. Solver produces three useful reports about the solution. Try it. Solver now also includes the ability to solve nonlinear programming problems and integer programming problems by using other solution methods available within it.

The following example was created by Professor Rick Wilson of Oklahoma State University to further illustrate the power of spreadsheet modeling for decision support.

The table in Figure 6.7 describes some hypothetical data and attributes of nine "swing states" for the 2016 election. Attributes of the nine states include their number of electoral votes, two regional descriptors (note that three states are classified as neither North nor South), and an estimated "influence function," which relates to increased candidate support per unit of campaign financial investment in that state.

For instance, influence function F1 shows that for every financial unit invested in that state, there will be a total of a 10-unit increase in voter support (let units stay general here), made up of an increase in young men support by 3 units, old men support by 1 unit, and young and old women each by 3 units.

The campaign has 1,050 financial units to invest in the nine states. It must invest at least 5% in each state of the total overall invested, but no more than 25% of the overall total invested can be in any one state. All 1,050 units do not have to be invested (your model must correctly deal with this).

The campaign has some other restrictions as well. From a financial investment standpoint, the West states (in total) must have campaign investments at levels that are at least 60% of the total invested in East states. In terms of people influenced, the decision

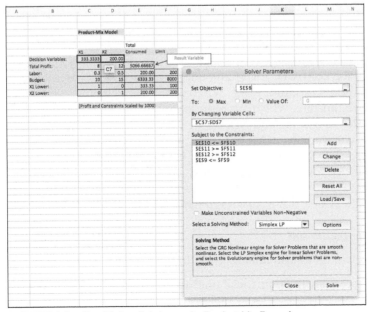

FIGURE 6.6   Excel Solver Solution to the Product-Mix Example.

	A	B	C	D	E	F	G	H
1								
2				Electoral			Influence	
3			State	Votes	W/E	N/S	Function	
4			NV	6	West		F1	
5			CO	9	West		F2	
6			IA	6	West	North	F3	
7			WI	10	West	North	F1	
8			OH	18	East	North	F2	
9			VA	13	East	South	F2	
10			NC	15	East	South	F1	
11			FL	29	East	South	F3	
12			NH	4	East		F3	
13								
14		F1	Young	Old				
15		Men	3	1	4			
16		Women	3	3	6			
17			6	4	10	Total		
18								
19		F2	Young	Old				
20		Men	1.5	2.5	4			
21		Women	2.5	1	3.5			
22			4	3.5	7.5	Total		
23								
24		F3	Young	Old				
25		Men	2.5	2.5	5			
26		Women	1	2	3			
27			3.5	4.5	8	Total		
28								

FIGURE 6.7   Data for Election Resource Allocation Example.

to allocate financial investments to states must lead to at least 9,200 total people influenced. Overall, the total number of females influenced must be greater than or equal to the total number of males influenced. Also, at least 46% of all people influenced must be "old."

Our task is to create an appropriate integer programming model that determines the optimal integer (i.e., whole number) allocation of financial units to states that maximizes the sum of the products of the electoral votes times units invested subject to the other aforementioned restrictions. (Thus, indirectly, this model is giving preference to states with higher numbers of electoral votes). Note that for ease of implementation by the campaign staff, all decisions for allocation in the model should lead to integer values.

The three aspects of the models can be categorized based on the following questions that they answer:

1. **What do we control?**   The amount invested in advertisements across the nine states, Nevada, Colorado, Iowa, Wisconsin, Ohio, Virginia, North Carolina, Florida, and New Hampshire, which are represented by the nine decision variables, NV, CO, IA, WI OH, VA, NC, FL, and NH.

2. **What do we want to achieve?**   We want to maximize the total number of electoral votes gains. We know the value of each electoral vote in each state (EV), so this amounts to EV*Investments aggregated over the nine states, that is,

   Max (6NV + 9CO + 6IA + 10WI + 18OH + 13VA + 15NC + 29FL + 4NH)

3. **What constrains us?**

   Following are the constraints as given in the problem description:

   a. No more than 1,050 financial units to invest into, i.e., NV + CO + IA + WI + OH + VA + NC + FL + NH <= 1,050.

   b. Invest at least 5% of the total in each state, that is,

$$NV >= 0.05 (NV + CO + IA + WI + OH + VA + NC + FL + NH)$$
$$CO >= 0.05 (NV + CO + IA + WI + OH + VA + NC + FL + NH)$$
$$IA >= 0.05 (NV + CO + IA + WI + OH + VA + NC + FL + NH)$$
$$WI >= 0.05 (NV + CO + IA + WI + OH + VA + NC + FL + NH)$$
$$OH >= 0.05 (NV + CO + IA + WI + OH + VA + NC + FL + NH)$$
$$VA >= 0.05 (NV + CO + IA + WI + OH + VA + NC + FL + NH)$$
$$NC >= 0.05 (NV + CO + IA + WI + OH + VA + NC + FL + NH)$$
$$FL >= 0.05 (NV + CO + IA + WI + OH + VA + NC + FL + NH)$$
$$NH >= 0.05 (NV + CO + IA + WI + OH + VA + NC + FL + NH)$$

We can implement these nine constraints in a variety of ways using Excel.

c. Invest no more than 25% of the total in each state.

   As with (b) we need nine individual constraints again because we do not know how much of the 1,050 we will invest. We must write the constraints in "general" terms.

$$NV <= 0.25 (NV + CO + IA + WI + OH + VA + NC + FL + NH)$$
$$CO <= 0.25 (NV + CO + IA + WI + OH + VA + NC + FL + NH)$$
$$IA <= 0.25 (NV + CO + IA + WI + OH + VA + NC + FL + NH)$$
$$WI <= 0.25 (NV + CO + IA + WI + OH + VA + NC + FL + NH)$$
$$OH <= 0.25 (NV + CO + IA + WI + OH + VA + NC + FL + NH)$$
$$VA <= 0.25 (NV + CO + IA + WI + OH + VA + NC + FL + NH)$$
$$NC <= 0.25 (NV + CO + IA + WI + OH + VA + NC + FL + NH)$$
$$FL <= 0.25 (NV + CO + IA + WI + OH + VA + NC + FL + NH)$$
$$NH <= 0.25 (NV + CO + IA + WI + OH + VA + NC + FL + NH)$$

d. Western states must have investment levels that are at least 60% of the Eastern states.

$$West\ States = NV + CO + IA + WI$$
$$East\ States = OH + VA + NC + FL + NH$$

   So, $(NV + CO + IA + WI) >= 0.60 (OH + VA + NC + FL + NH)$. Again we can implement this constraint in a variety of ways using Excel.

e. Influence at least 9,200 total people, that is,

$$(10NV + 7.5CO + 8IA + 10WI + 7.5OH + 7.5VA + 10\ NC + 8FL + 8\ NH) >= 9,200$$

f. Influence at least as many females as males. This requires transition of influence functions.

   F1 = 6 women influenced, F2 = 3.5 women
   F3 = 3 women influenced
   F1 = 4 men influenced, F2 = 4 men
   F3 = 5 men influenced

So, implementing females > = males, we get:

$$(6NV + 3.5CO + 3IA + 6WI + 3.5OH + 3.5VA + 6NC + 3FL + 3NH) >= (4NV + 4CO + 5IA + 4WI + 4OH + 4VA + 4NC + 5FL + 5NH)$$

As before, we can implement this in Excel in a couple of different ways.

g. At least 46% of all people influenced must be old.

All people influenced were on the left-hand side of the constraint (e). So, old people influenced would be:

$$(4NV + 3.5CO + 4.5IA + 4WI + 3.5OH + 3.5VA + 4NC + 4.5FL + 4.5NH)$$

This would be set >= 0.46* the left-hand side of constraint (e). (10NV + 7.5CO + 8IA + 10WI + 7.5OH + 7.5VA +10NC + 8FL + 8NH), which would give a right-hand side of

$$(0.46NV + 3.45CO + 3.68IA + 4.6WI + 3.45OH + 3.45VA + 4.6NC + 3.68FL + 3.68NH)$$

This is the last constraint other than to force all variables to be integers.

All told in algebraic terms, this integer programing model would have 9 decision variables and 24 constraints (one constraint for integer requirements).

Implementation

One approach would be to implement the model in strict "standard form," or a row-column form, where all constraints are written with decision variables on the left-hand side, a number on the right-hand side. Figure 6.8 shows such an implementation and displays the solved model.

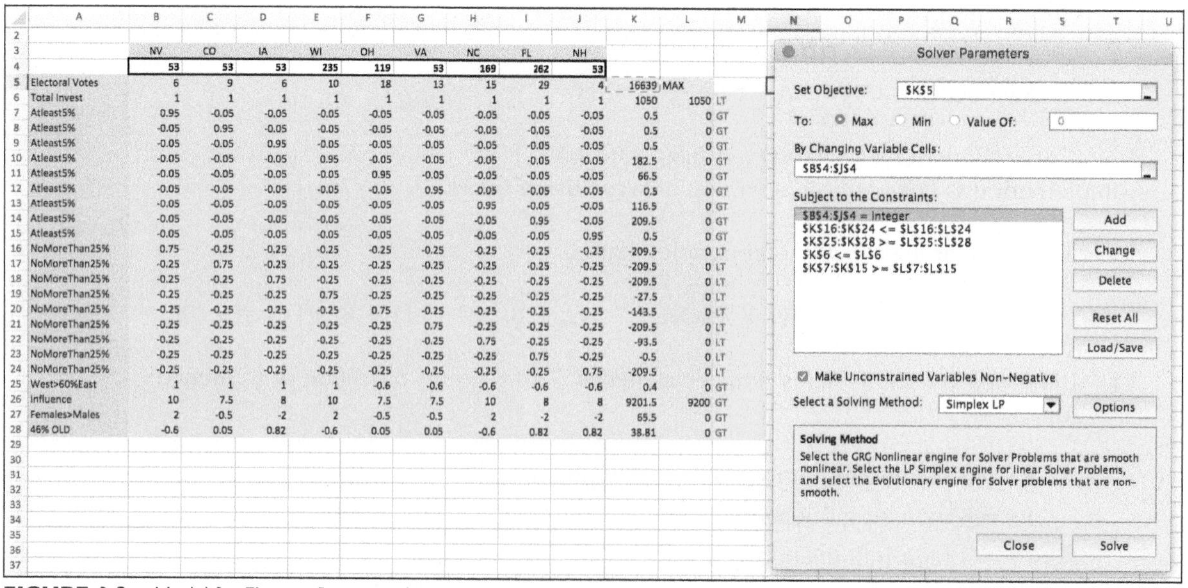

	A	B	C	D	E	F	G	H	I	J	K	L	M
2													
3		NV	CO	IA	WI	OH	VA	NC	FL	NH			
4		53	53	53	235	119	53	169	262	53			
5	Electoral Votes	6	9	6	10	18	13	15	29	4	16639	MAX	
6	Total Invest	1	1	1	1	1	1	1	1	1	1050	1050	LT
7	Atleast5%	0.95	-0.05	-0.05	-0.05	-0.05	-0.05	-0.05	-0.05	-0.05	0.5	0	GT
8	Atleast5%	-0.05	0.95	-0.05	-0.05	-0.05	-0.05	-0.05	-0.05	-0.05	0.5	0	GT
9	Atleast5%	-0.05	-0.05	0.95	-0.05	-0.05	-0.05	-0.05	-0.05	-0.05	0.5	0	GT
10	Atleast5%	-0.05	-0.05	-0.05	0.95	-0.05	-0.05	-0.05	-0.05	-0.05	182.5	0	GT
11	Atleast5%	-0.05	-0.05	-0.05	-0.05	0.95	-0.05	-0.05	-0.05	-0.05	66.5	0	GT
12	Atleast5%	-0.05	-0.05	-0.05	-0.05	-0.05	0.95	-0.05	-0.05	-0.05	0.5	0	GT
13	Atleast5%	-0.05	-0.05	-0.05	-0.05	-0.05	-0.05	0.95	-0.05	-0.05	116.5	0	GT
14	Atleast5%	-0.05	-0.05	-0.05	-0.05	-0.05	-0.05	-0.05	0.95	-0.05	209.5	0	GT
15	Atleast5%	-0.05	-0.05	-0.05	-0.05	-0.05	-0.05	-0.05	-0.05	0.95	0.5	0	GT
16	NoMoreThan25%	0.75	-0.25	-0.25	-0.25	-0.25	-0.25	-0.25	-0.25	-0.25	-209.5	0	LT
17	NoMoreThan25%	-0.25	0.75	-0.25	-0.25	-0.25	-0.25	-0.25	-0.25	-0.25	-209.5	0	LT
18	NoMoreThan25%	-0.25	-0.25	0.75	-0.25	-0.25	-0.25	-0.25	-0.25	-0.25	-209.5	0	LT
19	NoMoreThan25%	-0.25	-0.25	-0.25	0.75	-0.25	-0.25	-0.25	-0.25	-0.25	-27.5	0	LT
20	NoMoreThan25%	-0.25	-0.25	-0.25	-0.25	0.75	-0.25	-0.25	-0.25	-0.25	-143.5	0	LT
21	NoMoreThan25%	-0.25	-0.25	-0.25	-0.25	-0.25	0.75	-0.25	-0.25	-0.25	-209.5	0	LT
22	NoMoreThan25%	-0.25	-0.25	-0.25	-0.25	-0.25	-0.25	0.75	-0.25	-0.25	-93.5	0	LT
23	NoMoreThan25%	-0.25	-0.25	-0.25	-0.25	-0.25	-0.25	-0.25	0.75	-0.25	-0.5	0	LT
24	NoMoreThan25%	-0.25	-0.25	-0.25	-0.25	-0.25	-0.25	-0.25	-0.25	0.75	-209.5	0	LT
25	West>60%East	1	1	1	1	-0.6	-0.6	-0.6	-0.6	-0.6	0.4	0	GT
26	Influence	10	7.5	8	10	7.5	7.5	10	8	8	9201.5	9200	GT
27	Females>Males	2	-0.5	-2	2	-0.5	-0.5	2	-2	-2	65.5	0	GT
28	46% OLD	-0.6	0.05	0.82	-0.6	0.05	0.05	-0.6	0.82	0.82	38.81	0	GT

FIGURE 6.8 Model for Election Resource Allocation—Standard Version.

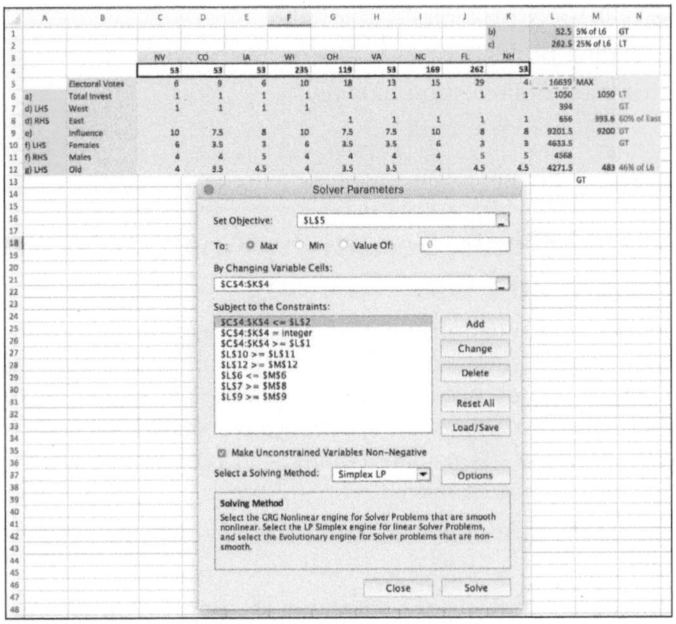

FIGURE 6.9 A Compact Formulation for Election Resource Allocation.

Alternatively, we could use the spreadsheet to calculate different parts of the model in a less rigid manner, as well as uniquely implementing the repetitive constraints (b) and (c), and have a much more concise (but not as transparent) spreadsheet. This is shown in Figure 6.9.

LP models (and their specializations and generalizations) can be also specified directly in a number of other user-friendly modeling systems. Two of the best known are Lindo and Lingo (Lindo Systems, Inc., lindo.com; demos are available). Lindo is an LP and integer programming system. Models are specified in essentially the same way that they are defined algebraically. Based on the success of Lindo, the company developed Lingo, a modeling language that includes the powerful Lindo optimizer and extensions for solving nonlinear problems. Many other modeling languages such as AMPL, AIMMS, MPL, XPRESS, and others are available.

The most common optimization models can be solved by a variety of mathematical programming methods, including the following:

- Assignment (best matching of objects)
- Dynamic programming
- Goal programming
- Investment (maximizing rate of return)
- Linear and integer programming
- Network models for planning and scheduling
- Nonlinear programming
- Replacement (capital budgeting)
- Simple inventory models (e.g., economic order quantity)
- Transportation (minimize cost of shipments)

SECTION 6.6 REVIEW QUESTIONS

1. List and explain the assumptions involved in LP.
2. List and explain the characteristics of LP.
3. Describe an allocation problem.

4. Define the product-mix problem.

5. Define the blending problem.

6. List several common optimization models.

6.7 Multiple Goals, Sensitivity Analysis, What-If Analysis, and Goal Seeking

Many, if not most, decision situations involve juggling between competing goals and alternatives. In addition, there is significant uncertainty about the assumptions and predictions being used in building a prescriptive analytics model. The following paragraphs simply recognize that these are also addressed in prescriptive analytics software and techniques. Coverage of these techniques is usually common in prescriptive analytics or operations research/management science courses.

Multiple Goals

The analysis of management decisions aims at evaluating, to the greatest possible extent, how far each alternative advances managers toward their goals. Unfortunately, managerial problems are seldom evaluated with a single simple goal, such as profit maximization. Today's management systems are much more complex, and one with a single goal is rare. Instead, managers want to attain *simultaneous goals*, some of which may conflict. Different stakeholders have different goals. Therefore, it is often necessary to analyze each alternative in light of its determination of each of several goals (see Koksalan & Zionts, 2001).

For example, consider a profit-making firm. In addition to earning money, the company wants to grow, develop its products and employees, provide job security to its workers, and serve the community. Managers want to satisfy the shareholders and at the same time enjoy high salaries and expense accounts, and employees want to increase their take-home pay and benefits. When a decision is to be made—say, about an investment project—some of these goals complement each other, whereas others conflict. Kearns (2004) described how the analytic hierarchy process (AHP) combined with integer programming, addresses multiple goals in evaluating information technology (IT) investments.

Many quantitative models of decision theory are based on comparing a single measure of effectiveness, generally some form of utility to the decision maker. Therefore, it is usually necessary to transform a multiple-goal problem into a single-measure-of-effectiveness problem before comparing the effects of the solutions. This is a common method for handling multiple goals in an LP model.

Certain difficulties may arise when analyzing multiple goals:

- It is usually difficult to obtain an explicit statement of the organization's goals.
- The decision maker may change the importance assigned to specific goals over time or for different decision scenarios.
- Goals and subgoals are viewed differently at various levels of the organization and within different departments.
- Goals change in response to changes in the organization and its environment.
- The relationship between alternatives and their role in determining goals may be difficult to quantify.
- Complex problems are solved by groups of decision makers, each of whom has a personal agenda.
- Participants assess the importance (priorities) of the various goals differently.

Several methods of handling multiple goals can be used when working with such situations. The most common ones are

- Utility theory
- Goal programming
- Expression of goals as constraints, using LP
- A points system

Sensitivity Analysis

A model builder makes predictions and assumptions regarding input data, many of which deal with the assessment of uncertain futures. When the model is solved, the results depend on these data. **Sensitivity analysis** attempts to assess the impact of a change in the input data or parameters on the proposed solution (i.e., the result variable).

Sensitivity analysis is extremely important in prescriptive analytics because it allows flexibility and adaptation to changing conditions and to the requirements of different decision-making situations, provides a better understanding of the model and the decision-making situation it attempts to describe, and permits the manager to input data to increase the confidence in the model. Sensitivity analysis tests relationships such as the following:

- The impact of changes in external (uncontrollable) variables and parameters on the outcome variable(s)
- The impact of changes in decision variables on the outcome variable(s)
- The effect of uncertainty in estimating external variables
- The effects of different dependent interactions among variables
- The robustness of decisions under changing conditions

Sensitivity analyses are used for:

- Revising models to eliminate too-large sensitivities
- Adding details about sensitive variables or scenarios
- Obtaining better estimates of sensitive external variables
- Altering a real-world system to reduce actual sensitivities
- Accepting and using the sensitive (and hence vulnerable) real world, leading to the continuous and close monitoring of actual results

The two types of sensitivity analyses are automatic and trial and error.

AUTOMATIC SENSITIVITY ANALYSIS   Automatic sensitivity analysis is performed in standard quantitative model implementations such as LP. For example, it reports the range within which a certain input variable or parameter value (e.g., unit cost) can vary without having any significant impact on the proposed solution. Automatic sensitivity analysis is usually limited to one change at a time, and only for certain variables. However, it is powerful because of its ability to establish ranges and limits very fast (and with little or no additional computational effort). Sensitivity analysis is provided by Solver and almost all other software packages such as Lindo. Consider the MBI Corporation example introduced previously. Sensitivity analysis could be used to determine that if the right-hand side of the marketing constraint on CC-8 could be decreased by one unit, then the net profit would increase by $1,333.33. This is valid for the right-hand side decreasing to zero. Significant additional analysis is possible along these lines.

TRIAL-AND-ERROR SENSITIVITY ANALYSIS   The impact of changes in any variable, or in several variables, can be determined through a simple trial-and-error approach. You change some input data and solve the problem again. When the changes are repeated several times, better and better solutions may be discovered. Such experimentation, which is easy to conduct when using appropriate modeling software, such as Excel, has two approaches: what-if analysis and goal seeking.

What-If Analysis

What-if analysis is structured as *What will happen to the solution if an input variable, an assumption, or a parameter value is changed?* Here are some examples:

- What will happen to the total inventory cost if the cost of carrying inventories increases by 10%?
- What will be the market share if the advertising budget increases by 5%?

With the appropriate user interface, it is easy for managers to ask a computer model these types of questions and get immediate answers. Furthermore, they can perform multiple cases and thereby change the percentage, or any other data in the question, as desired. The decision maker does all this directly, without a computer programmer.

Figure 6.10 shows a spreadsheet example of a what-if query for a cash flow problem. When the user changes the cells containing the initial sales (from 100 to 120) and the sales growth rate (from 3% to 4% per quarter), the program immediately recomputes the value of the annual net profit cell (from $127 to $182). At first, initial sales were 100, growing at 3% per quarter, yielding an annual net profit of $127. Changing the initial sales cell to 120 and the sales growth rate to 4% causes the annual net profit to rise to $182. What-if analysis is common in many decision systems. Users are given the opportunity to change their answers to some of the system's questions, and a revised recommendation is found.

Goal Seeking

Goal seeking calculates the values of the inputs necessary to achieve a desired level of an output (goal). It represents a backward solution approach. The following are some examples of goal seeking:

- What annual R&D budget is needed for an annual growth rate of 15% by 2018?
- How many nurses are needed to reduce the average waiting time of a patient in the emergency room to less than 10 minutes?

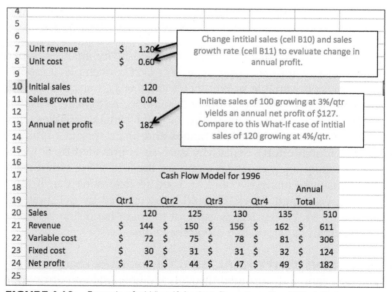

FIGURE 6.10   Example of a What-If Analysis Done in an Excel Worksheet.

5					
6					
7	Investment Problem		Initial Investment:		$ 1,000.00
8	Example of GoalSeeking		Interest Rate:		10%
9					
10	Find the Interest Rate		Annual	NPV	
11	(the Internal Rate of	Year	Returns	Calculations	
12	Return-IRR)	1	$ 120.00	$109.09	
13	that yields an NPV	2	$ 130.00	$118.18	
14	of $0	3	$ 140.00	$127.27	
15		4	$ 150.00	$136.36	
16		5	$ 160.00	$145.45	
17		6	$ 152.00	$138.18	
18		7	$ 144.40	$131.27	
19		8	$ 137.18	$124.71	
20		9	$ 130.32	$118.47	
21		10	$ 123.80	$112.55	
22					
23			The NPV Solutions:	$261.55	
24					

FIGURE 6.11   Goal-Seeking Analysis.

An example of goal seeking is shown in Figure 6.11. For example, in a financial planning model in Excel, the internal rate of return (IRR) is the interest rate that produces a net present value (NPV) of zero. Given a stream of annual returns in Column E, we can compute the NPV of planned investment. By applying goal seeking, we can determine the internal rate of return where the NPV is zero. The goal to be achieved is NPV equal to zero, which determines the internal rate of return of this cash flow, including the investment. We set the NPV cell to the value 0 by changing the interest rate cell. The answer is 38.77059%.

COMPUTING A BREAK-EVEN POINT BY USING GOAL SEEKING   Some modeling software packages can directly compute break-even points, which is an important application of goal seeking. This involves determining the value of the decision variables (e.g., quantity to produce) that generate zero profit.

In many general applications programs, it can be difficult to conduct sensitivity analysis because the prewritten routines usually present only a limited opportunity for asking what-if questions. In a DSS, the what-if and the goal-seeking options must be easy to perform.

SECTION 6.7 REVIEW QUESTIONS

1. List some difficulties that may arise when analyzing multiple goals.
2. List the reasons for performing sensitivity analysis.
3. Explain why a manager might perform what-if analysis.
4. Explain why a manager might use goal seeking.

6.8   Decision Analysis with Decision Tables and Decision Trees

Decision situations that involve a finite and usually not too large number of alternatives are modeled through an approach called **decision analysis** (see Arsham, 2006a,b; Decision Analysis Society, decision-analysis.society.informs.org). Using this approach, the alternatives are listed in a table or a graph, with their forecasted contributions to the goal(s) and the probability of obtaining the contribution. These can be evaluated to select the best alternative.

Single-goal situations can be modeled with *decision tables* or *decision trees*. Multiple goals (criteria) can be modeled with several other techniques, described later in this chapter.

Decision Tables

Decision tables conveniently organize information and knowledge in a systematic, tabular manner to prepare it for analysis. For example, say that an investment company is considering investing in one of three alternatives: bonds, stocks, or certificates of deposit (CDs). The company is interested in one goal: maximizing the yield on the investment after 1 year. If it were interested in other goals, such as safety or liquidity, the problem would be classified as one of *multicriteria decision analysis* (see Koksalan & Zionts, 2001).

The yield depends on the state of the economy sometime in the future (often called the *state of nature*), which can be in solid growth, stagnation, or inflation. Experts estimated the following annual yields:

- If there is solid growth in the economy, bonds will yield 12%, stocks 15%, and time deposits 6.5%.
- If stagnation prevails, bonds will yield 6%, stocks 3%, and time deposits 6.5%.
- If inflation prevails, bonds will yield 3%, stocks will bring a loss of 2%, and time deposits will yield 6.5%.

The problem is to select the one best investment alternative. These are assumed to be discrete alternatives. Combinations such as investing 50% in bonds and 50% in stocks must be treated as new alternatives.

The investment decision-making problem can be viewed as a *two-person game* (see Kelly, 2002). The investor makes a choice (i.e., a move), and then a state of nature occurs (i.e., makes a move). Table 6.3 shows the payoff of a mathematical model. The table includes *decision variables* (the alternatives), *uncontrollable variables* (the states of the economy; e.g., the environment), and *result variables* (the projected yield; e.g., outcomes). All the models in this section are structured in a spreadsheet framework.

If this were a decision-making problem under certainty, we would know what the economy would be and could easily choose the best investment. But that is not the case, so we must consider the two situations of uncertainty and risk. For uncertainty, we do not know the probabilities of each state of nature. For risk, we assume that we know the probabilities with which each state of nature will occur.

TREATING UNCERTAINTY Several methods are available for handling uncertainty. For example, the *optimistic approach* assumes that the best possible outcome of each alternative will occur and then selects the best of the best (i.e., stocks). The *pessimistic approach*

TABLE 6.3 Investment Problem Decision Table Model			
	State of Nature (Uncontrollable Variables)		
Alternative	Solid Growth (%)	Stagnation (%)	Inflation (%)
Bonds	12.0	6.0	3.0
Stocks	15.0	3.0	−2.0
CDs	6.5	6.5	6.5

assumes that the worst possible outcome for each alternative will occur and selects the best of these (i.e., CDs). Another approach simply assumes that all states of nature are equally possible (see Clemen & Reilly, 2000; Goodwin & Wright, 2000; Kontoghiorghes, Rustem, & Siokos, 2002). Every approach for handling uncertainty has serious problems. Whenever possible, the analyst should attempt to gather enough information so that the problem can be treated under assumed certainty or risk.

TREATING RISK   The most common method for solving this risk analysis problem is to select the alternative with the greatest expected value. Assume that experts estimate the chance of solid growth at 50%, the chance of stagnation at 30%, and the chance of inflation at 20%. The decision table is then rewritten with the known probabilities (see Table 6.3). An expected value is computed by multiplying the results (i.e., outcomes) by their respective probabilities and adding them. For example, investing in bonds yields an expected return of 12(0.5) + 6(0.3) + 3(0.2) = 8.4%.

This approach can sometimes be a dangerous strategy because the utility of each potential outcome may be different from the value. Even if there is an infinitesimal chance of a catastrophic loss, the expected value may seem reasonable, but the investor may not be willing to cover the loss. For example, suppose a financial advisor presents you with an "almost sure" investment of $1,000 that can double your money in one day, and then the advisor says, "Well, there is a 0.9999 probability that you will double your money, but unfortunately there is a 0.0001 probability that you will be liable for a $500,000 out-of-pocket loss." The expected value of this investment is as follows:

$$0.9999(\$2,000 - \$1,000) + .0001(-\$500,000 - \$1,000) = \$999.90 - \$50.10$$
$$= \$949.80$$

The potential loss could be catastrophic for any investor who is not a billionaire. Depending on the investor's ability to cover the loss, an investment has different expected utilities. Remember that the investor makes the decision only *once*.

Decision Trees

An alternative representation of the decision table is a decision tree (for examples, see Mind Tools Ltd., mindtools.com). A **decision tree** shows the relationships of the problem graphically and can handle complex situations in a compact form. However, a decision tree can be cumbersome if there are many alternatives or states of nature. TreeAge Pro (TreeAge Software Inc., treeage.com) and PrecisionTree (Palisade Corp., palisade.com) include powerful, intuitive, and sophisticated decision tree analysis systems. These vendors also provide excellent examples of decision trees used in practice. Note that the phrase *decision tree* has been used to describe two different types of models and algorithms. In the current context, decision trees refer to scenario analysis. On the other hand, some classification algorithms in predictive analysis (see Chapters 4 and 5) are also called decision tree algorithms.

TABLE 6.4 Multiple Goals			
Alternative	Yield (%)	Safety	Liquidity
Bonds	8.4	High	High
Stocks	8.0	Low	High
CDs	6.5	Very high	High

A simplified investment case of **multiple goals** (a decision situation in which alternatives are evaluated with several, sometimes conflicting, goals) is shown in Table 6.4. The three goals (criteria) are yield, safety, and liquidity. This situation is under assumed certainty; that is, only one possible consequence is projected for each alternative; the more complex cases of risk or uncertainty could be considered. Some of the results are qualitative (e.g., low, high) rather than numeric.

See Clemen and Reilly (2000), Goodwin and Wright (2000), and Decision Analysis Society (informs.org/Community/DAS) for more on decision analysis. Although doing so is quite complex, it is possible to apply mathematical programming directly to decision-making situations under risk. We discuss several other methods of treating risk later in the book. These include simulation, certainty factors, and fuzzy logic.

SECTION 6.8 REVIEW QUESTIONS

1. What is a decision table?
2. What is a decision tree?
3. How can a decision tree be used in decision making?
4. Describe what it means to have multiple goals.

6.9 Introduction to Simulation

In this section and the next we introduce a category of techniques that are used for supporting decision making. Very broadly, these methods fall under the umbrella of simulation. **Simulation** is the appearance of reality. In decision systems, simulation is a technique for conducting experiments (e.g., what-if analyses) with a computer on a model of a management system. Strictly speaking, simulation is a *descriptive* rather than a *prescriptive* method. There is no automatic search for an optimal solution. Instead, a simulation model describes or predicts the characteristics of a given system under different conditions. When the values of the characteristics are computed, the best of several alternatives can be selected. The simulation process usually repeats an experiment many times to obtain an estimate (and a variance) of the overall effect of certain actions. For most situations, a computer simulation is appropriate, but there are some well-known manual simulations (e.g., a city police department simulated its patrol car scheduling with a carnival game wheel).

Typically, real decision-making situations involve some randomness. Because many decision situations deal with semistructured or unstructured situations, reality is complex, which may not be easily represented by optimization or other models but can often be handled by simulation. Simulation is one of the most commonly used decision support methods. See Application Case 6.6 for an example. Application Case 6.7 illustrates the value of simulation in a setting where sufficient time is not available to perform clinical trials.

Major Characteristics of Simulation

Simulation typically involves building a model of reality to the extent practical. Simulation models may suffer from fewer assumptions about the decision situation as compared to other prescriptive analytic models. In addition, simulation is a technique for *conducting experiments*. Therefore, it involves testing specific values of the decision or uncontrollable variables in the model and observing the impact on the output variables.

Finally, simulation is normally used only when a problem is too complex to be treated using numerical optimization techniques. Complexity in this situation means

Application Case 6.7

Simulating Effects of Hepatitis B Interventions

Although the United States has made significant investments in healthcare, some problems seem to defy solution. For example, a sizable proportion of the Asian population in the United States is more prone than others to the Hepatitis B viral disease. In addition to the social problems associated with the disease (like isolation), one out of every four chronically infected individuals stands the risk of suffering from liver cancer or cirrhosis if the disease is not treated effectively. Managing this disease could be very costly. There are a number of control measures, including screening, vaccination, and treatment procedures. The government is reluctant to spend money on any method of control if it is not cost effective and there is no proof of increased health for people afflicted with the disease. Even though not all the control measures are optimal for all situations, the best method or combination of methods for combating the disease are not yet known.

Methodology/Solution

A multidisciplinary team consisting of those with medical, management science, and engineering backgrounds developed a mathematical model using operations research (OR) methods that determined the right combination of control measures to be used to combat Hepatitis B in the Asian and Pacific Island populations. Normally, clinical trials are used in the medical field to determine the best course of action in disease treatment and prevention. Complicating this situation is the unusually long period of time it takes Hepatitis B to progress. Because of the high cost that would accompany clinical trials in this situation, OR models and methods were used. A combination of Markov and decision models offered a more cost-effective way for determining what combination of control measures to use at any point in time. The decision model helps measure the economic and health benefits of the various possibilities of screening, treatment, and vaccination. The Markov model was used to model the progression of Hepatitis B. The new model was created based on past literature and expertise from one of the researchers and draws from actual current infection and treatment data. Policy makers built the new model using Microsoft Excel because it is user friendly.

Results/Benefits

The resultant model was analyzed vis-à-vis existing control programs in both the United States and China. In the United States, four strategies were developed and compared to the existing strategy. The four strategies are

a. All individuals are vaccinated.
b. Individuals are first screened to determine whether they have a chronic infection. If yes, then they are treated.
c. Individuals are first screened to determine whether they have a chronic infection. If they have the infection, they are treated. In addition, close associates of those infected are also screened and vaccinated, if necessary.
d. Individuals are first screened to determine whether they have a chronic infection or need a vaccination. If they are infected, they are treated. If they need a vaccination, they are vaccinated.

Results of the simulations indicated that performing blood tests to determine chronic infection and vaccinating associates of infected people are cost effective.

In China, the model helped design a catch-up vaccination policy for children and adolescents. This catch-up policy was compared with current coverage levels of Hepatitis B vaccination. It was concluded that when individuals under the age of 19 years are vaccinated, the health outcomes are improved in the long run. In fact, this policy was more financially cost effective than the current disease control policy in place at the time of the evaluation.

Questions for Discussion

1. Explain the advantage of OR methods such as simulation over clinical trial methods in determining the best control measure for Hepatitis B.

(Continued)

Application Case 6.7 (Continued)

2. In what ways do the decision and Markov models provide cost-effective ways of combating the disease?

3. Discuss how multidisciplinary background is an asset in finding a solution for the problem described in the case.

4. Besides healthcare, in what other domain could such a modeling approach help reduce cost?

Source: Adapted from Hutton, D. W., Brandeau, M. L., & So, S. K. (2011). Doing good with good OR: Supporting cost-effective Hepatitis B interventions. *Interfaces, 41*(3), 289–300.

either that the problem cannot be formulated for optimization (e.g., because the assumptions do not hold), that the formulation is too large, that there are too many interactions among the variables, or that the problem is stochastic in nature (i.e., exhibits risk or uncertainty).

Advantages of Simulation

Simulation is used in decision support modeling for the following reasons:

- The theory is fairly straightforward.
- A great amount of *time compression* can be attained, quickly giving a manager some feel as to the long-term (1- to 10-year) effects of many policies.
- Simulation is descriptive rather than normative. This allows the manager to pose what-if questions. Managers can use a trial-and-error approach to problem solving and can do so faster, at less expense, more accurately, and with less risk.
- A manager can experiment to determine which decision variables and which parts of the environment are really important, and with different alternatives.
- An accurate simulation model requires an intimate knowledge of the problem, thus forcing the model builder to constantly interact with the manager. This is desirable for DSS development because the developer and manager both gain a better understanding of the problem and the potential decisions available.
- The model is built from the manager's perspective.
- The simulation model is built for one particular problem and typically cannot solve any other problem. Thus, no generalized understanding is required of the manager; every component in the model corresponds to part of the real system.
- Simulation can handle an extremely wide variety of problem types, such as inventory and staffing, as well as higher-level managerial functions, such as long-range planning.
- Simulation generally can include the real complexities of problems; simplifications are not necessary. For example, simulation can use real probability distributions rather than approximate theoretical distributions.
- Simulation automatically produces many important performance measures.
- Simulation is often the only DSS modeling method that can readily handle relatively unstructured problems.
- Some relatively easy-to-use simulation packages (e.g., Monte Carlo simulation) are available. These include add-in spreadsheet packages (e.g., @RISK), influence diagram software, Java-based (and other Web development) packages, and the visual interactive simulation systems to be discussed shortly.

Disadvantages of Simulation

The primary disadvantages of simulation are as follows:

- An optimal solution cannot be guaranteed, but relatively good ones are generally found.
- Simulation model construction can be a slow and costly process, although newer modeling systems are easier to use than ever.
- Solutions and inferences from a simulation study are usually not transferable to other problems because the model incorporates unique problem factors.
- Simulation is sometimes so easy to explain to managers that analytic methods are often overlooked.
- Simulation software sometimes requires special skills because of the complexity of the formal solution method.

The Methodology of Simulation

Simulation involves setting up a model of a real system and conducting repetitive experiments on it. The methodology consists of the following steps, as shown in Figure 6.12:

1. ***Define the problem.*** We examine and classify the real-world problem, specifying why a simulation approach is appropriate. The system's boundaries, environment, and other such aspects of problem clarification are handled here.
2. ***Construct the simulation model.*** This step involves determination of the variables and their relationships, as well as data gathering. Often the process is described by using a flowchart, and then a computer program is written.
3. ***Test and validate the model.*** The simulation model must properly represent the system being studied. Testing and validation ensure this.
4. ***Design the experiment.*** When the model has been proven valid, an experiment is designed. Determining how long to run the simulation is part of this step. There are two important and conflicting objectives: accuracy and cost. It is also prudent to identify typical (e.g., mean and median cases for random variables), best-case (e.g., low-cost, high-revenue), and worst-case (e.g., high-cost, low-revenue) scenarios. These help establish the ranges of the decision variables and environment in which to work and also assist in debugging the simulation model.
5. ***Conduct the experiment.*** Conducting the experiment involves issues ranging from random-number generation to result presentation.

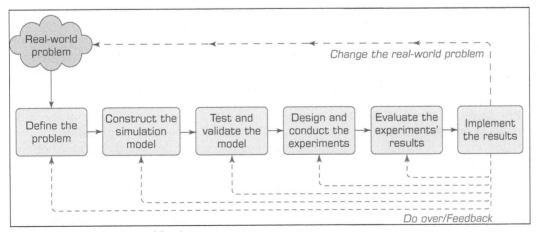

FIGURE 6.12 The Process of Simulation.

6. ***Evaluate the results.*** The results must be interpreted. In addition to standard statistical tools, sensitivity analyses can also be used.

7. ***Implement the results.*** The implementation of simulation results involves the same issues as any other implementation. However, the chances of success are better because the manager is usually more involved with the simulation process than with other models. Higher levels of managerial involvement generally lead to higher levels of implementation success.

Banks and Gibson (2009) presented some useful advice about simulation practices. For example, they list the following seven issues as the common mistakes committed by simulation modelers. The list, though not exhaustive, provides general directions for professionals working on simulation projects.

- Focusing more on the model than on the problem
- Providing point estimates
- Not knowing when to stop
- Reporting what the client wants to hear rather than what the model results say
- Lack of understanding of statistics
- Confusing cause and effect
- Failure to replicate reality

In a follow-up article they provide additional guidelines. You should consult this article: analytics-magazine.org/spring-2009/205-software-solutions-the-abcs-of-simulation-practice.html.

Simulation Types

As we have seen, simulation and modeling are used when pilot studies and experimenting with real systems are expensive or sometimes impossible. Simulation models allow us to investigate various interesting scenarios before making any investment. In fact, in simulations, the real-world operations are mapped into the simulation model. The model consists of relationships and, consequently, equations that all together present the real-world operations. The results of a simulation model, then, depend on the set of parameters given to the model as inputs.

There are various simulation paradigms such as Monte Carlo simulation, discrete event, agent based, or system dynamics. One of the factors that determine the type of simulation technique is the level of abstraction in the problem. Discrete events and agent-based models are usually used for middle or low levels of abstraction. They usually consider individual elements such as people, parts, and products in the simulation models, whereas systems dynamics is more appropriate for aggregate analysis.

In the following section, we introduce the major types of simulation: probabilistic simulation, time-dependent and time-independent simulation, and visual simulation. There are many other simulation techniques such as system dynamics modeling, and agent-based modeling. As has been noted before, the goal here is to make you aware of the potential of some of these techniques as opposed to make you an expert in using them.

PROBABILISTIC SIMULATION In probabilistic simulation, one or more of the independent variables (e.g., the demand in an inventory problem) are probabilistic. They follow certain probability distributions, which can be either discrete distributions or continuous distributions:

- *Discrete distributions* involve a situation with a limited number of events (or variables) that can take on only a finite number of values.
- *Continuous distributions* are situations with unlimited numbers of possible events that follow density functions, such as the normal distribution.

TABLE 6.5 Discrete versus Continuous Probability Distributions		
Daily Demand	Discrete Probability	Continuous Probability
5	0.10	Daily demand is normally distributed with a mean of 7 and a standard deviation of 1.2
6	0.15	
7	0.30	
8	0.25	
9	0.20	

The two types of distributions are shown in Table 6.5.

TIME-DEPENDENT VERSUS TIME-INDEPENDENT SIMULATION   *Time-independent* refers to a situation in which it is not important to know exactly when the event occurred. For example, we may know that the demand for a certain product is three units per day, but we do not care *when* during the day the item is demanded. In some situations, time may not be a factor in the simulation at all, such as in steady-state plant control design. However, in waiting-line problems applicable to e-commerce, it is important to know the precise time of arrival (to know whether the customer will have to wait). This is a *time-dependent* situation.

Monte Carlo Simulation

In most business decision problems, we usually employ one of the following two types of probabilistic simulations. The most common simulation method for business decision problems is the **Monte Carlo simulation**. This method usually begins with building a model of the decision problem without having to consider the uncertainty of any variables. Then we recognize that certain parameters or variables are uncertain or follow an assumed or estimated probability distribution. This estimation is based on analysis of past data. Then we begin running sampling experiments. Running sampling experiments consists of generating random values of uncertain parameters and then computing values of the variables that are impacted by such parameters or variables. These sampling experiments essentially amount to solving the same model hundreds or thousands of times. We can then analyze the behavior of these dependent or performance variables by examining their statistical distributions. This method has been used in simulations of physical as well as business systems. A good public tutorial on the Monte Carlo simulation method is available on Palisade.com (http://www.palisade.com/risk/monte_carlo_simulation.asp). Palisade markets a tool called @RISK, a popular spreadsheet-based Monte Carlo simulation software. Another popular software in this category is Crystal Ball, now marketed by Oracle as Oracle Crystal Ball. Of course, it is also possible to build and run Monte Carlo experiments within an Excel spreadsheet without using any add-on software such as the two just mentioned. But these tools make it more convenient to run such experiments in Excel-based models. Monte Carlo simulation models have been used in many commercial applications. Examples include Procter & Gamble using these models to determine hedging foreign-exchange risks; Lilly using the model for deciding optimal plant capacity; Abu Dhabi Water and Electricity Company using @Risk for forecasting water demand in Abu Dhabi; and literally thousands of other actual case studies. Each of the simulation software companies' Web sites include many such success stories.

Discrete Event Simulation

Discrete event simulation refers to building a model of a system where the interaction between different entities is studied. The simplest example of this is a shop consisting of a server and customers. By modeling the customers arriving at various rates and the server serving at various rates, we can estimate the average performance of the system, waiting time, the number of waiting customers, and so on. Such systems are viewed as collections of customers, queues, and servers. There are thousands of documented applications of discrete event simulation models in engineering, business, and so on. Tools for building discrete event simulation models have been around for a long time, but these have evolved to take advantage of developments in graphical capabilities for building and understanding the results of such simulation models. We will discuss this modeling method further in the next section. Application Case 6.8 gives an example of the use of such simulation in analyzing complexities of a supply chain that uses a visual simulation to be described in the next section.

Application Case 6.8

Cosan Improves Its Renewable Energy Supply Chain Using Simulation

Introduction

Cosan is a Brazil-based conglomerate that operates globally. One of its major activities is to grow and process sugar cane. Besides being a major source of sugar, sugar cane is now a major source of ethanol, a main ingredient in renewable energy. Because of the growing demand for renewable energy, ethanol production has become such a major activity for Cosan that it now operates two refineries in addition to 18 production plants, and of course, millions of hectares of sugar cane farms. According to recent data, it processed over 44 million tons of sugar cane, produced over 1.3 billion liters of ethanol, and produced 3.3 million tons of sugar. As one might imagine, operations of this scale lead to complex supply chains. So the logistics team was asked to make recommendations to the senior management to:

- Determine the optimum number of vehicles required in a fleet used to transport sugar cane to processing mills to preserve capital.
- Propose how to increase the actual capacity of sugar cane received at the sugar mills.
- Identify the production bottleneck problems to solve to improve the flow of sugar cane.

Methodology/Solution

The logistics team worked with Simio software and built a complex simulation model of the Cosan supply chain as it pertains to these issues. According to a Simio brief, "Over the course of three months, newly hired engineers collected data in the field and received hands-on training and modeling assistance from Paragon Consulting of San Palo."

To model agricultural operations to analyze the sugar cane's postharvest journey to production mills, the model objectives included details of the fleet of road transport sugar cane crop to Unity Costa Pinto, the actual capacity of reception of cane sugar mills, bottlenecks and points for improvement in the flow of CCT (cut-load-haul) of cane sugar, and so on.

The model parameters are as follows:

> Input Variables: 32
> Output Variables: 39
> Auxiliary Variables: 92
> Variable Entities: 8
> Input Tables: 19
> Simulated Days: 240 (1st season)
> Number of Entities: 12 (10 harvester compositional types for transport of sugar cane)

Results/Benefits

Analyses produced by these Simio models provided a good view of the risk of operation over the 240-day period due to various uncertainties. By analyzing the various bottlenecks and ways to mitigate those scenarios, the company was able to make better decisions and save over $500,000 from this modeling effort alone.

SECTION 6.9 REVIEW QUESTIONS

1. List the characteristics of simulation.
2. List the advantages and disadvantages of simulation.
3. List and describe the steps in the methodology of simulation.
4. List and describe the types of simulation.

6.10 Visual Interactive Simulation

We next examine methods that show a decision maker a representation of the decision-making situation in action as it runs through scenarios of the various alternatives. These powerful methods overcome some of the inadequacies of conventional methods and help build trust in the solution attained because they can be visualized directly.

Conventional Simulation Inadequacies

Simulation is a well-established, useful, descriptive, mathematics-based method for gaining insight into complex decision-making situations. However, simulation does not usually allow decision makers to see how a solution to a complex problem evolves over (compressed) time, nor can decision makers interact with the simulation (which would be useful for training purposes and teaching). Simulation generally reports statistical results at the end of a set of experiments. Decision makers are thus not an integral part of simulation development and experimentation, and their experience and judgment cannot be used directly. If the simulation results do not match the intuition or judgment of the decision maker, a *confidence gap* in the results can occur.

Visual Interactive Simulation

Visual interactive simulation (**VIS**), also known as **visual interactive modeling** (**VIM**) and *visual interactive problem solving*, is a simulation method that lets decision makers see what the model is doing and how it interacts with the decisions made, as they are made. This technique has been used with great success in operations analysis in many fields such as supply chain and healthcare. The user can employ his or her knowledge to determine and try different decision strategies while interacting with the model. Enhanced learning, about both the problem and the impact of the alternatives tested, can and does occur. Decision makers also contribute to model validation. Decision makers who use VIS generally support and trust their results.

VIS uses animated computer graphic displays to present the impact of different managerial decisions. It differs from regular graphics in that the user can adjust the decision-making process and see results of the intervention. A visual model is a graphic used as an integral part of decision making or problem solving, not just as a communication device. Some people respond better than others to graphical displays, and this type of interaction can help managers learn about the decision-making situation.

VIS can represent static or dynamic systems. Static models display a visual image of the result of one decision alternative at a time. Dynamic models display systems that evolve over time, and the evolution is represented by animation. The latest visual simulation technology has been coupled with the concept of virtual reality, where an artificial world is created for a number of purposes, from training to entertainment to viewing data in an artificial landscape. For example, the U.S. military uses VIS systems so that ground troops can gain familiarity with terrain or a city to very quickly orient themselves. Pilots also use VIS to gain familiarity with targets by simulating attack runs. The VIS software can also include GIS coordinates.

Visual Interactive Models and DSS

VIM in DSS has been used in several operations management decisions. The method consists of priming (like priming a water pump) a visual interactive model of a plant (or company) with its current status. The model then runs rapidly on a computer, allowing managers to observe how a plant is likely to operate in the future.

Waiting-line management (queuing) is a good example of VIM. Such a DSS usually computes several measures of performance for the various decision alternatives (e.g., waiting time in the system). Complex waiting-line problems require simulation. VIM can display the size of the waiting line as it changes during the simulation runs and can also graphically present the answers to what-if questions regarding changes in input variables. Application Case 6.9 gives an example of a visual simulation that was used to explore the applications of radio-frequency identification (RFID) technology in developing new scheduling rules in a manufacturing setting.

The VIM approach can also be used in conjunction with artificial intelligence. Integration of the two techniques adds several capabilities that range from the ability to build systems graphically to learning about the dynamics of the system. These systems, especially those developed for the military and the video-game industry, have "thinking" characters who can behave with a relatively high level of intelligence in their interactions with users.

Simulation Software

Hundreds of simulation packages are available for a variety of decision-making situations. Many run as Web-based systems. *ORMS Today* publishes a periodic review of simulation software. One recent review (current as of October 2015) is located at orms-today.org/surveys/Simulation/Simulation.html (accessed July 2016). PC software packages include Analytica (Lumina Decision Systems, lumina.com) and the Excel add-ins Crystal Ball (now sold by Oracle as Oracle Crystal Ball, oracle.com) and @RISK (Palisade Corp., palisade.com). A major commercial software for discrete event simulation has been Arena (sold

Application Case 6.9

Improving Job-Shop Scheduling Decisions through RFID: A Simulation-Based Assessment

A manufacturing services provider of complex optical and electromechanical components seeks to gain efficiency in its job-shop scheduling decision because the current shop-floor operations suffer from a few issues:

- There is no system to record when the work-in-process (WIP) items actually arrive at or leave operating workstations and how long those WIPs actually stay at each workstation.
- The current system cannot monitor or keep track of the movement of each WIP in the production line in real time.

As a result, the company is facing two main issues at this production line: high backlogs and high costs of overtime to meet the demand. In addition, the upstream cannot respond to unexpected incidents such as changes in demand or material shortages quickly enough and revise schedules in a cost-effective manner. The company is considering implementing RFID on a production line. However, the company does not know if going to this major expense of adding RFID chips on production boxes, installing RFID readers throughout the production line, and of course, the systems to process this information will result in any real gains. So one question is to explore any new production scheduling changes that may result by investing in RFID infrastructure.

Methodology

Because exploring the introduction of any new system in the physical production system can be extremely expensive or even disruptive, a discrete event simulation model was developed to examine how tracking and traceability through RFID can facilitate job-shop production scheduling activities. A visibility-based scheduling (VBS) rule that utilizes the real-time traceability systems to track those WIPs, parts and components, and raw materials in shop-floor operations was proposed. A simulation approach was applied to examine the benefit of the VBS rule against the classical scheduling rules: the first-in-first-out and earliest due date dispatching rules. The simulation model was developed using Simio. Simio is a 3-D simulation modeling software package that employs an object-oriented approach to modeling and has recently been used in many areas such as factories, supply chains, healthcare, airports, and service systems.

Figure 6.13 presents a screenshot of the Simio interface panel of this production line. The

FIGURE 6.13 Simio Interface View of the Simulation System.

(Continued)

Application Case 6.9 (Continued)

parameter estimates used for the initial state in the simulation model include weekly demand and forecast, process flow, number of workstations, number of shop-floor operators, and operating time at each workstation. In addition, parameters of some of the input data such as RFID tagging time, information retrieving time, or system updating time are estimated from a pilot study and from the subject matter experts. Figure 6.14 presents the process view

of the simulation model where specific simulation commands are implemented and coded. Figures 6.15 and 6.16 present the standard report view and pivot grid report of the simulation model. The standard report and pivot grid format provide a very quick method to find specific statistical results such as average, percent, total, maximum, or minimum values of variables assigned and captured as an output of the simulation model.

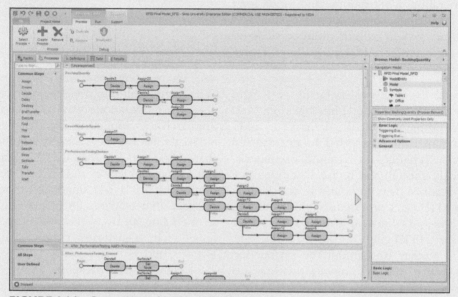

FIGURE 6.14 Process View of the Simulation Model.

FIGURE 6.15 Standard Report View.

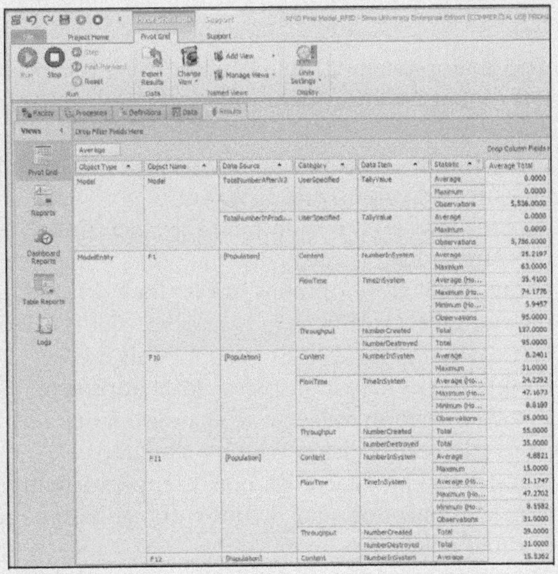

FIGURE 6.16 Pivot Grid Report from a Simio Run.

Results

The results of the simulation suggest that an RFID-based scheduling rule generates better performance compared to traditional scheduling rules with regard to processing time, production time, resource utilization, backlogs, and productivity. The company can take these productivity gains and perform cost/benefit analyses in making the final investment decisions.

QUESTIONS FOR DISCUSSION

1. In situations such as what this case depicts, what other approaches can one take to analyze investment decisions?
2. How would one save time if an RFID chip can tell the exact location of a product in process?
3. Research to learn about the applications of RFID sensors in other settings. Which one do you find most interesting?

Source: Based on Chongwatpol, J., & Sharda, R. (2013). RFID-enabled track and traceability in job-shop scheduling environment. *European Journal of Operational Research, 227*(3), 453–463, http://dx.doi.org/10.1016/j.ejor.2013.01.009.

by Rockwell Intl., arenasimulation.com). Original developers of Arena have now developed Simio (simio.com), a user-friendly VIS software. Another popular discrete event VIS software is ExtendSim (extendsim.com). SAS has a graphical analytics software package called JMP that also includes a simulation component in it.

For information about simulation software, see the Society for Modeling and Simulation International (scs.org) and the annual software surveys at *ORMS Today* (orms-today.com).

SECTION 6.10 REVIEW QUESTIONS

1. Define *visual simulation* and compare it to conventional simulation.
2. Describe the features of VIS (i.e., VIM) that make it attractive for decision makers.
3. How can VIS be used in operations management?
4. How is an animated film like a VIS application?

Chapter Highlights

- Models play a major role in DSS because they are used to describe real decision-making situations. There are several types of models.
- Models can be static (i.e., a single snapshot of a situation) or dynamic (i.e., multiperiod).
- Analysis is conducted under assumed certainty (which is most desirable), risk, or uncertainty (which is least desirable).
- Influence diagrams graphically show the inter-relationships of a model. They can be used to enhance the use of spreadsheet technology.
- Spreadsheets have many capabilities, including what-if analysis, goal seeking, programming, database management, optimization, and simulation.
- Decision tables and decision trees can model and solve simple decision-making problems.
- Mathematical programming is an important optimization method.
- LP is the most common mathematical programming method. It attempts to find an optimal allocation of limited resources under organizational constraints.

- The major parts of an LP model are the objective function, the decision variables, and the constraints.
- Multicriteria decision-making problems are difficult but not impossible to solve.
- What-if and goal seeking are the two most common methods of sensitivity analysis.
- Many DSS development tools include built-in quantitative models (e.g., financial, statistical) or can easily interface with such models.
- Simulation is a widely used DSS approach that involves experimentation with a model that represents the real decision-making situation.
- Simulation can deal with more complex situations than optimization, but it does not guarantee an optimal solution.
- There are many different simulation methods. Some that are important for decision making include Monte Carlo simulation and discrete event simulation.
- VIS/VIM allows a decision maker to interact directly with a model and shows results in an easily understood manner.

Key Terms

certainty
decision analysis
decision table
decision tree
decision variable
discrete event simulation
dynamic models
environmental scanning and analysis
forecasting

goal seeking
influence diagram
intermediate result variable
linear programming (LP)
mathematical programming
Monte Carlo simulation
multidimensional analysis (modeling)

multiple goals
optimal solution
parameter
quantitative model
result (outcome) variable
risk
risk analysis
sensitivity analysis
simulation
static models

uncertainty
uncontrollable variable
visual interactive modeling (VIM)
visual interactive simulation (VIS)
what-if analysis

Questions for Discussion

1. How does prescriptive analytics relate to descriptive and predictive analytics?
2. Explain the differences between static and dynamic models. How can one evolve into the other?
3. What is the difference between an optimistic approach and a pessimistic approach to decision making under assumed uncertainty?
4. Explain why solving problems under uncertainty sometimes involves assuming that the problem is to be solved under conditions of risk.
5. Excel is probably the most popular spreadsheet software for PCs. Why? What can we do with this package that makes it so attractive for modeling efforts?
6. Explain how decision trees work. How can a complex problem be solved by using a decision tree?
7. Explain how LP can solve allocation problems.
8. What are the advantages of using a spreadsheet package to create and solve LP models? What are the disadvantages?
9. What are the advantages of using an LP package to create and solve LP models? What are the disadvantages?
10. What is the difference between decision analysis with a single goal and decision analysis with multiple goals (i.e., criteria)? Explain the difficulties that may arise when analyzing multiple goals.
11. Explain how multiple goals can arise in practice.
12. Compare and contrast what-if analysis and goal seeking.
13. Describe the general process of simulation.
14. List some of the major advantages of simulation over optimization and vice versa.
15. Many computer games can be considered visual simulation. Explain why.
16. Explain why VIS is particularly helpful in implementing recommendations derived by computers.

Exercises

Teradata University Network (TUN) and Other Hands-on Exercises

1. Explore teradatauniversitynetwork.com, and determine how models are used in the BI cases and papers.
2. Create the spreadsheet models shown in Figures 6.3 and 6.4.
   a. What is the effect of a change in the interest rate from 8% to 10% in the spreadsheet model shown in Figure 6.3?
   b. For the original model in Figure 6.3, what interest rate is required to decrease the monthly payments by 20%? What change in the loan amount would have the same effect?
   c. In the spreadsheet shown in Figure 6.4, what is the effect of a prepayment of $200 per month? What prepayment would be necessary to pay off the loan in 25 years instead of 30 years?
3. Solve the MBI product-mix problem described in this chapter, using either Excel's Solver or a student version of an LP solver, such as Lindo. Lindo is available from Lindo Systems, Inc., at lindo.com; others are also available—search the Web. Examine the solution (output) reports for the answers and sensitivity report. Did you get the same results as reported in this chapter? Try the sensitivity analysis outlined in the chapter; that is, lower the right-hand side of the CC-8 marketing constraint by one unit, from 200 to 199. What happens to the solution when you solve this modified problem? Eliminate the CC-8 lower-bound constraint entirely (this can be done easily by either deleting it in Solver or setting the lower limit to zero) and re-solve the problem. What happens? Using the original formulation, try modifying the objective function coefficients and see what happens.
4. Investigate via a Web search how models and their solutions are used by the U.S. Department of Homeland Security in the "war against terrorism." Also investigate how other governments or government agencies are using models in their missions.
5. This problem was contributed by Dr. Rick Wilson of Oklahoma State University.

   The recent drought has hit farmers hard. Cows are eating candy corn!

   You are interested in creating a feed plan for the next week for your cattle using the following seven non-traditional feeding products: Chocolate Lucky Charms cereal, Butterfinger bars, Milk Duds, vanilla ice cream, Cap'n Crunch cereal, candy corn (because the real corn is all dead), and Chips Ahoy cookies.

	Choc Lucky Charms	Butterfinger	Milk Duds	Vanilla Ice Cream	Cap'n Crunch	Candy Corn	Chips Ahoy
$$/lb	2.15	7	4.25	6.35	5.25	4	6.75
Choc	YES	YES	YES	NO	NO	NO	YES
Protein	75	80	45	65	72	26	62
TDN	12	20	18	6	11	8	12
Calcium	3	4	4.5	12	2	1	5

Their per pound cost is shown, as is the protein units per pound they contribute, their total digestible nutrients (TDN) they contribute per pound, and the calcium units per pound.

You estimate that the total amount of nontraditional feeding products contribute the following amount of nutrients: at least 20,000 units of protein, at least 4,025 units of TDN, at least 1,000 but no more than 1,200 units of calcium.

There are some other miscellaneous requirements as well.

• The chocolate in your overall feed plan (in pounds) cannot exceed the amount of nonchocolate poundage. Whether a product is considered chocolate or not is shown in the table (YES = chocolate, NO = not chocolate).
• No one feeding product can make up more than 25% of the total pounds needed to create an acceptable feed mix.
• There are two cereals (Chocolate Lucky Charms and Cap'n Crunch). Combined, they can be no more than 40% (in pounds) of the total mix required to meet the mix requirements.

Determine the optimal levels of the seven products to create your weekly feed plan that minimizes cost. Note that all amounts of products must *not* have fractional values (whole numbered pounds only).

6. This exercise was contributed by Dr. Rick Wilson of Oklahoma State University to illustrate the modeling capabilities of Excel Solver.

You are working with a large set of temporary workers (collection of interns, retirees, etc.) to create a draft plan to staff a nighttime call center (for the near future). You also have a handful of full-time workers who are your "anchors"—but you have already placed them in the schedule, and this has led to your staffing requirements. They (full-time workers) are of no concern to you in the model.

These staffing requirements are by day: You need 15, 20, 19, 22, 7, 32, and 35 staff for M, T, W, Th, F, Sat, Sun (respectively).

You have between 8 and 10 of the pool who cannot work on the weekend (Saturday or Sunday).

For these "Weekday Only" folks, there are three shifts possible: They will work 4 of the 5 weekdays, one shift will have Tuesday off, one shift will have Wednesday off, and one shift will have Thursday off.

You must have at least eight people total assigned to these "Weekday Only" shifts.

For all other shifts (and you are not constrained by size of employee pool), a person works 4 of the 7 days each week. Workers will work 2 weekdays and both weekend days (a "2/2" shift). All possible "2"-day combinations of days are relevant shifts—except any combinations where workers have three consecutive days off; those are not allowed, and should not be in the model.

We are going with a very simple model—no costs. The objective of our model is to find the fewest number of workers that meet the stated minimum call center daily requirements *and* not have more than four extra workers (above min. requirements) assigned during any one day.

Also, all shifts ("Weekday Only" or the 2/2 shifts) can have no more than six people "allocated" to them.

Create a core model that satisfies these constraints and minimizes the total number of people needed to meet the minimum requirements. If it's an issue, yes, whole numbered people.

7. This exercise was also contributed by Dr. Rick Wilson of Oklahoma State University. The following simple scenario mimics the "Black Book" described in a *Business Week* article (http://www.businessweek.com/articles /2013-01-31/coke-engineers-its-orange-juice-with-an-algorithm, accessed February 2013) about Coca-Cola's production of orange juice. Create an appropriate LP model for this scenario.

For the next production period, there are five different batches of raw orange juice that can be blended together to make orange juice products, SunnyQ, GlowMorn, and OrenthalJames. In creating the optimal blend of the three products from the five different batches, an LP model should seek to maximize the net of the sales price per gallon of the products less the assessed per-gallon cost of the raw juice.

The five raw batches of orange juice are described here. Brix is a measure of sweetness, pulp, available stock, and cost—all self-explanatory:

Batch 1—Pineapple Orange A, brix = 16, pulp = 1.2, 250 gallons, $2.01/gallon

Batch 2—Pineapple Orange B, brix = 17, pulp = 0.9, 200 gallons, $2.32/gallon

Batch 3—Mid Sweet, brix = 20, pulp = 0.8, 175 gallons, $3.14/gallon

Batch 4—Valencia, brix = 18, pulp = 2.1, 300 gallons, $2.41/gallon

Batch 5—Temple Orange, brix = 14, pulp = 1.6, 265 gallons, $2.55/gallon

Note that to make sure that the raw juice doesn't get too "old" over time, one production requirement is that at least 50% of each batch's available stock must be used in blending the three orange juice products (obviously, more than what is available cannot be used).

From a product perspective, there must be at least 100 gallons of SunnyQ blended and at least 125 gallons each of GlowMorn and OrenthalJames. Likewise, the projected future demand for the products indicates that in this period, there should be a maximum of 400 gallons of SunnyQ, a maximum of 375 gallons of GlowMorn, and a maximum of 300 gallons of OrenthalJames produced. Also, when blending the products from the five batches, an individual batch can provide no more than 40% of the total amount of a given product. This is to be enforced individually on each product.

Attributes of the three products include sales price, the maximum average brix of the final mixed product, the minimum average brix of the final mixed product, and the maximum average pulp content. In the three "average" requirements, this implies the weighted average of all juice mixed together for that product must meet that specification.

SunnyQ—Sales = $3.92/gallon, Max Brix = 19, Min Brix = 18.5, Max Pulp = 1.6

GlowMorn—Sales = $4.13/gallon, Max Brix = 17, Min Brix = 16.75, Max Pulp = 1.8

OrenthalJames—Sales = $3.77/gallon, Max Brix = 17.75, Min Brix = 17.55, Max Pulp = 1.1

References

Arsham, H. (2006a). Modeling and simulation resources. home.ubalt.edu/ntsbarsh/Business-stat/RefSim.htm (accessed July 2016).

Arsham, H. (2006b). Decision science resources. home.ubalt .edu/ntsbarsh/Business-stat/Refop.htm (accessed July 2016).

Bailey, M. J., Snapp, J., Yetur, S., Stonebraker, J. S., Edwards, S. A., Davis, A., & Cox, R. (2011). Practice summaries: American Airlines uses should-cost modeling to assess the uncertainty of bids for its full-truckload shipment routes. *Interfaces, 41*(2), 194–196.

Banks, J., & Gibson, R. R. (2009). Seven sins of simulation practice. *INFORMS Analytics,* 24–27. www.analytics-magazine. org/summer-2009/193-strategic-problems-modeling-the-market-space (accessed July 2016).

Bowers, M. R., Noon, C. E., Wu, W., & Bass, J. K. (2016). Neonatal physician scheduling at the University of Tennessee Medical Center. *Interfaces, 46*(2), 168–182.

Businessweek.com. Coke engineers its orange juice—With an algorithm. www.businessweek.com/articles/2013-01-31/coke-engineers-its-orange-juice-with-an-algorithm (accessed July 2016).

Chongwatpol, J., & Sharda, R. (2013). RFID-enabled track and traceability in job-shop scheduling environment. *European Journal of Operational Research, 227*(3), 453–463, http://dx.doi.org/10.1016/j.ejor.2013.01.009.

Christiansen, M., Fagerholt, K., Hasle, G., Minsaas, A., & Nygreen, B. (2009, April). Maritime transport optimization: An ocean of opportunities. *OR/MS Today, 36*(2), 26–31.

Clemen, R. T., & Reilly, T. (2000). *Making hard decisions with Decision Tools Suite.* Belmont, MA: Duxbury Press.

Farasyn, I., Perkoz, K., & Van de Velde, W. (2008, July/August). Spreadsheet models for inventory target setting at Procter & Gamble. *Interfaces, 38*(4), 241–250.

Furman, K. C., Song, J. H., Kocis, G. R., McDonald, M. K., & Warrick, P. H. (2011). Feedstock routing in the ExxonMobil downstream sector. *Interfaces, 41*(2), 149–163.

Goodwin, P., & Wright, G. (2000). *Decision analysis for management judgment,* 2nd ed. New York: Wiley.

Hurley, W. J., & Balez, M. (2008, July/August). A spreadsheet implementation of an ammunition requirements planning model for the Canadian Army. *Interfaces, 38*(4), 271–280.

Hutton, D. W., Brandeau, M. L., & So, S. K. (2011). Do good with good OR: Supporting cost-effective Hepati interventions. *Interfaces, 41*(3), 289–300.

Kearns, G. S. (2004, January–March). A multi-objective criteria approach for evaluating IT investments from two case studies. *Information Resources M Journal, 17*(1), 37–62.

Kelly, A. (2002). *Decision making using gam introduction for managers.* Cambridge, U University Press.

Knight, F. H. (1933). *Risk, uncertainty an additional introductory essay hithe* London school of economics and poli

Koksalan, M., & Zionts, S. (Eds.). (ria decision making in the ne Springer-Verlag.

Kontoghiorghes, E. J., Rustem, B., & Siokos, S. (2002). *Computational methods in decision making, economics, and finance.* Boston: Kluwer.

Manikas, A. S., Kroes, J. R., & Gattiker, T. F. (2016). Metro Meals on Wheels Treasure Valley employs a low-cost routing tool to improve deliveries. *Interfaces, 46*(2), 154–167.

Mookherjee, R., Martineau, J., Xu, L., Gullo, M., Zhou, K., Hazlewood, A., Zhang, X., Griarte, F., & Li, N. (2016). End-to-end predictive analytics and optimization in Ingram Micro's two-tier distribution business. *Interfaces, 46*(1), 49–73; ingrammicrocommerce.com, "CUSTOMERS," https://www.ingrammicrocommerce.com/customers/ (accessed July 2016).

Ovchinnikov, A., & Milner, J. (2008, July/August). Spreadsheet model helps to assign medical residents at the University of Vermont's College of Medicine. *Interfaces, 38*(4), 311–323.

Simio.com. Agricultural operations simulation case study: Cosan. http://www.simio.com/case-studies/Cosan-agricultural-logistics-simulation-software-case-study/agricultural-simulation-software-case-study-video-cosan.php (accessed July 2016).

Simio.com. Cosan case study—Optimizing agricultural logistics operations. http://www.simio.com/case-studies/Cosan-agricultural-logistics-simulation-software-case-study/index.php (accessed July 2016).

Slaugh, V. W., Akan, M., Kesten, O., & Unver, M. U. (2016). The Pennsylvania Adoption Exchange improves its matching process. *Interfaces,* 462, 133–154.

Solver.com. Optimizing vendor contract awards gets an A+. solver.com/news/optimizing-vendor-contract-awards-gets (accessed July 2016).

Turban E., & Meredith, J. (1994). *Fundamentals of management science,* 6th ed. Richard D. Irwin, Inc.

Wikipedia.com. Cosan. https://en.wikipedia.org/w/index.php?title=Cosan&oldid=713298536 (accessed July 2016).

CHAPTER 7

Big Data Concepts and Tools

Big Data, which means many things to many people, is not a new technological fad. It has become a business priority that has the potential to profoundly change the competitive landscape in today's globally integrated economy. In addition to providing innovative solutions to enduring business challenges, Big Data and analytics instigate new ways to transform processes, organizations, entire industries, and even society altogether. Yet extensive media coverage makes it hard to distinguish hype from reality. This chapter aims to provide a comprehensive coverage of Big Data, its enabling technologies, and related analytics concepts to help understand the capabilities and limitations of this emerging technology. The chapter starts with a definition and related concepts of Big Data followed by the technical details of the enabling technologies, including Hadoop, MapReduce, and NoSQL. We provide a comparative analysis between data warehousing and Big Data analytics. The last part of the chapter is dedicated to stream analytics, which is one of the most promising value propositions of Big Data analytics. This chapter contains the following sections:

7.1 Opening Vignette: Analyzing Customer Churn in a Telecom Company Using Big Data Methods   370

7.2 Definition of Big Data   373

7.3 Fundamentals of Big Data Analytics   378

7.4 Big Data Technologies   383

7.5 Big Data and Data Warehousing   393

7.6 Big Data Vendors and Platforms   397

7.7 Big Data and Stream Analytics   406

7.8 Applications of Stream Analytics   409

7.1 OPENING VIGNETTE: Analyzing Customer Churn in a Telecom Company Using Big Data Methods

Background

A telecom company (named Access Telecom [AT] for privacy reasons) wanted to stem the tide of customers churning from its telecom services. Customer churn in the telecommunications industry is common. However, Access Telecom was losing customers at an alarming rate. Several reasons and potential solutions were attributed to this phenomenon. The management of the company realized that many cancellations involved communications between the customer service department and the customers. To this end, a task force comprising members from the customer relations office and the information technology (IT) department was assembled to explore the problem further. Their task was to explore how the problem of customer churn could be reduced based on an analysis of the customers' communication patterns (Asamoah, Sharda, Zadeh, & Kalgotra, 2016).

Big Data Hurdles

Whenever a customer had a problem about issues such as their bill, plan, and call quality, they would contact the company in multiple ways. These included a call center, company Web site (contact us links), and physical service center walk-ins. Customers could cancel an account through one of these listed interactions. The company wanted to see if analyzing these customer interactions could yield any insights about the questions the customers asked or the contact channel(s) they used before canceling their account. The data generated because of these interactions were in both text and audio. So, AT would have to combine all the data into one location. The company explored the use of traditional platforms for data management but soon found they were not versatile enough to handle advanced data analysis in the scenario where there were multiple formats of data from multiple sources (Thusoo, Shao, & Anthony, 2010).

There were two major challenges in analyzing this data: multiple data sources leading to a variety of data and also a large volume of data.

1. **Data from multiple sources:** Customers could connect with the company by accessing their accounts on the company's Web site, allowing AT to generate Web log information on customer activity. The Web log track allowed the company to identify if and when a customer reviewed his/her current plan, submitted a complaint, or checked the bill online. At the customer service center, customers could also lodge a service complaint, request a plan change, or cancel the service. These activities were logged into the company's transaction system and then the enterprise data warehouse. Last, a customer could call the customer service center on the phone and transact business just like he/she would do in person at a customer service center. Such transactions could involve a balance inquiry or an initiation of plan cancellation. Call logs were available in one system with a record of the reasons a customer was calling. For meaningful analysis to be performed, the individual data sets had to be converted into similar structured formats.

2. Data volume: The second challenge was the sheer quantity of data from the three sources that had to be extracted, cleaned, restructured, and analyzed. Although previous data analytics projects mostly utilized a small sample set of data for analysis, AT decided to leverage the multiple variety and sources of data as well as the large volume of data recorded to generate as many insights as possible.

An analytical approach that could make use of all the channels and sources of data, although huge, would have the potential of generating rich and in-depth insights from the data to help curb the churn.

Solution

Teradata Aster's unified Big Data architecture was utilized to manage and analyze the large multistructured data. We will introduce Teradata Aster in Section 7.6. A schematic of which data was combined is shown in Figure 7.1. Based on each data source, three tables were created with each table containing the following variables: customer ID, channel of communication, date/time stamp, and action taken. Prior to final cancellation of a service, the action-taken variable could be one or more of these 11 options (simplified for this case): present a bill dispute, request for plan upgrade, request for plan downgrade, perform profile update, view account summary, access customer support, view bill, review contract, access store locator function on the Web site, access frequently asked questions section on the Web site, or browse devices. The target of the analysis focused on finding the most common path resulting in a final service cancellation. The data was sessionized to group a string of events involving a particular customer into a defined time period (5 days over all the channels of communication) as one session. Finally Aster's nPath time sequence function (operationalized in an SQL-MapReduce framework) was used to analyze common trends that led to a cancellation.

Results

The initial results identified several routes that could lead to a request for service cancellation. The company determined thousands of routes that a customer may take to cancel service. A follow-up analysis was performed to identify the most frequent routes to cancellation requests. This was termed as the Golden Path. The top 20 most occurring paths

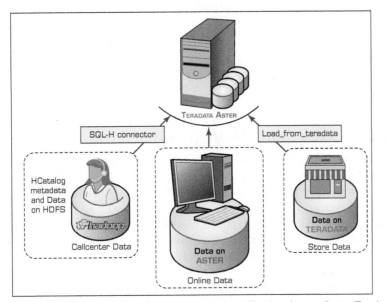

FIGURE 7.1 Multiple Data Sources Integrated into Teradata Aster. *Source:* Teradata Corp.

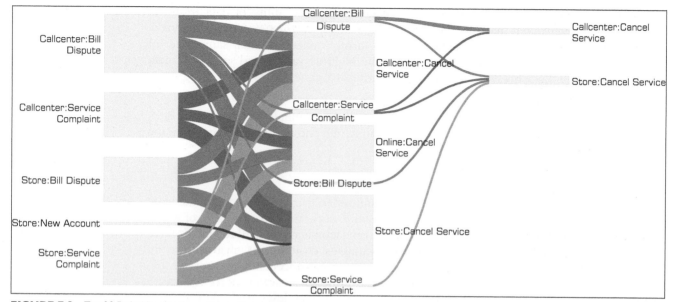

FIGURE 7.2   Top 20 Paths Visualization.   *Source:* Teradata Corp.

that led to a cancellation were identified in both short and long terms. A sample is shown in Figure 7.2.

This analysis helped the company identify a customer before they would cancel their service and offer incentives or at least escalate the problem resolution to a level where the customer's path to cancellation did not materialize.

QUESTIONS FOR THE OPENING VIGNETTE

1. What problem did customer service cancellation pose to AT's business survival?
2. Identify and explain the technical hurdles presented by the nature and characteristics of AT's data.
3. What is sessionizing? Why was it necessary for AT to sessionize its data?
4. Research other studies where customer churn models have been employed. What types of variables were used in those studies? How is this vignette different?
5. Besides Teradata Aster, identify other popular Big Data analytics platforms that could handle the analysis described in the preceding case.

What Can We Learn from This Vignette?

Not all business problems merit the use of a Big Data analytics platform. This situation presents a business case that warranted the use of a Big Data platform. The main challenge revolved around the characteristics of the data under consideration. The three different types of customer interaction data sets presented a challenge in analysis. The formats and fields of data generated in each of these systems was huge. And the volume was large as well. This made it imperative to use a platform that uses technologies to permit analysis of a large volume of data that comes in a variety of formats.

It is also worthwhile to note that AT aligned the questions asked of the data with the organization's business strategy. The questions also informed the type of analysis that was performed. It is important to understand that for any application of a Big Data architecture, the organization's business strategy and the generation of relevant questions are key to identifying the type of analysis to perform.

Sources: Asamoah, D., Sharda, R., Zadeh, A., & Kalgotra, P. (2016). Preparing a Big Data analytics professional: A pedagogic experience. In *DSI 2016 Conference*, Austin, TX. Thusoo, A., Shao, Z., & Anthony, S. (2010). Data warehousing and analytics infrastructure at Facebook. In *Proceedings of the 2010 ACM SIGMOD International Conference on Management of Data* (p. 1013). doi: 10.1145/1807167.1807278.

7.2 Definition of Big Data

Using data to understand customers/clients and business operations to sustain (and foster) growth and profitability is an increasingly challenging task for today's enterprises. As more and more data becomes available in various forms and fashions, timely processing of the data with traditional means becomes impractical. Nowadays, this phenomenon called Big Data, which is receiving substantial press coverage and drawing increasing interest from both business users and IT professionals. The result is that Big Data is becoming an overhyped and overused marketing buzzword.

Big Data means different things to people with different backgrounds and interests. Traditionally, the term *Big Data* has been used to describe the massive volumes of data analyzed by huge organizations like Google or research science projects at NASA. But for most businesses, it's a relative term: "Big" depends on an organization's size. The point is more about finding new value within and outside conventional data sources. Pushing the boundaries of data analytics uncovers new insights and opportunities, and "big" depends on where you start and how you proceed. Consider the popular description of Big Data: Big Data exceeds the reach of commonly used hardware environments and/or capabilities of software tools to capture, manage, and process it within a tolerable time span for its user population. **Big Data** has become a popular term to describe the exponential growth, availability, and use of information, both structured and unstructured. Much has been written on the Big Data trend and how it can serve as the basis for innovation, differentiation, and growth. Because of the technology challenges in managing the large volume of data coming from multiple sources, sometimes at a rapid speed, additional new technologies have been developed to overcome the technology challenges. Use of the term *Big Data* is usually associated with such technologies. Because a prime use of storing such data is generating insights through analytics, sometimes the term Big Data is expanded as Big Data analytics. But the term is becoming content free in that it can mean different things to different people. Because our goal is to introduce you to the large data sets and their potential in generating insights, we will use the original term in this chapter.

Where does Big Data come from? A simple answer is "everywhere." The sources that were ignored because of the technical limitations are now treated as gold mines. Big Data may come from Web logs, radio-frequency identification (RFID), global positioning systems (GPS), sensor networks, social networks, Internet-based text documents, Internet search indexes, detail call records, astronomy, atmospheric science, biology, genomics, nuclear physics, biochemical experiments, medical records, scientific research, military surveillance, photography archives, video archives, and large-scale e-commerce practices.

Big Data is not new. What is new is that the definition and the structure of Big Data constantly change. Companies have been storing and analyzing large volumes of data since the advent of the data warehouses in the early 1990s. Whereas terabytes used to be synonymous with Big Data warehouses, now it's exabytes, and the rate of growth in data volume continues to escalate as organizations seek to store and analyze greater levels of transaction details, as well as Web- and machine-generated data, to gain a better understanding of customer behavior and business drivers.

Many (academics and industry analysts/leaders alike) think that "Big Data" is a misnomer. What it says and what it means are not exactly the same. That is, Big Data is not just "big." The sheer volume of the data is only one of many characteristics that are often associated with Big Data, including variety, velocity, veracity, variability, and value proposition, among others.

The "V"s That Define Big Data

Big Data is typically defined by three "V"s: volume, variety, velocity. In addition to these three, we see some of the leading Big Data solution providers adding other "V"s, such as veracity (IBM), variability (SAS), and value proposition.

VOLUME   Volume is obviously the most common trait of Big Data. Many factors contributed to the exponential increase in data volume, such as transaction-based data stored through the years, text data constantly streaming in from social media, increasing amounts of sensor data being collected, automatically generated RFID and GPS data, and so on. In the past, excessive data volume created storage issues, both technical and financial. But with today's advanced technologies coupled with decreasing storage costs, these issues are no longer significant; instead, other issues have emerged, including how to determine relevance amid the large volumes of data and how to create value from data that is deemed to be relevant.

As mentioned before, *big* is a relative term. It changes over time and is perceived differently by different organizations. With the staggering increase in data volume, even the naming of the next Big Data echelon has been a challenge. The highest mass of data that used to be called petabytes (PB) has left its place to zettabytes (ZB), which is a trillion gigabytes (GB) or a billion terabytes (TB). Technology Insights 7.1 provides an overview of the size and naming of Big Data volumes.

From a short historical perspective, in 2009 the world had about 0.8 ZB of data; in 2010, it exceeded the 1 ZB mark; at the end of 2011, the number was 1.8 ZB. It is expected to be 44 ZB in 2020 (Adshead, 2014). With the growth of sensors and the Internet of Things (IoT—to be introduced in the next chapter), these forecasts could all be wrong. Though these numbers are astonishing in size, so are the challenges and opportunities that come with them.

VARIETY   Data today come in all types of formats—ranging from traditional databases to hierarchical data stores created by the end users and OLAP systems to text documents, e-mail, XML, meter-collected and sensor-captured data, to video, audio, and stock ticker data. By some estimates, 80 to 85% of all organizations' data are in some sort of unstructured or semi-structured format (a format that is not suitable for traditional database schemas). But there is no denying its value, and hence, it must be included in the analyses to support decision making.

VELOCITY   According to Gartner, velocity means both how fast data is being produced and how fast the data must be processed (i.e., captured, stored, and analyzed) to meet the need or demand. RFID tags, automated sensors, GPS devices, and smart meters are driving an increasing need to deal with torrents of data in near real time. Velocity is perhaps the most overlooked characteristic of Big Data. Reacting quickly enough to deal with velocity is a challenge to most organizations. For time-sensitive environments, the opportunity cost clock of the data starts ticking the moment the data is created. As time passes, the value proposition of the data degrades and eventually becomes worthless. Whether the subject matter is the health of a patient, the well-being of a traffic system, or the health of

TECHNOLOGY INSIGHTS 7.1
The Data Size Is Getting Big, Bigger, and Bigger

The measure of data size is having a hard time keeping up with new names. We all know kilobyte (KB, which is 1,000 bytes), megabyte (MB, which is 1,000,000 bytes), gigabyte (GB, which is 1,000,000,000 bytes), and terabyte (TB, which is 1,000,000,000,000 bytes). Beyond that, the names given to data sizes are relatively new to most of us. The following table shows what comes after terabyte and beyond.

Name	Symbol	Value
Kilobyte	kB	10^3
Megabyte	MB	10^6
Gigabyte	GB	10^9
Terabyte	TB	10^{12}
Petabyte	PB	10^{15}
Exabyte	EB	10^{18}
Zettabyte	ZB	10^{21}
Yottabyte	YB	10^{24}
Brontobyte*	BB	10^{27}
Gegobyte*	GeB	10^{30}

*Not an official SI (International System of Units) name/symbol, yet.

Consider that an exabyte of data is created on the Internet each day, which equates to 250 million DVDs' worth of information. And the idea of even larger amounts of data—a zettabyte—isn't too far off when it comes to the amount of information traversing the Web in any one year. In fact, industry experts are already estimating that we will see 1.3 zettabytes of traffic annually over the Internet by 2016—and it could jump to 2.3 zettabytes by 2020. By 2020, Internet traffic is expected to reach 300 GB per capita per year. When referring to yottabytes, some of the Big Data scientists often wonder about how much data the NSA or FBI have on people altogether. Put in terms of DVDs, a yottabyte would require 250 trillion of them. A brontobyte, which is not an official SI prefix but is apparently recognized by some people in the measurement community, is a 1 followed by 27 zeros. The size of such a magnitude can be used to describe the amount of sensor data that we will get from the Internet in the next decade, if not sooner.

A gegobyte is 10 to the power of 30. With respect to where the Big Data comes from, consider the following:

- The CERN Large Hadron Collider generates 1 petabyte per second.
- Sensors from a Boeing jet engine create 20 terabytes of data every hour.
- Every day, 600 terabytes of new data are ingested in Facebook databases.
- On YouTube, 300 hours of video are uploaded per minute, translating to 1 terabyte every minute.
- The proposed Square Kilometer Array telescope (the world's proposed biggest telescope) will generate an exabyte of data per day.

Sources: Higginbotham, S. (2012). As data gets bigger, what comes after a yottabyte? gigaom.com/2012/10/30/as-data-gets-bigger-what-comes-after-a-yottabyte (accessed August 2016).

Cisco. (2016). The zettabyte era: Trends and analysis. cisco.com/c/en/us/solutions/collateral/service-provider/visual-networking-index-vni/vni-hyperconnectivity-wp.pdf (accessed August 2016).

an investment portfolio, accessing the data and reacting faster to the circumstances will always create more advantageous outcomes.

In the Big Data storm that we are currently witnessing, almost everyone is fixated on at-rest analytics, using optimized software and hardware systems to mine large quantities of variant data sources. Although this is critically important and highly valuable, there is another class of analytics, driven from the velocity of Big Data, called "data stream analytics" or "in-motion analytics," which is evolving fast. If done correctly, data stream analytics can be as valuable, and in some business environments more valuable, than at-rest analytics. Later in this chapter we will cover this topic in more detail.

VERACITY *Veracity* is a term coined by IBM that is being used as the fourth "V" to describe Big Data. It refers to conformity to facts: accuracy, quality, truthfulness, or trustworthiness of the data. Tools and techniques are often used to handle Big Data's veracity by transforming the data into quality and trustworthy insights.

VARIABILITY In addition to the increasing velocities and varieties of data, data flows can be highly inconsistent with periodic peaks. Is something big trending in the social media? Perhaps there is a high-profile IPO looming. Maybe swimming with pigs in the Bahamas is suddenly the must-do vacation activity. Daily, seasonal, and event-triggered peak data loads can be highly variable and thus challenging to manage—especially with social media involved.

VALUE PROPOSITION The excitement around Big Data is its value proposition. A preconceived notion about "Big" data is that it contains (or has a greater potential to contain) more patterns and interesting anomalies than "small" data. Thus, by analyzing large and feature-rich data, organizations can gain greater business value that they may not have otherwise. Although users can detect the patterns in small data sets using simple statistical and machine-learning methods or ad hoc query and reporting tools, Big Data means "big" analytics. Big analytics means greater insight and better decisions, something that every organization needs.

Because the exact definition of Big Data (or its successor terms) is still a matter of ongoing discussion in academic and industrial circles, it is likely that more characteristics (perhaps more "V"s) are likely to be added to this list. Regardless of what happens, the importance and value proposition of Big Data is here to stay. Figure 7.3 shows a

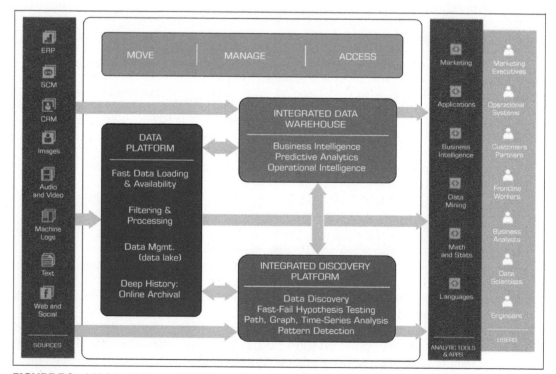

FIGURE 7.3 A High-Level Conceptual Architecture for Big Data Solutions. *Source:* AsterData—A Teradata Company.

conceptual architecture where Big Data (at the left side of the figure) is converted to business insight through the use of a combination of advanced analytics and delivered to a variety of different users/roles for faster/better decision making.

Another term that is being added to Big Data buzzwords is alternative data. Application Case 7.1 shows examples of multiple types of data in a number of different scenarios.

Application Case 7.1

Alternative Data for Market Analysis or Forecasts

Getting a good forecast and understanding of the situation is crucial for any scenario, but it is especially important to players in the investment industry. Being able to get an early indication of how a particular retailer's sales are doing can give an investor a leg up on whether to buy or sell that retailer's stock even before the earnings reports are released. The problem of forecasting economic activity or microclimates based on a variety of data beyond the usual retail data is a very recent phenomenon and has led to another buzzword—"alternative data." A major mix in this alternative data category is satellite imagery, but it also includes other data such as social media, government filings, job postings, traffic patterns, changes in parking lots or open spaces detected by satellite images, mobile phone usage patterns in any given location at any given time, search patterns on search engines, and so on. Facebook and other companies have invested in satellites to try to image the whole globe every day so that daily changes can be tracked at any location and the information can be used for forecasting. In the last 6 to 12 months, many interesting examples of more reliable and advanced forecasts have been reported. Indeed, this activity is being led by start-up companies. Here are some of the examples:

- Facebook used its image recognition engine to analyze over 14.6 billion images of every corner of the world to identify areas of low connectivity.
- RS Metrics monitored parking lots across the United States for various hedge funds. In 2015, based on an analysis of the parking lots, RS Metrics predicted a strong second quarter in 2015 for JC Penney. Its clients (mostly hedge funds) profited from this advanced insight. A similar story has been reported for Wal-Mart using car counts in its parking lots to forecast sales.
- Orbital Insights uses satellite imagery data to provide macroeconomic indicators for various industry sectors. For example, by analyzing shadows of the oil storage tanks around the world, it claims to have produced a better daily estimate of worldwide oil storage than is available from the International Energy Agency (IEA).
- Spaceknow keeps track of changes in factory surroundings for over 6,000 Chinese factory sites. Using this data, the company has been able to provide a better idea of China's industrial economic activity than what the Chinese government has been reporting.
- Descartes Labs uses satellite data to predict U.S. corn harvests with more accuracy than the U.S. Department of Agriculture does. Better forecasts can have huge financial impacts on futures trading. An older example of this was a company called Lanworth that also predicted corn crop estimates. Lanworth was acquired by Thomson Reuters and is integrated in their Eikon service.
- DigitalGlobe is able to analyze the size of a forest with more accuracy because its software can count every single tree in a forest. This results in a more accurate estimate because there is no need to use a representative sample.
- Kensho, a company backed by Goldman Sachs, is reportedly analyzing data from multiple sources (mentioned earlier) to build a trading engine.

These examples illustrate just a sample of ways data can be combined to generate new insights. Of course, there are privacy concerns in some cases. For example, a story in *the Wall Street Journal* in 2015 reported that Yodlee, a company that provides personal finance tools to many large banks and thus has access to millions of customers' credit card transactions, sells such data to other analytics firms that can use the information to develop early predictions of how sales are trending for a particular retailer.

(Continued)

Application Case 7.1 (Continued)

Such information is highly sought by stock market traders. This story led to an uproar about the customer information being used in ways not authorized. There is also a concern in some circles about the legality of developing such advanced predictions about a particular commodity or company. Although such concerns will eventually be resolved by policy makers, what is clear is that new and interesting ways of combining satellite data and many other data sources are spawning a new crop of analytics companies. All of these organizations are working with data that meets the three V's—variety, volume, and velocity characterizations. Some of these companies also work with another category of data—sensors. We will discuss those in the next chapter when we review emerging trends in analytics. But this group of companies certainly also falls under a group of innovative and emerging applications.

Sources: Dillow, C. (2016). What happens when you combine artificial intelligence and satellite imagery. fortune.com/2016/03/30/facebook-ai-satellite-imagery/ (accessed July 2016).

Ekster, G. (2015). Driving investment performance with alternative data. integrity-research.com/wp-content/uploads/2015/11/

Driving-Investment-Performance-With-Alternative-Data.pdf (accessed July 2016).

Hope, B. (2015). Provider of personal finance tools tracks bank cards, sells data to investors. wsj.com/articles/provider-of-personal-finance-tools-tracks-bank-cards-sells-data-to-investors-1438914620 (accessed July 2016).

Orbital Insight. World Oil Storage Index. orbitalinsight.com/solutions/world-oil-storage-index/ (accessed July 2016).

Shaw, C. (2016). Satellite companies moving markets. quandl.com/blog/alternative-data-satellite-companies (accessed July 2016).

Steiner, C. (2009). Sky high tips for crop traders. http://www.forbes.com/forbes/2009/0907/technology-software-satellites-sky-high-tips-for-crop-traders.html (accessed July 2016).

Turner, M. (2015). This is the future of investing, and you probably can't afford it. businessinsider.com/hedge-funds-are-analysing-data-to-get-an-edge-2015-8 (accessed July 2016).

Questions for Discussion

1. What is a common thread in the examples discussed in this application case?
2. Can you think of other data streams that might help give an early indication of sales at a retailer?
3. Can you think of other applications along the lines presented in this application case?

SECTION 7.2 REVIEW QUESTIONS

1. Why is Big Data important? What has changed to put it in the center of the analytics world?
2. How do you define Big Data? Why is it difficult to define?
3. Out of the "V"s that are used to define Big Data, in your opinion, which one is the most important? Why?
4. What do you think the future of Big Data will be like? Will it leave its popularity to something else? If so, what will it be?

7.3 Fundamentals of Big Data Analytics

Big Data by itself, regardless of the size, type, or speed, is worthless unless business users do something with it that delivers value to their organizations. That's where "big" analytics comes into the picture. Although organizations have always run reports and dashboards against data warehouses, most have not opened these repositories to in-depth on-demand exploration. This is partly because analysis tools are too complex for the average user but also because the repositories often do not contain all the data needed by the power user. But this is about to change (and has been changing, for some) in a dramatic fashion, thanks to the new Big Data analytics paradigm.

With the value proposition, Big Data also brought about big challenges for organizations. The traditional means for capturing, storing, and analyzing data are not capable of dealing with Big Data effectively and efficiently. Therefore, new breeds of technologies need to be developed (or purchased/hired/outsourced) to take on the Big Data challenge. Before making such an investment, organizations should justify the means. Here are some questions that may help shed light on this situation. If any of the following statements are true, then you need to seriously consider embarking on a Big Data journey.

- You can't process the amount of data that you want to because of the limitations posed by your current platform or environment.
- You want to involve new/contemporary data sources (e.g., social media, RFID, sensory, Web, GPS, textual data) into your analytics platform, but you can't because it does not comply with the data storage schema-defined rows and columns without sacrificing fidelity or the richness of the new data.
- You need to (or want to) integrate data as quickly as possible to be current on your analysis.
- You want to work with a schema-on-demand (as opposed to predetermined schema used in relational database management systems [RDBMSs]) data storage paradigm because the nature of the new data may not be known, or there may not be enough time to determine it and develop schema for it.
- The data is arriving so fast at your organization's doorstep that your traditional analytics platform cannot handle it.

As is the case with any other large IT investment, the success in Big Data analytics depends on a number of factors. Figure 7.4 shows a graphical depiction of the most critical success factors (Watson, 2012).

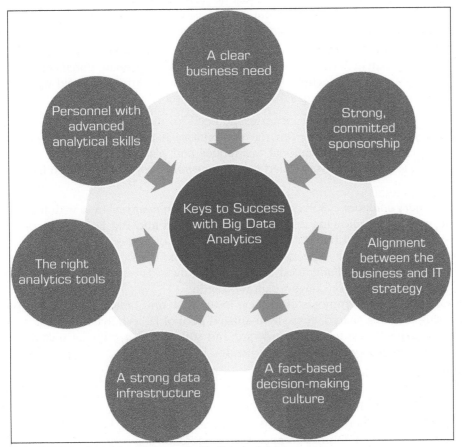

FIGURE 7.4 Critical Success Factors for Big Data Analytics.

The following are the most critical success factors for **Big Data analytics** (Watson, Sharda, & Schrader, 2012):

1. *A clear business need (alignment with the vision and the strategy).* Business investments ought to be made for the good of the business, not for the sake of mere technology advancements. Therefore, the main driver for Big Data analytics should be the needs of the business, at any level—strategic, tactical, and operations.

2. *Strong, committed sponsorship (executive champion).* It is a well-known fact that if you don't have strong, committed executive sponsorship, it is difficult (if not impossible) to succeed. If the scope is a single or a few analytical applications, the sponsorship can be at the departmental level. However, if the target is enterprise-wide organizational transformation, which is often the case for Big Data initiatives, sponsorship needs to be at the highest levels and organization wide.

3. *Alignment between the business and IT strategy.* It is essential to make sure that the analytics work is always supporting the business strategy, and not the other way around. Analytics should play the enabling role in successfully executing the business strategy.

4. *A fact-based decision-making culture.* In a fact-based decision-making culture, the numbers rather than intuition, gut feeling, or supposition drive decision making. There is also a culture of experimentation to see what works and what doesn't. To create a fact-based decision-making culture, senior management needs to:
   - Recognize that some people can't or won't adjust
   - Be a vocal supporter
   - Stress that outdated methods must be discontinued
   - Ask to see what analytics went into decisions
   - Link incentives and compensation to desired behaviors

5. *A strong data infrastructure.* Data warehouses have provided the data infrastructure for analytics. This infrastructure is changing and being enhanced in the Big Data era with new technologies. Success requires marrying the old with the new for a holistic infrastructure that works synergistically.

As the size and complexity increase, the need for more efficient analytical systems is also increasing. To keep up with the computational needs of Big Data, a number of new and innovative computational techniques and platforms have been developed. These techniques are collectively called *high-performance computing*, which includes the following:

- *In-memory analytics:* Solves complex problems in near real time with highly accurate insights by allowing analytical computations and Big Data to be processed in-memory and distributed across a dedicated set of nodes.
- *In-database analytics:* Speeds time to insights and enables better data governance by performing data integration and analytic functions inside the database so you won't have to move or convert data repeatedly.
- *Grid computing:* Promotes efficiency, lower cost, and better performance by processing jobs in a shared, centrally managed pool of IT resources.
- *Appliances:* Brings together hardware and software in a physical unit that is not only fast but also scalable on an as-needed basis.

Computational requirements are just a small part of the list of challenges that Big Data impose on today's enterprises. The following is a list of challenges that are found by business executives to have a significant impact on successful implementation of Big Data analytics. When considering Big Data projects and architecture, being mindful of these challenges will make the journey to analytics competency a less stressful one.

- *Data volume:* The ability to capture, store, and process a huge volume of data at an acceptable speed so that the latest information is available to decision makers when they need it.
- *Data integration:* The ability to combine data that is not similar in structure or source and to do so quickly and at a reasonable cost.
- *Processing capabilities:* The ability to process data quickly, as it is captured. The traditional way of collecting and processing data may not work. In many situations, data needs to be analyzed as soon as it is captured to leverage the most value. (This is called *stream analytics*, which will be covered later in this chapter.)
- *Data governance:* The ability to keep up with the security, privacy, ownership, and quality issues of Big Data. As the volume, variety (format and source), and velocity of data change, so should the capabilities of governance practices.
- *Skills availability:* Big Data is being harnessed with new tools and is being looked at in different ways. There is a shortage of people (often called *data scientists*) with skills to do the job.
- *Solution cost:* Because Big Data has opened up a world of possible business improvements, a great deal of experimentation and discovery is taking place to determine the patterns that matter and the insights that turn to value. To ensure a positive return on investment on a Big Data project, therefore, it is crucial to reduce the cost of the solutions used to find that value.

Though the challenges are real, so is the value proposition of Big Data analytics. Anything that you can do as a business analytics leader to help prove the value of new data sources to the business will move your organization beyond experimenting and exploring Big Data into adapting and embracing it as a differentiator. There is nothing wrong with exploration, but ultimately the value comes from putting those insights into action.

Business Problems Addressed by Big Data Analytics

The top business problems addressed by Big Data overall are process efficiency and cost reduction, as well as enhancing customer experience, but different priorities emerge when it is looked at by industry. Process efficiency and cost reduction are perhaps among the top-ranked problems that can be addressed with Big Data analytics for the manufacturing, government, energy and utilities, communications and media, transport, and healthcare sectors. Enhanced customer experience may be at the top of the list of problems addressed by insurance companies and retailers. Risk management usually is at the top of the list for companies in banking and education. Here is a partial list of problems that can be addressed using Big Data analytics:

- Process efficiency and cost reduction
- Brand management
- Revenue maximization, cross-selling, and up-selling
- Enhanced customer experience
- Churn identification, customer recruiting
- Improved customer service
- Identifying new products and market opportunities
- Risk management
- Regulatory compliance
- Enhanced security capabilities

Application Case 7.2 illustrates an excellent example in the banking industry, where disparate data sources are integrated into a Big Data infrastructure to achieve a single source of the truth.

Application Case 7.2

Top Five Investment Bank Achieves Single Source of the Truth

The bank's highly respected derivatives team is responsible for over one-third of the world's total derivatives trades. Their derivatives practice has a global footprint with teams that support credit, interest rates, and equity derivatives in every region of the world. The bank has earned numerous industry awards and is recognized for its product innovations.

Challenge

With its significant derivatives exposure, the bank's management recognized the importance of having a real-time global view of its positions. The existing system, based on a relational database, was comprised of multiple installations around the world. Due to the gradual expansions to accommodate the increasing data volume varieties, the legacy system was not fast enough to respond to growing business needs and requirements. It was unable to deliver real-time alerts to manage market and counterparty credit positions in the desired time frame.

Solution

The bank built a derivatives trade store based on the MarkLogic (a Big Data analytics solution provider) Server, replacing the incumbent technologies.

Replacing the 20 disparate batch-processing servers with a single operational trade store enabled the bank to know its market and credit counterparty positions in real time, providing the ability to act quickly to mitigate risk. The accuracy and completeness of the data allowed the bank and its regulators to confidently rely on the metrics and stress test results it reports.

The selection process included upgrading existing Oracle and Sybase technology. Meeting all the new regulatory requirements was also a major factor in the decision as the bank looked to maximize its investment. After the bank's careful investigation, the choice was clear—only MarkLogic could meet both needs plus provide better performance, scalability, faster development for future requirements and implementation, and a much lower total cost of ownership. Figure 7.5 illustrates the transformation from the old fragmented systems to the new unified system.

Results

MarkLogic was selected because existing systems would not provide the subsecond updating and analysis response times needed to effectively manage a

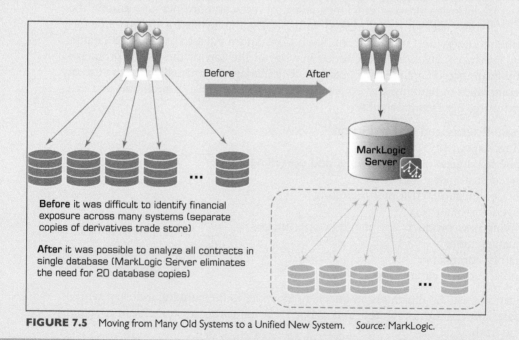

FIGURE 7.5 Moving from Many Old Systems to a Unified New System.   *Source:* MarkLogic.

derivatives trade book that represents nearly one-third of the global market. Trade data is now aggregated accurately across the bank's entire derivatives portfolio, allowing risk management stakeholders to know the true enterprise risk profile, to conduct predictive analyses using accurate data, and to adopt a forward-looking approach. Not only are hundreds of thousands of dollars of technology costs saved each year, but the bank does not need to add resources to meet regulators' escalating demands for more transparency and stress-testing frequency. Here are the highlights:

- An alerting feature keeps users appraised of up-to-the-minute market and counterparty credit changes so they can take appropriate actions.
- Derivatives are stored and traded in a single MarkLogic system requiring no downtime for maintenance, a significant competitive advantage.
- Complex changes can be made in hours versus days, weeks, and even months needed by competitors.
- Replacing Oracle and Sybase significantly reduced operations costs: one system versus 20, one database administrator instead of up to 10, and lower costs per trade.

Next Steps

The successful implementation and performance of the new system resulted in the bank's examination of other areas where it could extract more value from its Big Data—structured, unstructured, and/or polystructured. Two applications are under active discussion. Its equity research business sees an opportunity to significantly boost revenue with a platform that provides real-time research, repurposing, and content delivery. The bank also sees the power of centralizing customer data to improve onboarding, increase cross-selling opportunities, and support know-your-customer requirements.

QUESTIONS FOR DISCUSSION

1. How can Big Data benefit large-scale trading banks?
2. How did the MarkLogic infrastructure help ease the leveraging of Big Data?
3. What were the challenges, the proposed solution, and the obtained results?

Source: MarkLogic. (2012). Top 5 investment bank achieves single source of truth. marklogic.com/resources/top-5-derivatives-trading-bank-achieves-single-source-of-truth (accessed July 2016).

SECTION 7.3 REVIEW QUESTIONS

1. What is Big Data analytics? How does it differ from regular analytics?
2. What are the critical success factors for Big Data analytics?
3. What are the big challenges that one should be mindful of when considering implementation of Big Data analytics?
4. What are the common business problems addressed by Big Data analytics?

7.4 Big Data Technologies

There are a number of technologies for processing and analyzing Big Data, but most have some common characteristics (Kelly, 2012). Namely, they take advantage of commodity hardware to enable scale-out and parallel-processing techniques; employ nonrelational data storage capabilities to process unstructured and semistructured data; and apply advanced analytics and data visualization technology to Big Data to convey insights to end users. The three Big Data technologies that stand out that most believe will transform the business analytics and data management markets are MapReduce, Hadoop, and NoSQL.

MapReduce

MapReduce is a technique popularized by Google that distributes the processing of very large multistructured data files across a large cluster of machines. High performance is achieved by breaking the processing into small units of work that can be run in parallel across the hundreds, potentially thousands, of nodes in the cluster. To quote the seminal paper on MapReduce:

> MapReduce is a programming model and an associated implementation for processing and generating large data sets. Programs written in this functional style are automatically parallelized and executed on a large cluster of commodity machines. This allows programmers without any experience with parallel and distributed systems to easily utilize the resources of a large distributed system. (Dean & Ghemawat, 2004)

The key point to note from this quote is that MapReduce is a programming model, not a programming language, that is, it is designed to be used by programmers, rather than business users. The easiest way to describe how MapReduce works is through the use of an example—see the Colored Square Counter in Figure 7.6.

The input to the MapReduce process in Figure 7.6 is a set of colored squares. The objective is to count the number of squares of each color. The programmer in this example is responsible for coding the map and reducing programs; the remainder of the processing is handled by the software system implementing the MapReduce programming model.

The MapReduce system first reads the input file and splits it into multiple pieces. In this example, there are two splits, but in a real-life scenario, the number of splits would typically be much higher. These splits are then processed by multiple map programs running in parallel on the nodes of the cluster. The role of each map program in this case is to group the data in a split by color. The MapReduce system then takes the output from each map program and merges (shuffle/sort) the results for input to the reduce program,

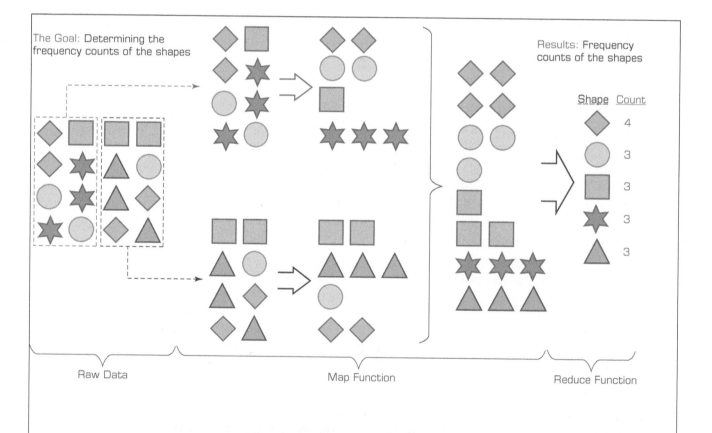

FIGURE 7.6 A Graphical Depiction of the MapReduce Process.

which calculates the sum of the number of squares of each color. In this example, only one copy of the reduce program is used, but there may be more in practice. To optimize performance, programmers can provide their own shuffle/sort program and can also deploy a combiner that combines local map output files to reduce the number of output files that have to be remotely accessed across the cluster by the shuffle/sort step.

Why Use MapReduce?

MapReduce aids organizations in processing and analyzing large volumes of multistructured data. Application examples include indexing and search, graph analysis, text analysis, machine learning, data transformation, and so forth. These types of applications are often difficult to implement using the standard SQL employed by relational DBMSs.

The procedural nature of MapReduce makes it easily understood by skilled programmers. It also has the advantage that developers do not have to be concerned with implementing parallel computing—this is handled transparently by the system. Although MapReduce is designed for programmers, nonprogrammers can exploit the value of prebuilt MapReduce applications and function libraries. Both commercial and open source MapReduce libraries are available that provide a wide range of analytic capabilities. Apache Mahout, for example, is an open source machine-learning library of "algorithms for clustering, classification and batch-based collaborative filtering" that are implemented using MapReduce.

Hadoop

Source: Hadoop.

Hadoop is an open source framework for processing, storing, and analyzing massive amounts of distributed, unstructured data. Originally created by Doug Cutting at Yahoo!, Hadoop was inspired by MapReduce, a user-defined function developed by Google in the early 2000s for indexing the Web. It was designed to handle petabytes and exabytes of data distributed over multiple nodes in parallel. Hadoop clusters run on inexpensive commodity hardware so projects can scale-out without breaking the bank. Hadoop is now a project of the Apache Software Foundation, where hundreds of contributors continuously improve the core technology. Fundamental concept: Rather than banging away at one huge block of data with a single machine, Hadoop breaks up Big Data into multiple parts so each part can be processed and analyzed at the same time.

How Does Hadoop Work?

A client accesses unstructured and semistructured data from sources including log files, social media feeds, and internal data stores. It breaks the data up into "parts," which are then loaded into a file system made up of multiple nodes running on commodity hardware. The default file store in Hadoop is the **Hadoop Distributed File System**, or **HDFS**. File systems such as HDFS are adept at storing large volumes of unstructured and semistructured data as they do not require data to be organized into relational rows and columns. Each "part" is replicated multiple times and loaded into the file system so that if a node fails, another node has a copy of the data contained on the failed node. A Name Node acts as facilitator, communicating back to the client information such as which nodes are available, where in the cluster certain data resides, and which nodes have failed.

Once the data is loaded into the cluster, it is ready to be analyzed via the MapReduce framework. The client submits a "Map" job—usually a query written in Java—to one of the nodes in the cluster known as the Job Tracker. The Job Tracker refers to the Name Node to determine which data it needs to access to complete the job and where in the cluster that data is located. Once determined, the Job Tracker submits the query to the relevant nodes. Rather than bringing all the data back into a central location for processing, the processing occurs at each node simultaneously, or in parallel. This is an essential characteristic of Hadoop.

When each node has finished processing its given job, it stores the results. The client initiates a "Reduce" job through the Job Tracker in which results of the map phase stored locally on individual nodes are aggregated to determine the "answer" to the original query, and then are loaded onto another node in the cluster. The client accesses these results, which can then be loaded into one of a number of analytic environments for analysis. The MapReduce job has now been completed.

Once the MapReduce phase is complete, the processed data is ready for further analysis by data scientists and others with advanced data analytics skills. **Data scientists** can manipulate and analyze the data using any of a number of tools for any number of uses, including searching for hidden insights and patterns, or use as the foundation for building user-facing analytic applications. The data can also be modeled and transferred from Hadoop clusters into existing relational databases, data warehouses, and other traditional IT systems for further analysis and/or to support transactional processing.

Hadoop Technical Components

A Hadoop "stack" is made up of a number of components, which include

- *Hadoop Distributed File System (HDFS):* The default storage layer in any given Hadoop cluster.
- *Name Node:* The node in a Hadoop cluster that provides the client information on where in the cluster particular data is stored and if any nodes fail.
- *Secondary Node:* A backup to the Name Node, it periodically replicates and stores data from the Name Node should it fail.
- *Job Tracker:* The node in a Hadoop cluster that initiates and coordinates MapReduce jobs or the processing of the data.
- *Slave Nodes:* The grunts of any Hadoop cluster, slave nodes store data and take direction to process it from the Job Tracker.

In addition to these components, the Hadoop ecosystem is made up of a number of complementary subprojects. NoSQL data stores like Cassandra and HBase are also used to store the results of MapReduce jobs in Hadoop. In addition to Java, some MapReduce jobs and other Hadoop functions are written in Pig, an open source language designed specifically for Hadoop. **Hive** is an open source data warehouse originally developed by Facebook that allows for analytic modeling within Hadoop. Here are the most commonly referenced subprojects for Hadoop.

HIVE Hive is a Hadoop-based data warehousing–like framework originally developed by Facebook. It allows users to write queries in an SQL-like language called HiveQL, which are then converted to MapReduce. This allows SQL programmers with no MapReduce experience to use the warehouse and makes it easier to integrate with business intelligence (BI) and visualization tools such as Microstrategy, Tableau, Revolutions Analytics, and so forth.

PIG Pig is a Hadoop-based query language developed by Yahoo! It is relatively easy to learn and is adept at very deep, very long data pipelines (a limitation of SQL).

HBASE HBase is a nonrelational database that allows for low-latency, quick lookups in Hadoop. It adds transactional capabilities to Hadoop, allowing users to conduct updates, inserts, and deletes. eBay and Facebook use HBase heavily.

FLUME Flume is a framework for populating Hadoop with data. Agents are populated throughout one's IT infrastructure—inside Web servers, application servers, and mobile devices, for example—to collect data and integrate it into Hadoop.

OOZIE Oozie is a workflow processing system that lets users define a series of jobs written in multiple languages—such as MapReduce, Pig, and Hive—and then intelligently link them to one another. Oozie allows users to specify, for example, that a particular query is only to be initiated after specified previous jobs on which it relies for data are completed.

AMBARI Ambari is a Web-based set of tools for deploying, administering, and monitoring Apache Hadoop clusters. Its development is being led by engineers from Hortonworks, which includes Ambari in its Hortonworks Data Platform.

AVRO Avro is a data serialization system that allows for encoding the schema of Hadoop files. It is adept at parsing data and performing removed procedure calls.

MAHOUT Mahout is a data mining library. It takes the most popular data mining algorithms for performing clustering, regression testing, and statistical modeling and implements them using the MapReduce model.

SQOOP Sqoop is a connectivity tool for moving data from non-Hadoop data stores—such as relational databases and data warehouses—into Hadoop. It allows users to specify the target location inside of Hadoop and instructs Sqoop to move data from Oracle, Teradata, or other relational databases to the target.

HCATALOG HCatalog is a centralized metadata management and sharing service for Apache Hadoop. It allows for a unified view of all data in Hadoop clusters and allows diverse tools, including Pig and Hive, to process any data elements without needing to know physically where in the cluster the data is stored.

Hadoop: The Pros and Cons

The main benefit of Hadoop is that it allows enterprises to process and analyze large volumes of unstructured and semistructured data, heretofore inaccessible to them, in a cost- and time-effective manner. Because Hadoop clusters can scale to petabytes and even exabytes of data, enterprises no longer must rely on sample data sets but can process and analyze *all* relevant data. Data scientists can apply an iterative approach to analysis, continually refining and testing queries to uncover previously unknown insights. It is also inexpensive to get started with Hadoop. Developers can download the Apache Hadoop distribution for free and begin experimenting with Hadoop in less than a day.

The downside to Hadoop and its myriad components is that they are immature and still developing. As with any young, raw technology, implementing and managing

Hadoop clusters and performing advanced analytics on large volumes of unstructured data require significant expertise, skill, and training. Unfortunately, there is currently a dearth of Hadoop developers and data scientists available, making it impractical for many enterprises to maintain and take advantage of complex Hadoop clusters. Further, as Hadoop's myriad components are improved on by the community and new components are created, there is, as with any immature open source technology/approach, a risk of forking. Finally, Hadoop is a batch-oriented framework, meaning it does not support real-time data processing and analysis.

The good news is that some of the brightest minds in IT are contributing to the Apache Hadoop project, and a new generation of Hadoop developers and data scientists is coming of age. As a result, the technology is advancing rapidly, becoming both more powerful and easier to implement and manage. An ecosystem of vendors, both Hadoop-focused start-ups like Cloudera and Hortonworks and well-worn IT stalwarts like IBM, Microsoft, Teradata, and Oracle are working to offer commercial, enterprise-ready Hadoop distributions, tools, and services to make deploying and managing the technology a practical reality for the traditional enterprise. Other bleeding edge start-ups are working to perfect NoSQL (Not Only SQL) data stores capable of delivering near–real-time insights in conjunction with Hadoop. Technology Insights 7.2 provides a few facts to clarify some misconceptions about Hadoop.

TECHNOLOGY INSIGHTS 7.2
A Few Demystifying Facts about Hadoop

Although Hadoop and related technologies have been around for more than 5 years now, most people still have several misconceptions about Hadoop and related technologies such as MapReduce and Hive. The following list of 10 facts intends to clarify what Hadoop is and does relative to BI, as well as in which business and technology situations Hadoop-based BI, data warehousing, and analytics can be useful (Russom, 2013).

Fact #1. Hadoop consists of multiple products. We talk about Hadoop as if it's one monolithic software, whereas it's actually a family of open source products and technologies overseen by the Apache Software Foundation (ASF). (Some Hadoop products are also available via vendor distributions; more on that later.)

The Apache Hadoop library includes (in BI priority order) HDFS, MapReduce, Hive, Hbase, Pig, Zookeeper, Flume, Sqoop, Oozie, Hue, and so on. You can combine these in various ways, but HDFS and MapReduce (perhaps with Hbase and Hive) constitute a useful technology stack for applications in BI, data warehousing, and analytics.

Fact #2. Hadoop is open source but available from vendors, too. Apache Hadoop's open source software library is available from ASF at **apache.org**. For users desiring a more enterprise-ready package, a few vendors now offer Hadoop distributions that include additional administrative tools and technical support.

Fact #3. Hadoop is an ecosystem, not a single product. In addition to products from Apache, the extended Hadoop ecosystem includes a growing list of vendor products that integrate with or expand Hadoop technologies. One minute on your favorite search engine will reveal these.

Fact #4. HDFS is a file system, not a database management system (DBMS). Hadoop is primarily a distributed file system and lacks capabilities we would associate with a DBMS, such as indexing, random access to data, and support for SQL. That's okay, because HDFS does things DBMSs cannot do.

Fact #5. Hive resembles SQL but is not standard SQL. Many of us are handcuffed to SQL because we know it well and our tools demand it. People who know SQL can quickly learn to hand-code Hive, but that doesn't solve compatibility issues with SQL-based tools. TDWI feels that over time, Hadoop products will support standard SQL, so this issue will soon be moot.

Fact #6. Hadoop and MapReduce are related but don't require each other. Developers at Google developed MapReduce before HDFS existed, and some variations of MapReduce work with a variety of storage technologies, including HDFS, other file systems, and some DBMSs.

Fact #7. MapReduce provides control for analytics, not analytics per se. MapReduce is a general-purpose execution engine that handles the complexities of network communication, parallel programming, and fault tolerance for any kind of application that you can hand code—not just analytics.

Fact #8. Hadoop is about data diversity, not just data volume. Theoretically, HDFS can manage the storage and access of any data type as long as you can put the data in a file and copy that file into HDFS. As outrageously simplistic as that sounds, it's largely true, and it's exactly what brings many users to Apache HDFS.

Fact #9. Hadoop complements a DW; it's rarely a replacement. Most organizations have designed their DW for structured, relational data, which makes it difficult to wring BI value from unstructured and semistructured data. Hadoop promises to complement DWs by handling the multistructured data types most DWs can't.

Fact #10. Hadoop enables many types of analytics, not just Web analytics. Hadoop gets a lot of press about how Internet companies use it for analyzing Web logs and other Web data, but other use cases exist. For example, consider the Big Data coming from sensory devices, such as robotics in manufacturing, RFID in retail, or grid monitoring in utilities. Older analytic applications that need large data samples—such as customer-base segmentation, fraud detection, and risk analysis—can benefit from the additional Big Data managed by Hadoop. Likewise, Hadoop's additional data can expand 360-degree views to create a more complete and granular view.

NoSQL

A related new style of database called **NoSQL** (Not Only SQL) has emerged to, like Hadoop, process large volumes of multistructured data. However, whereas Hadoop is adept at supporting large-scale, batch-style historical analysis, NoSQL databases are aimed, for the most part (though there are some important exceptions), at serving up discrete data stored among large volumes of multistructured data to end-user and automated Big Data applications. This capability is sorely lacking from relational database technology, which simply can't maintain needed application performance levels at a Big Data scale.

In some cases, NoSQL and Hadoop work in conjunction. The aforementioned HBase, for example, is a popular NoSQL database modeled after Google BigTable that is often deployed on top of HDFS, the Hadoop Distributed File System, to provide low-latency, quick lookups in Hadoop. The downside of most NoSQL databases today is that they trade ACID (atomicity, consistency, isolation, durability) compliance for performance and scalability. Many also lack mature management and monitoring tools. Both of these shortcomings are in the process of being overcome by the open source NoSQL communities and a handful of vendors that are attempting to commercialize the various NoSQL databases. NoSQL databases currently available include HBase, Cassandra, MongoDB, Accumulo, Riak, CouchDB, and DynamoDB, among others. Application Case 7.3 shows the use of NoSQL databases at eBay. Application Case 7.4 illustrates a social media application where the Hadoop infrastructure was used to compile a corpus of messages on Twitter to understand which types of users engage in which type of support for healthcare patients seeking information about chronic mental diseases.

Application Case 7.3

eBay's Big Data Solution

eBay is the world's largest online marketplace, enabling the buying and selling of practically anything. Founded in 1995, eBay connects a diverse and passionate community of individual buyers and sellers, as well as small businesses. eBay's collective impact on e-commerce is staggering: In 2012, the total value of goods sold on eBay was $75.4 billion. eBay currently serves over 112 million active users and 400+ million items for sale.

The Challenge: Supporting Data at an Extreme Scale

One of the keys to eBay's extraordinary success is its ability to turn the enormous volumes of data it generates into useful insights that its customers can glean directly from the pages they frequent. To accommodate eBay's explosive data growth—its data centers perform billions of reads and writes each day—and due to the increasing demand to process data at blistering speeds, eBay needed a solution that did not have the typical bottlenecks, scalability issues, and transactional constraints associated with common relational database approaches. The company also needed to perform rapid analysis on a broad assortment of the structured and unstructured data it captured.

The Solution: Integrated Real-Time Data and Analytics

Its Big Data requirements brought eBay to NoSQL technologies, specifically Apache Cassandra and DataStax Enterprise. Along with Cassandra and its high-velocity data capabilities, eBay was also drawn to the integrated Apache Hadoop analytics that come with DataStax Enterprise. The solution incorporates a scale-out architecture that enables eBay to deploy multiple DataStax Enterprise clusters across several different data centers using commodity hardware. The end result is that eBay is now able to more cost effectively process massive amounts of data at very high speeds, at very high velocities, and achieve far more than they were able to with the higher cost proprietary system they had been using. Currently,

eBay is managing a sizable portion of its data center needs—250TBs+ of storage—in Apache Cassandra and DataStax Enterprise clusters.

Additional technical factors that played a role in eBay's decision to deploy DataStax Enterprise so widely include the solution's linear scalability, high availability with no single point of failure, and outstanding write performance.

Handling Diverse Use Cases

eBay employs DataStax Enterprise for many different use cases. The following examples illustrate some of the ways the company is able to meet its Big Data needs with the extremely fast data handling and analytics capabilities the solution provides. Naturally, eBay experiences huge amounts of write traffic, which the Cassandra implementation in DataStax Enterprise handles more efficiently than any other RDBMS or NoSQL solution. eBay currently sees 6 billion+ writes per day across multiple Cassandra clusters and 5 billion+ reads (mostly offline) per day as well.

One use case supported by DataStax Enterprise involves quantifying the social data eBay displays on its product pages. The Cassandra distribution in DataStax Enterprise stores all the information needed to provide counts for "like," "own," and "want" data on eBay product pages. It also provides the same data for the eBay "Your Favorites" page that contains all the items a user likes, owns, or wants, with Cassandra serving up the entire "Your Favorites" page. eBay provides this data through Cassandra's scalable counters feature.

Load balancing and application availability are important aspects to this particular use case. The DataStax Enterprise solution gave eBay architects the flexibility they needed to design a system that enables any user request to go to any data center, with each data center having a single DataStax Enterprise cluster spanning those centers. This design feature helps balance the incoming user load and eliminates any possible threat to application downtime. In addition to the line of business data powering the Web pages its customers visit, eBay is

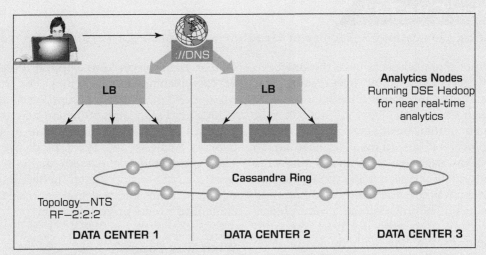

FIGURE 7.7   eBay's Multi–Data Center Deployment.   *Source:* DataStax.

also able to perform high-speed analysis with the ability to maintain a separate data center running Hadoop nodes of the same DataStax Enterprise ring (see Figure 7.7).

Another use case involves the Hunch (an eBay sister company) "taste graph" for eBay users and items, which provides customer recommendations based on user interests. eBay's Web site is essentially a graph between all users and the items for sale. All events (bid, buy, sell, and list) are captured by eBay's systems and stored as a graph in Cassandra. The application sees more than 200 million writes daily and holds more than 40 billion pieces of data.

eBay also uses DataStax Enterprise for many time-series use cases in which processing high-volume, real-time data is a foremost priority. These include mobile notification logging and tracking (every time eBay sends a notification to a mobile phone or device it is logged in Cassandra), fraud detection, SOA request/response payload logging, and RedLaser (another eBay sister company) server logs and analytics.

Across all of these use cases is the common requirement of uptime. eBay is acutely aware of the need to keep their business up and open for business, and DataStax Enterprise plays a key part in that through its support of high availability clusters. "We have to be ready for disaster recovery all the time. It's really great that Cassandra allows for active-active multiple data centers where we can read and write data anywhere, anytime," says eBay architect Jay Patel.

QUESTIONS FOR DISCUSSION

1. Why did eBay need a Big Data solution?
2. What were the challenges, the proposed solution, and the obtained results?

Source: DataStax. Customer case studies. datastax.com/resources/casestudies/eBay (accessed July 2016).

SECTION 7.4 REVIEW QUESTIONS

1. What are the common characteristics of emerging Big Data technologies?
2. What is MapReduce? What does it do? How does it do it?
3. What is Hadoop? How does it work?
4. What are the main Hadoop components? What functions do they perform?
5. What is NoSQL? How does it fit into the Big Data analytics picture?

Application Case 7.4

Understanding Quality and Reliability of Healthcare Support Information on Twitter

On the Internet today all users have the power to contribute as well as consume information. This power is used in many ways. On social network platforms such as Twitter, users are able to post information about their health condition as well as receive help on how best to manage those health conditions. Many users have wondered about the quality of information disseminated on social network platforms. Whereas the ability to author and disseminate health information on Twitter seems valuable to many users who use it to seek support for their disease, the authenticity of such information, especially when it originates from lay individuals, has been in doubt. Many users have asked, "How do I verify and trust information from nonexperts about how to manage a vital issue like my health condition?"

What types of users share and discuss what type of information? Do users with a large following discuss and share the same type of information as users with a smaller following? The number of followers of a user relate to the influence of a user. Characteristics of the information are measured in terms of quality and objectivity of the Tweet posted. A team of data scientists set out to explore the relationship between the number of followers a user had and the characteristics of information the user disseminated (Asamoah & Sharda, 2015).

Solution

Data was extracted from the Twitter platform using Twitter's API. The data scientists adapted the knowledge-discovery and data management model to manage and analyze this large set of data. The model was optimized for managing and analyzing Big Data derived from a social network platform and included phases for gaining domain knowledge, developing an appropriate Big Data platform, data acquisition and storage, data cleaning, data validation, data analysis, and results and deployment.

Technology Used

The tweets were extracted, managed, and analyzed using Cloudera's distribution of the Apache Hadoop. The Apache Hadoop framework has several subprojects that support different kinds of data management activities. For instance, the Apache Hive subproject supported the reading, writing, and managing of the large tweet data. Data analytics tools such as Gephi were used for social network analysis and R for predictive modeling. They conducted two parallel analyses; social network analysis to understand the influence network on the platform and text mining to understand the content of tweets posted by users.

What Was Found?

As noted earlier, tweets from both influential and noninfluential users were collected and analyzed. The results showed that the quality and objectivity of information disseminated by influential users was higher than that disseminated by noninfluential users. They also found that influential users controlled the flow of information in a network and that other users were more likely to follow their opinion on a subject. There was a clear difference between the type of information support provided by influential users versus the others. Influential users discussed more objective information regarding the disease management—things such as diagnoses, medications, formal therapies. Noninfluential users provided more information about emotional support and alternative ways of coping with such diseases. Thus a clear difference between influential users and the others was evident.

From the nonexperts' perspective, the data scientists portray how healthcare provision can be augmented by helping patients identify and use valuable resources on the Web for managing their disease condition. This work also helps identify how nonexperts can locate and filter healthcare information that may not necessarily be beneficial to the management of their health condition.

QUESTIONS FOR DISCUSSION

1. What was the data scientists' main concern regarding health information that is disseminated on the Twitter platform?
2. How did the data scientists ensure that nonexpert information disseminated on social media could indeed contain valuable health information?

3. Does it make sense that influential users would share more objective information whereas less influential users could focus more on subjective information? Why?

Sources: Asamoah, D., & Sharda, R. (2015). Adapting CRISP-DM process for social network analytics: Application to healthcare. In

AMCIS 2015 Proceedings. aisel.aisnet.org/amcis2015/BizAnalytics/ GeneralPresentations/33/ (accessed July 2016).

Sarasohn-Kahn, J. (2008). *The wisdom of patients: Health care meets online social media.* Oakland, CA: California HealthCare Foundation.

7.5   Big Data and Data Warehousing

There is no doubt that the emergence of Big Data has changed and will continue to change data warehousing in a significant way. Until recently, enterprise data warehouses (Chapters 2 and 3) were the centerpiece of all decision support technologies. Now, they have to share the spotlight with the newcomer, Big Data. The question that is popping up everywhere is whether Big Data and its enabling technologies such as Hadoop will replace data warehousing and its core technology RDBMS. Are we witnessing a data warehouse versus Big Data challenge (or from the technology standpoint, Hadoop versus RDBMS)? In this section we will explain why these questions have no basis—and at least justify that such an either-or choice is not a reflection of the reality at this point in time.

In the last decade or so, we have seen significant improvement in the area of computer-based decision support systems, which can largely be credited to data warehousing and technological advancements in both software and hardware to capture, store, and analyze data. As the size of the data increased, so did the capabilities of data warehouses. Some of these data warehousing advances included massively parallel processing (moving from one or few to many parallel processors), storage area networks (easily scalable storage solutions), solid-state storage, in-database processing, in-memory processing, and columnar (column-oriented) databases, just to name a few. These advancements helped keep the increasing size of data under control, while effectively serving analytics needs of the decision makers. What has changed the landscape in recent years is the variety and complexity of data, which made data warehouses incapable of keeping up. It is not the volume of the data but the variety and velocity that forced the world of IT to develop a new paradigm, which we now call "Big Data." Now that we have these two paradigms—data warehousing and Big Data—seemingly competing for the same job—turning data into actionable information—which one will prevail? Is this a fair question to ask? Or are we missing the big picture? In this section, we try to shed some light on this intriguing question.

As has been the case for many previous technology innovations, hype about Big Data and its enabling technologies like Hadoop and MapReduce is rampant. Nonpractitioners as well as practitioners are overwhelmed by diverse opinions. According to Awadallah and Graham (2012), people are missing the point in claiming that Hadoop replaces relational databases and is becoming the new data warehouse. It is easy to see where these claims originate because both Hadoop and data warehouse systems can run in parallel, scale-up to enormous data volumes, and have shared-nothing architectures. At a conceptual level, one would think they are interchangeable. The reality is that they are not, and the differences between the two overwhelm the similarities. If they are not interchangeable, then how do we decide when to deploy Hadoop and when to use a data warehouse?

Use Cases for Hadoop

As we have covered earlier in this chapter, Hadoop is the result of new developments in computer and storage grid technologies. Using commodity hardware as a foundation, Hadoop provides a layer of software that spans the entire grid, turning it into a single system. Consequently, some major differentiators are obvious in this architecture:

- Hadoop is the repository and refinery for raw data.
- Hadoop is a powerful, economical, and active archive.

Thus, Hadoop sits at both ends of the large-scale data life cycle—first when raw data is born, and finally when data is retiring, but is still occasionally needed.

1. *Hadoop as the repository and refinery.* As volumes of Big Data arrive from sources such as sensors, machines, social media, and clickstream interactions, the first step is to capture all the data reliably and cost effectively. When data volumes are huge, the traditional single-server strategy does not work for long. Pouring the data into HDFS gives architects much needed flexibility. Not only can they capture 100s of terabytes in a day, but they can also adjust the Hadoop configuration up or down to meet surges and lulls in data ingestion. This is accomplished at the lowest possible cost per gigabyte due to open source economics and leveraging commodity hardware.

   Because the data is stored on local storage instead of storage area networks, Hadoop data access is often much faster, and it does not clog the network with terabytes of data movement. Once the raw data is captured, Hadoop is used to refine it. Hadoop can act as a parallel "ETL engine on steroids," leveraging handwritten or commercial data transformation technologies. Many of these raw data transformations require the unraveling of complex freeform data into structured formats. This is particularly true with clickstreams (or Web logs) and complex sensor data formats. Consequently, a programmer needs to tease the wheat from the chaff, identifying the valuable signal in the noise.

2. *Hadoop as the active archive.* In a 2003 interview with ACM, Jim Gray claimed that hard disks could be treated as tape. Although it may take many more years for magnetic tape archives to be retired, today some portions of tape workloads are already being redirected to Hadoop clusters. This shift is occurring for two fundamental reasons. First, although it may appear inexpensive to store data on tape, the true cost comes with the difficulty of retrieval. Not only is the data stored offline, requiring hours if not days to restore, but tape cartridges themselves are also prone to degradation over time, making data loss a reality and forcing companies to factor in those costs. To make matters worse, tape formats change every couple of years, requiring organizations to either perform massive data migrations to the newest tape format or risk the inability to restore data from obsolete tapes.

   Second, it has been shown that there is value in keeping historical data online and accessible. As in the clickstream example, keeping raw data on a spinning disk for a longer duration makes it easy for companies to revisit data when the context changes and new constraints need to be applied. Searching thousands of disks with Hadoop is dramatically faster and easier than spinning through hundreds of magnetic tapes. In addition, as disk densities continue to double every 18 months, it becomes economically feasible for organizations to hold many years' worth of raw or refined data in HDFS. Thus, the Hadoop storage grid is useful both in the preprocessing of raw data and the long-term storage of data. It's a true "active archive" because it not only stores and protects the data, but also enables users to quickly, easily, and perpetually derive value from it.

Use Cases for Data Warehousing

After nearly 30 years of investment, refinement, and growth, the list of features available in a data warehouse is quite staggering. Built on relational database technology using schemas and integrating BI tools, the major differences in this architecture are

- Data warehouse performance
- Integrated data that provides business value
- Interactive BI tools for end users

1. **Data warehouse performance.**   Basic indexing, found in open source databases, such as MySQL or Postgres, is a standard feature used to improve query response times or enforce constraints on data. More advanced forms such as materialized views, aggregate join indexes, cube indexes, and sparse join indexes enable numerous performance gains in data warehouses. However, the most important performance enhancement to date is the cost-based optimizer. The optimizer examines incoming SQL and considers multiple plans for executing each query as fast as possible. It achieves this by comparing the SQL request to the database design and extensive data statistics that help identify the best combination of execution steps. In essence, the optimizer is like having a genius programmer examine every query and tune it for the best performance. Lacking an optimizer or data demographic statistics, a query that could run in minutes may take hours, even with many indexes. For this reason, database vendors are constantly adding new index types, partitioning, statistics, and optimizer features. For the past 30 years, every software release has been a performance release. As we will note at the end of his section, Hadoop is now gaining on traditional data warehouses in terms of query performance.

2. **Integrating data that provides business value.**   At the heart of any data warehouse is the promise to answer essential business questions. Integrated data is the unique foundation required to achieve this goal. Pulling data from multiple subject areas and numerous applications into one repository is the *raison d'être* for data warehouses. Data model designers and Extract, Transform, and Load (ETL) architects armed with metadata, data-cleansing tools, and patience must rationalize data formats, source systems, and semantic meaning of the data to make it understandable and trustworthy. This creates a common vocabulary within the corporation so that critical concepts such as "customer," "end of month," and "price elasticity" are uniformly measured and understood. Nowhere else in the entire IT data center is data collected, cleaned, and integrated as it is in the data warehouse.

3. **Interactive BI tools.**   BI tools such as MicroStrategy, Tableau, IBM Cognos, and others provide business users with direct access to data warehouse insights. First, the business user can create reports and complex analysis quickly and easily using these tools. As a result, there is a trend in many data warehouse sites toward end-user self-service. Business users can easily demand more reports than IT has staffing to provide. More important than self-service, however, is that the users become intimately familiar with the data. They can run a report, discover they missed a metric or filter, make an adjustment, and run their report again all within minutes. This process results in significant changes in business users' understanding of the business and their decision-making process. First, users stop asking trivial questions and start asking more complex strategic questions. Generally, the more complex and strategic the report, the more revenue and cost savings the user captures. This leads to some users becoming "power users" in a company. These individuals become wizards at teasing business value from the data and supplying valuable strategic information to the executive staff. Every data warehouse has anywhere from 2 to 20 power users.

The Gray Areas (Any One of the Two Would Do the Job)

Even though there are several areas that differentiate one from the other, there are also gray areas where the data warehouse and Hadoop cannot be clearly discerned. In these areas either tool could be the right solution—either doing an equally good or a not-so-good job on the task at hand. Choosing one over the other depends on the requirements and the preferences of the organization. In many cases, Hadoop and the data warehouse work together in an information supply chain, and just as often, one tool is better for a specific workload (Awadallah & Graham, 2012). Table 7.1 illustrates the preferred platform (one versus the other, or equally likely) under a number of commonly observed requirements.

TABLE 7.1 When to Use Which Platform—Hadoop versus DW

Requirement	Data Warehouse	Hadoop
Low latency, interactive reports, and OLAP	☑	
ANSI 2003 SQL compliance is required	☑	☑
Preprocessing or exploration of raw unstructured data		☑
Online archives alternative to tape		☑
High-quality cleansed and consistent data	☑	☑
100s to 1,000s of concurrent users	☑	☑
Discover unknown relationships in the data		☑
Parallel complex process logic	☑	☑
CPU intense analysis	☑	
System, users, and data governance		☑
Many flexible programming languages running in parallel		☑
Unrestricted, ungoverned sandbox explorations		☑
Analysis of provisional data	☑	
Extensive security and regulatory compliance	☑	☑

Coexistence of Hadoop and Data Warehouse

There are several possible scenarios under which using a combination of Hadoop and relational DBMS-based data warehousing technologies makes more sense. Here are some of those scenarios (White, 2012):

1. **Use Hadoop for storing and archiving multistructured data.** A connector to a relational DBMS can then be used to extract required data from Hadoop for analysis by the relational DBMS. If the relational DBMS supports MapReduce functions, these functions can be used to do the extraction. The Aster-Hadoop adaptor, for example, uses SQL-MapReduce functions to provide fast, two-way data loading between HDFS and the Aster Database. Data loaded into the Aster Database can then be analyzed using both SQL and MapReduce.
2. **Use Hadoop for filtering, transforming, and/or consolidating multistructured data.** A connector such as the Aster-Hadoop adaptor can be used to extract the results from Hadoop processing to the relational DBMS for analysis.
3. **Use Hadoop to analyze large volumes of multistructured data and publish the analytical results.** In this application, Hadoop serves as the analytics platform but the results can be posted back to the traditional data warehousing environment, a shared workgroup data store, or a common user interface.
4. **Use a relational DBMS that provides MapReduce capabilities as an investigative computing platform.** Data scientists can employ the relational DBMS (the Aster Database system, for example) to analyze a combination of structured data and multistructured data (loaded from Hadoop) using a mixture of SQL processing and MapReduce analytic functions.
5. **Use a front-end query tool to access and analyze data.** Here, the data are stored in both Hadoop and the relational DBMS.

These scenarios support an environment where the Hadoop and relational DBMSs are separate from each other and connectivity software is used to exchange data between the two systems (see Figure 7.8). The direction of the industry over the next few years will likely be moving toward more tightly coupled Hadoop and relational DBMS-based

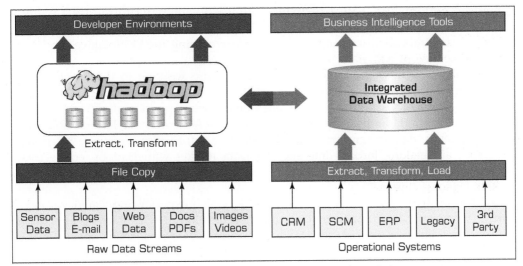

FIGURE 7.8 Coexistence of Hadoop and Data Warehouses.   *Source:* Teradata Corp.

data warehouse technologies—both software and hardware. Such integration provides many benefits, including eliminating the need to install and maintain multiple systems, reducing data movement, providing a single metadata store for application development, and providing a single interface for both business users and analytical tools. The opening vignette (Section 7.1) provided an example of how data from a traditional data warehouse and two different unstructured data sets stored on Hadoop were integrated to create an analytics application to gain insight into a customer's interactions with a company before canceling an account. As a manager, you care about the insights you can derive from the data, not whether the data is stored in a structured data warehouse or a Hadoop cluster.

SECTION 7.5 REVIEW QUESTIONS

1. What are the challenges facing data warehousing and Big Data? Are we witnessing the end of the data warehousing era? Why or why not?
2. What are the use cases for Big Data and Hadoop?
3. What are the use cases for data warehousing and RDBMS?
4. In what scenarios can Hadoop and RDBMS coexist?

7.6 Big Data Vendors and Platforms

As a relatively new technology area, the Big Data vendor landscape is developing very rapidly. A number of vendors have developed their own Hadoop distributions, most based on the Apache open source distribution but with various levels of proprietary customization. Two market leaders in terms of distribution seem to be Cloudera (cloudera.com) and Hortonworks (hortonworks.com). Cloudera was started by Big Data experts including Hadoop creator Doug Cutting and former Facebook data scientist Jeff Hammerbacher. Hortonworks was spun out of Yahoo! In addition to distribution, both companies offer paid enterprise-level training/services and proprietary Hadoop management software. MapR (mapr.com), another Valley start-up, offers its own Hadoop distribution that supplements HDFS with its proprietary network file system (NFS) for improved performance. EMC Greenplum partnered with MapR to release a partly proprietary Hadoop distribution of its own in May 2011. These are just a few of the many companies (established and start-ups) that are crowding the competitive landscape of tool and service providers for Hadoop technologies.

In the NoSQL world, a number of start-ups are working to deliver commercially supported versions of the various flavors of NoSQL. DataStax, for example, offers a commercial version of Cassandra that includes enterprise support and services, as well as integration with Hadoop and open source enterprise search via Lucene Solr. Most of the proprietary data integration vendors, including Informatica, Pervasive Software, and Syncsort, are making inroads into the Big Data market with Hadoop connectors and complementary tools aimed at making it easier for developers to move data around and within Hadoop clusters.

The analytics layer of the Big Data stack is also experiencing significant development. A start-up called Datameer, for example, is developing what it says is an "all-in-one" business intelligence platform for Hadoop, whereas data visualization specialist Tableau Software has added Hadoop and Next Generation Data Warehouse connectivity to its product suite. EMC Greenplum, meanwhile, has Chorus, a sort of playground for data scientists where they can mash-up, experiment with, and share large volumes of data for analysis. Other vendors focus on specific analytic use cases, such as ClickFox with its customer experience analytics engine. A number of traditional business intelligence vendors, most notably MicroStrategy, are working to incorporate Big Data analytic and reporting capabilities into their products.

Big Data application space is also growing. Many companies offer applications built to take advantage of the Hadoop cluster and MapReduce framework. Open-source tools such as R programming language has many implemented functions to take advantage of parallelizing execution through a cluster. For example, Treasata offers Big-Data-as-a-service applications for several industries.

Meanwhile, the next-generation data warehouse market has experienced significant consolidation recently. Four leading vendors in this space—Netezza, Greenplum, Vertica, and Aster Data—were acquired by IBM, EMC, HP, and Teradata, respectively. EMC itself has now been acquired by Dell. Mega-vendors Oracle and IBM also play in the Big Data space. Oracle has embraced the appliance approach to Big Data with its Exadata, Exalogic, and Big Data appliances. Its Big Data appliance incorporates Cloudera's Hadoop distribution with Oracle's NoSQL database and data integration tools. IBM's BigInsights platform is based on Apache Hadoop, but includes numerous proprietary modules including the Netezza database, InfoSphere Warehouse, Cognos business intelligence tools, and SPSS data mining capabilities. It also offers IBM InfoSphere Streams, a platform designed for streaming Big Data analysis. With the success of Watson analytics brand, IBM is folding many of its analytics offerings in general and Big Data offerings in particular under the Watson label. Teradata's acquisition of Aster has resulted in an impressive product offering in Teradata Aster that implements many of the commonly used analytics functions in the Big Data environment. We next briefly introduce IBM's InfoSphere and Teradata Aster environments and present a short application case for each. We chose to introduce these two platforms here because both are commercially successful platforms, and ample learning materials including downloadable software are available for them.

IBM InfoSphere BigInsights

Introduction IBM's InfoSphere BigInsights is a platform based on the open source Apache Hadoop project to analyze traditional structured data found in legacy databases along with semi- and unstructured data such as text, video, audio, images, social media, Web logs, and clickstreams. The platform incorporates many MapReduce implementations of analytics algorithms to run large-scale parallelized applications and is designed to provide advanced analytics on Hadoop technology specifically optimized for Big Data analysis requirements.

Architecture Figure 7.9 displays the various components of IBM InfoSphere BigInsights. In addition to the standard Apache Hadoop software, BigInsights provides IBM-unique technologies and programming languages with built-in analytics and application accelerators (e.g., text, geospatial, time series, data mining, finance, social media, telco event, and machine data) to efficiently perform specialized operations to meet Big Data analysis requirements. For example, *JSON Query Language* (*JAQL*) is designed to better support manipulation and analysis of semistructured *JavaScript Object Notation* (*JSON*) data. These functions are particularly useful in analyzing Twitter data streams. *BigSheets* is a spreadsheet-style tool that supports scalable data exploration and visualization directly on a Big SQL table residing on HDFS. *Annotation Query Language* (*AQL*) provides built-in libraries for advanced text analytics across vast amounts of semi- and unstructured documents. BigR is a platform for large-scale analytics on Hadoop that enables accessing, manipulating, analyzing, and visualizing data residing on HDFS from the R user interface. Last but not least, the InfoSphere BigInsights tools for Eclipse enable developers to develop programs to run on InfoSphere BigInsights. It includes wizards, code generators, and a test environment to simplify the application development efforts. With all these tools available in a single seamless platform, one can quickly develop and publish an application in the BigInsights Web-based catalog, then use a Web console to deploy the application on the Hadoop cluster and allow authorized users to access it.

How to Get Started BigInsights trials can be downloaded from the link: http://www.ibm.com/analytics/us/en/technology/hadoop/hadoop-trials.html.

The quick start edition of BigInsights is available to download for free via http://www.ibm.com/developerworks/downloads/im/biginsightsquick/.

It supports a single- or multinode cluster of open source Hadoop. It requires a system with a minimum of 16 GB RAM, 4-core processor, and 50 GB free disk space.

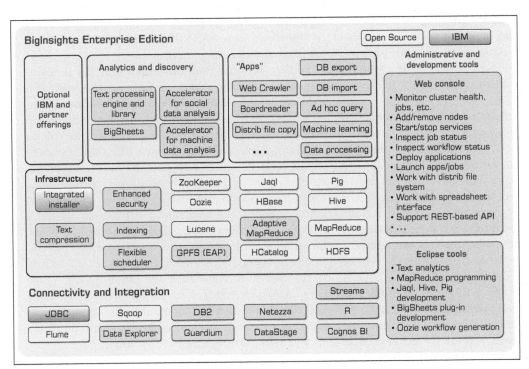

FIGURE 7.9 IBM InfoSphere Architecture.

The best place to start learning about InfoSphere BigInsights is through the IBM Knowledge Center:

http://www.ibm.com/support/knowledgecenter/SSPT3X_2.1.2/com.ibm.swg.im.InfoSphere.biginsights.tut.doc/doc/tut_Introduction.html.

Application Case 7.5 provides an example of how we were able to combine data from multiple sources to analyze reports of influenza.

Application Case 7.5

Using Social Media for Nowcasting the Flu Activity

Infectious diseases impose a significant burden to the U.S. public health system. The rise of HIV/AIDS in the late seventies, pandemic H1N1 flu in 2009, H3N2 epidemic during the 2012–2013 winter season, the Ebola virus disease outbreak in 2015, and the Zika virus scare in 2016, have demonstrated the susceptibility of people to such contagious diseases. Virtually each year influenza outbreaks happen in various forms and result in consequences of varying impacts. The annual impact of seasonal influenza outbreaks in the United States is reported to be an average of 610,660 undiscounted life-years lost, 3.1 million hospitalized days, 31.4 million outpatient visits, and a total of $87.1 billion in economic burden. As a result of this growing trend, new data analytics techniques and technologies capable of detecting, tracking, mapping, and managing such diseases have come on the scene in recent years. In particular, digital surveillance systems have shown promise in their capacity to discover public health seeking patterns and transform these discoveries into actionable strategies.

This project demonstrated that social media can be utilized as an effective method for early detection of influenza outbreaks. We used a Big Data platform to employ Twitter data to monitor influenza activity in the United States. Our Big Data analytics methods comprised temporal, spatial, and text mining. In the temporal analysis, we examined whether Twitter data could indeed be adapted for the nowcasting of influenza outbreaks. In spatial analysis, we mapped flu outbreaks to the geospatial property of Twitter data to identify influenza hotspots. Text analytics was performed to identify popular symptoms and treatments of flu that were mentioned in tweets.

The IBM InfoSphere BigInsights platform was employed to analyze two sets of flu activity data: Twitter data were used to monitor flu outbreaks in the United States, and Cerner HealthFacts data warehouse was used to track real-world clinical encounters. A huge volume of flu-related tweets was crawled from Twitter using Twitter Streaming API and was then ingested into a Hadoop cluster. Once the data were successfully imported, the JSON Query Language (JAQL) tool was used to manipulate and parse semistructured JavaScript Object Notation (JSON) data. Next, Hive was used to tabularize the text data and segregate the information for the spatial-temporal location analysis and visualization in R. The entire data mining process was implemented using MapReduce functions. We used the package BigR to submit the R scripts over the data stored in HDFS. The package BigR enabled us to benefit from the parallel computation of HDFS and to perform MapReduce operations. Google's Maps API libraries were used as a basic mapping tool to visualize the tweet locations.

Our findings demonstrated that the integration of social media and medical records can be a valuable supplement to the existing surveillance systems. Our results confirmed that flu-related traffic on social media is closely related with the actual flu outbreak. This has been shown by other researchers as well (St Louis & Zorlu, 2012; Broniatowski, Paul, & Dredze, 2013). We performed a time-series analysis to obtain the spatial-temporal cross-correlation between the two trends (91%) and observed that clinical flu encounters lag behind online posts. In addition, our location analysis revealed several public locations from which a majority of tweets were originated. These findings can help health officials and governments to develop more accurate and timely forecasting models during outbreaks and to inform individuals about the locations that they should avoid during that time period.

Sources: Zadeh, A. H., Zolbanin, H. M., Sharda, R., & Delen, D. (2015). Social media for nowcasting the flu activity: Spatial-temporal and text analysis. *Business Analytics Congress, Pre-ICIS Conference*, Fort Worth, TX.

Broniatowski, D. A., Paul, M. J., & Dredze, M. (2013). National and local influenza surveillance through Twitter: An analysis of the 2012–2013 influenza epidemic. *PloS One, 8*(12), e83672.

Moran, P. A. (1950). Notes on continuous stochastic phenomena. *Biometrika*, 17–23.

QUESTIONS FOR DISCUSSION

1. Why would social media be able to serve as an early predictor of flu outbreaks?
2. What other variables might help in predicting such outbreaks?
3. Why would this problem be a good problem to solve using Big Data technologies mentioned in this chapter?

Teradata Aster

Introduction Teradata Aster is a Big Data platform for distributed storage and processing of large multistructured data sets. It has been used for marketing optimization, fraud detection, sports analytics, social networking analysis, machine data analytics, energy analytics, healthcare analytics, and many other applications. Teradata Aster has parallelized many traditional and advanced analytics functions. It has in-built capabilities for performing time-series analysis, statistical analysis, cluster analysis, text mining, association rule mining, social network analysis, visual analytics, location analytics, and predictive analytics; all in a distributed manner. In addition to the traditional analytics packages, it also has several novel and unique analytics packages for path analysis. It is also compatible with other programming languages such as R, Python, and Java.

Architecture Teradata Aster has adapted the master–slave architecture of Apache Hadoop. It consists of a queen node and multiple worker nodes equivalent to the name node and data nodes in the Hadoop, respectively. Figure 7.10 presents the TD Aster architecture.

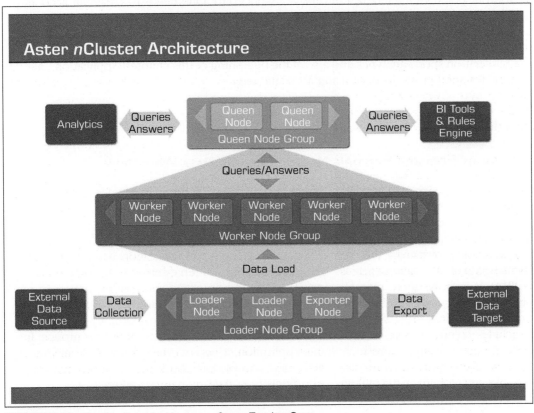

FIGURE 7.10 Teradata Aster Architecture. *Source:* Teradata Corp.

The queen node in the top tier manages the system, schema, error handling, and distribution of the computation across workers. It coordinates the queries and returns the query results. The middle tier of the architecture contains workers. The workers store the data with a replication factor assigned by the administrator, and thus, they are fault tolerant. The workers interact with each other to process the queries requested by the queen. The third tier of the architecture consists of the loader nodes that receive the data from third parties such as Informatics.

TD Aster architecture includes Aster File Store that can ingest multistructured data such as Web logs, sensor data, and machine log data. It is compatible with HDFS and other traditional file systems. The cluster can also be connected to other databases such as Oracle DB, Teradata Warehouse, and Hive through other available connecters.

For the data analysis, a user can write traditional SQL, SQL-MapReduce (SQL-MR), and SQL-Graph (SQL-GR) queries. SQL-MR is a TD Aster framework that enables the MapReduce execution of the analytics functions in the Aster Database. Similarly, SQL-GR is a framework for enabling Graph Engine processing in the Aster Database. The execution of the queries written in SQL, SQL-SQL-MR, or SQL-GR are automatically parallelized across the cluster. To access the databases and write queries, users can either use the Aster Command Tool (ACT) or a client-side application named Teradata Studio.

The complete package of TD Aster includes a Web browser-based tool for visualization called AppCenter. AppCenter can be used to create different types of visualizations such as a Sankey chart, sigma chart, chord chart, tree structure, hierarchical cluster chart, word cloud, bar chart, pie chart, and other traditional statistics charts.

How to Get Started The express version of Teradata Aster is available to download for free. One can download the TD Aster Express from the link (https://aster-community .teradata.com). It consists of two virtual machines: one queen and one worker. It requires a machine with minimum of 4 GB RAM. A user can upload a maximum of 17 GB of data in the Aster Express. A getting started guide can be accessed through the Teradata University Network portal (www.teradatauniversitynetwork.com). One needs to create an account on the TUN Web site to access the documentation, instructions, exercises, and data sets for learning Teradata Aster.

You have already seen examples of using Teradata Aster in the opening vignette in Chapter 1 on sports analytics and also at the beginning of this chapter. Application Case 7.6 provides another example of using Teradata Aster.

Application Case 7.6

Analyzing Disease Patterns from an Electronic Medical Records Data Warehouse

The Center for Health Systems Innovation at Oklahoma State University has been given a massive data warehouse by Cerner Corporation, a major electronic medical records (EMRs) provider, to help develop analytic applications. The data warehouse contains EMRs on the visits of more than 50 million unique patients across U.S. hospitals (1995–2014). It includes more than 84 million acute admissions and emergency and ambulatory visits. It is the largest and the industry's only relational database that includes comprehensive records with pharmacy, laboratory, clinical events, admissions, and billing data. The database also includes more than 2.4 billion laboratory results and more than 295 million orders for nearly 4,500 drugs by name and brand. It is one of the largest compilation of de-identified, real-world, HIPAA-compliant data of its type.

The EMRs can be used to develop multiple analytics applications. One application is to understand the relationships between diseases based on the information about the simultaneous diseases developed in the patients. When multiple diseases are present in a patient, the condition is called comorbidity. The comorbidities can be different across population groups. In this application, a research group at Oklahoma State University created a comparison of the comorbidities in patients from the urban and rural regions.

To compare the comorbidities, a network analysis approach was applied. A network is comprised of a defined set of items called nodes, which are linked to each other through edges. An edge represents a defined relationship between the nodes. A very common example of network is a friendship network in which individuals are connected to each other if they are friends. Similarly, other common networks are computer networks, Web page networks, road networks, and airport networks. To compare the comorbidities, networks of the diseases in the patients from rural and urban hospitals were developed. The information about the diseases developed by each patient during hospital visits was used to create a disease network. The total number of hospital visits in the urban hospitals were 66 million and in the rural hospitals were 1 million. To manage such a huge data set, Teradata Aster Big Data platform was used. To extract and prepare the network data, SQL, SQL-MR, and SQL-GR frameworks supported by Aster were utilized. To visualize the networks we used Aster AppCenter and Gephi.

Figure 7.11 presents the rural and urban comorbidity networks. In these networks, nodes represent different diseases classified as the *International Classification of Diseases*, Ninth Revision, Clinical Modification (ICD-9-CM), aggregated at the three-digit level. Two diseases were linked if they were significantly correlated or comorbid ($p < 0.01$). The larger the size of the node, the greater the comorbid is that disease. The urban comorbidity network is denser than the rural network. The number of nodes and edges in the urban network are 1,043 and 22,029, respectively, whereas the number of nodes and edges in the rural network are 993 and 2,073, respectively. This indicates that the patients in the rural hospitals are often diagnosed with fewer diseases simultaneously. The visualizations present a clear difference between the pattern of diseases developed in urban and rural patients. It presents many medical and social policy questions that require further research and analysis. On the other hand, we included this analysis to also raise awareness of another issue. We noted earlier that the data set used for this analysis included about 66 million urban patient encounters and only 1 million rural encounters. Such a whopping difference is because most rural hospitals probably could not afford the cost of a major electronic medical record system like Cerner, and thus the data are skewed toward urban hospitals. But any insights generated from such a sample would be questioned. As noted in Chapter 4, a proportional sample might have been drawn from the urban areas and have that be compared against the rural patient records.

The traditional database systems would be taxed in efficiently processing such a huge data set. The Teradata Aster made the analysis of data containing information on 84 million visits and 200 million records fairly fast and easy. Network analysis is often suggested as one method to analyze big data sets. It helps understand the data in one picture. In this application, the comorbidity network explains the relationship between diseases at one place.

QUESTIONS FOR DISCUSSION

1. Why could comorbidity of diseases be different between rural and urban hospitals?
2. What is the issue about the huge difference between rural and urban patient encounters?
3. What are the main components of a network?
4. Where else can you apply the network approach?

Source: Kalgotra, P., & Sharda, R. (2016). Rural versus urban comorbidity networks. Working Paper, Center for Health Systems and Innovation, Oklahoma State University.

The cloud is increasingly playing a role in the Big Data market as well. Amazon and Google support Hadoop deployments in their public cloud offerings. Amazon Elastic MapReduce and Google Compute Engine, respectively, enable users to easily scale-up and scale-down clusters as needed. Microsoft supports Hortonworks' Hadoop distribution on its Azure cloud. We will discuss cloud-based offerings in the next chapter.

There are also other vendors approaching Big Data from the visual analytics angle. As Gartner's latest Magic Quadrant indicates, a significant growth in business intelligence and analytics is in visual exploration and visual analytics. Large companies like SAS, SAP, and IBM, along with small but stable companies like Tableau, TIBCO, and QlikView, are making a strong case for high-performance analytics built into information visualization

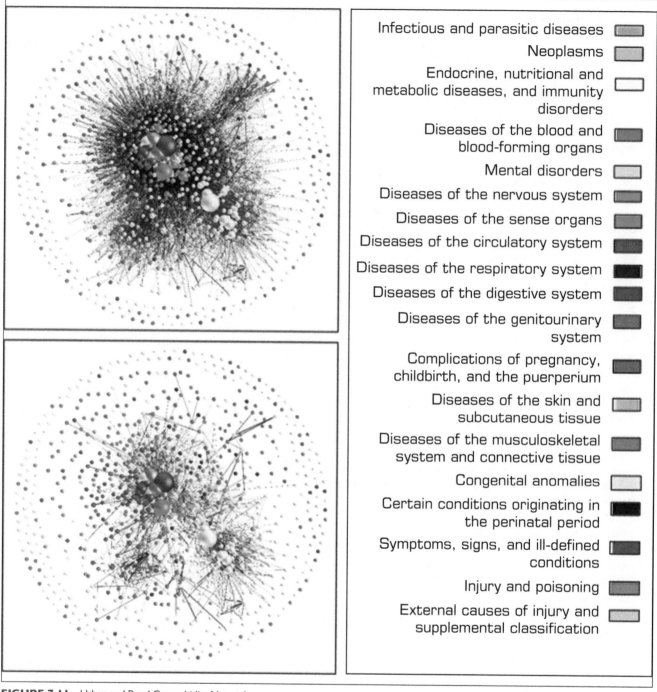

Infectious and parasitic diseases

Neoplasms

Endocrine, nutritional and metabolic diseases, and immunity disorders

Diseases of the blood and blood-forming organs

Mental disorders

Diseases of the nervous system

Diseases of the sense organs

Diseases of the circulatory system

Diseases of the respiratory system

Diseases of the digestive system

Diseases of the genitourinary system

Complications of pregnancy, childbirth, and the puerperium

Diseases of the skin and subcutaneous tissue

Diseases of the musculoskeletal system and connective tissue

Congenital anomalies

Certain conditions originating in the perinatal period

Symptoms, signs, and ill-defined conditions

Injury and poisoning

External causes of injury and supplemental classification

FIGURE 7.11 Urban and Rural Comorbidity Networks.

platforms. Technology Insights 7.4 provides a few key enablers to succeed with Big Data and visual analytics. SAS is perhaps the one pushing it harder than any other with its recently launched SAS Visual Analytics platform. It was introduced in Chapter 2. Using a multitude of computational enhancements, the SAS Visual Analytics platform is capable of turning tens of millions of data records into informational graphics in just a few seconds by using massively parallel processing (MPP) and in-memory computing.

TECHNOLOGY INSIGHTS 7.3
How to Succeed with Big Data

From the White House to your house, it's hard to find an organization or consumer who has less data today than a year ago. Database options proliferate, and business intelligence evolves to a new era of organization-wide analytics. And everything's mobile. Organizations that successfully adapt their data architecture and processes to address the three characteristics of Big Data—volume, variety, and velocity—are improving operational efficiency, growing revenues, and empowering new business models. With all the attention organizations are placing on innovating around data, the rate of change will only increase. So what should companies do to succeed with Big Data? Here are some of the industry testaments:

1. Simplify. It is hard to keep track of all of the new database vendors, open source projects, and Big Data service providers. It will be even more crowded and complicated in the years ahead. Therefore, there is a need for simplification. It is essential to take a strategic approach by extending your relational and online transaction processing systems to one or more of the new on-premise, hosted, or service-based database options that best reflect the needs of your industry and your organization, and then picking a real-time business intelligence platform that supports direct connections to many databases and file formats. Choosing the best mix of solution alternatives for every project (between connecting live to fast databases and importing data extracts into an in-memory analytics engine to offset the performance of slow or over-burdened databases) is critical to the success of any Big Data projects. For instance, eBay's Big Data analytics architecture is comprised of Teradata (one of the most popular data warehousing companies), Hadoop (the most promising solution to the Big Data challenge), and Tableau (one of the prolific visual analytics solution providers). eBay employees can visualize insights from more than 52 petabytes of data. eBay uses a visual analytics solution by Tableau to analyze search relevance and quality of the eBay.com site, monitor the latest customer feedback and meter sentiments on eBay.com, and achieve operational reporting for the data warehouse systems, all of which helped an analytic culture flourish within eBay.

2. Coexist. Using the strengths of each database platform and enabling them to coexist in your organization's data architecture are essential. There is ample literature that talks about the necessity of maintaining and nurturing the coexistence of traditional data warehouses with the capabilities of new platforms.

3. Visualize. According to leading analytics research companies like Forrester and Gartner, enterprises find advanced data visualization platforms to be essential tools that enable them to monitor business, find patterns, and take action to avoid threats and snatch opportunities. Visual analytics help organizations uncover trends, relationships, and anomalies by visually shifting through very large quantities of data. A visual analysis experience has certain characteristics. It allows you to do two things at any moment:

- Instantly change what data you are looking at. This is important because different questions require different data.
- Instantly change the way you are looking at the data. This is important because each view may answer different questions.

This combination creates the exploratory experience required for anyone to answer questions quickly. In essence, visualization becomes a natural extension of your experimental thought process.

4. Empower. Big Data and self-service business intelligence go hand in hand, according to Aberdeen Group's recently published "Maximizing the Value of Analytics and Big Data." Organizations with Big Data are over 70% more likely than other organizations to have BI/BA projects that are driven primarily by the business community, not by the IT group. Across a range of uses—from tackling new business problems, developing entirely new products and services, finding actionable intelligence in less than an hour, and blending data from disparate sources—Big Data has fired the imagination of what is possible through the application of analytics.

5. Integrate. Integrating and blending data from disparate sources for your organization is an essential part of Big Data analytics. Organizations that can blend different relational, semistructured, and raw data sources in real time, without expensive up-front integration costs, will be the ones that get the best value from Big Data. Once integrated and blended, the structure of the data (e.g., spreadsheets, a database, a data warehouse, an open source file system like Hadoop, or all of them at the same time) becomes unimportant;

(Continued)

TECHNOLOGY INSIGHTS 7.3 (Continued)
How to Succeed with Big Data

that is, you don't need to know the details of how data is stored to ask and answer questions against it. As we saw in Application Case 7.4, the Obama campaign found a way to integrate social media, technology, e-mail databases, fundraising databases, and consumer market data to create a competitive advantage.

6. Govern. Data governance has always been a challenging issue in IT, and it is getting even more puzzling with the advent of Big Data. More than 80 countries have data privacy laws. The European Union defines seven "safe harbor privacy principles" for the protection of their citizens' personal data. In Singapore, the personal data protection law took effect January 2013. In the United States, Sarbanes-Oxley affects all publicly listed companies, and HIPAA (Health Insurance Portability and Accountability Act) sets national standards in healthcare. The right balance between control and experimentation varies depending on the organization and industry. Use of master data management best practices seems to help manage the governance process.

7. Evangelize. With the backing of one or more executive sponsors, evangelists like yourself can get the ball rolling and instill a virtuous cycle: The more departments in your organization that realize actionable benefits, the more pervasive analytics becomes across your organization. Fast, easy-to-use visual analytics is the key that opens the door to organization-wide analytics adoption and collaboration.

Sources: Lampitt, A. (2012). Big data visualization: A big deal for eBay. infoworld.com/d/big-data/big-data-visualization-big-deal-ebay-208589 (accessed August 2016).

Tableau white paper. (2012). 7 Tips to Succeed with Big Data in 2013. cdnlarge.tableausoftware.com/sites/default/files/whitepapers/7-tips-to-succeed-with-big-data-in-2013.pdf (accessed August 2016).

SECTION 7.6 REVIEW QUESTIONS

1. What is special about the Big Data vendor landscape? Who are the big players?

2. How do you think the Big Data vendor landscape will change in the near future? Why?

3. What is the role of visual analytics in the world of Big Data?

7.7 Big Data and Stream Analytics

Along with volume and variety, as we have seen earlier in this chapter, one of the key characteristics that defines Big Data is velocity, which refers to the speed at which the data is created and streamed into the analytics environment. Organizations are looking for new means to process streaming data as it comes in to react quickly and accurately to problems and opportunities to please their customers and to gain a competitive advantage. In situations where data streams in rapidly and continuously, traditional analytics approaches that work with previously accumulated data (i.e., data at rest) often either arrive at the wrong decisions because of using too much out-of-context data, or they arrive at the correct decisions but too late to be of any use to the organization. Therefore, it is critical for a number of business situations to analyze the data soon after it is created and/or as soon as it is streamed into the analytics system.

The presumption that the vast majority of modern-day businesses are currently living by is that it is important and critical to record every piece of data because it might contain valuable information now or sometime in the near future. However, as long as the number of data sources increases, the "store-everything" approach becomes harder and harder and, in some cases, not even feasible. In fact, despite technological advances, current total storage capacity lags far behind the digital information being generated in the world. Moreover, in the constantly changing business environment, real-time detection of meaningful changes in data as well as of complex pattern variations within a given short time window are essential to come up with the actions that better fit with the new environment. These facts become the main triggers for a paradigm that we call *stream analytics*. The stream analytics paradigm was born as an answer to these challenges, namely, the unbounded flows of data that cannot be permanently stored to be subsequently analyzed, in a timely and efficient manner, and complex pattern variations that need to be detected and acted on as soon as they happen.

Stream analytics (also called *data-in-motion analytics* and *real-time data analytics,* among others) is a term commonly used for the analytic process of extracting actionable information from continuously flowing/streaming data. A stream is defined as a continuous sequence of data elements (Zikopoulos et al., 2013). The data elements in a stream are often called *tuples.* In a relational database sense, a tuple is similar to a row of data (a record, an object, an instance). However, in the context of semistructured or unstructured data, a tuple is an abstraction that represents a package of data, which can be characterized as a set of attributes for a given object. If a tuple by itself is not sufficiently informative for analysis or a correlation—or other collective relationships among tuples are needed—then a window of data that includes a set of tuples is used. A window of data is a finite number/sequence of tuples, where the windows are continuously updated as new data become available. The size of the window is determined based on the system being analyzed. Stream analytics is becoming increasingly more popular because of two things. First, time-to-action has become an ever-decreasing value, and second, we have the technological means to capture and process the data while it is created.

Some of the most impactful applications of stream analytics were developed in the energy industry, specifically for smart grid (electric power supply chain) systems. The new smart grids are capable of not only real-time creation and processing of multiple streams of data to determine optimal power distribution to fulfill real customer needs, but also generating accurate short-term predictions aimed at covering unexpected demand and renewable energy generation peaks. Figure 7.12 shows a depiction of a generic use case for streaming analytics in the energy industry (a typical smart grid application). The goal

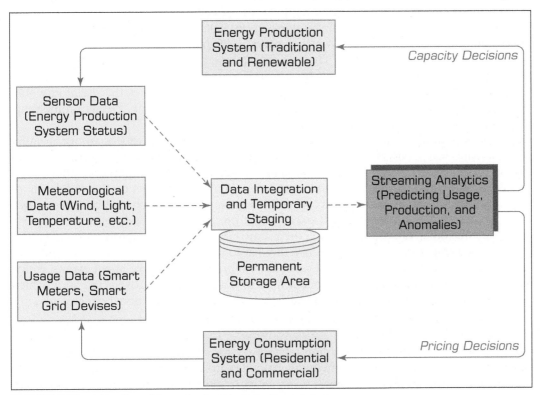

FIGURE 7.12   A Use Case of Streaming Analytics in the Energy Industry.

is to accurately predict electricity demand and production in real time by using streaming data that is coming from smart meters, production system sensors, and meteorological models. The ability to predict near future consumption/production trends and detect anomalies in real time can be used to optimize supply decisions (how much to produce, what sources of production to use, and optimally adjust production capacities) as well as to adjust smart meters to regulate consumption and favorable energy pricing.

Stream Analytics versus Perpetual Analytics

The terms *streaming* and *perpetual* probably sound like the same thing to most people, and in many cases they are used synonymously. However, in the context of intelligent systems, there is a difference (Jonas, 2007). Streaming analytics involves applying transaction-level logic to real-time observations. The rules applied to these observations take into account previous observations as long as they occurred in the prescribed window; these windows have some arbitrary size (e.g., last 5 seconds, last 10,000 observations). **Perpetual analytics**, on the other hand, evaluates every incoming observation against all prior observations, where there is no window size. Recognizing how the new observation relates to all prior observations enables the discovery of real-time insight.

Both streaming and perpetual analytics have their pros and cons and their respective places in the business analytics world. For example, sometimes transactional volumes are high and the time-to-decision is too short, favoring nonpersistence and small window sizes, which translates into using streaming analytics. However, when the mission is critical and transaction volumes can be managed in real time, then perpetual analytics is a better answer. That way, one can answer questions such as "How does what I just learned relate to what I have known?" "Does this matter?" and "Who needs to know?"

Critical Event Processing

Critical event processing is a method of capturing, tracking, and analyzing streams of data to detect events (out of normal happenings) of certain types that are worthy of the effort. Complex event processing is an application of stream analytics that combines data from multiple sources to infer events or patterns of interest either before they actually occur or as soon as they happen. The goal is to take rapid actions to prevent (or mitigate the negative effects of) these events (e.g., fraud or network intrusion) from occurring, or in the case of a short window of opportunity, take full advantage of the situation within the allowed time (based on user behavior on an e-commerce site, create promotional offers that they are more likely to respond to).

These critical events may be happening across the various layers of an organization such as sales leads, orders, or customer service calls. Or, more broadly, they may be news items, text messages, social media posts, stock market feeds, traffic reports, weather conditions, or other kinds of anomalies that may have a significant impact on the well-being of the organization. An event may also be defined generically as a "change of state," which may be detected as a measurement exceeding a predefined threshold of time, temperature, or some other value. Even though there is no denying the value proposition of critical event processing, one has to be selective in what to measure, when to measure, and how often to measure. Because of the vast amount of information available about events, which is sometimes referred to as the *event cloud*, there is a possibility of overdoing it, in which case as opposed to helping the organization, it may hurt the operational effectiveness.

Data Stream Mining

Data stream mining, as an enabling technology for stream analytics, is the process of extracting novel patterns and knowledge structures from continuous, rapid data records. As we saw in the data mining chapter (Chapter 4), traditional data mining methods require the data to be collected and organized in a proper file format, and then processed in a recursive manner to learn the underlying patterns. In contrast, a data stream is a continuous flow of an ordered sequence of instances that in many applications of data stream mining can be read/processed only once or a small number of times using limited computing and storage capabilities. Examples of data streams include sensor data, computer network traffic, phone conversations, ATM transactions, Web searches, and financial data. Data stream mining is considered a subfield of data mining, machine learning, and knowledge discovery.

In many data stream mining applications, the goal is to predict the class or value of new instances in the data stream given some knowledge about the class membership or values of previous instances in the data stream. Specialized machine-learning techniques (mostly derivative of traditional machine-learning techniques) can be used to learn this prediction task from labeled examples in an automated fashion. An example of such a prediction method was developed by Delen, Kletke, & Kim, (2005), where they gradually built and refined a decision tree model by using a subset of the data at a time.

SECTION 7.7 REVIEW QUESTIONS

1. What is a stream (in the Big Data world)?
2. What are the motivations for stream analytics?
3. What is stream analytics? How does it differ from regular analytics?
4. What is critical event processing? How does it relate to stream analytics?
5. Define *data stream mining*. What additional challenges are posed by data stream mining?

7.8 Applications of Stream Analytics

Because of its power to create insight instantly, helping decision makers to be on top of events as they unfold and allowing organizations to address issues before they become problems, the use of streaming analytics is on an exponentially increasing trend. The following are some of the application areas that have already benefited from stream analytics.

e-Commerce

Companies like Amazon and eBay (among many others) are trying to make the most out of the data that they collect while a customer is on their Web site. Every page visit, every product looked at, every search conducted, and every click made is recorded and analyzed to maximize the value gained from a user's visit. If done quickly, analysis of such a stream of data can turn browsers into buyers and buyers into shopaholics. When we visit an e-commerce Web site, even the ones where we are not a member, after a few clicks here and there we start to get very interesting product and bundle price offers. Behind the scenes, advanced analytics are crunching the real-time data coming from our clicks, and the clicks of thousands of others, to "understand" what it is that we are interested in (in some cases, even we do not know that) and make the most of that information by making creative offerings.

Telecommunications

The volume of data that come from call detail records (CDR) for telecommunications companies is astounding. Although this information has been used for billing purposes for quite some time now, there is a wealth of knowledge buried deep inside this Big Data that the telecommunications companies are just now realizing to tap. For instance, CDR data can be analyzed to prevent churn by identifying networks of callers, influencers, leaders, and followers within those networks and proactively acting on this information. As we all know, influencers and leaders have the effect of changing the perception of the followers within their network toward the service provider, either positively or negatively. Using social network analysis techniques, telecommunication companies are identifying the leaders and influencers and their network participants to better manage their customer base. In addition to churn analysis, such information can also be used to recruit new members and maximize the value of the existing members.

Continuous streams of data that come from CDR can be combined with social media data (sentiment analysis) to assess the effectiveness of marketing campaigns. Insight gained from these data streams can be used to rapidly react to adverse effects (which may lead to loss of customers) or boost the impact of positive effects (which may lead to maximizing purchases of existing customers and recruitment of new customers) observed in these campaigns. Furthermore, the process of gaining insight from CDR can be replicated for data networks using Internet protocol detail records. Because most telecommunications companies provide both of these service types, a holistic optimization of all offerings and marketing campaigns could lead to extraordinary market gains. Application Case 7.7 is an example of how Salesforce.com gets a better sense of its customers based upon an analysis of clickstreams.

Application Case 7.7

Salesforce Is Using Streaming Data to Enhance Customer Value

Salesforce has expanded their Marketing Cloud services to include Predictive Scores and Predictive Audience features called the Marketing Cloud Predictive Journey. This addition uses real-time streaming data to enhance the customer engagement online. First, the customers are given a Predictive Score unique to them. This score is calculated from several different factors, including how long their browsing history is, if they clicked an e-mail link, if they made a purchase, how much they spent, how long ago did they make a purchase, or if they have ever responded to an e-mail or ad campaign. Once customers have a score, they are then segmented into different groups. These groups are given different marketing objectives and plans based on the predictive behaviors assigned to them. The scores and segments are updated and changed daily and give companies a better road map to target and achieve a desired response. These marketing solutions are more accurate and create more personalized ways companies can accommodate their customer retention methods.

QUESTIONS FOR DISCUSSION

1. Are there areas in any industry where streaming data is irrelevant?

2. Besides customer retention, what are other benefits of using predictive analytics?

What Can We Learn from This Case?

Through the analysis of data acquired in the here and now, companies are able to make predictions and decisions about their consumers more rapidly. This ensures that businesses target, attract, and retain the right customers and maximize their value. Data acquired last week is not as beneficial as the data companies have today. Using relevant data makes our predictive analysis more accurate and efficient.

Sources: Amodio, M. (2015). *Salesforce adds predictive analytics to Marketing Cloud. Cloud Contact Center.* http://www.cloudcontactcenterzone.com/topics/cloud-contact-center/articles/413611-salesforce-adds-predictive-analytics-marketing-cloud.htm (accessed July 2016).

Davis, J. (2015). Salesforce adds new predictive analytics to Marketing Cloud. *Information Week.* http://www.informationweek.com/big-data/big-data-analytics/salesforce-adds-new-predictive-analytics-to-marketing-cloud/d/d-id/1323201 (accessed July 2016).

Henschen, D. (2016). Salesforce reboots Wave Analytics, preps IoT cloud. *ZD Net.* http://www.zdnet.com/article/salesforce-reboots-wave-analytics-preps-iot-cloud/ (accessed July 2016).

Law Enforcement and Cybersecurity

Streams of Big Data provide excellent opportunities for improved crime prevention, law enforcement, and enhanced security. They offer unmatched potential when it comes to security applications that can be built in the space, such as real-time situational awareness, multimodal surveillance, cyber-security detection, legal wiretapping, video surveillance, and face recognition (Zikopoulos et al., 2013). As an application of information assurance, enterprises can use streaming analytics to detect and prevent network intrusions, cyberattacks, and malicious activities by streaming and analyzing network logs and other Internet activity monitoring resources.

Power Industry

Because of the increasing use of smart meters, the amount of real-time data collected by power utilities is increasing exponentially. Moving from once a month to every 15 minutes (or more frequently), meter reading accumulates large quantities of invaluable data for power utilities. These smart meters and other sensors placed all around the power grid are sending information back to the control centers to be analyzed in real time. Such analyses help utility companies to optimize their supply chain decisions (e.g., capacity adjustments, distribution network options, real-time buying or selling) based on the up-to-the-minute consumer usage and demand patterns. In addition, utility companies can integrate weather and other natural conditions data into their analytics to optimize power generation from alternative sources (e.g., wind, solar) and to better forecast energy demand on different geographic granulations. Similar benefits also apply to other utilities such as water and natural gas.

Financial Services

Financial service companies are among the prime examples where analysis of Big Data streams can provide faster and better decisions, competitive advantage, and regulatory oversight. The ability to analyze fast-paced, high-volumes of trading data at very low latency across markets and countries offers a tremendous advantage to making the split-second buy/sell decisions that potentially translate into big financial gains. In addition to optimal buy/sell decisions, stream analytics can also help financial service companies in real-time trade monitoring to detect fraud and other illegal activities.

Health Sciences

Modern-era medical devices (e.g., electrocardiograms and equipment that measure blood pressure, blood oxygen level, blood sugar level, and body temperature) are capable of producing invaluable streaming diagnostic/sensory data at a very fast rate. Harnessing this data and analyzing it in real time offers benefits—the kind that we often call "life and death"—unlike any other field. In addition to helping healthcare companies become more effective and efficient (and hence more competitive and profitable), stream analytics is also improving patient conditions and saving lives.

Many hospital systems all around the world are developing care infrastructures and health systems that are futuristic. These systems aim to take full advantage of what the technology has to offer, and more. Using hardware devices that generate high-resolution data at a very rapid rate, coupled with super-fast computers that can synergistically analyze multiple streams of data, increases the chances of keeping patients safe by quickly detecting anomalies. These systems are meant to help human decision makers make faster and better decisions by being exposed to a multitude of information as soon as it becomes available.

Government

Governments around the world are trying to find ways to be more efficient (via optimal use of limited resources) and effective (providing the services that people need and want). As the practices for e-government become mainstream, coupled with widespread use and access to social media, very large quantities of data (both structured and unstructured) are at the disposal of government agencies. Proper and timely use of these Big Data streams differentiates proactive and highly efficient agencies from the ones who are still using traditional methods to react to situations as they unfold. Another way in which government agencies can leverage real-time analytics capabilities is to manage natural disasters such as snowstorms, hurricanes, tornadoes, and wildfires through a surveillance of streaming data coming from radar, sensors, and other smart detection devices. They can also use similar approaches to monitor water quality, air quality, and consumption patterns and detect anomalies before they become significant problems. Another area where government agencies use stream analytics is in traffic management in congested cities. By using the data coming from traffic flow cameras, GPS data coming from commercial vehicles, and traffic sensors embedded in roadways, agencies are able to change traffic light sequences and traffic flow lanes to ease the pain caused by traffic congestion problems.

SECTION 7.8 REVIEW QUESTIONS

1. What are the most fruitful industries for stream analytics?
2. How can stream analytics be used in e-commerce?
3. In addition to what is listed in this section, can you think of other industries and/or application areas where stream analytics can be used?
4. Compared to regular analytics, do you think stream analytics will have more (or less) use cases in the era of Big Data analytics? Why?

Chapter Highlights

- Big Data means different things to people with different backgrounds and interests.
- Big Data exceeds the reach of commonly used hardware environments and/or capabilities of software tools to capture, manage, and process it within a tolerable time span.
- Big Data is typically defined by three "V"s: volume, variety, velocity.
- MapReduce is a technique to distribute the processing of very large multistructured data files across a large cluster of machines.
- Hadoop is an open source framework for processing, storing, and analyzing massive amounts of distributed, unstructured data.
- Hive is a Hadoop-based data warehousing–like framework originally developed by Facebook.
- Pig is a Hadoop-based query language developed by Yahoo!
- NoSQL, which stands for Not Only SQL, is a new paradigm to store and process large volumes of unstructured, semistructured, and multistructured data.

- Data scientist is a new role or job commonly associated with Big Data or data science.
- Big Data and data warehouses are complementary (not competing) analytics technologies.
- As a relatively new area, the Big Data vendor landscape is developing very rapidly.
- Stream analytics is a term commonly used for extracting actionable information from continuously flowing/streaming data sources.
- Perpetual analytics evaluates every incoming observation against all prior observations.
- Critical event processing is a method of capturing, tracking, and analyzing streams of data to detect certain events (out of normal happenings) that are worthy of the effort.
- Data stream mining, as an enabling technology for stream analytics, is the process of extracting novel patterns and knowledge structures from continuous, rapid data records.

Key Terms

Big Data	data stream mining	Hive	Pig
Big Data analytics	Hadoop	MapReduce	stream analytics
critical event processing	Hadoop Distributed File	NoSQL	
data scientists	System (HDFS)	perpetual analytics	

Questions for Discussion

1. What is Big Data? Why is it important? Where does Big Data come from?
2. What do you think the future of Big Data will be? Will it lose its popularity to something else? If so, what will it be?
3. What is Big Data analytics? How does it differ from regular analytics?
4. What are the critical success factors for Big Data analytics?
5. What are the big challenges that one should be mindful of when considering implementation of Big Data analytics?
6. What are the common business problems addressed by Big Data analytics?
7. In the era of Big Data, are we about to witness the end of data warehousing? Why?
8. What are the use cases for Big Data/Hadoop and data warehousing/RDBMS?
9. What is stream analytics? How does it differ from regular analytics?
10. What are the most fruitful industries for stream analytics? What is common to those industries?
11. Compared to regular analytics, do you think stream analytics will have more (or less) use cases in the era of Big Data analytics? Why?

Exercises

Teradata University Network (TUN) and Other Hands-on Exercises

1. Go to teradatauniversitynetwork.com, and search for case studies. Read cases and white papers that talk about Big Data analytics. What is the common theme in those case studies?
2. At teradatauniversitynetwork.com, find the SAS Visual Analytics white papers, case studies, and hands-on exercises. Carry out the visual analytics exercises on large data sets and prepare a report to discuss your findings.
3. At teradatauniversitynetwork.com, go to the Sports Analytics page. Find applications of Big Data in sports. Summarize your findings.
4. Go to teradatauniversitynetwork.com, and search for BSI Videos that talk about Big Data. Review these BSI videos, and answer the case questions related to them.
5. Go to the teradata.com and/or asterdata.com Web sites. Find at least three customer case studies on Big Data, and write a report where you discuss the commonalities and differences of these cases.
6. Go to IBM.com. Find at least three customer case studies on Big Data, and write a report where you discuss the commonalities and differences of these cases.
7. Go to claudera.com. Find at least three customer case studies on Hadoop implementation, and write a report where you discuss the commonalities and differences of these cases.
8. Go to mapr.com. Find at least three customer case studies on Hadoop implementation, and write a report where you discuss the commonalities and differences of these cases.
9. Go to hortonworks.com. Find at least three customer case studies on Hadoop implementation, and write a report in which you discuss the commonalities and differences of these cases.
10. Go to marklogic.com. Find at least three customer case studies on Hadoop implementation, and write a report where you discuss the commonalities and differences of these cases.
11. Go to youtube.com. Search for videos on Big Data computing. Watch at least two. Summarize your findings.
12. Go to google.com/scholar, and search for articles on stream analytics. Find at least three related articles. Read and summarize your findings.
13. Enter google.com/scholar, and search for articles on data stream mining. Find at least three related articles. Read and summarize your findings.
14. Enter google.com/scholar, and search for articles that talk about Big Data versus data warehousing. Find at least five articles. Read and summarize your findings.

References

Adshead, A. (2014). Data set to grow 10-fold by 2020 as Internet of Things takes off. http://www.computerweekly.com/news/2240217788/Data-set-to-grow-10-fold-by-2020-as-internet-of-things-takes-off (accessed September 2016).

Amodio, M. (2015). Salesforce adds predictive analytics to Marketing Cloud. Cloud Contact Center.cloudcontactcenter-zone.com/topics/cloud-contact-center/articles/413611-salesforce-adds-predictive-analytics-marketing-cloud.htm (accessed August 2016).

Asamoah, D., Sharda, R., Zadeh, A., & Kalgotra, P. (2016). Preparing a Big Data analytics professional: A pedagogic experience. In *DSI 2016 Conference*, Austin, TX.

Asamoah, D., & Sharda, R. (2015). Adapting CRISP-DM process for social network analytics: Application to healthcare. *In AMCIS 2015 Proceedings*. aisel.aisnet.org/amcis2015/BizAnalytics/GeneralPresentations/33/ (accessed July 2016).

Awadallah, A., & Graham, D. (2012). Hadoop and the data warehouse: When to use which. teradata.com/white-papers/Hadoop-and-the-Data-Warehouse-When-to-Use-Which (accessed August 2016).

Broniatowski, D. A., Paul, M. J., & Dredze, M. (2013). National and local influenza surveillance through Twitter: An analysis of the 2012–2013 influenza epidemic. *PloS One, 8*(12), e83672.

Cisco. (2016). The zettabyte era: Trends and analysis. cisco.com/c/en/us/solutions/collateral/service-provider/visual-networking-index-vni/vni-hyperconnectivity-wp.pdf (accessed August 2016).

DataStax. Customer case studies. datastax.com/resources/case-studies/eBay (accessed July 2016).

Davis, J. (2015). Salesforce adds new predictive analytics to Marketing Cloud. Information Week. informationweek.com/big-data/big-data-analytics/salesforce-adds-new-predictive-analytics-to-marketing-cloud/d/d-id/1323201 (accessed August 2016).

Dean, J., & Ghemawat, S. (2004). MapReduce: Simplified data processing on large clusters. research.google.com/archive/mapreduce.html (accessed August 2016).

Delen, D., Kletke, M., & Kim, J. (2005). A scalable classification algorithm for very large datasets. *Journal of Information and Knowledge Management, 4*(2), 83–94.

Dillow, C. (2016). What happens when you combine artificial intelligence and satellite imagery. fortune.com/2016/03/30/facebook-ai-satellite-imagery/ (accessed July 2016).

Ekster, G. (2015). Driving investment performance with alternative data. integrity-research.com/wp-content/uploads/2015/11/Driving-Investment-Performance-With-Alternative-Data.pdf (accessed July 2016).

Henschen, D. (2016). Salesforce reboots Wave Analytics, preps IoT cloud. *ZD Net*. zdnet.com/article/salesforce-reboots-wave-analytics-preps-iot-cloud/ (accessed August 2016).

Higginbotham, S. (2012). As data gets bigger, what comes after a yottabyte? gigaom.com/2012/10/30/as-data-gets-bigger-what-comes-after-a-yottabyte (accessed August 2016).

Hope, B. (2015). Provider of personal finance tools tracks bank cards, sells data to investors. Wall Street Journal. wsj.com/articles/provider-of-personal-finance-tools-tracks-bank-cards-sells-data-to-investors-1438914620 (accessed July 2016).

Jonas, J. (2007). Streaming analytics vs. perpetual analytics (Advantages of Windowless Thinking). jeffjonas.typepad.com/jeff_jonas/2007/04/streaming_analy.html (accessed August 2016).

Kalgotra, P., & Sharda, R. (2016). Rural versus urban comorbidity networks. Working Paper, Center for Health Systems and Innovation, Oklahoma State University.

Kelly, L. (2012). Big data: Hadoop, business analytics, and beyond. wikibon.org/wiki/v/Big_Data:_Hadoop,_Business_Analytics_and_Beyond (accessed August 2016).

Lampitt, A. (2012). Big data visualization: A big deal for eBay. infoworld.com/d/big-data/big-data-visualization-big-deal-ebay-208589 (accessed August 2016).

MarkLogic. (2012). Top 5 investment bank achieves single source of truth. marklogic.com/resources/top-5-derivatives-trading-bank-achieves-single-source-of-truth (accessed July 2016).

Moran, P. A. (1950). Notes on continuous stochastic phenomena. *Biometrika*, 17–23.

Orbital Insight. World Oil Storage Index. orbitalinsight.com/solutions/world-oil-storage-index/ (accessed July 2016).

Russom, P. (2013). Busting 10 myths about Hadoop: The Big Data explosion. TDWI's *Best of Business Intelligence, 10*, 45–46.

Sarasohn-Kahn, J. (2008). *The wisdom of patients: Health care meets online social media*. Oakland, CA: California HealthCare Foundation.

Shaw, C. (2016). Satellite companies moving markets. quandl.com/blog/alternative-data-satellite-companies (accessed July 2016).

Steiner, C. (2009). Sky high tips for crop traders (accessed July 2016).

St Louis, C., & Zorlu, G. (2012). Can Twitter predict disease outbreaks? *BMJ*, 344.

Tableau white paper. (2012). 7 Tips to succeed with Big Data in 2013. cdnlarge.tableausoftware.com/sites/default/files/whitepapers/7-tips-to-succeed-with-big-data-in-2013.pdf (accessed August 2016).

Thusoo, A., Shao, Z., & Anthony, S. (2010). Data warehousing and analytics infrastructure at Facebook. In *Proceedings of the 2010 ACM SIGMOD International Conference on Management of Data* (p. 1013).

Turner, M. (2015). This is the future of investing, and you probably can't afford it. businessinsider

.com/hedge-funds-are-analysing-data-to-get-an-edge-2015-8 (accessed July 2016).

Watson, H. (2012). The requirements for being an analytics-based organization. *Business Intelligence Journal, 17*(2), 42–44.

Watson, H., Sharda, R., & Schrader, D. (2012). Big Data and how to teach it. *Workshop at AMCIS*, Seattle, WA.

White, C. (2012). MapReduce and the data scientist. Teradata Aster White Paper. teradata.com/white-paper/MapReduce-and-the-Data-Scientist (accessed August 2016).

Wikipedia.com. "Petabyte." en.wikipedia.org/wiki/Petabyte (accessed August 2016).

Zadeh, A. H., Zolbanin, H. M., Sharda, R., & Delen, D. (2015). Social media for nowcasting the flu activity: Spatial-temporal and text analysis. *Business Analytics Congress, Pre-ICIS Conference,* Fort Worth, TX.

Zikopoulos, P., DeRoos, D., Parasuraman, K., Deutsch, T., Corrigan, D., & Giles, J. (2013). *Harness the power of Big Data.* New York: McGraw-Hill.

8

Future Trends, Privacy and Managerial Considerations in Analytics

LEARNING OBJECTIVES

- Explore some of the emerging technologies that may impact analytics, business intelligence (BI), and decision support

- Describe the emerging Internet of Things (IoT) phenomenon, potential applications, and the IoT ecosystem

- Describe the current and future use of cloud computing in business analytics

- Describe how geospatial and location-based analytics are assisting organizations

- Describe the organizational impacts of analytics applications

- List and describe the major ethical and legal issues of analytics implementation

- Identify key characteristics of a successful data science professional

This chapter introduces several emerging technologies that are likely to have major impacts on the development and use of business intelligence (BI) applications. In a dynamic area such as analytics, the terms also evolve and overlap. As noted earlier, we can refer to these technologies as BI, analytics, data science, machine learning, artificial intelligence (AI), cognitive computing, Big Data, or by several other labels. Our goal is not to focus on subtle differences among each, but to look at the collection as one big constellation. We focus on some trends that have already been realized and others that are about to impact analytics further. Using a crystal ball is always a risky proposition, but this chapter provides an analysis of some growing areas. We introduce and explain some emerging technologies and explore their current applications. We then discuss the organizational, personal, legal, ethical, and societal impacts of analytical support systems and issues that should be of importance to managers and professionals in analytics. This chapter contains the following sections:

8.1 Opening Vignette: Analysis of Sensor Data Helps Siemens Avoid Train Failures   418

8.2 Internet of Things   419

8.3 Cloud Computing and Business Analytics   429

8.4 Location-Based Analytics for Organizations 441

8.5 Issues of Legality, Privacy, and Ethics 448

8.6 Impacts of Analytics in Organizations: An Overview 453

8.7 Data Scientist as a Profession 459

8.1 OPENING VIGNETTE: Analysis of Sensor Data Helps Siemens Avoid Train Failures

Siemens is the world's largest producer of energy-efficient, resource-saving technologies. The company is headquartered in Berlin, Germany, with an annual revenue of $93 billion. Siemens produces a variety of trains and infrastructure components like control systems and power systems.

Siemens' Mobility Data Services team believes that Big Data analytics and Internet of Things (IoT) can enable them to forecast component faults weeks in advance. They are exploring these techniques to make sure no train is left stranded on the tracks due to unforeseen technical failures. Siemens wants to move *from* reactive maintenance (after the incident) and preventive maintenance (with regular inspections) *to* predictive maintenance of trains.

Sensors connected to their trains' components measure the current situation of the components. Siemens collects the sensor data and analyzes it in near real time. If there is any anomaly found in the data, then it indicates a component is likely to fail. Thus, preventive measures can be taken accordingly.

According to the Teradata blog, Siemens' engineers leverage data from tens of thousands of sensors. Data from the trains and rails, repair process data, weather data, and data from the supply chain, all go into Siemens' Teradata Unified Data Architecture leveraging Hadoop, Teradata Aster, and the Teradata Data Warehouse. Gerhard Kress, Director, Siemens, Mobility Services, said, "We could not do what we're doing based on a different architecture because data volumes we're having are rather large. So, for example, for one fleet of vehicles from Europe, we just gather together all the data from sensors—it was about 100 billion lines of a table. If you want to run a machine learning algorithm on that it does not work on something that's not massively parallel."

Machine learning using all the sensor data enables Siemens' data scientists and engineers to quickly identify false positives (predicting a failure that doesn't really happen) and give a clear prediction of actual part failures. Because there are more false alarms than real ones, the organization is looking at work orders, serial numbers, the history of train and service data, diagnostic information, sensor data, repair processes, and supply chain data to help identify and resolve genuine part failures. By incorporating weather data, Siemens can differentiate what is more likely to fail on the high-speed train between Moscow and St. Petersburg in the frigid winter versus the high-speed train traveling in the hot Spain summers.

Spanish train operator RENFE uses key components of Siemens' high-speed train, Valero E, which are monitored continuously by Siemens. If the patterns of collected sensor data are abnormal, a team is dispatched to inspect these components, thus preventing failure of the train on the tracks. As a result, only one of 2,300 trains is noticeably delayed. Siemens also claims that the enhanced reliability of their trains has helped many train operators to improve their on-time performance. For example, Bangkok's trains reputably run only 1% late. And Siemens also estimates that the highly dependable train operations between Barcelona and Madrid have actually increased train ridership significantly and have reduced air traffic.

Thus, predictive modeling has given Siemens a new service opportunity. They are now established as a key service provider of tracking train failures. Selling these predictive services is becoming even more important than just the original equipment.

What Lessons Can We Learn from This Vignette?

Siemens is leading the way in developing additional services and value from large industrial products coming from relatively mature industries. By employing sensors that generate large amounts and varieties of data and merging those with other data sources such as weather, a company can build a better picture of how its products perform in the real environment. Further, analysis of such data can help a customer perform maintenance when it is really needed rather than on a timed schedule. Selling such analytic services has become a major new focus for all leading industrial equipment makers such as Siemens and General Electric. Selling services to perform analytics on products and predictive maintenance or repairs is an excellent example of creating new market opportunities for established products.

QUESTIONS FOR DISCUSSION

1. In industrial equipment such as trains, what parameters might one measure on a regular basis to estimate the equipment's current performance and future repair needs?
2. How would weather data be useful in analyzing a train's equipment status?
3. Estimate how much data you might collect in one month using, say, 1,000 sensors on a train. Each sensor might yield 1 KB data per second.
4. How would you propose to store such data sets?

Source: Adapted from Teradata.com. (2016). The Internet of trains. http://www.teradata .com/resources/case-studies (accessed August 2016); theit.org. (2016). Siemens tracks Big Data for trains that keep on running. http://eandt.theiet.org/magazine/2016/07/siemens-big-data-trains.cfm (accessed August 2016); Siemens.com. (2016). About Siemens. http://www.siemens.com/about/en/ (accessed August 2016).

8.2   Internet of Things

The opening vignette introduced an area that is currently experiencing explosive growth. **Internet of Things (IoT)** is the phenomenon of connecting the physical world to the Internet, in contrast to the Internet of people that connects us humans to each other through technology. In IoT, physical devices are connected to sensors that collect data on the operation, location, and state of a device. This data is processed using various analytics techniques for monitoring the device remotely from a central office or for predicting any upcoming faults in the device. Perhaps the most common example of the IoT is the upcoming self-driving car. To drive on its own, a car needs to have enough sensors that automatically monitor the situation around it and take appropriate actions to adjust any setting necessary, including the car's speed, direction, and so on. Another common example of the IoT is a fitness tracker device that allows a user to keep track of physical activities such as walking, running, and sleep. Another example that illustrates the IoT phenomenon is a company called Smartbin. Smartbin has developed trash containers that include sensors to detect the fill levels. The trash collection company can automatically be informed to empty a trash container when the sensor detects it to be nearly full. Of course, the most common example people give in illustrating IoT is the idea of your refrigerator automatically ordering milk when it detects that the milk has run out! Clorox just introduced a new Brita filter so that a Wi-Fi–enabled pitcher can order the water filters by itself when it detects the time to change. In all these examples, a human does not have to necessarily communicate with another human, or even with a machine in many cases. The machines can do the talking. That is why the term *Internet of Things* is used.

According to Juniper Research (2016) besides tablets, smartphones, and PCs, more than 38 billion things will be connected to the Internet by 2020. There are many reasons IoT is growing exponentially:

1. Hardware is smaller, affordable, and more powerful: Costs of actuators and sensors have decreased significantly in the last 10 years, resulting in a much cheaper sensor overall. Cheap mobility: Costs of data processing, bandwidth, and mobile devices have gone down by 97% since the last decade.
2. Availability of BI tools: Now more and more companies are offering their BI tools both on premise and in the cloud at cheaper rates. Big Data and BI tools are widely available and are highly sophisticated.
3. New and interesting use cases are emerging virtually every day.

We should also note that there is some disagreement about using the term *Internet of Things*. Some people also term this as the Web of Things. Others have argued to call it the Internet of Systems because in many ways it would be a combination of systems that would communicate with one another. However, we will continue to refer to this phenomenon as the Internet of Things (IoT) in this section for the sake of consistency.

Estimates vary widely about the growth of the IoT industry, but somewhere between nearly $6 trillion to $11 trillion will be spent on IoT solutions by 2020. It is one of the fastest-growing information technology (IT) sectors in general and a key component of the analytics industry. Application Cases 8.1 and 8.2 give two examples of IoT applications in different industries using two different technology platforms.

Application Case 8.1

SilverHook Powerboats Uses Real-Time Data Analysis to Inform Racers and Fans

SilverHook powerboats are one of the fastest, power efficient boats in the world manufactured by the company of the same name. SilverHook powerboats are used in powerboat racing around the world. High speeds of the boats pounding against saltwater pose a risk of failure of onboard equipment. Racers rely on telemetry data from their boats to make safety and strategy decisions. In some situations, biometric data of racers is also collected. Thus, racers receive a lot of information, making it difficult to track all of the data. SilverHook also noticed that powerboat racing fans were finding it hard to follow the racers in the ocean, as the boats moved quickly, decreasing engagement from fans. SilverHook powerboats

collected sensor data from 80 sensors but there was no easy way to get insights to improve decision-making abilities, make safety decisions, and enhance fan experience.

The SilverHook team employed IBM Bluemix Platform as a service (PaaS—see next section) to employ IBM SPSS analytics solutions and deliver insights in an understandable format to the users and fans. PaaS enabled SilverHook to build applications, pull data into the cloud, and perform required analytics on that data. IBM Bluemix, along with partner company Virtual Eye, used an IoT foundation to send sensor data generated from sensors and global positioning system (GPS) trackers to the cloud. Analysis on the sensor data was done using analytics tools present in IBM Bluemix. Virtual Eye delivered technical information alerts to the racing team and real-time representation of the race to the fans. Racers can now get real-time insights about the race, improving their decision making and competitiveness.

QUESTIONS FOR DISCUSSION

1. What type of information might the sensors on a race boat generate that would be important for the racers to know? What about for the fans?

2. Which other sports might benefit from similar technologies?

3. What technological challenges might you face in building such systems?

Sources: IBMbigdatahub.com. (2015). SilverHook Powerboats: Tracking fast-moving boats in real time. http://www.ibmbigdatahub.com/blog/silverhook-powerboats-tracking-fast-moving-powerboats-real-time (accessed August 2016); IBM.com. (2015). Case study: SilverHook Powerboats. http://www.ibm.com/cloud-computing/case-studies/silverhook-powerboats.html (accessed August 2016).

Application Case 8.2

Rockwell Automation Monitors Expensive Oil and Gas Exploration Assets

Rockwell Automation is one of the world's largest providers of industrial automation and information solutions. It has customers in more than 80 countries worldwide, and the company has around 22,500 employees. One of its business areas of focus is assisting oil and gas companies in exploration. An example is Hilcorp Energy, a company that drills oil in Alaska. The equipment used in drilling, extracting, and refining oil is very expensive. A single fault in the equipment can cost the oil and gas company around $100,000 to $300,000 per day in lost production. To deal with this problem, technology that can monitor the status of such equipment remotely and can predict issues that can likely happen well ahead of time is required.

Rockwell Automation considered it an opportunity to expand their business in oil and gas industries by gathering data from the exploration sites and analyzing it to improve efficiency and drive better performance. The company is bringing its vision of Connected Enterprise using Microsoft's IoT to provide monitoring and support of oil and gas equipment placed in remote areas. Rockwell is now providing solutions to predict failure of equipment along the petroleum supply chain, monitor their health and performance in real time, and help prevent their failure in the future. They are providing solutions in the following areas:

1. **Drilling:** Hilcorp Energy has its pumping equipment stationed in Alaska, where it drills

oil 24 hours a day. A single failure in equipment can cost Hilcorp a lot of money. Rockwell connected electrical variable drives of pumping equipment to the cloud (see next section), so that these machines can be controlled thousands of miles away from the control room in Ohio. Sensors capture data, and through Rockwell's control gateway, this data is passed on to Microsoft Azure Cloud and then reaches Hilcorp engineers through digital dashboards. Dashboards provide real-time information about pressure, temperature, flow rate, and dozens of other parameters that help engineers monitor health and performance of the equipment. These dashboards also display alerts about any likely issues. When one of Hilcorp's pieces of pumping equipment failed, it was identified, tracked, and repaired in less than an hour, saving 6 hours of tracing the failure and the cost involved in lost production.

2. **Building Smarter Gas Pumps:** Nowadays some delivery trucks use liquid natural gas (LNG) as fuel. Oil companies are updating their filling stations to incorporate LNG pumps. Rockwell Automation installed sensors and variable frequency drives at these pumps to collect real-time data about operations of equipment, inventory of fuel, and consumption rate. This data is transmitted to Rockwell's cloud platform. Rockwell then generates interactive

(Continued)

Application Case 8.2 (Continued)

dashboards and reports depicting these details using Microsoft Azure and sends it to the appropriate stakeholders. This gives their stakeholders a good idea about the health of their capital assets.

The Connected Enterprise solution by Rockwell has accelerated growth for many oil and gas companies like Hilcorp Energy by bringing their operations data to the cloud platform and helping them reduce costly downtime and maintenance. It has resulted in a new business opportunity for industrial age stalwarts like Rockwell Automation.

QUESTIONS FOR DISCUSSION

1. What type of information would likely be collected by an oil and gas drilling platform?
2. Does this application fit the three V's of Big Data (volume, variety, velocity)? Why or why not?
3. Which other industries could use similar operational measurements and dashboards?

Sources: Customers.microsoft.com. (2015). Rockwell Automation: Fueling the oil and gas industry with IOT. https://customers.microsoft.com/Pages/CustomerStory.aspx?recid=19922 (accessed August 2016); Microsoft.com. (n.d.). Customer stories | Rockwell Automation. https://www.microsoft.com/en-us/cloud-platform/customer-stories-rockwell-automation (accessed July 2016).

IoT Technology Infrastructure

From a bird's-eye view, IoT technology can be divided into four major blocks. Figure 8.1 illustrates these four blocks.

1. **Hardware:** It includes the physical devices, sensors, and actuators where data is produced and recorded. The device is the equipment that needs to be controlled, monitored, or tracked. IoT sensor devices could contain a processor or any computing device that parses incoming data.
2. **Connectivity:** There should be a base station or hub that collects data from the sensor-laden objects and sends that data to the cloud. Devices are connected to a network to communicate with each other or with other applications. These may be directly or indirectly connected to the Internet. A gateway enables devices that are not directly connected to Internet to reach the cloud platform.
3. **Software backend:** In this layer the data collected is managed. Software backend manages connected networks and devices and provides data integration. This may very well be in the cloud (again, see next section).
4. **Applications:** In this part of IoT, data is turned into meaningful information. Many of the applications may run on smartphones, tablets, and PCs and do something useful with the data. Other applications may run on the server and provide results or alerts through dashboards or messages to the stakeholders.

RFID Sensors

One of the earliest sensor technologies that has found a new life and is experiencing significant growth is **radio-frequency identification (RFID)**. RFID is a generic technology that refers to the use of radio-frequency waves to identify objects. Fundamentally, RFID is one example of a family of automatic identification technologies, which also includes the ubiquitous barcodes and magnetic strips. Since the mid-1970s, the retail supply chain (and many other areas) has used barcodes as the primary form of automatic identification. The potential advantages of RFID have prompted many companies (led by large retailers such as Wal-Mart, Target, and Dillard's) to aggressively pursue this technology as a way to improve their supply chain and thus reduce costs and increase sales.

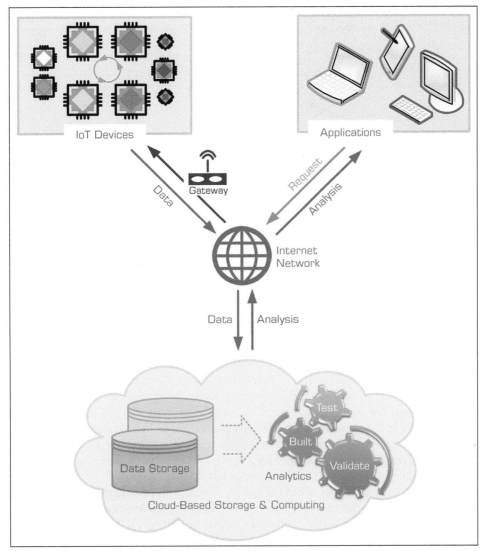

FIGURE 8.1 Building Blocks of IoT Technology Infrastructure.

How does RFID work? In its simplest form, an RFID system consists of a tag (attached to the product to be identified), an interrogator (i.e., reader), one or more antennae attached to the reader, and a computer (to control the reader and capture the data). At present, the retail supply chain has primarily been interested in using passive RFID tags. *Passive tags* receive energy from the electromagnetic field created by the interrogator (e.g., a reader) and backscatter information only when it is requested. The passive tag will remain energized only while it is within the interrogator's magnetic field.

In contrast, *active tags* have a battery on board to energize them. Because active tags have their own power source, they don't need a reader to energize them; instead they can initiate the data transmission process on their own. As compared to passive tags, active tags have a longer read range, better accuracy, more complex rewritable information storage, and richer processing capabilities (Moradpour & Bhuptani, 2005). On the negative side, due to the battery, active tags have a limited life span, are larger in size than passive tags, and are more expensive. Currently, most retail applications are designed and operated with passive tags. Active tags are most frequently found in defense or military

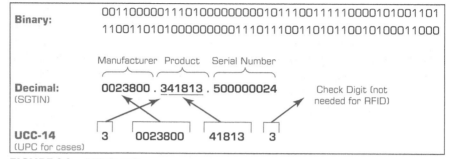

FIGURE 8.2 RFID Data Tag.

systems, yet they also appear in technologies such as EZ Pass, where tags are linked to a prepaid account, enabling drivers to pay tolls by driving past a reader rather than stopping to pay at a tollbooth.

The most commonly used data representation for RFID technology is the Electronic Product Code (EPC), which is viewed by many in the industry as the next generation of the Universal Product Code (UPC), most often represented by a barcode. Like the UPC, the EPC consists of a series of numbers that identifies product types and manufacturers across the supply chain. The EPC code also includes an extra set of digits to uniquely identify items.

Currently, most RFID tags contain 96 bits of data in the form of serialized global trade identification numbers (SGTINs) for identifying cases or serialized shipping container codes for identifying pallets (although SGTINs can also be used to identify pallets). The complete guide to tag data standards can be found on EPCglobal's Web site (epcglobalinc .org). EPCglobal, Inc., is a subscriber-driven organization of industry leaders and organizations focused on creating global standards for the EPC to support the use of RFID.

As illustrated in Figure 8.2, tag data, in its purest form, is a series of binary digits. This set of binary digits can then be converted to the SGTIN decimal equivalent. As shown, an SGTIN is essentially a UPC (UCC-14, for shipping-container identification) with a serial number. The serial number is the most important difference between the 14-digit UPC used today and the SGTIN contained on an RFID tag. With UPCs, companies can identify the product family to which a case belongs (e.g., 8-pack Charmin tissue), but they cannot distinguish one case from another. With an SGTIN, each case is uniquely identified. This provides visibility at the case level, rather than the product-family level.

One of the applications of the massive amounts of data that are generated by RFID is in supply-chain management (Delen, Hardgrave, & Sharda, 2007). RFID can also be used by companies to improve either the efficiency or effectiveness of various existing processes by incremental process change. For example, early evidence suggested that RFID can reduce the amount of time to receive product at a warehouse (Katz, 2006). Instead of scanning each case of product individually with a barcode scanner, an RFID-tagged product can be read automatically at a receiving-door portal. Gillette reported a reduction in pallet-receiving time at its distribution center from 20 to 5 seconds due to RFID and its tag-at-source strategy (Katz, 2006). The process of receiving did not drastically changed (i.e., forklifts unloaded the product as before). The only change was eliminating the need to manually scan the product. Thus, the process became more efficient. Processes can also be made more effective. For example, Wal-Mart found a 21% reduction in out-of-stocks by using RFID data to generate better lists of products to be replenished (Hardgrave, Langford, Waller, & Miller, 2008). The shelf replenishment process was not changed, but was improved by the use of RFID. RFID is also being used to reduce the number of errors, which improves inventory accuracy, ultimately leading to better forecasting and replenishment.

RFID data have been used in many other related applications. For example, perishable goods present some of the biggest challenges for supply-chain management due to the high number of variants with different perishability characteristics, requirements to account for the flow of goods in some supply chains, and large volumes of goods handled over long distances. Although food represents a major portion of the perishables portfolio, many other products, including fresh-cut flowers, pharmaceuticals, cosmetics, and auto parts, among others, require strict environmental controls to retain their quality. Due to the extremely large volume of goods handled, the likelihood for problems increases (Sahin, Babaï, Dallery, & Vaillant, 2007). The elimination of even a small percentage of spoilage, for example, adds up to a significant improvement to the supply chain. Therefore, the optimal management of the perishables supply chain is of paramount importance to businesses in this market segment.

The success of today's highly volatile perishables supply chain depends on the level (and timeliness) of product visibility. Visibility should provide answers to the questions of "Where is my product?" and "What is the condition of my product?" Already, several companies have begun experimenting with RFID for perishables. Consider the following examples:

- Samworth Brothers Distribution (UK; sandwiches, pastries, etc.) has implemented real-time temperature monitoring in its trucks (Swedberg, 2006a).
- Starbucks uses temperature tracking for food preparation products going to retail outlets (Swedberg, 2006b).
- Sysco uses RFID to check load conditions without opening doors (Collins, 2005).

Another example of the use of RFID in supply chains is in managing product quality. Studies using sensor-based RFID tags in refrigerated trucks carrying food items revealed that the temperature did not remain uniform as assumed. Indeed, it varied rather widely (Delen, Hardgrave, & Sharda, 2011). As a product moves through the supply chain, the environment can change, affecting the product quality and safety. RFID-enabled environmental sensors provide insight into the changing environmental conditions experienced by the product and provide the data necessary to determine to what extent those changes affect the quality or safety of the product. Without sensors, one can get various single-point estimations of the environmental conditions (e.g., temperature at the time of loading, temperature at time of delivery), but not have visibility between these points. In the sample applications, temperatures varied by position on the pallet (e.g., top, middle, bottom), by load configuration (i.e., the position of the pallets), by container type, by product type, and by packaging material (e.g., corrugated box versus plastic tote). The obvious impact of many variables suggests that continuous environmental monitoring is necessary to fully understand the conditions at the pallet and/or case level. Overall, RFID-enabled (temperature) sensors worked well and provided tremendous insights into the conditions faced by the product as it passed through the supply chain—insight that is not possible with single-point estimations. The overall lesson is that RFID technology generates massive amounts of data that can be analyzed to achieve great insights into a company's environment, a major purpose for the very existence of BI and decision support.

Fog Computing

One of the key issues in IoT is that the data produced by sensors is huge, and not all of it is useful. So how much should be uploaded to the cloud servers for analysis? A recent concept to address this question is the idea of fog computing. Fog extends the cloud to be closer to the things that produce and act on IoT data. These devices, called fog nodes, can be placed anywhere between the network connection. Any device with computing, storage, and network connectivity can be a fog node, for example, routers or switches. The following view illustrates this:

TABLE 8.1 Difference between Fog Nodes and a Cloud Platform	
Fog Nodes	Cloud Platform
Receive data from IoT devices	Receives and aggregates data from fog nodes
Run IoT real-time analytics in millisecond response time	Analysis is performed on huge amounts of business data and can take hours or weeks

Data Center/Cloud ------->> Fog device ------->> Physical device/Sensors generating data

Analyzing data close to the devices minimizes latency. It also conserves bandwidth, as sending data to the cloud requires large bandwidth. Fog computing is crucial in situations when data need to be analyzed in less than a second, as in the case of a cascading system failure. Table 8.1 identifies two simple differences between the cloud and fog.

Fog computing may also give better security, as fog nodes can be secured with the same security solution used in the other IT environments.

Source: **Cisco.com.** (2015). Fog computing and the Internet of Things: Extend the Cloud to where the things are. https://www.cisco.com/c/dam/en_us/solutions/trends/iot/docs/computing-overview.pdf (accessed August 2016).

IoT Platforms

Because IoT is still evolving, many domain-specific and application-specific technology platforms are also evolving. Not surprisingly, many of the major vendors of IoT platforms are the same vendors who provide analytics and data storage services for other application domains. These include Amazon AWS IoT, Microsoft Azure IoT Suite, Predix IoT Platform by General Electric (GE), and IBM Watson IoT solutions. Teradata Unified Data Architecture has similarly been applied by many customers in the IoT domain. An example was in the opening vignette. Application Case 8.3 provides an application of another major IoT platform being marketed by General Electric.

Application Case 8.3

Pitney Bowes Collaborates with General Electric IoT Platform to Optimize Production

Pitney Bowes, headquartered in Connecticut, is an American provider of e-commerce solutions and shipping and mailing products. The company's machines process or produce an average of 150 million mail pieces each day.

Pitney Bowes's "Enterprise Mail Business" develops, sells, and services large machines called Inserters. These machines help banks and healthcare providers put exactly the right piece of mail in the right-sized envelope. For one bank, such a machine assembled 900 million mail pieces in a year. Most of the machines produce 20,000 letters per hour. With this level of automated production, Pitney Bowes and its clients also produce a huge volume of data every day. Pitney Bowes wants to analyze data generated from these mailing machines to predict faults in the machines in advance to prevent any outage and fix machines before they break down.

Pitney Bowes adopted GE Predix, a cloud-based platform designed for the industrial Internet. The Predix platform analyzes sensor data of machines and by using real-time analytics, gives powerful insights that facilitate making decisions. Besides outage prevention, analytics by Predix help in reducing downtime and in increasing productivity. The overall analysis of sensor data by Predix increased productivity and the performance of the machines.

Sources: News.pb.com. (2015). GE and Pitney Bowes join forces to bring the power of the industrial Internet to the world of commerce. http://news.pb.com/article_display.cfm?article_id=5634 (accessed August 2016); GEreports.com. (2016). The power of Predix: An inside look at how Pitney Bowes is using the industrial Internet platform. http://www.gereports.com/the-power-of-predix-an-inside-look-at-how-pitney-bowes-has-been-using-the-industrial-internet-platform/; (accessed August 2016); GE.com. (2016). Making machines intelligent is smart business. http://www.ge.com/digital/sites/default/files/ge_digital_predix_pb_brochure.pdf; (accessed August 2016); GE.com. (2015). The industrial Internet, Pitney Bowes and GE. http://blogs.pb.com/corporate/2015/07/14/the-industrial-internet-pitney-bowes-and-ge/ (accessed August 2016).

IoT Start-Up Ecosystem

Many start-up companies are emerging in the field of IoT and in the next 3–4 years we will see a boom in the IoT industry. Venture capital in the IoT landscape is growing, from $1.8 billion in 2013, to $2.59 billion in 2014, and to $3.44 billion in 2015. Some of the prominent start-up companies in the IoT landscape are Sigfox, 3D Robotics, Canary, Athos, Greenwave, Jawbone, FreedomPop, Razer, and Ring.

One of the most successful start-up IoT firms is Fitbit. Fitbit is an American company that manufactures activity trackers, wireless-enabled technology devices that use sensors to determine the number of steps walked, heart rate, quality of sleep, steps climbed, and other personal health metrics.

Telecommunication companies have also been exploring and promoting IoT. Most of the big telecom players like AT&T want to take advantage of this technology. AT&T has partnered with 8 of the 10 U.S. car manufacturers to provide connectivity to the cars. Many telecom companies view their upcoming 5G networks as the backbone of IoT.

Google/Alphabet and Amazon are among notable players in the IoT ecosystem. Google with its Google cloud, SideWalk Labs (smart cities) and autonomous cars is a leading investor in several IoT initiatives. Amazon with its AWS (Amazon Web Services) has introduced a new IoT platform which can serve as the backend of the IoT. Figure 8.3 provides a concise view of the IoT ecosystem components. This includes various application areas, hardware manufacturers, connectivity providers, software developers, analytics consultants, and the like. It is adapted from an ecosystem diagram developed and maintained by Matt Turck at his blog site: http://mattturck.com/2016/03/28/2016-iot-landscape/ (accessed August 2016).

His detailed diagram includes a list of companies in each block. We reproduced a list of categories in Figure 8.3 rather than a list of companies in each section because those would be obsolete in no time in this fast-evolving area. However, Figure 8.3 makes it clear that IoT opportunities are evolving in three major sectors. The first major group includes companies that provide building blocks of IoT technologies and enablers (hardware, software, connectivity, and consultants/incubators/alliances/partners). The second group can be called service providers to IoT developers—horizontal sector. This group entails platforms, interfaces, and the recent 3D printing and allied technology/service providers. The third major cluster consists of industry verticals, the area that would be largely applications in various sectors—personal, home, vehicles, and in the enterprise. Figure 8.3 presents one view of this organization, and the blog site includes a different view that includes examples of companies in each of the subgroups identified here.

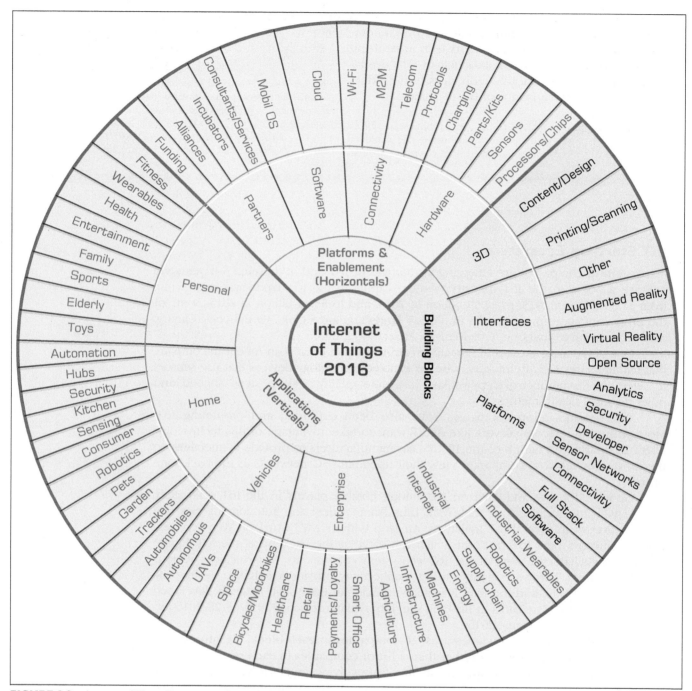

FIGURE 8.3 Internet of Things Ecosystem. *Source:* Adapted from Matt, T. (2016, March). Internet of Things: Are We There Yet? http://mattturck.com/2016/03/28/2016-iotlandscape/ (accessed August 2016).

Managerial Considerations in the Internet of Things

Although there is considerable excitement about the growth and the potential of IoT, there are also some concerns that managers should be aware of. McKinsey's Global Institute (2015) has put together an excellent *Executive's Guide to the Internet of Things*. This report identifies the following issues:

1. **Organizational Alignment**   Although it is true of many other technology initiatives, with IoT, the opportunities for operational improvements and creating new business opportunities means that IT and operational personnel have to work as one team rather than separate functions. As noted by the authors of the guide, "IoT will challenge other notions of organizational responsibilities. Chief financial, marketing, and operating officers, as well as leaders of business units, will have to be receptive to linking up their systems" (McKinsey, 2015).

2. **Interoperability Challenges**   Interoperability is a huge detriment thus far in the growth of these systems. All devices do not connect seamlessly with each another. Second, there are a lot of technology issues in connectivity. Many remote areas do not yet have proper Wi-Fi connections. Issues related to Big Data processing are also responsible for slow progress in IoT. Companies are trying to reduce data at the sensor level so that only minimal data goes into the cloud. The current infrastructure hardly supports the huge amount of data created by IoT. A related problem is also retrofitting sensors on devices to be able to gather and transmit data for analysis. It takes an average of 18 to 24 months for an IoT start-up to ship their product. And it takes a start-up an additional 1 to 2 years to distribute and sell their product in the market.

   In addition, it will take time for consumers to replace their analog objects with new IoT smart products. As an example, it is easier for people to replace mobile phones than replacing a car, kitchen appliances, locks, and other things that can benefit from having a sensor and being connected to IoT.

3. **Security**   Security of data is an issue in general, but it is an even bigger issue in the context of IoT. Each device that is connected to IoT becomes another entry point for malicious hackers to get into a large system, or at the very least, operate or corrupt the specific device. There are stories of hackers being able to breach into and control automated functions of a car, or controlling a garage door opener remotely. Such issues require that any large-scale adoption of IoT involves security considerations from the very beginning.

Notwithstanding these managerial considerations, the emerging growth of IoT and its potential to help us achieve the vision of smart cities, smart grid, smart *anything* is tantalizing. It is one of the wide open areas for creativity and entrepreneurship.

SECTION 8.2 REVIEW QUESTIONS

1. What are the major uses of IoT?
2. What are the technology building blocks of IoT?
3. What is RFID?
4. Search online for applications of RFID in healthcare, entertainment, and sports.
5. Identify some key players in the IoT ecosystem. Explore their offerings.
6. What are some of the major issues managers have to keep in mind in exploring IoT?

8.3   Cloud Computing and Business Analytics

Another emerging technology trend that business analytics users should be aware of is cloud computing. The National Institute of Standards and Technology (NIST) defines **cloud computing** as "a model for enabling convenient, on-demand network access to a shared pool of configurable computing resources (e.g., networks, servers, storage, and services) that can be rapidly provisioned and released with minimal management effort or service-provider interaction." Wikipedia (n.d., Cloud Computing) defines cloud computing as "a style of computing in which dynamically scalable and often virtualized resources are provided over the Internet. Users need not have knowledge of, experience in, or control over the technology infrastructures in the cloud that supports them." This definition is broad and comprehensive. In some ways, cloud computing is a new name for many previous, related trends: utility computing, application service provider grid computing, on-demand computing, software as a service (SaaS), and even older, centralized computing with dumb terminals. But the term *cloud computing* originates from a reference to the Internet as a "cloud" and represents an evolution of all of the previously shared/centralized computing trends. The Wikipedia entry also recognizes that cloud computing is a combination of several IT components as services. For example, *infrastructure as a service* (IaaS) refers to providing computing *platforms as a service* (PaaS), as well as all of the basic platform provisioning, such as management administration, security, and so on. It also includes SaaS, which includes applications to be delivered through a Web browser, whereas the data and the application programs are on some other server.

Although we do not typically look at Web-based e-mail as an example of cloud computing, it can be considered a basic cloud application. Typically, the e-mail application stores the data (e-mail messages) and the software (e-mail programs that let us process and manage e-mails). The e-mail provider also supplies the hardware/software and all of the basic infrastructure. As long as the Internet is available, one can access the e-mail application from anywhere in the cloud. When the application is updated by the e-mail provider (e.g., when Gmail updates its e-mail application), it becomes available to all customers without them having to download any new programs. Social networking Web sites like Facebook, Twitter, and LinkedIn, are also examples of cloud computing. Thus, any Web-based general application is in a way an example of a cloud application. Another example of a general cloud application is Google Docs and Spreadsheets. This application allows a user to create text documents or spreadsheets that are stored on Google's servers and are available to the users anywhere they have access to the Internet. Again, no programs need to be installed as "the application is in the cloud." The storage space is also "in the cloud."

A good general business example of cloud computing is Amazon.com's Web services. Amazon.com has developed an impressive technology infrastructure for e-commerce as well as for BI, customer relationship management, and supply-chain management. It has built major data centers to manage its own operations. However, through Amazon.com's cloud services, many other companies can employ these very same facilities to gain advantages of these technologies without having to make a similar investment. Like other cloud-computing services, a user can subscribe to any of the facilities on a pay-as-you-go basis. This model of letting someone else own the hardware and software but making use of the facilities on a pay-per-use basis is the cornerstone of cloud computing. A number of companies offer cloud-computing services, including Salesforce.com, IBM (Bluemix), Microsoft (Azure), Google, and many others.

Cloud computing, like many other IT trends, has resulted in new offerings in BI. These options permit an organization to scale up its data warehouse and pay only for what it uses. The end user of a cloud-based BI service may use one organization for analysis applications that, in turn, uses another firm for the platform or infrastructure. The next several paragraphs summarize the latest trends in the interface of cloud computing and BI/business analytics. A few of these statements are adapted from a paper written by Haluk Demirkan and one of the coauthors of this book (Demirkan & Delen, 2013).

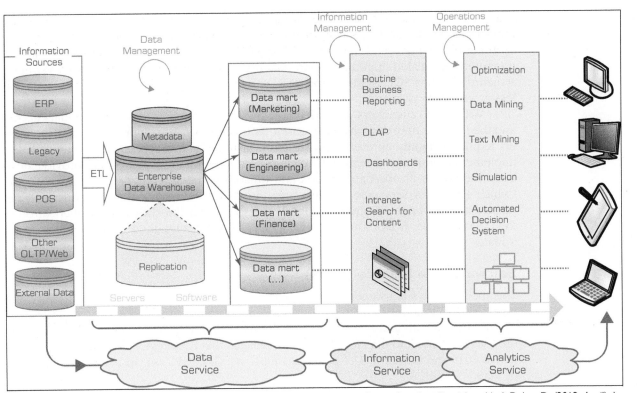

FIGURE 8.4 Conceptual Architecture of a Cloud-Oriented Support System. *Source:* Based on Demirkan, H., & Delen, D. (2013, April). Leveraging the capabilities of service-oriented decision support systems: Putting analytics and Big Data in cloud. *Decision Support Systems, 55*(1), 412–421.

Figure 8.4 illustrates a conceptual architecture of a service-oriented decision support environment, that is, a cloud-based analytics system. This figure superimposes the cloud-based services on the general analytics architecture presented in previous chapters.

In service-oriented decision support solutions, (1) operational systems, (2) data warehouses, (3) online analytic processing, and (4) end-user components can be obtained individually or bundled and provided to the users as service. Any or all of these services can be obtained through the cloud. Because the field of cloud computing is fast evolving and growing at a rapid pace, there is much confusion about the terminology being used by various vendors and users. The labels vary from Infrastructure, Platform, Software, Data, Information, and Analytics as a Service. In the following, we define these services. Then we summarize the current technology platforms and highlight applications of each through application cases.

Data as a Service (DaaS)

The concept of data as a service basically advocates the view that "where data lives"—the actual platform on which the data resides—doesn't matter. Data can reside in a local computer or in a server at a server farm inside a cloud-computing environment. With DaaS, any business process can access data wherever it resides. Data as a service began with the notion that data quality could happen in a centralized place, cleansing and enriching data and offering it to different systems, applications, or users, irrespective of where they were in the organization, computers, or on the network. This has now been replaced with master data management and customer data integration solutions, where the record of the customer (or product, or asset, etc.) may reside anywhere and is available as a service to any application that has the services allowing access to it. By applying a standard set of transformations to the various sources of data (for example, ensuring that gender fields containing different notation styles [e.g., M/F, Mr./Ms.] are all translated into male/female) and then enabling applications to access the data via open standards such as SQL, XQuery, and XML, service requestors can access the data regardless of vendor or system.

With DaaS, customers can move quickly thanks to the simplicity of the data access and the fact that they don't need extensive knowledge of the underlying data. If customers require a slightly different data structure or have location-specific requirements, the implementation is easy because the changes are minimal (agility). Second, providers can build the base with the data experts and outsource the analysis or presentation layers (which allows for very cost-effective user interfaces and makes change requests at the presentation layer much more feasible), and access to the data is controlled through the data services. It tends to improve data quality because there is a single point for updates.

Software as a Service (SaaS)

This model allows consumers to use applications and software that run on distant computers in the cloud infrastructure. Consumers need not worry about managing underlying cloud infrastructure and have to pay for the use of software only. All we need is a Web browser to connect to the cloud. Gartner estimates that SaaS revenue was around $32 billion in 2015 and is used in 77% of all organizations. Gmail, Picasa, and Flickr are examples of SaaS.

Platform as a Service (PaaS)

Using this model, companies can deploy their software and applications in the cloud so that their customers can use them. Companies don't have to manage resources needed to manage their applications in cloud-like networks, servers, storage, or operating systems. This reduces the cost of maintaining underlying infrastructure for running their software and also saves time for setting up this infrastructure. Now, users can focus on their business rather than focusing on managing infrastructure for running their software. Examples of PaaS are Microsoft Azure, Amazon EC2, and Google App Engine.

Infrastructure as a Service (IaaS)

In this model, infrastructure resources like networks, storage, servers, and other computing resources are provided to client companies. Clients can run their application and have administrative rights to use these resources but do not manage underlying infrastructure. Clients have to pay for usage of infrastructure. A good example of that is Amazon.com's Web services. Amazon.com has developed impressive technology infrastructure that includes data centers. Other companies can use Amazon.com's cloud services on a pay-per-use-basis without having to make similar investments.

We should note that there is considerable confusion and overlap in the use of cloud terminology. For example, some vendors also add information as a service (IaaS), which is an extension of DaaS. Clearly, IaaS is different from infrastructure as a service described earlier. Our goal here is to just recognize that there are varying degrees of services that an organization can subscribe to manage the analytics applications. Figure 8.5 highlights the level of service subscriptions a client uses in each of the three major types of cloud offerings. SaaS is clearly the highest level of cloud service that a client may get. For example, in using Office 365, an organization is using the software as a service. The client is only responsible for bringing in the data. Many of the analytics as a service application fall in this category as well.

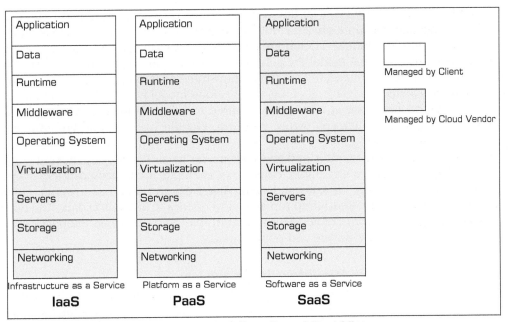

FIGURE 8.5 Technology Stack as a Service for Different Types of Cloud Offerings.

Essential Technologies for Cloud Computing

VIRTUALIZATION Virtualization is the creation of a virtual version of something like an operating system or server. A simple example of virtualization is the logical division of a hard drive to create two separate hard drives in a computer. Virtualization can be in all three areas of computing:

- **Network virtualization:** It is the splitting of available bandwidth into channels, which disguises complexity of the network by dividing it into manageable parts. Then each bandwidth can be allocated to a particular server or device in real time.
- **Storage virtualization:** It is the pooling of physical storage from multiple network storage devices into a single storage device that can be managed from a central console.
- **Server virtualization:** It is the masking of physical servers from server users. Users don't have to manage the actual servers or understand complicated details of server resources.

This difference in the level of virtualization directly relates to which cloud service one employs.

Cloud Deployment Models

Cloud services can be acquired in several ways, from building an entirely private infrastructure to sharing with others. The following three models are the most common.

- **Private cloud:** This can also be called internal cloud or corporate cloud. It is a more secure form of cloud service than public clouds like MS Azure and Google BigQuery. It is operated solely for a single organization having a mission critical workload and security concerns. It provides the same benefits as a public cloud-like service, scalability, changing computing resources on demand, and so on. Companies that have a private cloud have direct control over their data and applications. The disadvantage of having a private cloud is the cost of maintaining and managing the cloud because on-premise IT staff are responsible for managing it.

- **Public cloud:** In this model the subscriber uses the resources offered by service providers over the Internet. The cloud infrastructure is managed by the service provider. The main advantage of this public cloud model is saving time and money in setting up hardware and software required to run their business. Examples of public clouds are Microsoft Azure platform, Google App Engine, and Amazon AWS.

- **Hybrid cloud:** The hybrid cloud gives businesses great flexibility by moving workloads between private and public clouds. For example, a company can use hybrid cloud storage to store its sales and marketing data, and then use a public cloud platform like Amazon Redshift to run analytical queries to analyze its data. The main requirement is network connectivity and API (application program interface) compatibility between the private and public cloud.

Major Cloud Platform Providers in Analytics

This section first identifies some key cloud players that provide the infrastructure for analytics as a service, as well as selected analytics functionalities. Then we also mention representative analytics-as-a-service offerings that may even run on these cloud platforms.

Amazon Elastic Beanstalk: Amazon Elastic Beanstalk is a service offered from Amazon Web Services. It can deploy, manage, and scale Web applications. It supports the following programming languages: Java, Ruby, Python, PHP, and .NET on servers like Apache HTTP, Apache Tomcat, and IIS. A user has to upload the code for the application, and Elastic Beanstalk handles the deployment of the application, load balancing, and autoscaling and monitors the health of the application. So the user can focus on building Web sites, mobile applications, API backend, content management systems, SaaS, and so on, while the applications and infrastructure to manage them is taken care by Elastic Beanstalk. A user can use Amazon Web Services or an integrated development environment like Eclipse or Visual Studio to upload their application. A user has to pay for AWS resources needed to store and run the applications.

IBM Bluemix: IBM Bluemix is a cloud platform that allows a user to build apps using many open source computer technologies. Users can also deploy and manage hybrid applications using the software. With IBM Watson, whose services are available on IBM Bluemix, users can now create next-generation cognitive applications that can discover, innovate, and make decisions. IBM Watson services can be used for analyzing emotions and synthesizing natural-sounding speech from text. Watson uses the concept of cognitive computing to analyze text, video, and images. It supports programming languages like Java, Go, PHP, Ruby, and Python.

Microsoft Azure: Azure is a cloud platform created by Microsoft to build, deploy, and manage applications and services through a network of Microsoft data centers. It serves as both PaaS and IaaS and offers many solutions such as analytics, data warehousing, remote monitoring, and predictive maintenance.

Google App Engine: Google App Engine is Google's service cloud computing platform used for developing and hosting applications. Managed by Google's data centers, it supports developing apps in Python, Java, Ruby, and PHP programming languages. The BigQuery environment offers data warehouse services through the cloud.

OpenShift: OpenShift is Red Hat's cloud application platform based on a PaaS model. Through this model, application developers can deploy their applications on the cloud. There are two different models available for OpenShift. One serves as a public PaaS and the other serves as a private PaaS. OpenShift Online is Red Hat's public PaaS that offers development, build, hosting, and deployment of applications in the cloud. The private PaaS, OpenShift Enterprise, allows development, build, and deployment of applications on an internal server or a private cloud platform.

Analytics as a Service (AaaS)

Analytics and data-based managerial solutions—the applications that query data for use in business planning, problem solving, and decision support—are evolving rapidly and being used by almost every organization. Enterprises are being flooded with information, and getting insights from this data is a big challenge for them. Along with that, there are challenges related to data security, data quality, and compliance. AaaS is an extensible analytical platform using a cloud-based delivery model where various BI and data analytics tools can help companies in better decision making and get insights from their huge amount of data. The platform covers all functionality aspects from collecting data from physical devices to data visualization. AaaS provides an agile model for reporting and analytics to businesses so they can focus on what they do best. Customers can either run their own analytical applications in the cloud or they can put their data on the cloud and receive useful insights.

AaaS combines aspects of cloud computing with Big Data analytics and empowers data scientists and analysts by allowing them to access centrally managed information data sets. They can now explore information data sets more interactively and discover richer insights more rapidly, thus erasing many of the delays that they may face while discovering data trends. For example, a provider might offer access to a remote analytics platform for a fee. This allows the client to use analytics software for as long as it is needed. AaaS is a part of SaaS, PaaS, and IaaS, thus helping IT significantly reduce costs and compliance risk, while increasing productivity of users.

For example, eBay employees access a virtual slice of the main data warehouse server where they can store and analyze their own data sets. eBay's virtual private data marts have been quite successful with 50 to 100 in operation at any one time. The virtual data marts have eliminated the company's need for new physical data marts, which cost an estimated $1 million each and require the full-time attention of several skilled employees (Winter, 2008).

AaaS in the cloud has economies of scale and scope by providing many virtual analytical applications with better scalability and higher cost savings. With growing data volumes and dozens of virtual analytical applications, chances are that more of them leverage processing at different times, usage patterns, and frequencies (Kalakota, 2011).

Data and text mining is another very promising application of AaaS. The capabilities that a service orientation (along with cloud computing, pooled resources, and parallel processing) brings to the analytics world can also be used for large-scale optimization, highly complex multicriteria decision problems, and distributed simulation models. Next we identify selected cloud-based analytics offerings.

Representative Analytics as a Service Offerings

ASTER ANALYTICS AS A SERVICE Teradata Aster is a major player offering Analytics as a Service. Aster AaaS includes Aster MapReduce Analytics Foundation (allows data processing across massive data sets), and Aster Graph Analytics along with a host of other BI tools. With Aster AaaS, companies can get valuable insights from their data, which helps them in better decision making, without making any up-front infrastructure investment.

IBM WATSON ANALYTICS IBM is making all of its analytics offerings available through its cloud service, Bluemix. IBM Watson Analytics integrates most of the analytics features and capabilities that can be built and deployed through Bluemix. In addition, IBM Watson Cognitive has been a major cloud-based offering that employs text mining and deep learning at a very high level. It was introduced earlier in the context of text mining.

MINEMYTEXT.COM One of the areas of major growth in analytics is text mining. Text mining identifies high-level topics of documents, infers sentiments from reviews, and visualizes the document or term/concept relationships, as covered in the text mining chapter. A start-up called MineMyText.com offers these capabilities in the cloud through their Web site.

SAS VISUAL ANALYTICS AND VISUAL STATISTICS SAS Institute is making its analytics software offering available on demand through the cloud. Currently, SAS Visual Statistics is only available as a cloud service and is a competitor of Tableau.

TABLEAU Tableau, a major visualization software that was introduced in the context of descriptive analytics, is also available through the cloud.

SNOWFLAKE Snowflake is a cloud-based data warehouse solution. Users can bring together their data from multiple sources as one source and analyze it using Snowflake.

PREDIX BY GENERAL ELECTRIC Reportedly, General Electric is focusing on developing an IoT predictive analytics platform to help its customers better operate and manage industrial equipment and platforms. The company developed a new analytics offering called Predix (discussed in Application Case 8.3), which is available in the cloud though Amazon Web Services and will soon be available through Microsoft Azure.

Illustrative Analytics Applications Employing the Cloud Infrastructure

In this section we highlight several cloud analytics applications. We present them as one section as opposed to individual Application Cases.

MD Anderson Cancer Center Utilizes Cognitive Computing Capabilities of IBM Watson to Give Better Treatment to Cancer Patients

The University of Texas MD Anderson Cancer Center (colloquially MD Anderson Cancer Center) is one of the best cancer hospitals in the United States. Since 1941, MD Anderson Cancer Center has treated 900,000 cancer patients and has around 19,000 employees.

Every year, around 100,000 cancer patients are treated in MD Anderson and its surrounding regional and national network. As a result, the Center has accumulated a lot of clinical oncology data about their patients. The data include day-to-day patient care, clinical trials, and test results of patients, either in notes from researchers and clinicians or located in remote databases and files of other clinicians who treated these patients in the past. MD Anderson recognized that if this massive data set was collected in one source and analyzed, then it would help physicians with clinical trials and in determining the best treatment choices for their patients.

MD Anderson launched a program in 2012 called "Moon Shots" and implemented IBM Watson content analytics to find better cures for cancer. They developed a technology platform named APOLLO that aggregates all scattered unstructured data of patients into one electronic medical records (EMR) system. IBM Watson integrates seamlessly with the EMR system and uses content analytics to generate a comprehensive profile of each cancer patient in a structured format for clinicians. It helps physicians better evaluate a patient's condition and enables

them to conduct a comparison of patients based on a new range of data-driven attributes. Now, the MD Anderson physician team can compare a group of patients to identify those who respond differently to therapies and discover attributes that are responsible for these differences. Physicians can now offer patients to participate in clinical trials on novel therapies based on evidence and experience.

Sources: MDanderson.org. (2013). MD Anderson taps IBM Watson to power "Moon Shots" mission. https://www.mdanderson.org/newsroom/2013/10/md-anderson–ibm-watson-work-together-to-fight-cancer.html (accessed August 2016); IBM.com. (2015). Smarter care at MD Anderson. http://www-03.ibm.com/software/businesscasestudies/us/en/corp?synkey=H447240O66679Z38 (accessed August 2016); YouTube.com. (2014). Smarter care at MD Anderson. https://www.youtube.com/watch?v=savJ8VQ0kcA (accessed August 2016). Wikipedia.org. (n.d.). University of Texas MD Anderson Cancer Center. https://en.wikipedia.org/wiki/University_of_Texas_MD_Anderson_Cancer_Center (accessed August 2016).

Public School Education in Tacoma, Washington, Uses Microsoft Azure Machine Learning to Predict School Dropouts

Tacoma Public Schools is the main school district for Tacoma, Washington. It is composed of 35 elementary schools, 9 middle schools, and 9 high schools. It is the third-largest school district in the state of Washington, with more than 30,000 students and over 5,000 employees.

A study conducted in 2007 referred to five high schools of Tacoma Public Schools as "drop out factories." By 2010, the situation was even worse. Only 55% of the high school students earned their diploma on time, well below the national average of 88%. The school district had a lot of data related to students such as test scores, where students live, and which elementary school they attended. Using this data they wanted to find a solution to boost the graduation rates. Second, they also wanted to predict in advance which students are most likely to drop out, so they could give special attention to the child's problem and take preventive actions.

Tacoma Public Schools started exploring various BI solutions for analyzing their data. Microsoft

Consulting Services worked with the school district and built a data warehouse that captures information about a student's health, grades, attendance, and additional details from the school's student information systems. Microsoft Excel Services and SharePoint helped teachers to view historical data about their students and actions that had been taken on the observed metrics. This helped them to collectively measure a child's progress and determine how well the school was doing in helping kids move forward.

Second, the district wanted to predict which students were most likely to drop out of school, so they could help the students in advance and work closely with them. Again the school officials worked with Microsoft to create a proof-of-concept data model that is based on Microsoft's Azure Machine Learning (ML), a predictive analytics solution based on the Microsoft cloud platform. This model analyzed data uploaded to Azure from multiple on-campus information systems. The Azure Data Factory enabled

(Continued)

a predictive pipeline that uses the Azure ML model to predict whether a student is at risk of dropping out. Predictive results are put through the Microsoft Azure SQL database, from which staff members and district board members can view the results using Power BI dashboards. With the help of predictive analytics and the Microsoft Azure Machine Learning, the district was able to boost graduate rates from 55% in 2010 to 82.6% in 2016 for Tacoma Public Schools.

Sources: Blogs.technet.microsoft.com. (2015). ML predicts school dropout risk & boosts graduation rates. https://blogs.technet.microsoft.com/machinelearning/2015/06/04/ml-predicts-school-dropout-risk-boosts-graduation-rates/ (accessed August 2016); Customer.microsoft.com. (2015). Tacoma Public Schools: Predicting student dropout risks, increasing graduation rates with cloud analytics. https://customers.microsoft.com/Pages/CustomerStory.aspx?recid=20703 (accessed August 2016); YouTube.com. (2016). The saving power of data. https://www.youtube.com/watch?v=rfAoKs8XxzY (accessed August 2016).

Dartmouth-Hitchcock Medical Center Provides Personalized Proactive Healthcare Using Microsoft Cortana Analytics Suite

Dartmouth-Hitchcock Medical Center (DHMC) is located in Lebanon, New Hampshire. It is New Hampshire's only academic medical center and has about 400 beds. DHMC wants to proactively determine the health of people who are likely to fall sick and thus prevent them from falling ill. Their aim is to provide personalized healthcare at a lower cost. The nurses and health coaches track a patient's health status in real time, and data is collected using sensors that are attached to devices such as blood pressure cuffs, pulse oximeter devices, and activity trackers like Microsoft Band. This data is transmitted to the Azure cloud using smartphones. The data is then displayed on dashboards that are continuously monitored 24/7 by registered nurses using Microsoft Cortana Analytics Suite. Whenever the data of a patient crosses a safety limit, an alert is sent to nurses, who then contact the patient, thus avoiding risk of any serious problem to the patient. As a result of using this Microsoft technology, the health of the patient can be monitored remotely from a patient's home, helping reduce the cost of regular doctors' visits.

Sources: Blogs.microsoft.com. (2015). Dartmouth-Hitchcock ushers in a new age of proactive, personalized healthcare using Cortana Analytics Suite. http://blogs.microsoft.com/transform/2015/07/13/dartmouth-hitchcock-ushers-in-a-new-age-of-proactive-personalized-healthcare-using-cortana-analytics-suite/(accessed August 2016); Enterprise.microsoft.com. (2015). How Dartmouth-Hitchcock is challenging healthcare's status quo with Cortana Analytics. https://enterprise.microsoft.com/en-us/industries/health/how-dartmouth-hitchcock-is-challenging-healthcares-status-quo-with-cortana-analytics/(accessed August 2016); YouTube.com. (2015). Dartmouth-Hitchcock revolutionizes the U.S. healthcare system. https://www.youtube.com/watch?v=-wVeHZNn8aU (accessed August 2016).

Mankind Pharma Uses IBM Cloud Infrastructure to Reduce Application Implementation Time by 98%

Mankind Pharma is a pharmaceutical company based in New Delhi, India. With 11,000 employees and $600 million in revenue, it is the fourth-largest prescription drug producer in India. With its growing business, Mankind Pharma was searching for a cloud hosting environment to provide an infrastructure for its human resources (HR) platform and for other critical missions.

The Mankind technical team began using an IBM Cloud platform called Softlayer for this task.

Softlayer has data centers and bare metal servers placed all across the world, helping Mankind globally reach and fulfill their business critical missions. By using the infrastructure service of Softlayer, the company's application implementation time decreased by 98%. Now their application is available to customers in hours, versus the previous timeline of 15 days.

Sources: IBM.com. (2014). Softlayer hosting platform reduces application implementation time by 98%. http://www-03.ibm.com/software/businesscasestudies/us/en/corp?synkey=Y979749I50926G25 (accessed August 2016); CIO.in. (2015). Mankind Pharma finds an antidote in IBM solution for improving app implementation time (accessed August 2016). http://www.cio.in/solution-center/emc/55281; CxOtoday.com. (2014). Cloud platform to help Pharma Co accelerate growth. http://www.cxotoday.com/story/mankind-pharma-to-drive-growth-with-softlayers-cloud-platform/ (accessed August 2016); Wikipedia.org. (n.d.). Mankind Pharma. https://en.wikipedia.org/wiki/Mankind_Pharma (accessed August 2016); Mankindpharma.com. (n.d.). Overview. https://www.mankindpharma.com/company/companyoverview (accessed August 2016).

Gulf Air Uses Big Data to Get Deeper Customer Insight

Gulf Air is the national carrier of Bahrain. It is a major international carrier with 3,000 employees, serving 45 cities in 24 countries across 3 continents. Gulf Air is an industry leader in providing traditional Arabian hospitality to customers. To learn more about how their customers felt about their hospitality services, the airline wanted to know what their customers were saying on social media about the airline's hospitality. The challenge was analyzing all the comments and posts from their customers, as there were hundreds of thousands of posts every day. Monitoring these posts manually would be a time-consuming and daunting task and would also be prone to human error.

Gulf Air wanted to automate this task and analyze the data to learn of the emerging market trends. Along with that, the company wanted a robust infrastructure to host such a social media monitoring solution that would be available around the clock and agile across geographical boundaries.

Gulf Air developed a sentiment analysis solution, "Arabic Sentiment Analysis," that analyzes English and Arabic social media posts. The Arabic Sentiment Analysis tool is based on Cloudera's distribution of Hadoop Big Data framework. It runs on Gulf Air's private cloud environment and also uses the Red Hat JBoss Enterprise Application platform. The private cloud holds about 50 terabytes of data, and the Arabic Sentiment Analysis tool can analyze thousands of posts on social media, providing sentiment results in minutes.

Gulf Air achieved substantial cost savings by putting the "Arabic Sentiment Analysis" application on the company's existing private cloud environment as they didn't need to invest in setting up the infrastructure for deploying the application. "Arabic Sentiment Analysis" helps Gulf Air in deciding promotions and offers for their passengers on a timely basis and helps them stay ahead of their competitors. In case the master server fails, the airline created "ghost images" of the server that can be deployed quickly, and the image can start functioning in its place. The Big Data solution quickly and efficiently captures posts periodically and transforms them into reports, giving Gulf Air up-to-date views of any change in sentiment or shifts in demand, enabling them to respond quickly. Insights from the Big Data solution have had a positive impact on the work performed by the employees of Gulf Air.

Sources: RedHat.com. (2016). Gulf Air builds private cloud for Big Data innovation with Red Hat Technologies. https://www.redhat.com/en/about/press-releases/gulf-air-builds-private-cloud-big-data-innovation-red-hat-technologies; (accessed August 2016); RedHat.com. (2016). Gulf Air's Big Data innovation delivers deeper customer insight. https://www.redhat.com/en/success-stories(accessed August 2016); ComputerWeekly.com. (2016). Big-data and open source cloud technology help Gulf Air pin down customer sentiment. http://www.computerweekly.com/news/450297404/Big-data-and-open-source-cloud-technology-help-Gulf-Air-pin-down-customer-sentiment (accessed August 2016).

Chime Enhances Customer Experience Using Snowflake

Chime, a banking option, offers a Visa debit card, FDIC-insured spending and savings account, and a mobile application app that makes banking easier for people. Chime wanted to learn about their customer engagement. They wanted to analyze data across their mobile, Web, and backend platforms to help enhance the user experience. However, pulling and aggregating data from multiple sources such as ad services from Facebook and Google and events from other third-party analytics tools like JSON (JavaScript Object Notation) docs, was a laborious task. They wanted a solution that could aggregate data from these multiple sources and analyze the data set. Chime needed a solution that could process JSON data sources and query them using standard SQL database tables.

Chime started using Snowflake Elastic Data Warehouse solution. Snowflake pulled data from all 14 data sources of chime, including data like JSON docs from applications. Snowflake helped Chime analyze JSON data quickly to enhance member services and provide a more personalized banking experience to customers.

Source: Adapted from Snowflake.net. (n.d.). Chime delivers personalized customer experience using Chime. http://www.snowflake.net/product (accessed August 2016).

We are entering the "petabyte age," and traditional data and analytics approaches are beginning to show their limits. Cloud analytics is an emerging alternative solution for large-scale data analysis. Data-oriented cloud systems include storage and computing in a distributed and virtualized environment. A major advantage of these offerings is the rapid diffusion of advanced analysis tools among the users, without significant investment in technology acquisition. These solutions also come with many challenges, such as security, service level, and data governance. A number of concerns have been raised about cloud computing, including loss of control and privacy, legal liabilities, cross-border political issues, and so on. According to Cloud Security Alliance, the top three security threats in the cloud are data loss and leakage, hardware failure of equipment, and an insecure interface. All the data in the cloud is accessible by the service provider, so the service provider can unknowingly or deliberately alter the data or can pass the data to a third party for purposes of law without asking the company. Research is still limited in this area. As a result, there is ample opportunity to bring analytical, computational, and conceptual modeling into the context of service science, service orientation, and cloud intelligence. Nonetheless, cloud computing is an important initiative for an analytics professional to watch as it is a fast-growing area.

SECTION 8.3 REVIEW QUESTIONS

1. Define *cloud computing*. How does it relate to PaaS, SaaS, and IaaS?
2. Give examples of companies offering cloud services.
3. How does cloud computing affect BI?
4. How does DaaS change the way data is handled?
5. What are the different types of cloud platforms?
6. Why is AaaS cost effective?
7. Name at least three major cloud service providers.
8. Give at least three examples of analytics-as-a-service providers.

8.4   Location-Based Analytics for Organizations

Thus far, we have seen many examples of organizations employing analytical techniques to gain insights into their existing processes through informative reporting, predictive analytics, forecasting, and optimization techniques. In this section, we learn about a critical emerging trend—incorporation of location data in analytics. Figure 8.6 gives our classification of location-based analytic applications. We first review applications that make use of static location data that is usually called *geospatial data*. We then examine the explosive growth of applications that take advantage of all the location data being generated by today's devices. This section first focuses on analytics applications that are being developed by organizations to make better decisions in managing operations, targeting customers, promotions, and so forth. Then we will also explore analytics applications that are being developed to be used directly by a consumer, some of which also take advantage of the location data.

Geospatial Analytics

A consolidated view of the overall performance of an organization is usually represented through the visualization tools that provide actionable information. The information may include current and forecasted values of various business factors and key performance indicators (KPIs). Looking at the KPIs as overall numbers via various graphs and charts can be overwhelming. There is a high risk of missing potential growth opportunities or not identifying the problematic areas. As an alternative to simply viewing reports, organizations employ visual maps that are geographically mapped and based on the traditional location data, usually grouped by postal codes. These map-based visualizations have been used by organizations to view the aggregated data and get more meaningful location-based insights. The traditional location-based analytic techniques using geocoding of organizational locations and consumers hamper the organizations in understanding "true location-based" impacts. Locations based on postal codes offer an aggregate view of a large geographic area. This poor granularity may not help pinpoint the growth opportunities within a region, as the location of target customers can change rapidly. Thus, an organization's promotional campaigns may not target the right customers if it is

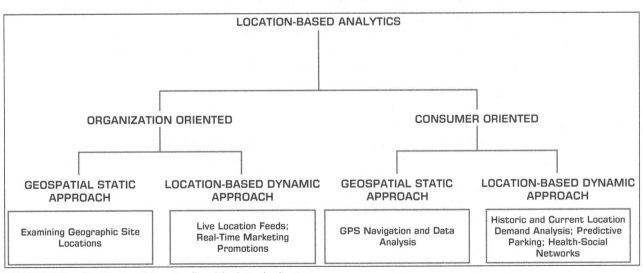

FIGURE 8.6   Classification of Location-Based Analytics Applications.

based on postal codes. To address these concerns, organizations are embracing location and spatial extensions to analytics (Gnau, 2010). The addition of location components based on latitudinal and longitudinal attributes to the traditional analytical techniques enables organizations to add a new dimension of "where" to their traditional business analyses, which currently answers the questions of "who," "what," "when," and "how much."

Location-based data are now readily available from **geographic information systems (GIS)**. These are used to capture, store, analyze, and manage data linked to a location using integrated sensor technologies, global positioning systems installed in smartphones, or through RFID deployments in the retail and healthcare industries.

By integrating information about the location with other critical business data, organizations are now creating location intelligence (Krivda, 2010). Location intelligence is enabling organizations to gain critical insights and make better decisions by optimizing important processes and applications. Organizations now create interactive maps that further drill down to details about any location, offering analysts the ability to investigate new trends and correlate location-specific factors across multiple KPIs. Analysts can now pinpoint trends and patterns in revenue, sales, and profitability across geographical areas.

By incorporating demographic details into locations, retailers can determine how sales vary by population level and proximity to other competitors; they can assess the demand and efficiency of supply-chain operations. Consumer product companies can identify the specific needs of customers and customer complaint locations and easily trace them back to the products. Sales reps can better target their prospects by analyzing their geography.

A company that is the market leader in providing GIS data is ESRI (esri.com). ESRI licenses its ArcGIS software to thousands of customers including commercial, government, and the military. It can take a book or more to highlight applications of ESRI's GIS database and software! Another company grindgis.com identifies over 60 categories of GIS applications (http://grindgis.com/blog/gis-applications-uses). A few examples that have not been mentioned yet include the following:

- **Agricultural applications:** By combining location, weather, soil, and crop-related data, very precise irrigation and fertilizer applications can be planned. Examples include companies such as sstsoftware.com and sensefly.com (they combine GIS and the latest information collected through drones, another emerging technology).
- **Crime analysis:** Superimposition of crime data including date, time, and type of crime onto the GIS data can provide significant insights into crime patterns and police staffing.
- **Disease spread prediction:** One of the first known examples of descriptive analytics is the analysis of the cholera outbreak in London in 1854. Dr. John Snow plotted the cases of cholera on a map and was able to refute the theory that the cholera outbreak was being caused by bad air. The map helped him pinpoint the outbreak to a bad water well. (TheGuardian.com, 2013). We have come a long way from needing to plot maps manually, but the idea of being able to track and then predict outbreaks of diseases, such as the flu, using GIS and other data has become a major field in itself. Chapter 7 gave an example of using social media data along with GIS data to pinpoint flu trends.

In addition, with location intelligence, organizations can quickly overlay weather and environmental effects and forecast the level of impact on critical business operations. With technology advancements, geospatial data is now being directly incorporated in enterprise data warehouses. Location-based in-database analytics enable organizations to perform complex calculations with increased efficiency and get a single view of all the spatially oriented data, revealing hidden trends and new opportunities. For example, Teradata's data warehouse supports the geospatial data feature based on the SQL/MM standard. The geospatial feature is captured as a new geometric data type called ST_GEOMETRY. It supports a large spectrum of shapes, from simple points, lines, and curves to complex polygons in representing the geographic areas. They are converting the nonspatial data of their operating business locations by incorporating the latitude and longitude coordinates. This process of geocoding is readily supported by service companies like NAVTEQ and Tele Atlas, which maintain worldwide databases of addresses with geospatial features and make use of address-cleansing tools like Informatica and Trillium, which support mapping of spatial coordinates to the addresses as part of extract, transform, and load functions.

Organizations across a variety of business sectors are employing geospatial analytics. We will review some examples next. Application Case 8.4 provides an example of how location-based information was used in making site selection decisions in expanding a company's footprint. Application Case 8.5 illustrates another application that goes beyond just the location decision.

Application Case 8.4

Great Clips Employs Spatial Analytics to Shave Time in Location Decisions

Great Clips, the world's largest and fastest-growing hair salon, has more than 3,000 salons throughout the United States and Canada. Great Clips franchise success depends on a growth strategy that is driven by rapidly opening new stores in the right locations and markets. The company needed to analyze the locations based on the requirements for a potential customer base, demographic trends, and sales impact on existing franchises in the target location. Choosing a good site is of utmost importance. The current processes took a long time to analyze a single site and a great deal of labor requiring intensive analyst resources to manually assess the data from multiple data sources.

With thousands of locations to analyze each year, the delay was risking the loss of prime sites to competitors and was proving expensive; Great Clips employed external contractors to cope with the delay. The company created a site-selection workflow application to evaluate the new salon site locations by using the geospatial analytical capabilities of Alteryx. A new site location was evaluated by its drive-time proximity and convenience for serving all the existing customers of the Great Clips network in the area. The Alteryx-based solution also enabled evaluation of each new location based on

demographics and consumer behavior data, aligning with existing Great Clips customer profiles and the potential impact of new site revenue on the existing sites. As a result of using location-based analytic techniques, Great Clips was able to reduce the time to assess new locations by nearly 95%. The labor-intensive analysis was automated and developed into a data collection analysis, mapping, and reporting application that could be easily used by the nontechnical real estate managers. Furthermore, it enabled the company to implement proactive predictive analytics for a new franchise location, as the whole process now took just a few minutes.

QUESTIONS FOR DISCUSSION

1. How is geospatial analytics employed at Great Clips?
2. What criteria should a company consider in evaluating sites for future locations?
3. Can you think of other applications where such geospatial data might be useful?

Source: Adapted from Alteryx.com. (n.d.). Great Clips. alteryx. com/sites/default/files/resources/files/case-study-great-chips.pdf (accessed August 2016).

Application Case 8.5

Starbucks Exploits GIS and Analytics to Grow Worldwide

One of the key challenges for any organization that is trying to grow its presence is deciding the location of its next store. Starbucks faces the same question. To identify new store locations, more than 700 Starbucks' employees (referred to as partners) in 15 countries use an ArcGIS-based market planning and BI solution called Atlas. Atlas provides partners with workflows, analysis, and store performance information so that local partners in the field can make decisions when identifying new business opportunities.

As reported in multiple sources, Atlas is employed by local decision makers to understand the population trends and demand. For example, in China, there are over 1,200 Starbucks' stores, and the company is opening a new store almost every day. Information such as trade areas, retail clusters and generators, traffic, and demographics is important in deciding the next store's location. After analyzing a new market and neighborhood, a manager can look at specific locations by zooming into an area in the city and identifying where three new office towers may be completed over the next 2 months, for example. After viewing this area on the map, a workflow window can be created that will help the manager move the new site through approval, permitting, construction, and eventually opening.

By integrating weather and other local data, one can also better manage demand and supply-chain operations. Starbucks is integrating its enterprise business systems with its GIS solutions in Web services to see the world and its business in new ways. For example, Starbucks integrates AccuWeather's forecasted real-feel temperature data. This forecasted temperature data can help localize marketing efforts. If a really hot week in Memphis is forthcoming, Starbucks' analysts can select a group of coffee houses and get detailed information on past and future weather patterns, as well as store characteristics. This knowledge can be used to design a localized promotion for Frappuccinos, for example, helping Starbucks anticipate what its customers will be wanting a week in advance.

Major events also have an impact on coffee houses. When 150,000 people descended on San Diego for the Pride Parade, local baristas served a lot of customers. To ensure the best possible customer experience, Starbucks used this local event knowledge to plan staffing and inventory at locations near the parade.

QUESTIONS FOR DISCUSSION

1. What type of demographics and GIS information would be relevant for deciding on a store location?

2. It has been mentioned that Starbucks encourages its customers to use its mobile app. What type of information might the company gather from the app to help it better plan operations?

3. Will the availability of free Wi-Fi at Starbucks' stores provide any information to Starbucks for better analytics?

Sources: Digit.HBS.org. (2015). Starbucks: Brewing up a data storm! https://digit.hbs.org/submission/starbucks-brewing-up-a-data-storm/ (accessed August 2016); Wheeler, C. (2014). Going big with GIS. http://www.esri.com/esri-news/arcwatch/0814/going-big-with-gis (accessed August 2016); Blogs.ESRI.com. From customers to CxOs, Starbucks delivers world-class service. (2014). https://blogs.esri.com/esri/ucinsider/2014/07/29/starbucks/ (accessed August 2016).

In addition to the retail transaction analysis applications highlighted here, there are many other applications of combining geographic information with other data being generated by an organization. For example, network operations and communication companies often generate massive amounts of data every day. The ability to analyze the data quickly with a high level of location-specific granularity can better identify the customer churn and help in formulating strategies specific to locations for increasing operational efficiency, quality of service, and revenue.

Geospatial analysis can enable communication companies to capture daily transactions from a network to identify the geographic areas experiencing a large number of failed connection attempts of voice, data, text, or Internet. Analytics can help determine the exact causes based on location and drill down to an individual customer to provide better customer service. You can see this in action by completing the following multimedia exercise.

A Multimedia Exercise in Analytics Employing Geospatial Analytics

Teradata University Network includes a BSI video on the case of dropped mobile calls. Please watch the video that appears on YouTube at the following link: http://www.teradatauniversitynetwork.com/Library/Items/ BSI–The-Case-of-the-Dropped-Mobile-Calls/.

A telecommunication company launches a new line of smartphones and faces problems with dropped calls. The new rollout is in trouble, and the northeast region is the worst hit region as they compare effects of dropped calls on the profits for the geographic region. The company hires BSI to analyze the problems arising due to defects in smartphone handsets, tower coverage, and software glitches. The entire northeast region data is divided into geographic clusters, and the company solves the problem by identifying the individual customer data. The BSI team employs geospatial analytics to identify the locations where network coverage was leading to dropped calls and suggests installing a few additional towers where unhappy customers are located.

After the video is complete, you can see how the analysis was prepared at: slideshare.net/teradata/bsi-teradata-the-case-of-the-dropped-mobile-calls.

This multimedia excursion provides an example of a combination of geospatial analytics along with Big Data analytics that assist in better decision making.

Real-Time Location Intelligence

Many devices in use by consumers and professionals are constantly sending out their location information. Cars, buses, taxis, mobile phones, cameras, and personal navigation devices all transmit their locations thanks to network-connected positioning technologies such as GPS, Wi-Fi, and cell tower triangulation. Millions of consumers and businesses use location-enabled devices for finding nearby services, locating friends and family, navigating, tracking assets and pets, dispatching, and engaging in sports, games, and hobbies. This surge in location-enabled services has resulted in a massive database of historical and real-time streaming location information. It is, of course, scattered and not very useful by itself. The automated data collection enabled through capture of cell phones and Wi-Fi hotspot access points presents an interesting new dimension in nonintrusive market research, data collection, and, of course, microanalysis of such massive data sets.

By analyzing and learning from these large-scale patterns of movement, it is possible to identify distinct classes of behaviors in specific contexts. This approach allows a business to better understand its customer patterns and make more informed decisions about promotions, pricing, and so on. By applying algorithms that reduce the dimensionality of location data, one can characterize places according to the activity and movement between them. From massive amounts of high-dimensional location data, these algorithms uncover trends, meaning, and relationships to eventually produce human-understandable representations. It then becomes possible to use such data to automatically make intelligent predictions and find important matches and similarities between places and people.

Location-based analytics finds its application in consumer-oriented marketing applications. Quiznos, a quick-service restaurant, used Sense Networks' platform to analyze location trails of mobile users based on geospatial data obtained from the GPS and targeted tech-savvy customers with coupons. See Application Case 8.6. This case illustrates

Application Case 8.6

Quiznos Targets Customers for Its Sandwiches

Quiznos, a franchised, quick-service restaurant, implemented a location-based mobile targeting campaign that targeted tech-savvy and busy consumers of Portland, Oregon. It made use of Sense Networks' platform, which analyzed the location trails of mobile users over detailed time periods and built anonymous profiles based on the behavioral attributes of their shopping habits.

With the application of predictive analytics on the user profiles, Quiznos employed location-based behavioral targeting to narrow the characteristics of users who were most likely to eat at a quick-service restaurant. Its advertising campaign ran for 2 months—November and December 2012—and targeted only potential customers who had been to quick-service restaurants over the past 30 days,

within a 3-mile radius of Quiznos, and between the ages of 18 and 34. It used relevant mobile advertisements of local coupons based on the customer's location. The campaign resulted in over 3.7 million new customers and a 20% increase in coupon redemptions within the Portland area.

QUESTIONS FOR DISCUSSION

1. How can location-based analytics help retailers in targeting customers?
2. Research similar applications of location-based analytics in the retail domain.

Source: Adapted from Mobilemarketer.com. (2013). Quiznos sees 20pc boost in coupon redemption via location-based mobile ad campaign. mobilemarketer.com/cms/news/advertising/14738.html (accessed August 2016).

the emerging trend in the retail space where companies are looking to improve efficiency of marketing campaigns—not just by targeting every customer based on real-time location, but by employing more sophisticated predictive analytics in real time on consumer behavioral profiles to find the right set of consumers for advertising campaigns.

Yet another extension of location-based analytics is to use augmented reality. In 2016, Pokémon GO became a market sensation. It is a location-sensing augmented reality-based game that encourages users to claim virtual items from select geographic locations. The user can start anywhere in a city and follow markers on the app to reach a specific item. Virtual items are visible through the app when the user points a phone's camera toward the virtual item. The user can then claim this item. Business applications of such technologies are also emerging. For example, an app called Candybar allows businesses to place these virtual items on a map using Google Maps. The placement of this item can be fine-tuned using Google's Street View. Once all virtual items have been configured with the information and location, the business can submit items, which are then visible to the user in real time. Candybar also provides usage analytics to the business to enable better targeting of virtual items. The virtual reality aspect of this app improves the experience of users, providing them with a "gaming" environment in real life. At the same time, it provides a powerful marketing platform for businesses to reach their customers.

As is evident from this section, location-based analytics and ensuing applications are perhaps the most important front in the near future for organizations. A common theme in this section was the use of operational or marketing data by organizations. We will next explore analytics applications that are directly targeted at users and sometimes take advantage of location information.

Analytics Applications for Consumers

The explosive growth of the apps industry for smartphone platforms (iOS, Android, Windows, and so forth) and the use of analytics are creating tremendous opportunities for developing apps where the consumers use analytics without ever realizing it. These apps differ from the previous category in that these are meant for direct use by a consumer, as opposed to an organization that is trying to mine a consumer's usage/purchase data to create a profile for marketing specific products or services. Predictably, these apps are meant for enabling consumers to make better decisions by employing specific analytics. We highlight two of these in the following examples.

Waze, a social Web app that assists users in identifying a navigation path and alerts users about potential issues such as accidents, police checkpoints, speed traps, and construction, based on other users' inputs, has become a very popular navigation app. Google acquired this app a few years ago and has enhanced it further. This app is an example of aggregating user-generated information and making it available for customers.

Many apps allow users to submit reviews and ratings for businesses, products, and so on, and then present those to the users in an aggregated form to help them make choices. These apps can also be identified as apps based on social data that are targeted at consumers where the data are generated by the consumers. One of the more popular apps in this category is Yelp.

Another transportation-related app that uses predictive analytics has been deployed in Pittsburgh, Pennsylvania. Developed in collaboration with Carnegie Mellon University, this app includes predictive capabilities to estimate parking availability. ParkPGH directs drivers to parking lots in areas where parking is available. It calculates the number of parking spaces available in 10 lots—over 5,300 spaces and 25% of the garage parking in downtown Pittsburgh. Available spaces are updated every 30 seconds, keeping the driver as close to the current availability as possible. Depending on historical demand and current events, the app is able to predict parking availability and provide information on which lots will have free space by the time the driver reaches the destination. The app's underlying algorithm uses data on current events around the area—for example, a basketball game—to predict an increase in demand for parking spaces later that day, thus saving the commuters valuable time searching for parking spaces in the busy city.

Analytics-based applications are emerging not just for fun and health, but also to enhance one's productivity. For example, Cloze is an app that manages in-boxes from multiple e-mail accounts as well as other social media accounts, CRM, and so on, in one place. It integrates social networks with e-mail contacts to learn which contacts are important and assigns a score—important contacts receive a higher score. E-mails with a higher score are shown first, thus filtering less important and irrelevant e-mails out of the way. Cloze stores the context of each conversation to save time when catching up on a pending conversation. Contacts are organized into groups based on how frequently they interact, helping users keep in touch with people with whom they may be losing contact. Users are able to set a Cloze score for people they want to get in touch with and work on improving that score. Cloze marks up the score whenever an attempt at connecting is made. On opening an e-mail, for example, Cloze provides several options, such as now, today, tomorrow, and next week, which automatically reminds the user to initiate contact at the scheduled time. This serves as a reminder for getting back to e-mails at a later point, without forgetting about them or marking them as "unread," which often leads to a cluttered in-box. Because Cloze is now being targeted as a business productivity app, its pricing as of right now is beyond a typical consumer's range.

As is evident from these examples of consumer-centric apps, predictive analytics is beginning to enable development of software that is directly used by a consumer. The *Wall Street Journal* (wsj.com/apps) estimates that the app industry has already become a $25 billion industry with more growth expected. We believe that the growth of consumer-oriented analytic applications will continue and create many entrepreneurial opportunities for the readers of this book.

One key concern in employing these technologies is the loss of privacy. If someone can track the movement of a cell phone, the privacy of that customer is a big issue. Some of the app developers claim that they only need to gather aggregate flow information, not individually identifiable information. But many stories appear in the media that highlight violations of this general principle. Both users and developers of such apps have to be very aware of the deleterious effect of giving out private information as well as collecting such information. We discuss this issue a bit further in Section 8.5.

SECTION 8.4 REVIEW QUESTIONS

1. How does traditional analytics make use of location-based data?
2. How can geocoded locations assist in better decision making?
3. What is the value provided by geospatial analytics?
4. Explore the use of geospatial analytics further by investigating its use across various sectors like government census tracking, consumer marketing, and so forth.
5. Search online for other applications of consumer-oriented analytical applications.
6. How can location-based analytics help individual consumers?
7. Explore more transportation applications that may employ location-based analytics.
8. What other applications can you imagine if you were able to access cell phone location data?

8.5   Issues of Legality, Privacy, and Ethics

As data science, analytics, cognitive computing, and AI grow in reach and pervasiveness, everyone is affected by these applications. Just because something is doable through technology, does not make it appropriate, legal, or ethical. Data science professionals and managers have to be very aware of these concerns. Several important legal, privacy, and ethical issues are related to analytics. Here we provide only representative examples and sources. Popular media is usually quite keen to report on such breaches of legal and ethical behavior, so this is one section where you may find even more recent examples online. As pointed out in Chapter 1, our goal here is only to give you an exposure to these issues. Your class teams should identify more recent cases and discuss those.

Legal Issues

The introduction of analytics may compound a host of legal issues already relevant to computer systems. For example, questions concerning liability for the actions of advice provided by intelligent machines are beginning to be considered.

In addition to resolving disputes about the unexpected and possibly damaging results of some analytics, other complex issues may surface. For example, who is liable if an enterprise finds itself bankrupt as a result of using the advice of an analytic application? Will the enterprise itself be held responsible for not testing the system adequately before entrusting it with sensitive issues? Will auditing and accounting firms share the liability for failing to apply adequate auditing tests? Will the software developers of intelligent systems be jointly liable? As self-driving cars become more common, who is liable for any damage or injury when a car's sensors, network, or the analytics fail to function as planned? A recent case involving a Tesla car accident where the driver died in a crash while the car was allegedly in "autopilot" mode has brought this issue to the front pages of newspapers and the legal profession.

Application Case 7.1 gave examples of the use of alternative data in using additional information to better forecast future crop output, sales for a company, and so on. Although these tools today do not pose the traditional insider trading restrictions because no one inside the company is sharing nonpublic information, there may still be issues about having information that is not publicly available. Ekster (2015) notes that any market trader using analytics and alternative data should be aware of information rules imposed by financial regulatory bodies. Typically, insights *derived* from public data are safe because they have not been *directly acquired* from insider sources.

Consider the following specific legal issues:

- What is the value of an expert opinion in court when the expertise is encoded in a computer?
- Who is liable for wrong advice (or information) provided by an intelligent application? For example, what happens if a physician accepts an incorrect diagnosis made by a computer and performs an act that results in the death of a patient?
- What happens if a manager enters an incorrect judgment value into an analytic application and the result is damage or a disaster?
- Who owns the knowledge in a knowledge base?
- Can management force experts to contribute their expertise?

Privacy

Privacy means different things to different people. In general, **privacy** is the right to be left alone and the right to be free from unreasonable personal intrusions. Privacy has long been a legal, ethical, and social issue in many countries. The right to privacy is recognized today in every state of the United States and by the federal government, either by statute or by common law. The definition of *privacy* can be interpreted quite broadly. However, the following two rules have been followed fairly closely in past court decisions: (1) the right of privacy is not absolute. Privacy must be balanced against the needs of society. (2) The public's right to know is superior to the individual's right to privacy. These two rules show why it is difficult, in some cases, to determine and enforce privacy regulations (see Peslak, 2005). Privacy issues online have specific characteristics and policies. One area where privacy may be jeopardized is discussed next. For privacy and security issues in the data warehouse environment, also see the paper by Elson and LeClerc (2005).

Collecting Information about Individuals

The complexity of collecting, sorting, filing, and accessing information manually from numerous government agencies was, in many cases, a built-in protection against the misuse of private information. It was simply too expensive, cumbersome, and complex to invade a person's privacy. The Internet, in combination with large-scale databases, has created an entirely new dimension of accessing and using data. The inherent power in systems that can access vast amounts of data can be used for the good of society. For example, by matching records with the aid of a computer, it is possible to eliminate or reduce fraud, crime, government mismanagement, tax evasion, welfare cheating, family-support filching, employment of illegal workers, and so on. However, what price must the individual pay in terms of loss of privacy so that the government can better apprehend criminals? The same is true on the corporate level. Private information about employees may aid in better decision making, but the employees' privacy may be affected. Similar issues are related to information about customers.

The implications for online privacy are significant. The USA PATRIOT Act also broadens the government's ability to access student information and personal financial information without any suspicion of wrongdoing by attesting that the information likely to be found is pertinent to an ongoing criminal investigation (see Electronic Privacy Information Center, 2005). Location information from devices has been used to locate victims as well as perpetrators in some cases, but at what point is the information not the property of the individual? The recent flap about the United States and other countries recording data about telephone calls, e-mail, and other electronic traffic has brought many of these issues to the forefront. In addition, the release of information from government communications by Wikileaks created a major storm over the last few years. Finally, Edward Snowden's disclosure of the U.S. government's data collection programs and mining of this information also resulted in major media discussion of invasion of privacy issues. Any search on these topics will yield a host of links and viewpoints. As a data science professional, you have to recognize that such issues can make a big difference in your organization's reputation.

Two effective tools for collecting information about individuals are cookies and spyware. Single-sign-on facilities that let a user access various services from a provider are beginning to raise some of the same concerns as cookies. Such services (Google, Yahoo!, MSN) let consumers permanently enter a profile of information along with a password and use this information and password repeatedly to access services at multiple sites. Critics say that such services create the same opportunities as cookies to invade an individual's privacy.

The use of AI technologies in the administration and enforcement of laws and regulations may increase public concern regarding privacy of information. These fears, generated by the perceived abilities of AI, will have to be addressed at the outset of almost any AI development effort.

Mobile User Privacy

Many users are unaware of the private information being tracked through their smartphone usage. Many apps collect user data that track each phone as it moves from one cell tower to another, from GPS-enabled devices that transmit users' locations, and from phones transmitting information at Wi-Fi hotspots. Major app developers claim they are extremely careful and protective of users' privacy, but it is interesting to note how much information is available through the use of a single device. A recent debate between Apple and the U.S. government about the U.S. government's demand to unlock an iPhone and Apple's refusal to modify its software to do so highlighted this issue. Apple claims to collect little to no information about its individual iPhone users. On the other hand, Google collects a lot of usage information to be able to give the users proactive information about their calendar, preferred restaurants, upcoming activities, and so on. Any analytics application developer has to keep privacy issues in mind.

Homeland Security and Individual Privacy

Using analytics technologies such as mining and interpreting the content of telephone calls, taking photos of people in certain places and identifying them, and using scanners to view your personal belongings are considered by many to be an invasion of privacy. However, many people recognize that analytic tools are an effective and efficient means to increase security, even though the privacy of many innocent people is compromised.

The U.S. government applies analytical technologies on a global scale in the war on terrorism. In the first year and a half after September 11, 2001, supermarket chains, home improvement stores, and other retailers voluntarily handed over massive amounts of customer records to federal law enforcement agencies, almost always in violation of their stated privacy policies. Many others responded to court orders for information, as required by law. The U.S. government has a right to gather corporate data under legislation passed after September 11, 2001. The FBI now mines enormous amounts of data, looking for activity that could indicate a terrorist plot or crime.

Privacy issues abound. Because the government is acquiring personal data to detect suspicious patterns of activity, there is the prospect of improper or illegal use of the data. Many see such gathering of data as a violation of citizens' freedoms and rights. They see the need for an oversight organization to "watch the watchers," to ensure that the Department of Homeland Security does not mindlessly acquire data. Instead, it should acquire only pertinent data and information that can be mined to identify patterns that could potentially lead to stopping terrorists' activities. This is not an easy task.

Recent Technology Issues in Privacy and Analytics

Most providers of Internet services such as Google, Facebook, Twitter, and others depend on monetizing their users' actions. They do so in many different ways, but all of these approaches in the end amount to understanding a user's profile or preferences on the basis of their usage. With the growth of Internet users in general and mobile device users in particular, many companies have been founded to employ advanced analytics to develop profiles of users on the basis of their device usage, movement, and the contacts of the users. The *Wall Street Journal* has an excellent collection of articles titled "What They Know" (WallStreetJournal.com, 2016). These articles are constantly updated to highlight the latest technology and privacy/ethical issues. One of the companies mentioned in this series included Rapleaf (now part of Towerdata). Rapleaf's technology claims to be able to provide a profile of a user just by knowing their e-mail address. Clearly, their technology enables them to gather significant information. Another company that aims to identify devices on the basis of their usage is BlueCava, which recently merged with Qualia (**Qualia.com**). Qualia's BlueCava technology attaches a personal profile to be able to recognize a user as one individual or household even though they may be using multiple mobile devices and laptops. All of these companies employ technologies such as clustering and association mining to develop profiles of users. Such analytics applications definitely raise thorny questions of privacy violation for the users. Of course, many of the analytics start-ups in this space claim to honor user privacy, but violations are often reported. For example, Rapleaf (as noted earlier, now merged with Towerdata) was collecting unauthorized user information from Facebook users and was subsequently banned from Facebook. A column in *Time* magazine by Joel Stein (2011) reported that an hour after he gave his e-mail address to a company that specializes in user information monitoring (reputation.com), they had already been able to discover his Social Security number. This number is a key to accessing private information about a user and could lead to identity theft. So, violations of privacy create fears of criminal conduct based on user information. This area is a big concern overall and needs careful study. This book's Web site will update new developments. The *Wall Street Journal* site, "What They Know," is a resource that ought to be consulted periodically. These examples not only illustrate the power of analytics in being able to learn more about target customers, but also serve as a warning to analytics professionals about being sensitive to privacy and ethical issues.

Another application area that combines organizational IT impact, Big Data, sensors, and privacy concerns is analyzing employee behaviors on the basis of data collected from sensors that the employees wear in a badge. One company, Humanyze, has reported several such applications of their sensor-embedded badges that the employees wear. These sensors track all movement of an employee. Of course, this creates major privacy issues. Should the companies be able to monitor their employees this intrusively? Humanyze has reported that its analytics are only reported on an aggregate basis to their clients. No individual user data is shared. They have noted that some employers want to get individual employee data, but their contract explicitly prohibits this type of sharing. In any case, sensors are leading to another level of surveillance and analytics, which poses interesting privacy, legal, and ethical questions.

Who Owns Our Private Data?

With the recent growth of data from our use of technology and companies' ability to access and mine it, the privacy debate also leads to the obvious question of whose property any user's data is. Welch (2016) highlighted this issue in a *Bloomberg Businessweek* column. Take an example of a relatively new car. The car is equipped with many sensors starting with tire pressure sensors to GPS trackers that can keep track of where you have gone, how fast you were driving, when you changed lanes, and so on. The car may even know the passenger's weight added to the front seat. As Welch notes, a car connected to the Internet (most new cars are!) can be a privacy nightmare for the owner or a data "gold mine" for whoever can possess this data. A major battle is brewing between automobile manufacturers and technology providers such as Apple (CarPlay) and Google (Android Auto) on who owns this data and who can get access to this data. This is becoming more crucial because as cars become more self-driving, the driver/passenger in the car could be a highly targeted prospective customer for specific products and services whose profile is very well known to the organization who is able to create that profile. For example, Google's Waze app collects user GPS data for over 50 million users to track traffic information and help users find the best route, but then displays pop-up ads on the users' screens. Yelp, Spotify, and other apps popularly used in the car have similar plans and applications.

A similar battle is also brewing about users' health and biometric data. Because of security concerns, many users are moving to biometric log-in authentication using fingerprints, touch screens, iris scans, and so on. Because this information is highly unique to an individual, future profiling of a user may become even more precise. Thus the battle to own and relate this information to other data gathered is growing as well. Similarly, hospitals, medical professionals, labs, and insurance companies collect a lot of information about our medical history. Although in the United States there are strict laws in place (e.g., HIPAA) to protect a user's privacy, compilation of this information is unleashing major advances in health analytics. The privacy challenge, however, is still very real.

Bottom line, as a data analytics professional, be very aware of the legal and ethical issues involved in collecting information that may be privileged or protected. A general question to ask yourself is—would you like your own information to be included for the application you are contemplating?

Ethics in Decision Making and Support

The last question brings us to several ethical issues that are related to analytics. Representative ethical issues that could be of interest in analytics implementations include the following:

- Electronic surveillance
- Ethics in DSS design (see Chae, Paradice, Courtney, & Cagle, 2005)
- Software piracy
- Invasion of individuals' privacy
- Use of proprietary databases
- Use of intellectual property such as knowledge and expertise
- Exposure of employees to unsafe environments related to computers
- Computer accessibility for workers with disabilities
- Accuracy of data, information, and knowledge
- Protection of the rights of users
- Accessibility to information
- Use of corporate computers for non-work-related purposes
- How much decision making to delegate to computers

Personal values constitute a major factor in the issue of ethical decision making. The study of ethical issues is complex because of its multidimensionality. Therefore, it makes sense to develop frameworks to describe ethics processes and systems. Mason, Mason, and Culnan (1995) explained how technology and innovation expand the size of the domain of ethics and discuss a model for ethical reasoning that involves four fundamental focusing questions: Who is the agent? What action was actually taken or is being contemplated? What are the results or consequences of the act? Is the result fair or just for all stakeholders? They also described a hierarchy of ethical reasoning in which each ethical judgment or action is based on rules and codes of ethics, which are based on principles, which in turn are grounded in ethical theory.

One story that made many users upset (although it was not illegal) some time back was Facebook's experiment to present different News Feeds to the users and monitor their emotional reactions as measured by replies, likes, sentiment analysis, and so on (for example, see Goel, 2014). Most companies, including technology companies, run user testing to identify the features most liked or disliked and fine-tune their product offerings. Because Facebook is so large, running this experiment without the users' informed consent was viewed as unethical. Indeed, Facebook acknowledged its error and instituted a more formal review through Internal Review Boards and other compliance mechanisms for future testing. Although they faced a lot of bad press initially, their timely response allowed them to recover quickly.

SECTION 8.5 REVIEW QUESTIONS

1. List some legal issues of analytics.
2. Describe privacy concerns in analytics.
3. In your view, who should own the data about your use of a car?
4. List ethical issues in analytics.

8.6 Impacts of Analytics in Organizations: An Overview

Analytic systems are important factors in the information and knowledge revolution. This is a cultural transformation with which most people are only now coming to terms. Unlike the slower revolutions of the past, such as the Industrial Revolution, this revolution is taking place very quickly and affecting every facet of our lives. Inherent in this rapid transformation are a host of managerial, economic, and social issues.

Separating the impact of analytics from that of other computerized systems is a difficult task, especially because of the trend toward integrating, or even embedding, analytics with other computer-based information systems. Analytics can have both micro and macro implications. Such systems can affect particular individuals and jobs, and they can also affect the work structures of departments and units within an organization. They can also have significant long-term effects on total organizational structures, entire industries, communities, and society as a whole (i.e., a macro impact).

Explosive growth in analytics, AI, and cognitive computing is going to have a major impact on the future of organizations. The impact of computers and analytics can be divided into three general categories: organizational, individual, and societal. In each of these, computers have had many impacts. We cannot possibly consider all of them in this section, so in the next paragraphs we touch on topics we feel are most relevant to analytics. Figure 8.7 highlights the general topics we plan to cover.

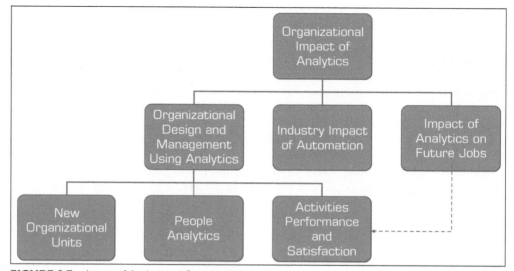

FIGURE 8.7 Impact of Analytics on Organizations.

New Organizational Units

One change in organizational structure is the possibility of creating an analytics department, a BI department, or a data science department in which analytics play a major role. This special unit can be combined with or replace a quantitative analysis unit, or it can be a completely new entity. Some large corporations have separate decision support units or departments. For example, many major banks have such departments in their financial services divisions. Many companies have small data science or BI/data warehouse units. These types of departments are usually involved in training in addition to consulting and application development activities. Others have empowered a chief technology officer over BI, intelligent systems, and e-commerce applications. Companies such as Target and Walmart have major investments in such units, which are constantly analyzing their data to determine the efficiency of marketing and supply-chain management by understanding their customer and supplier interactions. On the other hand, many companies are embedding analytics/data science specialties within functional areas such as marketing, finance, and operations. In general, this is one area where considerable job opportunities currently exist. We identified related job titles in Chapter 1, and present a general description of an ideal data scientist in the next section.

Growth of the BI industry has resulted in the formation of new units within IT provider companies as well. For example, a few years back IBM formed a new business unit focused on analytics. This group included units in BI, optimization models, data mining, and business performance. More important, the group is focused not just on software, but significantly more on services/consulting. As noted in previous sections, the enormous growth of the app industry has created many opportunities for new companies that can employ analytics and deliver innovative applications in any specific domain. We noted earlier how the traditional industrial age stalwarts such as General Electric and Siemens are retooling themselves to generate significant revenue from providing analytics services related to their products and services. This will change the organizational power structure because an organization power structure is typically derived from where the most income is generated.

Redesign of an Organization through the Use of Analytics

An emerging area of research and practice is employing the data science technologies for studying organizational dynamics, personnel behavior, and redesigning the organization to better achieve its goals. Indeed, such analytics applications are known as "People Analytics." For example, analytics are used by HR departments to identify ideal candidates from the pool that submit resumes to the organization, or even through broader pools such as LinkedIn. Applications have been developed to identify the best candidates who will likely not leave the organization. Retaining an employee is similar to retaining a customer, so minimizing "churn" internally is equally important to an organization's success.

A more interesting and recent application area relates to understanding employee behavior by monitoring their movements within the organization and using that information to redesign the layout or teams to achieve better performance. A company called Humanyze (previously known as Sociometric Solutions and mentioned in Section 8.5) has badges that include a GPS and a sensor. When employees wear these badges, all of their movement is recorded. Humanyze has reportedly been able to assist companies in predicting which types of employees are likely to stay with the company or leave on the basis of these employees' interactions with other employees. For example, those employees who stay in their own cubicles are less likely to progress up the corporate ladder than those who move about and interact with other employees extensively. Similar data collection and analysis has helped other companies determine the size of conference rooms needed or even the office layout to maximize efficiency. According to Humanyze's Web site, one company wanted to better understand characteristics of its leaders. By analyzing the data from these badges, the company was able to recognize that the successful leaders indeed have larger networks that they interact with, spend more time interacting with others, and are also physically active. The information gathered across team leaders was used to redesign the work space and help improve other leaders' performance. Clearly this leads to privacy issues, but within an organization such studies may be doable. Humanyze's Web site has several other interesting case studies that offer examples of how Big Data technologies can be used to develop more efficient team structures and organizational design.

Analytics Impact on Managers' Activities, Performance, and Job Satisfaction

Although many jobs may be substantially enriched by analytics, other jobs may become more routine and less satisfying. For example, more than 40 years ago, Argyris (1971) predicted that computer-based information systems would reduce managerial discretion in decision making and lead to managers being dissatisfied. However, in their study of automated decision systems, Davenport and Harris (2005) found that employees using such systems, especially those who are empowered by the systems, were more satisfied with their jobs. If the routine and mundane work can be done using an analytic system, then it should free up the managers and knowledge workers to do more challenging tasks.

The most important task of managers is making decisions. Analytics can change the manner in which many decisions are made and can consequently change managers' job responsibilities. For example, Perez-Cascante, Plaisent, Maguiraga, and Bernard (2002) found that a decision support system improved the performance of both existing and new managers as well as other employees. It helped managers gain more knowledge, experience, and expertise and consequently enhanced the quality of their decision making. Many managers report that computers have finally given them time to get out of the office and into the field. They have also found that they can spend more time planning activities instead of putting out fires because they can be alerted to potential problems well in advance thanks to intelligent agents and other analytical tools.

Another aspect of the managerial challenge lies in the ability of analytics to support the decision-making process in general, and strategic planning and control decisions in particular. Analytics could change the decision-making process and even decision-making styles. For example, information gathering for decision making is completed much more quickly when analytics are in use. Enterprise information systems are extremely useful in supporting strategic management. Data, text, and Web mining technologies are now used to improve the external environmental scanning of information. As a result, managers can change their approach to problem solving and improve on their decisions quickly. It is reported that Starbucks recently introduced a new coffee beverage and made the decision on pricing by trying several different prices and monitoring the social media feedback throughout the day. This implies that data collection methods for a manager could be drastically different now than in the past.

Research indicates that most managers tend to work on a large number of problems simultaneously, moving from one to another as they wait for more information on their current problem (see Mintzberg, Lampel, Quinn, & Ghoshal, 2002). Analytics technologies tend to reduce the time required to complete tasks in the decision-making process and eliminate some of the nonproductive waiting time by providing knowledge and information. Therefore, managers work on fewer tasks during each day but complete more of them. The reduction in start-up time associated with moving from task to task could be the most important source of increased managerial productivity.

Another possible impact of analytics on the manager's job could be a change in leadership requirements. What are now generally considered good leadership qualities may be significantly altered by the use of analytics. For example, face-to-face communication is frequently replaced by e-mail, wikis, and computerized conferencing; thus, leadership qualities attributed to physical appearance could become less important.

The following are some potential impacts of analytics on managers' jobs:

- Less expertise (experience) is required for making many decisions.
- Faster decision making is possible because of the availability of information and the automation of some phases in the decision-making process.
- Less reliance on experts and analysts is required to provide support to top executives; managers can do it by themselves with the help of intelligent systems.
- Power is being redistributed among managers. (The more information and analysis capability they possess, the more power they have.)
- Support for complex decisions makes them faster to develop and be of better quality.
- Information needed for high-level decision making is expedited or even self-generated.
- Automation of routine decisions or phases in the decision-making process (e.g., for frontline decision making and using ADS) may eliminate some managers.

In general, it has been found that the job of middle managers is the most likely job to be automated. Midlevel managers make fairly routine decisions, which can be fully automated. Managers at lower levels do not spend much time on decision making. Instead, they supervise, train, and motivate nonmanagers. Some of their routine decisions, such as scheduling, can be automated; other decisions that involve behavioral aspects cannot. However, even if we completely automate their decisional role, we could not automate their jobs. The Web provides an opportunity to automate certain tasks done by frontline employees; this empowers them, thus reducing the workload of approving managers. The job of top managers is the least routine and therefore the most difficult to automate.

Industrial Restructuring

A few authors have begun to speculate on the impact of AI, analytics, and cognitive computing on the future of industry. A few excellent recent resources to consult are Autor (2016), Ransbotham (2016), a special report by *The Economist* (Standage, 2016), and a book by Brynjolfsson and McAfee (2016). The report by *The Economist* is quite comprehensive and considers many dimensions of the impact of the current developments on industry and society. The main arguments are that the technology is now enabling more and more tasks that were done by humans to be done by the computers. This, of course, has happened before, in the Industrial Revolution. What makes the change this time around to be significantly more far reaching is that the technology is enabling many cognitive tasks to be done by machines. And the speed of change is so radical that the likely impact on organizations and society will be very significant and at times unpredictable. These authors do not agree in their predictions, of course. In this paragraph let us focus on the organizational impacts first. Ransbotham (2016) argues that cognitive computing will convert many jobs done by humans to be done by computers, thus reducing the costs for organizations. The quality of output may increase as well in cognitive work, which has been shown in several studies that compare a human's performance with a machine. Everyone is aware of IBM Watson having won in *Jeopardy!* or Google's system winning in the game of GO against human champions. But many other studies in specific domains such as speech recognition and medical image interpretation have also shown similar superiority of an automated system when the task is highly specialized and yet routine or repetitive. Also, because machines tend to be available at all hours and at all locations, an organization's reach may increase, resulting in easier scaling and thus greater competition between organizations. These organizational impacts mean that yesterday's top organizations may not remain at the top forever because cognitive computing and automation can challenge established players. This is also the case in the automotive industry. Although traditional car companies are trying fast to catch up, Google, Tesla, and other technology companies are disrupting the industry structure by challenging the leaders of the automotive age. Analytics is empowering many of these changes.

Automation's Impact on Jobs

Research reports identified in the previous paragraph are also debating the impact of advances in data science and AI on human jobs. As noted earlier, many knowledge worker tasks may now be doable by a machine. At the same time, technology does not always lead to fewer people being employed. As noted by Autor (2016), the number of automated teller machines (ATMs) has quadrupled from about 100,000 to 400,000 between 1995 and 2010, but during the same time the number of bank employees also increased from about half a million in 1980 to about 550,000 in 2010. What happened is that the routine part of the job was being done by the ATM machines, and the bank employees were better connected to customers and were now focused on cross-selling and up-selling services. Of course, some of these services can now also be offered through the analytics models identifying the appropriate customer for a specific opportunity. Ransbotham (2016) gives another example. Financial advising is typically considered a knowledge-intensive task. As data science technology provides customized support for a specific scenario, the costs of such services will go down. This will lead to more people opting to demand such services, and eventually needing more humans for advanced work.

Some of these authors argue that the automation due to cognitive computing and AI will accelerate what is called "polarization" of the labor market in the future. This entails significant job growth in top *and* bottom tiers of the labor market, but losses in the middle. Jobs requiring low skills—janitorial services, personal care, food preparation, and so on, are continuing to grow. Similarly, jobs that require very high skill levels—such as managerial, graphics design, and computational work, are also growing. But jobs that require "middle skills"—specialized knowledge that was applied over and over with some adaptation—are at the greatest risk of disappearing. Sometimes technology disintermediates itself! For example, IBM Watson Analytics now includes preliminary capabilities to begin asking questions that an analytics professional could ask of a data store and, obviously, provide answers. Other analytics-as-a-service offerings similarly may lead to fewer people needing to be proficient at using analytics software.

The Economist report notes that even if AI does not replace workers directly, it will certainly require them to acquire new skills to remain competitive. And the market disruption is always uncomfortable. The next few years will provide excellent opportunities for analytics professionals to shape the future. In the next section we identify some general traits of a data science professional.

Unintended Effects of Analytics

Besides the issues we have already discussed regarding privacy, ethics, security, and personal/organizational impacts of analytics, managers and data science professionals should be aware of the social and long-term effects of the models. A recent book by Cathy O'Neil (2016) has made these arguments very well and has been in the news. She is a Harvard PhD in mathematics and worked in finance and the data science industry. Her experiences and observations have led her to write a popular book titled *Weapons of Math Destruction: How Big Data Increases Inequality and Threatens Democracy.* We urge you to read the book, or at least her blog site at https://mathbabe.org/. Besides promoting her book, the blog site highlights social issues related to analytics. A good summary/review of the book is at this Web site: http://knowledge.wharton.upenn.edu/article/rogue-algorithms-dark-side-big-data/.

In her book, O'Neil argues that models must satisfy three conditions. Many mathematical models are not transparent. If the model is not understandable, its application can lead to unintended consequences. Second, the model must have clear objectives that are quantifiable. For example, the celebrated application of analytics in the book and movie *Moneyball*, the model was aimed at increasing the number of wins. And the input measures that were proposed were age-understandable as well. Rather than using the more commonly reported run base in (RBI) measure, the analyst proposed and used on base percentages and other measures (which were also easily calculated and understood by anyone with basic math skills). On the other hand, models built to assess the risk of mortgage-backed securities where no one fully understood the underlying assumptions but financial traders were trading the collateralized securities are widely blamed for leading the financial crisis of 2008. The third requirement is that the models must have a self-correcting mechanism and a process in place so that the models are audited regularly and new inputs and outputs are constantly being considered. This third issue is particularly critical in applying models in social settings. Otherwise, the models perpetuate the faulty assumptions inherent in the initial modeling stage. O'Neil discusses several situations where such is the case. For example, she describes the models built in the United States to identify underperforming teachers and reward better teachers. These models utilized the test scores of their pupils. She relates several examples where the models were used to fire "underperforming" teachers even though those teachers were loved by the students and parents. O'Neil also cites another example that is growing in importance in many organizations–workers' performance. Models are used to optimize scheduling of workers in many organizations. In many cases these schedules are developed to meet seasonal and daily demand variations, but she laments the fact that the models do not take into account the deleterious impacts of such variability in schedules on the families of these lower-income workers. Other such examples include credit score assessment models which are based on historical profiles and thus may negatively impact minorities. Without mechanisms to audit such models and their unintended effects, we can do more harm than good in the long term. So data science professionals need to be aware of such concerns.

SECTION 8.6 REVIEW QUESTIONS

1. List the impacts of analytics on decision making.

2. List the impacts of analytics on other managerial tasks.

3. Describe new organizational units that are created because of analytics.

4. Identify other examples of analytics applications to redesign work space or team behavior.

5. How is cognitive computing affecting industry structure?

6. Which jobs are most likely to change as a result of automation?

7. Study *The Economist* (Standage, 2016) report mentioned in this section. What other impacts of automation did you find interesting?

8.7 Data Scientist as a Profession

Data scientist is a role or a job frequently associated with Big Data. In a very short time it has become one of the most sought-out roles in the marketplace. In an article published in the October 2012 issue of the *Harvard Business Review,* authors Thomas H. Davenport and D. J. Patil called a data scientist "the sexiest job of the 21st century." In that article they specified data scientists' most basic, universal skill as the ability to write code (in the latest Big Data languages and platforms). Although this may be less true in the near future when many more people will have the title "data scientist" on their business cards, at this time it seems to be the most fundamental skill required from data scientists. A more enduring skill will be the need for data scientists to communicate in a language that all of their stakeholders understand—and to demonstrate the special skills involved in storytelling with data, whether verbally, visually, or—ideally—both (Davenport & Patil 2012).

Data scientists use a combination of their business and technical skills to *investigate* Big Data, looking for ways to improve current business analytics practices (from descriptive to predictive and prescriptive) and hence to improve decisions for new business opportunities. One of the biggest differences between a data scientist and a BI user—such as a business analyst—is that a data scientist investigates and looks for new possibilities, whereas a BI user analyzes existing business situations and operations.

One of the dominant traits expected from data scientists is an intense curiosity—a desire to go beneath the surface of a problem, find the questions at its heart, and distill them into a very clear set of hypotheses that can be tested. This often entails the associative thinking that characterizes the most creative scientists in any field. For example, we know of a data scientist studying a fraud problem who realized that it was analogous to a type of DNA sequencing problem (Davenport & Patil, 2012). By bringing together those disparate worlds, he and his team were able to craft a solution that dramatically reduced fraud losses.

Where Do Data Scientists Come From?

Although there is some disagreement about the use of *science* in the name, it is becoming less of a controversial issue. Real scientists use tools made by other scientists, or make them if they don't exist, as a means to expand knowledge. That is exactly what data scientists are expected to do. Experimental physicists, for example, have to design equipment, gather data, and conduct multiple experiments to discover knowledge and communicate their results. Even though they may not be wearing white coats and may not be living in a sterile lab environment, this is exactly what data scientists do: use creative tools and techniques to turn data into actionable information for others to use for better decision making.

There is no consensus on what educational background a data scientist should have. The usual suspects like Master of Science (or PhD) in Computer Science, Management Information Systems (MIS), Industrial Engineering, or the newly popularized postgraduate analytics degrees, may be necessary but not sufficient to call someone a data scientist. One of the most sought-out characteristics of a data scientist is expertise in technical as well as business application domains. In that sense, it somewhat resembles the professional engineer or project management professional roles, where experience is valued as much as (if not more than) technical skills and educational background. It would not be a huge surprise to see within the next few years a certification specifically designed for data scientists (perhaps called "Data Science Professional" or "DSP" for short).

Because it is a profession for a field that is still being defined, many of its practices are still experimental and far from being standardized. Thus, companies are overly sensitive about the experience dimension of a data scientist. As the profession matures, and practices are standardized, experience will be less of an issue when defining a data scientist. Nowadays, companies looking for people who have extensive experience in working with complex data have had good luck recruiting among those with educational and work backgrounds in the physical or social sciences. Some of the best and brightest data scientists have been PhDs in esoteric fields like ecology and systems biology (Davenport & Patil, 2012). Even though there is no consensus on where data scientists come from, there is a common understanding of what skills and qualities they are expected to possess. Figure 8.8 shows a high-level graphical illustration of these skills.

Data scientists are expected to have soft skills such as creativity, curiosity, communication/interpersonal, domain expertise, problem definition, and managerial (shown with green-background hexagons on the top and left side of the figure) as well as sound technical skills such as data manipulation, programming/hacking/scripting, and Internet and social

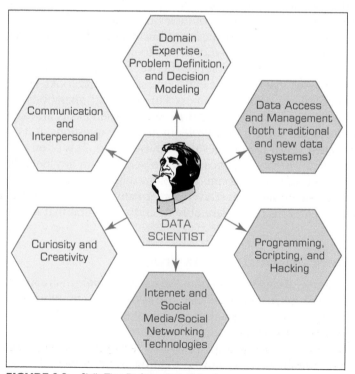

FIGURE 8.8   Skills That Define a Data Scientist.

TECHNOLOGY INSIGHTS 8.1
A Typical Job Post for Data Scientists

[Some company] is seeking a Data Scientist to join our Big Data Analytics team. Individuals in this role are expected to be comfortable working as a software engineer and a quantitative researcher. The ideal candidate will have a keen interest in the study of an online social network and a passion for identifying and answering questions that help us build the best products.

Responsibilities

- Work closely with a product engineering team to identify and answer important product questions
- Answer product questions by using appropriate statistical techniques on available data
- Communicate findings to product managers and engineers
- Drive the collection of new data and the refinement of existing data sources
- Analyze and interpret the results of product experiments
- Develop best practices for instrumentation and experimentation and communicate those to product engineering teams

Requirements

- MS or PhD in a relevant technical field, or 4+ years of experience in a relevant role
- Extensive experience solving analytical problems using quantitative approaches
- Comfort with manipulating and analyzing complex, high-volume, high-dimensionality data from varying sources
- A strong passion for empirical research and for answering hard questions with data
- A flexible analytic approach that allows for results at varying levels of precision
- Ability to communicate complex quantitative analysis in a clear, precise, and actionable manner
- Fluency with at least one scripting language such as Python or PHP
- Familiarity with relational databases and SQL
- Expert knowledge of an analysis tool such as R, Matlab, or SAS
- Experience working with large data sets, experience working with distributed computing tools a plus (MapReduce, Hadoop, Hive, etc.)

media/networking technologies (shown with gray-background hexagons on the bottom and right side of the figure). Technology Insights 8.1 is about a typical job advertisement for a data scientist.

People with this range of skills are rare, which explains why data scientists are in short supply. Because of the high demand for these relatively fewer individuals, the starting salaries for data scientists are well above six figures (in U.S. dollars), and for ones with ample experience and specific domain expertise, they are even higher. In most organizations, rather than looking for individuals with all of these capabilities, it will be necessary instead to build a team of people that collectively have these skills. Here are some recent statements about data scientists:

- Data scientists turn Big Data into big value, delivering products that delight users and insight that informs business decisions.
- A data scientist is not only proficient in working with data, but also appreciates data itself as an invaluable asset.
- By 2020 there will be 4.5 million new data scientist jobs, of which only one-third will be filled because of the lack of people available to fill them.
- Today's data scientists are the quants of the financial markets of the 1980s.

Use of data scientists is not limited to high-tech Internet companies. Many of the companies that do not have much of an Internet presence are also interested in highly qualified Big Data analytics professionals. Indeed, that is where much of the growth is being witnessed. Of course, as noted several times in the book, entrepreneurial opportunities still exist to develop the next "killer" application that would make a huge difference to an organization and its stakeholders and thus make you rich and famous!

SECTION 8.7 REVIEW QUESTIONS

1. What is a data scientist? What makes them so much in demand?
2. What are the common characteristics of data scientists? Which one is the most important?
3. Where do data scientists come from? What educational backgrounds do they have?
4. What do you think is the path to becoming a great data scientist?

Chapter Highlights

- Geospatial data can enhance analytics applications by incorporating location information.
- Real-time location information of users can be mined to develop promotion campaigns that are targeted at a specific user in real time.
- Location information from mobile phones can be used to create profiles of user behavior and movement. Such location information can enable users to find other people with similar interests and advertisers to customize their promotions.
- Location-based analytics can also benefit consumers directly rather than just businesses. Mobile apps are being developed to enable such innovative analytics applications.
- Internet of Things (IoT) is the next major frontier for the growth of analytics/data science. Some people also call it the industrial Internet.
- Applications of IoT are growing in every industry including medical, manufacturing, energy, and aviation.
- One popular category of IoT applications is in predictive maintenance to minimize unnecessary downtime of equipment and perform the required maintenance/repairs before these are necessary.
- Cloud computing offers the possibility of using software, hardware, platforms, and infrastructure, all on a service-subscription basis. Cloud

computing enables a more scalable investment on the part of a user.
- Cloud-computing–based analytic services offer organizations the latest technologies without significant up-front investment.
- Analytics can affect organizations in many ways, as stand-alone systems or integrated among themselves, or with other computer-based information systems.
- The impact of analytics on individuals varies—it can be positive, neutral, or negative.
- Serious legal issues may develop with the introduction of intelligent systems; liability and privacy are the dominant problem areas.
- Many positive social implications can be expected from analytics. These range from providing opportunities to disabled people to leading the fight against terrorism. Quality of life, both at work and at home, is likely to improve as a result of analytics. Of course, there are also negative issues to be concerned about.
- Growth of analytics is going to lead to major changes in industry structure and future employment.
- A major battle is brewing about who owns all the user data that is being generated from the use of smartphones, cars, and so on.

Key Terms

cloud computing

geographic information systems (GIS)

Internet of Things (IoT)

privacy

radio-frequency identification (RFID)

Questions for Discussion

1. What are the potential benefits of using geospatial data in analytics? Give examples.
2. What types of new applications can emerge from knowing locations of users in real time? What if you also knew what they have in their shopping cart, for example?
3. How can consumers benefit from using analytics, especially based on location information?
4. "Location-tracking–based profiling is powerful but also poses privacy threats." Comment.
5. Is cloud computing "just an old wine in a new bottle?" How is it similar to other initiatives? How is it different?
6. Discuss the relationship between mobile devices and social networking.
7. Some say that analytics in general dehumanize managerial activities, and others say they do not. Discuss arguments for both points of view.
8. Diagnosing infections and prescribing pharmaceuticals are the weak points of many practicing physicians

(according to E. H. Shortliffe, one of the developers of MYCIN). It seems, therefore, that society would be better served if analytics-based diagnosis systems were used by more physicians. Answer the following questions:
   a. Why do you think such systems are used minimally by physicians?
   b. Assume that you are a hospital administrator whose physicians are salaried and report to you. What would you do to persuade them to use the system?
   c. If the potential benefits to society are so great, can society do something that will increase doctors' use of such analytic systems?
9. What are some of the major privacy concerns in employing analytics on mobile data?
10. Identify new cases of violations of user privacy from current literature and their impacts on data science as a profession.

Exercises

Teradata University Network (TUN) and Other Hands-on Exercises

1. Go to teradatauniversitynetwork.com and search for case studies. Watch the BSI Video about the Case of Misconnected Passengers that you may have watched while reading Chapter 1. What new applications can you imagine with the level of detailed data an airline can capture today?
2. At teradatauniversitynetwork.com, go to the Podcasts Library Find podcasts of Pervasive BI submitted by Hugh Watson. Summarize the points made by the speaker.
3. Go to teradatauniversitynetwork.com and search for BSI videos. Review these BSI videos and answer case questions related to them.
4. Location-tracking–based clustering provides the potential for personalized services but challenges for privacy. Divide the class into two parts to argue for and against such applications.

5. Identify ethical issues related to managerial decision making. Search the Internet, join discussion groups/blogs, and read articles from the Internet. Prepare a report on your findings.
6. Search the Internet to find examples of how analytics systems can facilitate activities such as empowerment, mass customization, and teamwork.
7. Investigate the American Bar Association's Technology Resource Center (abanet.org/tech/ltrc/techethics.html) and nolo.com. What are the major legal and societal concerns and advances addressed there? How are they being dealt with?
8. Explore several sites related to healthcare (e.g., WebMD .com, who.int). Find issues related to analytics and privacy. Write a report on how these sites improve healthcare.
9. Visit Matt Turck's IoT Ecosystem blog at http://mattturck.com/2016/03/28/2016-iot-landscape/. Identify at least two companies in at least two vertical and two horizontal

sectors. Go to those companies' Web sites and prepare a report on their offerings and customer successes.

10. Enter YouTube.com. Search for videos on cloud computing, and watch at least two. Summarize your findings.

11. Enter Pandora.com. Find out how you can create and share music with friends. Explore how the site analyzes user preferences.

12. Enter Humanyze.com. Review various case studies and summarize one interesting application of sensors in understanding social exchanges in organizations.

13. The objective of the exercise is to familiarize you with the capabilities of smartphones to identify human activity.

The data set is available at archive.ics.uci.edu/ml/datasets/Human+Activity+Recognition+Using+Smartphones.

It contains accelerometer and gyroscope readings on 30 subjects who had the smartphone on their waist. The data is available in a raw format and involves some data preparation efforts. Your objective is to identify and classify these readings into activities like walking, running, climbing, and such. More information on the data set is available on the download page. You may use clustering for initial exploration and to gain an understanding of the data. You may use tools like R to prepare and analyze this data.

References

Alteryx.com. (n.d.). Great Clips. alteryx.com/sites/default/files/resources/files/case-study-great-chips.pdf (accessed August 2016).

Argyris, C. (1971). Management information systems: The challenge to rationality and emotionality. *Management Science, 17*(6), B-275.

Autor, D. H. (2016). The shifts—great and small—in workplace automation. sloanreview.mit.edu/article/the-shifts-great-and-small-in-workplace-automation/ (accessed August 2016).

Blogs.ESRI.com. (2014). From customers to CxOs, Starbucks delivers world-class service. blogs.esri.com/esri/ucinsider/2014/07/29/starbucks/ (accessed August 2016).

Blogs.microsoft.com. (2015). Dartmouth-Hitchcock ushers in a new age of proactive, personalized healthcare using Cortana Analytics Suite. microsoft.com/transform/2015/07/13/dartmouth-hitchcock-ushers-in-a-new-age-of-proactive-personalized-healthcare-using-cortana-analytics-suite/ (accessed August 2016).

Blogs.pb.com. (2015). The industrial Internet, Pitney Bowes and GE.blogs.pb.com/corporate/2015/07/14/the-industrial-internet-pitney-bowes-and-ge/ (accessed August 2016).

Blogs.technet.microsoft.com. (2015). ML predicts school dropout risk & boosts graduation rates. blogs.technet.microsoft.com/machinelearning/2015/06/04/ml-predicts-school-dropout-risk-boosts-graduation-rates/ (accessed August 2016).

Brynjolfsson, E., & McAfee, A. (2016). The second machine age. secondmachineage.com (accessed September 2016).

Chae, B., Paradice, D. B., Courtney, J. F., & Cagle, C. F. (2005). Incorporating an ethical perspective into problem formulation. *Decision Support Systems, 40*(2), 197–212.

CIO.in. (2015). Mankind Pharma finds an antidote in IBM solution for improving app implementation time. cio.in/solution-center/emc/55281 (accessed August 2016).

Collins, J. (2005, June). Sysco gets fresh with RFID. *RFID Journal.* rfidjournal.com/articles/view?1652 (accessed September 2016).

ComputerWeekly.com. (2016). Big-data and open source cloud technology help Gulf Air pin down customer sentiment. computerweekly.com/news/450297404/Big-data-and-open-source-cloud-technology-help-Gulf-Air-pin-down-customer-sentiment (accessed August 2016).

Customers.microsoft.com. (2015). Rockwell Automation: Fueling the oil and gas industry with IoT customers. microsoft.com/Pages/CustomerStory.aspx?recid=19922 (accessed August 2016).

Customers.microsoft.com. (2015). Tacoma Public Schools: Predicting student dropout risks, increasing graduation rates with cloud analytics. customers.microsoft.com/Pages/CustomerStory.aspx?recid=20703 (accessed August 2016).

CxOtoday.com. (2014). Cloud platform to help Pharma Co accelerate growth. cxotoday.com/story/mankind-pharma-to-drive-growth-with-softlayers-cloud-platform (accessed August 2016).

Davenport, T. H., & Harris, J. G. (2005). Automated decision making comes of age. *MIT Sloan Management Review, 46*(4), 83.

Davenport, T. H., & Patil, D. J. (2012, October). Data scientist. *Harvard Business Review,* 70–76.

Delen, D., Hardgrave, B., & Sharda, R. (2007). RFID for better supply-chain management through enhanced information visibility. *Production and Operations Management, 16*(5) 613–624.

Delen, D., Hardgrave, B. C., & Sharda, R. (2011, April). The promise of RFID-based sensors in the perishables supply chain. *IEEE Wireless Communications,* 1–8.

Demirkan, H., & Delen, D. (2013, April). Leveraging the capabilities of service-oriented decision support systems: Putting analytics and Big Data in cloud. *Decision*

Support Systems, 55(1), 412–421. dx.doi.org/10.1016/j .dss.2012.05.048 (accessed September 2016).

Digit.HBS.org. (2015). Starbucks: Brewing up a data storm! digit.hbs.org/submission/starbucks-brewing-up-a-data-storm/ (accessed August 2016).

Ekster, G. (2015). Driving investment performance with alternative data. integrity-research.com/wp-content/uploads/2015/11/ Driving-Investment-Performance-With-Alternative-Data.pdf (accessed September 2016).

Electronic Privacy Information Center. (2005). USA PATRIOT Act. epic.org/privacy/terrorism/usapatriot (accessed September 2016).

Elson, R. J., & LeClerc, R. (2005). Security and privacy concerns in the data warehouse environment. *Business Intelligence Journal, 10*(3), 51.

Enterprise.microsoft.com. (2015). How Dartmouth-Hitchcock is challenging healthcare's status quo with Cortana Analytics. enterprise.microsoft.com/en-us/industries/health/how-dartmouth-hitchcock-is-challenging-healthcares-status-quo-with-cortana-analytics/ (accessed August 2016).

Gartner.com (2016) Gartner Says Worldwide Public Cloud Services Market Is Forecast to Reach $204 Billion in 2016. http://www.gartner.com/newsroom/id/3188817 (Accessed November 2016)

GE.com. (2016). Making machines intelligent is smart business. ge.com/digital/sites/default/files/ge_digital_predix_ pb_brochure.pdf (accessed August 2016).

GEreports.com. (2016). The power of Predix: An inside look at how Pitney Bowes is using the industrial Internet platform. gereports.com/the-power-of-predix-an-inside-look-at-how-pitney-bowes-has-been-using-the-industrial-internet-platform (accessed August 2016).

Gnau, S. (2010). Find your edge. *Teradata Magazine Special Edition Location Intelligence.* teradata.com/articles/Teradata-Magazine-Special-Edition-Location-Intelligence-AR6270/?type=ART (accessed September 2016).

Goel, V. (2014, June 29). Facebook tinkers with users' emotions in news feed experiment, stirring outcry. *New York Times.* nytimes.com/2014/06/30/technology/facebook-tinkers-with-users-emotions-in-news-feed-experiment-stirring-outcry.html (accessed September 2016).

Hardgrave, B. C., Langford, S., Waller, M., & Miller, R. (2008). Measuring the impact of RFID on out of stocks at Wal-Mart. *MIS Quarterly Executive, 7*(4), 181–192.

IBMbigdatahub.com. (2015). SilverHook Powerboats: Tracking fast-moving boats in real time. http://www.ibm-bigdatahub.com/blog/silverhook-powerboats-tracking-fast-moving-powerboats-real-time (accessed August 2016).

IBM.com. (2015). Case study: SilverHook Powerboats develops a racing app 40 percent faster. ibm.com/ cloud-computing/case-studies/silverhook-powerboats .html (accessed August 2016).

IBM.com. (2014). Softlayer hosting platform reduces application implementation time by 98 percent. www-03 .ibm.com/software/businesscasestudies/us/en/ corp?synkey=Y979749I50926G25 (accessed August 2016).

IBM.com. (2015). Smarter care at MD Anderson. www-03.ibm.com/software/businesscasestudies/us/en/ corp?synkey=H447240O66679Z38 (accessed August 2016).

Juniper Research (2016). 'Internet of Things' connected devices to almost triple to over 38 billion units by 2020. http://www .juniperresearch.com/press/press-releases/iot-connected-devices-to-triple-to-38-bn-by-2020 (accessed September 2016).

Kalakota, R. (2011). Analytics-as-a-service: Understanding how Amazon.com is changing the rules. practicalanalytics. wordpress.com/2011/08/13/analytics-as-a-service-understanding-how-amazon-com-is-changing-the-rules (accessed September 2016).

Katz, J. (2006, February). Reaching for ROI on RFID. *Industry Week.* industryweek.com/companies-amp-executives/reaching-roi-rfid (accessed September 2016).

Krivda, C. D. (2010). Pinpoint opportunity. *Teradata Magazine Special Edition Location Intelligence.* teradata.com/articles/ Teradata-Magazine-Special-Edition-Location-Intelligence-AR6270/?type=ART (accessed September 2016).

Mankindpharma.com. (n.d.). Overview. mankindpharma .com/company/companyoverview (accessed August 2016).

Mason, R. O., Mason, F. M., & Culnan, M. J. (1995). *Ethics of information management.* Thousand Oaks, CA: Sage.

McKendrick, J. (2015). SilverHook Powerboats: Tracking fast-moving boats in real time. ibmbigdatahub.com/blog/ silverhook-powerboats-tracking-fast-moving-power-boats-real-time (accessed August 2016).

McKinsey.com. (2015). *An executive's guide to the Internet of Things.* mckinsey.com/business-functions/business-technology/our-insights/an-executives-guide-to-the-internet-of-things (accessed September 2016).

MDanderson.org. (2013). MD Anderson taps IBM Watson to power 'Moon Shots' mission. mdanderson.org/news-room/2013/10/md-anderson--ibm-watson-work-together-to-fight-cancer.html (accessed August 2016).

Microsoft.com. (n.d.). Customer stories | Rockwell Automation. microsoft.com/en-us/cloud-platform/customer-stories-rock-well-automation (accessed July 2016).

Mintzberg, H., Lampel, J. B., Quinn, J. B., & Ghoshel, S. (2002). *The strategy process,* 4th ed. Upper Saddle River, NJ: Prentice Hall.

Mobilemarketer.com. (2013). Quiznos sees 20pc boost in coupon redemption via location-based mobile ad campaign. mobilemarketer.com/cms/news/advertising/14738 .html (accessed September 2016).

Moradpour, S., & Bhuptani, M. (2005). *RFID field guide: Deploying radio frequency identification systems.* New York: Sun Microsystems Press.

News.pb.com. (2015). GE and Pitney Bowes join forces to bring the power of the industrial Internet to the world of commerce. news.pb.com/article_display.cfm?article_ id=5634 (accessed August 2016).

O'Neil, C. (2016). *Weapons of Math Destruction: How Big Data Increases Inequality and Threatens Democracy,* Crown, 2016 New York.

Perez-Cascante, L. P., Plaisent, M., Maguiraga, L., & Bernard, P. (2002). The impact of expert decision support systems on the performance of new employees. *Information Resources Management Journal 15*(4), 64–78.

Peslak, A. R. (2005). Internet privacy policies: A review and survey of the *Fortune 50*. *Information Resources Management Journal, 18*(1), 29–41.

Ransbotham, S. (2016). How will cognitive technologies affect your organization? sloanreview.mit.edu/article/how-will-cognitive-technologies-affect-your-organization/ (accessed September 2016).

RedHat.com. (2016). Gulf Air builds private cloud for big data innovation with Red Hat Technologies. redhat.com/en/about/press-releases/gulf-air-builds-private-cloud-big-data-innovation-red-hat-technologies (accessed August 2016).

RedHat.com. (2016). Gulf Air's Big Data innovation delivers deeper customer insight. redhat.com/en/success-stories (accessed August 2016).

Sahin, E., Babaï, M. A., Dallery, Y., & Vaillant, R. (2007). Ensuring supply chain safety through time temperature integrators. *The International Journal of Logistics Management, 18*(1), 102–124.

Snowflake.net. (n.d.). Chime delivers personalized customer experience using Chime. snowflake.net/product (accessed August 2016).

Standage, T. (2016). Special report by *The Economist*: The return of the machinery question. bit.ly/28X8cfD, economist.com/news/special-report/21700761-after-many-false-starts-artificial-intelligence-has-taken-will-it-cause-mass (accessed September 2016).

Stein, J. (2011). Data mining: How companies now know everything about you. *Time*. time.com/time/magazine/article/0,9171,2058205,00.html (accessed September 2016).

Swedberg, C. (2006a, October). Samworth keeps cool with RFID. *RFID Journal*. rfidjournal.com/article/articleview/2733/ (accessed September 2016).

Swedberg, C. (2006b, December). Starbucks keeps fresh with RFID. *RFID Journal*. rfidjournal.com/article/articleview/2890/ (accessed September 2016).

TheGuardian.com. (2013). John Snow's data journalism: The cholera map that changed the world. theguardian.com/news/datablog/2013/mar/15/john-snow-cholera-map (accessed August 2016).

Turck, M. (2016). Internet of Things: Are we there yet? (The 2016 IoT landscape). mattturck.com/2016/03/28/2016-iot-landscape/ (accessed August 2016).

WallStreetJournal.com. (2016). What they know. wsj.com/public/page/what-they-know-digital-privacy.html (accessed September 2016).

Welch, D. (2016, July 18–24). The battle for smart car data. *Bloomberg Business Week*. bloomberg.com/news/articles/2016-07-12/your-car-s-been-studying-you-closely-and-everyone-wants-the-data (accessed September 2016).

Wheeler, C. (2014). Going big with GIS. esri.com/esri-news/arcwatch/0814/going-big-with-gis (accessed August 2016).

Wikipedia.org. (n.d.). Cloud computing. en.wikipedia.org/wiki/cloud_computing (accessed August 2016).

Wikipedia.org. (n.d.). Mankind Pharma. wikipedia.org/wiki/Mankind_Pharma (accessed August 2016).

Wikipedia.org. (n.d.). University of Texas MD Anderson Cancer Center. wikipedia.org/wiki/University_of_Texas_MD_Anderson_Cancer_Center (accessed August 2016).

Winter, R. (2008). E-Bay turns to analytics as a service. information-week.com/news/software/info_management/210800736 (accessed September 2016).

YouTube.com. (2014). Smarter care at MD Anderson. youtube.com/watch?v=savJ8VQ0kcA (accessed August 2016).

YouTube.com. (2015). Dartmouth-Hitchcock revolutionizes the U.S. healthcare system. youtube.com/watch?v=wVeHZNn8aU (accessed August 2016).

YouTube.com. (2016). The saving power of data. youtube.com/watch?v=rfAoKs8XxzY (accessed August 2016).

Glossary

active data warehousing *See* real-time data warehousing.

ad hoc query A query that cannot be determined prior to the moment the query is issued.

algorithm A step-by-step search in which improvement is made at every step until the best solution is found.

analytical models Mathematical models into which data are loaded for analysis.

analytical techniques Methods that use mathematical formulas to derive an optimal solution directly or to predict a certain result, mainly in solving structured problems.

analytics The science of analysis.

analytics ecosystem A classification of sectors, technology/solution providers, and industry participants for analytics.

analytics ready A state of preparedness for analytics projects, especially as it relates to data acquisition and preparedness.

a priori algorithm The most commonly used algorithm to discover association rules by recursively identifying frequent itemsets.

area under the ROC curve A graphical assessment technique for binary classification models where the true positive rate is plotted on the y-axis and false positive rate is plotted on the x-axis.

arithmetic mean A descriptive statistics measure—a simple average of a given sample of numeric data points.

artificial intelligence The subfield of computer science concerned with symbolic reasoning and problem solving.

artificial neural network (ANN) Computer technology that attempts to build computers that operate like a human brain. The machines possess simultaneous memory storage and work with ambiguous information. Sometimes called, simply, a *neural network*.

association A category of data mining algorithm that establishes relationships about items that occur together in a given record.

authoritative pages Web pages that are identified as particularly popular based on links by other Web pages and directories.

balanced scorecard (BSC) A performance measurement and management methodology that helps translate an organization's financial, customer, internal process, and learning and growth objectives and targets into a set of actionable initiatives.

Big Data Data that is characterized by its volume, variety, and velocity that exceeds the reach of commonly used hardware environments and/or capabilities of software tools to process.

Big Data analytics Application of analytics methods and tools to Big Data.

bootstrapping A sampling technique where a fixed number of instances from the original data are sampled (with replacement) for training, and the rest of the data set is used for testing.

box plot A descriptive statistics tool that shows both central tendency and dispersion (quartiles) of a given sample of numeric data points in a graphical illustration.

business analyst An individual whose job is to analyze business processes and the support they receive (or need) from information technology.

business analytics (BA) The application of analytics to business problems/data.

business intelligence (BI) A conceptual framework for managerial decision support. It combines architecture, databases (or data warehouses), analytical tools, and applications.

business performance management (BPM) An advanced performance measurement and analysis approach that embraces planning and strategy.

business report Any communication artifact prepared with the specific intention of conveying information in a digestible form to whoever needs it, whenever and wherever they may need it.

categorical data Data that represent the labels of multiple classes used to divide a variable into specific groups.

centrality A group of metrics that aims to quantify the importance or influence (in a variety of senses) of a particular node (or group) within a network.

certainty The business situation where complete knowledge is available so that the decision maker knows exactly what the outcome of each course of action will be.

classification Supervised induction used to analyze the historical data stored in a database and to automatically generate a model that can predict future behavior.

clickstream analysis The analysis of data that occur in the Web environment.

cloud computing Information technology infrastructure (hardware, software, applications, and platform) that is available as a service, usually as virtualized resources.

clustering Partitioning a given data set into segments (natural groupings) in which the members of a segment share similar qualities.

confidence In association rules, the conditional probability of finding the RHS of the rule present in a list of transactions where the LHS of the rule exists.

corpus In linguistics, a large and structured set of texts (usually stored and processed electronically) prepared for the purpose of conducting knowledge discovery.

correlation A statistical measure that indicates the extent to which two or more variables change/fluctuate together.

CRISP-DM A cross-industry standardized process of conducting data mining projects, which is a sequence of six steps that starts with a good understanding of the business and the need for the data mining project (i.e., the application domain) and ends with the deployment of the solution that satisfied the specific business need.

critical event processing (CEP) A method of capturing, tracking, and analyzing streams of data to detect certain events (out of normal happenings) that are worthy of the effort.

critical success factors (CSFs) Key factors that delineate the things that an organization must excel at to be successful in its market space (may also be called key performance indicators, or KPIs in short).

dashboard A visual presentation of critical data for executives to view. It allows executives to see hot spots in seconds and explore the situation.

data Raw facts that are meaningless by themselves (e.g., names, numbers).

data cube A two-dimensional, three-dimensional, or higher-dimensional object in which each dimension of the data represents a measure of interest.

data integration Integration that comprises three major processes: data access, data federation, and change capture. When these three processes are correctly implemented, data can be accessed and made accessible to an array of ETL, analysis tools, and data warehousing environments.

data integrity A part of data quality where the accuracy of the data (as a whole) is maintained during any operation (such as transfer, storage, or retrieval).

data mart (DM) A departmental data warehouse that stores only relevant data.

data mining A process that uses statistical, mathematical, artificial intelligence, and machine-learning techniques to extract and identify useful information and subsequent knowledge from large databases.

data preprocessing A tedious process of converting raw data into an analytic ready state.

data quality The holistic quality of data, including their accuracy, precision, completeness, and relevance.

data scientist A new role/job/title commonly associated with Big Data or data science.

data security A set of protective measures taken to prevent unauthorized access to data/computers.

data stream mining The process of extracting novel patterns and knowledge structures from continuously streaming data records. *See* stream analytics.

data taxonomy A structured representation of the subgroups/subtypes of data.

data visualization A graphical, animation, or video presentation of data and the results of data analysis.

data warehouse (DW) A physical repository where relational data are specially organized to provide enterprise-wide, cleansed data in a standardized format.

data warehouse administrator (DWA) A person responsible for the administration and management of a data warehouse.

database A collection of files that is viewed as a single storage concept. The data are then available to a wide range of users.

database management system (DBMS) Software for establishing, updating, and querying (e.g., managing) a database.

datum A piece of information/fact; singular version of data.

deception detection A way of identifying deception (intentionally propagating beliefs that are not true) in voice, text, and/or body language of humans.

decision analysis A modeling approach that deals with decision situations that involve a finite and usually not too large number of alternatives.

decision making The action of selecting among alternatives.

decision or normative analytics Also called prescriptive analytics, is a type of analytics modeling that aims at identifying the best possible decision from a large set of alternatives.

decision support systems (DSS) A conceptual framework for a process of supporting managerial decision making, usually by modeling problems and employing quantitative models for solution analysis.

decision table A tabular representation of possible condition combinations and outcomes.

decision tree A graphical presentation of a sequence of interrelated decisions to be made under assumed risk. This technique classifies specific entities into particular classes based on the features of the entities; a root followed by internal nodes, each node (including root) is labeled with a question, and arcs associated with each node cover all possible responses.

decision variable The variable of interest.

dependent data mart A data mart that depends on the existence of a data warehouse.

descriptive (or reporting) analytics An earlier phase in analytics continuum that deals with describing the data—answering the question of what happened and why did it happen.

descriptive statistics A branch of statistical modeling that aims to describe a given sample of data (*also see* inferential statistics).

dimension tables In a data warehouse, surrounding the central fact tables (and linked via foreign keys) are called dimension tables.

dimensional modeling   A retrieval-based data querying system that supports high-volume, high-speed access to subsets of data.

dimensional reduction   An iterative/heuristic process of reducing the number of input variables to a manageable number—identifying the most prevalent/important/contributing variables to include in the modeling activities.

discrete event simulation   A type of simulation modeling where a system is studied based on the occurrence of events/interaction between different parts (entities/resources) of the system.

dispersion   A descriptive statistics measure where the spread of a given sample of numeric data points is assessed.

distance measure   A method used to calculate the closeness between pairs of items in most cluster analysis methods. Popular distance measures include Euclidian distance (the ordinary distance between two points that one would measure with a ruler) and Manhattan distance (also called the rectilinear distance, or taxicab distance, between two points).

DMAIC   A closed-loop business improvement model that includes the following steps: defining, measuring, analyzing, improving, and controlling a process.

drill down   The investigation of information in detail (e.g., finding not only total sales but also sales by region, by product, or by salesperson). Finding the detailed sources.

dynamic models   A modeling technique to capture/study systems that evolve over time.

ensemble modeling   A popular analytics technique where two or more models (or simply their outcomes) are combined to produce a more accurate/robust/reliable result (in predictive analytics it may also be called *model ensembles*).

enterprise application integration (EAI)   A technology that provides a vehicle for pushing data from source systems into a data warehouse.

enterprise data warehouse (EDW)   An organizational-level data warehouse developed for analytical purposes.

enterprise information integration (EII)   An evolving tool space that promises real-time data integration from a variety of sources, such as relational databases, Web services, and multidimensional databases.

entropy   A metric that measures the extent of uncertainty or randomness in a data set. If all the data in a subset belong to just one class, then there is no uncertainty or randomness in that data set, and therefore the entropy is zero.

environmental scanning and analysis   A continuous process of intelligence building—identification of problems and/or opportunities via acquisition and analysis of data/information.

extraction, transformation, and load (ETL)   A data warehousing process that consists of extraction (i.e., reading data from a database), transformation (i.e., converting the extracted data from its previous form into the form in which it needs to be so that it can be placed into a data warehouse or simply another database), and load (i.e., putting the data into the data warehouse).

forecasting   Using the data from the past to foresee the future values of a variable of interest.

geographical information system (GIS)   An information system capable of integrating, editing, analyzing, sharing, and displaying geographically referenced information.

Gini index   A metric that is used in economics to measure the diversity of the population. The same concept can be used to determine the purity of a specific class as a result of a decision to branch along a particular attribute/variable.

goal seeking   A prescriptive analytics method where first a goal (a target/desired value) is set, and then the satisfying set of input variable values is identified.

Hadoop   An open source framework for processing, storing, and analyzing massive amounts of distributed, unstructured data.

Hadoop Distributed File System (HDFS)   A distributed file management system that lends itself well to processing large volumes of unstructured data (i.e., Big Data).

heuristics   Informal, judgmental knowledge of an application area that constitutes the rules of good judgment in the field. Heuristics also encompasses the knowledge of how to solve problems efficiently and effectively, how to plan steps in solving a complex problem, how to improve performance, and so forth.

high-performance computing   A large-scale computing infrastructure to deal with Big Data.

histogram   A statistical chart that shows frequency of bins for a given sample of numeric data.

Hive   A Hadoop-based data warehousing–like framework originally developed by Facebook.

hub   One or more Web pages that provide a collection of links to authoritative pages.

hyperlink-induced topic search (HITS)   The most popular, publicly known, and referenced algorithm in Web mining, which is used to discover hubs and authorities.

IBM SPSS Modeler   A popular, commercially available, comprehensive data, text, and Web mining software suite developed by SPSS (formerly Clementine).

independent data mart   A small data warehouse designed for a strategic business unit or a department.

inferential statistics   A branch of statistical modeling that aims to draw inferences or conclusions about the characteristics of the population based on a given sample of data (*also see* descriptive statistics).

influence diagram   A graphical representation of a given mathematical model.

information gain   The splitting mechanism used in ID3 (a popular decision tree algorithm).

intelligent agent An expert or knowledge-based system embedded in computer-based information systems (or their components) to make them smarter.

intermediate results Intermediate outcomes in mathematical models.

Internet of Things (IoT) The technological phenomenon of connecting a variety of devices in the physical world to each other and to the computing systems via the Internet.

interval data Variables that can be measured on interval scales.

inverse document frequency A common and very useful transformation of indices in a term-by-document matrix that reflects both the specificity of words (document frequencies) as well as the overall frequencies of their occurrences (term frequencies).

key performance indicator (KPI) Measure of performance against a strategic objective and goal.

***k*-fold cross-validation** A popular accuracy assessment technique for prediction models where the complete data set is randomly split into *k* mutually exclusive subsets of approximately equal size. The classification model is trained and tested *k* times. Each time it is trained on all but one fold and then tested on the remaining single fold. The cross-validation estimate of the overall accuracy of a model is calculated by simply averaging the *k* individual accuracy measures.

KNIME A free, open source analytics software platform (can be accessed at knime.org).

knowledge Understanding, awareness, or familiarity acquired through education or experience; anything that has been learned, perceived, discovered, inferred, or understood; the ability to use information. In a knowledge management system, knowledge is information in action.

knowledge discovery in databases (KDD) A machine-learning process that performs rule induction or a related procedure to establish knowledge from large databases.

knowledge management The active management of the expertise in an organization. It involves collecting, categorizing, and disseminating knowledge.

kurtosis A statistical measure to characterize the shape of a unimodal distribution—characterizing the peak/tall/skinny nature of the distribution (*also see* skewness).

learning A process of self-improvement where the new knowledge is obtained through a process by using what is already known.

lift A goodness-of-fit measure for classification as well as association rule mining models.

linear programming (LP) A mathematical modeling technique used to represent and solve constraint optimization problems.

linear regression A relatively simple statistical technique to model the linear relationship between a response variable and one or more explanatory/input variables.

link analysis The linkage among many objects of interest is discovered automatically, such as the link between Web pages and referential relationships among groups of academic publication authors.

logistic regression A very popular, statistically sound, probability-based classification algorithm that employs supervised learning.

MapReduce A technique to distribute the processing of very large multistructured data files across a large cluster of machines.

mathematical programming A family of analytic tools designed to help solve managerial problems in which the decision maker must allocate scarce resources among competing activities to optimize a measurable goal.

mean absolute deviation An accuracy metric commonly used for regression-type prediction problems (e.g., time series forecasting) where the error is calculated as the average squared distance between the actuals and the predicted values.

median A central tendency measure in statistics that identifies the simple average of a given numeric data sample.

metadata Data about data. In a data warehouse, metadata describes the contents of a data warehouse and the manner of its use.

Microsoft Enterprise Consortium Worldwide source for access to Microsoft's SQL Server software suite for academic purposes—teaching and research.

Microsoft SQL Server A popular RDBM system developed by Microsoft.

mode A central tendency measure in statistics that identifies the value in the fiftieth percentile.

Monte Carlo simulation A simulation technique that relies on change/probability distribution to represent the uncertainty in the modeling of the decision problem.

multidimensional (modeling) analysis A modeling method that involves data analysis in several dimensions.

multiple goals Having more than just one goal to consider in an optimization problem.

natural language processing (NLP) Using a natural language processor to interface with a computer-based system.

neural network *See* artificial neural network (ANN).

nominal data A type of data that contains measurements of simple codes assigned to objects as labels, which are not measurements. For example, the variable *marital status* can be generally categorized as (1) single, (2) married, and (3) divorced.

NoSQL (Not Only SQL) A new paradigm to store and process large volumes of unstructured, semistructured, and multistructured data.

numeric data A type of data that represents the numeric values of specific variables. Examples of numerically valued variables include age, number of children, total household income (in U.S. dollars), travel distance (in miles), and temperature (in Fahrenheit degrees).

online analytical processing (OLAP) An information system that enables the user, while at a PC, to query the system, conduct an analysis, and so on. The result is generated in seconds.

online transaction processing (OLTP) Transaction system that is primarily responsible for capturing and storing data related to day-to-day business functions.

oper mart An operational data mart. An oper mart is a small-scale data mart typically used by a single department or functional area in an organization.

operational data store (ODS) A type of database often used as an interim area for a data warehouse, especially for customer information files.

optimal solution The best possible solution to a problem.

optimization The process of identifying the best possible solution to a problem.

ordinal data Data that contain codes assigned to objects or events as labels that also represent the rank order among them. For example, the variable *credit score* can be generally categorized as (1) low, (2) medium, and (3) high.

ordinary least squares (OLS) A method that relies on the square of the distance measure to identify the best filling line/plane/hyperplane in regression modeling.

PageRank A link analysis algorithm, named after Larry Page—one of the two founders of Google as a research project at Stanford University in 1996 and used by the Google Web search engine.

parameter Numeric constants used in mathematical modeling.

part-of-speech (POS) tagging The process of marking up the words in a text as corresponding to a particular part of speech (such as nouns, verbs, adjectives, adverbs) based on a word's definition and context of its use.

performance measurement systems Systematic methods of setting business goals together with periodic feedback reports that indicate progress against goals.

perpetual analytics An analytics practice that continuously evaluates every incoming data point (i.e., observation) against all prior observations to identify patterns/anomalies.

pie chart A graphical illustration of proportions.

Pig A Hadoop-based query language developed by Yahoo!.

polarity identification The process of identifying negative or positive connotations in text (in sentiment analysis).

polysemes Words also called *homonyms*; they are syntactically identical words (i.e., spelled exactly the same) with different meanings (e.g., *bow* can mean "to bend forward," "the front of the ship," "the weapon that shoots arrows," or "a kind of tied ribbon").

prediction The act of telling about the future.

predictive analytics A business analytical approach toward forecasting (e.g., demand, problems, opportunities) that is used instead of simply reporting data as they occur.

prescriptive analytics A branch of business analytics that deals with finding the best possible solution alternative for a given problem.

privacy In general, the right to be left alone and the right to be free of unreasonable personal intrusions. Information privacy is the right to determine when, and to what extent, information about oneself can be communicated to others.

quantitative model Mathematical models that rely on numeric/quantifiable measures.

quartile One-fourth (i.e., quarter) of a sorted numeric/ordinal data sample.

radio-frequency identification (RFID) A generic technology that refers to the use of radio-frequency waves to identify objects.

range A statistics measure for dispersion—the distance between the smallest and largest values within a given sample of numeric data points.

RapidMiner A popular, open source, free-of-charge data mining software suite that employs a graphically enhanced user interface, a rather large number of algorithms, and a variety of data visualization features.

ratio data Continuous data where both differences and ratios are interpretable. The distinguishing feature of a ratio scale is the possession of a nonarbitrary zero value.

real-time data warehousing (RDW) The process of loading and providing data via a data warehouse as they become available.

regression A data mining method for real-world prediction problems where the predicted values (i.e., the output variable or dependent variable) are numeric (e.g., predicting the temperature for tomorrow as 68°F).

report Any communication artifact prepared with the specific intention of conveying information in a presentable form.

result (outcome) variable A variable that expresses the result of a decision (e.g., one concerning profit), usually one of the goals of a decision-making problem.

risk A probabilistic or stochastic decision situation.

risk analysis Use of mathematical modeling to assess the nature of risk (variability) for a decision situation.

SAS Enterprise Miner A comprehensive, commercial data mining software tool developed by the SAS Institute.

scatter plot A graph in which the values of two variables are plotted along two axes to illustrate the relationship between them.

scorecard A visual display that is used to chart progress against strategic and tactical goals and targets.

search engine A program that finds and lists Web sites or pages (designated by URLs) that match some user-selected criteria.

search engine optimization (SEO) The intentional activity of affecting the visibility of an e-commerce site or a Web site in a search engine's natural (unpaid or organic) search results.

SEMMA An alternative process for data mining projects proposed by the SAS Institute. The acronym "SEMMA" stands for "sample, explore, modify, model, and assess."

sensitivity analysis A study of the effect of a change in one or more input variables on a proposed solution.

sentiment analysis The technique used to detect favorable and unfavorable opinions toward specific products and services using a large numbers of textual data sources (customer feedback in the form of Web postings).

SentiWordNet An extension of WordNet to be used for sentiment identification. *See* WordNet.

sequence mining A pattern discovery method where relationships among things are examined in terms of their order of occurrence to identify associations over time.

simple split Data is partitioned into two mutually exclusive subsets called a *training set* and a *test set* (or *holdout set*). It is common to designate two-thirds of the data as the training set and the remaining one-third as the test set.

simulation A technique for conducting experiments (e.g., what-if analyses) with a computer on a model of a real-world system.

singular value decomposition (SVD) Closely related to principal components analysis, it reduces the overall dimensionality of the input matrix (number of input documents by number of extracted terms) to a lower dimensional space, where each consecutive dimension represents the largest degree of variability (between words and documents).

Six Sigma A performance management methodology aimed at reducing the number of defects in a business process to as close to zero defects per million opportunities (DPMO) as possible.

skewness A statistical measure to characterize the shape of a unimodal distribution—characterizing the asymmetry (sway) of the distribution (*also see* kurtosis).

snowflake schema A logical arrangement of tables in a multidimensional database in such a way that the entity relationship diagram resembles a snowflake in shape.

social media analytics Application of analytics tools to social media and social network data.

social network analysis (SNA) The mapping and measuring of relationships and information flows among people, groups, organizations, computers, and other information- or knowledge-processing entities. The nodes in the network are the people and groups, whereas the links show relationships or flows between the nodes. SNAs provide both visual and mathematical analyses of relationships.

software as a service (SaaS) Software that is rented instead of sold.

speech analytics A growing field of science that allows users to analyze and extract information from both live and recorded conversations.

spider *See* Web crawler.

standard deviation A descriptive statistics measure for dispersion. It is the square root of the variance.

star schema Most commonly used and simplest style of dimensional modeling.

static models A model that captures a snapshot of the system, ignoring its dynamic features.

statistics A collection of mathematical techniques to characterize and interpret data.

stemming A process of reducing words to their respective root forms to better represent them in a text mining project.

stop words Words that are filtered out prior to or after processing of natural language data (i.e., text).

storytelling A case with rich information and episodes. Lessons may be derived from this kind of case in a case base.

stream analytics A term commonly used for extracting actionable information from continuously flowing/streaming data sources.

structured data Data that is formatted (often into tables with rows and columns) for computers to easily understand and process.

Structured Query Language (SQL) A data definition and management language for relational databases. SQL front-ends most relational DBMS.

support The measure of how often products and/or services appear together in the same transaction; that is, the proportion of transactions in the data set that contain all the products and/or services mentioned in a specific rule.

term–document matrix (TDM) A frequency matrix created from digitized and organized documents (the corpus) where the columns represent the terms and rows represent the individual documents.

text analytics A broader concept that includes information retrieval (e.g., searching and identifying relevant documents for a given set of key terms) as well as information extraction, data mining, and Web mining.

text mining The application of data mining to nonstructured or less structured text files. It entails the generation of meaningful numeric indices from the unstructured text and then processing those indices using various data mining algorithms.

time series forecasting A prediction model that relies solely on the past occurrences/values of the variable of interest to estimate/calculate the expected future values.

tokenizing Categorizing a block of text (token) according to the function it performs.

trend analysis The collecting of information and attempting to spot a pattern, or *trend*, in the information.

uncertainty A decision situation where there is a complete lack of information about what the parameter values are or what the future state of nature will be.

uncontrollable variable A mathematical modeling variable that has to be taken as given—not allowing changes/modifications.

unstructured data Data that do not have a predetermined format and are stored in the form of textual documents.

unsupervised learning A method of training artificial neural networks in which only input stimuli are shown to the network, which is self-organizing.

user interface The component of a computer system that allows bidirectional communication between the system and its user.

variable Any characteristics (number, symbol, or quantity) that can be measured or counted.

variable selection *See* dimensional reduction.

variance A descriptive statistics measure for dispersion. It is the square of standard deviation.

visual analytics An extension of data/information visualization that includes not only descriptive but also predictive analytics.

visual interactive modeling (VIM) A visual model representation technique that allows for user and other system interactions.

visual interactive simulation (VIS) A visual/animated simulation environment that allows for the end user to interact with the model parameters while the mode is running.

voice of the customer (VOC) Applications that focus on "who and how" questions by gathering and reporting direct feedback from site visitors, by benchmarking against other sites and offline channels, and by supporting predictive modeling of future visitor behavior.

Web analytics The application of business analytics activities to Web-based processes, including e-commerce.

Web content mining The extraction of useful information from Web pages.

Web crawler Also known as *spider* is an application used to swift/crawl/read through the content of a Web sites automatically.

Web mining The discovery and analysis of interesting and useful information from the Web, about the Web, and usually through Web-based tools.

Web service An architecture that enables assembly of distributed applications from software services and ties them together.

Web structure mining The development of useful information from the links included in Web documents.

Web usage mining The extraction of useful information from the data being generated through Web page visits, transactions, and so on.

Weka A popular, free-of-charge, open source suite of machine-learning software written in Java, developed at the University of Waikato.

what-if analysis It is an experimental process that helps determine what will happen to the solution/output if an input variable, an assumption, or a parameter value is changed.

WordNet A popular general-purpose lexicon created at Princeton University.

Index

A

AaaS. *See* analytics-as-a-service (AaaS)
AARP, Inc., 173–175
abandoned shopping carts, 297–298
abandonment rates, 303
Aberdeen Group, 405
absolutist approach, 140
academic applications, 266–267
academic institutions, 44–45
accessibility, 59, 310
accidental falls, 29–30
accounting, 329t
accuracy, 59, 217, 217t, 313
accuracy rate, 216
acquisitions, 146
acronyms, 16
active tags, 423–424
Acxiom, 43, 237
ad hoc data mining, 162
AdaBoosting, 220
advanced analytics, 170, 311
affective computing, 276
affinity analysis, 227
agent-based models, 356
agglomerative classes, 226
aggregated information, 132
aggregation, 66, 284
agile BI environment, 174
agility, 167
agricultural applications, 442
AI. *See* artificial intelligence (AI)
airlines, 204–205
alerts, 162
algorithms
    see also specific algorithms
    Apriori algorithm, 211, 229–230, 230f
    association rule mining, 202, 229
    classification modeling, 219–220
    clustering algorithms, 226–227
    data mining task, 209
    decision trees, 221–222
    in-database processing technology, 169
    machine learning algorithms, 62
    optimization via, 326t
    search engines, 296
    sentiment classifiers, 285
Alhea, 296
All England Lawn Tennis Club (AELTC), 277–280
alternative data, 377–378
Alteryx, 41–42
Amazon, 25, 33, 35, 409, 427, 430, 432
Amazon Elastic, 403
Amazon Elastic Beanstalk, 434
Ambari, 387
ambassadors, 44
AMC Networks, 257–260
American Airlines, Inc., 332
American Cancer Society, 209
analysis, 19, 28
analysts, 43–44
analytic processing, 19–20
analytic ready, 58
analytical processing activities, 131
analytical support, 12
analytics, 19, 22–23
    see also business analytics
    applications, selected domains, 29–35

Big Data analytics. *See* Big Data analytics
decision analytics, 27
department, 454
descriptive (or reporting) analytics, 24
    see also descriptive analytics
developments, 11–12
different domains, application to, 27–28
evolution of computerized decision support, 13–15, 13f
evolving needs for, 11–12
healthcare domain, examples, 29–33
impact of, in organizations, 453–458, 454f
levels of, 23, 23f
management, impact on, 455–456
normative analytics, 27
organizational redesign, 455
overview, 22–29
predictive analytics, 25–26
    see also predictive analytics
prescriptive analytics. *See* prescriptive analytics
retail value chain, examples, 33–35, 34t
unintended effects, 458
vs. data science, 28–29
analytics ambassadors, 44
analytics ecosystem, 37, 38f
    academic institutions, 44–45
    analysts, 43–44
    analytics user organizations, 45–46
    analytics-focused software developers, 41–42
    application developers, 42–43
    certification agencies, 44–45
    data generation infrastructure providers, 39
    data management infrastructure providers, 39–40
    data service providers, 40–41
    data warehouse providers, 40
    flower metaphor, 38
    general application developers, 42–43
    industry specific application developers, 42–43
    influencers, 43–44
    middleware providers, 40
    overview, 37–39
    policy makers, 45
    regulators, 45
analytics evangelists, 44
analytics influencers. *See* influencers
Analytics Leadership Award, 30
Analytics magazine, 322
analytics user organizations, 45–46
analytics-as-a-service (AaaS), 435–436
analytics-focused software developers, 41–42
Annotation Query Language (AQL), 399
antecedent, 229
AOL Search, 296
Apache, 36, 199
Apache Cassandra, 390–391
Apache Hadoop, 388–389, 392
    see also Hadoop
Apache Hive, 392
Apache Software Foundation (ASF), 388
Apple, 450
appliances, 380
application cases
    AARP, Inc., 173–175
    abandoned shopping carts, 297–298
    alternative data, 377–378

AMC Networks, 257–260
American Airlines, Inc., 332
athletic injuries, 26
BP Lubricants, 146–147
cancer research, 209–210
Cary, North Carolina, 84–85
CenterPoint Energy, 37
cloud infrastructure applications, 436–440
Cosan, 358–359
Czech Insurers' Bureau (CIB), 254–255
Dallas Cowboys, 118
Dell, 198–199
disease patterns, 402–403
eBay, 390–391
Electrabel GDF SUEZ, 119–120
Expedia.com, 182–183
ExxonMobil, 323
Federal Emergency Management Agency (FEMA), 100
flu activity, 400–401
Great Clips, 443
Hepatitis B interventions, 353–354
Hollywood movies, 233–236
Influence Health, 223–225
Ingram Micro, 325–326
Instrumentation Laboratory, 63–65
investment bank, 382–383
job-shop scheduling decisions, 361–363
Lenovo, 266–267
lies, 262–264
Lotte.com, 297–298
Macfarlan Smith, 103–105
Metro Meals on Wheels Treasure Valley, 334–335
Michigan Department of Technology, Management and Budget, 163
mobile service providers, 135–137
NCAA Bowl Game outcomes, 91–96
Pennsylvania Adoption Exchange, 333–334
Pitney Bowes and General Electric, 426–427
Quiznos, 446
research literature survey, 273–275
Rockwell Automation, 421–422
Sabre, 18–19
Salesforce, 410
Siemens, 25
Silvaris Corporation, 24
SilverHook, 420–421
specialty steel bar company, and available-to-promise dates, 27
Starbucks, 444
student attrition, 68–74
Target, 238
Teradata® Analytics, 151–153
terrorist funding, 205–206
Tito's Handmade Vodka, 305–308
Twitter, 392–393
University of Tennessee Medical Center, 337–338
Visa, 194–195
visual analytics, 119–120
Wimbledon, 277–280
applied mathematics, 28
appraisal extraction, 276
Apriori algorithm, 211, 229–230, 230f
ArcGIS, 444
archival public records, 196
area under the ROC curve, 219

ARIMA, 97
arithmetic mean, 76–77
artificial intelligence (AI), 16, 450, 457
Ask, 296
association, 198, 202, 272
Association for Information Systems, 44
association rule, 272
association rule learning, 202
association rule mining, 211, 227–230
assumed risk, 331
Aster analytics-as-a-service, 435–436
Aster Graph Analytics, 435–436
Aster MapReduce Analytics Foundation, 435–436
astronomy, 194
@RISK, 357
athletic injuries, 26
Atlas, 444
AT&T, 164, 427
attributes, 221
augmented reality, 446
authoritative pages, 290
authority, 290
automatic sensitivity analysis, 347
automatic summarization, 260
automation, 457–458
available-to-promise (ATP) decisions, 27
average, 76–77
average page views per visitor, 300
averaging methods, 97
Avro, 387

B

back-office business analytics, 5
bagging-type decision tree ensembles, 220
bag-of-words model, 255
"The Balanced Scorecard: Measures that Drive Performance" (Kaplan and Norton), 177
The Balanced Scorecard: Translating Strategy into Action (Kaplan and Norton), 177
balanced scorecard (BSC), 176–177, 179
    balance, meaning of, 179
    balanced scorecard–type reports, 99
    customer perspective, 177–178
    financial perspective, 178
    four perspectives, 177–178
    internal business processes perspective, 178
    learning and growing perspective, 178
    vs. Six Sigma, 180, 181f
BAM. *See* business activity management (BAM)
banking industry, 204, 382–383
banking services, 228
bar charts, 106
barcode, 424
basic indexing, 395
Bayesian classifiers, 220
Beane, Billy, 5
benchmark, 176
Bernoulli trial, 90
Bertin, Jacques, 101
best-of-breed components, 22
beyond the brand, 312
BI. *See* business intelligence (BI)
BI Competency Center, 20–21
bias, 66
Big Data, 15, 53, 57, 133, 373
    see also Big Data analytics
    Big Data platform, 40
    and data warehousing, 393–397
    definition of, 373–377
    high-level conceptual architecture, 376f
    management of, 11–12

meaning of, 35–37
    and stream analytics, 406–409
    succeeding with, 405–406
    technologies, 383–391
    value proposition, 376–377, 378–379
    variability, 376
    variety, 374
    velocity, 374–376
    vendors and platforms, 397–406
    veracity, 376
    volume, 374
Big Data analytics, 35–36, 379f, 418
    see also Big Data
    business problems addressed by, 381
    challenges, 380–381
    critical success factors, 379f, 380
    fundamentals of, 378–383
    high-performance computing, 380
    need for, 379
Big Data technologies, 383–391
    Hadoop, 385–388
    MapReduce, 383–385, 384f
    NoSQL, 389–391
BigSheets, 399
Bing, 296
biomedical applications, 264–265
biometric data, 452
black holes, 20
black-hat SEO, 295, 296
Bloomberg Businessweek, 452
BlueCava, 451
BM SPSS Modeler, 26
boosting-type decision tree ensembles, 220
bootstrapping, 218
bottom-up approach, 229–230
box plot, 79–80
box-and-whiskers plot, 79–80, 79f
BP Lubricants, 146–147
BPM. *See* business performance management (BPM)
branch, 221
brand management, 281
break-even point, 349
bridge, 308
brokerages, 204
brontobytes (BB), 375
Broussard, Bruce, 32
BSC. *See* balanced scorecard (BSC)
BSI Videos (Business Scenario Investigations), 19
bubble charts, 107
Building the Data Warehouse (Inmon), 133
bullet graphs, 108
BureauNet, 100
Burt, Ronald, 309
bus architecture. *See* data mart bus architecture
business, 20
business activity management (BAM), 21
business analytics, 16
    see also analytics
    back-office business analytics, 5
    and business intelligence, 130, 131f
    cloud computing. *See* cloud computing
    front-office business analytics, 5
    statistical modeling, 74–85
business data warehouse, 133
business intelligence (BI), 15, 16, 130
    acquisition of BI systems, 21–22
    architecture of, 16, 17f
    BI systems, 14
    and business analytics, 130, 131f
    business strategy, alignment with, 20–21
    cost–benefit analysis, 22

definitions of BI, 16
    department, 454
    development of BI systems, 21–22
    drivers of, 16–17
    evolution of, 13f
    framework for, 15–22
    high-level architecture, 17f
    history of, 16
    integration of systems and applications, 22
    justification, 22
    multimedia exercise in, 19
    origins of, 16–17
    planning, 20–21
    privacy, 22
    real-time, on-demand BI, 21
    real-time BI applications, 21
    security, 22
    tax fraud, targeting, 128–130
    transaction processing *vs.* analytic processing, 19–20
business need, 380
business objective, 207
Business Objects, 133, 139, 154t
business performance management (BPM), 16, 170
    closed-loop BPM cycle, 171–175, 171f
    key components, 170–171
business process management, 98
business reporting, 98–100
business reports, 98
business rules, 149
business strategy, 20–21
business-user comments, 122
buzzwords, 16, 27

C

C4.5, 222
C5, 222
calculated risk, 331
calculation rules, 149
California Institute of Technology (Caltech), 132
call detail records (CDR), 409–410
cancer research, 209–210
candidate generation, 229–230
Candybar, 446
capacities, 338
capacity, 161
Cary, North Carolina, 84–85
cascaded decision tree model, 7, 7f
case-based reasoning, 219
cases. *See* application cases
catastrophic loss, 351
categorical data, 61, 202, 208
categorical representation, 62
categorization, 252, 271
CDR. *See* call detail records (CDR)
Center for Health Systems Innovation, 402
CenterPoint Energy, 37
Centers for Disease Control and Prevention (CDC), 30, 31
central fact tables, 157
Central Intelligence Agency (CIA), 262
centrality, 80, 308
centralized data warehouse, 142, 143f, 145
centroid, 227
CEP. *See* complex event processing (CEP) engines
Cerner, 42
Cerner Corporation, 402
certainty, 330–331
certificate programs, 44
certification agencies, 44–45

Certified Analytics Professional certificate program, 44
The Championships, 277–280
change capture, 146
changing business environments, 11–12
channel analysis, 34t
charts
  see also graphs
  bar charts, 106
  basic charts, 106
  bubble charts, 107
  choice of, 108–109
  Gantt charts, 107
  line charts, 106
  PERT charts, 107
  pie charts, 106
  specialized charts, 107–108
  taxonomy, 108, 109f
Chime, 440
chi-squared automatic interaction detector (CHAID), 222
CIO Insight, 48
Citibank, 132
class label, 221
classical statistical techniques, 41
classification, 200–223, 271, 326
  accuracy of classification model, 216–219, 217f
  area under the ROC curve, 219
  Bayesian classifiers, 220
  bootstrapping, 218
  case-based reasoning, 219
  common accuracy metrics, 217f
  decision tree analysis, 219
  genetic algorithms, 200
  jackknifing, 218
  k-fold cross-validation, 218
  leave-one-out, 218
  neural networks, 219
  N–P polarity classification, 282–283
  rough sets, 200
  simple split, 217–218, 217f
  statistical analysis, 219
  techniques, 219–220
classification and regression trees (CART), 222, 232t
classification matrix, 216
classification tools, 200
class/response variable, 90
click map, 301
click paths, 301
ClickFox, 398
clickstream, 394
clickstream analysis, 298–299
client/server architecture, 139
cliques, 309
closed-circuit television (CCTV), 35
closed-loop BPM cycle, 171–175, 171f
cloud, 403
cloud analytics, 440
cloud computing, 39–40, 165–166, 429–430
  analytics-as-a-service (AaaS), 435–436
  cloud deployment models, 433–434
  cloud oriented support system, 431f
  data-as-a-service (DaaS), 431–432
  essential technologies, 433
  illustrative analytics applications, 436–440
  infrastructure-as-a-service (IaaS), 430, 432–433
  major cloud providers, 434–435
  platform-as-a-service (PaaS), 430, 432
  software-as-a-service (SaaS), 432
  technology stack as a service, 433f
  virtualization, 433

cloud deployment models, 433–434
cloud platform, 426t
cloud-based systems, 11
Cloudera, 392, 439
Cloze, 447
cluster analysis, 202, 225–227
clustering, 202, 253, 271–272, 274, 326
clustering algorithms, 25, 226
clustering coefficient, 309
clusters, 38, 43, 200, 225, 271
CNN, 163
cognitive limits, 12
Cognos, 18, 133
cohesion, 309
collaboration, 11
collection, 284
columnar database, 168
column-oriented database management system, 168
communication networks, 304–305
community networks, 305
comorbidity networks, 404f
comparative measures, 119
competitive advantage, 203
complex event processing (CEP), 408
complex event processing (CEP) engines, 42
components, 38
comprehensive database, 138
comprehensiveness, 59
Computer Associates, 154t
computer hardware and software, 204
computer science, 28
Computer Sciences Corporation (CSC), 100
Comscore, 41
concept hierarchies, 67
concept linking, 253
concepts, 253
conclusions, 75
condition-based maintenance, 204
confidence, 229
confidence gap, 359
confusion matrix, 216, 216f
Congressional Floor-Debate Transcripts, 286
connections, 308
consequent, 229
consistency, 64
consistent data, 59
constant variance (of errors), 90
constraints, 268, 329, 338
consumer-centric apps, 447–448
Contenko, 296
content groupings, 302
contextual metadata, 121
contingency table, 216
continuous distributions, 356, 357t
conversion statistics, 302–303
conversions, 303
cookies, 450
Cornell Movie-Review Data Sets, 286
corporate cloud, 433
corporate information factory. *See* hub-and-spoke architecture
corpus, 253, 269
correlation, 86
Cosan, 358–359
cost reduction, 136, 381
cost–benefit analysis, 22, 27
credibility assessment, 262
credit card transactions, 228
Credit score and classification reporting companies, 43

crime analysis, 442
criminal networks, 305
CRISP-DM (Cross-Industry Standard Process for Data Mining), 26, 207, 207f, 268
critical event processing, 408
CRM. *See* customer relationship management (CRM)
cross-linking, 295
Crystal Ball, 357
cube, 159
currency, 60
customer acquisition, 136
customer buying patterns, 238
customer churn, 370–373
customer churn analysis, 34t
customer experience, 381
customer objective, 179
customer performance, 176
customer perspective, 177–178
customer relationship management (CRM), 5, 20, 203–204, 257, 261
customer retention, 136
customer value, 410
Cutting, Doug, 397
cybersecurity, 411
Czech Insurers' Bureau (CIB), 254–255

D
DaaS. *See* data-as-a-service (DaaS)
Dallas Cowboys, 118
Dartmouth-Hitchcock Medical Center, 438
Dashboard Spy Web, 119
dashboards, 11, 16, 117–122
  analysis, 119
  benchmarks, 121
  best practices in dashboard design, 121
  business-user comments, 122
  characteristics, 121
  contextual metadata, 121
  design, 119
  guided analytics, 122
  management, 119
  monitoring, 119
  presentation of information, 122
  prioritization of alerts/exceptions, 122
  ranking of alerts/exceptions, 122
  usability specialist, 122
  visual construct, 122
  Web analytics, 303f
dashboard-type reports, 99
data, 13, 41, 61
  see also specific types of data
  Big Data. *See* Big Data
  data size, 375
  data to knowledge continuum, 57, 58f
  data-related tasks, 59
  dirty data, 65
  identification and selection, 208
  integration, 395
  nature of data, 57–60
  readiness level of data, 59–60
  representation schemas, 63
  shape of a distribution, 80–81
  simple taxonomy of data, 61–63, 61f
  storytelling with, 113–114, 114f
  transportation of, 148
  types of data, 61–62
  value proposition, 58
  variable types, 63
data access, 146
data accessibility, 59
data acquisition (back-end) software, 139
Data Advantage Group, 154t

data analysis, 141
data analyst, 28
data archaeology, 196
    see also data mining
data cleansing, 65–66, 68t, 161
data concertation, 76
data consistency, 59
data consolidation, 65, 68t
data content accuracy, 59
data currency/data timeliness, 60
data dredging, 196
    see also data mining
data extraction, 138
data federation, 146
data generation infrastructure providers, 39
data governance, 381, 406
data granularity, 60
data infrastructure, 380
data integration, 146–148, 381
data lakes, 166–168
data loading, 138
data management, 335
  improved data management, and decisions, 11
  infrastructure providers, 39–40
  technologies and practices, 169
data mart (DM), 134
data mart approach, 154–155
data mart bus architecture, 142, 143f, 145
data migration, 141, 149
data mining, 11, 14, 25, 190, 196, 200
  applications, 193–203, 203–206
  association, 202
  benefits, 196–197
  blend of multiple disciplines, 197f
  characteristics, 196–197
  classification, 200–202
  clustering, 202
  concepts, 193–203
  definitions, 196
  how data mining works, 197–198
  ideas behind, 194
  methods, 215–231
  myths and blunders, 238–241, 239f
  objectives, 196–197
  other names associated with, 196
  predictions, 200
  privacy issues, 237
  process, 206–215, 207f, 213f, 214f
  software tools, 231–233, 232f
  tasks, categories of, 200–202
  taxonomy for tasks, methods, and algorithms, 201f
  time-series forecasting, 203
  use of term, 193–194
  value proposition, 239
  visualization, 203
  vs. statistics, 203
data mining applications, 203–206
data mining methods, 215–231
  association rule mining, 227–230
  classification, 200–223
  cluster analysis, 225–227
  decision trees. *See* decision trees
  ensemble models, 220–221
data mining process, 206–215
  business understanding, 207
  CRISP-DM, 207, 207f
  data preparation, 208–209
  data understanding, 208
  deployment, 212
  evaluation, 212

model building, 209–211
  other standardized processes and methodologies, 212–214
  ranking of processes and methodologies, 214f
  testing, 212
data mining software tools, 231–233, 232f
data mining techniques, 41
data modeling, 162
data preparation, 208–209, 239
  see also data preprocessing
data preprocessing, 65, 208–209
  art and science of, 65–74
  essence of, 67, 68t
  purpose of, 208–209
  steps, 66f
  value proposition of, 67
data privacy, 59
data quality, 57–58, 149
data reduction, 67, 68t
data relevancy, 60
data retrieval, 141
data richness, 59
data science, 19, 324
  department, 454
  vs. analytics, 28–29
Data Science Central, 35, 47
data scientists, 386, 459–462
data scrubbing, 65
data security, 59
data service providers, 40–41
data source reliability, 59
data sources, 138, 149
data stream analytics, 375–376
data stream mining, 408–409
data taxonomy, 61–63, 61f
data transformation, 66–67, 68t, 138
data transformation tools, 149
data validity, 60
data visualization, 101
  dashboards. *See* dashboards
  data mining and, 203
  future of, 103
  history of, 101–103
  storytelling, 113–114, 114f
  tools, 41
  visual tools, need for, 103
data volume, 381
data warehouse (DW), 19–20, 127, 131
  see also data warehousing
  centralized data warehouse, 142, 143f
  as component of BI system, 16
  data analysis, 158
  data from, 14
  data mart (DM), 134
  data mart approach, 154–155
  data migration tools, 141
  data-driven decision making, 138f
  development, 150–160
  development approaches, 153–155
  direct benefits, 150
  DW model of traditional BI systems, 21
  DW solutions, 40
  DW-driven DSSs, 14
  EDW approach, 153, 154, 155t, 156t
  enterprise data warehouse (EDW), 135
  enterprise-wide data warehouse (EDW), 142
  federated data warehouse, 142–144
  framework and views, 138f
  giant data warehouses, 11–12, 162–164
  hosted data warehouse, 157
  hub-and-spoke architecture, 142, 143f, 144
  indirect benefits, 150

  management of giant data warehouses, 11–12
  manager, 161
  migration of data, 149
  performance, 395
  providers, 40
  representation of data, 156–158
  scalability, 162–164
  vs. data lake, 167t
  vs. Hadoop, 393–396
  wide variety of data, 20
data warehouse administrator (DWA), 164
data warehouse appliance, 168–169
The Data Warehouse Toolkit (Kimball), 133
data warehousing, 11, 16, 40
  see also data warehouse (DW)
  administration, 164–165
  all-in-one solutions, 168
  architectures, 139–145, 139f, 140f, 141f, 143f
  and Big Data, 393–397
  business value of, 155
  characteristics of, 133–134
  client/server architecture, 134
  future of, 165–170
  historical perspective, 132–133, 132f
  implementation issues, 160–164
  infrastructure, 168
  integration, 134
  metadata, 134
  modern approaches, origins of, 16
  multidimensional structure, 134
  nonvolatile, 134
  privacy, 164
  process, 137–139
  real time, 134
  real-time data warehousing (RDW), 14, 168
  relational structure, 134
  right-time data warehousing, 14
  risks, 161
  security issues, 164–165
  sourcing, 165–166
  subject orientation, 133–134
  tax fraud, targeting, 128–130
  time variant (time series), 134
  use cases, 394–395
  user participation, 162
  vendors, 154t
  Web-based applications, 134
data warehousing architectures, 139–145, 139f, 140f, 141f, 143f
The Data Warehousing Institute, 22, 44, 47, 153, 159
data-as-a-service (DaaS), 431–432
database management system (DBMS), 141, 170
data-driven decision making, 138f
data-driven marketing, 54–56
data-in-motion analytics, 407
  see also stream analytics
Datameer, 398
DataMirror, 154t
data-oriented cloud systems, 440
DataStax Enterprise, 390–391, 398
datum, 61
  see also data
Davenport, Thomas H., 5, 193, 459
DB2, 141
deception detection, 262–264, 264t
decision analysis, 349
  decision tables, 350–351
  decision trees. *See* decision trees
decision analytics, 27
decision making

analytics, support of, 456
certainty, 330–331
decision modeling with spreadsheets, 331–336
ethics, 452–453
probabilistic decision-making situation, 331
risk, 331
stochastic decision-making situation, 331
uncertainty, 331, 350–351
zones of decision making, 330f
decision modeling with spreadsheets, 331–336
decision support
developments, 11–12
ethics, 452–453
evolution of computerized decision support, 13–15, 13f
evolving needs for, 11–12
decision support mathematical models
components of, 329–330, 329t
decision variables, 328
intermediate result variables, 329
profit model, 329
result (outcome) variables, 328
structure of, 328–330
uncontrollable variables, 328
decision support systems (DSSs), 12, 13
add-ins, 332–333
DW-driven DSSs, 14
and visual interactive models, 360
Decision Support Systems (journal), 48
decision tables, 350–351
decision tree analysis, 219
decision tree models, 25
decision tree software, 42
decision trees, 200, 202, 211, 221–225, 351–352
algorithms, 221–222
cascaded decision tree model, 7, 7f
decision variables, 328, 338, 350
dedicated URL, 301
deep knowledge, 249
Deep Learning tools, 233
DeepQA, 249, 250f
defects, 180
defects per million opportunities (DPMO), 180
defense, 204
Dell, 154t, 198–199, 254, 398
Dell Statistica, 63–65, 199, 232t
Demirkan, Haluk, 430
demographic data, 40–41
demographic details, 442
demos, 48
denial of service (DDoS) attacks, 279
density, 308
Department for Homeland Security, 262, 450–451
dependent data mart, 134
dependent variables, 328
deployment, 212
Descartes Labs, 377
descriptive analytics, 24, 41, 98, 130–131, 311
branches of, 75
business intelligence. *See* business intelligence (BI)
data warehousing. *See* data warehousing
descriptive statistics, 75–76
online analytical processing (OLAP). *See* online analytical processing (OLAP)
statistical methods, 74
statistics, 75
descriptive statistics, 75–76, 81
arithmetic mean, 76–77
box-and-whiskers plot, 79–80, 79f
for descriptive analytics, 75–76

interquartile range, 78–79
mean absolute deviation, 78
measures of centrality tendency, 76
measures of dispersion, 77
median, 77
Microsoft Excel, 82–84
mode, 77
quartiles, 78–79
ranges, 78
role in business analytics, 75–76
shape of a distribution, 80–81
standard deviation, 78, 80
variance, 78
Devlin, Barry, 133
dice, 159
dictionary, 269
DigitalGlobe, 377
dimension tables, 157
dimensional modeling, 156
dimensional reduction, 67
direct searches, 301
dirty data, 65
discrete distributions, 356, 357t
discrete event simulation, 356, 358–359
discretization, 66, 202
discriminant analysis, 74, 200
disease patterns, 402–403
disease spread prediction, 442
dispersion, 77, 81f
distance, 308
distance measure, 226
distributed database management system, 132–133
distributions, 308–309
divisive classes, 226
DM approach, 153, 155t, 156t
DMAIC, 180
DNA microarray analysis, 264
document hierarchy, 289
document indexer, 293
document matcher/ranker, 294
Dogpile, 296
domain experts, 14
domain of interest, 269
domain-specific analytics solutions, 43
downloads, 300
DPMO. *See* defects per million opportunities (DPMO)
drill down/up, 159
drivers, 176
DSS. *See* decision support systems (DSSs)
DSS Resources, 48
DuckDuckGo, 296
Dundas BI, 25
DW. *See* data warehouse (DW)
DWA. *See* data warehouse administrator (DWA)
dynamic advertisements, 282
dynamic data, 62
dynamic models, 324, 360
dynamic pricing, 6, 6f

E

EAI. *See* enterprise application integration (EAI)
eBay, 390–391, 409, 435
ECHELON surveillance system, 261–262
e-commerce, 282, 297, 299–300, 409
Economining, 286
The Economist, 456–457, 458
EDW. *See* enterprise data warehouse (EDW)
EDW approach, 153, 154, 155t, 156t
EEE approach, 3
EII. *See* enterprise information integration (EII)
EIS. *See* executive information systems (EISs)

Electrabel GDF SUEZ, 119–120
Electronic Product Code (EPC), 424
Embarcadero Technologies, 154t
EMC Greenplum, 115, 398
encodings, 176
end-user modeling tool, 333
energy industry, 407f
ensemble models, 220–221
enterprise application integration (EAI), 147
enterprise data warehouse (EDW), 135
enterprise information integration (EII), 147, 148
enterprise resource planning (ERP), 14, 20
enterprise-wide data warehouse (EDW), 142
entertainment industry, 205
entropy, 223
environmental effects, 442
environmental scanning and analysis, 324
EPC. *See* Electronic Product Code (EPC)
EPCglobal, Inc., 424
ERP. *See* enterprise resource planning (ERP)
errors, 97
ESRI, 41, 442
ethics, 452–453
ETL. *See* extraction, transformation, and load (ETL)
EUROPOL, 262
evangelists, 44, 406
event cloud, 408
evidence-based medicine, 255–256
exabytes (EB), 373–374, 375
Excel. *See* Microsoft Excel
The Execution Premium (Kaplan and Norton), 177
executive champion, 380
executive dashboard, 117–118, 117f
see also dashboards
executive information systems (EISs), 14, 16
Executive's Guide to the Internet of Things, 428–429
exit rates, 303
expectations, 161
Expedia.com, 181, 182–183
Experian, 41
experience, 3
experimentation, 28
explanatory variable, 87
explanatory variables, 90
explicit sentiment, 277
explore, 3
exponential smoothing, 97
exposure, 3
"The Extended ASP Model," 165
eXtensible Markup Language (XML)–based tools, 142, 148
external data, 161
external data sources, 40
extraction, 148, 149
extraction, transformation, and load (ETL), 98, 147, 148–150, 148f
extract/transfer/load batch update, 21
extranet, 140
ExxonMobil, 323

F

Facebook, 43, 377, 386, 451, 453
fact-based decision-making culture, 380
falls, 29–30
Federal Communications Commission (FCC), 45
Federal Emergency Management Agency (FEMA), 100

Federal Trade Commission (FTC), 45
federated architecture, 143f, 145
federated data warehouse, 142–144
FICO, 42
FICO Decision Management, 232t
finance sectors, 194
financial investment, 329t
financial markets, 36, 281
financial model, 329
financial perspective, 178
financial planning and budgeting process, 172
financial services, 411
FirstMark, 39
flu activity, 400–401
Flume, 387
fog computing, 425–426
fog nodes, 425–426, 426t
fool's gold, 240
forecasting, 86, 200, 324
forecasts, 377–378
foreign language reading, 260
foreign language writing, 260
Forrester, 44, 405
fraud
  fraud detection, 225
  fraud detection engine, 42–43
  fraud reduction, 194–195
  tax fraud, 128–130
frequency, 310
frequency plot, 80
friendship network, 403
front-end query tool, 396
Frontline Systems, Inc., 42, 321
front-office business analytics, 5
functionality, 20
fuzzy logic, 226

G

Galton, Francis, 86
Gantt charts, 107
Gapminder, 109, 110f
"garbage in garbage out–GIGO" concept/principle, 53
Gartner, Inc., 20, 110, 111–112, 304, 374, 403, 405, 432
Gartner Group, 16, 44
GE Predix, 426–427, 436
gegobytes (GeB), 375
gene/protein interaction identification, 264–265, 265f
General Electric, 426–427
genetic algorithms, 200, 220, 226
genomic data, 194
geocoding, 443
geographic information system (GIS) solutions, 444
geographic information systems (GIS), 107, 442
geographic maps, 107
geography, 302
geospatial analytics, 441–445
geospatial data, 441
Gephi, 41, 392
GhostMiner, 232t
giant data warehouses, 11–12, 162–164
gigabytes (GB), 374, 375
Gillette, 424
Gini index, 222–223
GIS. *See* geographic information systems (GIS)
goal seeking, 335, 348–349, 349f
Goldman Sachs, 377
good scalability, 163
Google, 36, 41, 291, 296, 447, 450, 457
Google Analytics, 41, 299

Google App Engine, 434
Google Compute Engine, 403
Google Maps, 103
Google/Alphabet, 427
Gopal, Vipin, 29
government, 204, 412
government intelligence, 281–282
Gramm-Leach-Bliley privacy and safeguards rules, 164
granularity, 60
graphical user interface (GUI), 140
graphics developers, 44
graphs
  see also charts; maps
  basic graphs, 106
  bullet graphs, 108
  choice of, 108–109
  highlight tables, 108
  histogram, 80, 107
  scatter plots, 87f, 106
  specialized graphs, 107–108
  taxonomy, 108, 109f
Gray, Jim, 394
Great Clips, 443
Greenplum, 154t
grid computing, 380
Grimes, Seth, 110
grindgis.com, 442
group collaboration, 11
group communication, 11
guessing, 200
guided analytics, 122
Gulf Air, 439

H

Hadoop, 385–388, 393–394, 396–397
Hadoop clusters, 387–388
Hadoop Distributed File System (HDFS), 36, 385, 386
Hadoop MapReduce, 36
Hadoop/Big Data tools, 232, 233
Hammerbacher, Jeff, 397
Harte-Hanks, 154t
Harvard Business Review, 459
Harvard Business Review Analytic Services, 311
Hbase, 387
HCatalog, 387
health data, 39
Health Insurance Portability and Accountability Act (HIPAA), 59, 164
health insurers, 32
health services, 411
healthcare, 29–33, 205
healthcare sectors, 33–35
Healthy Days metric, 31
heat maps, 7, 8f, 108
Hepatitis B interventions, 353–354
heterogeneous model ensembles, 220–221
heuristics, 13–14, 326t
highlight tables, 108
high-performance computing, 112, 380
high-volume query access, 156
Hilcorp Energy, 421–422
HIPAA. *See* Health Insurance Portability and Accountability Act (HIPAA)
histogram, 80, 107
historical data, 134
Hive, 386
holdout, 217
Hollywood movies, 233–236
homeland security, 205–206, 450–451
homonyms, 253
homophily, 308

Hortonworks, 397, 403
hospital systems, 411
hosted data warehouse, 157
hotels/resorts, 204–205
HP, 154t
hub-and-spoke architecture, 142, 143f, 144, 145
hubs, 290
Humana, Inc., 29–33
Humanyze, 451, 455
Hummingbird Ltd., 154t
Hunch, 391
hybrid BAM-middleware providers, 21
hybrid cloud, 434
Hyperion Solutions, 133, 154t
hyperlink-induced topic search (HITS), 290
hyperlinks, 290
hypothesis testing, 86

I

IaaS. *See* infrastructure-as-a-service (IaaS)
IBM Bluemix, 434
IBM Corporation, 40, 42–43, 133, 141, 163, 224, 277–280, 376, 398, 420–421, 438–439
IBM InfoSphere BigInsights, 154t, 398–401, 399f
IBM Ireland, 133
IBM SPSS Modeler, 232t, 235–236
IBM Watson, 12, 43, 232t, 248–250, 279, 436–437, 457–458
ID3, 62–63, 222
if–then–else rules, 13–14
imagery data, 62
immediacy, 310
imperfect input, 256
implicit sentiment, 277
include terms, 269
in-database analytics, 169, 380
in-database processing technology, 169
independence, 200
independence (of errors), 89
independent data mart, 134, 142, 143f, 145
Indiana University Kelly School of Business, 30
indices, 270
individual impacts, 144
industrial restructuring, 456–457
Industry standards, 121
industry-specific data aggregators and distributors, 41
infectious diseases, 400
inferences, 75
inferential statistics, 75, 81, 86–97
influence diagram, 327
Influence Health, 223–225
influencers, 43–44, 312–313
Info, 296
Informatica, 154t
Information Builders, 100, 153
information dashboards. *See* dashboards
information extraction, 252
information fusion models, 221
information gain, 223
information harvesting, 196
  see also data mining
information quality, 144
information reporting, 98–100
Information Systems Research (ISR), 273–275
information visualization. *See* data visualization
information-as-a-service (IaaS), 432
INFORMS. *See* Institute for Operations Research and the Management Sciences (INFORMS)
Infospace, 296
infrastructure, 20, 168

infrastructure-as-a-service (IaaS), 14–15, 430, 432–433
Ingram Micro, 325–326
in-memory analytics, 195, 380
in-memory computing, 404
in-memory storage technology, 169–170
Inmon, Bill, 133, 144, 153, 154, 156t
in-motion analytics, 376
innovation networks, 305
INPRIME, 325
input/output (technology) coefficients, 338
Insightful Miner, 232t
Instagram, 306, 307
Institute for Operations Research and the Management Sciences (INFORMS), 23, 38, 44, 322, 327
Instrumentation Laboratory, 63–65
insurance, 204
insurance service products, 228
integration, 405
 business intelligence (BI), 22–23
 of data, 395
 data warehousing, 134
 integration technologies, 147
intelligent agents, 21
interactive BI tools, 395
intercept, 88
Interfaces, 322
intermediate result variables, 329
internal business process objective, 179
internal business processes perspective, 178
internal cloud, 433
internal record-oriented data, 161
International Classification of Diseases, 403
International Energy Agency (IEA), 377
International Telecommunication Union (ITU), 45
Internet, 140, 449
 see also Web analytics; Web mining
Internet marketing strategy, 295
Internet of Things (IoT), 39, 43, 247, 418, 419
 fog computing, 425–426
 growth of, 420
 managerial considerations, 428–429
 platforms, 426
 RFID sensors, 422–425
 start-up ecosystem, 427, 428f
 technology infrastructure, 422, 423f
 use of term, 420
interoperability, 429
interpretability, 216
interquartile range, 78–79
interval data, 62, 202
intranet, 140
inventory optimization, 34t
investment bank, 382–383
IoT. *See* Internet of Things (IoT)
irregular input, 256
islands of data, 132
IT strategy, 380
ixQuick, 296

J
jackknifing, 218
JavaScript Object Notation (JSON), 399, 400
JC Penney, 377
jeopardy, 248–250
JetBlue Airlines, 237
job tracker, 386
job-shop scheduling decisions, 361–363
Journal of Management Information Systems (JMIS), 273–275
JSON Query Language (JAQL), 399, 400

Juniper Research, 420

K
kaggle.org, 220
Kalido, 147
KDD. *See* knowledge discovery in databases (KDD)
KDnuggets.com, 232–233
Kensho, 377
key performance indicators (KPIs), 99, 121, 131, 171, 172, 175–176, 181, 441
keywords, 302
k-fold cross-validation, 218
kilobytes (KB), 375
Kimball, Ralph, 133, 144, 153, 154–155, 156t
k-means, 202, 211, 226, 227
k-means clustering, 74
k-modes, 226
KNIME, 41–42, 231
knowledge, 57
knowledge discovery in databases (KDD), 213, 214f
knowledge discovery in textual databases. *See* text mining
knowledge extraction, 196
 see also data mining
knowledge management, 12
knowledge management systems, 12
Knowledge Miner, 232t
knowledge-based modeling, 326
KPIs. *See* key performance indicators (KPIs)
kurtosis, 81

L
labor market, 457
lagging indicators, 176
landing page profiles, 302
Lanworth, 377
large data, 203
latent semantic indexing, 254
law enforcement, 205–206, 411
leadership, 456
leading indicators, 176
leads, 302
leaf node, 221
Lean Manufacturing (Lean Production), 180
learning, 90
learning and growing objective, 179
learning and growing perspective, 178
leave-one-out, 218
LeClaire, Brian, 29
left-hand side (LHS), 229
legal issues, 448–449
legislation, 16
Lenovo, 266–267
Lewis, Michael, 5
lexicon, 284–285
LHS. *See* left-hand side (LHS)
lies, 262–264
lift, 229
line charts, 106
linear discriminant analysis, 90
linear programming (LP), 336
linear programming model, 338–344
linear programming software, 42
linear regression, 88
 see also linear regression model
linear regression line, 87f
linear regression model
 see also regression modeling
 development of, 87–88

effectiveness of, 88
 important assumptions, 89–90
linearity, 89
link analysis, 202
LinkedIn, 28, 43
links, 47–48
load, 148
location analytics, 43
location information, 450
location intelligence, 442
location-based analytics
 classification, 441f
 consumer analytics applications, 446–448
 geospatial analytics, 441–445
 real-time location intelligence, 445–446
logistic function, 91, 91f
logistic regression, 25, 74, 90–96, 200
logistic regression coefficients, 91
logistics, 204
Lotte.com, 297–298
LP. *See* linear programming (LP)

M
Macfarlan Smith, 103–105
machine learning, 418
machine learning algorithms, 62
machine translation, 260
macros, 335
MAE. *See* mean absolute error (MAE)
magic bullet syndrome, 239
Magic Quadrant for Business Intelligence and Analytics Platforms, 44, 110, 111–112, 403
Mahout, 387
mainframes, 132
Major League Baseball, 206
management, 455–456
management information systems (MIS), 13
management science research software, 42
Mankind Pharma, 438–439
manual methods, 132
manual quality checks, 64
manufacturers, 204
manufacturing, 204, 329t
MAPE. *See* mean absolute percent error (MAPE)
MapR, 397
MapReduce, 36, 383–385, 384f, 389, 396, 400, 403
maps
 see also graphs
 geographic maps, 107
 heat maps, 7, 8f, 108
 tree maps, 108
market analysis, 377–378
market basket analysis, 34t, 35
market segmentation, 225
market-basket analysis, 202, 227, 228
marketing, 329t
marketing applications, 261
MarkLogic Server, 382–383
Mars, Forrest, 45
Mars Chocolate Empire, 45
Maryland, 128–129
mass spectrometry proteomics, 264
massive parallelism, 249
massively parallel processing (MPP), 404
mathematical models, 340f
 decision support mathematical models. *See* decision support mathematical models
 implementation, 344–345
 linear programming model, 338–344
 mathematical programming optimization, 336–345

mathematical programming, 336
mathematical programming optimization, 336–345
mathematical representation, 76
matrix size, 270–271
McKinsey, 44
McKinsey's Global Institute, 428–429
MD Anderson Cancer Center, 436–437
Meals on Wheels America, 334–335
mean, 76–77, 80
mean absolute deviation, 78
mean absolute error (MAE), 97
mean absolute percent error (MAPE), 97
mean squared error (MSE), 97
measures of centrality tendency, 76
measures of dispersion, 77
measures of location or centrality, 76
measures of spread decentrality, 77
median, 76, 77, 80
medical devices, 411
medical records, 228
Medicare Advantage, 30, 32
medicine, 205
megabytes (MB), 375
mergers, 146
message feature mining, 263
metadata, 134, 135, 139
metric management reports, 99
Metro Meals on Wheels Treasure Valley, 334–335
Miami-Dade Police Department, 190–193
Michigan Department of Technology, Management and Budget, 163
Microsoft, 41, 133, 154t, 421–422
Microsoft Azure, 434, 437–438
Microsoft Cortana Analytics Suite, 438
Microsoft Enterprise Consortium, 48, 231–232
Microsoft Excel, 81, 82–84, 334–335, 335, 335f, 336f, 340–341, 357
Microsoft SQL Server. *See* SQL Server
MicroStrategy, 398
middleware providers, 40
middleware tools, 139
Minard, Charles Joseph, 101
MineMyText.com, 436
MIS. *See* management information systems (MIS)
MIS Quarterly (MISQ), 273–275
missing values, 65
mixed integer programming software, 42
mixed-integer programming model, 337–338
mobile service providers, 135–137
mobile user privacy, 450
mode, 76, 77
model building, 209–211
model categories, 324–327, 326t
model management, 326
model-based decision making, 322–327
  current trends in modeling, 327
  environmental scanning and analysis, 324
  knowledge-based modeling, 326
  model categories, 324–327, 326t
  model management, 326
  prescriptive analytics model examples, 322–324
  problem identification, 324
models, 13, 197
Moneyball (Lewis), 5, 458
monitoring, 172
Monte Carlo simulation, 356, 357
morphology, 253
Motorola, Inc., 149
moving average, 97

MPQA Corpus, 286
MSE. *See* mean squared error (MSE)
multicollinearity, 90
multicriteria decision analysis, 350
multidimensional analysis (modeling), 327
multiple databases, 137
multiple goals, 346–347, 351t, 352
multiple linear regression, 88
multiple models, 221
multiple regression, 74, 87
Multiple-Aspect Restaurant Reviews, 286
multiplexity, 308
multistructured data, 396
Murphy, Paul, 133
Musixmatch, 43
mutuality, 308
MyWebSearch, 296

N

name node, 386
Napoleon's Army, 102f
National Basketball Association (NBA), 206
National Centre for Text Mining, 266
National Collegiate Athletic Association (NCAA), 206
National Flood Insurance Program (NFIP), 100
National Institute of Standards and Technology (NIST), 45, 429
National Institutes of Health, 266
natural language generation, 260
natural language processing (NLP), 251, 255–261, 279
natural language understanding, 260
Nature, 266
NCAA Bowl Game outcomes, 91–96
Netezza, 154t
network closure, 308
network diagrams, 107
network science, 28
network virtualization, 433
neural network models, 26
Neural Network software, 42
neural networks, 25, 200, 201–202, 219, 226
NeuroDimensions, 42
new organizational units, 454
new store analysis, 34t
new visitors, 302
newness, 167
next-generation data warehouse market, 398
Nielsen, 41
Nike, 43
NLP. *See* natural language processing (NLP)
nodes, 403
noise words, 253
nominal data, 61, 208
nonfinancial objectives, 179
normal distribution, 80, 81f
normality, 200
normality (of errors), 90
normative analytics, 27
NoSQL, 388, 389–391, 398
novelty, 167
N–P polarity classification, 282–283
n-tiered architectures, 139
nuclear physics, 194
numeric data, 62, 76, 208
numeric representation, 62

O

objective function, 338
objective function coefficients, 338
obsolete data, 134

occurrence matrix, 254
ODS. *See* operational data store (ODS)
offline campaigns, 301
oil and gas exploration assets, 421–422
Oklahoma State University, 26, 45
OLAP. *See* online analytical processing (OLAP)
OLTP. *See* online transaction processing (OLTP)
Omniture, 41
O'Neil, Cathy, 458
online analytical processing (OLAP), 11, 20, 75, 98, 158–159, 159f, 335
online campaigns, 301
online transaction processing (OLTP), 19, 98, 149, 158–159, 159f
on-site Web analytics, 299–300
Oozie, 387
open source software, 165
opening vignettes
  customer churn, 370–373
  IBM Watson, 248–249
  Miami-Dade Police Department, 190–193
  School District of Philadelphia, 320–321
  Siemens, 418–419
  SiriusXM Radio, 54–56
  sports analytics, 4–10
  tax fraud, 128–130
OpenShift, 435
oper marts, 135
operational data store (ODS), 135
operational databases, 19
operational KPIs, 176
operational plan, 172
operations research (OR), 13
  mathematical model, development of, 353
  OR models, 13
  software, 42
opinion mining, 276
opinion-oriented search engines, 282
optical character recognition, 260
optimal solution, 338
optimistic approach, 350
optimization
  algorithms, 326t
  analytic formula, 326t
  mathematical programming optimization, 336–345
optimization software, 42
OR. *See* operations research (OR)
Oracle Corporation, 18, 40, 133, 141, 154t, 357, 382, 398
Oracle Data Mining (ODM), 232t
Orange Data Mining Tool, 232t
Orbital Insights, 377
ordinal data, 62, 208
ordinal multiple logistic regression, 62
ordinary least squares (OLS), 88
organization, 20
organizational alignment, 429
organizational impacts, 144
organizational redesign, 455
organizational structure, 454
ORMS Today, 322, 360
O–S Polarity (Objectivity–Subjectivity Polarity), 282
outcomes, 176
outliers, 76–77, 79
output variable, 86
Overall Analysis System for Intelligence Support (OASIS), 262
overall classifier accuracy, 216
overall F-test, 88

P

PaaS. *See* platform-as-a-service (PaaS)
page views, 300
page-loading speed, 140
Palisade.com, 357
parallel processing, 141, 163–164
partitioning, 141
ParkPGH, 447
part-of-speech tagging, 253, 256, 265
passive tags, 423
Patil, D. J., 28, 459
pattern analysis, 196
    see also data mining
pattern searching, 196
    see also data mining
Pearson, Karl, 86
Pennsylvania Adoption Exchange, 333–334
Penzias, Arno, 193
per class accuracy rates, 216
performance dashboards. *See* dashboards
performance management system, 176
performance measurement, effective, 181
performance measurement systems, 175,
    176–177
    balanced scorecard (BSC), 176–177
    key performance indicators (KPIs). *See* key
        performance indicators (KPIs)
    Six Sigma, 179–183
    vs. performance management system, 176
periodic reporting, 162
periodicals, 48
perishables, 425
perpetual analytics, 408
personal values, 453
PERT charts, 107
pervasive confidence estimation, 249
pessimistic approach, 350–351
"petabyte age," 440
petabytes (PB), 164, 374, 375
petals, 38
physical data integration, 148
pie charts, 106
Pig, 387
Pitney Bowes, 426–427
pivot, 159
planning, 20–21, 172, 313
platform-as-a-service (PaaS), 430, 432
Playfair, William, 101, 102f
Pokémon Go, 446
polarity identification, 284
"polarization" of the labor market, 457
policy makers, 45
politically naive behavior, 161
politics, 281
PolyAnalyst, 232t
polysemes, 253
power industry, 411
power users, 395
precision, 217t
predictions, 86, 198, 200
predictive accuracy, 215–216
predictive analytics, 25–26, 41–42, 62, 324, 446,
    447
    see also data mining
    data mining. *See* data mining
    data types, 62–63
    ensemble models, 220–221
    social analytics. *See* social analytics
    social media analytics. *See* social media
        analytics
    statistical methods, 74
    text analytics. *See* text analytics
    Web analytics. *See* Web analytics

predictive analytics algorithms, 62
predictive models, 32–33, 326t
predictor variables, 90
prescriptive analytics, 26–27, 42, 320–321
    decision analysis. *See* decision analysis
    goal seeking, 335, 348–349
    model examples, 322–324
    model-based decision making, 322–327
    multiple goals, 346–347
    optimization. *See* optimization
    sensitivity analysis, 347–348
    simulation. *See* simulation
    what-if analysis, 335, 348f
price elasticity, 34t
pricing decisions, 325–326
primary data, 203
privacy, 448, 449
    business intelligence (BI), 22
    collection of information, 449–450
    data mining, 237
    data privacy, 59
    data warehousing, 164
    homeland security, 450–451
    mobile user privacy, 450
    ownership of private data, 452
    recent technology issues, 451
privacy lawsuits, 237
private cloud, 433–434
probabilistic decision-making situation, 331
probabilistic simulation, 356–357
problem identification, 324
process efficiency, 12, 381
processing capabilities, 381
ProClarity, 133
production, 204
productivity, 447
products, 48
profit model, 329
program, 338
programmability, 335
programming languages, 149, 233
propinquity, 308
proprietary data integration vendors, 398
public cloud, 434
pure-play BAM, 21

Q

Qualia, 43, 451
qualitative data, 208
quality, 309–310
quantitative data, 208
quantitative models, 328, 328f, 346
quartiles, 78–79
query analyzer, 294
query-specific clustering, 272
question answering, 253, 260
queuing, 360
Quiznos, 445, 446

R

R (open source platforms), 41–42, 232, 392
R^2 (*R*-squared), 88
radio-frequency identification data (RFID), 21,
    204, 360, 361–363, 422–425
Random Forest, 220, 232t
ranges, 78, 176
RapidMiner, 41–42, 231, 232
Rapleaf, 451
Rathi, Abhishek, 33
ratio data, 62
RDBM. *See* relational database management
    (RDBM)

reach, 310
real-time BI applications, 21
real-time computing and analysis,
    161
real-time data analysis, 420–421
real-time data analytics, 407
    see also stream analytics
real-time data warehousing (RDW), 14, 168
real-time location intelligence, 445–446
real-world data, 65
recall, 217t
recession, 165
reciprocity, 308
Red Brick Systems, 133
Red Hat JBoss Enterprise Application platform,
    439
referral Web sites, 301
Regional Neonatal Associates, 337
regression, 86, 215
    see also regression modeling
regression modeling, 86–98
    correlation *versus* regression, 86
    effectiveness of model, 88
    evaluation of fit, 88
    linear regression model, development of,
        87–88
    linear regression model, important assump-
        tions in, 89–90
    logistic regression, 90–96
    simple *vs.* multiple regression, 87
    time series forecasting, 96–97
regulation, 16
regulators, 45
regulatory compliance, 64
regulatory requirements, 146
relational database management (RDBM), 14,
    133, 141, 168, 169, 393
relational DBMS-based data warehouse tech-
    nologies, 396–397
relational triads, 308
relevancy, 60
reliability, 59
RENFE, 418
rental car companies, 204–205
report, 98
reporting analytics, 24, 41
research literature survey, 273–275
resources, 47–48
response variable, 86, 87
result (outcome) variables, 328
retail sector, 33–35, 194
retail value chain, 33–35, 33f, 34t
retailing, 204
retrieval speed, 166
return on investment (ROI), 145, 174, 198–199,
    300
returning visitors, 302
review-oriented search engines, 282
Revolution Analytics, 41
RFID. *See* radio-frequency identification data
    (RFID)
RFID-enabled (temperature) sensors,
    425
RHS. *See* right-hand side (RHS)
richness, 59
right-hand side (RHS), 229
right-time data warehousing, 14
ripple effect, 312
risk, 331
    calculated risk, 331
    catastrophic loss, 351
    data warehousing, 161
    treating risk, 351

risk analysis, 331
risk management, 254–255, 381
RMSE. *See* Root Mean Square Error (RMSE)
robustness, 216
ROC curve, 219, 219f
Rockwell Automation, 421–422
ROI. *See* return on investment (ROI)
ROI approach, 150
roll-up, 159
Root Mean Square Error (RMSE), 88
rotation estimation, 218
rough sets, 200, 220
RS Metrics, 377
rule induction, 202
Rulequest, 42
Russian campaign (1812), 102f

S

SaaS. *See* software-as-a-service (SaaS)
Sabre Corporation, 18
Sabre Technologies, 43
sales, 303
sales forecast, 176
sales operations, 176
sales plan, 176
sales transactions, 228
Salesforce, 410
Sam M. Walton College of Business, 232
Samworth Brothers Distribution, 425
SAP, 40, 151–153
SAP InfiniteInsight (KXEN), 232t
Sarbanes-Oxley Act, 16
SAS Enterprise Miner, 232t
SAS Institute, Inc., 23, 40, 41, 42, 85, 112, 115, 133, 146, 154t, 195, 212, 266, 267, 297–298, 404
SAS Visual Analytics, 112, 115, 115f, 116, 116f, 120, 404, 436
SAS Visual Statistics, 436
satellite imagery data, 377
scalability, 161, 162–164, 216
scatter plots, 87f, 106
scatter/gather clustering, 272
Schmidt, Eric, 296
School District of Philadelphia, 320–321
SCM. *See* supply chain management (SCM)
search, 290
search engine optimization (SEO), 294–297
search engine poisoning, 295
search engine spam, 295
search engines, 291–298, 301
    algorithms, 296
    anatomy of a search engine, 292–294
    development cycle, 292–293
    document indexer, 293
    document matcher/ranker, 294
    effectiveness, 292
    efficiency, 292
    evaluation metrics, 291–292
    most popular search engines, 296
    and organic search traffic, 296
    query analyzer, 294
    response cycle, 294
    search engine optimization (SEO), 294–297
    Web crawlers, 292–293
search precision, 272
search recall, 272
search spam, 295
secondary data, 203
secondary node, 386
sectors, 38
Securities and Exchange Commission, 99

securities trading, 204
security, 429
    business intelligence (BI), 22
    cybersecurity, 411
    data security, 59
    data warehousing, 164, 167
security applications, 261–264
security threats, 279
seeds, 293
segmentation, 309
self-organizing maps, 202
semantic orientation, 286
semistructured data, 61
SEMMA, 212–213, 213f
seniors, 29–30
sensitivity analysis, 236, 347–348
sensor data, 418–419
sensors, 39
sensory data, 204
sentiment analysis, 257, 276–286, 410, 439
    aggregation, 284
    applications, 280–282
    brand management, 281
    collection, 284
    financial markets, 281
    government intelligence, 281–282
    lexicon, 284–285
    N–P polarity classification, 282–283
    polarity identification, 284
    politics, 281
    process, 282–284, 283f
    semantic orientation, 286
    sentiment detection, 282
    target identification, 283–284
    training documents, 285
    voice of the customer (VOC), 280–281
    voice of the employee (VOE), 281
    voice of the market (VOM), 281
sentiment detection, 282
SentiWordNet, 285
sequence mining, 202
sequential relationships, 200
serial analysis of gene expression (SAGE), 264
serialized global trade identification numbers (SGTIN), 424
server capacity, 140
server virtualization, 433
service performance, 176
service-oriented architecture (SOA), 14–15, 147
services, 329t
SGTIN. *See* serialized global trade identification numbers (SGTIN)
shallow knowledge, 249
shallow-parsing, 265
shared economy providers, 43
Shazam, 43
shells, 21–22
shopper analytics, 35
shopper insight, 34t
should-cost modeling, 332
Siemens, 25, 154t, 418–419
Silvaris Corporation, 24
SilverHook, 420–421
simple average, 97
simple present-value cash flow model, 329–330
simple regression, 87
simple regression analysis, 87–88
simple split, 217–218, 217f
simplification, 405
simulation, 326t, 352
    advantages, 354
    characteristics, 352–354
    disadvantages, 355

discrete event simulation, 356, 358–359
    experiments, conduct of, 352
    inadequacies, 359
    methodology, 355–356
    Monte Carlo simulation, 356
    packages, 354
    probabilistic simulation, 356–357
    process, 355f
    software, 42, 360–363
    time-dependent simulation, 357
    time-independent simulation, 357
    types, 356–358
    visual interactive simulation (VIS), 359–363
Simulmedia, 43
simultaneous goals, 346
singular value decomposition (SVD), 254, 271
SiriusXM Radio, 54–56
Six Sigma, 179–183
Six Sigma Business Scorecard (Gupta), 180
skewed data, 77
skewness, 80
skills availability, 381
SKUs, 35
slave nodes, 386
slice, 159, 160f
"slice and dice," 159
slope, 88
SmartBin, 43
smartphone platforms, 446–447
smartphones, 43
Snowden, Edward, 450
Snowflake, 436, 440
snowflakes schema, 156, 158, 158f
SOA. *See* service-oriented architecture (SOA)
SOA coarse-grained services, 147
social analytics, 304–313
    connections, 308
    distributions, 308–309
    segmentation, 309
    social media analytics. *See* social media analytics
    social network analysis, 304–305
social capital, 309
social circles, 309
social media, 36, 43, 165, 400–401
social media analytics, 43, 309–310
    accuracy of analytic tool, 313
    accuracy of text analysis, 312
    best practices, 311–313
    beyond the brand, 312
    elusive sentiment, tracking, 312
    influencers, 312–313
    measurement of social media impact, 311
    not rating system, 311–312
    planning, 313
    ripple effect, 312
    users, 310–311, 310f
social monitoring, 306
social network analysis, 42, 304–305, 311
social network analysis metrics, 305–308
social networking, 136
social networking Web sites, 430
social networks, 304
soft data, 196
Softlayer, 438–439
software monitors, 21
software-as-a-service (SaaS), 165, 432
solution, 338
solution cost, 381
Sonatica, 117
Soundhound, 43
Spaceknow, 377
spam filtering, 255

spamdexing, 295
spatial analytics, 443
spatial data, 62
Special Interest Group on Decision Support and Analytics, 44
specialized data collection, aggregation, and distribution, 41
speech acts, 256
speech recognition, 260
speech synthesis, 260
speed, 216
spiders, 289, 292
split point, 221
sponsorship, 380
sponsorship chain, 161
sport analytics, 28, 91
sports, 206
sports analytics, 4–10, 43
sports industry, 39
Sportvision, 43
spreadsheets, 331–336
SPRINT (Scalable PaRallelizable INduction of Decision Trees), 222
Sprout, 306–308
spyware, 450
SQL queries, 139
SQL Server, 39, 231
SQL Server BI toolkit, 41
SQL Server Data Mining, 232t
Sqoop, 387
standard deviation, 78, 80
standardization of encoded attributes, 149
Stanford University, 257
Stanford—Large Movie Review Data Set, 286
star schema, 156, 157–158, 158f
Starbucks, 425, 444
state of nature, 350
static data, 21, 62
static models, 324, 360
Statistica Data Miner, 254
statistical analysis, 219
statistical modeling, 28, 74–85
statistical software companies, 41
statistics, 28, 74, 75
    descriptive statistics. *See* descriptive statistics
    inferential statistics, 75, 81, 86–97
    statistical software packages, 81
    vs. data mining, 203
statistics-based classification techniques, 200
Stein, Joel, 451
stemming, 253, 270
ST_GEOMETRY, 443
stochastic decision-making situation, 331
stop terms, 269
stop words, 253, 269
storage
    and cognitive limits, 12
    data warehouses, 167
storage virtualization, 433
store layout, 34t
stories, 113–114
story structure, 113–114
storytelling, 113–114
strategic plan, 172
strategy, 20–21, 171–172, 175, 380
Strategy Maps: Converting Intangible Assets into Tangible Outcomes (Kaplan and Norton), 177
The Strategy-Focused Organization: How Balanced Scorecard Companies Thrive in the New Business Environment (Kaplan and Norton), 177
stream analytics, 381, 407, 407f

applications, 409–412
and Big Data, 406–409
critical event processing, 408
cybersecurity, 411
data stream mining, 408–409
e-commerce, 409
financial services, 411
government, 412
health services, 411
law enforcement, 411
power industry, 411
telecommunications, 409–410
use case, 407f
vs. perpetual analytics, 408
stream mining, 42
structural holes, 309
structured data, 61, 253
student attrition, 68–74
subject matter experts, 240
subject orientation, 133–134
subjectivity analysis, 276
summarization, 252
summarization rules, 149
supervised induction, 200–202
supply chain management (SCM), 20
supply chain monitoring, 64
support, 12, 229
support vector machines (SVMs), 200
SVD. *See* singular value decomposition (SVD)
SVMs. *See* support vector machines (SVMs)
Sybase, 154t, 382
synonyms, 253, 269
syntactic ambiguity, 256
Sysco, 425
system dynamics, 356
system quality, 144

T
Tableau, 24, 40, 41, 114f, 118, 398, 436
Tacoma Public Schools, 437–438
Target, 238
target identification, 283–284
targets, 175
tax fraud, 128–130
TDWI.org, 40, 44
Teknion, 118
telecommunication companies (TELCOs), 135–137
telecommunications, 228, 409–410
terabytes (TB), 163, 373–374, 374
Teradata, 18, 55–56, 115, 132, 133, 141, 154t, 168, 398, 418
Teradata® Analytics, 151–153
Teradata Aster, 42, 199, 371, 401–406, 403, 435–436
Teradata University Network (TUN), 10, 19, 44, 48
Teradata Warehouse Miner, 232t
term, 253
term dictionary, 253
term-by-document matrix, 254, 293
term–document matrix (TDM), 269–271, 270f
terrorism, 450–451
terrorist funding, 205–206
test sample estimation, 217
test set, 217
text analytics, 12, 27–28, 251–253, 251f
    see also text mining
text categorization, 271
text data mining. *See* text mining
text mining, 14, 252
    application areas, 252–253

applications, 261–267
bag-of-words model, 255
benefits of, 252
biomedical applications, 264–265
and customer relationship management (CRM), 261
marketing applications, 261
natural language processing (NLP), 255–261
process, 268–275
security applications, 261–264
terminology, 253–254
text mining process, 268–275
    association, 272
    classification, 271
    clustering, 271–272
    context diagram, 268f
    corpus, establishment of, 269
    extraction of knowledge, 271–273
    reduction of dimensionality of matrix, 270–271
    representation of indices, 270
    term–document matrix (TDM), 269–271, 270f
    three-step/task, 269f
    trend analysis, 272–273
text proofing, 260
text segmentation, 256
text-based deception-detection process, 263f
text-to-speech, 260
textual data, 62, 285–286
Thomson Reuters, 377
three-tier data warehouse, 139–140, 139f
tie strength, 309
time compression, 354
time frames, 176
Time magazine, 451
time of day, 302
time on site, 300
time series analytics, 7, 8f
time series data, 97f
time series forecasting, 96–97, 203
time series line chart, 102f
time-dependent simulation, 357
time-independent simulation, 357
timelines, 60
time-sensitive environments, 374
time-series forecasting, 203
Tito's Handmade Vodka, 305–308
Toad software suite, 199
tokenizing, 253
topic tracking, 252
Torch Concepts, 237
Towerdata, 43
traders, 204
traffic management, 39
traffic sources, 301
training, 310
training documents, 285
training set, 217
transaction, 20
transaction processing systems, 19–20
transactional database design, 161
transformation, 148
transformation-tool approach, 149
transitivity, 308
transportation, 329t
travel industry, 204–205
Treasata, 398
tree maps, 108
trend analysis, 272–273
trial-and-error sensitivity analysis, 347–348
true negative rate, 217t
true positive rate, 217t
Tufte, Edward, 101

Tukey, John W., 79
TUN. *See* Teradata University Network (TUN)
tuples, 407
TurboRouter, 322
Turck, Matt, 39, 427
Twitter, 43, 306, 307, 392–393, 399, 400
two-person game, 350
two-tier data warehouse, 139, 140f

U

uncertainty, 331, 350–351
uncontrollable parameters, 328
uncontrollable variables, 328, 350
"understanding the customer," 193
unimodal distribution, 81
Universal Product Code (UPC), 424
universities, 44
University of Arkansas, 232
University of California, Berkeley, 266
University of Liverpool, 266
University of Manchester, 266
University of Tennessee Medical Center, 337–338
Unmetric, 43
unstructured data, 61, 253
UPC. *See* Universal Product Code (UPC)
updatability, 310
urban sociology, 305
U.S. Census, 138
U.S. Department of Agriculture, 377
U.S. Department of Commerce, 206
U.S. Department of Defense, 163
U.S. Department of Education, Center for Educational Statistics, 68
U.S. Department of Homeland Security, 205
U.S. Federal Bureau of Investigation (FBI), 262
U.S. government, 164
US PATRIOT Act, 205, 449–450
usability, 300–301, 310
usability specialist, 122
user interface, 16
users, 167

V

validity, 60
value drivers, 176
variability, 180, 376
variable identification, 324
variable selection, 67
variables, 328
    class/response variable, 90
    decision variables, 328, 338, 350
    dependent variables, 328
    explanatory variable, 87
    explanatory/predictor variables, 90
    intermediate result variables, 329
    output variable, 86
    predictor variables, 90
    response variable, 86, 87

result (outcome) variables, 328
    uncontrollable variables, 328, 350
variance, 78
variety, 374, 378
vCreaTek, LLC, 33
velocity, 374–376, 378
vendors, 48
veracity, 376
video analytics, 34t, 35
video data, 62
vignettes. *See* opening vignettes
virtualization, 433
VIS. *See* visual interactive simulation (VIS)
Visa, 194–195
vision, 380
visitor profiles, 302
visual analytics, 112, 203
    application case, 119–120
    emergence of, 110–116
    high-powered visual analytics environments, 112–116
visual interactive modeling (VIM), 359
    see also visual interactive simulation (VIS)
visual interactive problem solving, 359
    see also visual interactive simulation (VIS)
visual interactive simulation (VIS), 359–363
visualization. *See* data visualization
visualization tools, 24, 196
visualizations, 26, 41, 203, 405
voice data, 62
voice of the customer (VOC), 280–281
voice of the employee (VOE), 281
voice of the market (VOM), 281
voice recognition tools, 43
volume, 374, 378

W

waiting-line management, 360
Wall Street Journal, 377, 447, 451
Walmart, 163, 424
warehousing strategy, 153
Watson. *See* IBM Watson
Waze, 43, 447, 452
Weapons of Math Destruction: How Big Data Increases Inequality and Threatens Democracy (O'Neil), 458
wearables, 9
weather data, 40–41
weather effects, 442
Web analytics, 27–28, 43, 288, 298–303
    see also Web mining
    conversion statistics, 302–303
    dashboard, 303f
    metrics, 300–303
    on-site Web analytics, 299–300
    technologies, 299–300
    traffic sources, 301
    visitor profiles, 302
    Web site usability, 300–301

Web browser, 140
Web content mining, 288, 289–291
Web crawlers, 289, 292–293
Web mining, 287–291
    challenges, 287–288
    taxonomy of, 289f
    Web content mining, 288, 289–291
    Web structure mining, 288, 289–291, 291
    Web usage mining, 288, 298–303
Web services, 21
Web site usability, 300–301
Web spiders, 292
Web structure mining, 288, 289–291, 291
Web usage mining, 288, 298–303
    see also Web analytics
Web-based data management tools, 146
Web-based data warehouses, 140, 141f, 162
Web-based e-mail, 430
Web-based KPI scorecard system, 181–183
WebCrawler, 296
WebFOCUS software, 100
Webhousing, 162
Web-oriented languages, 28
weighted averages, 226–227
weighted moving average, 97
Weka, 231
Wells Fargo Bank, 133
"What They Know," 451
what-if analysis, 335, 348, 348f
white-hat SEO, 295
Wi-Fi hotspots, 450
Wikileaks, 450
Wikipedia, 430
Wimbledon, 277–280
word frequency, 253
word sense disambiguation, 256
WordNet, 257, 284–285
WordNet-Affect, 285
World Wide Web, 287
Wow, 296

X

XLMiner, 232t

Y

Yahoo! Search, 296
yield management, 204
Yodlee, 377
yottabytes (YB), 375
Young, John, 63–65
YP.com, 43

Z

Zementis Predictive Analytics, 232t
zettabytes (ZB), 374, 375